Conducting and Rehearsing the Instrumental Music Ensemble

Scenarios, Priorities, Strategies, Essentials, and Repertoire

John F. Colson

THE SCARECROW PRESS, INC.
Lanham • Toronto • Plymouth, UK
2012

Published by Scarecrow Press, Inc.
A wholly owned subsidary of The Rowman & Littlefield Publishing Group, Inc.
4501 Forbes Boulevard, Suite 200, Lanham, Maryland 20706
www.rowman.com

10 Thornbury Road, Plymouth PL6 7PP, United Kingdom

British Library Cataloguing in Publication Information Available

Library of Congress Cataloging-in-Publication Data

Colson, John F.
  Conducting and rehearsing the instrumental music ensemble : scenarios, priorities, strategies,
essentials, and repertoire / John F. Colson.
        p. cm.
  Includes bibliographical references and index.
  ISBN 978-0-8108-8260-7 (pbk. : alk. paper) — ISBN 978-0-8108-8261-4 (ebook)
  1. Conducting. 2. Instrumental music—Instruction and study. I. Title.
  MT85.C73 2012
  784.145—dc23   2012011681

Printed in the United States of America

Contents

Preface

ABOUT THIS BOOK

After teaching instrumental conducting as well as conducting various instrumental music ensembles for more than 40 years, I believe there exists a major deficiency in the teaching of this area of musical performance. There are many excellent textbooks and treatises on the subject of conducting technique. These books cover the basic elements of conducting technique thoroughly as well as focusing on many of the other important aspects of conducting. However, most of these books contain a chapter or less about what is really involved with the rehearsing of the instrumental music ensemble. There are also many other books available for continuing and supplementing the music education of the maturing conductor. Again, these books contain little specific information directed toward the actual rehearsal process. Ironically, however, I believe that most conductors would concur that *being able to conduct and rehearse the instrumental music ensemble effectively and efficiently* is the most important characteristic for being a successful conductor.

The realization of this apparent void in the teaching of conducting often appears during the student teaching or intern experience in college or at the outset of the first conducting employment. When developing conductors were asked what was not being covered adequately in the conducting classes, the response overwhelmingly was that when stopping the ensemble in the rehearsal process, *the conductors were not always comfortable or decisive about what they should do or say*—and this involves the conducting technique, the rehearsal scenario, the rehearsal essentials, the rehearsal priorities, the rehearsal teaching strategies, and also selecting the appropriate concert repertoire.

The premise of this book is that it is possible to raise the competency level for maturing conductors through specific training in how to conduct and rehearse the instrumental music ensemble. In this way, these conductors will be better prepared to be effective in the actual rehearsal process. The main emphasis of this book is to present ideas and suggestions for designing teaching strategies that will work in the various rehearsal scenarios. I hope that this book will fashion some realistic principles for the developing conductor to follow in preparing for and guiding the ensemble in the rehearsal process. The whole focus of this book is knowing what to do or say in the rehearsal process to achieve success with the instrumental music ensemble. The conducting technique is usually in place, but rehearsing skills tend to be left to practical experience in front of the ensemble. A secondary aspect, but very important for the maturing conductor, *is that of selecting repertoire* for the performing ensemble. This book provides lists of some standard music material for the various instrumental music ensembles (see Appendix A). Often, advanced conductors are left on their own in acquiring the appropriate repertoire for concert performances. I offer suggestions on how to research and collect this information on music material in chapter 3: The Ten Essentials of the Rehearsal Process Scenario (under Essential No. 2: Music Material).

The problem with most advanced conducting curricula is that the focus is on certain selected conducting problems with very few opportunities to actually conduct or rehearse an instrumental music ensemble, and therefore, with limited regard for either the evaluation or improvement of the conducting student (see Appendix F). What I have tried to do with this book is to develop a flexible curriculum with many options for the conducting teacher in providing the conducting student with the background to conduct and rehearse the instrumental music ensemble. It is based on the *ideas of apprenticeship and hands-on work as opposed to attending class and absorbing some miscellaneous ideas about conducting and rehearsing.* The reality is that the student conductor must have the opportunity to stand in front of an ensemble and pursue many of these multifaceted aspects of instrumental music conducting and rehearsing, thereby producing the music and experiencing what is involved with being a competent conductor.

The conducting teacher has good information but does not necessarily have the organized activities to deliver this information. *This study guide suggests and offers these organized activities* (see Appendix I). These activities require a great deal of advance planning. For example, if extra players are used from beyond the conducting class, then the music should be given to these players in advance of the class to prepare their parts. If the players are sight-reading this music, it will not be a good experience in terms of either conducting or rehearsing such an ensemble. This is also true for the conducting classroom, where the students must have read the assigned material in order to contribute to a quality discussion of the material and to participate in the activities involving the conducting class. The conducting class needs to be free of egocentricity in order to profit from these activities. There must be *a sense of freedom to try various things* without embarrassment or self-consciousness. If these ideas are fostered then there should be some real improvement with the conducting students during these activities.

The Purpose of This Book

The purpose of this book is to continue the education of the maturing conductor beyond the initial stages of the basic conducting technique course into that of the varied approaches for conducting and rehearsing the instrumental music ensemble. It is assumed that the following competencies have been achieved or are being developed and refined by the advancing conductor: (1) conducting patterns, (2) preparatory beats, (3) releases,

(4) conducting pattern subdivisions, (5) conducting the basic styles, (6) handling fermatas, (7) cueing properly, (8) using the left hand effectively, (9) conducting the various meters and meter changes, (10) indicating tempos and tempo changes, (11) indicating dynamic and nuance variations, and (12) acquiring background in clefs, transpositions, and musical terms or symbols to expedite score reading and study. All of these items are generally covered in the beginning collegiate conducting course.

This book offers information and ideas for the maturing conductor who has developed these basic conducting skills, but needs to grow into a leader capable of conducting and rehearsing the instrumental music ensemble. The general performance goals for any conductor should be (1) to build a cohesive, musical ensemble; (2) to sustain a climate for individual and ensemble growth; and (3) to prepare the ensemble to produce exciting, musical performances. The bottom line for the inclusion of information in this book is the relevancy to the advanced conductor's progress and what he or she needs to know to be successful. These ideas are offered to provide a basis for the student conductor in creating and designing the appropriate rehearsal teaching strategies for producing a quality ensemble, for enhancing the musical growth of the individual players and the ensemble as a whole, and for achieving superior instrumental music ensemble performances.

Is there an educational gap after the basic conducting skills are in place? The answer would appear to be that there is an educational gap and it is mainly concerned with the stated void of competently rehearsing (and conducting) the instrumental music ensemble. In many instances after the initial conducting course, the college conducting curriculum tends to fragment into the study of a few selected musical works or one of random content about certain conducting techniques and problems. Simply articulated, the purpose of this book is to organize the conducting curriculum, beyond the initial conducting course, whereby the developing conductor will gain the skills and acquire the information necessary to successfully conduct and rehearse the instrumental music ensemble. For this reason, the subtitle of this book is *A Study Guide for Advanced Instrumental Conducting.*

The Limitations of This Book

In general, there is minimal information provided here covering the multifaceted areas of score reading, study, and preparation. These areas I leave to the continued study, research, and practical experience of the conductor. (The omission of this information in no way diminishes the importance of these musical activities. Some basic ideas concerning score reading, study, and preparation have been included in chapter 5.) Guidance in these areas is offered in numerous books and is also in the domain of other collegiate music courses such as music theory, music history and literature, music composition, and orchestration. *Score reading and study are fostered and improved through concentrated work in this area.* The rationale behind score study is that the conductor is able to assimilate the details in the score of a particular work with the objective being to conduct and rehearse the music properly. Score preparation involves the conductor devoting the necessary time and effort to study, learn, and mark the score thoroughly and meticulously before the rehearsal process begins. Musical interpretation of specific repertoire is a topic generally relegated to the course content of graduate conducting offerings at the collegiate level and in regional or national conducting seminars. Certainly the pursuit of information about musical interpretation continues throughout the entire career of the conductor. Musical selections suggested at the end of the chapters starting with chapter 4 could be used for conducting/rehearsing projects, score study, and/or program building. The conducting teacher must decide if these suggested musical selections are of value for these various purposes in the conducting class. I include alternative selections in Appendix A.

Likewise, this book does not attempt *to scrutinize the rehearsal process unique to the jazz ensemble or marching band.* The jazz ensemble rehearsal process would necessitate working on certain stylistic and phrasing considerations along with improvisation, and the marching band rehearsals would need to underscore the personnel movement on the field (or in parade) in addition to the technical and musical problems that surface during the rehearsal process. Musically speaking, however, there should be considerable carry-over in the rehearsal process from the concert ensemble to that of the jazz ensemble or marching band.

This book is intended to be a continuation of the basic conducting course, or depending on the curriculum sequence, in the second year (or semester) of conducting study. In most college conducting curricula, after the basic conducting course is completed, the student would select either an instrumental or a vocal emphasis. *The focus of this book is intended for the instrumental music conductor in the conducting curriculum.* The book is not necessarily a textbook for a music education methods course or in an instrumental pedagogy course, even though some of the information included would be a part of these courses. Certainly, the maturing conductor will need teaching strategies and pedagogical information in order to rehearse the instrumental music ensemble effectively.

TEACHING THE ART OF CONDUCTING AND REHEARSING

Conducting and Rehearsing Can Be Taught

There are specific elements in conducting and rehearsing that certainly can be taught. The basic conducting patterns and gestures are examples of such elements. Likewise, rehearsal scenarios, rehearsal essentials, rehearsal priorities, and rehearsal teaching strategies can be suggested, demonstrated, and creatively developed as part of the education of the conducting student. Also, the understanding of various interpretive aspects of conducting and rehearsing can be emphasized. In the reality of the conducting classroom and rehearsal process lab environment, the conducting teacher should try to convey information and ideas *that can actually be employed in the rehearsal process.* In addition to this, the conducting teacher should provide practical opportunities for the students to develop the conducting technique and rehearsing skills by creating rehearsal process lab environments (see Appendix H).

It is crucial that the presentation of these rehearsal scenarios, priorities, essentials, and teaching strategies for the maturing conductor be a part of the conducting curriculum. Only in this way can the association of conducting and rehearsing be related, as it should be in the actual rehearsal process. *The conducting technique is an interlocking part of the rehearsal process*, and this should not be disassociated from the actual rehearsing of an ensemble. The teaching aspect in the rehearsal process should be accomplished in conjunction with both the conducting and rehearsing of the ensemble. In other words, the conductor should integrate all of these conducting and rehearsing elements in order to be effective in the rehearsal process. This book makes an effort to identify these various conducting and rehearsing elements within the conducting curriculum. There are limits as to what can be taught in the two areas of conducting technique and rehearsing skills. In reality, much of what transpires in the rehearsal process will require the conductor to be creative and musical. However, it would seem that in many of the college curricula, insufficient or at least disorganized content has been taught in such conducting courses in the past. The focus of this book is to provide the needed information and skill development in an organized fashion for developing conductors as they move confidently toward the podium in the rehearsal process scenario.

There is a time when the conductor should become quite self-reliant. Eventually, the maturing conductor will personalize the conducting technique and rehearsing, select repertoire based on an extensive knowledge of the literature, and guide ensembles in successful musical performances. Beyond a certain point, the background, talent, and creativity of the maturing conductor will come into play. (This is not to say that the education of the developing conductor stops when formal education is completed.) The conductor must continue to grow throughout his or her career. The struggle to discover and improve goes on.

Being a Successful Conductor

In many instances, the developing conductor has a distorted or "fuzzy" view of what it takes to be a successful conductor. The initial training of the conductor must center on conducting patterns and gestures. There is no question that the development and correct execution of these patterns and gestures are an important part of the conducting curriculum, and serve as a foundation for the developing conductor's growth. However, these basic elements of conducting begin to pale in comparison to the other skills that the conductor must develop and the knowledge that he or she must acquire in order to be a successful conductor.

The conductor of a professional ensemble will devote most of his or her efforts to the musical interpretation of the selected repertoire, although there are also many related duties such as organizing, selecting personnel, programming, and public relations. In reality, the conductor in an educational scenario has all of these above responsibilities plus the added tasks of promoting music reading with the ensemble, encouraging the development of technical skills, and fostering collective musicianship within the instrumental music ensemble environment.

A very important part of being a successful conductor is that of being a good musician. Musicianship development is contingent on the training and industry of the developing conductor as well as the continued exposure to quality musical performances. Serious study on a musical instrument with a competent teacher is the initial step in this musicianship development. Musicianship is an all-encompassing term and must be pursued diligently throughout the conductor's career. Private study with a master conductor would provide insights into musicianship development as well. It is important to realize that when there is an "artistic" performance presented by an ensemble, *it is usually because the conductor possesses this higher level of musicality.*

Some conductors will choose to be elementary school, middle school, or high school music directors, while others will continue on into graduate school programs to become college and university conductors. Others may wish to conduct on a semi-professional (community orchestras or bands) or on the professional level. I intend this book to present information and ideas that are usable at all of these levels. When the conducting student begins to make decisions about which level to pursue, I hope this background of conducting and rehearsing will serve as a solid foundation for the continued study in the specific direction.

Likewise, the choice of the type of ensemble to conduct (concert band, wind ensemble, brass band, orchestra, chamber orchestra, string orchestra, pit orchestra, contemporary music ensemble, woodwind ensemble, brass ensemble, percussion ensemble, and other mixed ensembles) will influence this preparation for the maturing conductor. In the beginning, these conducting goals may not be clearly defined or differentiated. Later on, however, such conducting aspirations may become quite specialized. In some circumstances, the conductor may find it advantageous to prepare for several of these avenues of performance.

The maturing conductor must realize that *the development of good conducting technique* is an important part of the preparation necessary to becoming a competent conductor. Subsequently, there is a great deal more preparation to be done in order to reach this level of conducting competency. With these thoughts in mind, I have attempted to disseminate the following information as well as offer some specific ideas that the instrumental music conductor should grasp on the way to achieving this competency as a conductor. Because of the diversity of knowledge and skills required in being a conductor, the task is continuous. For example, knowing the literature and keeping up with new works necessitates investigation, constant research, and continual exposure to fine musical performances. At the beginning, the conductor should accept most conducting opportunities to gain experience in this area of musical performance and then continue to study scores and develop the conducting technique and rehearsing skills in preparation for future opportunities.

In summary, the maturing conductor should nurture a number of specific qualities in the quest to be a successful conductor. These qualities include (1) a congenial personality, (2) effective leadership and organizational skills, (3) superior musicianship, (4) meticulous attention to details in score study and preparations, (5) clear conducting technique, and (6) effective and efficient rehearsing skills. Conducting classes are very important in the conductor's training and education, because this is what conductors will be spending much of their careers doing, that is, conducting and rehearsing! Consequently, conducting students need realistic opportunities to conduct and rehearse an instrumental music ensemble in the conducting curriculum (see Appendix H).

The Training and Education of the Conductor

Courses in basic conducting and score reading, music theory, counterpoint, form and analysis, music history and literature, orchestration, and musical interpretation are all important ingredients in the education of the developing conductor. I recommend that keyboard study, orchestra/band instrument study, and solfège instruction (sight-singing and ear-training) are included in the background of the conducting student. Additionally, such areas as languages, acoustics, visual arts, theater, dance, literature, poetry, architecture, and extensive travel would definitely broaden and enhance the education of the maturing conductor.

As a culmination or outcome of all of this study, the evolving conductor *must strive to develop the mastery for critical listening* so that the time spent on the podium in the rehearsal process translates into good performance productivity. Hearing acutely from the podium is a crucial part of being a conductor. This skill will not develop instantly when the advanced conductor steps on the podium, but unless there is a concerted effort toward and focused sensitivity regarding this important aspect, proper development will simply turn into toleration and moderation from what actually should be heard during the rehearsal process.

I also strongly recommend that *the maturing conductor consider the study of composition and orchestration* as a part of the conductor's education because it will help the conductor to understand the creative process. Specifically with composition and orchestration study, the conductor will recognize good voice leading, have a better understanding of the harmonic analysis, have a precise grasp on the rhythmic and formal structures, and become more fully aware of the elements of orchestration. By dealing with these aspects in actual practice, the conductor will deepen his or her insights in terms of score study and with the realization of what the composer was attempting to communicate musically.

Perhaps one of the most relevant parts of the developing conductor's education is that of being a competent ensemble performer. Until the maturing conductor has had considerable performance experience in a quality ensemble, the musicianship and musical sensitivity needed to lead or perform with others will be lacking. In order to transfer these two qualities into conducting and rehearsing an ensemble effectively, the conductor must have had this practical experience of performing in such instrumental music ensembles. In addition to this, chamber music performance and keyboard accompanying would also greatly enhance these two qualities. Finally, during the conducting classes offered, the developing conductor should *become aware of the standard instrumental ensemble repertoire* in preparation for program building. The conductor needs to develop a perspective about this instrumental music ensemble literature.

SEGMENTS, PROCEDURES, PRIORITIES, AND TEACHING STRATEGIES

Rehearsal Segments and Procedures

Conducting teachers often assume that students have played in various concert bands, orchestras, and other instrumental ensembles rehearsed by a conductor and have learned about rehearsal segments and procedures through this exposure. Obviously, this is not always so. As players, the ensemble members probably focus less on what the conductor is actually doing in the rehearsal process, and are more concerned with the playing of their individual ensemble parts. Acquiring adequate conducting technique and rehearsing skills along with the awareness of the various rehearsal segments and procedures is a continued investigative, developmental, and hands-on process.

Learning about rehearsal segments and procedures involves serious study and observation of the rehearsal process managed by successful and established conductors. *The maturing conductor needs to observe quality conductors and ensembles in the rehearsal process.* Only in this way will the developing conductor begin to feel confident about standing in front of an ensemble and making it all happen successfully. Maturing conductors must seek out opportunities to improve rehearsing skills by making an effort to discover and devise these rehearsal segments and procedures usable in many dissimilar scenarios.

Rehearsal Segments and Procedures Are Somewhat Personal

It is important to realize that this whole area of rehearsal segments and procedures is an individual and somewhat personal one. Perhaps such a book as this has not been brought forth previously because of the very nature of the content. Subsequently, the approach to rehearsing the instrumental music ensemble for the conductor is greatly influenced by his or her personality, the performance level of the ensemble being conducted, and the amount of rehearsal time available before the next concert performance.

However, it may be time to face the reality that many conductors are expected to conduct and rehearse an ensemble with less than adequate background. With trial and error, some of these conductors may succeed in spite of this lack of background. Other conductors will fail miserably in realizing the performance potential of the ensemble. I hope that this book will provide information and direction in the development of this crucial rehearsal process background. *Ultimately, the conductor should progress into a "personal" style of rehearsing based upon a solid rehearsal approach, thoughtful planning, and meticulous preparations.*

Rehearsal Priorities

The maturing conductor should *be aware of the numerous rehearsal priorities* involved within the instrumental music ensemble rehearsal process scenario. The conductor must determine which rehearsal priorities are most important in achieving the formulated rehearsal process objectives and ensemble performance goals. These priorities shift constantly throughout a single rehearsal and from rehearsal to rehearsal. This is expectable while rehearsing the selected concert repertoire with the ensemble. Many of these priorities will become evident by the performance level of the ensemble rehearsing. The conductor should be aware of the strengths and weaknesses of the ensemble and then adjust the rehearsal priorities to meet the needs of the players and the ensemble as a whole.

It is impractical to try to list the many and varied approaches to rehearsing an instrumental music ensemble because the priorities keep changing constantly. Chapters 8 through 16 deal with the various priorities and teaching strategies. The conductor should use these priorities as a basis for designing teaching strategies. For example, if a section in the ensemble seems to be weak in the area of intonation, then the conductor must confront this particular priority with the appropriate teaching strategies.

Teaching Strategy Designing for the Rehearsal Process

The intentions of this book are not to dictate specific rehearsal teaching strategies based on a researched or comprehensive collection of successfully employed methods from the past, or to conclude empirically that specific procedures or teaching strategies should be employed in the instrumental music rehearsal process. Rather, many suggestions and options are presented that can be applied to teaching strategy design in the resolution of technical or musical problems that confront the conductor in the instrumental music rehearsal process. With these ideas in mind, the conducting teacher and students are encouraged to expand these strategy lists (found in chapters 8 through 16) *with their own creative ideas.* These teaching strategy tables at the end of the various chapters advance the idea of opening up discussions on the designing of these teaching strategies.

The Rehearsal Plan and Schedule and Teaching Strategies

The conductor must develop a rehearsal plan and schedule (or general strategy) as well as acquire many teaching strategies to rehearse effectively the instrumental music ensemble. First, the conductor should develop a comprehensive plan or strategy for the rehearsal process that also involves the progression of the rehearsals that follow (that is, an overall rehearsal plan). It is not enough to just study the musical score and then react to what happens during the rehearsal process. The conductor must have a plan and vision to anticipate what is needed to be done in the rehearsal process. *Unless the conductor conceives this planning carefully, the rehearsal process will have little or no direction.*

The conductor comes to the rehearsal process as a teacher and conductor. A rehearsal plan and schedule allows the conductor to teach in a sequential way, and through the various teaching strategies, improve the technical and musical priorities for the ensemble performance. Teaching strategies are important in solving the problems that might occur during the rehearsal process. Varying these teaching strategies should also make for a more interesting and effective rehearsal process for the players.

The comprehensive rehearsal plan and the teaching strategies are designed and revised through careful score study, planning, and preparations before each rehearsal process. As the conductor studies the score, he or she should design teaching strategies to solve specific problems for the upcoming rehearsal process. It is the purpose of this book to offer ideas and suggestions for the designing of these teaching strategies.

Too often, the conductor comes to the rehearsal process totally unprepared to rehearse the instrumental music ensemble. There may be some score study done, but as far as preparing to rehearse the ensemble, the conductor has given little consideration as to how to accomplish this. If the conductor expects to rehearse effectively and efficiently the instrumental music ensemble, *this plan and schedule must be in place.*

THE STRUCTURE OF THIS BOOK

For Class Discussions, Class Demonstrations, and Class Assignments

Sections called *Practical Application (Discussion/Demonstration)* will, I hope, stimulate class discussion, encourage teaching strategy designing, and crystallize ideas to be used in the rehearsal process. They can serve for class discussion or demonstration of the material contained in each chapter. They could also serve as a basis for written examination questions over the various chapters.

Sections called *In the Rehearsal Process (Lab) Environment* provide an opportunity to design teaching strategies for use by the advanced conductor in the rehearsal process. These sessions also stand as a mock instrumental music rehearsal process in which the conducting teacher and/or the conducting students can replicate what might happen during the rehearsal process.

The Demonstration sections at the end of selected paragraphs in chapter 4 (Conducting Technique) offer possibilities for use by the conducting teacher in demonstrating for the conducting students certain aspects of the conducting technique. The conducting teacher through speaking, counting, or singing while simultaneously showing these conducting patterns and gestures could enhance these demonstrations. Starting with the premise that "a picture is worth a thousand words" and that the conducting technique is a "silent art," the conducting teacher may be more effective with the conducting students, in many instances, through demonstrations as opposed to that of simple verbalization. The idea of these demonstrations may then be employed by the conducting teacher in having the students show their understanding of the particular conducting technique or rehearsing skill through their own conducting or rehearsing demonstrations.

At the end of chapters 8 through 16, there are *Teaching Strategy Tables* relating to the material in those chapters. The conducting teacher can use these tables to advance various ideas and suggestions with the conducting student in developing teaching strategies for the rehearsal process. At the bottom of each table, there is a challenge to the conducting teacher and conducting students to come up with other ideas and suggestions in developing these teaching strategies for use in the rehearsal process.

Suggestions for Student Conducting/Rehearsing Projects, Listening Assignments, and Score Study Analysis Assignments are found at the end of each chapter starting with chapter 4: Conducting Technique. The use of these lists by the conducting teacher may be tempered by the availability of the scores and the ensemble music. If recordings are the alternative to the live ensemble, then this may also be a somewhat limiting factor. *A reasonable number of conducting/rehearsing projects should be assigned for student evaluation throughout the semester (or year).* In Appendix F, there are performance area comments and score sheets to evaluate these Student Conducting/Rehearsing Projects by the conducting teacher.

Appendix G provides assignment forms for both CD listening assignments and score study analysis assignments. I suggest that the conducting student should begin to become familiar with some of the standard ensemble literature by being exposed through the listening aspect as well as that of the basic score study analysis. The conducting teacher may ask for these forms to be completed by the end of the semester (or sooner) for the academic grading process.

Appendix H offers ways of creating a rehearsal process (lab) environment so that the students have an opportunity to stand in front of an ensemble and conduct and rehearse. Within these rehearsal environments, the conducting teacher for the purpose of evaluating, maintaining, or improving the conducting technique and the rehearsing skills, can then view and critique these developing conducting students, and use the performance area comments and score sheets found in Appendix F for the various Student Conducting/Rehearsing Projects.

Appendix I lists possible class activities, projects, discussions, demonstrations, and assignments for the conducting teacher and student conductors using this book. The conducting teacher would decide this sequence of events for the maximum benefit of the conducting students. These various activities could then be a basis for the academic grading process.

The Many Uses of This Book

Finally, this book could be used in various advanced conducting courses as well as in many other ways:

1. As a continuation undergraduate instrumental conducting course textbook following the initial (or beginning) conducting course.
2. As a semester instrumental conducting course textbook or as a full-year (or more) instrumental conducting course textbook.
3. As material for conducting master classes in which topics discussed or demonstrated could be selected based on need depending on the participants involved. (The Power-Point presentation that accompanies this book, www.advancedconducting.com, could be effective here.)
4. As a study guide for pursuing a master's degree in orchestral or wind-percussion ensemble conducting.
5. As a study guide for pursuing a doctoral degree in orchestral or wind-percussion ensemble conducting.
6. As a review for conductors who have been away from the academic areas of conducting and rehearsing for some time.
7. As a general review for all conductors by exploring the Recommended Reading at the end of each chapter, by becoming more familiar with the Standard Ensemble Repertoire found in Appendix A, and by viewing some of the Conducting/Rehearsing Videos listed in Appendix E.
8. As a library reference concerning the conducting and rehearsing of the instrumental music ensemble
9. To enhance one's personal and professional growth as a teacher, musician and conductor.

What is involved here—no matter at what level of competency—is that the conductor should always find himself or herself striving to improve the conducting and rehearsing. With this idea in mind, the conductor's success will only be realized if he or she is producing better ensembles, musicians, and performances. It is a continuous struggle. However, the "joy of music" and the "thrill of music" are certainly immeasurable!

Such items as organization, score study, conducting technique, rehearsing skills, phrasing, musicality, listening, sensitivity, communication, and musical interpretation can all continue to be improved through the efforts of the conductor. Advanced conductors might periodically review chapter 17: Conductor Profile and Self-Evaluation to remind themselves of those areas that may need to be improved.

As you begin to work your way through this book, keep in mind that the conducting and rehearsing information and the skills acquired will depend on how diligent and creative you are in applying this information within the given scenario. Since conducting and rehearsing are unique areas of study, *strive to always share your musicianship with others* and be ready to grasp all you can learn from the conducting teacher and through your own individual study.

CONCLUSION: AN EXCITING CAREER AHEAD

The humorous work by Paul Dukas, "A Sorcerer's Apprentice," which became well known through the Walt Disney film, *Fantasia* (or *Fantasia 2000*) offers some food for thought about how things can get out of control if the main character (the conductor) does not understand what should be done (or is incapable of conducting and rehearsing the instrumental music ensemble in an effective and efficient manner). The "Conductor's Apprentice" (or the developing conductor) will find that this can happen in front of an ensemble unless there is adequate score study, careful planning, and meticulous preparation. I hope that this book will give maturing conductors the needed practical information and options for conducting and rehearsing the instrumental music ensemble as they begin an exciting career in music. I also intend this book to serve as a reminder to the experienced conductor of the possibilities that exist for creative leadership. In summary, it is my intent to put forth ideas that will assist and guide the developing conductor in organizing the rehearsal process, selecting appropriate music material, and effectively and efficiently conducting and rehearsing the instrumental music ensemble to produce exciting musical performances. Therefore, the focus of this book is to offer these insights and this guidance in the preparation for a successful conducting career. The following information is the next step on an exciting journey to becoming a competent instrumental music conductor!

Acknowledgments

To Nancy Colson—my wife, who through more than thirty years allowed me to work on this book and listened to my thoughts on the various topics. I am deeply grateful to her for all of her patience and understanding along with our four wonderful children and our seven delightful grandchildren!

To my conducting teachers—Anne Forbes, who started me on the road to being a conductor while in high school and taught me well; Professor William Gower Sr., who taught undergraduate conducting at the University of Iowa and gave me a solid background in conducting; Professor James Dixon (assistant conductor of the Minnesota Symphony, conductor of the University of Iowa Symphony Orchestra, and conductor of the Quad-City Symphony Orchestra), who took us graduate students through all of the nine Beethoven Symphonies in great detail and related his conducting and rehearsing background from Maestro Dimitri Mitropoulos (former conductor of the Minneapolis Symphony and the New York Philharmonic).

To my conducting students and players—A few hundred conducting students and players during my teaching and conducting career have provided inspiration for this book and challenges for me in my fifty-some years of teaching, conducting, and rehearsing. Thanks to all of them for their talent and kindness.

To my book helpers—Many of my friends and colleagues, and especially my two sons, Peter and David, assisted me with this book by providing technological help, proofreading, editing, and suggesting many changes. I also wish to thank Dr. Richard Lee, Professor Emeritus of Journalism, who provided considerable insight into the realization of this book as well as other knowledgeable, kind, and gracious people who have helped in various ways with this book.

Finally, to Bennett Graff, Senior Acquisitions Editor at Scarecrow Press, and his staff for their continued advice and expertise during this publication process.

Part I

THE REHEARSAL SCENARIO

Interlochen Arts Camp World Youth Symphony Orchestra; Jung-Ho Pak, Music Director and Conductor

Chapter One

The Rehearsal Scenario
Infrastructure and Process

THE REHEARSAL INFRASTRUCTURE

The rehearsal scenario should have a solid infrastructure on which to conceive and build an effective rehearsal process. The rehearsal process needs to have this architecture or framework to guide the conductor in the formulation of the various rehearsal segments, rehearsal procedures, rehearsal priorities, rehearsal plan and schedule, and rehearsal teaching strategies. *The rehearsal process should not simply be structured based on conducting and rehearsing the selected concert music*; this will achieve only a part of the necessary rehearsal objectives for the ensemble. Rather, envision the rehearsal process as a whole in which the ensemble performance goals and the rehearsal process objectives can serve as the foundation for the formulation and realization of a successful rehearsal process scenario.

The rehearsal process *infrastructure components* will help the maturing conductor to effectively organize and execute the segments and procedures in the instrumental music ensemble rehearsal process. These infrastructure components are as follows:

1. Ensemble Performance Goals
2. Rehearsal Process Objectives
3. Rehearsal Essentials
4. Rehearsal Priorities
5. Rehearsal Plan and Schedule
6. Rehearsal Teaching Strategies

All of these components must be integrated into a whole—the rehearsal process scenario. The conductor needs to consider these components as he or she formulates what should happen in the rehearsal process. The rehearsal process objectives should connect with the ensemble performance goals in a very real way. The ten rehearsal essentials must become a major part of any rehearsal preparation and rehearsal process. At this point, the rehearsal priorities that need attention in the rehearsal process will begin to surface. Only when the conductor has conceived a rehearsal plan and schedule will it be possible to anticipate the possible problems encountered in the rehearsal process.

The rehearsal teaching strategies are then important for the resolution of these technical and musical problems and for the refinement of these various rehearsal priorities.

Ensemble Performance Goals and Rehearsal Process Objectives

The instrumental music rehearsal process scenario involves the planning and execution of the segments and procedures in the rehearsal process; that is, what should actually happen during the ensemble rehearsal process. Ensemble performance goals and rehearsal process objectives are important parts of this planning and execution. The difference between the goals and the objectives tends to become a "gray area" in many publications. In his book, *Teaching Music*, Dr. Darwin Walker defines a goal as "to be considered long-range in scope, broad in direction, and can be regarded as general in nature" (Walker 1998, 2). However, he defines a rehearsal process objective as "an accomplishment that is short-term in scope, is easily verified and specific in direction, and when properly implemented supports progress toward goal achievement" (3). I use these definitions throughout the book *to differentiate between ensemble performance goals and rehearsal process objectives.*

Formulate ensemble performance goals based on the given scenario. *The goals should be realistic and achievable.* In the final analysis, these goals are a conception of what the conductor wants to realize and achieve with the ensemble. The rehearsal process objectives are formulated based on these ensemble performance goals. These ensemble performance goals are achieved through well-conceived rehearsal process objectives. The rehearsal process objectives are the means to the end (of the ensemble performance goals). The conductor must come to the rehearsal process with clearly defined rehearsal process objectives. Failure to do this will result in a poorly organized rehearsal process and very little accomplished during the rehearsal process.

The three general ensemble performance goals for any instrumental music ensemble as stated previously in the preface are (1) to develop a cohesive, musical ensemble; (2) to improve the performance of the individual players and the ensemble as a whole, both technically and musically; and (3) to prepare repertoire for an authentic, musical, and exciting performance. Certainly, along with these three main goals, the ideas of musical sensitivity, artistic playing, and aesthetic awareness must be fostered. *Other more specific ensemble performance goals conceived and designed by the conductor would depend largely on the given scenario.*

Goals are viewed as important achievements; in most cases they are long-range in scope. (These are not to be confused with rehearsal process objectives, which are short-term in nature, but eventually lead to the achievement of the ensemble performance goals.) In addition to skill development and the dissemination of information in the rehearsal process, other factors in designing goals should include the cooperative attitude of the individual players and the aesthetic aspects of music performance in general. *Specifically, goal formulation involves what the conductor intends to do with and for the ensemble.* How these goals are achieved will vary depending on the conductor, the maturity and performance level of the ensemble, and the timetable of rehearsals and performances. In all cases, formulate these goals for the particular scenario. Evaluate goals periodically to determine the future direction and achievements for the ensemble.

The conductor must conceive and delineate rehearsal process objectives for the players. These objectives should go far beyond simply selecting the music. They must include what the rehearsal process should achieve through the specific music material. *These rehearsal process objectives then act as stepping-stones to the various formulated ensemble performance goals.* The objectives should inherently lead to achieving these ensemble performance goals. Without these clearly defined rehearsal process objectives, the rehearsal process lacks focus and organization. When these objectives are well conceived and defined for the ensemble, positive results should occur in the rehearsal process. The conductor should conceive these rehearsal process objectives before the rehearsal process begins. When the conductor states these rehearsal objectives during the rehearsal process, the players feel that they are a part of a cooperative effort, rather than simply following what the conductor might dictate. If the players understand what is to be accomplished in the rehearsal process, they will "be of one mind" with the conductor. Design rehearsal objectives so that they are achievable during the rehearsal process, that is, by being conceived realistically.

One of the objectives of any rehearsal process is for the players to understand the basis of the particular work. Another is for the conductor to make clear to the players what is expected of them in terms of achievement in the rehearsal process. This assumes that the conductor knows what the ensemble is able to accomplish in a single rehearsal process. By having these specific rehearsal process objectives formulated, the conductor should be able to plan the rehearsal more precisely and measure the results more accurately. With the formulation of these rehearsal process objectives, the conductor can illuminate problems and solutions for the players. In general, some of the rehearsal process objectives might be to (1) acquaint the players with the selected music, (2) solve specific technical and musical problems, (3) capture the beauty, essence, and spirit of the works being rehearsed, and (4) further the progress of the ensemble by concentrating on certain rehearsal priorities that need attention. Having specific rehearsal process objectives should also help keep the rehearsal process moving forward as well as ensure the musical progress of the ensemble.

The rehearsal process objectives of a specific rehearsal defy a listing. There are too many variables involved in a given scenario to make such a listing of any consequence. This is not to say that the conductor should avoid or ignore the formulation of these rehearsal process objectives in the planning of the rehearsal process. On the contrary, this is one of the most important parts of the rehearsal preparation. Without rehearsal process objectives, the rehearsal will lack direction and the steady progress of the ensemble will be curtailed during the rehearsal process. *Carefully formulate, and then subsequently evaluate these specific rehearsal process objectives in terms of achievement after the rehearsal process.*

Some examples of rehearsal process objectives (depending on the situation) include (1) the rehearsing of specific repertoire for the concert performance, (2) the development of reading ability, (3) developing good precision with the ensemble, (4) improving the musical sensitivity of the ensemble, (5) strengthening specific weaknesses within the ensemble, and (6) playing in-tune (intonation). Then, from these general rehearsal process objectives, the conductor should formulate more specific ones that serve the ensemble's needs in the given rehearsal scenario. These detailed rehearsal process objectives are formulated with the consideration of the rehearsal essentials (chapter 3) and the rehearsal priorities along with rehearsal teaching strategies (chapters 8–16).

Rehearsal Essentials

Rehearsal essentials represent the necessary ingredients in any rehearsal scenario. Some of these are part of the planning and preparation before or after the rehearsal process (ensemble personnel, music material, and rehearsal time) and others (pacing the rehearsal, warm-up routine, tuning, listening, sensitivity, communication, music reading, detecting errors, and striving for musicality) occur during the rehearsal process. The essentials during the rehearsal process will also need some advance planning and preparation. I delineate these ten essentials below. They represent those areas that one should consider a part of the basic development of any successful instrumental music ensemble program.

The ten essentials of the rehearsal process scenario are an important part of the infrastructure of the rehearsal process. These essentials serve as a basis for the conductor in organizing, preparing, and executing the rehearsal process effectively. I detail the following ten rehearsal essentials in chapter 3:

1. Selecting and Evaluating Ensemble Personnel—Performance Level, Maturity Level, and the Growth Factor
2. Selecting Appropriate Music Material (see Appendix A)
3. Utilizing Rehearsal Time and the Continuity Factor
4. Pacing the Rehearsal Process
5. Conceiving and Executing the Warm-up/Tuning Period with the Ensemble during the Rehearsal Process
6. Promoting Listening and Sensitivity with the Ensemble during the Rehearsal Process
7. Communication with the Ensemble during the Rehearsal Process
8. Developing Music Reading Skills with the Ensemble during the Rehearsal Process
9. Detecting and Correcting Errors with the Ensemble during the Rehearsal Process
10. Striving for Musicality with the Ensemble during the Rehearsal Process

The planning of the whole rehearsal process is critical in formulating rehearsal process objectives and in planning rehearsal segments and procedures. The conductor must see to it that these preparations take place before or after the rehearsal process (wherein memory can aid in anticipating problems for the following rehearsal process). The essentials during the rehearsal process can be accomplished only if this planning and preparation have been done before the rehearsal process begins. This will require the conductor to be highly organized and willing to spend sufficient planning and preparation time before or after the rehearsal process.

Some of the rehearsal essentials that the conductor should consider and execute before and during the rehearsal process may require this advance planning and preparation. For example, pacing the rehearsal will be successful only if there is a rehearsal plan and schedule in place and the conductor has thoroughly studied the musical scores. The conductor will need to determine selection of music material for the warm-up/tuning period before the rehearsal process begins. Likewise, there must be a plan as to how to implement ideas such as listening and sensitivity in the rehearsal process. Communication with the ensemble during rehearsal process will require the conductor to have studied the score and prepared to make the players aware of the many performance aspects and provide solutions for various performance problems. Selection of the musical material for sight-reading and the improvement of the music reading process will also need some pre-rehearsal planning. The detection and correction of errors can be accomplished only if the conductor has assimilated the score and is ready to conduct the ensemble properly through the selections. Again, if the conductor has not prepared the scores well, the idea of striving for musicality will be impossible during the rehearsal process. *The conductor should be prepared technically and musically in order to gain credibility with the ensemble.*

Rehearsal Priorities

Rehearsal priorities are those performance aspects that one needs to confront with the idea of improving and refining these priorities during the rehearsal process. The conductor needs to consider these rehearsal priorities so there is direction, progression, and ultimately, ensemble improvement during the rehearsal process. If the conductor carefully identifies these rehearsal priorities, then he or she can anticipate and implement the rehearsal plan and teaching strategies properly. The conductor has a clear responsibility for training players in all of the various performance aspects during the rehearsal process. Only if the conductor identifies and addresses these priorities in the rehearsal process will the ensemble begin to show real and steady progress toward achieving the rehearsal process objectives and the ensemble performance goals.

The identification of specific rehearsal priorities to be addressed in the rehearsal process will depend greatly on the particular scenario; the conductor should determine in what order these priorities are addressed beyond the actual rehearsing of the selected repertoire. To some extent, the repertoire may dictate the priorities. However, the performance level of the ensemble, the maturity level of the ensemble, and the rehearsal time available will affect which priorities need to be addressed immediately in the rehearsal process. *The conductor should confront these priorities.* I have divided these priorities into technical and musical priorities for better definition. Here are my formulated rehearsal priorities:

Technical Priorities

- Intonation and tuning
- Rhythms and rhythm patterns
- Ensemble sonority elements: tone, balance, blend, color, and texture
- Articulation and bowings

Musical Priorities

- Tempo and ensemble precision
- Phrasing and the musical line
- Style and musical interpretation
- Dynamics, nuances, and musical expression

Once the conductor confirms and ranks these rehearsal priorities, it then becomes necessary to identify in a particular rehearsal scenario the specific reason behind such rehearsal problems (priorities involved). The conductor should then implement solutions to these problems for the improvement of the ensemble. Some examples of such rehearsal problems might include:

- Flute intonation problems in the upper register
- The performance of certain rhythms and rhythm patterns with the ensemble
- Dynamic levels in the brass sections or percussion section
- Blend and balance problems within the trumpet section
- Slurring (legato tongue technique) in the trombone section
- Phrasing problems in relationship to breathing or bowing
- Style in the saxophone section concerning the articulation and/or vibrato
- Improvement of precision within the whole ensemble or with a particular section of the ensemble (such as the French horn section that tends to respond somewhat late because of the tone production aspect)

This list of priorities and problems could run on in relationship to the performance level of the ensemble and difficulty of the selected repertoire. *The more specifically the conductor can identify these rehearsal problem areas, the more efficient and effective the rehearsal process can be.*

How I group these priorities in this book may be a point of contention with other conductors and musicians, but what really is important is that these groupings provide an organizational basis for rehearsing the instrumental music ensemble. Some conductors might consider the various ensemble sonority elements (tone, balance, blend, color, and texture) individually. Likewise, they might consider tempo and ensemble precision separately. However, the categorizing of these priorities is not as critical as the fact that all of these priorities must be dealt with (at some point) during the instrumental music ensemble rehearsal process.

The conductor must formulate and clarify specific rehearsal objectives based on these priorities. The rehearsal segments and procedures should connect with the priorities that need attention in the rehearsal process. As players, we have all suffered through rehearsals that went nowhere and accomplished very little. To make progress in the rehearsal process, *the conductor must establish these priorities in order to plan the rehearsal teaching strategies.* Likewise, the conductor must keep adjusting these priorities to meet the needs of the ensemble. It is difficult to work on musical priorities such as phrasing and style in the rehearsal process when the ensemble focuses on "chasing notes and rhythms." With such a situation, the conductor must evaluate whether the ensemble is ready for the technical or musical challenges of the selected repertoire. The conductor should treat these priorities with flexibility depending on what occurs in the rehearsal process. Only by identifying the top priorities for the rehearsal process can the conductor then devise the segments and procedures for the rehearsal process, including those priorities that need more immediate attention. As rehearsals continue, the top priorities may change with the ensemble's development and improvement.

Looking at these priorities, the conductor must decide which are the most important of these priorities in a given scenario. Certainly, working on these priorities is necessary in developing a cohesive, musical ensemble. *Which priorities demand immediate attention is a decision the conductor must make.* In general, some conductors might feel that the rhythmic aspect is most important while others might emphasize the importance of style, balance, or intonation. The conductor must strongly determine top priority (or priorities) by the actual performance level and the maturity of the ensemble. As rehearsals proceed, he or she must evaluate these priorities according to the ensemble progress and in terms of what the performance of the selected repertoire dictates.

When the conductor works with the ensemble in the rehearsal process, the selected priorities should match with the problem areas that continually occur during the rehearsal process. If intonation is one of the main problems, then the conductor should include in the rehearsal process teaching strategies and procedures to improve this performance aspect. *Only by confronting this problem will the intonation be improved.* As a specific example, part of the solution might be a more effective tuning procedure to establish pitch level. Other solutions for this problem might be making the players more aware of what to listen for or how to adjust the pitch on their instruments. Only by identifying the specific rehearsal problem areas and working on the solutions to these performance priorities in the rehearsal process will the ensemble ultimately realize its potential.

Some of the problems, such as rhythm patterns, intonation, articulation, balance and blend, could be worked on during the warm-up period with school groups. Other problems might be best resolved in the rehearsal process through the performance of the selected repertoire. In general, rehearsals are for improving these priorities with the ensemble, solving the technical and musical problems, and bringing the ensemble to the highest possible performance level. The level of the ensemble performance, technically and musically, is ultimately determined by *what is accomplished in improving these priorities in the rehearsal process.* Every time a selection is played, there should be some noticeable improvement over the last playing of this selection.

Rehearsal Plan and Schedule and the Teaching Strategies

The rehearsal plan/schedule and the teaching strategies are two aspects that will improve the performance level of the ensemble in the rehearsal process. There needs to be careful planning by the conductor in devising a rehearsal plan and schedule along with these teaching strategies. The rehearsal strategy is a general plan (or outline) of what the conductor wants to happen during the rehearsal process. *Rehearsal process objectives are a part of this plan.* This plan and schedule also involve the warm-up period, the tuning segment, rehearsing of selected repertoire, and other rehearsal segments and procedures as needed. The teaching strategies would be designed based on score study and the anticipation of technical or musical problems as well as what actually occurs during the rehearsal process. The rehearsal plan and schedule and the teaching strategies vary greatly depending on the particular scenario.

There is a continuum of rehearsal preparation for the conductor before the rehearsal process begins, which should include:

• Score study (preparing to conduct and rehearse the music)
• Conceptualizing the musical interpretation (of the various works)
• Discovering the conducting problems (and solving them)
• Anticipating the playing problems (before the rehearsal process begins)
• Preparation of the parts (marking the parts for the bowings, breathing, phrasing, and many other performance aspects)
• Conceiving and planning the rehearsal process (plan and schedule)
• Designing applicable teaching strategies before the rehearsal process begins

I address the last two items on this continuum of rehearsal preparation in this section. The rehearsal plan and schedule is an outline of what should happen in the rehearsal process and *this should influence what happens in subsequent rehearsals.* This involves the segments, procedures, and sequence of events in the rehearsal process. The teaching strategies are the approaches used by the conductor to improve the performance level of the ensemble and to solve specific problems that occur during the rehearsal process. The conductor should be prepared to adapt the various teaching strategies within the context of the particular scenario.

The rehearsal plan and schedule needs to be considered beyond the single rehearsal to the subsequent rehearsals and should be revised throughout the rehearsal timetable to maximize performance achievement and ensemble improvement. The conductor should constantly evaluate and revise the rehearsal process to meet the needs and progress of the ensemble. In general, the rehearsal process must be devoted to realizing the potential of the players and that of the ensemble as a whole. A carefully conceived rehearsal plan and schedule allows the conductor to formulate the rehearsal objectives to be achieved during the rehearsal process (and to design teaching strategies). *The conductor must consider the specific timing of the various rehearsal segments so that sufficient rehearsal time can be devoted to each work.* Finally, the rehearsal plan and schedule should give purpose and direction to the entire rehearsal process.

The rehearsal plan and schedule represents a plan of action for the conductor to use in the rehearsal process. It allows the conductor to determine the segments, procedures, and sequence of events in the rehearsal process. The starting point for the plan is the musical material selected for rehearsal. From here, the conductor must decide what to cover in each particular rehearsal segment. Perhaps the ensemble cannot play and/or rehearse the entire concert repertoire in a single rehearsal. *The assumption is that there will be a warm-up period and a tuning period before the rehearsing of repertoire begins.* The music material used in the warm-up period should be determined in advance and the exact procedure for tuning planned. Each selection may require a different approach because of the various stages of preparation. Some specific details for each of the selections need to be spelled out so that the impression is one of organization and direction in the rehearsal process. Of course, there should be some flexibility if the reality of the rehearsal process takes a different turn than expected. (It is a questionable rehearsal strategy for the conductor to decide to work on some priority at a given rehearsal without relating it to the selected repertoire being rehearsed.) Finally, the conductor may need to change the rehearsal plan for the subsequent rehearsals, depending on what has occurred in the previous rehearsal process.

In developing a rehearsal plan and schedule and in designing the various teaching strategies, the conductor should evaluate the previous rehearsal process. If these teaching strategies do not receive some careful consideration, the conductor may find serious problems and ineffective results in the rehearsal process. The conductor must evaluate the actual ensemble performance level in advance in order to know what he or she can demand or expect of the individual players and the total ensemble. The maturity level will determine the approach (or rehearsal strategy) that the conductor should employ. The conductor should evaluate and anticipate what the realistic potential and expectations are for the specific group before and during the rehearsal process.

The conductor needs to be creative when designing teaching strategies for the rehearsal process. The key to designing these teaching strategies is to have a wide range of options for use in a particular scenario. Teaching strategies are designed by careful planning, by consideration of what works and what does not work, and by rehearsal experience in front of the ensemble. By gradually accumulating numerous teaching strategies over time, the conductor will be prepared to lead the ensemble effectively and efficiently in the rehearsal process. *The conductor must continue to experiment during the rehearsal process to find new ways to solve problems as well.* In the following chapters, I offer ideas and suggestions to help the maturing conductor in devising these teaching strategies in alliance with the rehearsal priorities.

Teaching strategies involve both conducting the ensemble and verbally explaining, modeling, or demonstrating the necessary performance aspects during the rehearsal process. The better the conducting technique, the less need there will be for the conductor to stop the ensemble for explanation, modeling, or demonstration. *The only way that the conductor can be effective in using the various teaching strategies is to have the undivided attention of the ensemble throughout the rehearsal process.* The players must learn to watch the conductor and to follow the conducting patterns and gestures meticulously. When it is necessary for the conductor to stop the ensemble, the conductor should be ready to proceed with the selected teaching strategy and then to immediately indicate to the ensemble where to begin again. Unless the ensemble focuses strongly, the teaching strategies (conducting or verbal) cannot be implemented successfully. Specifically, chapters 8–16 offer ideas and suggestions for designing these teaching strategies within the parameters of the various performance priorities and problem areas.

THE REHEARSAL PROCESS

Specifically, the rehearsal process scenario is an abstract of the segments, the procedures, and the sequence of events in the rehearsal process. The segments in the rehearsal process might consist of announcements, warm-up period, tuning, rehearsing concert repertoire, reading and/or rehearsing new repertoire, sight-reading, and solving the various technical and musical problems. The rehearsal procedures involve the strategy or the course of action to achieve the objectives of the rehearsal process. *The sequence of events in the rehearsal process is the order of segments and procedures as determined by the conductor.* These segments and procedures are very important for the success of the rehearsal process. The conductor should give considerable thought to planning the sequence of events before the rehearsal process begins. There are many factors involved in determining this order.

Many conductors allow an hour or so before the rehearsal to prepare. This is essential especially in terms of preparing the physical aspects (chairs, stands, music, equipment, etc.). However, it is definitely insufficient time for score study along with these other preparations. *The most important preparation is that of score study.* There will need to be other times scheduled for score study. Some conductors may prefer time after the rehearsal to review what has transpired in the rehearsal process and to prepare for the next rehearsal. If you have recorded the rehearsal process, evaluate the taping at this time. In reviewing the tape, write specific notations in anticipation of the next rehearsal process. It is also a time for some serious self-evaluation concerning the conductor's role and his or her effectiveness during the rehearsal process.

The actual conducting of the repertoire and the solving of technical and musical problems should be a large part of the rehearsal process. If this is the focus in the rehearsal process, then there is good reason to believe that the conductor is getting things done. Focusing on these two aspects will avoid too much talking by the conductor and keep the ensemble working on solving problems. The conductor must avoid getting distracted from these two main areas during the rehearsal process. If the conductor has carefully conceived the rehearsal plan and has planned the segments and procedures in rehearsing the ensemble, the conducting and the solving of problems should be a very natural part of the rehearsal process. Unexpected problems that surface in the rehearsal process may be taken care of immediately or else may need to be deferred (and written down) by the conductor in order for these problems to be resolved in future rehearsals. However, the conductor must be careful not to overlook these items at the following rehearsal; these technical or musical errors *would then become reinforced without the proper solutions.*

Segments and Procedures in the Rehearsal Process

By devising a list of segments and procedures similar to the lists below, the developing conductor can use it as a checklist of options during rehearsal, and then subsequently to evaluate the productivity of the rehearsal process. Below is a partial list of some rehearsal segments and procedures that the conductor could employ during the rehearsal process:

Rehearsal Segments

- Warm-up period
- Tuning and periodic tuning
- Conducting and playing

- Modeling and imitation (by the conductor or player)
- Vocalizing or playing for demonstration purposes (by the conductor)
- Ensemble detailed work (and feedback by conductor)
- Employing teaching strategies during the rehearsal process
- Music reading (and sight-reading)
- Problem-solving during the rehearsal process
- Fostering listening and musical sensitivity during the rehearsal process
- Fostering musicianship and artistry during the rehearsal process

Rehearsal Procedures

- Conducting and playing
- Teaching performance concepts
- Teaching for learning transfer
- Making players aware of various performance aspects
- Verbal explanations
- Tuning procedures
- Listening and musical sensitivity procedures
- Training the ensemble to watch the conductor
- Repetition of passages (detailed work)
- Modeling and imitation
- Demonstrations by the conductor
- Rehearsing for details and continuity
- Questioning players for understanding
- Providing players with feedback
- Confrontation and persistence in solving technical and musical problems

The rehearsal process should have a shape and design. Coming to the rehearsal process without a rehearsal plan and schedule can only lead to a less-than-constructive rehearsal process, void of direction and purpose. The segments of the rehearsal process will involve both technical and musical considerations and will vary from detailed rehearsing to playing repertoire straight through to establish continuity. This planning should act as an outline to guide the conductor throughout the rehearsal process. There should be room for flexibility with the rehearsal segments and procedures. However, simply reacting to what might occur during the rehearsal process will not provide sufficient direction for a productive rehearsal process.

All of the items listed above show the kind of segments and procedures that might transpire in the rehearsal process. Psychologically and musically, there are undoubtedly many omissions with these lists. However, this does present a variety of usable options that the maturing conductor should consider in planning the segments and procedures of the rehearsal process. Only by accumulating these usable options through score study, practical rehearsal experience, and observations of other conductors and ensembles will the evolving conductor grow into becoming an effective conductor of the instrumental music ensemble. The advanced conductor should grasp as many opportunities as possible to watch and hear other conductors and ensembles in the rehearsal process *in order to acquire these usable options.*

Variables in the Rehearsal Process Scenario

It would be a simple task to prepare the advanced conductor to be successful if every instrumental ensemble scenario were similar. However, there are numerous variables in the rehearsal scenario including the performance level of the ensemble, the difficulty of the selected repertoire, and the rehearsal time available before the concert performance. Likewise, if it is the very first rehearsal, then the rehearsal segments and procedures might be quite different than if it were the final dress rehearsal before the concert performance. The rehearsal process will vary considerably depending on many factors involved in the given scenario. The segments, the procedures, and the sequence of these events are all dependent largely on the succession of rehearsals in relationship to that of the concert performance.

The conductor should do preliminary research to determine the technical and musical level and aptitude of the ensemble. Questions need to be asked in order to evaluate the given scenario properly. For example, is this a guest-conducting situation or is the regular conductor rehearsing this ensemble? Is this a school ensemble as opposed to a semi-professional or professional group? Is the ensemble cooperative or is it somewhat hostile and undisciplined? Is the ensemble of superior quality or in need of remedial attention? All of these questions plus many more need to be answered so that the conductor *is aware of these variable scenarios.* How the conductor approaches the rehearsal process is extremely important for the success of the ensemble performance and the instrumental program as a whole. No matter what the scenario might be, the conductor needs to consider these variables and plan carefully.

Specifically, the conductor needs to be concerned about the performance level and the maturity level of the ensemble. In addition, the difficulty of the selected repertoire is a variable factor in terms of the approach to the rehearsal process. The amount of rehearsal time available before the concert performance influences the conductor in evaluating and adjusting the rehearsal process schedule. The conductor must approach the rehearsal process based on the technical and musical background and experience of the players in the ensemble. Adjustments to these rehearsal variables might include the pacing of the rehearsal process, the expectations of the conductor, and the planning of the rehearsal segments and procedures. These rehearsal process variables also affect the priorities addressed and the teaching strategies employed.

Rehearsal Format, Timetable, and Progression

Many of the conducting books touching on the subject of rehearsal segments and procedures concentrate on presenting a specific format for the rehearsal process. This is rather restrictive and perhaps not too imaginative. Creatively, the conductor needs to proceed according to a preconceived schedule without being locked into a strict format of rehearsal segments and procedures. Specific rehearsal objectives will need to be formulated, and thereby, guide the conductor throughout the rehearsal process. *It is important to have some routine in the rehearsal process*, but not to the extent that it is predictable or that it leads to loss of interest and concentration on the part of the players.

The "opening" and "closing" of the rehearsal process are important considerations. *The opening will set the focus and concentration level for the rest of the rehearsal process.* This is why the warm-up period is so crucial in establishing this concentration and focus for the school ensemble. Likewise, the opening should reflect the planning and conceived rehearsal process objectives as well as the sequence of events in the rehearsal process. *The "closure" planning will also help conclude the rehearsal process satisfactorily.* Even if there have been some unexpected changes in the rehearsal process, the conductor should strive to bring the rehearsal process to this "closure." In this way, the players will leave the rehearsal with enthusiasm and excitement in anticipation of the next rehearsal process. This will also encourage the players to practice their parts outside of the rehearsal process.

As mentioned above, *the conductor should design an exact timetable* not only for planning a single rehearsal process but also to be conscious of the continuity of rehearsals leading up to the concert performance. In many cases, this timetable may need revision as rehearsals go forward. The pace of this progression will be somewhat dependent on the frequency, spacing, and continuity of these rehearsals. Continuity of rehearsals is an impacting factor on the success of the ensemble. If there is only one rehearsal per week as opposed to two or three, then the approach to rehearsing might need to be designed differently. With one rehearsal per week, the conductor will probably want to cover the entire concert repertoire at each rehearsal; otherwise the players might only rehearse a selection every two weeks. This would lead to considerable loss of memory as to what had occurred in the previous rehearsals.

Finally, the conductor must carefully plan the progression of rehearsals to ensure that the ensemble has accomplished the technical and musical performance aspects by the time the scheduled performance arrives. *It is very easy to misjudge this progression.* The results will then be a less-than-satisfying concert performance. The conductor should know exactly the length of each piece so that the rehearsal schedule can be determined properly. If the work is a difficult one, then the conductor must allow for additional detailed work and repetition on that particular work during the rehearsal process. As the conductor and ensemble approach the concert performance time, they should place more emphasis on the musical aspects of the concert performance.

There is always a lurking danger of under-rehearsing or over-rehearsing the ensemble for a concert performance. The conductor needs to evaluate the performance level and potential of the ensemble, so that the rehearsal preparation is adequate for the concert performance. Under-rehearsing usually results in an erratic performance and over-rehearsing causes a lack of freshness and vitality in the concert performance. This is why it is so important to plan carefully and continue to revise the overall rehearsal plan to avoid either of these pitfalls. Continuity between rehearsals is a factor to consider in the problems of under-rehearsing or over-rehearsing. In a sense, there is never enough rehearsal time, so the danger of over-rehearsing is less than that of under-rehearsing. In the final analysis, the conductor must devote the rehearsal process to those priorities and performance problems that need attention.

While preparing for the concert performance, the conductor should continually strive to raise the performance level of the ensemble during the rehearsal process. This is where the rehearsal priorities (listed earlier in this chapter) become important factors in raising the level of the ensemble performance. *Most ensembles have weaknesses that need to be confronted and improved.* The conductor should determine the priorities that need to be refined with the particular ensemble, and subsequently devote more rehearsal time to those priorities. For example, such priorities as intonation and precision are crucial to raising the ensemble performance level. By focusing on these rehearsal essentials and rehearsal priorities, the conductor and ensemble should be able to achieve this higher performance level.

Unpredictable Events and Problems in the Rehearsal Process

Realistically, some of the events and problems that may occur in the rehearsal process are unpredictable. The better the conductor knows the score and the ensemble's performance potential, the less will these unpredictable events and problems impact. *In a sense, the conductor must be ready for any such eventualities.* How does the conductor do this? The answer is in good preparation. The main consideration must be the music; this involves careful score study, good rehearsal planning, and meticulous preparation. If the conductor comes into the rehearsal process unprepared, the ensemble will not make much progress. Through careful score study, planning, and preparation, the conductor can guide and instruct the ensemble, resulting in a productive rehearsal in spite of unpredictable events and problems.

These unpredictable events during the rehearsal process are probably too numerous to mention. However, most of these events concern the music being rehearsed. The absence of specific players would curtail the rehearsing of certain repertoire. There may be unavailable instruments or equipment. In both of these instances, good rehearsal planning prevents such negative events. There might be events that are uncontrollable by the conductor, in which case the conductor should simply proceed on to Plan B. When these unpredictable events do occur, *the conductor must show some flexibility and patience in dealing with these particular events.* Such circumstances will present an opportunity for the conductor to remain calm and continue in a creative manner. The ensemble players will appreciate this kind of a response rather than one of frustration or possibly anger from the conductor.

One of the main reasons for having rehearsals at all is solving technical and musical problems in preparation for the concert performance. The experienced teacher and/or "master" conductor will have anticipated these problems in the rehearsal process. *The maturing conductor will need to consider such problems as a learning experience in the early years of his or her conducting career.* If he or she views the experience in this manner, the advanced conductor will soon find that there are fewer unpredictable problems occurring in the rehearsal process. The maturing conductor should prepare as well as possible for the rehearsal process, and when confronted with the unpredictable problems in the rehearsal process, proceed by trying to solve these problems or delay them until a proper solution can be devised for the next rehearsal process. The players will respect the conductor more if the conductor defers solving these problems immediately, as opposed to "covering up" such deficiencies during the rehearsal process.

In the final analysis, the conductor must "be in charge" during the rehearsal process. The conductor must be assertive, and thereby, determine the direction of the rehearsal process. If unpredictable events or problems do occur, the conductor should decide whether to solve them immediately in the best interest of the ensemble during the rehearsal process. If not, then the conductor must find a way to return to the planned events quickly and effectively. If a problem warrants an immediate solution, the conductor can resolve it and return to the planned rehearsal process. Unpredictable events or problems must not distract or interfere with the rehearsal process. Wasting time in the rehearsal process will result in a loss of conductor credibility and will curtail preparation for the concert performance. I discuss this area of guiding the rehearsal process by the conductor in more detail in Chapter 3: Ten Rehearsal Essentials (specifically Essential No. 3—Rehearsal Time and Essential No. 4—Pacing the Rehearsal Process).

Keeping Records of Progress and Noting the Problems in the Rehearsal Process

Conductors should keep good records of what transpired from one rehearsal process to the next. This can be done in two basic ways: (1) If the conductor feels that memory is strong, then he or she can immediately following the rehearsal process note what needs to be taken care of for the next rehearsal process (I recommend that this be done soon after this rehearsal process), or (2) either an audio recording or an audio/visual recording of the rehearsal process can make a more permanent record of the problems encountered. The use of superior recording equipment will result in a more realistic "picture" of what occurred particularly in terms of precision, intonation, balance, blend, articulation, phrasing, etc. and this will dictate where more work is needed. The recording of rehearsals can be very beneficial for the conductor in checking tempos, rehearsal decorum, discipline, and the results achieved from the conducting technique. *Recording the rehearsal process will provide another evaluation tool for the conductor.*

Tape-recording the rehearsal process allows the conductor to listen, and then evaluate the results of the rehearsal process. In many instances, the conductor will find that he or she has overlooked certain items during the rehearsal process. *Because there are so many things occurring at the same time in the rehearsal process*, the conductor will focus on a specific problem and may be distracted from other problems that have surfaced. With the recording, the conductor can listen to the rehearsal process in a less complicated environment and prepare more meticulously for the next rehearsal process. After the conductor has had considerable experience in front of the ensemble, the need to record all of the rehearsals may be somewhat mitigated. However, if the rehearsals are intermittent or occur infrequently, the conductor may need to record the rehearsal process so as not to overlook important items during the intervening time but use them to prepare for the next rehearsal process. The conductor should make thorough notes from the recording in preparation for the following rehearsal process.

Reviewing the tapes of the preceding rehearsal process in preparation for the upcoming one allows the conductor to revise the rehearsal process objectives, determine the future segments and procedures, organize the sequence of rehearsal events, design teaching strategies for learning efficiency in the next rehearsal process, and realize musical interpretation. Also, the conductor should keep these rehearsal notes for comparison with previous rehearsals and evaluations. The conductor should continue to study the score to discover more details, such as subtle nuances, and to improve the musical interpretation of the concert repertoire. *The conductor should continually evaluate the preparation status of each work in readiness for the concert performance.*

Teaching for Learning Transfer in the Rehearsal Process

In the rehearsal process, the conductor becomes a teacher. To be an effective teacher, the conductor must accumulate and design teaching strategies. Daniel Kohut gives two options about teaching music in the rehearsal process: (1) teaching through demonstration, and (2) analytical teaching (1996, 9). This implies that the conductor must make careful preparation to ensure that effective teaching and learning take place. *The "hands-on" approach of instrumental music performance by the conductor will maximize learning and skill development in the rehearsal process.* Finally, it is important to remember that teaching and learning are most effective in a positive rehearsal environment. If there is sound teaching, then learning transfer occurs in the rehearsal process. Effective teaching involves learning that will transfer from one situation to another; rote learning procedures do not accomplished this. In any good teaching and learning situation, there must be an understanding of these music performance concepts that will transfer to other rehearsals, performances, and ensembles.

The conductor must teach performance concepts for the transfer of playing skills and the acquisition of information for future repertoire and in other music environments. In this way, by teaching for learning transfer, the players will become less dependent on the conductor (teacher) and will begin to make their own valid musical decisions. As the players begin to make such decisions, the conductor can bring the ensemble to the next higher level of performance. Likewise, when the players respond properly to the conductor's patterns and gestures, the ensemble will begin to move from one rehearsal to the next with a real sense of progress.

The conductor should be disseminating information *in the form of performance concepts as much as possible in the rehearsal process.* A concept is an idea or group of ideas summarized into a statement that will apply to situations beyond the immediate concern. Teaching by concepts encourages players to solve technical and musical problems by themselves. When the conductor makes a correction, the players should be aware of and understand the concept and its application in other performance scenarios. The players need some latitude in solving performance problems. Verbal comments or musical demonstrations by the conductor concerning either a technical or musical problem should also get a response from the players that may apply to more than the immediate problem or situation. In most scenarios, the players are there because they want to improve the performance level of the ensemble; the conductor should realize this and approach the rehearsal process from this standpoint. The conductor should guide the players in making their own musical decisions through the teaching of performance concepts in the rehearsal process.

Sound teaching in the rehearsal process involves the fundamental elements of instrumental performance as well as those of musicianship. These two basic components of sound teaching will carry the conductor through the rehearsal process and prepare the players for artistic performances. However, the conductor who is constantly under pressure to produce the next performance *will tend to manage the rehearsal process for expediency*, thereby ignoring the more valuable teaching aspects of the rehearsal process. The conductor will be forced to proceed in a manner that will negate sound teaching of the music fundamentals and the transfer of information and skills in such scenarios. Only if there is sufficient time in the rehearsal process will the conductor be able to teach soundly in a calm and focused atmosphere. The conductor should not try to cover too much repertoire in one rehearsal process. It may be necessary for the conductor to evaluate the schedule and repertoire selection, and then revise the schedule or repertoire so that sufficient time is allowed for sound teaching in the rehearsal process.

Rehearsal efficiency improves by finding some similar items to pursue during the rehearsal process. If the problem in the rehearsal process is a particular rhythm pattern, all of the players that have that particular rhythm pattern in the selection can rehearse. This will require the conductor to grasp where in the score all of these rhythm patterns exist and who is playing these patterns. Such an example can be found in Beethoven's *Seventh Symphony* with the performance of the dotted-eighth, sixteenth, and eighth-note rhythm pattern. This is an example of the kind of rehearsing that will make the players realize that the conductor is well prepared and trying to be as efficient as possible in the rehearsal process. *Throughout the rehearsal process, the conductor should also try to keep the whole ensemble involved in the rehearsal process so that player concentration does not wane.*

Dr. Edwin Gordon defines aptitude as a product of innate potential and musical exposure (1971, 25). The idea of teaching concepts will only be effective if the aptitude of the players is such as to understand these conceptual statements and their application for later use in their musical performance. *The conductor can only make effective demands on the ensemble if the aptitude of the players is sufficient to comprehend these concepts.* In many instances, the conductor's comments should suggest a transfer or progression to the next similar occurrence in future rehearsals. The conductor must work at this in the rehearsal process by reinforcing performance concepts with the specific intent of the player transferring these concepts to other rehearsals and performances. In summary, the conducting patterns and gestures of the conductor along with verbal comments on performance concepts should act as stimuli for the players during the rehearsal process, and thereby, carry these concepts over to these other rehearsals, performances, and ensembles.

Miscellaneous Items in the Rehearsal Process

During the rehearsal process, no matter how carefully the conductor has studied the score, *there are interpretation details to confirm.* This is not to say that the conductor should come to the rehearsal process in order to practice on the ensemble. The conductor needs to come to the rehearsal totally prepared musically. However, in the rehearsal process, the conductor should constantly be comparing his or her conception of the musical interpretation to exactly what is occurring. Only in this way can the conductor bring the ensemble to a reality that is in agreement with that of the previous score study. During the rehearsal process, the conductor may also discover a better interpretation of the passage than originally conceived. Then this change of musical interpretation needs to be reinforced with the ensemble in the subsequent rehearsals. Another situation to confirm in the rehearsal process is tempo. Even though the conductor may have decided on the tempo(s) for the work, it may become apparent in the rehearsal process that this tempo will be impossible for the clean execution of a particular passage. The conductor will have to reconsider these tempo decisions. There are numerous other ways whereby the actual rehearsal process may confirm or change the conceived musical interpretation somewhat.

The conductor should consider the rehearsal plan and schedule in light of the repertoire to be rehearsed. He or she should come to the rehearsal process with a plan and schedule of segments and procedures written out. This plan and schedule should also show the estimated time to be spent on a particular work, and where and what will be rehearsed in detail. The total length of each piece may influence some of the rehearsal plan. There may be some digression from this plan and schedule if it is warranted during the rehearsal process. The conductor should devise this plan and schedule beforehand and revise it after the rehearsal process in anticipation of the next rehearsal. *Simply rehearsing by going from one selection to the next* is an indication to the players that the conductor does not have a rehearsal plan and schedule. The players will notice this quickly and the conductor's credibility will certainly suffer.

When certain personnel are no longer needed during the rehearsal process, *players may be excused from the rehearsal process.* The conductor should try to arrange the schedule to accommodate the larger ensemble instrumentation at the beginning of the rehearsal process. This will occur more often with the orchestral ensemble, because instrumentation varies from one musical period to another. The players do appreciate this consideration by the conductor so that they can pursue other activities or obligations in their otherwise busy schedules. This also helps build respect and credibility for the conductor, who then appears to be organized and sensitive to the needs of the players. If the ensemble members are in a school situation, however, it may not be possible to excuse the players from the school schedule.

BUILDING A COHESIVE, MUSICAL ENSEMBLE

Building a cohesive, musical ensemble must be a continuous performance goal of the conductor. This is a long-range goal in most cases. If possible, during each rehearsal process, devote some time to pursuing this goal. This performance goal may be interspersed in conjunction with the solving of technical and musical problems and the rehearsing of the concert repertoire. *Certainly, formulate the rehearsal objectives with the idea of building this cohesive, musical ensemble.* These rehearsal components must exist if the ensemble is to grow to the next level of performance. In all of this, it is important for the conductor to gauge how much can be expected of the ensemble at any given time. If these expectations are unrealistic, then the conductor and ensemble will experience considerable frustration in the rehearsal process. The two important factors in achieving this main goal of a cohesive, musical ensemble *are ensemble precision and musicianship.*

The factor of uniformity is also important in the rehearsal process; this involves many performance aspects such as tone quality, balance, blend, intonation, articulation, and bowing as well as those of dynamics, style, and phrasing. In developing a cohesive, musical ensemble, the conductor must consider this idea of uniformity because without it, the ensemble will tend to sound erratic and inconsistent. Much of the rehearsal time must be devoted to the development and achievement of this uniformity. For example, uniform bowing in an orchestral ensemble will immediately make the ensemble more cohesive. Another aspect of uniformity involves watching the conductor. Unless the entire ensemble is watching the conductor and striving for this uniformity, the quality of the performance will be less than desirable. Only by reinforcing this uniformity idea in the rehearsal process can the concert performance be successful.

In building a cohesive ensemble, the conductor should focus on ensemble precision. It is important to realize that without good ensemble precision many of the other performance aspects will be difficult to improve. Everything must be performed together before such aspects as intonation, rhythm, balance, blend, articulation, phrasing, and style can be adjusted properly in the ensemble rehearsal process. To achieve good ensemble precision, the players must watch the conductor as well as listen to the rest of the ensemble. The attacks at the beginning of phrases and the releases at the end of the phrases are important performance areas that will need constant attention. *The conducting technique should be so clear that the players are confident about these attacks and releases.* I address details of ensemble precision in Chapter 12: Tempo and Ensemble Precision, and details on listening and musical sensitivity in Chapter 3: The Ten Essentials of the Rehearsal Process Scenario, Essential No. 6.

There can be little hope for fine leadership of an instrumental music ensemble unless the conductor has proper training. Unfortunately, there are too many poorly trained conductors or "time-beaters" in the profession. In some cases, the would-be conductor has no conducting background whatsoever. The reality of this situation is that many musicians find themselves on the podium without a sufficient background in conducting technique and/or without adequate rehearsing skills. They have gained this "conductor" status by being fine musicians in an ensemble or as an instrumental soloist or music teacher, *but have not studied the art and craft of conducting.* Conducting involves developing this conducting technique in the same way as a player would on the specific instrument. The second leadership problem is that many conductors do not allow sufficient time to study the score, and therefore, depend almost totally on learning the score during the rehearsal process. *This makes effective communication with the ensemble impossible.* With this lack of communication, poor and unmusical playing will result both during the rehearsal process and in the concert performance.

If the ensemble is aware of both the technical and musical problems of a particular work, the ensemble will then tend to project itself to a higher performance level. This awareness must come forth based on the conductor's musicianship and leadership. The authentic interpretation of a work requires continuous score study and the designing of teaching strategies by the conductor to communicate *the composer's intentions to the ensemble.* It cannot be stressed too strongly how important the conductor's musicianship and leadership are in the rehearsal process. Even during the rehearsal process, the players should be experiencing an expressive and musical performance; the conductor has the responsibility of seeing to it that this happens. In the rehearsal process, the conductor should strive to inspire the players. Unless the conductor has shown this musicianship and leadership in the rehearsal process, the ensemble will not reflect this inspiration during the concert performance.

Unity or cohesiveness is the key to developing a fine instrumental ensemble. Add to this the qualities of musicianship and musical sensitivity and the rehearsal process begins to move in a very meaningful direction. The conductor should try to give the players as much insight into what is involved in a "musical" performance as possible during the rehearsal process. Certainly one of the aspects that the conductor must stress is practicing the music before the rehearsals, so that the rehearsal process can then be devoted to ensemble considerations rather than to just "chasing notes and rhythms." *The conductor can help this expectation by providing a schedule for the following rehearsal or rehearsals, so that players will know what they are expected to practice.* On occasion, the conductor might distribute a detailed sheet to the players delineating those places that need practice and improvement in their parts. The conductor must strive to create an atmosphere of musicality and musical sensitivity in the rehearsal process. This will require the conductor to be creative and ask the question, What could be more important in the rehearsal process than to focus on musicianship and musical sensitivity?

In summary, *ensemble precision, musicianship, musical sensitivity, communication, and uniformity* during the rehearsal process will happen only if the conductor is well prepared through meticulous score study and the organizational aspects have been put in place before the rehearsal process begins. It is crucial for the conductor to realize that a great deal of preparation must go into all of this before the actual rehearsal process will be successful. During the rehearsal process, there should be an integration of these five elements as the rehearsal progresses. The musicianship and leadership of the conductor should be very evident in every rehearsal process.

PRACTICAL APPLICATION (DISCUSSION/DEMONSTRATION)

1. Make a list of some ensemble performance goals to achieve within a specific rehearsal scenario.
2. What are some rehearsal objectives that the ensemble might achieve immediately in the rehearsal process? What rehearsal objectives might take more time to achieve?
3. What would you (as a conductor) want the rehearsal process scenario to be like? (How would you get this done?)
4. Review and discuss briefly the Ten Essentials of the Rehearsal Scenario as outlined above (see chapter 3 for details also).
5. What items should the conductor note in studying the score that would anticipate conducting and playing problems?
6. What are the eight (technical and musical) rehearsal priorities? What might your top priorities be in a given scenario? Why?

7. How would the rehearsal priorities dictate the teaching strategies in the rehearsal process? What is the reason behind the problem?
8. What items would you include in the rehearsal process schedule and plan?
9. What are some of the rehearsal segments and procedures to you would use in the rehearsal process as listed in this chapter? (Discuss these areas briefly.)
10. What are some of the rehearsal variables present and/or unpredictable events and problems that might occur in the rehearsal process?
11. How would you proceed to keep records of ensemble progress and begin to solve problems for the next rehearsal process?
12. How should the conductor approach teaching for awareness and learning transfer in the rehearsal process?
13. What are some specific factors involved in building a cohesive, musical ensemble?
14. Discuss the ideas of leadership and musicianship for the conductor in the rehearsal process.
15. Discuss briefly some of these conductor leadership characteristics: score study, rehearsal preparation, organization, conviction, confidence, punctuality, cooperation, persistence, enthusiasm, credibility, patience, consistency, flexibility, spontaneity, creativity, and musicality.
16. Begin to gain familiarity with the standard repertoire found in Appendix A of this book through CD listening, score study, and guidance from the conducting teacher. (See Appendix G for assignment forms.)

RECOMMENDED READING

Farkas, Philip, *The Art of Musicianship.* Areas covered include musicianship, phrasing, dynamics, tempo, rhythm, articulation, expression marks, intonation, ensemble playing, relationship with colleagues, and conducting.

Gordon, Edwin E., *The Psychology of Music Teaching.* Part one covers musical aptitude and part two is concerned with musical achievement.

Green, Barry, and W. Timothy Gallwey, *The Inner Game of Music.* Chapter 10: Teaching and Learning with the Natural Learning Process.

Kohut, Daniel L., *Instrumental Music Pedagogy* (paperback version). Chapter 8: Ensemble Rehearsal Procedures addresses areas to consider in the rehearsal process.

Kohut, Daniel L., *Musical Performance: Learning Theory and Pedagogy.* Part 2 of this book emphasizes basic principles and methods of teaching.

Labuta, Joseph A., *Teaching Musicianship in the High School Band.* The book is about the rehearsal process and improving the musicality of the high school instrumental music ensemble.

Lisk, Edward S., *The Creative Director: Alternative Rehearsal Techniques.* Chapter 1: Rehearsal Structure with the Director Awareness Scale Instructional Process graph at the end of the chapter.

Long, R. Gerry, *The Conductor's Workshop: A Workbook on Instrumental Conducting.* This workbook supplies the conducting student with many short, but well-conceived exercises for conducting technique.

Peters, G. David, and Robert F. Miller, *Music Teaching and Learning.* Chapter 10: Assessment (personal and professional) addresses the school music conductor.

Schleuter, Stanley L., *A Sound Approach to Teaching Instrumentalists*. Chapter 4: Teaching Rhythmic Feeling adheres to the Edwin E. Gordon thesis of tempo beats, meter beats, and melodic rhythm patterns.

Walker, Darwin E., *Teaching Music: Managing the Successful Music Program*, 2nd ed. Among other items, the book covers the areas of leadership, motivation, discipline, housing, equipment, and the music library.

Chapter Two

Creating the Rehearsal Environment and Climate

Creating the rehearsal environment and climate involves three distinct categories: the physical aspect, the psychological aspect, and the musical aspect. These three aspects require careful planning and thorough preparation. To a greater or lesser extent and depending on the given scenario, *the conductor is responsible for the planning and execution of all three of these aspects.* The rehearsal environment and climate should reflect the conductor's organizational ability. Pre-rehearsal planning might include among other things such items as meetings about bowings (with the concertmaster or section principals), conferences with staff members as well as players, run-through with the soloist, and guidance for the librarian and equipment manager by the conductor. In addition, the planning and preparation should also include everything that would ensure a successful rehearsal process.

The rehearsal environment and climate may seem like rather similar terms. Specifically, the rehearsal environment refers to the scenario in a physical sense. The idea behind the rehearsal climate (or aura) is the "prevailing quality in thought, behavior or attitude of the people participating in the rehearsal process" (Roget's *Thesaurus*, 1988). *The climate relates more to the psychological and musical aspects of the environment.* Establishing a good rehearsal scenario by the conductor allows the players to realize their potential and ensures the improvement of the ensemble. A disorganized, ill-equipped, poorly disciplined, or unmusical environment would all contribute negatively to any rehearsal process. Two of the most important items in creating the rehearsal environment and climate are the planning and preparation.

To establish this "right" environment and climate is a critical part of the conductor's work. Progressing as an ensemble involves raising the performance level. An environment and climate that is not conducive to concentrated and focused rehearsing will fail to produce this higher performance level. The ensemble will not realize the rehearsal process objectives and performance goals unless the "right" environment and climate exist. *The conductor must be in charge of this rehearsal process.* The ensemble must be cooperative and ready to respond to the conductor's patterns and gestures, to go forward with the rehearsal procedures selected, and to understand the explanations and teaching strategies employed during the rehearsal process.

A UTOPIAN REHEARSAL ENVIRONMENT AND CLIMATE

The ideal (or utopian) rehearsal environment and climate can be realized only through the efforts and guidance of the conductor. It will not happen automatically or instantly. However, if after some length of time this "right" environment and climate are not well established, the conductor may need to reconsider what is happening that prevents the rehearsal process from approaching this utopian rehearsal environment and climate. Then it is up to the conductor to make some changes in the scenario so that the ensemble members will achieve their highest possible performance level and realize their potential.

The conductor must envision exactly what the rehearsal environment and climate should be in the particular scenario. It is the conductor's responsibility to implement this before, during, and after the rehearsal process. Here are some considerations:

1. Is there good organization in the rehearsal environment?
2. Is the ensemble of one mind as to what to accomplish in the rehearsal process?
3. Is the conductor prepared for the rehearsal process?
4. Have the players prepared their parts well before the rehearsal process?
5. Are the conductor and players ready to concentrate intensely during the rehearsal process?
6. Have the players progressed to the point of playing sensitively and musically with the other members of the ensemble?
7. Are all of the players in the ensemble watching the conductor to respond to the nuances and subtleties of the musical interpretation?
8. How much should the conductor tolerate in the rehearsal process in terms of talking, distractions, and other possible losses of concentration?

Certainly, in order to achieve a utopian-type environment and climate in the rehearsal process, much long-range planning and careful preparations are necessary. Not every rehearsal process will be perfect; such a rehearsal environment and climate will take time to evolve, and in some circumstances may never quite be realized. However, as time goes on, the conductor with some concerted effort in these various rehearsal aspects should see improvement within the rehearsal scenario. The following sections cover the specific aspects that will lead to this kind of a rehearsal environment and climate—now let us consider the physical aspect, the psychological aspect, and the musical aspect in detail.

THE PHYSICAL ASPECT

The conductor must consider the necessary preparations of the physical aspects of the rehearsal environment. The physical aspects include the chairs, the music stands, seating arrangements, the music, the music library, the music folders (with pencils), the folio cabinet or rack, the chalkboard or other visual displays, the tuner and other electronic devices (including recording equipment), lighting, temperature/humidity/

ventilation control, instrument storage, access to special instruments and equipment (such as harp, synthesizer, metronome, mutes, etc.) and risers, shells, podium, a rehearsal resource center as well as other equipment needed to enhance the rehearsal environment. Even though many of these physical aspects seem rather pedestrian, these are items that should be anticipated; the conductor will need to spend time and effort in planning and seeing that these physical aspects are available and "in place" for the rehearsal process.

The chairs and music stands can be considered together. With some instruments, it will be one chair and one stand, but generally it is two chairs and one stand. (There should never be three players on one stand; this will prevent at least one of the players from watching the conductor because of poor sight lines.) One of the main considerations with chairs and stands is that there is *adequate performance space for the various instruments.* Some players physically need more space than others, due to the size and technical nature of the particular instrument. String players need more space than do the wind instrumentalists in most instances, because of the motion of the bow. Cellists and bassists in particular need more space because of the size of the instrument along with the bow motion. (Usually the bassist will be most comfortable with one on a stand; however, this could hamper difficult page turns.) French horn players and flutists also need space because of the way in which they hold the instrument to the side. The percussion section, depending on the kind and number of instruments, generally requires a large amount of space as well as careful organization. Space requirements here are concerned with music stands and the various percussion instruments; most percussion playing takes place in a standing position (exceptions are the timpani and trap set). Percussionists need many separate stands because of the size and spacing of instruments; they also need music stands to keep sticks, mallets, and other equipment handy. When using a music stand as a table to lay this equipment on, it is advisable to have a protective carpet, towel, or cloth to eliminate the possible noise of placing sticks, mallets, and other equipment on these stands.

Instruments needing additional space in a seating plan include flute, bassoon, saxophone, horn, trombone, tuba, and string instruments (for bowing). If the rehearsal hall or concert stage will allow it, the conductor should experiment with opening up the spacing between players to enhance the sound of the ensemble. Besides the sound aspect, *the visual aspect is an important factor in the successful performance of the ensemble.* The view of the ensemble should give the impression of planned organization and neatness within the ensemble. As mentioned previously, risers and platforms can help the sound and visibility of the ensemble for the audience in a performance. In consideration of chairs and stands, here are some thoughts about ensemble seating:

1. Players should have the stands at a height and placement that will allow good sight lines to the conductor and yet be able to read the music without the constant adjustment of the eyes or head.
2. Conductors should experiment with space between chairs; Dr. John Paynter, late Director of Bands at Northwestern University, recommended placing chairs some distance apart to allow the sound to reverberate, in contrast to those conductors who choose to compact the ensemble (supposedly) for security purposes.

3. Use risers and platforms for both audio and visual advantages. The riser or plat-
   form will expose the ensemble for better visibility to the audience and aid the players in watching the conducting patterns and gestures. Woodwind sounds tend to
   be buried in the orchestral ensemble unless they are placed on a higher level with
   risers or platforms.
4. Horns need to have some reflection of their sound either against a wall or with
   some material placed behind these players.
5. Do not point directional instruments within a section at a 90-degree angle to
   each other; this will negate the sound and cause some unevenness in terms of the
   sectional balance.

At this point, it would seem proper to discuss the positioning of the various instruments in a specific seating plan or arrangement. There are many published seating
diagrams, and therefore, a repeat of this material would be redundant. Sources listed
at the end of this chapter contain some examples of these diagrams. This does not
mean that such matters are unimportant. Decisions regarding the placement of the
instruments are crucial in terms of ensemble tone, balance, blend, precision, and
the general performance success of the ensemble. *The conductor is responsible
for the instrument placement in the ensemble.* The conductor should use standard
seating arrangements until he or she finds a more suitable one for the ensemble. On
pp. 391–94 in *The Art of Conducting*, Hunsberger and Ernst present some standard
seating diagrams.

The final decisions about the seating arrangement are best left to the discretion
of the conductor based on (1) previously published seating charts, (2) standard or
traditional seating plans, (3) the creativity of the conductor, (4) the acoustics of the
rehearsal and performance halls (including curtains and shells), (5) the size of the
ensemble, (6) such practical performance considerations as strengths and weaknesses
within the ensemble, and (7) the placement of the directional instruments. Some
experimentation may be necessary to determine the most effective seating plan. The
available space in the particular performance facility may be a contributing factor in
this instrument placement. Duplicate this placement in the rehearsal hall.

The orchestra seating is standard with some slight variations. These variations
include the interchange of the viola and cello sections and the placement of first and
second violins on opposite sides of the conductor. Occasionally, the string basses are
placed in a slightly different position. The woodwinds have a standard placement with
the principal players together to improve hearing among these parts. There are sometimes slight changes in the brass and percussion families due to space availability.
The placement of special instruments, such as harp, piano, celesta, and saxophones,
tends to be determined by the prominence of their parts in the musical context of the
ensemble. Piccolo, English horn, bass clarinet, and contrabassoon are usually placed
at the end of their respective sections.

The concert band traditionally has shown more flexibility in instrument placement.
Because much of the concert band instrumentation consists of wind instruments, the
conductor must take care to place the various instruments in a position that will enhance the balance and blend of the ensemble. Some of the instruments, such as the

trumpets and trombones, are directional instruments and can pose balance problems in relationship to instruments that have less projection potential. For example, one could place these directional instruments in a straight line and played toward the conductor. If some of these directional instruments are placed so that they are playing directly into each other, there will be a cancellation of the sound. The strengths and weaknesses of the various sections of the ensemble in a given scenario could also be determining factors in the concert band seating arrangement.

The wind ensemble instrumentation tends to be placed in straight lines facing out toward the conductor and audience rather than in the semi-circle arrangement of the band and orchestra. This is because the wind ensemble as constituted has many parts with only one musician on a part (or two musicians depending on the projection potential of the instrument), and the point is that the conductor with this ensemble should be concerned with good clarity of the lines and balance of the parts. Positioning the instruments may require some experimentation to discover what will work best for the particular ensemble and the selected repertoire. Risers and platforms can enhance the wind ensemble performances.

Smaller combinations of instruments could be based on the orchestra or band alignment with adjustments to suit the selections and the ensemble space. In some works for special ensembles, the composer may provide a seating plan within the score. Particularly in contemporary music, the composer may wish to space or group the instruments in such a way as to enhance a certain combination of instruments. On occasion, there may be a need to place the instruments in an antiphonal situation to realize the composer's intentions. There are many ways to configure this seating. Smaller ensembles may need to use shells.

Base the decision about instrument placement in the ensemble on five main points: (1) the directional sound of the particular instruments, (2) the proximity of the related voice parts to each other (such as soprano, alto, tenor, and bass), (3) the family of instruments, (4) similarity of parts, and (5) the overall balance and blend of the ensemble. Certainly the volume of sound that potentially can be produced by the specific instruments, and the placement of instruments with unique considerations, such as the French horn where the sound is delivered backward, or the percussion section (although they may be the most visually attractive instruments in the performance), seem to be relegated to the back of the ensemble or to the conductor's left side and these should also be considered in terms of placement. The percussion section can also benefit from having more space so that the taller instruments do not obstruct the vision of the players toward the conductor. Seating of the ensemble can be problematic because of weak sections, balance problems, and general acoustics. The conductor might experiment with various seating arrangements from time to time. Therefore, the conductor should carefully plan the physical rehearsal environment (such as positioning the strings somewhat obliquely so that all of these players can see the conductor better).

Dealing with the Music

Obtaining the music can be problematic in certain situations. A knowledgeable and efficient music dealer can be of great help for the instrumental conductor in locating the various selections. These music dealers are in constant contact with the publishers and distributors, and are able to locate the desired composition. Likewise, the conductor *can search the Internet for* music material through large music establishments or by the specific selection. Particularly with the orchestra, much of the repertoire is available through rental. The standard orchestral repertoire is available for purchase or through rental from Edwin F. Kalmus, a music publisher in Florida, or Luck's Music Library in Michigan. In some instances, the individual composer or publisher of the work may need to be contacted directly to obtain the specific music. There are also other publishers and outlets such as Educational Music Service, Boosey and Hawkes Rental Library, G. Schirmer, Inc., Presser Music Company, and Broude Brothers that handle music above and beyond this standard repertoire. With more recent works, the conductor may need to do some research to find who is publishing or handling the newer compositions. In many cases, the publisher will be able to furnish perusal scores to help the instrumental music conductor decide on the particular selection before making the purchase or rental. An important source for orchestra repertoire is David Daniels's *Orchestral Music: A Handbook*, 4th ed. For the concert band, Frank L. Battisti's *The Winds of Change* is one of the current literature resources.

The music, music folders, music cabinet or sorting rack, and the music library are considerations in establishing the physical rehearsal environment. The conductor who does not have the music "ready to go" before the rehearsal process risks losing some respect from the players because of the obvious lack of good organization. This also involves some advance planning and preparation of the music. These items include selecting the music, obtaining the music (purchase or rental), marking the music, having it placed in the music folders or assigned to players, and then organizing the folders in a cabinet, sorting rack, or another system for quick access. (In some scenarios, the music librarian is responsible for having this music in the folders or placed on the proper music stand before the rehearsals begins.) Especially with orchestra music, the conductor and/or librarian needs to be knowledgeable about instrument names in foreign languages for the correct organization of the music into the folders (such as fagotto, cor, tromba, tamburo, pauken, gross trommel, and many other foreign words for the various instruments).

Along with score study, the conductor may find it necessary to mark the parts with bowings and fingerings (positions), meter changes, key changes, dynamics, articulations, accents, phrasing (breathing and bowing), balance changes, and vertical marks for both pulse identification and style indications before they are placed in the folders. In addition, the conductor could highlight certain instructions such as pizzicato, arco, mute, open, clef changes, cuts, repeats, special effect markings, and many other kinds of indications. Marking the parts before the rehearsal in this manner will save time during the rehearsal process. The conductor must take into consideration the maturity level of the players when deciding which items in the parts to mark. Student and amateur groups probably need more help than does the professional ensemble in this regard.

Check rehearsal numbers or letters to determine that there is a sufficient amount of these numbers or letters as this will save considerable time in locating specific measures during the rehearsal process. Sometimes having each measure numbered can be beneficial in identifying the spot. Likewise, score and parts comparison can detect printing errors or omissions. Having music folios with a pencil pocket and pencil can provide for the quick marking of parts during the rehearsal process. Inevitably, some marking will be necessary during the rehearsal process as the occasion arises.

The music library must be well organized *with cross-indexing of the composer and the selection for efficient access.* Today most music libraries are cataloged on database software. With this technology, the conductor or music librarian can now organize music into many different categories and access it quickly for consideration. A large sorting table, a music sorting rack, or a music folio cabinet will make it easier to organize and distribute the music. Keep the music in score order. (This requires that the music librarian knows score order for the particular ensemble.) Replace lost or damaged parts and scores immediately. In some cases, the musical scores may be indexed and kept in a separate place for conductor access.

Visual Strategy

The attractiveness and organization of the rehearsal room is an important consideration for the conductor. Chalkboards, bulletin boards, or other ways of displaying material and disseminating information in the rehearsal room or hall are appropriate in organizing the rehearsal environment. Visual strategy should also be aesthetically pleasing to enhance the environment. Colorful (and musical) posters or pictures add to the aura of the rehearsal facility. In educational settings, display playing and rehearsal concepts in large print as a reminder to the players—such as "Listen!" The rehearsal area should be clean, neat, and organized to reflect the efficiency of the conductor. *In this way, the conductor has the opportunity to be creative and enhance this visual environment.*

All kinds of important announcements can be displayed in the rehearsal environment to reinforce what the conductor might otherwise announce during the rehearsal process. This could save some valuable rehearsal time by simply calling these announcements to the attention of the players for them to follow up after the rehearsal process, with a reminder if needed. Likewise, the conductor should list the order of pieces for the rehearsal process with not only the title, but also the composer and other significant musical information. This is so that the ensemble is ready for the next selection in the rehearsal process. A PowerPoint presentation might be a possibility to display these important announcements or the repertoire.

The chalkboards or bulletin boards in the rehearsal environment could be used to show (1) the order of selections to be rehearsed, (2) a list of scheduled coming events, (3) other important announcements and reminders for the ensemble, and (4) the displaying of this needed information as a teaching tool (on a lined chalkboard) during the rehearsal process. Chalkboards, bulletin boards, charts, pictures, posters, and other wall displays serve to inform the participating musicians of important items and at the same time keep the surroundings attractive. PowerPoint technology (if this equipment is available) in the rehearsal hall could certainly be an effective means to use for visual strategy. By listing the repertoire for the upcoming rehearsal process on the chalkboard, the players can be ready to rehearse the next selection. *This is particularly helpful for the percussion section* because they must organize the various instruments. Such a listing also indicates to the ensemble that the conductor is organized and prepared for the rehearsal process.

Special Instruments and Equipment

An electronic tuner, recording equipment, and other necessary devices should be available in the rehearsal area. In addition, there should be access to special instruments, such as piano, harp, synthesizer, and unusual percussion instruments (wind machine, thunder sheet, bell tree, etc.). Special equipment such as a metronome, mutes, and video equipment should also be a part of the rehearsal environment. In the orchestra rehearsal area, there are such items as bass chairs or stools, cello boards or stoppers, available strings, and storage racks for cello and bass. In the band and orchestra rehearsal area, the percussion instruments and equipment would predominate in terms of special needs. Organize sticks and mallets for quick access during the rehearsal process. In both ensembles (orchestra and band), there might be a need for special mutes for brass instruments or for reeds and pads for the woodwind instruments. The more permanent equipment found in the rehearsal environment could be obtained through the Wenger Corporation in Owatonna, Minnesota.

There are numerous tuners available for use in the rehearsal process. The stroboconn, strobotuner, Johnson tuner 520 model, and the Korg AT-12 are examples of these tuners. I recommend employing a tuner that sounds the pitches (tone-generated) before the tuner that visually indicates pitches as flat, sharp, or in-tune. If the common procedure is for a particular instrument (and player) to sound a pitch in establishing a pitch level for the ensemble, it is important for that player to have a tuner available to secure the accuracy of the pitch. Then another tuner could also be available for the players to check individual pitches before the rehearsal process begins.

The recording equipment needed in the rehearsal process should include a stereo playback system, along with a turntable, CD player, double cassette deck with remote control, high-quality speakers, and good microphones. *The quality and placement of microphones* in the rehearsal environment will greatly enhance the recording fidelity of the ensemble during the rehearsal process. A review of this rehearsal tape by the conductor can help to evaluate the ensemble progress in the rehearsal process and be a rehearsal evaluation tool in general. Recording the rehearsal process can be of tremendous value in preparing for future rehearsals and the concert performance. Consideration of the recorded quality is important to the conductor during this evaluation of the rehearsal process.

Since the percussion section comprises so many and varied instruments, this is also a consideration for the conductor in having the needed instruments and equipment available in the rehearsal environment. The percussion section leader should be the driving force in seeing that the instruments and equipment are organized, maintained, and available as requested by the conductor and as needed for the work at hand. Cymbal stand, percussion workstation, timpani mallets, concert snare drum sticks, gong mallet, bell mallets, chime hammers, and much more are all part of this percussion equipment. It is crucial that all of these percussion instruments and equipment are organized and in satisfactory playing condition. Contemporary music demands a great variety and number of percussion instruments as well as the auxiliary equipment to be available. The percussionist should be encouraged to purchase some of these sticks and mallets and to be able to wrap mallets and maintain this equipment.

Risers or Platforms, Shells, and Conductor's Podium/Stand

The permanent or portable equipment such as risers or platforms, shells, and the conductor's podium/stand are important components in the rehearsal hall or room. Having these items available and integrated properly into the particular environment helps instrumental ensemble players to hear each other and see the conductor. *Portable risers or platforms, movable shells, and the adjustable conductor's podium/stand are better for the obvious reasons that they can be adapted to the various situations.* Duplicate this same setup as much as possible in the concert hall to avoid conductor or player disorientation. Risers or platforms for some of the instruments such as woodwinds and brass can enhance both the visual and audio aspects for the ensemble.

The conductor's podium and stand come in a variety of forms. The podium and stand differ in that the stand has little or no resemblance to the podium, and in many cases, involves a regular music stand that moves easily. In all instances, the conductor's stand needs to be adjusted to the desired height. One of the most important considerations is the height of the podium as conductors come in various sizes from short to tall. Some conductors may need no podium at all, while others will require a rather high one. The crucial concern is always the sight lines of the players, so the conductor is able to communicate visually with the ensemble. Place the conductor's podium and stand somewhat beyond the ensemble so that the conducting patterns and gestures are clear to all of the players. (In the rehearsal process, an additional stand could be positioned by the conductor's stand to hold extra music or the rehearsal plan and schedule. The conductor's stand may also have a shelf below.) A conductor's chair or stool on the podium may need adjustment for a clear view of patterns and gestures.

The use of risers, platforms, or staging will enhance the ensemble visually and audibly both in the rehearsal process and in the concert performance. I recommend portable risers on a flat floor above permanent, built-in risers. This allows for flexibility in positioning the various instrumental sections. The acoustical shells or panel system will reflect the sound of the ensemble forward to the audience and in most cases help the players hear the rest of the ensemble better. As mentioned previously, adjust and place the conductor's podium and stand properly to achieve maximum visibility of the conductor by the players. In doing this, the main consideration is for the players to be able to see the conductor's beat patterns and gestures comfortably.

Room Controls, Instrument Storage, Instrument Repair Room, Practice Rooms, Office Space, and a Rehearsal Resource Center

Temperature, humidity, and ventilation control and accessible instrument storage are essential aspects in making the rehearsal area as pleasant and comfortable as possible for the participants. Temperature and humidity control are absolutely necessary in places where stringed instruments, harpsichord, piano, and woodwind instruments are played and/or stored. Ventilation (air-conditioning and heating) control is important for the player's comfort, especially in the rehearsing of large ensembles. Instrument storage should be secure, with convenient and easy access to the rehearsal area. All of this will help provide a rehearsal environment in which the players can concentrate and respond well.

Lighting should be above or behind the ensemble and not in the eyes of the players (which often occurs with lighting trees). Ventilation (blowers or fans) should be controllable and silent during the rehearsal process. Instrument and other storage such as a percussion cabinet, string instrument storage racks (especially for cellos and basses), and other instrument and equipment storage should be a part of the rehearsal environment. There are many storage units available for these instruments and equipment.

Instrument repair facility (containing repair equipment, workbench, supplies, etc.), practice rooms, office space, and a rehearsal resource center are important auxiliary parts to the rehearsal environment. To upgrade such an environment that presently does not have these facilities may take some long-range planning and persuasion between the administrative personnel and the conductor concerning the necessity for these changes. Purchase portable practice modules with environmental control of the acoustics if space and financial resources are available. Other larger adjoining rooms (soundproofed) can provide for smaller ensembles and sectional rehearsal space. In most instances, an office for the conductor and the music library should be in close proximity to the rehearsal facility if possible. The rehearsal resource center might contain the stereo system with speakers, turntable, cassette player, and CD player, a keyboard and a computer.

Audio Characteristics

Having considered all of these physical aspects above, the bottom line *is whether the conductor can hear the players from the podium* in terms of what is being produced in the rehearsal process. If the conductor cannot hear the various players of the ensemble with a true perspective of the sound, the efforts put forth by the players and conductor will depreciate. The acoustical characteristics of the rehearsal room are significant for performance success. The proper application of acoustical tile or panels, floor material, carpeting, adjustable curtains, adjustable doors, ceiling height, and so on are all very important elements in the physical rehearsal environment.

I must stress two considerations here: (1) the acoustics in the rehearsal environment must be adequate so that the players can hear what is happening within the surrounding sonority, and (2) the conductor must foster in the rehearsal process *the ideas of listening and musical sensitivity.* If the players cannot hear each other because of poor acoustics or distortions in the room, then much rehearsal time will be wasted. (The recommended reverberation time is 1.50–2.00, although this might vary with the size and makeup of the instrumental ensemble.) If these two considerations are not present, then the ensemble will have great difficulty in achieving finesse in terms of intonation, balance, blend, and precision in the rehearsal process. I discuss this in depth in Chapter 3: The Ten Essentials of the Rehearsal Process Scenario—Essential No. 6: Listening and Sensitivity.

If the concert is held in a different location from most of the rehearsals, then a rehearsal or two should be allowed in the concert hall before the performance. Failure to do this will mean that the players may be somewhat uneasy about playing in the new location and the performance will suffer. Most of the adjustments pertain to the acoustics in the performance facility. It will require some time and careful listening in the performance hall to achieve this desired precision, balance, blend, and intonation. With a performance hall that is considerably different from the rehearsal facility, such performance aspects as tempo, style, and dynamics may need adjustment before the concert performance. Sound checks for the ensemble before the performance will be absolutely necessary.

THE PSYCHOLOGICAL ASPECT

Creating a good climate psychologically is not nearly as concrete or easily accomplished as the physical aspects of the rehearsal environment. In essence, the various messages that the conductor sends to the players constitute *the psychological aspect in the rehearsal environment.* The conductor needs to convince the players that they are there for the improvement of the total ensemble as well as for their individual progress as players. The attitude and verbal feedback of the conductor in the rehearsal process should help the players become more confident about making some of their own musical decisions. Psychological messages, which should permeate the rehearsal environment and climate, *are those of excitement, challenges, accomplishments, and especially musicality.* The following are some of the messages that the conductor needs to transmit to the players during the rehearsal process:

- I (the conductor) am interested in making this ensemble as cohesive and musical as the potential will allow.
- I respect your ability and musicianship as players.
- I have prepared well and I expect you to do likewise.
- I do not intend to waste time in the rehearsal process.
- I want to help you as individuals and as a group to play better.
- I want to establish a rehearsal process that is efficient and effective.
- I want to make you aware of the ensemble sonority and the relationship among the various parts (expressive and structural features).
- I want this ensemble to be based on sound, fundamental musicianship (tone, rhythms/rhythm patterns, articulation/bowing, style, phrasing, intonation, tempo, balance/blend, dynamics/nuances/musical expression, and precision).
- I want this ensemble grounded on the proper fundamental techniques of posture, embouchure, breath control (winds), bow control (strings), stick control (percussion), articulation, finger technique, etc.
- I want you to feel a sense of accomplishment in the rehearsal process. Your contribution is important to the ensemble.
- I want you to grow as a musician and ensemble member through intense concentration in this rehearsal process.

- I want you to feel the "joy" and "thrill" of playing in this rehearsal process.
- My praise or criticism of your performance is sincere and stated for constructive purposes only.
- I want you always to strive to do your best.
- I want you to feel self-confident about your playing. (The conductor should send the message that he or she has confidence in the players to make good decisions.)
- This is a cooperative venture between the conductor and the ensemble.

The conductor should deliver these and many more in a way in which the players are not getting mixed messages. This involves the quality of consistency from the conductor. In summary, in the rehearsal process, the conductor should create this positive, comfortable environment and a climate of cooperation and mutual respect with the players. This will contribute to the rehearsal process objectives and ensemble performance goals that are to build a cohesive, musical ensemble, to prepare for a musical performance, and to help realize each individual player's potential, technically and musically. It is important to realize that in the rehearsal process, *there are always elements of confrontation and compromise.* This is inevitable in the process of solving rehearsal problems. How the conductor handles these problems with the ensemble will greatly determine the success or failure of the ensemble and its conductor.

It is important in the rehearsal process that the players respond in a positive way toward the conductor and what is happening in the rehearsal process. This is not necessarily an immediate response in every scenario. However, over time this positive response must be sustained in the rehearsal environment. Otherwise, the conductor must somehow "change the game plan" so that the players' attitude and work ethic will show this positive response. This attitude involves a number of aspects I discuss later in this chapter, such as motivation, enthusiasm, concentration, and discipline. This is necessary for the rehearsal process to be productive, resulting in the improvement of the ensemble, for the progress of the players and for the preparation of the concert repertoire. For example, if the response from the players is such that the conductor is unable to be productive in the rehearsal process, then the conductor must evaluate and discover what he or she can do to change this scenario. Leaving this situation as it exists will only cause frustration with the players and "burn-out" for the conductor.

Motivating the Ensemble

Motivation will be accomplished in many different ways. Every conductor must find his or her way to motivate the players in a given scenario. With good preparation for the rehearsal process, the conductor will gain considerable credibility with the ensemble. Much depends on the ensemble maturity and the formulated ensemble performance goals as to what the successful approach will be in motivating the ensemble. One very important reason in motivating any ensemble is to attain from each player individual practice outside of the rehearsal process, and thereby to maintain and improve the performance level of the ensemble, technically and musically. In the rehearsal process, the conductor should constantly strive to challenge the group to play better. Gear these motivational techniques to the level of the ensemble. The conductor should hold out the "carrot" so that the players are always striving for a higher performance level. This can be done in many different ways before, during, and after the rehearsal process.

Rapport, cooperation, and mutual respect—all of these terms relate to motivation. The conductor must initiate this motivation. The eventual goal is to achieve self-motivation from the players. The quality of leadership in motivating players at every level becomes evident in the final product. This is not to imply that if the performance is good that the method of motivation is necessarily proper and valid. Fear and guilt—the great motivators—may achieve a good performance, but will probably not realize a great performance. Especially at the educational level, if not in the professional ranks, there needs to be some consideration given to how the players feel about the means to the end. The conductor, in most instances, should know the names of the players and call them by first names in the rehearsal process. *The selection of music can certainly be a motivational factor with most ensembles.* If they feel that the music is worth rehearsing and playing, they will work more intensely in the rehearsal process and practice the music outside of the rehearsal process more diligently. The challenge is in playing the music at the highest possible performance level, and not in winning superior ratings, plaques, or trophies.

Daniel L. Kohut (1985, 90–91) recommends the following techniques for external motivation (in the school environment):

1. Gain the respect of your students by demonstrating your knowledge of music and ability as a musician.
2. Praise the students when they deserve it, and do it enthusiastically and sincerely.
3. Give the students specific performance goals to work toward; provide them with a sense of purpose.
4. Give your students a sense of achievement.
5. The best motivator should be the music itself.
6. Schedule enough public student performances so that students always have a concrete goal—a real reason to practice and improve.
7. Probably most important is to stress small ensembles.
8. Invite guest conductors to rehearse your ensembles, and guest clinicians to give master classes to your students.
9. Provide a good balance between the study and practice of fundamentals and real music.

At the professional level, much will depend on the musicality of the conductor; it will take a very short amount of time for the players to evaluate the conductor. This positive evaluation will motivate the professional player to cooperate and achieve a great performance. The professional conductor must come before the ensemble *totally prepared musically* and proceed in a straightforward, businesslike manner. There may be exceptions to this approach such as Sir Thomas Beecham, who was able, through his sheer personality and uniquely humorous nature, to gain respect from the professional ensemble. (In a television interview with the young Maestro Leonard Slatkin, I asked whether he ever felt intimidated by players twice his age. His reply was that

within a few minutes after the rehearsal process begins, the players will make a judgment in terms of respect and cooperation.) There is no need to present yourself in any
other way than "to be yourself" and to be well prepared musically. The ensemble will
make an individual and collective judgment regarding your leadership and musical
qualifications. The conductor's musical interpretation can certainly be a motivational
factor for the professional ensemble.

Concentration, Discipline, and Enthusiasm

Rehearsal concentration involves the lack of distractions and an ensemble intensity
that the conductor must initiate in the rehearsal environment. It is worth contem-
plating that frequent stops to make corrections in the rehearsal process may lead
to these distractions and a loss of concentration. Frederick Fennell stated that in a
conducting seminar with the famous Eastman Wind Ensemble, he kept rehearsals to
a minimum, but the concentration level was always very high. (In some situations,
this might even mean taking away a visible clock as a distraction in preventing
"clock-watching.") How the rehearsal process begins is a factor that the conductor
should consider. Likewise, the conductor should find ways of involving most of the
players in the rehearsal process to avoid lapses in concentration. He or she can effectively pursue this rehearsal concentration during the warm-up and tuning periods
of the rehearsal process. One of the main goals for the conductor is keeping the
ensemble alert for the entire rehearsal process. Discipline within the instrumental
music ensemble encompasses two areas:

1. The usual idea of not allowing talking, inattention, or other distractions to occur in
   the rehearsal process
2. The mental discipline in music performance necessary to play well throughout the
   rehearsal process

There are many points to discuss in the area of discipline. In the instrumental music
ensemble rehearsal process, the conductor should acquire a sense of group dynamics;
this is just as important as a psychological approach with the individual player. This
is because the conductor is dealing with the whole group. The use of psychology in
the instrumental music rehearsal process involves a massive amount of material; I do
not attempt to include this information here. The eventual goal with any ensemble is
for the members of the group to develop into a strongly self-disciplined ensemble. The
conductor should avoid embarrassment to the players whenever possible; this can foster a belligerent attitude from the players or, in some cases, intimidation and a loss of
self-confidence. *By making the rehearsal process a cooperative effort, the conductor
can diminish discipline problems considerably.* The rehearsal environment needs to be
a quiet, thoughtful one in character. This does not necessarily mean absolutely no talking by the players, but it depends on the scenario and whether this talking would detract from teaching and learning in the rehearsal process. The conductor should speak
softly, not loudly, to get the attention of the players. If the atmosphere of the rehearsal
process is one of talking or distraction, the conductor must find ways to eliminate this

behavior. If the rehearsal environment will not allow for this concentration, teaching, learning, and musical improvement, then it must be changed.

One of the keys to discipline problems in the educational rehearsal environment is consistency. The conductor must be consistent in discipline procedures and the treatment of the players. The conductor should not send mixed messages by being inconsistent from rehearsal to rehearsal. The expectations of the conductor with the players should reflect this consistency. *The conductor must treat the players with respect and yet firmness.* The conductor should always be consistent about his or her performance evaluations of the players. The bottom line for discipline or classroom management in the educational rehearsal environment is what the conductor will tolerate, and this should be at an attention level that will allow for effective teaching, learning, and wonderful music making. Below are some ideas proposed by Dr. Darwin Walker (1998, 57) concerning discipline principles applicable to school ensembles:

1. Be sure that the students understand the reasons why certain behavior is expected and what that behavior is.
2. Be generous with praise.
3. Young people need to be needed. Make them part of the ensemble.
4. Young people who are interested and active are rarely behavioral problems.
5. Keep class activities moving.
6. Be firm, be fair, and "mean what you say."
7. Be consistent.

Enthusiasm in the instrumental ensemble rehearsal is an important ingredient in maintaining concentration and discipline. In selecting the music to rehearse and perform, consideration must be given to repertoire in which the conductor can generate strong interest and enthusiasm for the music. *Initially, the conductor needs to be excited about the repertoire.* Then the ensemble, in the way that the music is presented to them by the conductor, will "catch fire." Closure is important at the end of the rehearsal process to give the impression of good planning in order to retain the enthusiasm for the music and for what has transpired in the rehearsal process. Enthusiasm for what is going on in the rehearsal process can decline if the conductor is constantly stopping for corrections or for detailed work that tends to disrupt the flow of the rehearsal process. If the music is too difficult presently for the ensemble, it will necessitate the conductor stopping frequently. In such circumstances, the conductor may need to consider different repertoire. *Likewise, a generally negative attitude on the part of the conductor can curtail rehearsal enthusiasm as well.* The conductor needs to stimulate interest and enthusiasm through various procedures in the rehearsal process and be an inspiration to the ensemble. The rehearsal process should be a rewarding experience for the players.

Attitudes in the Rehearsal Process

Finally, in the discussion of the psychological aspect of creating a rehearsal environment and climate, the prevailing attitude of the conductor and players becomes an important factor. The conductor must come before the group in a professional way with the thought of accomplishing as much as possible to improve the ensemble performance. The conductor's preparations for the rehearsal process are paramount in "getting things done." The conductor's attitude must be a positive one and consistent from rehearsal to rehearsal. This preparation involves meticulous score study along with all of the other physical preparations discussed previously. The final ingredient would then be the musical aspect that follows this section.

Likewise, this positive attitude by the conductor should pervade the entire rehearsal environment and climate, so that the players are motivated to acquire this same attitude. The conductor comes before the ensemble under the presumption *that the players are also there to achieve the planned rehearsal process objectives.* The conductor must state these rehearsal objectives clearly to the players during the rehearsal process. The development of good player attitude is both a long-range and short-term situation. The development of this attitude involves many factors before, during, and after the rehearsal process. Certainly, the personality and preparation of the conductor are important factors here. The conductor can only expect a positive attitude from the ensemble if there is rapport, cooperation, and mutual respect. Every conductor should sense how the ensemble is responding to the conductor and make changes if the response is not a positive one.

The player's attitude registers in various ways not only during the rehearsal process but also before and after the rehearsal. The conductor will need to observe this in the way the players behave and approach the rehearsal process. If the player seems to be intent on getting the instrument out of the case and adjusting the instrument for the beginning of the warm-up period in a constructive way, it is a good indication that the player has the right attitude. If the warm-up is done (or begun) individually, the conductor should observe whether the player executes this warm-up properly. If the ensemble warm-up is executed as a group, the conductor should observe the demeanor and attitude of the players in terms of alertness, concentration, and cooperation. The end of the rehearsal process should be one in which the conductor feels that the individual players are leaving the rehearsals enthusiastically and with a sense of accomplishment. Here, there may be some individual or section playing just to clear up a passage. There may be some discussion about the music or the whole rehearsal process in general. I hope the players are not running for the door to escape because of what has transpired during the rehearsal process!

Teacher-Student and Conductor-Player Relationship

Both the teacher-student and the conductor-player relationship need to be fostered carefully. Although there are similarities between these two relationships of teacher-student and conductor-player, there are obvious and yet subtle differences. In the classroom, the teacher-student relationship will vary considerably based on the philosophy of the teacher and the approach to classroom instruction that the teacher finds to be effective. The classroom teacher is dealing mostly with cognitive information and individual student evaluation as opposed to the conductor, who is trying to develop performance skills and musicianship with the ensemble in addition to the informational aspect of teaching and learning in the rehearsal scenario.

In the conductor-player relationship, rapport, cooperation, and mutual respect must predominate. Without these qualities present in the rehearsal process, the rehearsal process objectives and ensemble performance goals cannot be achieved. With the conductor-player relationship, the development of performance skills and musicianship is a gradual task and the achievement takes place over an extended period. The conductor should evaluate where each player is in the developmental process and provide the necessary guidance for this continued development. The conductor must find the way in any given situation to impose on the players a sense of self-responsibility in order to realize this continued development in the rehearsal environment. To attempt to list ways of fostering this relationship would involve at least another volume on the psychology of conducting and teaching. This will only to suffice to say that these positive relationships are a necessary part of the conducting, the teaching, and the whole ensemble rehearsal process.

The developing conductor must realize that these relationships between the conductor and players need to be fostered carefully. *Especially for the advanced conductor, he or she must guard against being too flippant or for wanting everyone to like the conductor immediately.* This relationship will need to be fostered over time and be based on respect and credibility. If the conductor has prepared well and treats people with dignity, the players will eventually respond in a positive way. This may require considerable patience on the part of the conductor in a given scenario. Again, the conductor should evaluate the progress periodically in fostering this relationship with the players, and if needed, make an effort to change the approach.

Presence and Aura

The rehearsal environment should have a presence that fosters this rapport, cooperation, and mutual respect. The conductor must set the tone for the rehearsal environment and climate *by allowing the players to ask questions and have the freedom to be creative.* However, the conductor at the same time should control this psychological environment to maintain the concentration and discipline needed in the rehearsal process. This involves both the physical aspects and the psychological aspects discussed above. The psychological environment should not be threatening or hostile to the players; otherwise, the players will not respond positively in the rehearsal process. This presence involves the conductor's personality and attitude as well as many other physical and psychological factors in the given rehearsal scenario.

In addition to this psychological aspect, an aura or ambience of musicality should pervade the rehearsal process. The conductor, of course, is mainly responsible for fostering this aura of musicality. This is accomplished through the conductor's musical approach and by making musicianship and musical sensitivity the primary goals in the rehearsal process and the concert performance. In the final analysis, this will happen only if the conductor's musicianship is on a very high level, and he or she is able to communicate this musicality and musical sensitivity to the ensemble during the rehearsal process. In the rehearsal process, the conductor accomplishes this communication through the conducting patterns and gestures along with verbal comments and demonstrations.

The conductor should make every effort to enhance the surroundings musically. The rehearsal process must not deteriorate into just "chasing notes and rhythms," as this will only be a very small part of what is to be accomplished in the rehearsal process. Such an approach will definitely overlook the goals of building a cohesive, musical ensemble, providing the players and ensemble with an environment for growth, and preparing the ensemble for a quality concert performance. Many performances show this lack of musicality. Most of the blame dwells with the conductor unless there are extenuating circumstances beyond his or her control. If this is the situation, the conductor must then evaluate and change the rehearsal process to improve the rehearsal surroundings musically in time. This brings us to the third aspect of establishing the rehearsal environment and climate—the musical aspect.

THE MUSICAL ASPECT

The third aspect within the rehearsal environment and climate is one of musicality. *The ensemble will reflect what the conductor does musically in the rehearsal process.* If the conductor shows little concern for the musicality of the composition being rehearsed or displays a general lack of musicianship while rehearsing the ensemble, the players will tend to ignore such performance elements as style, dynamics, phrasing, nuances, and musical interpretation. It is very easy for the conductor (especially with school groups) to become enamored with only having the ensemble play together and realize most of the notes and rhythms. Too often, the musical concerns are ignored in the rehearsal process.

Even a simple term such as "fortissimo" expressed by the conductor will tend to create a better musical climate than just saying "very loud." Another example is the use of famous composer's names such as Beethoven for rehearsal letter "B" or Mozart for rehearsal letter "M" to reinforce and to identify alphabetically rehearsal letters (avoiding misinterpretation of the first consonant) in the music during the rehearsal process. These two cited examples of promoting musicality may seem insignificant, *but this sort of creative activity will foster a more musical scenario.* The initial step for the conductor, through score study, is to assimilate the musical content of the works to be rehearsed. The conductor must communicate to the ensemble the essence, spirit, and musical details of the work in the rehearsal process. Then the rehearsal process will begin to take on a climate wherein producing music becomes an effort by the ensemble to play as musically and expressively as possible.

Musical Conception of the Work

To foster this musical aspect in the rehearsal environment, the conductor *should be mainly concerned about presenting the composer's intentions* and in realizing his or her conception of the musical interpretation with the players. This is why careful score study becomes so essential for the conductor. Coming to the rehearsal process without a clear and musical conception of how the work should sound will waste rehearsal time and make little progress toward the concert preparation. The players will quickly discover in the rehearsal process whether the conductor has done his or her homework. Without this score study and preparation by the conductor, only the notes and rhythms will be a concern for the ensemble in the rehearsal process. The conductor will need to be ready to communicate these musical aspects to the ensemble or risk losing credibility with the players in the rehearsal process. Chapters 12–15 (Part IV: Musical Priorities and Teaching Strategies) contain additional material on musical interpretation and the various musical aspects to be pursued within the rehearsal process.

The conductor must come to the first rehearsal totally prepared to communicate this conception of a work to the ensemble. *The conductor cannot be learning the score while conducting it in the rehearsal process.* If the conductor has not spent the necessary time in score study to have a clear conception of the work, what results is a rather groping approach on the part of the conductor to discover even the essence and spirit of the work. The conducting technique will be unable to express the conception because of the lack of score study. The conductor will not have anticipated the conducting or rehearsal problems, let alone have teaching strategies available for solutions to these problems. This, of course, leads to wasted rehearsal time because the conductor does not know how the work will really sound or how to approach what needs to be done in the rehearsal process. Taking care of the details in the rehearsal process will not occur if the conductor is inept or unprepared in comparing the ensemble performance with the conceived musical interpretation.

The musical interpretation conceived in score study should be the major step toward arriving at the final concert performance. However, this conception may change somewhat as the rehearsals progress. *The conductor should be open to these musical interpretation changes.* Many factors may influence the conductor to revise the original musical interpretation. For example, the conductor might reconsider tempo in the light of the technical prowess of the ensemble, or the performance facility acoustics may prove to be an influence on the tempo. During the rehearsal process, the conductor may find some passages in which certain conceptions do not work, and this will demand a change in the musical interpretation. Of course, the more mature ensemble will be able to produce the musical interpretation conceived by the conductor with fewer changes because of their technical and musical advancement. However, the conductor can benefit from the rehearsal process in that this conception may change if in the judgment of the conductor the musical interpretation will be enhanced. It is obviously important to make these changes early in the rehearsal progression and not just before the concert performance.

Ensemble Awareness

One of the primary duties of the conductor is to make the ensemble members aware of what is happening around them. *This is done in a number of ways.* The conductor can call attention in the rehearsal process to certain lines, doublings, phrases, and so on, thereby identifying for the players what they should be listening for at any given point. Likewise, attention needs to be directed toward improvement of such priorities as intonation, balance, blend, articulation, and tone, and many of the other priorities in order to enhance the ensemble's performance in the rehearsal process. The conductor can promote this awareness through:

1. Isolating technical and musical problems: Discover the problem and isolate the passage or phrase that needs attention. Then integrate this correction back into the phrase, section, or composition during the rehearsal process.
2. Slowing the tempo of a passage so there is more time to listen and discover the problem that needs a solution.
3. Using a model (either one of the players or the conductor) to improve many performance aspects. Imitation is an effective teaching procedure in musical performance. However, it must be used judiciously and not as a rote method of teaching for expediency.
4. Devising ways to make the players aware of the surrounding sounds and the relationships among the parts.
5. Conducting musically and expressively. This will do more toward creating the musical climate than almost any other single procedure introduced during the rehearsal process.
6. Establishing good communication between the conductor and the ensemble. This can only happen if the conductor knows the score and the ensemble is watching the conductor and responding to this guidance during the rehearsal process.

Awareness of what is happening in terms of the surrounding sound is vital in the development of sensitive playing. The conductor is at least partially responsible for making the players aware of the surrounding sound. A simple example is for the conductor to isolate a passage and have certain players perform their parts so the rest of the ensemble can hear what is happening in relationship to their own individual parts. *Both the conductor and the players need to be listening and adjusting constantly on several levels at the same time.* The more listening that occurs within an ensemble, the more sensitive and musical the performance will be. Peripheral listening and watching by the players is necessary to fit their parts properly in the ensemble fabric. The conductor should approach the large ensemble rehearsal process with the idea of instilling in the players a sense of chamber music performance. With this approach, the players must listen to each other and be more aware of the rest of the ensemble. When the player first comes to be in an ensemble, it is a very different musical experience than with his or her individual instrument study and practice. Suddenly, the player must adjust to what is happening with the rest of the ensemble. This involves musical sensitivity toward elements such as intonation, balance, blend, precision, style, articulation, phrasing, and musical expression. *All of this musical sensitivity is contingent on the player listening and reacting to the surrounding sound.*

One of the specific activities in the rehearsal process should be *demonstrating or explaining the essence and spirit of the work* (see chapter 14). This will certainly aid in the understanding of the work by the players and thus enhance the musical interpretation. Two of the psychological activities in the rehearsal environment are making musical decisions and solving both technical and musical problems that arise during the rehearsal process. Teaching players about musicianship, especially with less mature players, is a necessary part of the rehearsal process. Beyond the actual rehearsal process, the conductor should announce to the players upcoming musical events and encourage them to attend. Likewise, encourage the players to join other quality groups that may provide a different experience than the one in which they are presently participating. The conductor can encourage the player to study privately with a fine teacher. Many conductor-teachers are reluctant to encourage players to study with other teachers, but this can only be a win-win situation in improving the ensemble. It certainly would not be a negative reflection on the conductor. In many other ways, the conductor can be helpful and motivating in furthering the musicianship of the players in the ensemble and in stimulating a musical climate!

PRACTICAL APPLICATION
(CLASS DISCUSSION/DEMONSTRATION)

1. Discuss what you would envision as a utopian rehearsal environment and climate. (Consider the physical, the psychological, and the musical aspects).
2. Diagram the seating plans for the various ensembles (such as orchestra, wind ensemble, and concert band).
3. How would you set up the band or orchestra? Why? What other factors might be involved in the instrument placement within the ensemble?
4. What are the responsibilities of the conductor in dealing with the music, the visual strategies, and the special instruments and equipment needed?
5. Discuss the kind of messages that the conductor should send to the players to enhance the psychological aspect of the rehearsal climate and environment.
6. Discuss ideas on concentration, discipline, and enthusiasm in establishing the right rehearsal climate. How are these three items connected?
7. List ways of motivating the instrumental music ensemble (considering the maturity and performance level of the ensemble).
8. What could you do to enhance the rehearsal hall physically?
9. How would you go about establishing the right presence and aura in the rehearsal environment?
10. List some items that the conductor should note in score study for the preparation of the rehearsal process.
11. How would you stimulate a musical approach in the rehearsal process?
12. How would you go about communicating your musical conception of a given work to the ensemble? (Should this be done mostly with the conducting technique or verbally or both?)
13. Begin to gain familiarity with the standard repertoire found in Appendix A of this book through CD listening, score study, and guidance from the conducting teacher. (See Appendix G for assignment forms.)

RECOMMENDED READING

Casey, Joseph L., *Teaching Techniques and Insights for Instrumental Music Educators.* A comprehensive book that covers many aspects needed by the conductor in the rehearsal process.

Dalby, Max F., *Band Rehearsal Techniques: A Handbook for New Directors.* Chapter 5: Rehearsal Psychology on the topic of discipline.

Fuchs, Peter Paul, *The Psychology of Conducting.* Chapter 5: The Rehearsal is especially enlightening in terms of what should happen between the conductor and players in the rehearsal environment.

Harris, Frederick Jr., *Conducting with Feeling.* Chapter 5: Communicating Musical Feeling addresses the psychological and musical environment.

Kohut, Daniel L., and Joe W. Grant, *Learning to Conduct and Rehearse.* Chapter 5: Beyond Manual Technique discusses the ideas of leadership and self-confidence in being a successful conductor.

Moses, Don V., Robert W. Demaree, and Allen F. Ohmes, *Face to Face with an Orchestra.* Chapter 3: Preparing for Rehearsals, Chapter 4: Adjusting your Baton Technique, and Chapter 5: Rehearsing the Orchestra.

Walker, Darwin E., *Teaching Music*, 2nd ed. Specifically under Part Three: Within the School Environment delineates many aspects of the environment and climate in the rehearsal process.

Weerts, Richard, *Handbook of Rehearsal Techniques for the High School Band.* Under Chapter 1: Preparing the Physical Plant, Instruments, Uniforms and Music offers some ideas about the rehearsal process physical environment.

Chapter Three

The Ten Essentials of the Rehearsal Process Scenario

ESSENTIAL NO. 1: ENSEMBLE PERSONNEL

Selecting and Evaluating Ensemble Personnel

The ensemble whose members are at similar performance level will present fewer real problems in the rehearsal process than the group that has great diversity in player background. This diversity of background will determine the performance level of the ensemble as well as the ensemble's ultimate potential. Likewise, this diversity may reflect in a more obvious way what the weaknesses are in the ensemble's performance. The conductor may find it necessary to make some different priority adjustments and design unique teaching strategies in such diverse scenarios. This diversity will limit the selection of the repertoire as well. At any rate, the ideal ensemble is one in which all of the players have been auditioned and evaluated.

The performance level of the group defines the actual present achievement of the ensemble. The conductor must continually evaluate the performance level of the ensemble in order to select the proper rehearsal priorities and teaching strategies. It is important for the conductor to know this performance level so that the demands made upon the players are realistic. Asking for more from the players than they can deliver only leads to frustration on the part of the conductor and the players. Likewise, the conductor must select the concert repertoire based on this present performance level. Consider also the idea of challenging the players slightly to bring the ensemble to a higher performance level. However, there is some inherent danger here that the selection of repertoire may over-estimate the performance level, causing both the conductor and the ensemble to feel inadequate.

The maturity level of the group involves age, innate ability, the musical background of the individual players, and the history of their ensemble training. The conductor will need to evaluate the maturity level and the collective understanding of the various musical performance aspects within the ensemble. Most conductors during their career will have the opportunity to work with different levels of ensemble maturity. This will span from the very young school group to semi-professional or professional ensembles. This means that to be effective, the conductor will need to adjust the priorities, teaching strategies, and music material for these diverse groups.

There are many factors to consider in evaluating just *how much growth to expect* from the individual players and the particular ensemble. Unrealistic expectations will only lead to frustration on the part of the conductor and the ensemble. Likewise, the conductor is certainly a major factor in how much the ensemble can achieve. (In some instances, the conductor can even be detrimental to the progress of the ensemble!) In a sense, the growth factor is difficult to evaluate because there would never be a point where one would judge the level as the ultimate. The conductor and ensemble should always be striving for a higher level of performance. Since both the artistry and the growth factors are difficult to define and evaluate specifically, the conductor must continue to rehearse the ensemble to the best of his or her ability. The main goal is for the conductor to bring the ensemble to its highest possible performance level.

Conductor-Ensemble Relationship

The relationship between the conductor and the ensemble influences strongly achieving the rehearsal process objectives and the ensemble performance goals. The conductor must adjust to the various ensemble levels. In this regard, the adjustments must be in the application of teaching strategies and the selection of repertoire. The teaching strategies employed in the rehearsal process will vary tremendously among these diverse groups. A basic rehearsal strategy (or plan) and a minimal number of teaching strategies will not suffice for the conductor to cover the difference in the performance levels, maturity levels, or growth factors. This is why I offer many suggestions and options for designing these teaching strategies. I present these teaching strategy options and suggestions throughout all of the various chapters on rehearsal priorities and teaching strategies in Parts III and IV of this book. The selection of repertoire is extremely important for the conductor and the ensemble. The selection of repertoire is addressed in this chapter (Essential No. 2) and also in Appendix A.

The age of the players, the length of the rehearsal period, the difficulty of repertoire, the amount of rehearsal time before the concert performance, and the actual performance level of the ensemble are all factors to consider in the rehearsal process. Because of these considerations, the conductor will have to constantly adjust the priorities and teaching strategies in order to efficiently and effectively rehearse the instrumental music ensemble. Much will depend on where each selection is in the preparation for the concert performance as well as for the refinement of the various priorities in determining what approach to employ within each particular rehearsal process.

The conductor must determine the best approach for the particular ensemble. The younger ensemble will need a different approach from that of the more mature ensemble. The conductor should be realistic about the expectations and demands made upon the various ensembles. The selection of music is a vital consideration in the success of any ensemble performance. The amount of rehearsal time available is a crucial factor in terms of ensemble development and progress. The priorities considered and the teaching strategies employed vary with the performance level and maturity level of the ensemble. The conductor should make all of these decisions through evaluation and thoughtful judgment.

Personnel Selection

The selection of personnel will have definite impact on the rehearsal process as well as on the ensemble performance level. The selection of personnel for the ensemble will vary depending on whether it is an educational group, an amateur group, or a professional group. This selection process also depends upon the performance goals of the ensemble. The conductor must determine the choice of informal or formal auditions. Likewise, the preliminary procedures before the audition vary in terms of notification of interested musicians, selection of judges, announcement of the audition date, time, and place, and the musical material to prepare for the audition.

In an educational scenario, make *the audition announcement* to the interested students with a specific indication of what you expect of them on the audition. The conductor should select the musical passages for the audition. Adjudication by unbiased or "outside" judges would allow the players (and parents) to feel that the students are being evaluated more objectively. If employing an outside judge(s), then the main consideration is to place the players in ability order, and perhaps configure the placement within the various sections. The conductor may see fit to shift the personnel around within the section to improve the performance strength and leadership within the ensemble before finalizing these audition results.

In a semi-professional or professional scenario, publicize *the audition announcement* for a considerable length of time. Interested musicians would then contact the administration of the ensemble to secure the musical material to be prepared and to ascertain the date, time, and place of the audition. These auditions often take place behind a screen or curtain in order to be as objective and impartial as possible. The conductor, concertmaster, and the principal player of the particular instrument or section involved would then hear the audition(s). Usually, the conductor will want to be involved with personnel selection because of the impact that the new player will have on the ensemble performance. In certain circumstances, professional auditions come about only through invitation.

In addition to the selection of ensemble personnel through the audition process, the evaluators might be requested to select the chair placement in the particular section. In the professional scenario, this chair placement is usually determined in advance of the audition such as a principal or section player specification. In the educational scenario, a general audition usually will result in a specific order of personnel within a section. Here the conductor may determine the placement of the personnel after the audition to ensure that each section has a leader and/or strong player. Part assignments are important for good balance and blend within the ensemble. Leadership is an important criterion for the principal player of a section. In some instances, the chair placement in the section occurs on a rotating basis. In professional ensembles, there may be a designation of assistant principal as well. There should be some consideration at every level to rotate the players within a section. This is easiest if all the players were at about the same performance level; this would give all the players more of a sense of responsibility and satisfaction.

Other Ensemble Personnel Factors

Within many scenarios, the conductor must not only find the best technically proficient players for the ensemble, but should consider the factors of cooperation and dedication as well as the level of artistry. With chamber music ensembles, this relationship among the players is crucial; with the conducted ensemble, these working relationships between the players and conductor are also very important for the success of the ensemble. The players must be willing to submit to the wishes of the conductor in matters of musical interpretation; otherwise, the ensemble would lack the necessary cohesiveness and musicality in the concert performance. The working relationship is important in terms of producing these successful music performances.

The selection of the principal players in most ensembles is an important decision for the conductor. There must be cooperation and mutual respect between the principal players and the conductor. The principal players can exert strong leadership over the various sections of the ensemble. The principal players can suggest, with the blessing and guidance of the conductor, how the ensemble might best play a certain passage. In the string section, the principal player in consultation with the conductor should see that the section is bowing in similar directions, preferred positions, and with the proper bowing style. In the wind and percussion sections, the principal player might listen for consistency of articulation, intonation, balance, blend, phrasing, and style. Certainly, the conductor has the final word on musical interpretation, but the principal players should be of great service to the conductor in refining their respective sections of the ensemble.

The artistic factor is an important consideration in the selection of ensemble personnel. Much depends on the actual performance level of the ensemble in terms of what the conductor could expect artistically from the players. These expectations vary considerably from one ensemble to another. However, the serious conductor wants to strive for the highest level of artistic performance possible from the ensemble. In this regard, an ensemble in which the personnel is able to read music fluently and accurately on the first reading of a work can then be expected to achieve a relatively high level of artistic performance during the rehearsal process and concert performance. One cannot disregard or gloss over as unimportant fluent and accurate music reading by each member of the ensemble to the artistic success in the rehearsal process or the concert performance. In this way, the ensemble can begin rehearsing immediately on an artistic level, rather than spending considerable rehearsal time on just the notes, rhythms, or articulations/bowings.

ESSENTIAL NO. 2: MUSIC MATERIAL

Selecting Appropriate Music Material

The conductor, generally, must take full responsibility for the selection of program material for the concert performances. There may be situations where others might have input (such as an artistic committee), but in the final analysis the conductor must decide. The selecting of appropriate music material is based on a number of considerations that include (1) the ensemble performance level, (2) the quality and difficulty of the selected music, (3) the strengths and weaknesses of the ensemble, (4) the suitability for the ensemble, (5) the available players and instrumentation of the ensemble, (6) the continuity and number of rehearsals before the concert performance, (7) the type of listening audience, (8) the reason or occasion for the performance, and (9) the program repertoire, which should have unity, contrast, and variety. Factors involved in selecting the program material are quality, challenge, appropriateness, strengths, weaknesses, keys, rhythmic prowess, and the range demands made on the players (especially for the brass players). The conductor should strive to reflect broad musical taste in the selection of program material. The availability of special instruments might limit the selection of certain repertoire. (Examples of this are the requirement for two harps in a Debussy selection or that of English horn or contrabassoon in romantic or contemporary selections.) These kinds of instrument requirements in the concert band might be less severe as opposed to those of the orchestral ensemble; the band instrumentation is more standardized and is usually cross-cued with most band ensemble compositions. In selecting and formatting program material, the conductor should also think in terms of the variety of colors and textures within this repertoire for the concert performance.

Above everything else, the material should be of the highest musical quality. The conductor must judge this quality, considering the composer, arranger, editor, publisher, and the music itself. This selection of quality music should include contrasting styles as well as the various musical periods. Especially in the band area, there seems to be a trend toward performing only the latest contemporary music, in this way avoiding any precedence as to how to interpret the music. The band conductor should program orchestra transcriptions as well as original works for band. The band conductor should consider the use of early wind music in concerts (which involves less instrumentation) and in this way vary the texture of the program. Just as a soloist can give relief from the full ensemble sound, the variance of texture in a concert program is crucial for the listener. The orchestra conductor tends to stay with the proven repertoire rather than trying to discover quality music that is infrequently played but may be worthy of exposure to the audience. Many professional orchestra conductors also tend to avoid extremely dissonant contemporary music because of the fear of displeasing the paying audience.

The selected pieces should challenge the music ensemble both technically and musically. If the music is technically too difficult for the performance level of the ensemble, then the group will get discouraged. (Developing conductors tend to select music that they performed in college, and thereby impose this on a less mature ensemble.) The conductor must be careful that the selected music is not much beyond the present performance level of the ensemble. Some mistakes that conductors frequently make relate to only the technical challenges rather than selecting music that will emphasize the musicality of the ensemble. The conductor must find challenges for the players in the rehearsal process and concert performance that require good tone, consistent tone control, good intonation, sensitive balance, good blend, and musical phrasing. By selecting the appropriate pieces for the ensemble, the conductor can devote time and effort to developing this musicality and musical sensitivity during the rehearsal process.

Many conductors and musicians have indicated to me on numerous occasions how very important they feel the selecting of good music material is to the success of the instrumental music ensemble and the total instrumental program. The conductor should select music that will allow the ensemble to improve their technical performance level and the ensemble's collective musicality. The music must be challenging to the particular ensemble and also musically worthwhile. Selecting music is comparable to casting a play or movie in that the selection of characters must hinge on many factors, not just how they look or how they might deliver the lines. Selecting music involves knowing the literature and then with some careful consideration choosing the appropriate material for the specific scenario with the idea of enhancing the total instrumental music program. Selecting repertoire that exceeds the technical or musical limits of the players leads to player frustration and poor performance. There really is so much fine music material at all levels of performance available, that there is *no reason for selecting music of poor quality*. This is one reason that it is so important for the conductor to know the literature.

The process by which the conductor selects the music for the instrumental music ensemble needs to be a thoughtful one. Many factors come into play here. Not least among them is that the conductor must like the music; it should be attractive for ensemble members as well. If it is a school group, then consider what will benefit the ensemble most technically and musically. If it is a professional ensemble, consider the repertoire that will appeal to (or stretch) the paying audience. The selection of repertoire for the ensemble is an important factor for the credibility of the conductor. The conductor needs to know the standard repertoire and be constantly exploring the literature for new works or for less familiar repertoire. (I offer Appendix A: Score Study and Program Building with Standard Repertoire in this book as a basis for knowing much of the standard ensemble literature.) When the thoughtful selection of music material, careful preparation of the scores by the conductor, and the many other rehearsal preparations are in place, the rehearsal process should then become one of excellent music making in preparation for the concert performance.

Concert Programming

Programs are conceived in many different ways and presented in various formats. The advanced conductor should be *constantly thinking about programming* and be as creative as possible in this regard. A special occasion might strongly dictate the program. Likewise, a guest soloist may significantly influence the selection of the entire program. The kind of audience may also be a determining factor. The conductor must be realistic about selecting music for concert performances. The conductor should consider the strengths and weaknesses of the ensemble while selecting music for the concert performance. Instrumental solos and important exposed parts in the ensemble music must be played well in the concert performance or otherwise the total impression left with the audience is a negative one. The conductor must be committed to the music being performed and put forth his or her best effort in the rehearsal process to communicate the conceived musical interpretation to the players. The program should fit together, and the program order is quite critical in producing a satisfying concert.

There are numerous types of instrumental concert programs: theme concerts, historical (or chronological) concerts, concerts emphasizing a particular composer or composers, soloist concerts, pops concerts, young people's concerts, family concerts, holiday or season celebration concerts, concerts featuring special repertoire, music of a particular country (nationalistic) or area, ballet music concerts and dance concerts, concerto-aria concerts, concerts of operatic works, choral-orchestra (or choral-band) concerts, concerts featuring commissioned works or premieres, and prism or collage concerts (switching from one ensemble to another with no applause until the intermission and/or the end of the concert). The list could go on and on as creatively configured by the conductor. All of these concert programs need variation in tempos, musical periods, styles, moods, keys, dynamics, tone colors, and textures.

The rule of thumb in concert programming is to select music that the particular ensemble can "adequately" read the first time through. In many instances, the conductor reasons that things can be worked out, with the result of spending rehearsal time "chasing notes and rhythms" without ever getting to the musical aspects of the performance. The conductor should consider many selections before making decisions about the concert program. One of the main factors here is the actual music time involved. It is probably better to under-program than to present a program that resembles a marathon. Mature ensembles can keep the attention of the audience much longer than less refined ensembles. The program order should have a sense of organization and one of a well-conceived format. In some cases, the logistics of the ensemble setup (or changes) may determine the order of the program as well as the various selections. In addition, base program building on the rehearsal time available.

There are many concert season programming considerations for the conductor. Much will depend on the given scenario, but base them upon the formulated ensemble performance goals. There should be variation in musical periods and compositional styles. Consider such decisions in terms of the players and the audience. Especially in the educational scenario, give thought to the performance of the standard repertoire periodically to expose the players to this music material as background before moving on to other ensembles in the future. Playing the standard repertoire is very important for the conductor, players, and audience. There must be a mixture between standard works and contemporary selections. In many scenarios, the soloists or the specific occasional music will influence these program decisions as well. In the final analysis, the need for balancing the concert season is crucial for the success of the ensemble and the total instrumental program.

The length or duration of the program is certainly an important consideration. Some ensembles because of their maturity and high performance level will be able to sustain audience interest longer than a young, less proficient ensemble. Physical and mental endurance will be a problem for the younger ensemble. When programming, the conductor should be concerned about the timing of each work in order to evaluate the total program length. Also within the concert program, the conductor must allow time for intermission, applause, bows, entrances, exits, and the physical logistics between selections. A change of the texture in programming can be important in that variations of this factor can sustain the audience's attention longer than if the major portion of the concert is a constant "tutti" sound by the full ensemble. (An example of texture change here is that of using a soloist with the ensemble or a separate smaller ensemble to add variety to the total sonority of the concert program.)

The program format or order has many different looks. The bottom line is that the format must appear organized, not haphazard. In all of this, the conductor must make the selection of repertoire and decisions on program format in the context of the existing scenario. Programs should have organization, direction, and shape. The program order above everything else must be logical and geared to enhancing the total effect of the concert performance. In some cases, the order will be influenced by where the soloist is placed in the program. For example, if you select the soloist from within the ensemble, consider the physical endurance factor (especially with the high brass instruments) and place the solo early in the program. Another example of the placement of the soloist in the program is the traditional way of placing the soloist just before intermission and at the beginning of the second half of the concert (when more than one selection is played by the soloist) and then to finish the concert with a full ensemble performance.

The conductor's selection of music for the instrumental music ensemble will depend largely on the conductor's knowledge of the repertoire, the programming philosophy, and the quality of the conductor's musical experiences. This is not good news for the maturing conductor who lacks this knowledge, background, or experience. In the case of the evolving conductor, he or she must work hard to "catch up." Likewise, the experienced conductor may need a refresher course in the literature area as well. If he or she puts forth a genuine effort, there is no reason that the developing conductor cannot gain rapidly on this standard literature deficiency. There are numerous sources of information for the maturing conductor to utilize in becoming more familiar with the standard literature as well as in discovering more recent and new works through:

- The examination of various instrumental ensemble printed programs
- Lists of repertoire (provided by numerous organizations)—most helpfully, lists annotated and graded by difficulty
- Books on the standard ensemble repertoire (see Recommended Reading)
- New music reviews in periodicals (such as *The Instrumentalist* magazine)
- Live concert performances
- Recordings (listening to as much recorded music as possible and building and indexing your own CD library)
- Music reading sessions (associated with conventions or sponsored by music companies, schools, etc.)
- Discussions with music colleagues and friends
- Discussions with other conductors
- Composers (commissions and premieres)
- Music ensemble libraries (in schools, colleges, etc.)
- Music store inventories
- Publishers' catalogs and newsletters
- Perusal scores requested from publishers and music libraries (as possible selections for programming)
- Sample scores provided by publishers for programming consideration
- Selected web sites (if some information is known about the specific composition)

One can use all of the sources of information listed above to produce a personal file of ensemble literature for future reference. Annotated and graded lists are more helpful than just a simple listing of ensemble literature. Keep this information in card files, notebooks, or on soft copy. This search will continue for the duration of the conductor's career. The advanced conductor should refer to Appendix A in this book for a representative list of the standard instrumental ensemble literature. Attendance at live performances and listening to recordings by the developing conductor will accelerate the accumulation of entries for these literature lists. It is also very important for the conductor, when exposed to this literature, to become as cognizant as possible about the composer, the musical period involved, the compositional style, the main themes or form, soloists needed, and other detailed and essential information to reinforce the characteristics and the uniqueness of the particular composition.

ESSENTIAL NO. 3: REHEARSAL TIME

Utilizing Rehearsal Time and the Continuity Factor

The amount of rehearsal time, the continuity of rehearsals, and the work to accomplish during each rehearsal process are crucial aspects in determining which priorities to stress and what teaching strategies to employ. The performance level of the ensemble, the difficulty of the selected music, and the amount of rehearsal time available before the concert performance are all-important considerations in making good decisions about these priorities and teaching strategies. In the planning of a concert season or for the school-year performances, conceive and frequently review a rehearsal and concert schedule. The conductor should plan the number of rehearsals before a concert performance so that he or she can adjust the preparation for each selection as needed.

If the instrumental music ensemble rehearses every day or every other day during the week, the continuity problem certainly lessens in comparison to the ensemble that rehearses once a week. There is definitely some loss in rehearsal progress when there is a lapse of a week or longer between rehearsals. Consider this in terms of the rehearsal priorities and teaching strategies employed as well. The ensemble players simply retain more if rehearsals occur closer together. With frequent rehearsals, there is less repetition of effort in solving the problems from one rehearsal process to another. The conductor must estimate the amount of time required to rehearse each selection; this may change somewhat during the various rehearsals. One of the first considerations in planning the rehearsal process or the subsequent performance is to know the playing time of each selection. This will allow the conductor to plan the rehearsal preparation more objectively. Reviewing these selections in the rehearsal process to keep them ready for performance may be necessary and this does involve how some of the time is spent in the rehearsal process.

It is very easy to neglect a second aspect of continuity during the rehearsal process as well because the conductor is intent on taking care of the details of the performance. This can result in many stops and starts in the rehearsal process with considerable disregard for the continuity within each selection. The conductor can avoid some of this by not stopping so much to work on details. Particularly as the concert performance nears, there should be more concentration on this continuity factor in the rehearsal process. The conductor should begin to rehearse longer sections of the music without stopping. If the conductor ignores this continuity factor, several serious errors or problems may occur during the concert performance. Another approach might be for the conductor to "seam" various sections through a process of starting before a troublesome passage and working forward into this section. This "reversal" process can reinforce the connection between one section of a piece and the next.

If rehearsal time seems insufficient in preparing for the next concert performance, the conductor should consider the following changes or adjustments:

- Fewer concert performances in the season
- Additional rehearsal time with the full ensemble
- Sectional rehearsals
- Less difficult repertoire for the ensemble
- Evaluation of the whole rehearsal process by the conductor

Saving and Wasting Time in the Rehearsal Process

The conductor seldom feels that there is sufficient rehearsal time available. There are always priorities and problems that need attention during the rehearsal process that may require more rehearsal time for preparation of the repertoire before a concert performance. This suggests that the conductor must find ways of "saving time" in the rehearsal process or at the very least avoid "wasting time" in the rehearsal process. Wasting time in the rehearsal process leads to player frustration and a loss of credibility for the conductor. In the following listings are some ideas and options about efficiency and inefficiency in the rehearsal process. Here are some ways to save time:

- The conductor has studied the musical scores in detail.
- The conductor has conceived the musical interpretation.
- An atmosphere of intensity and concentration exists in the rehearsal process.
- The parts are marked before the rehearsal process begins.
- Players have their parts prepared before the rehearsals.
- The players are watching the conductor in the rehearsal process.
- The conductor provides clear and musical conducting technique.
- Well-designed teaching strategies are in place.
- Priorities shift based on the ensemble's needs.
- Rehearsal process objectives are clear to the players during the rehearsal process.
- Rehearsal pacing relies on pre-rehearsal planning (a rehearsal plan).
- The conductor is specific when making corrections and improvements during the rehearsal process. (General comments tend to be useless.)
- The conductor speaks audibly when verbalizing to the players in the rehearsal process.
- The conductor uses verbal comments in advance warning of approaching problems in the rehearsal process (especially with mature ensembles).
- The conductor schedules sectional rehearsals when needed.
- The conductor works with individual players outside of the rehearsal process when needed.

- The conductor is consistent in conducting patterns and gestures in every rehearsal process and then from the rehearsals to the concert performance.

And some ways to waste time:

- There is too much talking during the rehearsal process (conductor and players).
- There are too many distractions during the rehearsal process.
- There is a lack of clear rehearsal process objectives.
- There is a lack of score preparation by the conductor.
- Players are unprepared to play their parts correctly in the rehearsal process.
- The conductor has not designed (or even considered) good rehearsal teaching strategies.
- Players are not watching the conductor.
- The conductor displays poor or inadequate conducting technique in the rehearsal process.
- Poor manuscript or parts with errors (especially with new works or musical production parts) cause players some frustration and time wasted.
- Rehearsal letters or numbers in the score and parts are insufficient.
- The conductor has edited or marked the music poorly.
- The conductor has neglected other preparations before the rehearsal process.
- The conductor repeats a passage without stating the reason for this repetition.
- The conductor makes too many verbal comments, causing pacing problems.
- Rehearsals become dull and/or lack positive direction.
- There is poor pacing and momentum in the rehearsal process due to the conductor's lack of planning or score study.
- The conductor has not taken care of necessary tasks outside of the full rehearsal process.

Solutions to Rehearsal Time Problems

The conductor should schedule *sectional rehearsals* for the convenience of the players if possible; these would be considered extra rehearsals beyond the formulated rehearsal schedule. The danger is in scheduling the sectional rehearsal for too many players or with too many problems for the limited time available. It may be best to have these sectional rehearsals immediately before or after the full ensemble rehearsal process. Determine the sectional rehearsals largely by the needs of the ensemble. In some cases, it might be the entire brass section or it might be just one instrumental section, such as the trumpet section. Sometimes, sectional rehearsals can run simultaneously with the full rehearsal or at the same time as other sectional rehearsals, depending on the available facilities, time involved, and the needed leadership. The performance level of the ensemble and the difficulty of the selected repertoire will dictate the personnel makeup of the sectionals and the number of sectional rehearsals scheduled. These sectional rehearsals should result in full ensemble rehearsal time saved and equated with much-improved full rehearsals and concert performance.

Sectional rehearsals should have specific objectives. The whole idea of sectional rehearsals is to deal with details that the full ensemble rehearsal process cannot cover.

The sectional rehearsal gives the conductor the opportunity to stress sectional balance and blend. It also provides the opportunity to work more with the section's tone color and intonation. Sectional rehearsals allow the players and conductor to hear the section as a unit. Sectional rehearsals can produce an environment more conducive to working on very basic aspects of performance that would not be possible in the full ensemble rehearsal process. In many cases, technical and musical problems arise in the sectional rehearsal that the conductor may have overlooked or not even considered in the full ensemble rehearsal process.

Periodically it is more efficient to schedule a time for an individual player to receive additional instruction or help from the conductor or other instrumental specialists outside of the full ensemble rehearsal process. Using the full ensemble rehearsal time to work with an individual player is certainly not an efficient approach for any full rehearsal process. The wasted time is obvious to the other players in the ensemble. It may be a case where a solo passage or other passages need attention with the individual players. There may be circumstances where the individual player is simply not producing the part correctly or musically and needs the insight of the conductor or another teacher. Whatever the reason for working with the player individually, the conductor must not waste valuable full ensemble rehearsal time. He or she should use the full ensemble rehearsal process for the benefit of the entire ensemble.

The conductor will usually select music material that will require members of the ensemble to practice their parts outside of the full ensemble rehearsal process. If this is not the case, then the conductor is probably not challenging the ensemble with the program selections. It is not unreasonable for the conductor to expect the players to prepare their parts to the best of their abilities, just as the conductor is expected to prepare for rehearsals with detailed and thorough score study. If the players come to the rehearsal process unprepared, then most of the rehearsal time will be spent on notes, rhythms, or articulations and bowings. This situation will delay confronting the most important aspect of the rehearsal process (i.e., the musicality aspect)!

ESSENTIAL NO. 4: PACING THE REHEARSAL PROCESS

The pacing of the rehearsal process is an important consideration. I define pacing as the speed and variance with which the conductor might move from one rehearsal segment or procedure to another during the rehearsal process. This also involves how much time he or she spends talking as opposed to actual playing. When the conductor possesses good conducting technique, is well prepared (through score study), and ensures that the players are watching carefully, then more playing time (and less talking time) should occur in the rehearsal process. The amount of stopping and starting will affect the pacing of the rehearsal process. The conductor should pace the rehearsal process so that there are infrequent periods of working with just one section of the ensemble, leaving this for sectional rehearsals or individual work. A well-planned rehearsal process will help avoid this poor pacing and enhance the progress of the ensemble.

Much depends on the personality of the conductor as to the pacing of the rehearsal process. However, the conductor must strive to keep the rehearsal process moving forward and to vary the segments and procedures for maximum player interest and concentration. The conductor's personality should reflect enthusiasm for the music, for the rehearsal itself, and for the progress of the group. An indifferent or suave attitude from the conductor throughout a rehearsal process will not generate the kind of pace that is needed. The conductor should sense when "enough is enough" in working with one section for an extended period. The conductor must strive to keep all the players interested in the rehearsal process. Gear the pacing to the maturity level of the ensemble and always with concern for the players and their technical and musical development and improvement.

The pacing must be realistic in the rehearsal process. Pacing does not simply mean moving at a frantic speed. There are times when the players need "space" mentally. The conductor should sense this and back away from the otherwise furious pace of the rehearsal process. Pacing involves the rehearsal atmosphere of intensity and relaxation. There must be recovery time for the players during the rehearsal process. The conductor should keep events moving in the rehearsal process, but avoid going always at a rapid pace; this will not necessarily lead to positive rehearsal results or effective learning, especially with the young ensemble. Pacing in the rehearsal process should not mean talking fast and moving from one problem to another quickly; rather if a point is worth making, make it in a manner that will allow the players to absorb its worth and significance or it will be unusable as learning transfer. There are times in a rehearsal process when the conductor should consider how the players are reacting to the pacing of the rehearsal process, and thereby, evaluate the effectiveness of this pacing.

Rehearsal Pacing Problems

The conductor can minimize discipline problems by keeping the players interested and the rehearsal process moving forward. If distractions do occur, the conductor should let the ensemble know that he or she will not tolerate this. Changing the segments and/ or procedures in terms of the rehearsal pacing may help keep the players at a higher level of concentration. At least part of the problem of discipline in the rehearsal process relates to the attention span of the players, and this relates directly to the maturity of the ensemble. However, do not tolerate an uncontrolled rehearsal scenario because the teaching, the learning transfer, and the playing sensitivity in the rehearsal process are then affected negatively.

The conductor must guard against the problems of physical endurance, especially with the high brass players. The deterioration factor in playing brass instruments is most evident in younger ensembles. This physical endurance problem becomes critical in a dress rehearsal when followed immediately by the concert performance. The conductor should be aware of this problem and allow sufficient time for the brass players to rest by backing away from the high register and loud dynamic passages; nothing is accomplished by causing such embouchure fatigue. In a long rehearsal process, it might be wise for the conductor to allow the players to take a break to avoid a lack of concentration as well as physical fatigue. In some cases, asking the ensemble to stand, stretch, or exercise physically for a moment to break the tension of a long, continuous rehearsal period may be in order. Proper rehearsal pacing is an important consideration in counteracting physical or mental endurance problems in the rehearsal process.

There never seems to be enough rehearsal time to take care of all of the details before the concert performance. This leads the conductor to try to cover too much repertoire in a single rehearsal process. Rather, the conductor should attempt to be thorough in what is covered without overwhelming the players. If one addresses too many problems in a single rehearsal process, the ensemble will tend to react negatively. If the ensemble frantically rehearses the repertoire during a single rehearsal process, it will diminish the effectiveness of the rehearsal process and result in careless playing and preparation. Little progress or learning transfer will occur here.

In many cases, the pacing problems in the rehearsal process are due to the lack of conductor preparation. The unprepared conductor will immediately be at odds in the rehearsal process because he or she has no focus or direction established. The physical environment, the score study, the marking of the parts, the conducting problems, and the solutions and the anticipation of playing problems are the conductor's preparations before the rehearsal process begins. If he or she has neglected these items, the conductor will find that the rehearsal pacing is erratic and uneven. The rehearsal process can achieve much more if the conductor has carefully prepared.

Solutions to Rehearsal Pacing Problems

Beyond the meticulous study of the scores, the conductor should design teaching strategies based on the score study and his or her knowledge of the strengths and weaknesses of the ensemble. Only if the conductor can anticipate what will happen in the rehearsal process will the proper pacing of the rehearsal process be possible. During the rehearsal process, the conductor should spend most of the rehearsal time solving problems. If the conductor prepares well for the rehearsal process, then the pacing problems should be resolved quite easily. The conductor needs to be sensitive to the response of the ensemble and when necessary slow down or speed up the pacing of the rehearsal process. This can transpire only if the conductor knows the scores and has anticipated the technical and musical problems. If the conductor spends an inordinate amount of time on one passage or with one section of the ensemble, the pacing of the rehearsal process may become a problem. The rehearsal process should involve the full ensemble most of the time; otherwise the pacing will begin to stagnate. With careful planning, these problems can be avoided either by returning to the passage or section in a later rehearsal process or by scheduling sectional rehearsals to address the other specific problems.

Long periods of working with one section of the ensemble will cause the other sections to lose interest in the proceedings. This can easily occur during a tuning period in which the majority of the players are uninvolved. To avert this situation, the conductor should spot check the pitch level during the rehearsal process, but not try to tune the entire ensemble during a single rehearsal process. In the situation where certain sections need attention, the solution may be the scheduling of sectional rehearsals outside of the regular rehearsals or at the beginning or end of the regularly scheduled rehearsal process. This will also allow the players to come to rehearsals when needed or leave when they are not involved.

A segment such as sight-reading or other variances in the rehearsal process can act as a change of pace. This will give the players a break from the usual routine of the rehearsal process. The conductor must sense when the rehearsal begins to lose intensity; a change of pace may need to be instituted. The conductor might change the pace by working on different music, even without the intentions of programming this repertoire. Ways of changing the pace in the rehearsal process might include the use of humor or short stories (preferably related to the music), simply slowing down or speeding up the pace, changing the focus, changing the mood, or taking a break. Changes of pace in the rehearsal process might come about through intense rehearsing and then playing works requiring less intensity. Pacing and stopping for corrections by the conductor may be influenced by how the ensemble is responding at a certain point in the rehearsal process. The conductor should sense a lack of progress in the rehearsal process and determine what to change. The conductor should always be in control and should know how to bring the group back to a more intense level of concentration at any given time.

ESSENTIAL NO. 5: THE WARM-UP/TUNING PERIOD

Conceiving and Executing the Warm-up/Tuning Period

With most school ensembles, there is a strong need for a warm-up period. The main reason for the warm-up period is for the players to begin to focus and concentrate on the task. The conductor can address many specific priorities during this time also. For example, intonation, tone production, attacks, releases, balance, blend, articulation, rhythm patterns, style, and many other performance aspects can come under scrutiny. The warm-up material, for the most part, should relate to the music that is played during the rehearsal process. By using original material in the warm-up period, the conductor can tailor it to the specific needs of the ensemble and address the priorities deemed necessary for improvement. The conductor can design exercises to solve specific performance problems. Later I provide a list of warm-up material to use over time to achieve a continuity of material; the conductor can control these variations to avoid monotony in the warm-up period. Sometimes during the warm-up period, have the ensemble play without a conductor; this encourages listening and the feeling for chamber music playing. Try playing as a brass choir, a string choir, or a woodwind choir in the warm-up period to establish this listening connection with the players.

The conductor should formulate specific objectives for the warm-up period. Otherwise, this time will become routine with decreased value for the ensemble. The conductor will need to plan and vary the warm-up exercises carefully to sustain interest during this time and to achieve the objectives of the warm-up period. What the warm-up period accomplishes should continue into the rehearsal process, such as listening and watching. Viewed in this light, the warm-up period becomes extremely important. The conductor needs to teach concepts in the warm-up period so there will be learning transfer into the actual rehearsal process as well as in the rehearsals that follow. During the warm-up period, the ensemble can address some of the technical and musical problems and their solutions. Tuning can also be a part of the warm-up period.

The warm-up period should not be a time to try to fix everything at once. Rather, a little time spent on several performance aspects during the warm-up and then moving on to the regular rehearsal process should be the rule. Keep in mind what the purposes of the warm-up period are *to confirm and reinforce the rehearsal process objectives.* The warm-up period should be a time to solidify the fundamentals, improve playing skills, and concentrate on musicianship. Explain to the players why you chose a particular exercise. The focus in the warm-up period should be on tone production, articulation, basic styles, listening, watching, intonation, and rhythm. One of the most important purposes of the warm-up period is to establish concentration with the ensemble and settle the players into the rehearsal process. Another purpose of the warm-up is to establish good playing habits, such as the synchronized breath on initial attacks, balance within a section and among the various sections, proper articulation and bowing, and so on. Hand out sheets during the warm-up for individual use to improve such areas as rhythm and intonation. Use quarter-note drills to encourage the players to watch the conductor by varying the tempos, dynamics, and styles. The warm-up period needs to focus on listening, watching, and adjusting, and in general, relating musically to the rest of the ensemble. After the ensemble has been "warmed up," implement the tuning period. The exception here is that the strings must be tuned before beginning the warm-up period so that there is pitch consensus before playing together. In some cases, the winds may want to do a preliminary tuning before the warm-up as well.

Above everything else, *this warm-up period must not become humdrum*, and thereby lack purpose, promote boredom, and cause careless playing within the ensemble. As mentioned previously, the conductor needs to let the players know the reason for playing the music material in the warm-up period. For example, if the purpose of playing a chorale is to concentrate on the improvement of the intonation, then the conductor must tell the players to listen and adjust to improve the intonation of the ensemble. Specific items to improve in the warm-up period include concentration, sensitivity, listening, watching, breathing, balance, blend, tone production, and intonation. Also during the warm-up period, the conductor can evaluate how the players are responding to the conducting technique. The conductor needs to stress the idea of playing with a beautiful, characteristic sound on the instrument. It may be necessary, depending on the age level of the ensemble, to emphasize certain pedagogical aspects, such as breath use, embouchure, posture, equipment, and so on. Playing long tone exercises, performing lyric passages, and stressing the art of phrasing in the warm-up period will all contribute to the improvement of the ensemble tone quality and tone control. The conductor may need to isolate rhythms and rhythm patterns for detailed work. There are many other reasons for warming up properly that I could advance here.

Music Material in the Warm-up Period

Below are some of the various kinds of music material to use in the warm-up period:

- Long tones (unison and chords)
- Series of chords (major, minor, 7th, etc.)
- Scales (major, minor, chromatic, etc.)
- Arpeggios (string, woodwind, brass, and mallet percussion)

- Intervals (string, woodwind, brass, and mallet percussion)
- Lip slur exercises (for brass instruments)
- Tonguing exercises (for all winds)
- Bowing and bowing style exercises (for strings)
- Intonation exercises (for all players except percussion)
- Rhythm pattern exercises (string, woodwind, brass, and percussion)
- Technical exercises (only after tonal exercises are well established)

Below are some variations to apply to the music material listed above for the warm-up period:

- Tempo change (sudden)
- Tempo change (gradual)
- Dynamic change (sudden)
- Dynamic change (gradual)
- Articulation (tonguing and slurring)
- Bowing and bowing styles
- Stylistic changes (staccato, legato, tenuto, and marcato)
- Change of meters (simple, compound, changing, and asymmetrical)
- Use of rubato (to encourage watching the conductor)

Below are some of the performance areas to develop and refine during the warm-up period:

- Attacks
- Releases
- Dynamic levels, dynamic range, and tone control
- Variations in articulation and bowing
- Balance
- Blend
- Intonation (tuning)
- Precision
- Rhythm and rhythm patterns
- Phrasing
- Listening (call and response, improvisation, and unison playing of melodies without the printed music)

Below are some recommended music material ideas with specific performance areas identified for use during the warm-up period:

- Unison and harmonized scales (major, minor, and chromatic scale)
- Chorales (intonation, balance, blend, attack, and release)
- Sustained (unison/octave) tones; half and whole steps down and up; use hand signals (for intonation improvement and for the sustained musical line; take a breath when needed)

- Lip slur and flexibility exercises (for brass flexibility: tongued and slurred)
- Rhythmic exercises (rhythms and for the improvement of ensemble precision)
- Tonguing exercises (articulation, multiple tonguing, and tonguing speed)
- Bowing exercises (bow control, unison bowing, and bowing styles)
- Long tone exercises (tone development, balance, and blend)
- Interval exercises (intonation and technical accuracy)
- Arpeggiated chords (fingering and technical accuracy)
- Technical drills (beyond the interval exercises and arpeggiated chords)

Below is a list of some published warm-up material to employ creatively during the warm-up period:

- Curnow-Smith: *Chorales*
- Raymond C. Fussell: *Exercises for Ensemble Drill*
- Leonard B. Smith: *Treasury of Scales for Band and Orchestra*
- Edward Lisk: *Alternative Rehearsal Techniques* (student books 1 and 2)
- Claude T. Smith: *Symphonic Warm-ups for Band*
- Yoder-Gillette: *Thirty-five Famous Chorales for Band*
- Merle J. Isaac: *Orchestral Exercises* (in three books)
- Allen-Hanna: *Daily Warm-ups for Full Orchestra*
- Frank Erickson: *Festive & Famous Chorales for Band*
- Frank Erickson: *Technique Through Melody for Band*
- Williams-King: *Foundations for Superior Performances*
- McLeod-Staska: *Rhythm Etudes*
- Jack Bullock: *Rhythm & Technique*
- J. S. Bach (Lake): *Sixteen Chorales for Band*
- James Swearingen: *Strictly Technique for Band*
- Rhodes-Bierschenk: *Symphonic Band Technique*

There are many *advantages in writing original warm-up materials* to fit the needs of the ensemble. With this approach, the conductor can focus on specific performance aspects that the ensemble needs for improvement. The materials should be tailored to the performance level of the ensemble and also to offer challenges for their improvement. Numerous playing aspects can be improved on during the warm-up period. The conductor can incorporate such areas as tone, intonation, interval flexibility, precision, balance, blend, articulation, and dynamic control into the warm-up period by writing this original material for the ensemble. This also gives the conductor a further extension in order to be creative in the leadership of the instrumental music ensemble.

The Length and Type of the Warm-up Period

The conductor, based on the needs of the ensemble, must determine the length of the warm-up period. Some warming up should always take place before attempting to establish a pitch level (except strings, which must tune before the warm-up). Tuning may also be a part of the warm-up period, as well as a separate segment during the rehearsal process. However, avoid an inordinate amount of tuning in the warm-up period; this will take away from the other purposes of the warm-up period. An extremely long warm-up will mean slighting the repertoire being prepared for a concert performance. In other words, the conductor must carefully balance the warm-up period and the rest of the rehearsal process for maximum ensemble progress.

With the semi-professional or professional ensemble, each of the players warms up as an individual activity. The usual procedure is then to continue by sounding a concert A (440), concert B-flat (456), or concert F, thereby carefully establishing the pitch level to the sounding tone. An individual warm-up is valid only if the players know how to warm up properly. Certainly, professional players are very aware of what they must do on the instrument before the rehearsal process begins or they would never have achieved the necessary performance level to be considered a professional player.

The conductor may choose to have an individual warm-up by the players first and then proceed to a group warm-up period. This will be profitable only if the players are mature enough to handle the warm-up individually. If it becomes a chaotic situation with the individual warm-up, then the conductor must impose the group approach immediately. The main benefit from the warm-up period is to establish player focus and concentration. Few school ensembles are mature enough to use the individual player warm-up. Therefore, the group warm-up period, in most cases, is crucial for the success of the rehearsal process, and certainly for the improvement of the ensemble performance level. The group warm-up should be creative and varied. *The warm-up period should not be the same music material and routine at the beginning of every rehearsal process!*

In all cases, whether it is an educational or a professional ensemble, the reasons for warming up individually or as a group activity are as follows:

1. Limbering up muscles (embouchure, tongue, arm, hands, fingers, etc.)
2. Getting the breath mechanism working properly (winds)
3. Promoting focus and concentration for the rehearsal process
4. Adjusting the instrument (pitch level, reeds, keys, bridge, pegs, etc.)
5. Improving various performance aspects (tone production, articulation, rhythm patterns, intonation, musical expression, etc.)
6. Listening to improve the intonation, balance, and blend produced by the ensemble (group warm-up)
7. Establishing various dynamic levels with the ensemble (group warm-up)
8. Training the ensemble to watch the conductor by varying the tempo, style, and dynamics with the conducting patterns and gestures (group warm-up)
9. Reminding the players about such tone production fundamentals as breathing, tonguing, embouchure, instrument and hand positions, bow use, right hand position in the French horn bell, posture, etc. (group warm-up)
10. To give the percussion section the time to organize, set up, and adjust instruments and equipment (group warm-up)
11. To develop the sensitivity toward a specific style such as staccato, legato, tenuto, and marcato (group warm-up)
12. To establish a high intensity level for the ensemble during the rehearsal process (group warm-up)
13. To check the pitch level and confirm the ensemble intonation (refer to Chapter 8: Intonation and Tuning for more details here)

ESSENTIAL NO. 6: LISTENING AND SENSITIVITY

Promoting Listening during the Rehearsal Process

The conductor must be *an astute listener* in the rehearsal process. This ability separates the fine conductor from an average one. This kind of listening does not necessarily occur immediately when a person steps on the podium in front of an ensemble. The maturing conductor will find too many other items holding his or her attention such as conducting patterns, correct tempo, changes of tempo, fermatas, releases, preparatory beats, dynamic indications, and so on. This is why the conductor must practice and sharpen technique seriously and continually so that the patterns and gestures become automatic, comfortable, and ambidextrous. The conductor needs to be free of the technical aspects in the conducting technique to concentrate on the musical aspects and to hear what is actually happening in the rehearsal process. Throughout the rehearsal process, he or she must make numerous musical decisions on the podium based on what is heard from the ensemble. In this reality, the conductor should certainly be listening to make the necessary changes for the improvement of the ensemble performance during the rehearsal process. The conductor should be listening "across" the ensemble!

The conductor must convince the players to confront the smallest detail in the rehearsal process. During the rehearsal process, the conductor should address these details to the degree that the players are aware that the conductor is prepared and is listening to what the ensemble is producing. When the players are convinced that the conductor is hearing the smallest inflections and nuances, the players will begin to listen more and correct problems on their own. It is the conductor's duty to make the players aware of what to listen for in dealing with such elements as intonation, precision, balance, blend, and phrasing. During the rehearsal process, the conductor can ask questions to motivate the players to listen more to the ensemble sonority. *Especially, intonation will improve only through meticulous listening by the conductor and the players in the rehearsal process.* In conducting classes, the teacher and conducting students should be concerned with developing the aural skills on which effective rehearsing depends. The aural element in the rehearsal process is foremost for both the conductor and the players.

In the rehearsal process, the conductor detects note and rhythm errors, adjusts balance and blend, refines articulation, solves intonation problems, and makes many other needed corrections. Without careful listening and detection, these problems remain unresolved and the performance will suffer. The auditory imagery from score study and these rehearsal preparations serve as a basis for comparison with what is actually occurring in the ensemble rehearsal process, *and thereby the conductor can hear the digressions from his or her conception of the musical score.* By recording the rehearsal process, the conductor will be able to bring this reality back into focus. The developing conductor has a basic problem at the beginning of his or her career—one of listening to what the ensemble is producing. Because of the many distractions, nervousness, and self-consciousness, the evolving conductor can become overwhelmed at first. However, with meticulous score study and preparations, the conductor will begin to gain confidence in front of the ensemble and will be able to hear what is actually happening during the rehearsal process.

The players need to develop the ability to listen critically to what is happening around them. It is not enough to simply watch the conductor's beat and play their parts. The performance must conform to the total ensemble sound. *The players should realize what the function and importance of their parts are at any given moment and how they fit with the rest of the ensemble.* The conductor must continually remind the players about listening to each other and playing their parts within the context of this total ensemble setting. The conductor should strive to achieve this kind of focus from the whole ensemble—that is, intense listening to the other parts. The conductor can foster this in many ways during the rehearsal process. To encourage players to listen more, stop conducting and thereby put the responsibility on the players to listen to each other in maintaining the precision and musical sensitivity. This procedure will not necessarily work in rubato passages or in selections where tempo changes occur frequently. When working with a section of the ensemble, the conductor should keep the rest of the group involved by having them listen to see how their individual parts fit. In the rehearsal process, it is necessary for the conductor to do more than simply keep saying periodically "listen to each other." At various times the conductor must isolate and dissect passages to show the players specific things to listen for in the music. To foster the idea of listening, the conductor might ask the players at a certain point, "Who are you playing this passage with?" The answer may require the players to make an adjustment in terms of the tone quality, articulation, balance, intonation, or style.

Promoting Musical Sensitivity during the Rehearsal Process

In individual practice, the players should listen to themselves, but in the rehearsal process, the players must watch the conductor and listen to the other players as well. There is no way for an instrumentalist to play with musical sensitivity unless he or she is listening to the rest of the ensemble. Musical sensitivity involves good tone quality, proper articulation, exacting intonation, correct balance, well-conceived phrasing, and perfect precision. Dynamics and nuances, tone color, vibrato, and other various musical expressions all play a part in a musically sensitive performance. All of this musical sensitivity is dependent on being able to hear the other players. *The feedback from listening to the other players should greatly improve the ensemble's performance.* The development of sensitive playing in the ensemble is a long-range goal. As an example of sensitivity development in the rehearsal process, the percussion section must be aware of such items as cymbal diameter, types of sticks or mallets, and stroke placement on the instrument as possible options available to enhance the musicality of the percussion section performance. Along with this, the conductor should also be aware of the variety of sounds that all of the various percussion instruments can produce. The conductor can foster this musical sensitivity in the ensemble rehearsal process by encouraging players to listen to as many fine performances as possible.

Musical sensitivity on the part of the conductor is developed by becoming a proficient instrumentalist and sensitive musician, having developed a clear, precise conducting technique and through continuous study in the area of musical interpretation. Unless the conductor can produce a fine performance on his or her instrument, it would be difficult to know exactly what to do or say in improving the musical sensitivity of an ensemble.

In the rehearsal process, the conductor should be a model and guide in terms of this musical sensitivity. If the conducting technique is secure, the conductor can show this finesse and musicality with patterns and gestures. The study of musical interpretation as an instrumental musician and conductor is an important factor in delivering the authenticity and musical interpretation to the ensemble in the rehearsal process and then to the audience during the concert performance.

Listening and developing musical sensitivity in ensemble performance is a cooperative effort by the conductor and the players. There must be an intense desire on the part of the musicians to get to this next level of performance. Certainly, in terms of musical sensitivity, the ensemble should arrive at a point where the eye contact and musicality resemble that realized by a fine string quartet, with most of the eye contact directed toward the conductor. In the final analysis, it comes down to listening to each other with the goal of developing a musically sensitive, cohesive ensemble. Teamwork on the part of the conductor and players is essential for this to happen. Poor discipline and the lack of concentration in the rehearsal process will not result in this careful listening, the musical sensitivity among the various parts or with the surrounding sounds that are being produced. Poor discipline or the lack of concentration in the rehearsal process environment will always disallow the final product of an excellent concert performance. The goal that the conductor and players should pursue throughout the rehearsal process is that of listening in order to produce this musically sensitive performance.

ESSENTIAL NO. 7: COMMUNICATION DURING THE REHEARSAL PROCESS

Silent Communication (Conducting) with the Ensemble

Most communication with the ensemble in the rehearsal process should be that of the conducting technique. The conductor initiates and sustains this silent communication by (1) *knowing the score thoroughly* (which results in good eye contact with the ensemble), (2) clear, meaningful conducting technique that will assure better communication with the ensemble, and (3) constant reminders by the conductor (if needed) that it is crucial to watch the conductor in the rehearsal process and in the concert performance. The conductor, using verbal communication, modeling, or demonstration in the rehearsal process may then supplement this silent communication with the ensemble.

The conductor could have superb conducting technique, but it would be all in vain unless the players are watching. *Watching the conductor* is assuming that the players have good sight lines to the podium and are able to see the conductor's patterns and gestures without constant eye or head movement. The use of good peripheral vision is the key to watching the conductor. (Players see general motion in the conducting gestures, but the conductor must psychologically conduct as if the tip of the baton or hand, if no baton is used, is the focus of the patterns.) This silent communication between conductor and players is a two-way street. The conductor must know the score so that he or she is able to have frequent eye contact with the ensemble, and the players must be able to interpret the patterns and gestures of the conductor. In this way, the players will become more confident in playing precisely, making proper entrances, responding to dynamic gestures, and producing their parts in a musically sensitive manner. You can tell by the ensemble precision whether the players are watching the conductor.

In the rehearsal process, the conductor can encourage the players to watch the conducting patterns and gestures more by:

1. Occasionally changing the tempo in the rehearsal process unexpectedly to keep the players alert (avoid being deceptive too much of the time, however)
2. Verbally reminding the ensemble of the need to watch
3. Training the ensemble to watch through the various activities and exercises during the warm-up period
4. Playing repertoire that requires flexibility and rubato
5. Showing musical sensitivity in conducting patterns and gestures to give players a reason for watching the conductor
6. Emphasizing precision, phrasing, and musicality in the rehearsal process
7. Using good eye contact with the ensemble (not allowing the eyes to continually look at the score), and giving good cues

Watching the conductor should be a "routine" experience for instrumental music ensembles. The development of this watching should begin as soon as the young musician becomes a member of an ensemble. As the ensemble matures, "reading the stick" will involve more than starting together, playing together, and ending together. Eventually almost every beat should show the player the conductor's intentions. (A relatively young student was lauding the conductor of a summer music camp orchestra when she said, "If I lost my place in the music, I only need to look at the conductor and I will be able to tell where I should be in the music." This may be a slight exaggeration, but it elucidates the importance of conducting with clarity, variation, and emotion along with insisting that the players watch the conductor.) I cover additional information concerning this conductor/player silent communication elsewhere in this book.

The Other Procedures for Communication in the Rehearsal Process

Verbal communication with the ensemble is a necessary part of the rehearsal process. Seldom would a conductor go through an entire rehearsal process without some comments concerning the performance of the selected repertoire. (However, it is a worthwhile reminder to the conductor that if he or she keeps the verbal communication to a minimum in the rehearsal process, the conductor could still communicate effectively with good conducting technique.) The conductor who has adequate conducting technique and is able to show precisely what is intended with the conducting patterns and gestures will find this to be much more effective and efficient in the rehearsing of the instrumental music ensemble. This approach, of course, is assuming that the players are watching the conductor and responding appropriately to the patterns and gestures. A good check on the verbal aspect of the rehearsal process is to record the rehearsal process and then replay the recording to discover just how much of the rehearsal time is spent communicating verbally. As a basic guideline, if half of the time in the rehearsal process is spent verbalizing, the conductor should question the value of this approach. (It might even be necessary to use a stopwatch on the replay to really prove that this much time is spent verbalizing to the ensemble.)

Modeling would involve verbalizing and playing and/or singing passages to the ensemble for the purposes of improving the performance of the ensemble. It is also an effective tool for a selected player in the ensemble to demonstrate passages for the rest of the ensemble. (Caution: Spread the player selection around so that it does not appear that there is favoritism on the part of the conductor, which would lead to some resentment by other members of the ensemble.) Imitation in music has always been one of the most effective approaches. In most instances, it is much more efficient and effective than long verbal explanations concerning the development of performance skills or in fostering musicianship. Modeling and imitation and rote learning are sometimes confused. Rote learning really involves the frequent repetition of a passage repeatedly, while modeling and imitation are based not on repetition but on careful listening to the model and then a quality performance of the example by imitation. Particularly, the conductor can teach such items as tone quality, articulation or bowing, phrasing, style, and musical expression very effectively through modeling and imitation in the rehearsal process.

Demonstrations by the conductor either played or sung with some verbal explanation can be effective for communicating with the ensemble in the rehearsal process. The demonstration may be a positive one in which the conductor shows exactly how to play a given passage or correct a problem. There also may be circumstances in which the conductor will choose to demonstrate how *not to play* a particular passage. From that demonstration, the conductor might then move to showing what he or she expects from the player or the ensemble. In this way, the players understand the solution more immediately. This approach would then clarify and reinforce the proper solution to the performance problem. The question of whether to use a positive or negative approach in demonstrating depends on the particular problem and the given scenario. The conductor must make this decision based on the specific rehearsal situation. In the reality of the rehearsal process, singing would probably be the best method for demonstration in most cases, just because the voice is there and ready. Using an instrument would probably involve some movement or logistics in getting to the particular instrument to produce this demonstration. The demonstration should be secure and musical on the part of the conductor or this could reflect on the poor technical prowess and/or musicality of the conductor. Conductor credibility would be at risk in such a situation.

ESSENTIAL NO. 8: MUSIC READING

Developing Music Reading Skills during the Rehearsal Process

Developing the ability to read music accurately and fluently must be an essential part of the ensemble rehearsal process scenario. If in the rehearsal process, most of the music has to be "worked out," much rehearsal time is wasted. The rehearsal process should be devoted mainly to solving technical and musical problems as an ensemble, and not trying to learn to read the notes, rhythms, and articulations. The private teacher and the conductor must strongly encourage players to become good music readers. If all of the players in the ensemble are good readers, they can cover more music material in the rehearsal process, and the ensemble will play with much better accuracy and fluency. (Sight-reading skill prowess is also critical for most instrumental music ensemble auditions.) Too many players in educational ensembles are dependent on the teacher, the conductor, or the other ensemble members to show them how a particular piece should sound. This promotes music illiteracy among student musicians. In such scenarios, every time the ensemble begins to read a new work, it starts very close to zero!

Consequently, how does one develop and foster reading ability in the ensemble rehearsal process? Largely, the development will be a matter for the individual player. The player, through good instruction, serious application, and maturation, should become a proficient music reader. (It is very unfortunate that all young players are not provided with a workable rhythmic system and encouraged to become independent readers.) Some work can and should take place during the ensemble rehearsal process. The sight-reading experience should be a frequent activity in the rehearsal process. The conductor must try to provide some additional opportunities for sight-reading beyond the initial reading of the concert repertoire. The conductor must make a strong effort in the rehearsal process to improve this music reading aspect. He or she should encourage the players to develop these skills and instill good sight-reading habits for their individual practice. The conductor should expect (or even demand) that players continue to work on and improve their reading ability. Unfortunately, if the responsibility for developing music reading ability falls on the conductor during the rehearsal process, then some rehearsal time will have to be diverted from the real focus of the rehearsal process.

From time to time during the rehearsal process, the conductor should read unfamiliar music and challenge the players "to play it correctly the first time." Likewise, in the initial reading of any work during the rehearsal process, the ensemble should make every effort to play as accurately as possible. Both of these ideas merit utilization by the conductor and the ensemble. If slower tempos will obtain better reading accuracy, then this should be the rule. Playing a work on the initial reading at the specified tempo in the music may cause technical and musical errors, and send a wrong message to the players that music reading is a matter of somehow getting through the piece. *The point is that good reading ability means playing with accuracy.* By playing accurately, the ensemble will improve their music reading and eventually solve the problem of reading at the specified tempo.

The collective ability of the ensemble to read an unfamiliar piece with good accuracy is very important because the ensemble can then begin to achieve those performance aspects that will lead to the three main performance goals. If every time the conductor places a new work before the ensemble and they spend considerable time "chasing the notes and rhythms," then the rehearsals will deteriorate into mainly rote learning. With most ensembles, the actual music is delivered to the players in advance of the rehearsal process and it becomes their responsibility to come to the rehearsal ready to play their parts accurately. *Rehearsals are not really the time for learning notes and rhythms.* This idea should be inculcated within any serious music ensemble. Preparation is expected of the conductor (in score study), and therefore, it should also be expected of the ensemble players to know their parts when they arrive at the rehearsal process. However, they can achieve this only if they are capable of *playing correctly in their individual practice.* The players must become independent readers. This reading involves the playing skills, rhythmic development, key signatures and scales, accidentals, various articulations, seeing the various note groups, musical patterns, and intervals, as well as many other aspects of this music reading.

Problems in Developing Music Reading Skills

In a very large percentage of cases, rhythm is the main obstacle confronting the player in music reading. In a sense, the notes are not variables; they are absolutes. B-flat will always be B-flat on a particular instrument! What changes constantly is the rhythm and articulation (or bowings). When the player has progressed to a somewhat advanced level, he or she can play the actual notes without much thought. However, if the player still tends to focus on the notes, then rhythm becomes secondary and the result is a decrease in both note and rhythmic accuracy. The late Dr. Philip Greeley Clapp, Orchestra Conductor at the University of Iowa for many years, offered sage advice on this matter by stating numerous times during the rehearsal process, *"Keep the rhythm and let the notes fall where they may!"* By focusing on the rhythm, the player now begins to see groups of notes that are necessary for good reading fluency.

Articulation is a problem in music reading in terms of awareness. With wind instruments, the concern is about tonguing and slurring as indicated in the music. Generally, two situations exist with this music reading aspect: (1) With the young player, the articulation markings are ignored or at best played erratically, and (2) when the player focuses on the articulation, then other reading problems may appear. Here is where slow practice to confirm the articulation is beneficial to the player. Fast practice leads to carelessness of articulation in reading music. These articulations pertain to stylistic considerations on wind instruments and bow movement and bowing style on the string instruments. This does encumber the fluency and accuracy of music reading. Again slow practice is the answer to this problem, but not so slow that other problems in controlling the air or the bow then appear. Fundamentally, the player should read in note groups and look for musical patterns to improve the sight-reading of the articulations and bowings. As a conductor, do not allow the players to play the articulations or bowings carelessly. This may mean that occasionally the conductor will have to isolate passages and make sure that the players are performing these articulations or bowings correctly in the rehearsal process.

Especially in the orchestral ensemble, the players must develop the ability *to transpose parts and read in various clefs* at sight. The main wind instruments involved in these transposition activities are the clarinets, trumpets, and French horns. Likewise, the following players need to learn to play in more than the usual clef: bass clarinet in bass clef, bassoon in tenor clef, French horn in bass clef, viola in treble clef, cello in tenor and treble clefs, trombone in tenor and alto clefs, and contrabass in tenor clef.

The players involved must strive to develop reading proficiency with these transposed parts and with the additional clefs. In this same regard, the conductor must know transposition both in terms of sounding pitch produced from the written note and also know the transpositions required for the various instruments in the ensemble. Especially with a young ensemble, it may be necessary for the conductor to instruct the players concerning the interval of transposition and the key signature that the player must think in order to execute the part in question. Usually the tessitura of the part will dictate whether to play the transposition up or down. On occasion, the composer will indicate this with terms such as basso and alto (meaning to transpose down). With most transpositions, the smallest interval of transposition is used, although there are some exceptions to this rule. Once the interval of transposition is determined, then the key signature can be figured by calculating the same interval from C major (no sharps or flats); for example, playing on the B-flat trumpet a trumpet part in D will be played a major third higher and in the key of E major (4 sharps) because the player is thinking up a major third from C major. The written key signature must also be a consideration. In this regard, flats and sharps will be added or subtracted from the original key signature.

Key signatures do pose a problem in music reading especially regarding two aspects: (1) remembering the key signature and being aware of when this changes in the piece, and (2) having the technical facility on the instrument and the familiarity with the key to produce the altered notes involved with the particular key signature. When doing individual practice, it might help to play the major or minor scales and the arpeggios before playing the exercise or the repertoire in that key. This would also familiarize the player with the various keys and key signatures. The players must understand what notes are altered in the particular key signature. Accidentals are usually only problematic because they carry through the measure. In this circumstance, the player tends to forget to carry the accidental through the measure. It would be well for the player to have the mindset that when an accidental appears, the possibility exists that it may occur again in the same measure. There is also the problem of the accidental applying at the octave without the printed music indicating this octave application.

Accuracy of partials on the brass instruments is definitely a reading problem that the instrumental music ensemble needs to confront. The problem is that the brass player can produce the different partials of the harmonic series without the use of valve changes or slide position changes (on the trombone). This is not problematic on the woodwind instruments with the correct fingerings. (The only exception here is the flute that over-blows at the octave if the player does not adjust embouchure and air properly.) The brass player must produce the particular pitch needed with the adjustment of the embouchure and the air stream. Each pitch of the harmonic series has its own special feel that the player needs to acquire in order to improve the accuracy of partials. Large interval skips are likewise a problem on the brass instruments for the same reason as that of the harmonic series partials. However, in addition to this, the brass player in producing a large interval is required to adjust the embouchure and air stream dramatically. This can lead to both inaccuracy and unevenness in tone production. The brass player will need to develop the ability to produce these large interval skips with ease and *maintain even tone quality* as well as play with good technical accuracy. All brass players must develop lip slurs using the "tah-oo-ee" technique. The trombonist should develop the legato tongue technique to negotiate the slurred passages.

To improve music reading ability in the ensemble rehearsal process, the player must physically feel the beat (or pulse); when the length of one beat is known, then the next beat can be anticipated precisely. There are numerous methods of counting. The teacher (or conductor) must provide the student with a systematic method. Too many teachers simply let the student guess about rhythms and rhythm patterns. This, of course, carries over into the ensemble rehearsal process and the performance. In the rehearsal process, the conductor visually provides the beat (or pulse) for the ensemble with the conducting patterns, but the player still needs to feel the beat physically. This is the only way in which the player can accurately subdivide each beat. If this procedure is not implemented, the player becomes dependent on these conducting patterns or the other players in the ensemble for reading proficiency. This then leads to guessing on the part of the player in the rehearsal process as well as during their individual practice.

In the Rehearsal Process

If the conductor will foster music reading in the rehearsal process, the players should benefit greatly in the development of this aspect. In the rehearsal process, the conductor should direct attention to such elements as meter, rhythms, rhythm patterns, note and rest accuracy, correct articulation, and so on. If the player consciously applies what is said or demonstrated in the rehearsal process, ensemble reading improvement should occur. The warm-up period can promote music reading as well as fostering other performance elements. A specific segment of the rehearsal process could be devoted to music reading. However, it is important to emphasize that developing music reading ability must be primarily the player's responsibility. This development, of course, can be strongly encouraged and helped by the conductor.

The conductor *needs to keep the conducting clear and expressive* during the sight-reading experience with the ensemble. The conductor may conclude that the main duty is to keep everyone playing together during this activity, but if the conductor does not conduct clearly and expressively, the ensemble will decide that the main consideration is to be the notes and rhythms. In such a circumstance, the players will stop watching the conductor and then even the notes and rhythms will not be together. The conductor should conduct as if giving a performance and the players will be stimulated to play as expressively and perfectly as possible on the very first reading. This, therefore, assumes that the conductor has studied the score carefully and is prepared to conduct and lead the ensemble in this manner. Players who are not only able to play the notes and rhythms correctly but are aware of the expressive qualities in the music will be much better readers and players than those who do not.

Playing selections up to the prescribed tempo when sight-reading can be somewhat discouraging, especially for young players. It sends the wrong message that it is fine to "plow through" the piece rather than to try to play it accurately on the initial reading. *Instead, the conductor should moderate the tempos* to allow the players to be successful on the first few attempts. At times during the reading of new material, it may be necessary during the reading to indicate verbally the rehearsal letters or numbers to gather the ensemble back together and reassure the group that they are indeed in the right place. By using this procedure, the conductor will not disrupt the continuity and flow of the piece by stopping. The conductor should select music for sight-reading that will allow the players a successful experience. In sight-reading, the emphasis must be on accuracy and playing the work "nearly perfect" the very first time. In this regard, the players should become independent readers and not rely on other players (or even the conductor) for this guidance. If necessary, the conductor should teach the players "how to practice" and "how to improve reading ability" in the rehearsal process in addition to what performance aspects or musical passages might need their attention. Likewise, the conductor needs to encourage the player to read in note groups (the music itself should dictate these groupings) to avoid being surprised. With this procedure, the player begins to read in these "groups" and this will improve fluency.

The conductor can consider the first read-through of program repertoire to be sight-reading material and approach it in this same manner. Before sight-reading a work, the conductor might make the players aware of various details such as the key signature, change of key signature, tempo, change of tempo, meter, style, articulation, dynamics, difficult rhythm patterns, large interval skips, repeat signs, awkward fingerings, accidentals, phrasing, and so on. (I suggest having a separate folder for sight-reading materials. In this way, the ensemble will consider sight-reading a unique or special activity.) The conductor can instruct about techniques that will improve the various aspects of performance, such as reading in note groups, focusing on the rhythm, familiarity with keys, accidentals carrying through the measure, stressing accuracy, as well as many other performance aspects. *Chamber music and/or small ensemble participation* will help reading prowess, because the "one on a part" scenario will put the responsibility directly on the individual player. During the rehearsal process, the conductor should encourage and foster this type of participation.

In summary, for the players to become better sight-readers, the ensemble should spend time in the rehearsal process on this activity if needed. The conductor must be prepared in terms of score study. (There should never be any reason for the conductor to sight-read the score in the rehearsal process.) The conductor can help this process by preparing the material in advance of the reading by circling key signatures, tempo changes, clef changes, and other musical indications that the player might miss in the sight-reading of a work. With a pencil in hand, the players or the conductor can use a vertical line to mark the pulse (especially on difficult rhythmic passages) during the rehearsal process or before the sight-reading begins. Do not deliver conducting patterns and gestures in a routine or indifferent manner during the sight-reading process, but execute them in a clear and expressive way to enhance the reading experience. This procedure indicates to the players that the conductor is interested in achieving more than notes and rhythms in the first reading. He or she should conduct the selection at a tempo in which accuracy is the main concern. At some point, the prescribed tempo will be a factor, but not necessarily on the first reading of a piece. The conductor should select reading material that will foster accuracy but not overwhelm the ensemble. Later, as reading prowess improves, the technical and musical challenges can be increased for the sight-reading experience.

ESSENTIAL NO. 9: DETECTING AND CORRECTING ERRORS

In the rehearsal process, one of the main duties of the conductor is the detection and correction of errors. These errors are found in all of the various elements of the musical performance. The detection of these errors is greatly dependent on the conductor's good score study and *discerned listening during the rehearsal process*. Considered in Rehearsal Essential No. 6 of this chapter, the emphasis was on how important it is for the maturing conductor to develop into being a good listener. In essence, the success of the rehearsal process depends on detecting and correcting errors. If the psychological climate is not conducive to hearing what is happening in the rehearsal environment, then make changes. After the rehearsal process, the conductor should consider what has transpired to prepare for the next rehearsal process. The conductor should consider solutions to these rehearsal errors and problems in preparation for the following rehearsal process.

When an error or problem is perceived, the conductor must consider whether to stop the ensemble during the rehearsal process. In many instances, the player(s) will also detect the error and on the next reading will correct the problem without help from the conductor. Continuing to play will save rehearsal time in many scenarios. Especially with the more mature ensemble, the players should be given ample opportunity to make these corrections without stopping. However, if the error persists, then the conductor should resolve the problem. Stopping the ensemble in order to correct a performance error or problem takes great care and consideration. Here are some of the questions that a conductor might ask before stopping the ensemble to make these corrections:

- Will the player(s) take care of this error?
- At what point should I interrupt the flow to make the correction?
- Is this a major error or an incidental one?
- Does this error need immediate attention?
- What was the reason behind this error?
- Does the error involve a basic performance concept that will continue to cause problems unless corrected?

The point of the questions above is that the conductor must make a decision about stopping the ensemble. *It is a judgment call.* There are a number of different philosophies concerning these important decisions. Some conductors will feel that they need to immediately stop and make the correction. Other conductors feel that stopping destroys rehearsal continuity and the correction should take place at the end of the section, movement, or the entire piece. Some errors need immediate attention while others through repetition will correct themselves. The conductor should realize that these critical decisions affect the entire climate and pacing of the rehearsal process.

When the conductor stops the ensemble to make a correction, the following activities generally occur:

1. The conductor stops the ensemble.
2. The conductor states what the problem or reason behind the error is.
3. The conductor verbalizes, models, or demonstrates the correct performance.
4. The conductor asks for repetition (detailed work) of the passage.
5. The conductor provides feedback to the ensemble.
6. The conductor may then repeat the passage to incorporate the corrected error or problem within the context of the passage.
7. With a specific indication from the conductor, the ensemble continues or else returns to (2) through (6) until the passage is correctly and securely played.

The list above indicates the amount of time spent when stopping the ensemble to make a correction. It is important that the conductor not stop too frequently, to avoid squandering rehearsal time. When stopping the ensemble simply quit conducting; the ensemble should be trained to stop with this. (This may also be an indication that some players are not watching.) If the ensemble does not immediately stop, then the conductor should make it quite clear how the ensemble should react when the conductor stops conducting. Do not allow talking when stopping. The conductor should be ready to speak and rehearse immediately after stopping.

The Rehearsal Time Factor

If you follow the above sequence of activities, a single stop for correction does involve a considerable amount of time. In some cases, if the conductor is insistent on a perfect rendition before proceeding, this activity could involve as much as five to ten minutes of rehearsal time. Therefore, the conductor must carefully consider stopping an ensemble for a correction, so that the available rehearsal time is well spent and there is sufficient rehearsal time to cover the repertoire before the concert performance. There needs to be a balance maintained in stopping the ensemble for corrections or continuing with the idea of the players making the necessary corrections. In some cases, it might be judicious to return to the error or the performance problem at the next rehearsal process.

Alternatives to stopping for corrections with the ensemble include:

1. Continuing with simultaneous verbal comments directed at the player(s) or section involved. This can be an effective procedure, especially with a mature ensemble.
2. Waiting until a stopping place occurs in the music and then making the corrections for the entire passage or section. This also works well for the mature ensembles.
3. Not stopping the ensemble until the end of the work and then returning to those passages that need attention. If the conductor's memory is strong, this can be a very effective procedure.
4. Assuming that the player or players have heard the error also and will correct it on the next repetition or two and deciding to continue.

5. Preparing the score well so that the decision by the conductor to stop or not stop the ensemble is a valid one.
6. Having a clear conducting technique that will guide the players and promote reading accuracy and fluency with the ensemble.
7. Selecting repertoire that is within the prowess range of the ensemble. Otherwise, the conductor will need to stop too frequently for these corrections.

Valid reasons for stopping for corrections with the ensemble are:

- To correct errors and solve technical and musical problems
- To send the message to the players that the conductor wants the ensemble performance to be correct and musical
- So the players will realize that the conductor has heard the error(s) and wants to provide a solution
- So that verbal instruction, modeling, or demonstration can improve ensemble performance and/or clarify the composer's intentions

Valid reasons for not stopping for corrections with the ensemble are:

- To avoid a loss of concentration by the players (especially true for those players who are not directly involved with the correction)
- To prevent an interruption in the musical continuity of the work
- To avoid spending valuable rehearsal time in stopping the ensemble
- To depend more on conducting technique and less on verbal instruction during the rehearsal process
- To train the ensemble to watch the conductor, thereby causing fewer reasons for stopping

Correcting Errors in the Rehearsal Process

When verbal instructions, modeling, or demonstrations are necessary, consider the following ideas:

1. Speak clearly in a voice that can be heard by the player farthest away.
2. Be brief and concise. Long explanations, rarely necessary, will waste rehearsal time.
3. Avoid sarcasm, emotional outburst, and non-constructive comments.
4. Use musical terms and vocabulary. If required, define these terms.
5. Use concise terms, such as louder, softer, more staccato, more legato, etc., as opposed to long, colorful, and time-consuming explanations.
6. With younger ensembles, you may need to make the correction in terms of how (technically) as well as what and where.
7. Remember that you are giving constructive criticism to help the group play better. Personal verbal attacks on players are completely out of line.

8. Clearly identify the place in which the error has occurred with measures, count(s), and players involved.
9. Clearly identify where you wish to begin after you explain, model, or demonstrate the correction, by counting measures backward or forward from a rehearsal letter or number. Always identify this letter or number before counting so that the players can count with the conductor and save some valuable rehearsal time.
10. Comment directly and specifically to the individual or section; general comments to the whole ensemble are usually quite ineffective.

The conductor should direct verbal comments to the players involved in the correction. There should be no confusion as to who needs to solve these performance problems. A general comment to the entire ensemble is less effective. When the conductor stops to make a correction, he or she should make comments immediately so there is no time for concentration loss. Keep verbal comments relevant, musical, and concise when making these corrections. The use of a duplicated sheet to point out problems for specific players to practice may be an efficient means of correcting errors. (The conductor can be very specific about these problems after listening to the recording of the previous rehearsals.) With these instructions expressed in "black and white" for later player practice, the conductor will assume that the individual players will take care of these problems. This procedure, perhaps, is most effective when used for a continuous group of rehearsals so the player can solve these problems as rehearsals go forward and within the context of the ensemble rehearsal process.

When the conductor detects an error that needs attention, he or she must decide upon the best approach for solving the problem with the minimum amount of rehearsal time involved. If the conductor decides to repeat the passage to correct the error, he or she should note the error and state the solution before the detailed work on the passage begins. In some cases, the conductor might choose to model the passage by singing it, playing it, or having a member of the ensemble play it. Detailed work on the passage would follow this modeling procedure. Reinforce this work with feedback to assure the ensemble that they performed the passage correctly in the procedure; the rehearsal process can then move forward. Be sure to do the detailed work rhythmically and slowly in order to achieve this accuracy.

The taping of the rehearsal process can be important to the conductor in preparation for the following rehearsals. Even if the conductor has a "fine ear" for detecting errors and problems, there is always the chance of missing something that needs correcting during the subsequent rehearsals. The conductor should not become dependent on the recorder, but it helps in developing a more meticulous and thorough rehearsal preparation. It is easy to disregard or overlook problems in the rehearsal process because of other things happening at the same moment. The use of recordings can be of great value to the conductor in discovering and recalling these overlooked errors and problems. Conductors, when listening to the recording after the rehearsal process, should ask themselves questions about the various performance aspects. This procedure is a valid reason for recording rehearsals so that in the "quiet" of their home, office, or studio, the conductor can note these problems, design teaching strategies, and provide solutions at the next rehearsal process.

ESSENTIAL NO. 10: STRIVING FOR MUSICALITY

Striving for Musicality during the Rehearsal Process

The elements of musicianship include tempo, changes of tempo, balance, blend, color, texture, articulation/bowing, phrasing, style, dynamics, nuances, and general musical expression. This list of musicianship elements could be expanded and detailed somewhat, but for the sake of simplicity and recall, this is a usable checklist for the advanced conductor. With these elements in mind, the conductor should come to the rehearsal process prepared to nurture these performance aspects with the ensemble. In many instances when trying to produce the rhythms and notes precisely, the conductor (and subsequently by the players) dismiss or ignore some of these musicianship elements in the rehearsal process. Only through striving for musicality during the rehearsal process will the conductor be able to achieve the kind of musical performance desired.

The conductor must bring to the rehearsal process all of the musical background, experience, and sensitivity possible. The score study and preparation before the rehearsal process must focus on this musicality. If the conductor simply learns the score based on keeping the ensemble together to present a clean, precise performance, there will certainly be a lack of musicality in the concert performance. Rather, the maturing conductor must devote much of the preparation time to musical concerns and for conveying the composer's intentions to the ensemble. In the rehearsal process, the conductor needs to cultivate this attitude of musicality among the players. For many ensembles, the focus could be on the musical aspects immediately, because the technical aspects will take care of themselves in most cases.

In thinking about this attitude of musicality, the conductor must bring to the rehearsal process the elements of dynamics, nuances, phrasing, tempo, and tempo changes, and then reinforce these elements during the rehearsal process. The general dynamic level as well as the balance and blend (dynamically) should be a constant concern for the conductor. Likewise, the conductor should always be aware of the phrasing as this communicates to the players and audience the meaning of the music. Certainly the tempo is a special concern for the conductor, but changes of tempo (including the idea of rubato) are particularly significant in the interpretation of the musical composition. In reality, if the players are watching, the conductor should have complete control over changes of tempo. Finally, the nuances bring everything together in the rehearsal process and also in the concert performance. The definition of nuances is, perhaps, a rather nebulous one, but the essence of expressive music is in this idea of nuances. Without this factor, music would not have "soul" or much meaning for the listener.

Musicality in the Concert Performance

Frequently the developing conductor during the concert performance will begin to think about the musicality and this causes the conducting to change considerably from what happened in the rehearsal process. This can lead to disaster; the players are not expecting these changes. The rehearsal process is the time for the conductor to reinforce this musicality in preparation for the concert performance. Therefore, the conductor must be consistent from the rehearsal process to the concert performance. If the ensemble is mature and sensitive enough, the conductor may be able to communicate certain subtleties to the players during the concert performance, but the general rule must be to avoid changes from the rehearsal process to the concert performance. See Chapter 18: Coda: From Rehearsal Process to Concert Performance.

Once the performance begins, *there is little that the conductor can do to communicate except through the conducting technique.* The rehearsal process is over and what the conductor established in the rehearsal process remains to be projected to the audience. Even if the conductor does not have great finesse in conducting technique, the musicality of the conductor should project from the rehearsal process through the response of the ensemble into the concert performance. The conducting technique should be adequate to convey this musicality. The conductor must always be thinking and promoting the elements of musicianship in the rehearsal process with the ensemble. Musicianship is not something that will automatically appear when the rhythm and notes are in place; only if the conductor during the rehearsal process insists on the consciousness of this musicality will such musical performances succeed.

The point is that whatever is produced in the concert performance has to have been reinforced during the rehearsal process. Therefore, such musical items as phrasing, balance, style, dynamics, nuances, and musical expression should be shown in the conducting and rehearsing of these performance aspects in order to come to fruition in the concert performance. The conductor should not assume that these musical performance aspects are just going to happen in the concert performance. The conductor must reinforce these musicality aspects in the rehearsal process. The final dress rehearsal is not the time for this reinforcement. The attitude of musicality must begin at the first rehearsal process and continue throughout the remaining rehearsals in order to reinforce this musicality. While all of this is going on in the rehearsal process in preparation for the concert performance, the players should be improving as individual musicians as well as progressing toward this higher ensemble performance level.

PRACTICAL APPLICATION
(CLASS DISCUSSION/DEMONSTRATION)

1. What ways and means would you use in selecting personnel for a particular ensemble? How would you decide on chair placement?
2. What criteria would you use in selecting music materials for performance?
3. Discuss ways of saving time in the rehearsal process. What would waste time in the rehearsal process?
4. Discuss what is meant by "realistic pacing" in the rehearsal process.
5. Discuss the kind of musical materials to use and the type of musical activities to foster during the warm-up period.
6. What performance aspects should the conductor consider to improve listening and sensitivity in the rehearsal process?

7. What techniques or procedures would you use in getting the players to watch the conductor during the rehearsal process?
8. What should you emphasize in the rehearsal process to improve music reading?
9. When you stop the ensemble to correct an error or solve a problem (of intonation, rhythm, meter, sonority, articulation, precision, phrasing, style, or musical expression), what would you say or do? Choose a performance area and discuss the various approaches in solving the problem.
10. How could the maturity of the ensemble temper your demeanor in making a correction or adjustment? Set up a specific situation.
11. Why is flexibility and adaptability so important for the conductor in the rehearsal process?
12. In striving for the improvement of musicality with the instrumental ensemble in the rehearsal process, what performance areas do you need to cover?
13. Begin to gain familiarity with the standard repertoire found in Appendix A of this book through CD listening, score study, and guidance from the conducting teacher. (See Appendix G for assignment forms.)

RECOMMENDED READING

Bailey, Wayne, *Aural Skills for Conductors*. This workbook stresses the importance of listening by the conductor in the rehearsal process.

Battisti, Frank L., *The Winds of Change: The Evolution of the Contemporary American Wind Band/Ensemble and its Conductor*. This book is a historical and comprehensive listing of the standard and new literature for the wind ensemble.

Bernstein, Leonard, *Young People's Concerts*. Starting on page 345 there is a chronological list of 53 young people's concert repertoire with Leonard Bernstein.

Butts, Carrol M., *Troubleshooting the High School Band: How to Detect and Correct Common and Uncommon Performance Problems*. This textbook covers many of the performance problems found in the band rehearsal process.

Camphouse, Mark, *Composers on Composing for Band*. The organization of this book is based on 11 contemporary band composers and their works.

Casey, Joseph L., *Teaching Techniques and Insights for Instrumental Music Educators*. Section V, Part One is on the process of audiation and Section V, Part Three makes a strong case for the importance of being able to read music fluently.

Dalby, Max F., *Band Rehearsal Techniques*. Chapter 1: Getting Organized gives the band conductor some ideas about a new instrumental program. Chapter 2: Rehearsal Objectives summarizes what should be happening in the rehearsal.

Daniels, David. *Orchestral Music: A Handbook*, 4th ed. This is the most comprehensive listing of orchestral repertoire available.

Fennell, Frederick. *Time and the Winds*. An early compendium of the concert band and wind ensemble repertoire. This is a good introduction to some of the basic standard repertoire for this medium.

Goldman, Richard Franko. *The Wind Band (Its Literature and Technique)*. An early, but significant listing of the standard concert band repertoire. This book traces the repertoire of the band to 1960 under the category of Original Band Music.

Green, Barry, and W. Timothy Gallwey, *The Inner Game of Music.* Chapter 4: The Power of Awareness has important information. Chapter 11: The Inner Game Listener emphasizes its relationship to the awareness strategy.

Holmes, Malcolm H., *Conducting an Amateur Orchestra.* In Chapter 10: Sight Reading, the author makes a strong case for developing the ability to sight-read music fluently in the rehearsal process.

Instrumentalist: Band Music Guide. This book lists compositions alphabetically by title. It also lists some solos and ensembles with band accompaniment.

Instrumentalist: Orchestra Music Guide. This book lists compositions alphabetically by title. It also lists some solos and ensembles with orchestral accompaniment.

Janzen, Eldon R., *The Band Director's Survival Guide: Planning and Conducting the Successful School Band Program.* Chapter 10: Musical Expression in Band Performance and Chapter 11: Evaluating Performance.

Kahn, Emil, *Conducting.* A selected list of annotated and graded orchestra repertoire for school or amateur orchestras is included in the Appendix of this book.

Kohut, Daniel L., *Musical Performance: Learning Theory and Pedagogy.* Chapter Eight: Developmental and Remedial Teaching deal with basic error-detection and -correction procedures in the rehearsal process.

Lisk, Edward S., *The Creative Director: Alternative Rehearsal Techniques.* Both Chapter 3: Creating an Aural and Visual Image of Sound and Chapter 7: The Conductor pertain to listening in the rehearsal process.

Moore, E.C., *Playing at Sight.* This pamphlet was published by G. Leblanc Corporation. The main point of this publication is dealing with music reading.

Prausnitz, Frederik, *Score and Podium.* In the Conclusion of this book and starting on page 513 the author titles this section, A Unique Way of Being a Musician.

Spradling, Robert, *Error Detection: Exercises for the Instrumental Conductor.* This recent workbook (2010) supplies scores and altered parts for the maturing conductor to find errors during the rehearsal process.

Whitwell, David, *A New History of Wind Music.* A revolutionary book for its time (1972) concerning the concert band literature starting with the wind music from the baroque period and going forward from there.

Wittry, Diane, *Beyond the Baton: What Every Conductor Needs to Know.* There are listings of orchestral literature categorized in various ways. This is a very recent book (2007) on repertoire and programming for the symphony orchestra.

Part II

THE CONDUCTOR IN THE REHEARSAL PROCESS

Butler Eitel, Conductor of High School, University, Professional, Military Bands and Orchestras (Charcoal sketches by Elizabeth Eitel Schaefer)

Chapter Four

Conducting Technique

I define conducting technique as the conducting patterns, conducting gestures (hand, wrist, and arm movement), body language, and facial expressions along with the mental and musical activities in controlling these physical aspects that the conductor uses in guiding the ensemble through the rehearsal process and the concert performance. Some refer to conducting technique as baton technique; however, this is somewhat misleading because some conductors prefer not to use a baton, and conducting involves more than just the baton itself. Others have referred to this part of conducting as the manual technique. This term seems to refer only to the physical aspects of the conducting technique; perhaps such a term discounts the mental and aesthetic aspects implied in the conducting technique. By acquiring adequate conducting technique, the conductor can clearly communicate many of the performance aspects as well as the conceived musical interpretation to the ensemble silently.

The development of a clear conducting technique is of paramount importance for the maturing conductor. Just as the ballet dancer or the mime attempts to communicate specifically but silently to the audience, the conductor needs to communicate with the players through these patterns and gestures as well as other means in the instrumental music ensemble rehearsal process and in the concert performance. It is crucial that a clear conducting technique be consistent from the rehearsal process through the concert performance. The conducting patterns and gestures should always be visible to the players to ensure this communication. Two important qualities that the developing conductor should strive to achieve from the beginning of the conducting technique development are: (1) to be comfortable with the conducting patterns and gestures, and (2) to be graceful with these conducting motions. In achieving these two fundamental qualities, the ensemble will tend to respond accordingly in its performance. Along with these qualities are the ideas of clarity, precision, musicality, and authority. Conducting technique must be practiced and developed to become automatic, so that the conductor can place focus on the various aspects of the musicality. The development of this clear conducting technique must also be maintained and continually improved throughout the conductor's career.

The basic elements of the conducting technique need to be seriously studied and developed as background in readiness for leading the instrumental music ensemble. These basic elements are:

1. Conducting the various patterns and the subdivision of these patterns
2. Conducting meters (simple, compound, changing, and asymmetrical)
3. Executing preparatory beats properly
4. Indicating releases clearly
5. Handling fermatas
6. Cueing as needed
7. Indicating dynamic levels, nuances, and ensemble balance
8. Showing styles, accents, phrasing, and musical expression
9. Using the left hand effectively
10. Studying the score in order to implement this conducting technique

The first conducting course offered at the collegiate level usually covers these elements. In some cases, this first exposure to conducting will come before entrance into college; the earlier the better, if these elements are taught correctly. This allows the student more time to work on and develop these conducting motor skills. The student conductor in a high school program can be of great assistance to the instrumental director if these elements are adequately taught and developed. Some of the following paragraphs present ideas on demonstration of the conducting technique by the conducting teacher for the students to emulate.

The reason for the conductor to use conducting patterns is to indicate to the player *what beat is being shown in the prescribed meter*; otherwise, it would be unnecessary to show patterns, if all that were needed was the pulse beat (or ictus). The conductor could then indicate all beats by a simple downbeat. However, it is important for the player to know which beat of the pattern the conductor is showing. In this way, the entire ensemble has a certain confidence that all of the players are on the same beat of the measure. In some instances, the conductor might erroneously show more than one count repeatedly in the same place on the conducting plane and this leads to confusion on the part of the players. *It is extremely important that the conductor show these counts separated and differentiated from each other.* If the conductor learns the patterns well and continues throughout his or her career to show these patterns clearly, the conducted ensemble will respond securely and precisely to these patterns. A key aspect in showing these beats clearly is the speed and motion between the beats, that is, the rebound of the beat. The rebound is where the conductor actually indicates the variation in the beat length and weight. However, large rebounds do tend to distort the conducting patterns. **Demonstration: Showing each pattern clearly with the conducting technique.**

The maturing conductor should avoid becoming "too fancy or fussy" with the conducting patterns and gestures. Likewise, these conducting patterns and gestures must never appear to be executed without a definite purpose. Especially in a concert performance, the presence of the audience may motivate the conductor to become more theatrical or even worse, virtuosic; consequently, the patterns and gestures may become exaggerated to the point of being unclear. Avoid meaningless gestures; to be effective gestures need to impact on the players in a precise manner. A meaningless gesture only confuses and usually occurs when the conductor is trying to show too many things in the conducting technique. The players will greatly appreciate very clear conducting patterns and gestures; this will significantly influence the quality and precision of their performance. **Demonstration: Showing fancy or fussy conducting patterns.**

In the development of the conducting technique, place an emphasis on the idea of "flow" and good communication with patterns and gestures. The observation of successful conductors will confirm this flow aspect in the conducting technique. The idea behind the conducting flow is that the players will always respond to expected gestures. This flow keeps the players from being confused by choppy, unclear motion between beats. The conducting flow equates with the feeling of forward motion in the musical line. The conductor accomplishes this flow by having the score prepared in order to be free from constantly looking at the score; likewise, the players will be watching the conductor to reflect this flow in their playing. In order for the conducting technique to be effective, the conductor should clearly communicate both physically and psychologically with the ensemble through these patterns and gestures. Finally, the idea of "flow" is one of predictability in terms of communicating the next beat to the instrumental music ensemble. **Demonstration: Conducting flow to improve communication.**

Expressive conducting certainly connects with the idea of conducting flow. Beyond this, there are many other ideas about expressive conducting. The music itself largely dictates expressive conducting. Some of these expressive aspects include dynamics, accents, tempo, style, phrasing, and musical interpretation. It is impossible to describe these expressive gestures without the relationship to specific music. When the conductor prepares a musical work, the idea of expressive conducting relates to the minute details of the composition. The point is, to be expressive, the conductor should vary these conducting patterns and gestures in order to show how to perform each beat, measure, or phrase. *From this premise, the conductor now begins to change the conducting technique according to the music being rehearsed or performed.* This means that some beats will be stronger than others, some beat duration will be stretched, and the conducting patterns will need to be adjusted constantly. The rebounds of the pattern must show the specific style of the composition. The end of phrases will need to be conducted to allow for the release of tension, and perhaps, a slight pause rhythmically. All of these items and many more elements will be involved in what we refer to as expressive conducting. **Demonstration: Expressive conducting as related to the music.**

The conductor needs to evaluate constantly the conducting technique to ensure effective communication with the ensemble. Especially on difficult passages involving fermatas, tempo changes, meter changes, releases, and so on, the conductor needs to evaluate this effectiveness. The conductor must practice as one would practice a musical instrument in order to improve his or her technique. The conductor should work to control the ensemble and make every effort to obtain the desired response from the group. In other words, the conductor's main goal must be to influence the ensemble. In the rehearsal process, the conductor should give clear conducting technique a chance in communicating with the ensemble before employing verbal comments and demonstrations. The conductor should think of conducting as if having to produce the music tonally and rhythmically (as in inner singing or inner hearing). The conductor should keep the head and eyes out of the musical score, so there is no loss of communication with the ensemble. All conducting technique aspects should be periodically critiqued and evaluated. Below I offer a checklist of these important conducting technique aspects.

SIX IMPORTANT FUNDAMENTAL ASPECTS
OF THE CONDUCTING TECHNIQUE

In the initial conducting course, considerable time should have been devoted to practicing the patterns and gestures until they become clear, comfortable, graceful, authoritative, and above all else, automatic. Establishing these conducting fundamentals needs to be done, because most of the conductor's focus should be on musical matters and in solving the technical and musical problems that surface during the rehearsal process. The idea of developing good conducting fundamentals and believing in the effect and impact that these can have on the ensemble is the rationale for teaching conducting beyond the basic elements. Unless these conducting fundamentals are in place, there can be no basis for building sound conducting technique or for trying to obtain the desired musicality from the ensemble. Therefore, the conductor must not ignore a conducting fundamental such as keeping the palm of the right hand parallel to the floor at any point. Twisting or turning the right hand in the conducting patterns distorts the conducting plane and patterns. **Demonstration: Emphasizing conducting fundamentals.**

The proper holding of the baton when conducting is important to the basic look of the conducting technique. Hold the baton between the thumb and forefinger of the right hand with the forefinger curled around at both the first and second knuckle. Place this grip with the thumb and forefinger just beyond the baton handle and place the baton comfortably between the thumb and the forefinger. There should be little or no space between the thumb and forefinger. The other three fingers of the right hand should only curl around the handle of the baton in a controlling fashion, without gripping or a feeling of rigidity. What often happens is that the conductor feels the baton should be an extension of the right arm and hand, and tries to keep the baton in a straight line with the forearm and hand. This positioning causes the wrist to be inflexible and the conducting technique then lacks good flow. *The conductor should allow the baton to point somewhat to the left* so that the wrist is free to flow with a comfortable up and down motion in producing conducting patterns and gestures. The wrist should show some flexibility without being "floppy." **Demonstration: Holding the baton and wrist flexibility.**

Many experienced conductors, as well as maturing conductors, need to evaluate their conducting position and stance. If the conductor can establish a good position right away, this will carry through during his or her entire conducting career. At first, this conducting position may not seem to be important, but eventually conducting clarity suffers from a poor conducting position. Mainly, the problem here is that *the hands and arms do not extend far enough from the body*. This results in the hand and arm motion moving toward the player rather than showing the patterns vertically. When the elbow is too close to the body (which projects an acute angle from the side view), then the hand and arm motion will be directed toward the player. At this point, it is difficult for the players to determine exactly where the ictus of the beat is. The side view between the upper arm and the forearm should display an obtuse angle. In this way, the elbow remains higher and the forearm and hand are parallel to the floor. Likewise, there can be a problem of conducting regarding the face and head area where the patterns and gestures again move toward the player rather than showing the vertical pattern to define where the conducting plane is. In this conducting position, it is difficult for the players to judge where the beat (or ictus) actually occurs. Finally, evaluate the conducting stance periodically so that poor habits such as bending the knees, placing weight mostly on one leg, or tapping the foot does not creep into this conducting stance. **Demonstration: Arm and hand position in relationship to the body.**

When the beginning conductor first learns and develops the conducting patterns and gestures without the association of the musical score, he or she can readily establish the conducting position. However, as the conducting student starts to conduct an ensemble and read the musical score, the conducting position may deteriorate through the lack of focus on this position aspect. Several negative things may occur in the process. The right elbow may drop too low and toward the body, causing a complete change in the conducting position and subsequently in the clarity of the patterns or gestures. The conducting patterns will become less centered and focused. The right arm, due to the elbow position change, will show motion toward the players instead of defining the ictus of the conducting pattern. Likewise, the left arm and hand may assume a position too close to the body and make such gestures as showing the crescendo or diminuendo to be less effective for the players. Most of the problem in this regard may be that the arms and hands now extend over the musical score, and *this may result in some visibility difficulties in reading the score*. This position problem makes a strong case for studying and preparing the musical score rather than relying on constant reading of the score while conducting over the stand during rehearsal process or in the concert performance. **Demonstration: Conducting position while reading from the score and conducting the instrumental music ensemble.**

The attention position for the conductor is crucial in alerting the players that the music is about to begin and also in dictating the conducting position. The conductor allowing the arms to spread out in opposite directions does not give the ensemble a focused look at the conductor. In many instances, this attention position (especially from the audience view) is rather grotesque in appearance. The conductor in this rather bizarre position will then need to bring the hands into the center for the ensemble before executing the preparatory beat and downbeat. Even this bit of adjusted movement in centering the hands may be a deceptive motion as to the intentions of the conductor. When the conductor has the hands at approximately 18 inches apart, then he or she should scan the ensemble to see that all of the players are alert and ready to play. With this activity, the conductor should not wait for too long or too little a time before executing the preparatory beat. If the players become sensitized to a longer wait, they will not respond to the playing position as rapidly. If the wait in scanning the ensemble is too short, not all of the players will be ready to play, and this will lead to considerable frustration on the part of the ensemble members. **Demonstration: Assume the attention position, scan the ensemble, and then execute the preparatory beat.**

The conductor must always show that the meter *divides into either 2s or 3s.* With the preparatory beat, the conductor must define this subdivision and show this distinction with this passive gesture. The conductor will tend to conduct more in the subdivision of 2s as found in simple meter (2/4, 3/4, and 4/4). In this situation, the preparatory beat and the downbeat will be reflected with fairly even speed unless the musical expression is a factor at any given point. However, when conducting compound meter (3/8, 6/8, 9/8, and 12/8 or one beat in 3/4 meter as in a waltz), the motion and feel of the preparatory beat and the downbeat need to vary in speed in order to indicate to the ensemble this subdivision into 3s. In this situation, the motion will accelerate at the bottom of the beat and then slow at the top of the beat to indicate the subdivision into the three parts. When conducting compound meter (3/8 in a one-pattern, 6/8 in a two-pattern, 9/8 in a three-pattern, and 12/8 in a four-pattern) the conductor must show each beat dividing into 3s. Pattern time in the subdivision of 3s is gained by showing a slower upward motion. Once the rebound begins to descend toward the next downbeat, the conductor has committed precisely to where the beat will occur. Conducting in one beat per measure (as in 3/4 meter) must show that the beat divides into 3s. **Demonstration: Showing the meter beats clearly for the ensemble.**

For the conducting technique to be effective, the players in the ensemble must learn to watch the conductor and the conducting patterns and gestures in order to respond properly. The players often ignore conducting patterns and gestures for a number of reasons: (1) the lack of eye contact between the conductor and the players, (2) the conducting patterns and gestures are unclear, (3) music reading problems may take precedence over watching the conductor, (4) the technical problems encountered by the players interfere with watching the conductor, and (5) the players discount the importance of watching the conductor. In many instances, the players have not learned or been trained to "read the stick." The players will watch the conductor only if there is a reason for doing so. The primary reason behind watching the conductor, of course, is to enhance communication between the conductor and the players. If the players learn the music by rote or mostly through repetition, watching the conductor becomes less important; the chances of good communication between the conductor and the players are reduced in such a rehearsal process environment. **Demonstration: Proper communication between the conductor and players.**

If the conductor appears to be constantly looking at the score at the beginning, the players' reaction is to do the same with their individual parts, resulting in a lack of communication between the conductor and players. The musical score should be a reference when conducting and rehearsing, not a "security blanket" or a "magnet." Because of the fear of losing their place in the musical score or the lack of score study and preparation, conductors continue to watch the score rather than communicate with the ensemble. Conducting teachers frequently suggest to their students that they memorize the first few measures of a musical work so that they can establish eye contact with the players. What items will the conductor need to have memorized at the beginning of a work in order to assure eye contact and communication with the ensemble? The answer is, "Surprisingly, very little!" Tempo, meter, starting count, attack, dynamic level, and the basic style of the work are the essential items. Interestingly enough, these are the very items required to execute the initial preparatory beat properly. **Demonstration: Immediate eye contact for communication at the beginning.**

What can the conductor do to counteract this communication problem? First, he or she must know the musical score so that eye contact with the ensemble is consistent throughout. Second, remind the ensemble to watch and respond precisely. The conductor should encourage players to watch, especially at critical places such as at the beginning, tempo changes, fermatas, phrase endings, sudden dynamics, and so on. The reason for watching the conductor is for guidance, and accomplishing this with an ensemble involves being insistent that the ensemble is actually watching. Another suggestion for establishing this important communication between the conductor and ensemble is to have the group count verbally as the conductor shows patterns and gestures to indicate tempos, tempo changes, dynamics, and styles. The conductor can promote this activity during the warm-up period as well as in the rehearsal process proper. In this procedure of "conduct and count," the players will become more aware of the conductor's patterns. Finally, if the conductor is very clear and expressive with the patterns and gestures, this will certainly lead to a better response from the ensemble. However, the conducting patterns and gestures must vary; monotonous "time beating" will cause the players to stop watching these conducting patterns and gestures. **Demonstration: Verbal counting by the players as a reminder to watch the conductor.**

Such a conducting procedure as changing tempo unexpectedly will show if the players are watching. (Use caution here in not overdoing this "alertness" procedure; it will lead to frustration and indifference on the part of the players. Players do not appreciate constant deception in the conducting technique.) To some extent, the conductor can reinforce and improve the routine of watching by varying the tempo, dynamics, and style during the warm-up period. Also in the warm-up period, playing without music or with hand signals and gestures by the conductor will free the players from the written music and reinforce the idea of watching the conductor. Smaller gestures, at times, may also alert the players about watching the conductor; the players will need to be more observant in such a situation. (Perhaps the most telling evidence that the players are not watching is the conductor's intuitive sense of being disregarded musically, and in general, having a lack of good control over the ensemble.) As mentioned previously, if the conductor shows good eye contact and clear, expressive patterns and gestures, the ensemble now has a reason for watching the conductor; this will be reciprocated in the rehearsal process by the players responding sensitively and expressively. **Demonstration: Showing expressive gestures through good eye contact with the ensemble.**

ADEQUATE CONDUCTING TECHNIQUE

If the players find it difficult to follow the conductor's patterns or gestures, several things may occur. First, the players simply give up trying to follow the conductor. All is lost. Second, if the ensemble valiantly tries to follow poor conducting technique, the results may be even worse than not watching at all. Third, respect and credibility for the conductor decreases as the player frustration level rises. To be successful in the rehearsal process, the conductor must have control of the ensemble with adequate conducting technique as a prerequisite to effectively rehearsing the ensemble. It is important for the developing conductor to realize that he or she will be able to control many performance aspects silently during the rehearsal process with adequate conducting technique. (By taping the rehearsal process, the conductor will be able to tell if the players are watching the conductor consistently.) **Demonstration: Adequate conducting technique in order to control the ensemble.**

Conducting technique, like most skill areas, is dependent on the acquisition of knowledge and then the application of this information. Even if the conducting technique is adequate or better, there may be circumstances in the rehearsal process when the conductor will need to stop the ensemble to explain the conducting patterns or gestures. This explanation will ultimately save time by resolving the confusion existing between the conductor and the players. (When explaining the conducting patterns and gestures, the conductor may find it beneficial to sing and conduct the passage simultaneously.) Of course, the conductor must sense or hear when this confusion occurs. Examples of such confusion are the manner in which a fermata is handled, how an initial tempo is established when beginning on a fraction of a beat, how a sudden change of tempo is indicated, how an accent is shown (gesture of syncopation), or perhaps how a passage is being conducted involving the subdivision of the beat. Once the confusion is resolved, the conducting technique should suffice for the players. From that point on, the conductor should keep the conducting technique of that passage consistent throughout the rehearsal process and into the concert performance. If the conductor decides to change the conducting technique after that, then he or she must reinforce the change during the rehearsal process. **Demonstration: Explanation and/or demonstration of how to conduct a particular passage.**

This automatic conducting technique comes about by having developed secure conducting patterns and gestures, having studied the score carefully, and having practiced conducting the work at hand. This involves considerable time and preparation on the part of the conductor. When this score study and the preparation are realized, then the conductor's concentration can be placed almost entirely on the musical interpretation of the work and in the detection and resolution of performance problems as they occur in the rehearsal process. There is a lurking danger in all of this, however, in the sense that the conductor must continue to audit and evaluate the conducting technique so that it continues to be meaningful, precise and above all else, musical. **Demonstration: The importance of automatic conducting technique in order to show the musical interpretation.**

The developing conductor must believe that through good conducting technique, he or she can significantly influence the ensemble. If the conductor does not accept this premise, then the intense study of conducting holds little worth for the maturing conductor. It is apparent with many conductors that they are indifferent to this idea and to the positive effect that good conducting can or will make on the performance of an ensemble. Conducting in the rehearsal process or in the concert performance cannot be a casual activity in which the conductor does little more than show the pulse for the ensemble. (This kind of conductor is often labeled "a time-beater.") The conductor must prepare and conduct the ensemble in the rehearsal process exactly as he or she desires to present the ensemble to the audience in the concert performance. **Demonstration: Good conducting technique will influence the performance of the ensemble.**

One way of varying the patterns and gestures is for the conductor to be aware of *the use of passive and active gestures*. The active gestures indicate to the ensemble that a musical response should happen. This type of gesture says to the ensemble "play in a certain way"—such as staccato, marcato, tenuto, or legato. The passive gestures say to the ensemble "do not play yet." The passive gestures are preparatory beats, beats to indicate rests, or other beats that should not elicit an immediate response from the ensemble. *The gesture of syncopation* in which the conductor changes the speed of the pattern in order to achieve a particular response from the ensemble is another example of a way to vary the conducting patterns in order to show these syncopations, entrances, and accents. In executing the gesture of syncopation for an on-the-beat accent, for a syncopation figure, or for an off-the-beat entrance, the pattern must stop on the previous rebound and then arrive in time at the following beat. For off-the-beat accents, the conductor must produce a strong on-the-beat gesture before the accent occurs. Above everything else, the music itself will be the catalyst as to how the conductor varies the patterns and gestures. It is always important for the conductor to realize that the active gesture will only be effective, however, if the preparatory gesture is executed correctly before the actual musical response is expected. **Demonstration: Varying the patterns and gestures; showing the gesture of syncopation.**

With adequate conducting technique, the conductor should have control over two basic aspects in the rehearsal process and the concert performance. The ensemble must *play together precisely*, and *project musicianship* during the rehearsal process as well as in the concert performance. The conductor should reinforce these two elements in the rehearsal process. It is well for the conductor to keep in mind that what is done in the rehearsal process will be reflected exactly in the concert performance. The conducting technique must be such that the ensemble is able to respond properly to what the conductor is indicating. If the conducting technique is inadequate to show this precision and/or musicality to the ensemble, what will happen in both the rehearsal process and the concert performance will be a pronounced absence of these performance qualities. What is needed to guarantee the communication of precision and musicality with the ensemble are (1) good score study and preparation by the conductor, (2) adequate conducting technique, (3) effective rehearsing skills, (4) the reinforcement of these aspects in the rehearsal process, and (5) a mutual attitude of alertness and musicality by both the conductor and the players in the rehearsal process and in the concert performance. **Demonstration: Controlling the precision and musicality of the ensemble.**

OVER-CONDUCTING

One of the common problems in the conducting technique is over-conducting, in which the conducting patterns and gestures become too large, exaggerated, or uncontrolled.

The results are a loss of clarity in the precision of the beat, and subsequently poor communication with the ensemble. The conductor should train the ensemble to respond to gestures precisely without using excessive motions. Then the problems of over-conducting will be nonexistent, and thereby, unnecessary to employ such patterns at any point in the rehearsal process or in the concert performance. The conductor cannot expect the ensemble to play with any distinct contrast unless he or she shows variations in these patterns and gestures. For example, *it is difficult to achieve dynamic contrast if the gestures are all large and exaggerated.* If the conductor does not over-conduct but shows this dynamic contrast in the patterns and gestures, players should respond in a positive manner. **Demonstration: Disruption of precision and musicality of the ensemble with exaggerated patterns and gestures.**

The conductor usually resorts to exaggerated gestures when the ensemble does not respond to normal-sized patterns and gestures. This leads to even more expansive patterns on the part of the conductor. The continuation of these large conducting motions in the rehearsal process will cause conductor fatigue and a lack of clarity in these patterns. Conducting indications of dynamics, phrasing, and style depend somewhat on the size of the beat patterns and gestures; do these according to the demands of the music and in the spirit of the work. Not only in terms of dynamics will large gestures and constant motion tend to blur the clarity of the conducting technique, but also the ensemble will become less sensitive to the many other subtle changes indicated by the conductor in the music. Over-conducting creates more problems than it solves, such as heavy playing, unwanted accents, uncontrolled dynamics, and above all else, poor precision. It is good to use energy and weight in the conducting technique, but not to the detriment of the conducting clarity. Over-conducting also causes the players *to depend too much on the conductor.* **Demonstration: The loss of clarity and musical sensitivity with exaggerated patterns and gestures.**

The conductor must guard against ineffective patterns and gestures used in an effort to "draw the music from the ensemble." Many times, these exaggerated gestures develop rather unconsciously with the conductor. Trying to do too much or showing too many things (i.e., too many cues, too many dynamic indications, too many beats in a measure, and too much emotion) may cause over-conducting and are examples of such over-conducting and negative leadership. This causes the conductor to look "fussy" and the ensemble to respond nervously and insecurely. If the conductor feels that all of these patterns or gestures are necessary to bring the work to fruition, it might be well to question whether the ensemble is ready at this time to perform such concert repertoire at this level of technical or musical difficulty. **Demonstration: Trying to do too much with the conducting technique.**

Poor posture and irritating mannerisms by the conductor can be distractions along with over-conducting. The conductor should realize that the ensemble (in the rehearsal process and concert performance) and the audience (in the concert performance) are viewing the conductor. Exaggerated gestures and other distractions such as facial grimacing or knee bending by the conductor will in no way improve the musical performance of the ensemble or the audience appreciation for the performance. In the rehearsal process and concert performance, the conductor must eliminate distracting mannerisms such as foot tapping, pointing to the ear for intonation improvement, bouncing around on the podium, or in general displaying poor conducting posture. This poor posture exists far too often with the conductor in both the rehearsal process and the concert performance. The conductor should recall the main reason behind the idea of conducting: to influence the ensemble into producing the best possible performance. For the most part, the players and the audience are unimpressed by these irrational mannerisms and peculiar gyrations, such as lunging toward a section for a cue or other such postured affectations. **Demonstration: Poor posture and irritating mannerisms while conducting (foot tapping, knee bending, or facial grimacing).**

It is helpful for the conductor to observe the conducting motions, pattern clarity, left hand use, facial expressions, and many other items considered over-conducting in front of a mirror, or better yet *by videotaping the conductor in the rehearsal process.* This taping can be accomplished by conducting to recordings (although this has some limitations, such as tempo indications, handling fermatas, preparatory beats, etc.) or silently through inner singing (which seems to be the most effective means for the experienced conductor). Likewise, this videotaping of the rehearsal process for self-evaluation can be a revealing experience for the conductor. In this situation, place the camera at the back of the ensemble facing toward the conductor and locate the microphones in front of the ensemble for the best sound coverage. At times, it might be advantageous to bring a "master conductor" into observe the rehearsal process and the conducting technique. This might be difficult for the conductor's ego but would certainly be profitable for the conductor. Chapter 17: Conductor Profile and Self-Evaluation covers some of these areas of the conducting and rehearsing evaluation.

OTHER CONDUCTING TECHNIQUE PROBLEMS

Small patterns and gestures can lead to a definite loss of clarity in the conducting technique and cause frustration on the part of the players trying to follow the conductor. If the patterns and gestures are too small to be discernible, the player will again give up trying to follow the conductor's indications. There might be occasions when the conductor would use small patterns and gestures to show extremely soft dynamics, but not for long. The conductor must realize that what the players see is general motion in the patterns and gestures. If that motion is minimal or microscopic in nature, the visual aspect for the player becomes unclear. However, in fast tempos, the conductor may reduce the size of the conducting patterns to cover the space between beats. If the speed of these patterns becomes too great to show good clarity, then the conductor should decrease the number of beats in each measure. **Demonstration: Using small patterns and gestures continuously that result in poor ensemble precision.**

As mentioned in the preceding paragraph, the players respond to the general motion of the conductor's patterns and gestures. The patterns must move from one beat to the next with sufficient space for the players *to differentiate each beat.* There may be times when the players will need less guidance from the conductor concerning the pulse. In these circumstances, the conductor can use a small or even minute pattern. However, if this curtailed motion in the conducting pattern is used frequently or continuously, the players will tend to watch these conducting patterns and gestures less and then the necessary communication with the ensemble will become questionable. Indeed, with the younger ensemble, the players should have a clear indication of the pulse all of the time. In summary, small patterns will be ineffective when the motion of the gestures is visually difficult to see and/or impossible to comprehend. **Demonstration: The loss of clarity in showing the pulse with small patterns.**

With a mature ensemble, there are specific circumstances where there is less need for showing the pulse of the music and the conductor can turn to being more expressive. However, *in rhythmically complex sections or passages,* any ensemble will want to see the indication of the pulse clearly by the conductor to execute the subdivision of the beat precisely. In other words, there are times when the conductor must execute the pattern very clearly in order for the ensemble to subdivide the beat as well as to produce a clear indication of which beat the conductor is showing. In such a circumstance, the conductor may find it necessary to resort to a slightly larger gesture even though the dynamic level requested by the composer in the music is quite soft. It may then be necessary, during the rehearsal process, to rehearse and reinforce this indicated dynamic level to coincide with the composer's intentions or the conductor's realization of the musical interpretation. **Demonstration: Clear patterns shown when the players need to subdivide the beat precisely.**

KEEPING PATTERNS AND GESTURES FOCUSED

Controlling the instrumental music ensemble requires that the conductor keep the patterns and gestures focused. Certainly, over-conducting and extremely small gestures will detract from this clear focus. The ensemble responds best to expected patterns and gestures, not to vague or nebulous conducting. If this focus of the conducting patterns and gestures is inconsistent, then confusion, poor precision, and the absence of musical expression will result in the ensemble performance. The conductor must be aware that the patterns and gestures are controlled and kept within the confines of the "conducting box." *This conducting box is an area where the players can expect to see the conducting motions.* The conducting box should move with the conductor if the conductor turns slightly to the right or left. Ask yourself the following question: "What is the purpose or worth of showing any of these patterns and gestures when the players cannot see them clearly or interpret them correctly?" **Demonstration: Keeping the patterns and gestures focused within the conducting box.**

Design the players' sight lines for the rehearsal process and concert performance so that the players will see all of these patterns and gestures comfortably and the communication with the ensemble is in no way obstructed. If the players have to adjust their head or playing position (for eye contact) in order to see the conductor's patterns and gestures, they will soon tire of this visual game. The players should be able to view the conductor *through peripheral vision and/or with direct eye contact* during certain specific situations in the music, such as initial attacks, the beginning of the phrases, tempo changes, fermatas, sudden dynamics, and so on. The conductor must make certain that the stand is low enough so that all of the players can see the bottom of the beat (or ictus). With younger ensembles, the conductor may need to remind the players to adjust their chairs and stands for easy viewing of these conducting patterns and gestures. In this regard, there should never be more than two players on a stand because the sight-line angles from the players to the conductor will then become somewhat obscured. **Demonstration: Achieving good sight lines from the players to the conductor.**

The conducting teacher and the student conductor must see that the arms and hands stay centered and not allow them to spread apart or lower to the point where it would become difficult for the players to see the patterns and gestures when they look toward the conductor on the podium. If the maturing conductor does not solidify this "centered" position initially, then there will be a tendency to continue this conducting problem indefinitely. Keeping the patterns and gestures centered lessens the chance of an over-conducting problem. If the conductor keeps the patterns and gestures confined and centered, the players will be able to see these motions clearly. In particular, the two-pattern and the three-pattern tend to be too far to the right because these patterns never move to the left of center at any point theoretically. **Demonstration: Centering the two-pattern and the three-pattern.**

The positioning of the conductor in relationship to the ensemble physically is a consideration in terms of the placement of the conducting plane. If the conductor is extremely tall, a podium may not be necessary. However, if the conductor were relatively short, he or she would need a podium. Never show the bottom of the conductor's beat (placement of the ictus) or the conducting plane below the sight lines of the players. This can also occur if the conductor's stand is adjusted too high, causing a loss of visibility between the players and the conducting plane. In some instances, it may be necessary for the conductor to move away from the ensemble so that the angle of the player's sight line is improved. If not, the players in the first or second row of the ensemble will constantly have to adjust the head and eyes in order to see the patterns and gestures. Another option is for the conductor to lower or raise the conducting plane by adjusting the patterns and gestures. There is some danger in this adjustment, however, in that the conductor may forget to continue this throughout the rehearsal process or even in the concert performance. Finally, the conducting plane should remain quite consistent in height except for showing sudden soft dynamic indications. In this situation, the conducting plane may be somewhat higher. **Demonstration: Defining and adjusting the conducting plane.**

PREPARATORY BEATS

The key to effective conducting technique is in the preparation. In general, the preparatory gestures should always precede the beat of execution with initial attacks, cues, accents, sudden dynamic changes, and sudden tempo changes. The conductor must always show a preparatory gesture before the time the players should respond. In most cases, make this anticipatory gesture only an instant before the response is required. An example of this is the indication of an accent where the conductor makes the preparatory gesture the instant before the accent is played. The conductor must show the off-the-beat accent with a strong placement on the beat. Another example of this preparation idea is extending the length of a beat by delaying the preparation and then after that doing the release/preparation into the next beat. There are many more examples that I could cite here, but the idea of preparation in conducting should have received considerable attention in the initial conducting course and textbook. **Demonstration: The off-the-beat accent shown with a strong placement on the beat.**

The conductor should train and sensitize the ensemble to watch for the preparatory beat and respond correctly and precisely. The conductor should avoid, even during the rehearsal process, starting the ensemble by verbally counting or by showing two or more preparatory beats (preferably, one preparatory beat). Counting or saying "ready, play" during the rehearsal process to begin a section should be infrequent so that it does not establish a "crutch" for the conductor or the ensemble. Of course, the conductor should not use any verbal indications during the concert performance. The preparatory gesture should also reflect the meter beat, that is, the subdivision of the beat into 2s or 3s. Only by showing this preparatory subdivision of one beat clearly can the conductor hold the ensemble responsible for the subdivision of the first beat of music as well as the subsequent beats. Also, the preparatory beat should be within the confines of the conducting box for the players to respond securely. **Demonstration: Executing the preparatory beat properly.**

To accomplish a precise attack at the beginning of a selection, section, or phrase, the conductor should insist that the players breathe in time with the preparatory beat. When all players do this, the chances are excellent that good precision on the attack will result. Therefore, even string players, keyboard players, and percussionists need to be encouraged to breathe with the preparatory beat. The success of the preparatory beat secures the psychological communication between the conductor and players. The conductor will accomplish this clear preparatory beat and downbeat by also breathing with the ensemble as well as indicating this with eye contact and/or a nod of the head. The conductor must execute the gesture in a synchronized fashion so there is no doubt about where the ictus is placed or what will be the conceived tempo of the music. To go one step further, principal players can show motions for the particular section to synchronize this attack. The string sections often perform this function because of the bow motion that will parallel the body motion. **Demonstration: Breathing with the preparatory beat.**

In some instances when the conductor wants a precise attack, it becomes natural and habitual for the conductor to stop at the top of the preparatory beat to indicate this precision of the attack; unfortunately, the exact opposite results occur. The player is now confused about where the attack should be placed. With preparatory beats on an isolated attack, with pizzicato placement, or even with the staccato style, the conductor must keep the right hand moving; otherwise it misrepresents to the player where the downbeat will fall. The meter beat must be showing 2s or 3s. The tempo should be shown by the speed of the preparatory beat motion. The conductor must indicate with a flick of the wrist as to when this preparatory beat motion begins and then continue this through to the downbeat. The length of one beat (or the basic unit to be conducted) is shown by the conductor and expected by the players. The dynamic level is shown by the size of the preparatory beat and the intensity of the downbeat. In showing the basic style with the preparatory beat and downbeat, the variation in speed and the tension (or relaxation) of the preparatory beat will show how these notes should be articulated stylistically. *Remember: Good preparatory gestures are necessary to ensure a precise attack and the desired response from the ensemble.* **Demonstration: The preparatory beat showing attack, meter beat, tempo, dynamic level, and the basic style.**

The musical significance of the preparatory beat connects with the idea of the essence and spirit of the music. I present more information concerning the essence and spirit of the music in Chapter 14: Style and Musical Interpretation. The conductor should have discovered this essence and spirit of a given work or section so that the preparatory beat reflects these important musical qualities. The essence is the basic or fundamental nature of the work. The spirit is the vitality or driving force of the work. Unless the conductor has studied the score and discovered this essence and spirit, even the initial start of the piece will lack valid communication with the players, and then subsequently with the audience. It is not really all that surprising that so many musical interpretations are boring and unimaginative when the conductor has failed to grasp this essence and spirit of the music being performed and fails to show this with the initial preparatory beat to the ensemble. **Demonstration: Showing the essence and spirit of the music with the preparatory beat.**

When starting on beats other than beat one in the measure, the rule is that the preparatory beat always precedes the beat on which the music begins (beat of execution). Therefore, if the piece starts on beat three, the preparatory beat is beat two in the designated meter. In a few instances where the tempo is relatively fast, there might be reason to show more than one preparatory beat to ensure establishment of the tempo. In showing this initial preparatory beat, the motion must be clear and not anticipated with a slight motion before the preparatory beat. In such a situation, the players might erroneously try to play on the preparatory beat. Show this preparatory beat in the proper direction for the players to understand which beat is the beat of execution. The one exception to this rule is the preparatory beat occurring on beat one wherein this conducting gesture is straight down theoretically. This vertical motion may confuse the players into thinking that this is a beat of execution. To avoid this problem, the conductor may simply want to show the preparatory beat in the opposite direction of the beat of execution, and thereby eliminate this possible confusion. **Demonstration: Starting on beats other than beat one of the indicated meter.**

Starting on the fractions of the beat presents special problems for the conductor in that not all the players may subdivide the initial beat properly. By using only one beat preceding this fraction of a beat as the preparatory beat, the conductor has not shown the ensemble one full beat to subdivide precisely. The players are then guessing as to the proper subdivision or the desired tempo of the conductor. If the conductor and players have rehearsed together for a considerable length of time, it may be possible to achieve the necessary precision in playing on the fractions of the beat with just one preparatory beat, but even here, there may be some hesitation as to exactly where to place the first note. Therefore, *the recommendation is for giving two preparatory beats*, thereby showing the length of one full beat before having to subdivide the beat. This can be accomplished in one of two ways: (1) the preparatory beats will simply be the two preceding beats before the fraction of the beat begins, or (2) the left hand can flick downward to show the first of the two preparatory beats and the right hand will then execute the preparatory beat before the fraction of the beat begins. In both conducting procedures, one full beat is shown before the players must enter and subdivide the beat properly. There may be circumstances in which the conductor will have insufficient time musically to execute two preparatory beats, and will then need to reinforce this in the rehearsal process. **Demonstration: Starting on the fractions of the beat in the indicated meter.**

SPECIAL AREAS OF THE CONDUCTING TECHNIQUE

Areas of concern in refining the conducting technique include the handling of fermatas, changes of tempo, subdivision and merging (transitional patterns), supermetric and melded gestures, releases, cueing, and the effective uses of the left hand. Even though the conducting fundamentals course or textbook may have addressed these conducting problems, they need the conductor's constant and special attention later in executing these basic elements of the conducting technique. The conductor should continuously evaluate these problems in terms of conducting clarity. The use of videotaping and/or a mirror should reveal the clarity of such patterns and gestures. Likewise, when studying the score, these conducting problems need to receive special consideration by the conductor. In most instances, the conductor will need to consider these patterns and gestures while performing inner singing (or inner hearing) during this initial score study and certainly during the individual conducting practice.

Fermatas require a clear understanding on the part of the conductor. *Each fermata presents a unique situation.* In reality, a fermata indicates a cessation of the rhythmic aspect of the music. However, the conductor in most situations may want the musical pulse to continue in his or her mind to dictate a logical release of the note and/or the continuation of the music. First, the conductor must make a musical judgment about a tempo change or no tempo change before arriving at the fermata. Then he or she must consider the length of the fermata. (Beginning conductors tend not to hold fermatas long enough.) Finally, the release of the fermata and preparation for what follows the fermata must be determined. Even if the conducting technique is good, the conductor on certain occasion may need to explain the gestures used in handling a fermata in order to guarantee good precision from the ensemble. The options following a fermata are (1) no break, (2) one beat break, and (3) more than one beat break. These options are problematic when the music continues after the fermata. In the final analysis, the conductor must decide on the musical and dramatic aspect of the fermata as well as the placement and the flow of the beats in order to avoid any awkward look with the conducting release. The release needs to be executed by a clockwise or counterclockwise downward motion depending on the continuation of the music and placement of the following beat. **Demonstration: Handling the fermata musically (three ways).**

The conductor frequently executes these sudden tempo changes very poorly. Generally, the problem with sudden tempo changes lies *not in making these exact tempo changes*, but rather in making a gradual or late one. The important aspect here is in the preparation for the change of tempo. The conductor must show this preparation as a preparatory beat into the new tempo. The danger here is that of poor ensemble precision due to unclear conducting gestures or the lack of alertness on the part of the players. I expand these ideas in Chapter 12: Tempo and Ensemble Precision. The conductor must measure and gauge gradual changes of tempo so that the eventual tempo is achieved at the proper time. Accelerando, stringendo, poco a poco animando, ritardando, and rallentando are all terms that indicate these gradual tempo changes and require a smooth change in tempo. The conductor must make these gradual tempo changes consistently and reinforce them during the rehearsal process. **Demonstration: Conducting sudden and gradual tempo changes.**

When the conductor finds it necessary to change the number of pulses between measures, either *by subdividing or by merging,* he or she must take care to keep the musical flow. Below are some basic rules to follow regarding the subdivision and the merging of patterns:

1. The subdivided beat should move in the opposite direction to the next main beat.
2. Execute the subdivided beat (mostly with the wrist) smaller in order to keep the basic pattern clearly shown.
3. The initial preparatory beat is always the basic unit to show one beat before the beat of execution. For example, if the 8th note is conducted then the preparatory beat is the length of one 8th note.
4. The subdivision of the conducting pattern will divide into either 2s or 3s.
5. Execute both the subdivision and the merging very smoothly.

The conductor should calculate and execute these transitions of the conducting patterns in merging, such as 6 into 2, 3 into 1, or even 4 into 2. Conductors often employ these changes of conducting patterns in accommodating tempos that fall in the middle of a so-called in-between tempo with either of the patterns or else are due to a gradual or sudden tempo change indicated by the composer. Examples of this "in-between" tempo in either pattern would be found in the fast 3/4 section (3 into 1) in the Beethoven *Egmont Overture* and also the concluding alla breve section (2 into 4) in this same work. The conductor must decide how many beats should be in a measure depending on the tempo and the flow of the piece. This can involve either subdivision or merging of the various patterns. When there is a tempo change indicated by the composer, the tempo change might employ an abridged or transitional pattern by the conductor between the two regular patterns to achieve this required smoothness. Such an example would be the transitional pattern from three into one where the pattern would gradually merge from the three-pattern into the one-pattern or the reverse. **Demonstration: Subdivision and merging patterns.**

There are also the conducting techniques of *supermetrics and melded gestures* in which two or more beats may be grouped under one gesture to improve the flow of the music. The conductor should not overdo supermetrics but use them effectively to enhance the musical expression and flow in the ensemble performance. Supermetric conducting is imposed on larger groupings of the metric measure. Melded gestures are used in the same way as supermetrics, and are perhaps more frequently employed. The conductor should look for these various applications of supermetrics and melded gestures during score study and mark these in the musical score for consistent usage in the rehearsal process and the concert performance. **Demonstration: Supermetrics and melded gestures.**

Even though releases are a basic part of the conducting technique, many experienced conductors still find it difficult to execute releases properly so that the players release together and with the desired nuance. There are several items concerning releases that need to be reinforced: (1) there must always be a preparation to the actual release, (2) the release must be shown on a beat (trying to release on the fraction of a beat leads to surprises for the players and usually results in poor precision on the release), (3) in general, the release must be done in tempo (many conductors, in an effort to give a precise release, speed up the actual preparation/release motion and this causes confusion with the players), (4) the "character" or intensity of the release must be given careful consideration and executed to reflect the desired nuance of the release, (5) the use of the left hand in making the release can be done so that the right hand will remain in the proper position for the continuation of the music, and (6) releases may be executed as part of the pattern or as a distinct preparation and release motion. A final point is that the instrumental music ensemble conductor needs to be concerned about releases during both the rehearsal process and in the concert performance. Too often, the release is ignored or given minor consideration by many instrumental music conductors, which places the responsibility totally on the players; this usually results in poor ensemble precision on the release. The release will be a clockwise or counterclockwise downward release depending where the gesture will need to be at the end of the release for the music continuation. I discuss the release aspect in more detail in Chapter 12: Tempo and Ensemble Precision. **Demonstration: Various nuances on the conducting release.**

Largely, *cueing is a problem of preparation and alertness*. It is a matter not only of giving a preparation just before the entrance, but also of using eye contact and body language to alert the individual or section that the entrance is approaching. In this way, the preparation of the cue becomes a reminder to the player (that is, a confidence-builder) as well as a stylistic and dynamic indication. Cueing should show the character as well as the precision of the entrance. The other question concerning cueing is how many cues to give. If entrances come rapidly, perhaps the conductor should proceed by simply showing a clear beat pattern and place the responsibility on the players to enter according to the indicated pulses. For the conductor to attempt to indicate all of the rapid entrances may be more confusing than helpful. Too much cueing takes away from the conductor showing the phrasing, dynamics, and other important musical details of the performance. During the practice time in conducting, the "imaginary" ensemble for the conductor should provide a mental picture of where the various instruments are located. Cueing should be conceived during the conductor's score study and practice time, and then adjusted in the rehearsal process to meet the needs of the ensemble. Above all else, the conductor must not let the players become dependent on cues during the rehearsal process or in the concert performance. It is a good idea, on occasion, to go through the entire rehearsal process without cueing to see that the players are not relying on the conductor to show all of these various entrances. **Demonstration: Preparing the ensemble to respond to cueing.**

The use of the left hand in conducting has always been a somewhat perplexing problem for the evolving conductor. Ambidextrous conducting is a term used to call attention to the idea of independence between the right hand and left hand. The conductor should realize that much of the effective conducting could be done with the right hand alone. Therefore, the left hand becomes an independent factor, as a reinforcing agent with some special duties. These left-hand special duties are usually detailed in most conducting textbooks and include (1) crescendo, (2) diminuendo, (3) cueing, (4) releases, (5) phrasing, (6) adjusting balance, (7) reinforcement of the basic style, (8) controlling dynamic levels, (9) general musical expression through specific emphasis, and (10) turning the pages of the score. The constant mirroring of the right hand with the left hand in the rehearsal process will cease to impact on the ensemble if done continuously. It is also important to realize that the left hand needs to move in contrary motion to the right hand and not in parallel motion with the right hand. **Demonstration: Left-hand use for the various special duties.**

The positioning and motion of the left hand must be comfortable for the conductor and likewise appear to be so for the players. In many cases, the left hand is positioned too close to the body, and therefore, becomes rather ineffective as far as the ensemble is concerned. Extend the left hand outward just as with the right hand. This may, at times, clutter what the right hand is doing, but this is a good reason for not using the left hand much of the time. When you are not using the left hand for a specific purpose, then it should remain in front of the body in a "ready" position, but not touching the body. In terms of the development of the left-hand technique, practice certain motions such as the crescendo and diminuendo motions. With these specific duties, the conductor needs to develop a smooth, consistent motion in which the left hand looks very natural and not poised or contrived. Practice using the left hand in conjunction with the right hand in its development, so that the left hand is independent of the conducting pattern motions of the right hand. **Demonstration: Positioning and motion of the left hand on crescendo/diminuendo.**

CREATIVE CONDUCTING TECHNIQUE

There are many ways for the conductor *to show creativity in the conducting technique.* The patterns and gestures need to reflect what the conductor is trying to do musically. Not only will the patterns indicate the pulse variance at times, but also the motion between the pulses should indicate what the conductor really wants to have happen with the music. The conductor, based on tempo, flow, or musical emphasis, should determine the number of pulses in a measure. Certainly, the fluctuation of the number of pulses in a measure (subdivision and merging) will strongly affect the actual performance of the music. The conductor should place fewer pulses in each measure if more flow is desired and more pulses if rhythmic stability is needed. As a caution and general rule for the maturing conductor, the creativity in the conducting technique *should not, however, over-shadow the clarity of the conducting patterns and gestures.* For example, the conductor may need to improve the symmetry of the 3/4 patterns by having the motion to the third beat come "up and over" rather than retracing the second beat; also in the 4/4 pattern the motion to the fourth beat should not retrace the third beat, but should come "up and over" also. The one-pattern must show whether the beat divides into either 2s or 3s; this is important for players in executing the subdivision of the beat. The variance in the speed of the rebound will show these compound meters in the triple subdivision. **Demonstration: Varying the number of pulses in the designated meter.**

Passive and active gestures are a very important part of the conducting technique. The creativity of these conducting patterns and gestures involves the speed variance and intensity of the conducting motion (that is, active and passive gestures). Passive gestures include conducting rests, showing preparatory beat, and other musical situations in which the conductor requires no sound from the ensemble. The active gestures say to the ensemble—"play." These include legato, staccato, marcato, and tenuto. The active gestures must draw from the ensemble the actual and immediate musical sounds. These active gestures should show considerable intensity in the conducting motion as opposed to the passive gestures that say to the ensemble— "do not play, yet." It is particularly important to indicate to the ensemble when they should or should not play. An example of this is at the end of a lengthy composition when there is a repetition of the final chords interspersed with rests. The conductor should show these active and passive gestures to prevent ensemble members from playing during the rests. **Demonstration: Alternation of passive and active gestures to clarify precision.**

The flow and clicking of the conducting pattern to make the beats "come alive" is a part of the creative conducting process. The creative use of the left hand by showing dynamics, nuances, and musical expression is also an important part of the conducting technique. Any way the conductor can create a more musical atmosphere should be encouraged. The conductor's gestures need to communicate to the players the composer's intentions. Some other examples of the creative conducting technique are (1) facial expression can be helpful in showing this expressiveness; however, this should not be overdone to the point of grimacing, (2) the conductor's facial expression should reflect the mood of the music through the facial intensity and relaxation in reinforcing the patterns and gestures, (3) the conductor in the rehearsal process can pronounce silently (or audibly) various syllables that give the correct idea of the intended articulation, and (4) when breathing with the preparatory beat, the conductor can indicate precisely by closing the lips where the attack should be placed. The creative conducting possibilities are infinite and valid as long as they produce the desired musical results. **Demonstration: Conducting creatively in order to achieve musical expression.**

MAINTAINING AND IMPROVING THE CONDUCTING TECHNIQUE

Developing the conducting technique is one thing, but maintaining and improving it is another. *It is easy to develop bad habits in conducting over time, such as meaningless gestures with the left hand.* Unconsciously, the conductor can develop unclear technique by trying to do too many things or by becoming too "fancy" with the patterns and gestures. Examples of this are wherein the conducting pattern "curls around" or "bounces between beats," causing the ictus and pattern to become obscured. Below are some suggestions for keeping the conducting technique clear and meaningful:

- Continue to study conducting textbooks.
- Avoid "bouncing" between beats, usually caused by a tense right wrist and forearm.
- Observe other (preferably good) conductors by attending rehearsals and concerts; also check out the videos listed in Appendix E.
- Videotape yourself by conducting with recordings and then critique yourself (or have others critique your conducting as well).
- Practice conducting (with inner singing) in front of a mirror; this forces you to "get out of the score."
- Attend workshops and symposiums on conducting.
- Do advanced study with a "master teacher" of conducting.
- Record or videotape rehearsals and performances to analyze your conducting effectiveness with the ensemble. (Is the ensemble "noticeably" responsive to the patterns and gestures or does the ensemble seem to be ignoring the conductor's patterns and gestures?)
- See Appendix F in this book for performance area comments and score sheets used for evaluating the student conducting/rehearsing projects.

The conductor must realize that he or she is controlling the sound of the ensemble, and not simply conducting the meters, rhythms, and notes from the printed score. This affects many aspects of the conducting technique. For example, eye contact with the ensemble, general communication with the players, and fostering musicality could all improve if the conductor focused on controlling the sound, rather than getting "tied-up" in the score. Even very experienced conductors are guilty of this problem at times. The lack of score study and score preparation are the main reasons for this occurrence. The conductor should videotape the conducting occasionally and discern if the patterns and gestures are reflecting what the music should be depicting or expressing. Above all else, the conductor must not let the eyes and head stay in the score, but must maintain communication and eye contact with the players in order to guide the ensemble precisely and musically. *The key to this situation is whether the conductor is listening carefully to the ensemble in the rehearsal process and making the necessary adjustments in preparation for the concert performance.*

CONDUCTING TECHNIQUE, REHEARSING SKILLS, AND LEADERSHIP

Frequently, one can observe in the rehearsal process and/or in live concert performances that there is a definite lack of musicality with the specific conductor. In many instances, the problem really is that the conductor does not have the necessary background in conducting or rehearsing skills even though the conductor may have spent many years as a professional musician in a quality ensemble or as an instrumental music teaching specialist. The conducting skills have not been developed through serious study, expert guidance, and intense practice. It is assumed that because a musician has played under many competent conductors that the transition from player to conductor is easily accomplished and certain to be successful. This is not to say that a superior musician cannot become a fine conductor. Just as with any skill development, the conductor must develop good conducting technique to communicate through the patterns and gestures to the players. If the conductor has developed conducting technique and rehearsing skills properly, then he or she will be able to communicate the musicality as well as realize the conceived musical interpretation with the ensemble.

Conducting technique must be developed through this serious study, good instruction, and intense practice just as in learning to play an instrument well. In many cases, the conductor assumes that he or she fostered the conducting technique and rehearsing skills through playing in various ensembles. *In general, this is an erroneous assumption.* (What happens with an ensemble player in the rehearsal process is that the player's concentration and focus is on the performance of the individual part, not on how the conductor is achieving the objectives in the rehearsal process.)

The only way for the conductor to be able to communicate the conceived musical interpretation to the players is with adequate conducting technique and carefully developed rehearsing skills. Even though the musicianship may be superb, the conductor may not be able to show this musicality through the specific patterns and gestures while rehearsing the ensemble. This conductor learning process would seem to be overlooked by many conductors who turn to the podium after considerable music ensemble performance, solo work, chamber music performance, or music teaching experience.

Leadership

Leadership is defined as the act of guiding. The conductor must impose his or her decisions on the ensemble. This involves being clear and expressive with the conducting technique. The beat must have a "live" quality to it. Some conducting teachers suggest that the physical feeling is one of "baton weight." A further suggestion for the conductor is having wrist snap or "clicking" on the pulse. In the final analysis, the conducting technique should be able to indicate exactly how the conductor wishes the ensemble to play and sound. *The two important goals in the rehearsal process should be ensemble precision and musicality.* The conductor must constantly foster and practice clarity of conducting technique throughout the career. The conducting patterns and gestures must speak distinctly to the players. If there is a lack of this leadership, due to poor conducting clarity or the lack of good rehearsing skills, then the ensemble's performance will certainly be disappointing for both the players and the audience.

Besides being expressive and precise with the conducting technique, the conductor must also realize that there are times when "getting out of the way" is more effective than interfering with the flow of the ensemble performance. The conductor can hamper the ensemble performance with the conducting technique in trying to do too many things; this can lead to poor precision, ensemble confusion, and a general feeling of "fussiness" within the ensemble. The ensemble should be allowed to take the initiative in specific passages (under the watchful eyes, ears, patterns, and gestures of the conductor). However, the conductor needs to show that he or she has real confidence in the collective musicianship of the ensemble in the rehearsal process and in the concert performance.

The ensemble must learn to respond to expressive conducting technique; this will then suggest that the conductor is a sensitive musician and leader. Another indication of leadership is how much gets accomplished during the rehearsal process. Leadership implies that the conductor must be "in charge" during the rehearsal process. The conductor, as a leader, should strive to make the rehearsal process and the concert performance exciting, interesting, and, above all, musical for the ensemble as well as for the audience (during the concert performance). Subsequently, the conductor should acknowledge that it is the players who produce the "sounds of music," as conducting is a silent art. In this regard, leadership involves letting the players know periodically that the conductor appreciates their work in the rehearsal process, and the conductor should recognize the achievements of the ensemble after the concert performance.

Assuming that the conductor has already acquired good conducting technique, the development of rehearsing skills is essential in producing a fine instrumental music ensemble. At this specific juncture, *the development of these rehearsal skills* should be one of the most important goals in the maturing conductor's education and development. The planned segments of the rehearsal process, efficient rehearsal procedures, effective teaching strategies, and the proper sequencing of these segments, procedures, and teaching strategies are the ingredients necessary to produce a fine ensemble and exciting, musical performances. The conductor should always begin rehearsing with the idea that there is never enough rehearsal time, and therefore make good use of the available time in the rehearsal process. Good conducting technique can enhance this efficiency during the rehearsal process.

Common sense, creativity, and flexibility are all factors in the rehearsal process. Careful consideration of the maturity level of the ensemble and their potential achievement level will help the conductor formulate realistic expectations and determine the proper rehearsal teaching strategies. The conducting technique creativity will vary somewhat depending on the performance level of the ensemble, the maturity level of the ensemble, and where in the rehearsal process the ensemble has progressed with the selected repertoire. The conductor should show some flexibility in the rehearsal process in relation to the given scenario. The expectations and teaching strategies by the conductor in the rehearsal process will always require this common sense, creativity, and flexibility with almost every ensemble.

In preparing to conduct musically in the rehearsal process and the concert performance, some items to include are:

- Detailed score study (for a distinctive and authentic musical interpretation)
- Researching the composer, the musical period, and the specific composition if possible (in an effort to capture the essence and spirit of the work)
- Practicing the work to be rehearsed (through inner singing)

- Practicing the difficult conducting spots (such as those involving fermatas, tempo changes, style contrast, sudden dynamic changes, starting on the fraction of the beat, etc.)
- Anticipating performance problems that may need resolution and conceiving the appropriate teaching strategies to employ in the rehearsal process
- Preparing for and utilizing a musical approach throughout the rehearsal process
- Being as precise and expressive with conducting patterns and gestures as possible during the rehearsal process and into the concert performance

PRACTICAL APPLICATION (DISCUSSION/DEMONSTRATION)

1. What attributes should the conducting technique show in the patterns and gestures?
2. What are the basic elements of the conducting technique as noted in this chapter?
3. What are some of the variations of the conducting patterns and gestures?
4. Cite some musical examples of how adequate conducting technique can avoid frequent stops during the rehearsal process.
5. By demonstration, determine the parameters of the largest pattern and the smallest pattern (using a video recording or a mirror to view these decisions). Is there a distinct lack of clarity in these extreme patterns?
6. "Fancy" and meaningless patterns and gestures will affect negatively the conducting technique clarity. Demonstrate this.
7. Conducting "flow" equals good communication with the ensemble. Discuss this conducting flow aspect in detail and then demonstrate.
8. What are the various elements involved with "expressive conducting?"
9. Describe and demonstrate the proper baton grip, wrist action, and arm position in conducting with good clarity.
10. Why is the "attention" position so important in the conducting technique?
11. Discuss the execution problems and the precise impact of the preparatory beat on both simple and compound meter patterns.
12. Why are the concepts of the preparatory beats and of rehearsal preparations so important for the conductor and the ensemble?
13. What is involved in "reading the stick" for both the conductor and the players?
14. Discuss and demonstrate the idea of verbal counting with the ensemble during the rehearsal process. When and how would you use this procedure?
15. Discuss the problems of over-conducting as well as that with small patterns and gestures in the conducting technique.
16. What is involved in keeping the patterns and gestures focused for the ensemble?
17. What can you do to maintain and improve the conducting technique throughout your career?
18. Discuss the principles of leadership that are involved specifically with the conducting technique.
19. Discuss the idea and the application of the passive and active gestures in the conducting technique.

20. Having discussed the above items, now go back to the beginning of this chapter and study and practice the various conducting demonstrations (shown in bold print) at the end of many paragraphs. *The conducting teacher may choose to demonstrate these items and then have the conducting students emulate these demonstrations for the conducting teacher.*
21. Begin to gain familiarity with the standard repertoire found in Appendix A through CD listening, score study, and guidance from the conducting teacher. (See Appendix G for assignment forms).

RECOMMENDED READING

Atherton, Leonard, *Vertical Plane Focal Point Conducting.* This brief book presents a slightly different approach to the basic conducting patterns in that the beats cross through an X in the conducting patterns.

Boult, Adrian Cedric, *A Handbook on the Technique of Conducting.* Even though this is a brief book on conducting technique, it is well worth reviewing Sections 1 through 6.

Curtis, Larry G., and David L. Kuehn, *A Guide to Successful Instrumental Conducting.* This textbook covers the basic conducting technique and then supplies basic and intermediate etudes for practicing these techniques.

Green, Elizabeth A. H., *The Dynamic Orchestra.* Chapter 4: The Rehearsal covers many of the aspects of the conducting technique and rehearsing skills.

Green, Elizabeth A. H., *The Modern Conductor*, 6th ed. Chapter 1: So You Want to Be a Conductor and Chapter 11: The Virtuoso Technique cover the areas of conducting technique thoroughly.

Green, Elizabeth A. H., *The Modern Conductor Workbook.* This workbook provides full scores for some standard orchestral repertoire.

Hunsberger, Donald, and Roy E. Ernst, *The Art of Conducting*, 2nd ed. Chapters 1, 2, 3, and 4 show many photographs and conducting diagrams with musical examples to reinforce the various aspects of the conducting technique.

Kahn, Emil, *Conducting.* There are many good ideas presented in this book on conducting technique and rehearsing.

Kohut, Daniel L., and Joe W. Grant, *Learning to Conduct and Rehearse.* Chapter 2: Standard Conducting Gestures, Chapter 3: Intermediate Techniques and Chapter 4: Advanced Techniques cover the physical aspects of conducting.

Labuta, Joseph A., *Basic Conducting Techniques*, 5th ed. The strength of this book is in the many musical examples that can be played with almost any size group from the conducting class.

Long, R. Gerry, *The Conductor's Workshop: A Workbook on Instrumental Conducting.* Part 2 of this workbook, Baton Technique and its Application, supplies many exercises for developing the various aspects of the conducting technique.

Maiello, Anthony, *Conducting: A Hands-On Approach.* This textbook covers the conducting technique quite thoroughly. In addition, a real strength of the book is in the musical examples presented.

Malko, Nicolai, *The Conductor and his Baton.* Chapter 2: Physical Training provides exercises for the conductor in developing the conducting technique.

McBeth, W. Francis, *Effective Performance of Band Music: Solutions to Specific Problems in the Performance of 20th Century Band Music.* Solution VI: Effective Podium Technique deals with the conducting and rehearsing of contemporary band music.

McElheran, Brock, *Conducting Technique for Beginners and Professionals.* This small text-book allows the conducting teacher to expand into the various areas of the more advanced conducting technique and musicianship.

Phillips, Kenneth H., *Basic Techniques of Conducting.* Even though this is a basic conducting textbook, some of the examples could be useful in an advanced conducting class.

Ross, Allan A., *Techniques for Beginning Conductors.* This is a beginning textbook on conducting, but there is strong emphasis on score reading and terminology with each chapter.

Rudolf, Max, *The Grammar of Conducting*, 3rd ed. Part 1 covers the basic conducting techniques. Part 2 covers the application of these conducting techniques.

Scherchen, Hermann, *Handbook of Conducting.* This book is considered one of the milestones in conducting technique and rehearsing.

Shepherd, William, *A Conducting Workbook with CD-Rom Video.* This textbook has many single- or double-line exercises for conducting practice.

Vermeil, Jean, *Conversations with Boulez (Thoughts on Conducting).* Chapter 4: On Gestures and Chapter 6: Rehearsing.

Wood, Sir Henry, *About Conducting.* "My Points for the Would-be Conductor" starting on page 19.

REPERTOIRE FOR PROJECTS AND ASSIGNMENTS

Below are suggestions for the conducting/rehearsing projects, for listening assignments, and also for the score study analysis assignments. (The conducting teacher should assign these conducting/rehearsing projects throughout the semester or year.) Executing these conducting/rehearsing projects with a live ensemble is much more beneficial for the student than with recordings. However, this is not always possible because of the difficulty in scheduling such an ensemble for this purpose. There are definite limitations in conducting with a recording such as in showing preparatory beats, initial attacks, fermatas, tempos, tempo changes, and releases. Therefore, it is better to have some sessions with a live, full ensemble and supplement these projects with the other rehearsal environments (see Appendix H). It is essential to have a live ensemble in order to learn how to proceed in rehearsing the instrumental ensemble.

Below are listed ensemble repertoire suggestions for use with either live groups or recordings. Starting with this chapter and continuing through chapter 16 is a listing of repertoire that moves from less complicated conducting and performance problems to much more demanding repertoire. The conducting teacher can select the conducting/rehearsing projects for the individual student conductor from these listings or from Appendix A. Also, the listening and score study analysis assignments can be assigned from these lists over the entire semester (or year) to acquaint the developing conductor with the standard repertoire (see Appendix G).

Full Orchestra, Chamber Orchestra, or String Orchestra

Mascagni: Intermezzo from "Cavalliera Rusticana"
Grieg: The Last Spring (from Two Elegiac Melodies)
Bach: Brandenburg Concerto No. 3 (first movement)

Beethoven: Symphony No. 1 (first movement)
Dvořák: Symphony No. 9 "New World" (second movement)

Concert Band or Wind Ensemble

Holst: Second Suite in F (first movement)
Vaughan Williams: English Folk Song Suite (third movement)
Daehn: With Quiet Courage
Carter: Symphonic Overture for Band
Erickson: Toccata for Band

Miscellaneous or Small Ensembles

Dukas: Fanfare from "La Peri" (brass ensemble or trumpet ensemble)
Weinberger: Concerto for Timpani (4 trumpets, 4 trombones, or with tuba)

Chapter Five

Score Study, Music Imagery, and Inner Singing

SCORE READING, STUDY, AND PREPARATION

The conducting teacher should incorporate score reading, study, and preparation into the curriculum for the developing conductor at some point (and before the assigned student conducting/rehearsing projects). In this regard, the basic items involved in reading a score are clefs, transpositions, instrumentation, and orchestration. Beyond these perfunctory aspects and the musical knowledge involved, the reading and study of the score will encompass all of the student's previous background in music theory, form, and analysis as well as instrumental study and pedagogy. Just as the conductor must bring to the rehearsal process all of his or her experience and background, the conductor in reading and studying a score must draw upon much of the previously accumulated knowledge about music, instrumental pedagogy, and musical interpretation. In studying a score in preparation for the rehearsal process, the evolving conductor should strive to develop a melodic memory, that is to say, linearly; music is always moving forward in time. This is not to say that the conductor should ignore the tonal (pitch), rhythmic (time), or harmonic (vertical) aspects when reading and studying a score, but the conductor must always be aware of what is coming up next in the music. I address the preparation aspect of the musical score later in this chapter and involve the marking of the score and attention to the many details of the composition.

Through score reading and study, the conductor should acquire a clear image of the work involved. With this image, the conductor in the rehearsal process can then compare this music imagery with what the ensemble actually plays in the rehearsal process. In preparation for the rehearsal process, the conductor needs to consider the following items in this basic order:

- Synthesis (general outline of the work)
- Analysis (details of the work)
- Second synthesis (looking at the work as a whole with the details)
- Conducting problems (that need to be solved and practiced)
- Playing problems (solutions that may need to be anticipated)
- Designing of teaching strategies (to solve these playing problems)

As the above items are implemented, the conductor will continue to study the scores by marking the score and preparing the parts with the idea of saving time in the rehearsal process. The only way to become truly competent at score reading, study, and preparation is to spend enough concentrated time doing these activities. The conductor must come before the ensemble ready to conduct and rehearse the instrumental music ensemble effectively and efficiently.

Below are some specific items to consider in the reading, study, and preparation of the musical score:

1. Synthesis: Analysis: Synthesis (SAS) in score study
2. The essence and spirit of the music (the basic character and vitality)
3. Clefs and transpositions as indicated on the first page of the score; thereafter, there may be changes in clefs (treble, alto, tenor, and bass) and transposition changes later on in the score as well
4. Instrumentation and orchestration (2222-4331-perc-str) that affects the sonority, tone, balance, blend, tone color, and texture)
5. Form, themes, and structure (how the music unfolds)
6. Harmonic system, keys, key modulations, key changes, cadences, etc.)
7. Counterpoint (how the parts fit together)
8. Rhythm (meter, pulse, tempo, accents, rhythms, rhythm patterns, etc.)
9. Phrasing (climax, contour, breathing, bowing, articulation, musical line, dynamics, performance practice, period style, etc.)
10. Dynamics, nuances, accents, and musical expression (written or implied)
11. Designing of flow charts and/or bar grouping to help the conductor realize the details and the order involved in the score study
12. Conducting problems (tempo, tempo changes, preparatory beats, releases, fermatas, meter changes, asymmetrical meters, etc.)
13. Playing problems (anticipating technical and musical problems in the rehearsal process)
14. Assimilating the details of the score (ask yourself questions about the music; why did the composer do this here?)
15. Marking the score (for your comprehension)
16. Editing and marking the parts (to save time in the rehearsal process)
17. Teaching strategies (during score study the various teaching strategies need to be conceived in preparation for the rehearsal process)
18. Style and the musical interpretation (putting it all together)

Memorization of the score can be helpful in bringing out the musicality of the ensemble during the rehearsal process and in the concert performance, enhancing the communication with the ensemble, and achieving the proper musical interpretation of the repertoire. If these are the purposes for this memorization, then it is worth the time involved in memorizing the score. However, the memorization of the score to impress the players or the audience that the conductor can memorize the score is not a valid reason. If the conductor is not proficient at score memorization, it might be a waste of valuable time that could be devoted to other matters, and in the final analysis, poor memorization might cause the conductor to omit many of the important details in the rehearsal process or spell disaster in a concert performance. However, the conductor should attempt to know the score so well that an occasional glance at the music will provide the necessary confidence and at the same time retain communication with the ensemble.

SCORE STUDY

One might think that with a younger ensemble or even with a professional group, the conductor could come to the rehearsal process without much score study, preparation, or rehearsal planning and still be quite effective. With any of these scenarios, wasted time and diminished effectiveness result. Much more can be accomplished with any level of ensemble if the conductor *comes to the rehearsal process totally prepared.* With this meticulous score study, the conductor is able to compare the musical conception with the reality in the rehearsal process. Preparations for the rehearsal process should include detailed score study, research about the composers and the repertoire being performed, solutions to conducting problems, anticipation of playing problems, and designing of teaching strategies. The conductor should contemplate all of these preparations before the first rehearsal and then adapt and revise as the rehearsals continue. *During the score study the conductor must develop the interpretive conception, to reinforce with the ensemble during the rehearsal process.*

Even though score study is not an integral part of this book, the importance of it for the success of the conductor is immeasurable. *Score study should be the number one priority for any serious conductor.* The conductor needs to come out of the score study sessions with a clear image of the work(s) and how to accomplish the conceived musical interpretation in the rehearsal process. Only then can the conductor in the rehearsal process compare this image with what the ensemble is actually playing in the rehearsal process. First, the conductor should study the score thoroughly, and only after this preparation begin to listen to recordings to gain a perspective on the work. Initially, the conductor is looking to discover the structure of the piece through score study. At some point, the conductor should begin to ask all sorts of questions about what the composer intended at any given place in the score. Only after these procedures can the conductor start to practice conducting the score and anticipating the rehearsal and playing problems. What might be considered a rather insignificant detail in the initial score reading may eventually hold the key in how to rehearse and interpret the work.

The progression of score study should be a continuous one from the beginning (before the first rehearsal process) until the final performance of the work. The score study must start with the conductor becoming familiar with the music, followed by the search for all of the details of the musical performance. At this point, the conception of the musical interpretation needs to be confirmed before the first rehearsal process. As the rehearsals continue, the conductor should again study the score and strive to reinforce and confirm this interpretative conception. The rehearsing of the work should eventually culminate in an exciting and musical concert performance.

CONCERT PERFORMANCE

CONCEPTION **REHEARSING**

Figure 5.1. Score Study

Figure 5.1 shows a triangle in the progressive relationship of conception (in score study), rehearsing (process), and performance (concert). All three of these are connected and should result in a successful concert performance with this serious score study.

SCORE STUDY AND TEACHING STRATEGIES

Some conductors may believe that if they carefully studied and prepared the score, the main consideration is to react to what may occur in the rehearsal process. This idea might be somewhat of a valid approach in the rehearsal process, especially with the experienced conductor. However, any conductor can be more effective if a general strategy (rehearsal plan) is conceived and teaching strategies are designed in anticipation of the specific rehearsal problems. When the conductor studies the score, attention should be given to how this particular work should be approached in the rehearsal process. During score study, the conductor should anticipate the possible performance problems and design the teaching strategies in order to solve these problems.

Especially for the maturing conductor, the above ideas are an effective approach. As they gain experience and confidence in rehearsing, conductors may call upon their accumulated backgrounds for effective rehearsal procedures and teaching strategies. This is not to say that planned teaching strategies are then unnecessary. The developing conductor should make a conscious effort to acquire as many ways as possible to solve problems in the rehearsal process. The acquisition of this background assumes meticulous score study, observation of master conductors in the rehearsal process, and considerable experience in front of the ensemble. By noting what is effective or ineffective in the rehearsal process, the maturing conductor can begin to build an arsenal of teaching strategies that will then work in various rehearsal scenarios.

SCORE AND REHEARSAL PREPARATION

Marking the score must be done by and for the conductor. The conductor marks those items that need to be remembered in score study, in conducting practice, and throughout the overall rehearsal process. Some conductors will use a variety of colored pencils to differentiate the various items such as tempo changes, cues, dynamics, phrasing, and so on. (This approach may prove to be somewhat confusing as it simply adds another problem of color selection to marking the score.) However, most conductors will limit the marking of the score to one or two colors. A single red and blue pencil has a definite efficiency in marking the score. Use the red end for everything except cues; mark the cues in blue with an abbreviated instrument name if needed. The red marking would include the boxing in or circling of tempo terms, key changes, and meter changes. Use the red color to reinforce dynamic indications and call attention to special conducting or performance problems (such as handling fermatas). The blue end of the pencil could then in contrast show the necessary cues. There are many different ways to mark the spots in the score with arrows, diagrams, brackets, circles, boxes, and slashes. The evolving conductor should develop a consistent system in marking the score that will help in studying the score, conducting the music, and rehearsing the ensemble.

In score preparation, *the idea of bar groupings* is based on the four-bar phrase. One can then decrease or increase this bar grouping according to the dictates of the music. There may be times when the grouping is indicated by the orchestration as well as dictated by the phrase. This bar grouping can be shown at the top of the score with brackets or a check at the beginning of each grouping. A more obvious bar grouping procedure would be to draw a line vertically in color at the end of each bar grouping. If the bar grouping length is more or less than a four-bar phrase, the number of bars in the grouping could be indicated by a number at the beginning of the bar grouping. This bar grouping would be particularly helpful when conducting in one to a bar, so that mentally the conductor can keep track of fast-moving music even when all of the beats are downbeats. (Two examples of this are the scherzo movement of a Beethoven Symphony or in the final movement of the Rimsky-Korsakov *Scheherazade* in the 2/8 sections.) With one beat to a measure, the conductor can envision a four-pattern to coincide with the four-bar grouping but keep all the beats in the conducting pattern as downbeats. When a three-bar phrase appears, enlist the three-pattern. Such a procedure could also enhance the phrasing and musical expression in the sense that, for example, the beat of the third bar with an accent could be executed on the third downbeat of the imagined four-pattern.

One of the most efficient ways of identifying problematic places for rehearsal purposes is with small "stick-on" or "Post-it" sheets (about ½ by 2 inches), which allow sufficient space to notate the problem and can then be easily removed and discarded when the problem no longer exists. This prevents having to write on the score and erase these places thereafter. These notes may also serve as a reminder in reviewing the rehearsals before the concert performance. (On these little sheets, it is important to identify the place in relationship to the rehearsal letters or numbers.) Such place identification can save time in the rehearsal process as the conductor can immediately communicate to the ensemble the need to rehearse certain sections without referring to the separate rehearsal plan and schedule. This is just one more way for the conductor to gain credibility with the players in the rehearsal process. It also shows the ensemble that the conductor has done the necessary homework.

In score study, the conductor must spend enough time to assimilate the musical details. If the conductor simply reads the score for familiarity (as in the initial synthesis in score study) before the rehearsal process, then the musical details would not be a consideration for the conductor during the rehearsal process. In many instances, the conductor will not be able to take care of all the details in one rehearsal process, but must be prepared to address these as the rehearsals go forward. By having studied these details *through the designing of these flow charts*, the conductor will have a better grasp of the musical interpretation. These flow charts can include many different aspects in the score. (See Battisti and Garofalo 1990, 33: Flow Charting.) The analysis part of score study (SAS) must be the time in which the conductor considers these musical details. The final synthesis then brings back the total picture for the conductor in preparation for the rehearsal process and the concert performance.

MUSIC IMAGERY AND INNER SINGING

Among many other items, the conductor studies the score in order to conceive the musical interpretation of a particular work. This study in determining the musical interpretation is done through the music imagery of the conductor. The conductor's music imagery will improve with time spent in score study. The conductor must imagine what a passage will sound like and then compare this image to the reality of the music (and sound) produced in the rehearsal process. Music imagery certainly involves the musical interpretation on the part of the conductor. In the rehearsal process, the conductor must move the ensemble precisely in the direction of this conceived musical interpretation. In essence, this interpretive focus should be the main reason for having the rehearsal process. The concert performance will definitely reflect this music imagery and the creativity of the conductor during the rehearsal process.

Music imagery and inner singing—these two mental-physical activities are essential in realizing the musical interpretation of a work. *In serious score study, these two activities are interlaced.* The process of music imagery is a large part of score study in that the mental process involved here is then reinforced through inner singing. Inner singing will aid the conductor in arriving at the desired musical interpretation. The eyes send the message to the brain to produce the musical imagery that motivates the inner singing of the conductor. This inner singing can be a guide for the conducting patterns and gestures the conductor uses in the rehearsal process and in the concert performance. This inner singing may be audible in score study, but in the rehearsal process and the concert performance, it needs to be silent in order to avoid distracting the players or the audience.

Music imagery will help focus, clarify, and emphasize the elements of the musical interpretation during score study. Inner singing is a mental (and, perhaps in some cases, vocal) activity used by the conductor to reproduce what is seen in the score. It involves the entire mental process of assimilating the score. Music imagery and inner singing (or inner hearing) skills are important in score study and during the rehearsal process as well as in the concert performance. With practice, the conductor's conception of the work through music imagery and inner singing will bring the reality of the sounds heard by the conductor to coincide with the ensemble in both the rehearsal process and the concert performance.

MUSIC IMAGERY

With both the conductor and the players, imagination should play a large part in the musical interpretation. Music imagery is a right brain function, as opposed to verbal and analytical concepts from the left brain. The more vivid the music image is, the better the conductor will be able to share this with the players in the rehearsal process and the audience (through the ensemble) in the concert performance. If the conductor's music image is unclear, the conducting will not translate into an exciting interpretation during the rehearsal process. For the conductor it is very important to come to the rehearsal process with *this precise image of the music*; only then can the conductor begin to shape the work in the rehearsal process to correspond with the music imagery. There must be a musically sensitive communication between the conductor and the players to achieve this proper interpretation during the rehearsal process. The conductor, in order to capture the essence and spirit of the music, may use some verbal descriptions, analogies, and metaphors in explaining these musical interpretive aspects. A handout to improve the interpretation of a work may be of value in certain instances.

Music imagery is a visual-audio-mental-musical process whereby the conductor during score study conceives the essence and spirit of the work as well as the style and the musical interpretation. In this score study, the conductor visualizes in his or her mind the work at hand and allows the imagination to bring this work to fruition mentally, physically, and musically. Because the music is always moving forward, the conductor must hear mentally and/or sing the music (inner singing) as the score study continues to evolve into the conceived musical interpretation. Just as in rehearsing the ensemble, the conductor should conceive through score study this musical interpretation rhythmically, harmonically, structurally, and tonally. If the conductor is weak in rhythmic reading, this should be improved as quickly as possible to enhance the music imagery process. It follows that the rehearsing of the work then converts this conception into the reality of the musical performance.

One definition of image is "that which exists in the mind as the product of careful mental activity" (Roget's *Thesaurus*, 1988). Music imagery raises the question of how it should sound. The conception or music imagery that the conductor is able to bring to the rehearsal process will determine largely the eventual performance level achieved in the production of an exciting, musical performance. This assumes that the conductor has done careful score study and knows what he or she wants to do with the piece in terms of the style and the musical interpretation. A clear image or conception of the musical score and just how it should sound are the most important preparations for the conductor to have accomplished before the rehearsal process begins. The conductor then must impose this conception on the ensemble through the conducting technique and the rehearsing skills during the rehearsal process.

In the instrumental music ensemble rehearsal process, the conductor must impose his or her conceived interpretation on the group to achieve this exciting and musical performance. Without this music imagery, the conductor and players in the rehearsal process are reproducing the notes and rhythms written by the composer, and not much else. A priority such as phrase contour or the flow of the musical line would be mostly ignored unless the music imagery is activated by the conductor and subsequently with the players in the rehearsal process. *Through audiation*, the conductor should know what the phrase will sound like before it is actually played by the ensemble. During the rehearsal process, the conductor will need to proceed with this idea of imposing and reinforcing this conceived musical interpretation on the ensemble in anticipation of the concert performance.

Through careful score study, the conductor conceives "how this should sound." Musically speaking, it would be difficult to achieve much in the ensemble rehearsal process unless the conductor has done this score study and is prepared to communicate this conception to the players. Here is where the idea of teaching strategies becomes important. Subsequently, if the conductor has a clear image of the music, but has not produced a rehearsal plan or teaching strategies for communicating this to the players either through gestures or verbally in the rehearsal process, the results will be less than positive for the ensemble and certainly unsatisfactory for the audience (in the concert performance). As much as possible, the conductor should present specific images to the ensemble in the rehearsal process. In other words, the player must be aware of the possibilities involved in the musical interpretation and take an artistic attitude with the performance of the music. The conductor could use some descriptive words (such as murky, misty, mysterious, brilliant, sparkling, shimmering, etc.) to enhance the understanding of the music. Sometimes, the conductor might cite a particularly familiar activity in the rehearsal process to clarify the specific performance or stylistic aspect. (Examples of such analogies are a sports activity or a school event). *The music imagery and inner singing must connect with the arms, hands, and baton in conducting*; this connection is tremendously important in achieving the musical conception with the ensemble.

INNER SINGING

Inner singing is a procedure or technique for solidifying the conductor's music imagery in score study. During the study of a specific score, the conductor will better understand the phrasing and music interpretation by using inner singing. Most score study and conducting practice in preparation for the rehearsal process or the concert performance should take place with inner singing. By inner singing, the conductor is able to feel and reproduce the music, and thereby, physically translate this inner singing into the conducting patterns and gestures that will communicate the conceived musical interpretation in the rehearsal process and in the concert performance. In front of the ensemble, this inner singing must be done silently so as not to interfere with or detract from the produced sounds of the ensemble. Hermann Scherchen, who advocates inner singing strongly in his book, *Handbook of Conducting*, guides the conductor by advising "singing it within himself," (1989, 15) and later says, "the song that gives inward life to musical sounds" (29). In rehearsing under and in watching Dimitri Mitropoulos (Conductor, New York Philharmonic) both in the rehearsal and in the concert performance, I determined that he was using music imagery and inner singing because when the music became very intense his head would begin to shake rapidly.

The conductor should listen to a number of different recordings of a work after studying the score in detail. Recordings will give the conductor several perspectives and some insights into the musical interpretation. Contrarily, the value of listening to recordings during score study and conducting practice is minimal. In the final analysis, the conductor must determine the musical interpretation of a specific work; more is gained in score study and conducting practice through inner singing of the score than through the available recorded representations. The conductor should study the score thoroughly and diligently before actually doing any conducting practice. In most cases, what needs to be considered for the conducting practice are the difficult places, such as fermatas, tempo changes, meter changes, asymmetrical meter, sudden dynamic changes, and so on. It is also very important to stand up for this conducting practice in order *to maintain a good conducting position and stance.*

During the rehearsal process and the concert performance, inner singing can act as a catalyst in producing what the conductor has conceived in score study and with the conducting practice. Therefore the purpose of inner singing is threefold: (1) to help the score study in determining tempo, style, phrasing, etc., (2) to provide the basis for the conducting practice, and (3) to encourage and reinforce the emotional content and musicality in both the rehearsal process and the concert performance. Inner singing can be performed with actual sounds as in singing or humming of the melodic line; the tempo and the rhythmic structure should be maintained as well in score study. However, the inner singing should take place mentally and silently in the rehearsal process and in the concert performance to avoid any distraction for either the players or the audience.

The late Sir Georg Solti, conductor of the Chicago Symphony for many years, emphatically stated that he depends on inner hearing, not inner singing. Inner singing may very likely progress to inner hearing as the conductor acquires experience both in score reading and conducting the instrumental music ensemble. The idea of inner hearing can be just as beneficial to the conductor as that of inner singing. Inner hearing will certainly allow the experienced conductor to compare the conceived musical interpretation with the actual sounds produced in the rehearsal process. In performance, the conductor should employ either inner singing or inner hearing as a means of controlling the ensemble. Therefore, in the initial stages with the evolving conductor, the idea of inner singing may be most helpful in score study and conducting practice. *With experience, the conductor may find that inner hearing produces the same results as inner singing.*

The conductor will conceive the musical interpretation and then in the rehearsal process and concert performance impose this conception with the conducting technique. The connection between this musical conception and the conducting and rehearsing of the ensemble in the rehearsal process is a crucial one. Of course, it would be impossible to show the ensemble the proper patterns and gestures if the conductor has not conceived the musical interpretation carefully in score study. If the conducting technique is adequate, the conductor should be able to bring forth this conception in the rehearsal process with the ensemble. All of this connection depends on the score study of the conductor, the musical conception, the rehearsing of the ensemble, and finally in the concert performance *through the adequacy of the conducting technique.*

PRACTICAL APPLICATION (DISCUSSION/DEMONSTRATION)

1. Consider the various clefs used in a full score (for orchestra and band) and also the transpositions involved in two ways: (a) written pitch vs. sounding pitch and (b) transposing from a different pitched instrumental part (than the usual) for the purposes of score reading and player transposition information.
2. Discuss the instrumentation and orchestration parts for orchestra and band.
3. Discuss the idea of SAS (Synthesis-Analysis-Synthesis) with score study.
4. What kind of conducting or playing problems might occur in the rehearsal process as noted during score study? (Check Appendixes B and C.)
5. The conductor should mark what items in the score before the rehearsal process begins? How should these items be marked?
6. Discuss the idea of bar grouping for score study, during the rehearsal process, and in the concert performance. Connect this with flow charting.
7. Score study should promote teaching strategies used in the rehearsal process. Give some specific examples.
8. Why are the details in score study so important for the conductor before the rehearsal process begins? During conducting class, take a score and after considerable study, discuss some of these details.
9. Discuss music imagery for the conductor. How is it applied in score study?
10. How would the conductor use music imagery during the rehearsal process and in the concert performance?
11. Why is it so important for the conductor to use and impose this music imagery conception on the ensemble in the rehearsal process?
12. Discuss the ideas of inner singing (or inner hearing) in score study and also its application in the rehearsal process and during the concert performance.
13. Begin to gain familiarity with the standard repertoire found in Appendix A through CD listening, score study, and guidance from the conducting teacher. (See Appendix G for assignment forms).

RECOMMENDED READING

Battista, Frank, and Robert Garofalo, *Guide to Score Study for the Wind Band Conductor.* This book focuses on the Percy Grainger's *Irish Tune from County Derry* and the various aspects of score study.

Boult, Adrian Cedric, *A Handbook on the Technique of Conducting.* Section 7: Preparing a Score delivers some thoughtful suggestions on score preparation.

Copland, Aaron, *Music and Imagination.* The last chapter of *Music and Imagination* could act as a summation for the rehearsing of contemporary music.

Green, Elizabeth A. H., *The Conductor and his Score.* This brief book covers many of the aspects of score reading, score study, and score preparation.

Green, Elizabeth A. H., *The Modern Conductor*, 6th ed. Chapters 12, 13, and 14 address score study from the standpoint of the orchestra and band.

Hunsberger, Donald, and Roy E. Ernst, *The Art of Conducting*, 2nd ed. Chapter 5: Score Study and Rehearsals contains material on score study, clefs, transpositions, and instrument terminology.

Jacob, Gordon, *How to Read a Score*. Chapter V: Special Effects introduces the advanced conductor to the whole area of special effects that are demanded with the contemporary composer.

Kohut, Daniel L., and Joe W. Grant, *Learning to Conduct and Rehearse*. Chapter 7: Music Selection, Score Study and Preparation covers many aspects of this score study and preparation.

Leinsdorf, Erich, *The Composer's Advocate: A Radical Orthodoxy for Musicians*. The author makes many good points about conductor preparation and score study throughout.

Nowak, Jerry, and Henry Nowak, *Conducting the Music, Not the Musicians*. Chapter 22: Preparing the Score delves into the various ideas of score reading and score preparation.

Prausnitz, Frederik, *Score and Podium: A Complete Guide to Conducting*. There are many worthwhile points made about score study in chapter 12.

Rudolf, Max, *The Grammar of Conducting*, 3rd ed. Chapter 27 provides a viewpoint on score study, marking the score, preparation of the orchestra parts, and bow markings.

Scherchen, Hermann, *Handbook of Conducting*. In several sections of this book the author stresses the importance of singing, as on page 5, where he says, "Live music always becomes sung music."

Wagner, Richard, *On Conducting*. The idea of inner singing is emphasized here starting on page 15. "In finding the correct tempo, you must learn to sing the melody in all its aspects."

Weisberg, Arthur, *Performing Twentieth-Century Music: A Handbook for Conductors and Instrumentalists*. Chapter 5: Preparing the Score offers some valuable insights into score study and the rehearsal preparations of contemporary music.

REPERTOIRE FOR PROJECTS AND ASSIGNMENTS

Full Orchestra, Chamber Orchestra or String Orchestra

Mozart: Eine Kleine Nachtmusik (Strings) (various movements)
Borodin: In the Steppes of Central Asia
Dello Joio: Five Images for Orchestra
Elgar: Serenade in E minor for Strings (various movements)
Handel: Water Music Suite (Hardy, arr.) (various movements)

Concert Band or Wind Ensemble

Giannini: Fantasia for Band
Grainger: Irish Tune from County Derry
Grundman: American Folk Rhapsody No. 2
Holsinger: On a Hymnsong of Lowell Mason
Hermann: Belmont Overture

Miscellaneous or Small Ensembles

Mozart: Serenade No. 10 in B-flat "Gran Partita" (2 oboes, 2 clarinets, 3 bassoons or contrabass as a substitute for contrabassoon, 4 horns, and 2 bassett horns)
Copland: Fanfare for the Common Man (3 trumpets, 4 horns, 3 trombones, tuba, and 2 percussion)

Chapter Six

Rehearsal Segments and Procedures

REHEARSAL SEGMENTS AND PROCEDURES DEFINED

I define rehearsal segments as those parts of the rehearsal process that the conductor has advocated and/or established for improving the ensemble performance. The conductor should not base such segments only on the concert repertoire to be rehearsed. These rehearsal segments include announcements, warm-up period, tuning, the reading of unfamiliar music, detailed work on passages that need attention, problem solving, and other such segments that are generated through the priorities and teaching strategies as determined by the conductor. Unless the conductor carefully plans these segments, the rehearsal process will lack focus and the proper direction for the continued progress of the ensemble. I discuss many of these segments in chapters 8–15 of this book concerning priorities and teaching strategies.

I define rehearsal procedures as those courses of action that the conductor employs as a means of improving the ensemble's performance during the rehearsal process. These rehearsal procedures include conducting, playing, verbalizing, modeling (and imitation), demonstrations, providing feedback, and teaching concepts for awareness and learning transfer. These procedures will vary greatly depending on (1) the selected repertoire, (2) the rehearsal priorities that need improvement, (3) the maturity and performance level of the ensemble, (4) the rehearsal objectives to be realized, and (5) the performance goals to be achieved. The procedures employed by the conductor in the rehearsal process should serve as specific approaches along with the teaching strategies for the improvement of the ensemble performance. Initially, a rehearsal plan and schedule should be in place to help guide the conductor in establishing these efficient and productive rehearsal segments and procedures.

The beginning conductor generally comprehends the basic conducting course content quite well; however, a very important part of the conductor's education is frequently neglected or taught without practical considerations for rehearsing the instrumental music ensemble. In many cases, after the basic conducting technique is acquired, the advanced conductor finds the remainder of his or her education in the conducting curriculum centered around score study, the conducting of a few selected works, or a curriculum totally focused on musical interpretation without much regard for the background necessary to be an effective leader in front of an ensemble. Music education methods courses sometimes discuss rehearsal procedures briefly. If the evolving conductor is in a music education curriculum, much of the emphasis seems to be on the various aspects of being a competent teacher. This emphasis is extremely important and necessary, but in reality tends to end abruptly the relationship of the conductor and the ensemble in the rehearsal scenario in favor of becoming an effective music teacher. The thinking behind this book is to combine and incorporate the teaching approaches in the rehearsal process along with providing the advanced conductor the needed background to be an effective leader. If the conducting curriculum does not instill these rehearsal segments and procedures, much background falls to self-education and practical experience later. The rehearsing process should combine with the various teaching aspects in an ensemble setting. The conducting technique, the development of rehearsing skills, and those skills involved in the actual rehearsal process should *be in the conducting curriculum and nurtured within the rehearsal process (lab) scenario.*

The technical priorities listed previously (Intonation and Tuning, Rhythms and Rhythm Patterns, Ensemble Sonority Elements, and Articulation and Bowing) and the musical priorities also listed previously (Tempo and Ensemble Precision, Phrasing and Musical Line, Style and Musical Interpretation, and Dynamics, Nuances and Musical Expression) are all factors in the rehearsal process. The selected segments and procedures in moving the rehearsal process along and improving the ensemble performance are strongly determined through the priorities that need attention with the particular ensemble. The conductor must decide which priorities need this remedial work and refinement. In many instances, these performance priorities become apparent as to the degree of prowess lacking through the concert repertoire being rehearsed. The conductor *must then design the segments and procedures for the rehearsal process* in order to improve and refine these priorities.

The development of these rehearsal segments and procedures is a somewhat individual and personal one. Adequate pre-rehearsal planning will help to ensure that the rehearsal process holds to solving problems, improving musicianship, and properly interpreting the repertoire. Anticipating these segments and procedures will help make for much greater effectiveness and efficiency in the rehearsal process. The experience of facing the ensemble in the rehearsal process will be the "best teacher" for the conductor but only if this actual experience translates into the development of these teaching strategies for future rehearsals. The conductor must continue to grow in this development and in the designing of these various teaching strategies.

REHEARSAL SEGMENTS

The given scenario will determine many of these specific rehearsal segments. However, these segments will be a part of almost every rehearsal process. These segments will vary in content and approach from one rehearsal process to another, but the general rehearsal segment format will be quite similar. The bottom line is to organize these segments to yield progress with the ensemble in the rehearsal process. The conductor should reevaluate a specific segment that does not allow for this progress, and perhaps, change in favor of a more productive segment.

Below are eight specific rehearsal segments to incorporate in the rehearsal process:

1. Announcements (keep them brief)
2. Warm-up period and routine
3. Tuning and periodic tuning
4. Reading unfamiliar music
5. Rehearsing concert repertoire
6. Detailed work on passages that need attention
7. Solving problems in the rehearsal process
8. Other segments generated by the rehearsal priorities and solved through teaching strategies.

I will discuss these specific rehearsal segments individually in the following paragraphs.

Announcements, even though they may seem mundane at times, are necessary to keep the ensemble members on the same page with the conductor. The number and kind of announcements will vary greatly from one rehearsal process to the next. Some of the announcements will pertain to upcoming musical events, while others may reinforce the rehearsal schedule for the ensemble. Whatever the reason may be for the announcements, these announcements should be concise and clear to the players. It is important for the conductor to understand that the players are there to rehearse music and not to listen to long announcements from the conductor. There may be situations in which there are numerous announcements to communicate to the ensemble, in which case, it might be best to distribute these announcements in "black and white" so that the players will be able to refer back to them as needed. Another approach is to post them and then make sure the players are responsible for attending to them before or after the rehearsal process.

I discussed *the warm-up period and routine* in some detail in Chapter 3: The Ten Essentials of the Rehearsal Process Scenario. The warm-up routine is an important segment in the rehearsal process. The conductor should not eliminate this segment because he or she wants to get on with rehearsing the concert repertoire. Many performance aspects can be improved in the warm-up period, as well as getting the ensemble to focus and concentrate for the rest of the rehearsal process. The quality of the rehearsal process that follows will be strongly dependent on this warm-up segment. Through careful planning of the activities in this rehearsal segment, the conductor can effectively prepare the ensemble for the remainder of the rehearsal process. Certainly, the brass player is in dire need of a warm-up because of the way in which the tone is produced and the reality of the brass embouchure deterioration factor. Especially with educational or amateur groups, the warm-up period for the brass player is crucial in establishing a responsive embouchure. Most of the other players need the warm-up routine because of the needed adjustments to the instrument or for such items as the intonation factor. *In general, the warm-up routine creates the psychological and musical climate for the rehearsal process.*

The conductor must establish a pitch level at the beginning and maintain it throughout the rehearsal process. This may involve *both an initial tuning as well as periodic tuning* throughout the rehearsal process. This segment is essential for the improvement and maintenance of good intonation with the ensemble. Exactly how this is accomplished and with what degree of expectation will depend on the given scenario. There must be an effort and awareness on the part of the conductor and players to continually check this pitch level and maintain it during the rehearsal process. The problems of intonation in the rehearsal process never go away. By listening and adjusting, the player will be able to play in tune with the rest of the ensemble. I discuss intonation problems in detail in Chapter 8: Intonation and Tuning.

Reading unfamiliar music involves both sight-reading and rehearsing a work that is unfamiliar to the players in the ensemble. The conductor will have prepared the scores in advance of the rehearsal process. The players should be developing reading skills to improve their ability to read unfamiliar music with a certain degree of perfection on the first reading and to improve independently on subsequent readings. Developing this ability to sight-read and read music accurately is most essential. If the conductor does not foster this segment in the ensemble rehearsal process, it will mean that every time a new selection is presented, the process of familiarizing the ensemble with the music will start over again. This will only slow the progress of the ensemble and result in wasted time during the rehearsal process. I discussed ways to improve music reading in chapter 3, Essential No. 8.

In many instances, the conductor may view *rehearsing concert repertoire* as the main part of any rehearsal process, if not the only one. Of course, in the preparation stages, this involves the selection of repertoire, score study, conceiving the concert program format, and many other preparations on the part of the conductor. However, if rehearsing concert repertoire is the only rehearsal process objective, it is doubtful that the conductor will accomplish the needed rehearsal process objectives or move the ensemble forward. Rehearsing the concert repertoire certainly gives the ensemble the motivation to prepare for a concert performance, but does not necessarily improve the ensemble in terms of a higher performance level. In formulating ensemble rehearsal objectives, the conductor should include those items that will improve the ensemble performance level in a continuous manner. Simply having achieved the performance of a demanding work does not necessarily bring the ensemble to a higher performance level.

Detailed work on various passages should predominate in most educational ensemble rehearsals. If the conductor does not spend a large percentage of the rehearsal process with this segment, the players will soon question if the conductor is credible. Simply playing through selections without stopping for detailed work on passages that need attention will cause the players to wonder if the conductor has prepared properly for the rehearsal process and/or if he or she is able to detect and correct errors. Passages must be "taken apart" and specific problems addressed in the rehearsal process. In a concert performance, it becomes obvious if the conductor has not done detailed work on passages that need attention. An example of this is an exposed passage in which the intonation produced is faulty. These kinds of passages will improve only if the conductor devotes the needed rehearsal time to correcting these problems. In other words, the conductor must confront these problems and insist that they are rehearsed properly until improvement is shown during the rehearsal process.

The segment of problem solving in the rehearsal process may or may not involve detailed work on passages. The solution may be understanding the problem and then employing teaching strategies as opposed to the detailed work process. However, when the conductor realizes the particular problem, it may be necessary to proceed with detailed work on the passage. The conductor should come prepared to offer solutions to problems that surface during the rehearsal process. This requires that the conductor has studied the score thoroughly and has anticipated at least some of these problems. The conductor needs to be ready with viable solutions. In some instances, the conductor will need to delay the solving of a particular problem if the solution is not apparent during the rehearsal process. The conductor then must make sure that he or she comes to the next rehearsal process "armed" with teaching strategies for resolving this problem.

As the various priorities that need attention surface during the rehearsal process and become evident, *other rehearsal segments may be generated by these rehearsal priorities* in need of resolution through teaching strategies. These priorities might include intonation, rhythm, tone production, articulation, precision, phrasing, style, interpretation, and musical expression. These priorities would then dictate the rehearsal segments needed in the rehearsal process to resolve the particular performance problem. The conductor should accompany these various rehearsal segments with teaching strategies to implement the resolution of the problem or the refinement of the targeted priority. In almost all cases, the conductor should discover these problems and priorities through acute listening during the rehearsal process.

REHEARSAL PROCEDURES

Rehearsal procedures employed in a given scenario are many and varied. Much depends on the creativity of the conductor as to the effectiveness and appropriateness of these specific procedures. However, the advanced conductor needs to be provided with a basis for rehearsing the ensemble, and in this sense, be aware of six specific procedures that can be used to enhance the progress of the instrumental music ensemble. I have enumerated and elaborated on these six procedures in the following paragraphs so that the maturing conductor will have a certain confidence about rehearsing the ensemble. These six specific rehearsal procedures employed by the conductor are as follows:

1. Conducting (non-verbal communication)
2. Verbalizing (or singing) by the conductor
3. Modeling and imitation (by conductor or players)
4. Demonstration by the conductor
5. Providing feedback by the conductor
6. Teaching by concepts for awareness and learning transfer

Conducting should be the dominant procedure in the rehearsal process for the conductor. If the conducting technique is clear and musical, it will be unnecessary for the conductor to stop frequently for corrections and adjustments. There should be a balance between conducting and verbal rehearsing, but most of the time should be spent conducting in the rehearsal process. If the ensemble learns to watch the conductor, the responsibility then lies with the conductor to communicate through these conducting patterns and gestures in terms of the precision and musicality. If the conductor finds that much of the rehearsal time is spent in verbalizing or demonstrating, the conductor should question the balance between the conducting technique and verbal procedures. In the rehearsal process, the players must watch the conductor, listen to what is happening around them, and relate their part to the rest of the ensemble. It is the conductor's duty to see that these activities are occurring.

A word of caution is necessary here concerning *the idea of verbalizing in the rehearsal process.* It is extremely important that the conductor should avoid long periods of talking in the rehearsal process. Second, the conductor should not become so anxious about taking care of the details that much of the rehearsal time is spent talking and consequently the actual playing and the factor of continuity becomes secondary. The conductor should keep remarks concise in the rehearsal process and avoid straying from the immediate performance problems. Third, with podium experience there is a tendency for the conductor to talk too much in the rehearsal process. Players learn best when the conductor employs the "hands-on" approach of playing as opposed to "lecturing" in the rehearsal process. When verbalizing in the rehearsal process, look at the players and not at the score or above the ensemble so that there is no lack of communication with the ensemble. Finally, the conductor should also be cautious about using verbal imagery, analogy, or long explanations that simply waste valuable rehearsal time.

The modeling procedure by either the conductor or a selected player can be very effective in the rehearsal process. The conductor should model by either singing or playing on an instrument. The conductor must be competent on the instrument or the player's imitation may become distorted. In modeling, the players must listen carefully to the model performance so that their imitation is a precise and correct playing of the model. If the conductor is not a good singer, the model sung could still be effective in most instances, depending on what the conductor is trying to achieve. This is saying to the advanced conductor, do not be inhibited if your vocal skills are imperfect. One can successfully model many performance aspects, such as rhythm, articulation, phrasing, style, and musical expression, without great vocal skills. Having a member of the ensemble model the passage can also be a very effective procedure in the rehearsal process, or having one section play for the rest of the ensemble can also extend this modeling procedure.

The conductor usually accompanies *the procedure of demonstration* with an explanation. In some cases, this procedure may cross the line into modeling and imitation. However, the important consideration here is that the conductor's message gets across to the players and the demonstration is effective in improving the ensemble performance. The demonstration may be either a positive one in the sense of what should be done or take on the negative quality as to what should not be done with a particular aspect of the musical performance. The demonstration by the conductor should be concise and to the point. The rehearsal process will then continue with the repetition of the passage to show the results of the demonstration or more repetition until attaining the proper results. The conductor should always provide feedback concerning the success or failure of the demonstration procedure.

Feedback is a crucial procedure during the rehearsal process; the players psychologically need to know if they have learned the passage to the satisfaction of the conductor. The conductor can express this feedback in many different ways. The feedback may only be a simple positive affirmation from the conductor or it may require further explanation to let the ensemble know the status of the passage in question. If the conductor does not provide feedback, the players will have a sense of incompleteness or, at least, be confused about whether to put additional work into the passage. A lack of feedback sends the message to the players that either the conductor does not know what to do or else is satisfied with a lower standard of performance from the ensemble. In most instances, the player does want to know from the conductor, "how am I doing?" If the passage is played satisfactorily, a simple "thank you" may be a polite way of expressing this to the ensemble. If more remedial work needs to be done, then the conductor should proceed to work on improving the passage. When asking the ensemble to start again, avoid repeating letters or numbers as the ensemble will begin to expect this, resulting in rehearsal time wasted. (Likewise, players should indicate and respond to the conductor when asked to play a certain way by nodding the head to clarify that they understand or else ask a question if they are confused.)

The procedures of teaching by concepts for awareness and learning transfer pertain to the perceptiveness and creativity on the part of the conductor in building a cohesive, musical ensemble. If the conductor spends all of the rehearsal time trying to prepare the repertoire for the next concert performance, then the ideas of teaching by concepts for awareness and learning transfer in the rehearsal process must be set aside. However, if the conductor views the rehearsal process as a learning experience in which performance concepts are promoted, then the rehearsal process becomes an environment for exciting music-making and ensemble improvement. Likewise, the awareness idea fosters listening and musical sensitivity in the rehearsal process and the results will be a more musical environment. This learning transfer means that the players will carry over to the other rehearsals, performances, and ensembles those performance skills and other musical considerations that they previously addressed. The advantages of learning transfer will be obvious in terms of the ensemble improvement. In this regard, the players begin to take care of performance aspects without the help of the conductor in the rehearsal process. This approach should then lead to accelerated improvement on the part of the whole ensemble.

Largely, the selected repertoire and the maturity of the ensemble will dictate how the conductor will rehearse. These rehearsal segments and procedures involve detailed score study, careful planning, and meticulous rehearsal preparations. The maturity of the ensemble will determine the pace of the rehearsal process, the segments selected, procedures employed, and the teaching strategies implemented. Especially with the educational groups, the conductor must *have pedagogical knowledge about the instruments of the ensemble.* If the conducting technique is clear and the conductor is able to communicate the composer's intentions to the ensemble, then successful musical performances will result. In the final analysis, conducting and rehearsing the instrumental music ensemble effectively and efficiently are certainly the most critical aspects for any conductor.

As mentioned above, the conducting technique is a very important part of rehearsing the ensemble. Considerable time can be saved in the rehearsal process if the conductor has a clear conducting technique; then there is less need for stopping the ensemble for corrections or demonstrations. Good conducting technique, along with effective rehearsal procedures, will allow the conductor to communicate the conceived musical interpretation to the ensemble more efficiently. In many cases, the conducting technique can replace or enhance the rehearsal procedures. For example, when offering a solution to a specific problem, the conductor might vocalize as a model, while at the same time conducting the passage for the ensemble. *The combination of the conducting technique and the rehearsal procedure* can reinforce each other in many instances during the rehearsal process.

PROCEDURAL OPTIONS IN THE REHEARSAL PROCESS

There are three basic procedural options in rehearsing any given work. The conductor must determine which rehearsal procedural option to employ. Below are the three basic options for rehearsing the concert repertoire:

1. Play all the way through the work (without stopping if possible) and then return to places that need attention.
2. Start at the beginning and when corrections need to be made, stop and work on these places.
3. Select places to rehearse and later play through the entire piece or section for continuity and confirmation.

In the rehearsal process, one or more of these options will be used depending on the particular preparation timetable the conductor has conceived. Careful planning on the part of the conductor is necessary for the effective use of these three options. The first option is reading a work initially and then continuing to rehearse the work thereafter. The second option is discovering where the various passages are that need attention during the rehearsal process and work on these passages as they occur. The third option is very effective and efficient when the conductor, through careful score study or from previous rehearsals, *knows what needs to be done.* The conductor may also combine these options or change from one option to another in the rehearsal process.

Technical and musical problems tend to occur within the context of the music being rehearsed. To solve these problems, the conductor must isolate the particular problem, and thereafter, return the solved problem to the musical context of the passage. Likewise, phrases and sections are a fractional part of the musical composition, and in the rehearsing of the ensemble, the conductor must not lose sight of this when working on details. *The underlying idea here is continuity.* At times, the conductor will become so enamored with the details of a work that the "big picture" gets lost for the ensemble. At least on the initial reading and during subsequent rehearsals along with the last run-through (during the dress rehearsal process), the idea of continuity is very important. However, the conductor should avoid getting into the habit of simply playing through one piece after another in the rehearsal process for the sake of continuity. He or she must address the details as well. A creative procedure for working on continuity is to change from the regular rehearsal procedures by starting close to the end of the piece and then gradually working backward to the beginning to help "seam" the various sections of the work together.

The SAS (synthesis-analysis-synthesis) procedure applies here in the rehearsing of a new work. The initial reading is the first synthesis, that of acquainting the ensemble with the music. Rehearsing to perfect the details of the performance during the analysis part follows the initial reading of the work. Finally, the second synthesis brings all the details back into focus by presenting the "big picture" for the ensemble. Some conductors have suggested in the initial reading to play the most attractive parts of the work to promote player enthusiasm. Other conductors have suggested playing through the more accessible parts of a piece, rather than discouraging the players with the difficult places initially. This procedure will help build confidence with the players so they feel capable of playing the selected repertoire. With these procedures, the conductor should also provide the players with a sense of the essence and spirit of the work (see Chapter 14: Style and Musical Interpretation).

In the professional ensemble environment, the approach is more businesslike, and if the works to be rehearsed are standard repertoire, the ensemble will not expect or need a complete run-through of each work. With the professional ensemble, time is money, and the amount of rehearsal time is limited. Instead, the conductor must be prepared to rehearse only those passages that are problematic or in need of reinforcement due to the conductor's preference or through the imagination in the musical interpretation of the work. If the repertoire is new, however, the familiarity, details, and continuity factors are important for the professional ensemble as well.

It is extremely important for the educational ensemble to have rehearsed the details of the performance thoroughly before presenting it in concert performance. Also, because music is always based on the forward motion of the musical line, continuity and sequence are always important factors in the rehearsal process. However, the players must experience this continuity and sequencing of the music in the rehearsal process. If not, many surprises may occur in the concert performance and the results could even be disastrous. Only by achieving this continuity and sequencing will the players grasp the essence and spirit of the music throughout the rehearsal process and then project this to the audience in the concert performance.

THREE MISCELLANEOUS PROCEDURAL CONSIDERATIONS IN THE REHEARSAL PROCESS

To do *detailed work on passages* in the rehearsal process, isolate the problems, probably slowing the passages down and making sure to play them rhythmically. Unless it is a problem of checking intonation or balancing of a chord where there might be some value of sustaining each note to check these performance aspects, always rehearse with a rhythmic feel. The point here is that music is rhythmic and notes must fall when they occur at the selected tempo and indicated pulse—no matter how slow the tempo may be. Later on, increasing the tempo will not be a problem when the ensemble has rehearsed the passage securely and rhythmically. If you do not complete this task in the rehearsal process, there is a false sense of having rehearsed the passage but little or no improvement will actually have occurred.

It is valid to repeat passages for reinforcement in the rehearsal process, but the conductor should let the ensemble know the reason behind such repetition. Otherwise, the players will consider it a waste of time and tend to become hostile and belligerent. In such an instance, the players will not profit from repeating the passage. There may be times when the ensemble, in the judgment of the conductor, needs to repeat a passage for security or continuity purposes. These are valid reasons for repeating a passage. Whatever the reason might be, let the players know. Do not repeat passages for conductor practice. The conductor should better prepare for the rehearsal process if this is the case. Otherwise, players will become resentful about such a procedure.

Many times, *players think that they can remember changes* made during the rehearsal process. However, either in the following rehearsals or in the concert performance, the player's memory may fail, or through some other distraction the player will miss the change made in the rehearsal process unless it is notated in the music. Always make these notations with a pencil (no ink) so that you can erase them later. It is necessary to do this with rental music. The conductor should see to it that a pencil is provided at rehearsals for the players to mark the conductor's decisions, correct mistakes in the parts, indicate where the pulse will occur in passages of rhythmic complexity, and other such items that may occur throughout the rehearsal process. In many situations, the player should bring a pencil to the rehearsal process for this marking purpose. The conductor can anticipate some of these changes and mark the parts before the rehearsal process begins. If these changes are not marked in the music during the rehearsal process, the same items may need reexamination in the following rehearsal, and of course, this will mean some rehearsal time wasted. With younger ensembles, the conductor may need to show or indicate to the players how to mark these corrections or changes.

The information contained in this book, along with continued study of other sources cited below, should enhance the education of the advanced conductor and allow for the development of effective rehearsal segments and procedures. This creative development does require considerable application by the conductor in the areas of selecting the music material, the conducting technique, the score study, and the musical interpretation. Effective rehearsal segments and procedures are acquired through evaluating the achievement during the rehearsal process and then continuing to design these segments and procedures for the following rehearsals. The maturing conductor must come to the rehearsal process with specific ideas in mind and implement them as the rehearsal process continues. It is quite easy in the rehearsal process to use segments and procedures that do not really work or reap much improvement from the ensemble. The conductor must constantly be asking himself or herself, "Was this really effective in the rehearsal process?"

THE MAIN DUTY OF THE CONDUCTOR

If this general question were posed: "What is the conductor trying to do in the rehearsal process (or concert performance)?" the answer is to help the group play better. *This is the main duty of the conductor.* (In some cases, the conductor may even be detrimental to the ensemble performance unless clear conducting technique has been well developed and coupled with effective rehearsal skills and procedures.) Clear conducting patterns, expressive gestures, meaningful facial expressions, and natural body language will help the players perform better. In the rehearsal process the conductor should help the players both individually and collectively to play better. In the final analysis, in the rehearsal process (or concert performance) the conductor should influence the performance of the ensemble in a constructive and positive way. The conductor should always implement and reinforce the concert performance during the rehearsal process. This is why the effectiveness and efficiency of the conductor is so important in the rehearsal process.

With a school ensemble, the task is threefold in that the conductor must devote efforts not only to solving technical problems and developing musicianship fundamentals, but also to producing superior musical performances of the selected repertoire. The focus of this book from chapters 8–15 (Priorities and Strategies) is to provide ideas and suggestions for the advanced conductor in solving these technical and musical problems. I have not attempted to present specific interpretations of selected works. This must fall to later study in other advanced or graduate conducting courses. However, in the Appendix A of this book, I list some standard repertoire for orchestra, string orchestra, chamber orchestra, concert band, wind ensemble, woodwind choirs, brass choirs, miscellaneous ensembles, opera orchestras, musical orchestras, and ballet orchestras. This list could serve as a basis for the selection of repertoire, for score study, and for program building by the advanced conductor. The conductor must always be concerned *about fostering the musicality and authenticity of these selections in the rehearsal process, and subsequently in the concert performance.*

The professional conductor and ensemble concentrate mostly on the interpretative aspects. The professional player is hired to technically and musically reproduce the part. The conductor of a professional ensemble dictates the conceived interpretation and the players respond technically and musically to these requests. The conductor of a professional ensemble should be able to tell the players exactly how he wants the music interpreted. The professional player is ready to do exactly as the conductor wishes if the conductor is able to communicate this interpretation to the ensemble. However, the conductor must have a clear concept of "how the music should sound" and then be able to communicate this effectively to the players through clear conducting technique and effective rehearsal procedures during the rehearsal process.

In between the very youthful school ensemble and the highly professional ensemble, there are many levels of performance and maturity. In the rehearsal process, the conductor must *adjust the approach to these various levels in numerous ways.* For example, the conductor must decide when to affect the ensemble directly and when to let the ensemble have some freedom with the musical flow in the rehearsal process and concert performance. How sensitively the conductor does this will greatly determine the rehearsal process efficiency and the performance success of the ensemble. In adapting to the maturity level of the ensemble, the conductor should show some flexibility in moving from one level to another. The choice of words and the conductor's expectations of the group involved are factors in this flexibility and adaptability. In all cases, the conductor must strive to bring out the best qualities possible in the particular group—that is, help the group to play better.

COMMUNICATION IN THE REHEARSAL PROCESS

The conductor, through conducting technique and rehearsing skills, communicates his or her musical interpretation to the ensemble. On the surface, this may seem obvious; however, the conductor who spends most of the rehearsal time keeping everyone somewhat together is probably not getting a musical response from the ensemble or showing the intentions of the composer. It is important to realize that when the conductor looks at the musical score for even a very few seconds at a time during the rehearsal process, communication with the ensemble is diminished. If the conductor allows, the score will tend to attract his or her eyes. Rather, the musical sound should be the focus and not the printed notes of the score. It is important for the maturing conductor to have a clear conception of the work and then compare this conception with what is actually occurring within the ensemble during the rehearsal process. The conductor should try communicating with conducting patterns and gestures before using verbal communication. In communicating verbally, the conductor should always be straightforward and concise. The use of carefully selected words or phrases can enhance communication with the ensemble and save time during the rehearsal process.

There is really no debate here as to which is more important—conducting technique or rehearsing skills. *They are both important!* In chapters 8–15, I identify the priorities that need attention in the rehearsal process. The conducting technique will enter into this discussion because with many of the suggestions presented for the designing of teaching strategies, the adequacy of the conducting technique is a factor in rehearsing the instrumental music ensemble effectively. It is impossible to determine specifically where conducting technique might become secondary and rehearsing skills or teaching strategies should take over in the rehearsal process. The conductor must realize that in the rehearsal process, there is a mental duality involved: (1) thinking ahead in anticipation of what is needed to properly conduct and interpret the music, and (2) listening for technical and musical problems that may need resolution through the rehearsing skills and/or teaching strategies. Because of this duality, the conductor is combining both conducting technique and rehearsing skills throughout the rehearsal process.

The conductor and the ensemble communicate during the rehearsal process in numerous ways:

- Clear conducting patterns and gestures
- Eye contact, body language, and facial expression directed toward the ensemble members
- Players watching the conductor (and then responding sensitively and appropriately)

- Succinct verbal explanations and comments (speaking concisely, looking at the players, not at the music)
- Modeling and imitation by the conductor or the players
- Demonstrations by the conductor (by singing, playing, explaining, modeling, or conducting)
- Asking the players questions for feedback to improve the communication between the conductor and players (within a controlled situation)
- Creating a rehearsal environment and climate that is conducive to ensemble intensity, concentration, teamwork, cooperation, sensitivity, and musicality

The conductor should generally concentrate on one problem at a time. The conductor should not give the impression of hurrying or trying to do too many things at once in the rehearsal process. *If this happens, the players will feel that the rehearsal process is cluttered, and perhaps, that the conductor is disorganized.* Likewise, the conductor should present his comments for improvement in an emphatic manner and with a sense of credibility and authority. An effective technique for the conductor when explaining something to the ensemble is using both verbal comments (or singing) and conducting patterns and gestures simultaneously to make a sound and visual connection with the ensemble. I present more detailed information about the pacing of the rehearsal process and communicating with the ensemble in chapter 3, Essential No. 4: Pacing the Rehearsal Process.

PRACTICAL APPLICATION (DISCUSSION/DEMONSTRATION)

1. List the various segments to use in the rehearsal process as outlined in the book.
2. List the various procedures to use in the rehearsal process as outlined in the book.
3. What are the three basic procedural rehearsal options outlined in the book?
4. Why is rehearsing for both details and continuity so very important for the conductor and the players during the rehearsal process?
5. Why is it necessary to continue the conductor's education within the conducting curriculum and within the rehearsal process environment?
6. List and discuss the technical and musical priorities that you may need to confront in the rehearsal process. (This is a more detailed review of the rehearsal priorities discussed earlier.)
7. Discuss the employment of teaching strategies as a part of the procedures within the rehearsal process. How can one vary these teaching strategies?
8. Why is feedback from the conductor so important for the ensemble in the rehearsal process?
9. Cite some musical examples of how the conducting technique employed and a rehearsal procedure might complement each other.
10. What are some ideas concerning how to present and rehearse a new work with the ensemble in the rehearsal process?
11. How does the mature or professional ensemble differ from the educational ensemble in the rehearsal process?

12. Why rehearse rhythmically and why rehearse slowly?
13. What are some of the various ways in which to communicate with the instrumental ensemble during the rehearsal process?
14. Begin to gain familiarity with the standard repertoire found in Appendix A through CD listening, score study, and guidance from the conducting teacher. (See Appendix G for assignment forms).

RECOMMENDED READING

Dalby, Max F., *Band Rehearsal Techniques: A Handbook for New Directors.* In this book, there are chapters on Rehearsal Objectives, Rehearsal Procedures, and Rehearsal Psychology that would be relevant for the maturing band director.

Fuchs, Peter Paul, *The Psychology of Conducting.* This book addresses many of the various issues in being a conductor that would follow the basic conducting course in the curriculum.

Green, Elizabeth A. H., *The Dynamic Orchestra.* Chapter Four: The Rehearsal takes a unique approach to the rehearsal segments and procedures.

Kahn, Emil, *Workbook for Conducting.* This is an interesting format with full scores for various orchestra, band, and choral works as well as succinct conducting comments.

Kohut, Daniel L., and Joe W. Grant, *Learning to Conduct and Rehearse.* Chapter 8: Rehearsal Procedures addresses the various segments and procedures in the rehearsal process.

Kohut, Daniel L., *Musical Performance: Learning Theory and Pedagogy.* Part III: Principles, Methods and Theories of Tone Production focuses on the whole matter of tone production in chapters 9–12.

Long, R. Gerry, *The Conductor's Workshop: A Workbook on Instrumental Conducting.* Part I of this workbook discusses the various aspects confronting the conductor in the rehearsal process.

McBeth, W. Francis, *Effective Performance of Band Music: Solutions to Specific Problems in the Performance of Band Music.* The first five Solutions addressed are: Ensemble Pitch and Balance, Dynamic and Articulation Markings, Interpretation of Asymmetrical Meters, Subdivision, and Percussion Techniques.

Taubman, Howard, *The Maestro: The Life of Arturo Toscanini.* Part Two of this book has four chapters entitled Conducting: A Way of Life, Rehearsals, It is Mutual, and Musical Values as proposed by Arturo Toscanini.

REPERTOIRE FOR PROJECTS AND ASSIGNMENTS

Full Orchestra, Chamber Orchestra, or String Orchestra

Gounod: Faust Ballet Suite (various movements)
Grieg: Peer Gynt Suite No. 1 (various movements)
Holst: Brook Green Suite (for strings)
Khatchaturian: Three Dances from the "Gayaneh" Ballet
Mozart: The Marriage of Figaro Overture

Concert Band or Wind Ensemble

Bach: Fantasia in G Major (Goldman, arr.)
Benson: The Leaves are Falling
Camphouse: Three London Miniatures
Jacob: William Byrd Suite (various movements)
Lo Presti: Elegy for a Young American

Miscellaneous or Small Ensembles

Strauss, R.: Serenade for 13 Winds (2 flutes, 2 oboes, 2 clarinets, 3 bassoons or double bass as a substitute for contrabassoon, and four horns)
Husa: Divertimento for Brass and Percussion (2 horns, 3 trumpets, 3 trombones, tuba, and 2 percussion)

Chapter Seven

An Integrated Approach to Rehearsing

INTEGRATING THE REHEARSAL PROCESS ELEMENTS

The elements of the rehearsal process include conducting and playing, the rehearsal process essentials, the technical and musical priorities, the rehearsal segments and procedures, the rehearsal plan and schedule, and the rehearsal teaching strategies as well as other items that the conductor might deem necessary for the improvement of the ensemble. This integration, of course, assumes that meticulous score study, careful rehearsal planning, and various preparations on the part of the conductor have been accomplished. In numerous scenarios, conductors come into the rehearsal process unprepared to help the ensemble play better. They simply proceed through the rehearsal process with little or no direction except for the repetition of the repertoire to be prepared for a concert performance. The experienced conductor might be able to rehearse a younger or less mature ensemble without this intense score study, planning, and preparations, but the rehearsal results will never be as productive as they would be with good score study, careful planning, and meticulous preparations. If the evolving conductor tries to do without these elements, the results in the rehearsal process will tend to be quite unsatisfactory.

The integration of these rehearsal process elements will ultimately determine the success or failure of the ensemble's performance. *The rehearsal process must have a focus and direction that the conductor plans.* The conductor should decide how to integrate these elements and how much emphasis to place on the various rehearsal process elements. The conductor might create a checklist of these rehearsal process elements that will confirm whether these rehearsal preparations are completed. The initial preparatory step is the selection of music material for the rehearsal process. Determining the segments in the rehearsal process and the music materials and procedures to use in the warm-up/tuning period follows this selection of music material. In most instances, this planning involves the rehearsing of the concert repertoire, but it could also include some sight-reading material, working on certain fundamentals in the warm-up period, or the improvement or refinement of specific priorities during the rehearsal process. The conductor should design a rehearsal plan and schedule, and, guided by careful score study of each of the concert selections, then consider the procedural options and the selected teaching strategies to use in the rehearsal process.

A DETAILED LOOK AT THESE REHEARSAL PROCESS ELEMENTS

Conducting and playing should be the main and most significant parts of the rehearsal process. The conductor, with adequate conducting technique, should be able to control the following performance aspects: tempo, changes of tempo, precision, rhythm (showing the pulse), style, phrasing, and musical interpretation. The conductor should also have some control over the balance, blend, articulation, and the musical expression (including dynamics and nuances) with the conducting technique. The proper response of the ensemble to the conductor's patterns and gestures assumes that the players have learned to watch the conductor and that the conducting technique is clear and meaningful to the ensemble. If the conductor does not show clearly through the conducting patterns and gestures, facial expressions, or body language what is wanted from the ensemble, players will be unable to respond accordingly. To build a cohesive, musical ensemble, the conductor must show these meaningful conducting patterns and gestures, have trained the players to watch, and come to the rehearsal process totally prepared to conduct musically.

The first three essentials of the rehearsal scenario—personnel, music material, and rehearsal time—must be established before the rehearsal process begins. Then the *pacing of the rehearsal process* involves proceeding in a manner to keep the rehearsal moving forward and using the rehearsal time profitably with the ensemble. Carefully plan the *warm-up/tuning period* in terms of music material and activities. Then *listening, musical sensitivity, and communication* should be a part of the entire rehearsal process. Incorporate *music reading* throughout the rehearsal process and frequently make it a separate part of the rehearsal process for the improvement of this performance aspect. *Detecting and correcting errors* during the rehearsal process is one of the main reasons for the rehearsal process. Finally, the idea of *striving for musicality* with the ensemble is the most important of all these essentials.

The integration of the technical and musical priorities into the rehearsal process allows for an effective and precise direction for the rehearsal process to evolve. Unless the conductor has determined these priorities with the ensemble, the rehearsal process will not make substantial progress. In most instances, these priority problems will be decided by: (1) the performance level of the ensemble, (2) the strengths and weaknesses within the ensemble, and (3) the repertoire being rehearsed. Which of these priorities merit attention in the rehearsal process? Formulate these priorities based on the reality of the scenario. If the conductor determines that the ensemble is playing certain rhythm patterns poorly, then address this rhythm priority in the rehearsal process. Depending on the circumstances, you may solve this priority weakness quickly, or it may require continued rehearsal time to correct. Such priorities as intonation will need constant vigilance on the part of both the conductor and the players.

Varying the segments and procedures in the rehearsal process can add interest and keep the players focused. In general, such variance should intensify the rehearsal process. Rehearsals should not become routine and predictable. Rehearsal segments, perhaps, have some limitations in terms of variation, but the rehearsal procedures available are infinite depending on the imagination of the conductor. When the rehearsal process seems to be going nowhere in improving the performance of the ensemble or solving problems with the players, the conductor may need to consider other options in terms of the rehearsal segments and procedures. This is where the post-evaluation of the rehearsal process becomes important. The conductor should evaluate the rehearsal process and determine whether maximum progress is being made with the ensemble. If the answer is no, then the conductor must conclude that it is necessary to institute a change in the rehearsal process. In many instances, this may involve the variance of the rehearsal segments and procedures. In general, the rehearsal segments and procedure variance will depend strongly on the reasons behind the particular technical or musical problems encountered in the rehearsal process.

The rehearsal plan and schedule should vary from one rehearsal process to the next. Much will depend on the ensemble progress from the previous rehearsal. The main consideration is that the conductor has a plan formulated before the rehearsal process begins. Unless this happens, the rehearsal process will lack the needed direction and focus. The players will detect this situation almost immediately and the conductor's credibility will become suspect. This plan may take on a general outline such as *announcements, warm-up period, tuning, rehearsing the selected repertoire, sight-reading activity, detailed work on passages, solving problems, and closure.* The conductor should at least estimate the time that each activity will take. In the reality of the rehearsal process, these times may not work out quite as the outline was conceived. However, the conductor may have to decide during the rehearsal process whether to alter the schedule. Second, the conductor should decide on the rehearsal process objectives (before the rehearsal process) and strive to incorporate these objectives into the rehearsal plan. In other words, the conductor should plan precisely as to what the ensemble should accomplish during the rehearsal process and *then proceed to get it done.* This will mainly affect the rehearsal items to be emphasized and the rehearsal process objectives to be achieved.

After formulating the rehearsal plan and schedule, the conductor should now be prepared to execute this plan. This will involve serious score study on the part of the conductor. On occasions, the conductor may find it necessary to change the plan as formulated before the rehearsal process begins, but should have "memorized" the main points, and only when necessary, refer to the written plan and schedule for specific details. The musical scores then become the main outline for the conductor to follow (beyond the general outline of the rehearsal process objectives, segments, and procedures) during the rehearsal process. *The conductor must keep the selected priorities in mind* with a plan as to how to implement these priorities with the designed teaching strategies. How successful the rehearsal process will be depends on what the conductor can bring to the rehearsal process in terms of this score preparation, his or her musicianship, and the appropriately designed teaching strategies.

In most instances, *the application of the teaching strategies* will appear in the rehearsal process during the time that the conductor is working on concert repertoire. In some cases, the conductor can employ these teaching strategies during the warm-up period to improve a variety of technical priorities or problems that may have surfaced in the previous rehearsal process. To repeat, these technical priorities include intonation and tuning, rhythm and rhythm patterns, ensemble sonority elements (tone, balance, blend, color and texture), and articulation and bowing. The conductor will need to employ these teaching strategies in solving problems and improving the technical priorities during the rehearsal process. The conductor should continually think about designing new teaching strategies for use in the rehearsal process. Chapters 8–11 contain information concerning these technical priorities and the related teaching strategies.

Likewise, the application of teaching strategies will also occur in the rehearsal process *while trying to solve musical problems* that occur in the concert repertoire. Again, these teaching strategies may be employed during the warm-up period in solving these musical problems, and thereby, improving these musical priorities. These musical priorities include tempo and ensemble precision, phrasing and the musical line, style and interpretation, and dynamics, nuances, and musical expression. Just as with the technical priorities and problems, the conductor must stockpile teaching strategies to solve these musical priorities and problems. Chapters 12–15 cover these musical priorities and the related teaching strategies.

REHEARSING THE INSTRUMENTAL MUSIC ENSEMBLE

The Relationship of the Conducting Technique in the Rehearsal Process

Many of the problems occurring in the rehearsal process *relate directly to the area of the conducting technique.* As a basic example, the clarity of the preparatory beat will greatly influence the initial attack, the exact tempo executed, and the precision of the ensemble. I could cite many other examples here. Conductors should rely strongly on their conducting technique and resort to verbal comments, explanations, and demonstrations only if the problems cannot be resolved through the conducting patterns and gestures. This, of course, assumes that the members of the ensemble are watching the conductor. By depending on the conducting technique, there will be less need to stop, and less time wasted during the rehearsal process.

Although the main concern of this book is to present ideas and suggestions about the rehearsal process, the conducting technique adequacy is a crucial part of the rehearsal process. The point is that the conductor must develop this conducting technique to enhance his or her effectiveness in the rehearsal process (and in the concert performance). This involves serious study and practice by the conductor to acquire good conducting technique. This book assumes that conducting technique has been studied, and is being developed and refined by the evolving conductor. Once the ensemble learns to watch and respond to even adequate conducting technique, the rehearsal process should equate with measurable ensemble progress.

There are times in the rehearsal process when the only solution is for the conductor to stop and verbalize to the players. The conductor must make these rehearsal choices: *To stop or not to stop, that is the question!* However, long periods of rehearsal time devoted to verbalizing will probably do little in achieving these rehearsal process objectives that have been formulated for the rehearsal process. When verbal explanations or demonstrations are necessary, keep them concise and employ them infrequently. One of the most important duties in the rehearsal process is to keep the players interested, involved, and focused; only by doing this will the rehearsal objectives be realized. Stopping frequently will tend to cause the players a loss of concentration, making them unable to stay involved in the rehearsal process.

Good conducting technique can save time and avoid frustration in the rehearsal process. The gesture is more efficient than taking the time for verbal comments. When the conductor stops the ensemble to make corrections, to present concepts, or improve various performance aspects, valuable rehearsal time may pass during somewhat frequent interruptions. In the actual stopping of the ensemble, considerable time is spent making the necessary adjustments, repeating the passage, presenting feedback to the players, and then continuing to the next problem in the rehearsal process. The conductor should keep this foremost in mind when rehearsing. *The conductor should be ready to state immediately the reason for stopping.* Efficiency in the rehearsal process depends on a proper balance between the use of conducting and that of verbalizing. In many scenarios, asking questions of the players (or allowing the players to ask questions) during the rehearsal process is a more efficient approach than simply telling them what to do.

Conducting and rehearsing is not unlike driving a car. The driver needs to be aware of the traffic, road signs, weather conditions, road construction signs, map directions, and gas gauge reading. In the rehearsal process, the conductor must be watching (and listening) for potential problems, technical or musical errors, changes of tempo, dynamic contrast, style consistency, ensemble precision, ensemble balance, ensemble blend, and the list goes on and on. In the rehearsal process, the conductor must be listening and reacting to what is actually happening on many different levels. Good conducting technique and alertness on the part of the players can avoid most of these rehearsal problems. The conductor must make musical decisions constantly throughout the rehearsal process, not unlike driving the car, especially in congested city traffic or even down the interstate with large vehicles looming!

WHAT SHOULD HAPPEN IN THE REHEARSAL PROCESS

There needs to be intensity with both the conductor and the ensemble during the rehearsal period. The environment should have a sense of trying to accomplish certain specific rehearsal objectives. Without this intensity, the rehearsal process will lose its purpose. This does not mean that the rehearsal process needs to be "high stress" throughout the whole rehearsal time. The conductor must sense when the ensemble needs some relief from this intensity. However, if this intensity does not exist in the ensemble rehearsal process, there will be a loss of interest as well as concentration on the part of the players. Only if this intensity is present in the rehearsal process will the ensemble be focused. In an environment where this intensity is missing, several psychological aspects are noticeably absent: concentration, focus, discipline, enthusiasm, and self-motivation on the part of the ensemble.

As with all endeavors of an academic or artistic nature, *concentration is an absolute necessity* in order to achieve the rehearsal objectives and eventually the ensemble performance goals. Concentration in the rehearsal process can be fostered only in an environment that is relatively free of distractions and has developed into the scenario where discipline is self-imposed with the players (in teaching terms this is known as classroom management). If the total ensemble is concentrating, the progress in the rehearsal process should be quite remarkable. However, the opposite will be the case if the rehearsal environment is such that the players are unable to focus their attention on the matters at hand during the rehearsal process. The conductor must insist that the ensemble maintain this concentration in any rehearsal scenario. *The emphasis on listening* in the rehearsal process can help foster this needed concentration.

The conductor will communicate with the ensemble in the rehearsal process in numerous ways. *This communication is essential in raising the ensemble performance level.* The most common is communicating with conducting patterns and gestures. However, the verbalization and various other procedures used during the rehearsal process are also important means of communicating with the ensemble. Beyond these obvious means of communication, there are even more subtle avenues of communication between the conductor and the ensemble as well. I have discussed this communication in the rehearsal process throughout the book. The conductor must employ all of these procedures in the rehearsal process with the ultimate goal of building a cohesive, musical ensemble.

Not unlike those of communication, the conductor must incorporate *the various ideas concerning listening and musical sensitivity* into the rehearsal process scenario. The conductor must do everything possible to promote this listening and sensitivity in the rehearsal process. It is important for the conductor to point out to the players continually what to listen for in the rehearsal process. This awareness procedure comes about by isolating passages, asking various players to perform their parts individually, or calling attention to passages that need the players to listen carefully. Likewise, the conductor must show with the conducting patterns and gestures the kind of performance sensitivity that is characteristic of a fine ensemble. Only when the players are intensely aware of the surrounding sound are they able to fit their part into the ensemble fabric and then begin to realize improvement in the intonation, balance, blend, precision, and musicality associated with superior ensemble performances.

There must be persistence on the part of both the conductor and the ensemble in the rehearsal process to get things done correctly and musically. This will not always work quickly, but the conductor must lead the way in promoting the importance of this persistence in the rehearsal process. Like enthusiasm, the conductor's attitude must prevail in this situation. If the players observe through participation in the rehearsal process that the conductor wants things to be correct and musical, they will respond positively. However, if the conductor is not insistent and persistent, the message to the players is one of apathy or indifference. This persistence will not always make for the most interesting and exciting times in the rehearsal process, but this striving for perfection and for wonderful musicality must prevail in the rehearsal process in order to improve the performance level of the ensemble and present outstanding performances.

There is probably no other activity *that needs teamwork and cooperation* more than that of a music ensemble. When all of the elements involved in the rehearsal process or concert performance are considered, these two qualities are the most important aspects to ensemble performance success. This teamwork includes such items as mutual respect, striving together toward the rehearsal process objectives and ensemble performance goals, and in particular, a willingness to be a team player. For example, the player must subjugate the written dynamic level to the importance of the part within the ensemble. This may seem rather simple in concept, but this is critical to the elements of balance and blend. I could bring forth many other musical ideas concerning teamwork and cooperation, but the main point is that this cooperative attitude must exist and prevail in the rehearsal process. With a younger ensemble in the rehearsal process, for example, the conductor might physically move directly into a section to give the impression of this teamwork with the players.

THE CONDUCTOR IN THE REHEARSAL PROCESS

Bringing It All Together

The ensemble should spend most of the rehearsal process in conducting and rehearsing. Within this framework, the conductor must focus on improving the level of performance in some way and/or on preparing the instrumental music ensemble for a concert performance. This should be what the rehearsal process is all about. The segments and procedures of the rehearsal process will vary greatly depending on the individual scenario, the conductor, the difficulty of the repertoire, and the maturity and performance level of the ensemble. The conductor must plan and prepare in order to use the rehearsal process in a productive manner. However, all of this planning and preparation for the rehearsal process is strongly contingent on the repertoire to be rehearsed and the diligent score study of the conductor.

In the rehearsal process, the conductor must keep in mind the rehearsal process objectives and the ensemble performance goals as the rehearsals continue. Of an immediate nature, the rehearsal process objectives need to be achieved and then evaluated following the rehearsal process. The ensemble will reach its performance goals if the formulated rehearsal process objectives are consistent with these goals. The conductor in the rehearsal process must keep evaluating these objectives, and if necessary, revise these rehearsal process objectives to achieve the ensemble performance goals. From rehearsal process to rehearsal process, the conductor may begin to realize that the ensemble cannot or will not achieve certain rehearsal objectives on schedule. This evaluation may lead to a revision of the rehearsal plan. These important items of the ensemble performance goals, the rehearsal objectives, and the rehearsal plan must be in place *so that the rehearsal process is organized.* In rehearsing the ensemble, the conductor should start with the basic performance aspects and then eventually move to musicality aspects.

The selected concert repertoire will strongly determine the segments and procedures employed in the rehearsal process. The repertoire largely will dictate what happens in the rehearsal process. Each selection may be at a different stage of readiness for the upcoming concert performance. The conductor will have to pace the progress in the rehearsal process *so that all the selections are prepared well for the concert performance.* This involves careful planning and constant evaluation as to where each selection stands in the rehearsal process; then the conductor should devote the necessary rehearsal time to the selections that need the most attention. The conductor should be aware of the timetable for each rehearsal and of the number of rehearsals remaining before the concert performance. In some circumstances, the conductor may need to change the repertoire after evaluating how the ensemble is progressing toward the concert performance. If a repertoire change is inevitable, the earlier the better should be the rule for the conductor in making these changes.

Some of the rehearsal essentials discussed in chapter 3 are a part of the actual rehearsal process. Specifically, pacing the rehearsal process, the warm-up/tuning period, promoting listening and sensitivity, communicating with the ensemble, music reading development, detecting and correcting errors, and striving for musicality are all within the scope of the rehearsal process. Pacing the rehearsal would be included in all these aspects during the rehearsal process. The warm-up/tuning period would occur at the beginning of the rehearsal process. The promoting of listening and sensitivity, as well as communication between the conductor and the ensemble, should continue throughout the rehearsal process. Music reading skills development would occur (as needed) at specific points during the rehearsal process. *Likewise, detecting and correcting errors would be an ongoing activity in the rehearsal process.* Striving for musicality would also be continuous throughout the rehearsal process.

During the rehearsal process, *the conductor must keep the technical and musical priorities foremost in mind.* In this regard, the conductor must know these various priorities from memory and be listening to correct or refine these priorities within the reality of the rehearsal process. These priorities will surface as the rehearsals progress and the conductor will need to confront these for the improvement of the ensemble. For example, the appearance of compound meter may confuse a younger ensemble and require the conductor to explain the subdivision of the beat into three parts (in contrast to duple subdivision). I could cite many other examples concerning the priorities within the rehearsal process. Various conductors have suggested placing a list of these technical and musical priorities on the conductor's stand for referral and as a reminder throughout the rehearsal process. Please note that I have shown these various priorities on the Rehearsal Plan and Schedule contained in this chapter.

During the rehearsal process, the conductor must be ready to employ various teaching strategies as the situation dictates. In many cases, the conductor will be able to anticipate the specific performance problem and have a teaching strategy ready to improve the ensemble performance. In other instances, the conductor may be "surprised" by the problem and will need to devise a teaching strategy creatively to remedy the particular problem. If the conductor cannot find such a solution immediately, then he or she should note this and be ready at the next rehearsal process to confront the problem. In most instances, the experienced conductor will be able to find the solution by having an arsenal of teaching strategies from the past. The maturing conductor with less teaching experience may have to delay the solution until the following rehearsal process. *There are many options to utilize as teaching strategies in the rehearsal process.* (See the Teaching Strategy Tables at the end of the chapters that follow.)

THE CONDUCTOR'S BASIC RESPONSIBILITIES IN THE REHEARSAL PROCESS

Score preparation involves score reading, score study, marking the score (to aid in the rehearsing), solving conducting problems, and preparing the parts. Initially, the conductor must read the score to discover the composer's intentions and to conceive an authentic and musical interpretation of the work. Following this, the conductor must execute serious and long-term study in order to assimilate the details of the score in preparation for the rehearsal process. *The conductor must be ready to conduct properly the selections to be rehearsed.* This means that the conductor understands and has practiced such areas of conducting as tempo, changes of tempo, phrasing, fermatas, releases, preparatory beats, and other such conducting techniques so that time is not wasted in the rehearsal process because of the lack of preparation on the part of the conductor. The conductor must mark the score for his or her own benefit. Marking involves those details in the score that he or she must remember as well as mentally organizing the score in terms of the form, the phrasing, and the musical interpretation. When the conductor has assimilated the score well and marked the score for details, the preparation of the parts can then begin. *Marking details in the instrumental parts before the rehearsal process begins can also save considerable rehearsal time.*

These conducting preparations include having developed adequate conducting technique, knowing the score thoroughly, being prepared to conduct the selected repertoire, and *anticipating rehearsal problems and providing the solutions.* The development of adequate conducting technique in order to project the conceived musical interpretation to the ensemble and eventually to the listening audience is crucial in the preparation and background for the conductor. Without this adequate conducting technique, the conductor will waste valuable time in the rehearsal process and be unable to communicate the composer's intentions to the ensemble precisely.

Knowing the score thoroughly is a matter of the conductor spending the necessary time to learn the score and having the musical background to capture the essence and spirit of the work. Being prepared to conduct the selected repertoire focuses on the idea that the conductor has studied and practiced conducting the music at hand and is able to communicate this silently to the ensemble with patterns and gestures. Finally, the conductor must anticipate the technical and musical problems that may arise during the rehearsal process and offer some solutions to these performance problems. The conductor must be prepared to do whatever is necessary in the rehearsal process to improve the performance level of the ensemble.

In addition to the conducting and rehearsing preparations, *the conductor must oversee the other items that should be in readiness for the rehearsal process.* These include such items as personnel concerns, preparing the music, the physical rehearsal environment, and the organization of the rehearsal process. The personnel concerns may be many and varied. Much will depend on the given scenario as to the extent of these personnel concerns. Preparing the music must be at the top of the agenda for the conductor, because so many performance aspects are dependent on the preparation of the music to be rehearsed and produced. The physical rehearsal environment must be "ready to go" before each rehearsal process, and this may require the conductor to supervise this preparation. The general organization of the rehearsal process may involve numerous preparations, but these preparations specifically center around the idea that the conductor comes to the rehearsal process prepared to conduct and rehearse the selected repertoire. All of these important preparations will ensure that the rehearsal proceeds efficiently and effectively.

The organization of the rehearsal process definitely includes the rehearsal plan and schedule and the various teaching strategies to improve the ensemble performance. The rehearsal plan will help the pacing of the rehearsal process and will allow the conductor to distribute the time in the rehearsal schedule so that the ensemble rehearses the concert repertoire adequately. Without this rehearsal plan and schedule, the rehearsal process will lack organization and focus. It does not take very long for the players in an ensemble to discover that the conductor is disorganized and unprepared. This leads to some loss of conductor credibility. The conductor must also be prepared to offer solutions for the technical and musical problems that surface in the rehearsal process. Through careful score study, the conductor will anticipate many of these technical and musical problems and can devise the teaching strategies and solutions to these problems before the rehearsal process ever begins.

ABOUT THE REHEARSAL PLAN AND SCHEDULE AND THE OVERALL REHEARSAL PLAN

I present a *Rehearsal Plan and Schedule* form below (see Textbox 7.1). The conductor should employ this form (or a similar plan and schedule) to achieve an organized approach to the rehearsal process. This allows for the formulation of rehearsal process objectives and teaching strategies before the rehearsal begins. The rehearsal process will then have a focus and direction. This also acts as a reminder in terms of the technical and musical priorities in the rehearsal process. The conductor should evaluate the rehearsal process immediately following the rehearsal process and write down important issues on the reverse side of this form. The rehearsal process evaluation could wait if there is a recording made of the rehearsal process.

The Overall Rehearsal Plan worksheet will provide a guide for the conductor over the course of a specific number of rehearsals in preparation for the concert performance. This also serves as a record for what may have happened in the rehearsal process and for what the ensemble needs to accomplish in the following rehearsals. This worksheet will allow the conductor to gauge what to do in the following rehearsals in preparation for a successful concert performance. The conductor can use this Overall Rehearsal Plan (see Textbox 7.2) worksheet to visualize what adjustments might be necessary before the concert performance and note the essentials, priorities, and teaching strategies on the back of the form.

Textbox 7.1.

REHEARSAL PLAN AND SCHEDULE (Date: / /)

Time:

_____ ANNOUNCEMENTS:

1. _____
2. _____
3. _____
4. _____

_____ WARM-UP ROUTINE:
      MUSIC MATERIAL:
      PERFORMANCE ASPECTS TO BE COVERED:
      OBJECTIVES:

_____ TUNING PROCEDURES TO BE USED:
_____ CONCERT REPERTOIRE TO BE REHEARSED:
      SPECIFIC SELECTION (and passages):
      SPECIFIC SELECTION (and passages):
      SPECIFIC SELECTION (and passages):
      SPECIFIC SELECTION (and passages):
_____ READING NEW MATERIAL (as determined by the conductor):

REHEARSAL OBJECTIVES AND TEACHING STRATEGIES (before the rehearsal):

EVALUATION OF THE REHEARSAL PROCESS (after the rehearsal—use the reverse side of this sheet for noting specific problems):

(Circle priorities for consideration during the rehearsal process):

TECHNICAL PRIORITIES: INTONATION AND TUNING / RHYTHM AND RHYTHM PATTERNS / ENSEMBLE SONORITY ELEMENTS: TONE, BALANCE, BLEND, COLOR AND TEXTURE / ARTICULATION AND BOWING

MUSICAL PRIORITIES: TEMPO AND ENSEMBLE PRECISION / PHRASING AND THE MUSICAL LINE / STYLE AND INTERPRETATION / DYNAMICS, NUANCES AND THE MUSICAL EXPRESSION

This page may be duplicated for rehearsal planning.

Textbox 7.2.

OVERALL REHEARSAL PLAN (for preparation of the concert performance)

Warm-up procedures (needs of the ensemble):

_____

_____

Tuning procedures (depending on the accuracy of the pitch level):

_____

_____

Concert selections (timings) and details to be rehearsed:

1. _____ (   )

_____

2. _____ (   )

_____

3. _____ (   )

_____

4. _____ (   )

_____

5. _____ (   )

_____

6. _____ (   )

_____

7. _____ (   )

_____

8. _____ (   )

_____

Essentials to be considered: On reverse side of this sheet
Priorities to be considered: On reverse side of this sheet

Teaching strategies to be considered: On reverse side of this sheet
The number of rehearsals before the performance: 1 2 3 4 5 6 7 8 9 10 11 12

This page may be duplicated for rehearsal planning.

CONDUCTING AND REHEARSING
WITH THE ACCOMPANYING ENSEMBLE

During the conductor's career, there will be numerous opportunities to provide ensemble accompaniments for soloists or small ensembles. There is a somewhat different approach needed than in preparing regular ensemble repertoire for the concert performance. Accompaniments usually involve some reassessment of balance, dynamics, flexibility, and precision. Below are some of the aspects that are unique to this endeavor:

- Before the ensemble rehearses with the soloist, *the conductor should have a preliminary session with the soloist(s)* in which such matters as tempo, tempo changes, style, and phrasing are agreed upon. This procedure avoids wasting time on these details with the soloist during the rehearsal process. In almost all instances, the accompaniment should be rehearsed meticulously before the soloist (or small ensemble) rehearses with the accompanying ensemble.
- The conductor should realize that his or her main duty is to lead the ensemble to enhance the soloist's performance. The soloist must be heard prominently. In most instances, the conductor will make many of the necessary changes when the soloist appears at the rehearsal process. Interludes are also an important part of the performance; these should highlight the ensemble and give the audience relief from the intensity of the solo performance. In general, there should be a feeling of ease in accompanying the soloist. The ensemble should applaud the soloist at the end of his or her portion of the rehearsal process.
- There are times in which the conductor must dictate to either the soloist or the small ensemble in order to maintain good precision. This is a time for collaboration. (Examples of this are initial attacks, fermatas, tempo changes, phrase releases, and so on.)
- Balance is a critical aspect when accompanying the soloist. The music itself must determine the balance (as to the importance of the part) and then be modified by the general acoustics of the performance hall.
- Sudden or gradual changes in dynamics (crescendo or diminuendo) must be gauged among the various instruments so that these changes are sudden, gradual, balanced and dramatic, but for support without overpowering the soloist.
- Flexibility on the part of the conductor and ensemble is the key to following the soloist. (This becomes very apparent and particularly true in opera or musical production conducting.) There needs to be some "give and take" between the soloist (or small ensemble) and the accompanying ensemble.
- In accompanying the soloist, the conductor should conduct the ensemble, not the soloist. The soloist wants the freedom and flexibility to interpret the music. However, there should be no "surprises" by the soloist in the concert performance.
- Realize that the downward motion of the beat is a commitment to the anticipated ictus and cannot be revoked once the motion has started. The conductor must be certain that it is time to go on before showing the downward motion of the following beat and/or of the preparatory beat.

- The use of the "sliding" fermata can be helpful in terms of accompanying in that the baton motion should be in the direction of the next pulse. See a more detailed explanation of this technique in the following paragraph.

The "sliding" fermata technique is effective in accompanying the soloist. This technique allows the soloist freedom to proceed without losing the conductor or the accompanying ensemble. The conductor simply moves toward the next pulse in the pattern while waiting for the soloist to come off a fermata or tenuto and then when the soloist indicates (through subtle inflection) the desire to go on, the conductor will slide through the beat and show the (in-tempo) preparatory motion for the next pulse. The experienced soloist realizes that the conductor must give a preparatory beat before the ensemble will respond precisely. Young or student soloists should be made aware of this fact concerning the needed preparatory beat. The idea of the "sliding" fermata is particularly applicable in opera and musical production conducting scenarios. *With cadenzas, there is usually a slight ritardando and spacing of notes into the cadenza* by the orchestra or band. The conductor and soloist must work out how the orchestra or band will return precisely with the soloist at the end of the cadenza.

There are many instances while accompanying the soloist, in which the conductor must *be aware of the tonal or rhythmic patterns* involved in order to be precise in following the soloist. In the majority of these cases, this awareness should be concerned with duple and triple subdivision of the single beat. An example of this is on a fast run in the solo part where the ensemble must come in exactly on time at the end of the soloist's run. In such instances, it is crucial that the conductor understands and feels the rhythmic pattern and/or hears the tonal pattern to indicate for the ensemble where to place the entrance. There are many examples of such patterns found in major concertos for the piano, violin, viola, and cello as well as with numerous wind instrument solo pieces. Opera arias and musical show songs frequently present similar problems. *In conducting recitatives*, the conductor must anticipate where the next chord with the ensemble will occur, so that the proper preparatory beat is shown precisely for the ensemble entrance.

In general, the conductor and the ensemble will need to be *thinking about softer dynamics when accompanying a soloist.* This requires more musical sensitivity on the part of the players in the ensemble. The dynamic range of the ensemble, in most cases, is curtailed somewhat so that the accompaniment does not overpower the soloist. Finally, the factor of balance is important in enhancing the soloist's performance. The soloist, in most cases, would need to predominate above the ensemble. The conductor has the responsibility to see that the ensemble does not cover the soloist dynamically and consider when studying the score where the dynamics or the orchestration might be problematic in maintaining this proper balance. There could be places in the accompaniment where the moving line might need projection, especially when the soloist is not playing or singing. In the rehearsal process with the soloist, these problems should become evident and be adjusted by the conductor between the soloist and the ensemble.

With an accompanying ensemble, the conductor must be cognizant of the fact that the ensemble player has only a single part. By looking at the score, the conductor can relate to all the parts, while the player does not have this luxury. *Therefore, the conductor must show all of the beats.* This is certainly true in musical theater and opera conducting as well as solo (or small ensemble) accompanying. The conductor must not take for granted that the players know which beat or measure is being shown, unless the beats or measures preceding the entrance have been indicated clearly in some fashion. The conductor must not create a situation in which the players are guessing about where to begin playing their individual parts. Even when the beats or measures in the music are rests, these beats need to be shown so that the players will be confident about their entrances.

Important factors in accompanying soloists (or small ensembles) include precision with the soloist (or small ensemble), balance with the soloist (or small ensemble), and response to the musical expression and rubato of the soloist (or small ensemble), as well as being ready for unexpected events that may even occur in the concert performance. *The reason for meticulous rehearsing is to avoid these unexpected events.* However, because the soloist has a certain freedom to interpret the work and the emotions of the moment in a concert performance, the soloist may decide to decrease or increase the tempo slightly, hold on to a fermata longer than rehearsed, sustain a dramatic pause, or change any number of other performance aspects. The conductor must be ready to adjust (within reason) to keep the ensemble intact and with the soloist (or small ensemble). The conductor cannot or should not expect the players to actually skip beats in such a situation if the unexpected does occur in the performance. Rather, the conductor must remain calm and try to "catch up" to the soloist, but retain the ensemble precision. It is somewhat easier for the conductor to "put on the brakes" if needed as opposed to "catching up." In some cases, a strategic cue can sort out a panic situation if the players are watching and alert for this necessary change.

Conducting and Rehearsing the Various Media

The assumption of this book is that the conductor will have the opportunity during his or her career to rehearse and conduct various instrumental music ensembles as well as the combinations of instrumental, dance, and vocal groups. Here is a list of the ensembles and combined groups that the conductor may be obligated to prepare and conduct for a concert performance: orchestra; chamber orchestra; string orchestra; concert band; wind ensemble; brass band; brass choir; woodwind choir; percussion ensemble; miscellaneous ensembles of strings, winds, and percussion; orchestra with soloist (or small ensemble); band with soloist (or small ensemble); orchestra and chorus; band and chorus; musical theater (pit orchestra); opera (pit orchestra); ballet (pit orchestra); modern dance (pit orchestra); theater presentations with orchestra; and various avant-garde ensembles (which may involve unusual instrumentation and/or placement of personnel) as well as other multimedia ensemble combinations.

All of these media will have their problems to solve in terms of precision, balance, blend, articulation, and phrasing. An example of this is the balance between the soloist and accompanying ensemble. *However, there will also be great similarity among the various media as to the rehearsal and performance requirements.* In all cases, the conductor will be dealing with the musicality of the ensemble throughout the rehearsal process and concert performance. In attempting to identify the problems faced by the conductor in rehearsing and conducting the various media, this situation would immediately call forth all sorts of omissions. Rather, the conductor when confronting the various media should proceed in the following manner:

1. Analyze the problematic differences inherent in the specific instrumentation and voices involved.
2. Research available material for guidance in handling these various ensembles and combinations (such as orchestra or band with chorus).
3. Compare and contrast the unusual media with an ensemble familiar to the conductor.
4. Confront the technical problems (with teaching strategies).
5. Confront the musical problems (with teaching strategies).
6. Study the musical score in detail and be prepared for the opening rehearsal process.

Especially in contemporary instrumental ensemble music, coping with the use of unusual instrumentation is commonplace. Because of the variation in ensemble instrumentation, ensemble numbers, and seating placement, the conductor should set up the imaginary group for conducting practice as there will need to be some adjustments made from the normal instrumentation and seating arrangements. *The cueing of entrances will need to be conceived carefully because of the placement of the players in these unique ensembles.* In some instances, the composer will indicate the seating arrangements in the score. However, in other instances, the seating may be at the discretion of the conductor. As a general guide, the conductor could or should organize the players in approximately the same positions as with the seating arrangements for the standard instrumental ensembles.

Balance is difficult with opera and musical productions because the accompanying ensemble is often asked to play too softly in order to balance the voices; at least three major problems then occur: (1) loss of intensity in the orchestration, (2) insecure tone production, and (3) therefore, poor intonation in the accompanying ensemble occurs. An orchestra pit is of absolute necessity in such presentations. A superior amplifying system on stage might help with musical show productions, but even this would result in less than satisfactory acoustical balance. The use of video technology in certain situations could help place the accompanying ensemble for proper balance between voices and instruments. In opera and musical theater productions, the conductor must be prepared to be more flexible in the conducting technique while following the singers or dancers than in rehearsing the standard instrumental music ensemble. The conductor is now dealing with both the instrumental ensemble and what is transpiring on the stage. The conductor's duties now become multifaceted because of having to coordinate the singers, chorus, actors, and dancers with the instrumental music ensemble. However, the focus for the conductor in the cast rehearsals and in the performances must be on the stage. I provide a list of score study repertoire for operas and musical productions in Appendix A.

In ballet and modern dance accompaniment, the conductor must strive for consistency of tempo between the rehearsals and the performance. It is extremely important that the dancers are comfortable with the selected pace of the music. Ensemble precision is, likewise, a critical aspect for both the dancers and the accompanying group. Exact tempos and definitive styles will greatly enhance the ballet performance. Balance problems are no longer a factor except within the accompanying ensemble itself in the presentation of the music for the dancers or the audience. Some of the most technically difficult music is found in the ballet repertoire, such as the three famous Igor Stravinsky ballets. The conductor must realize that ballet music is written for dance, and the fluctuation of tempo in the musical interpretation could destroy the authenticity of the dance performance. Modern dance accompaniments are, perhaps, less restrictive in terms of tempo and tempo changes, because the repertoire is usually freely selected by the artistic directors of the dance companies. However, the tempo consistency factor between the rehearsals and the performance is still critically important in the modern dance presentations. The score study repertoire for ballets is in Appendix A.

Multimedia presentations may involve actors, slides, film or video, prerecorded tapes, dancers, and the list goes on. Such presentations are at the discretion and imagination of the composer. Sometimes the musicians may be placed or moved around differently from the normal concert presentation. This may call for differences in the conducting technique and rehearsing or even the use of more than one conductor. All of this will require more study on the part of the conductor in the presentation of such works. Some avant-garde works may, likewise, be multimedia presentations. *Avant-garde works (or new music)* in many instances may be difficult technically and rhythmically. Such performances may mean that more rehearsal time must be devoted to these works. There are several musical examples listed in Appendix A that fall under the multimedia or avant-garde (or new music) compositions.

PRACTICAL APPLICATION (DISCUSSION/DEMONSTRATION)

1. What are some of the basic segments and procedures employed during the rehearsal process? Review these ideas in chapters 1 and 6.
2. In preparing for the rehearsal process, what items should be included in these unique and special preparations? (Make a checklist of these items.)
3. What might be your top priority or priorities with a given ensemble? Be specific as to why.
4. Discuss the idea of musical demonstrations by the conductor during the rehearsal process. Could modeling and imitation also be a part of this procedure?
5. How can you vary segments and procedures throughout the rehearsal process?
6. Why is the rehearsal plan and schedule so critical to the success of the rehearsal process scenario?
7. Discuss the idea of score study as a means for designing teaching strategies.
8. Discuss what should happen when stopping the ensemble to make needed corrections and/or adjustments during the rehearsal process.
9. How would you (as a conductor) promote the ideas of listening and sensitivity with the ensemble in the rehearsal process?

10. How would you (as a conductor) begin to achieve intensity and concentration from the ensemble in the rehearsal process?
11. What would be some of the real values of conductor persistence and ensemble teamwork in the rehearsal process? Discuss these two ideas.
12. How does repertoire selection and score study affect conducting and rehearsing during the rehearsal process?
13. What are the conductor's basic responsibilities in the rehearsal process scenario as noted in this chapter of the book?
14. What means does the conductor have available to communicate this essence and spirit of the music with the ensemble?
15. What are some of the problems involved in the conducting technique and in rehearsing the accompanying ensemble with a soloist (or small group)?
16. What are some of the problems involved in the conducting technique and in the rehearsing of the various performance media (with smaller instrumental ensembles, opera or musical productions, ballet or dance productions, music theater, new music, or avant-garde works)?
17. Begin to gain familiarity with the standard repertoire found in Appendix A through CD listening, score study, and guidance from the conducting teacher. (See Appendix G for assignment forms).

RECOMMENDED READING

Adey, Christopher, *Orchestral Performance: A Guide for Conductors and Players.* Part IV, No. 20 under The Orchestra as a Whole: Rehearsal covers many important aspects of the orchestral ensemble rehearsal process.

Boult, Adrian Cedric, *A Handbook on The Technique of Conducting.* Section 10: Accompaniments offers some good advice on how to accompany soloists or small ensembles.

Casey, Joseph L., *Teaching Techniques and Insights for Instrumental Music Educators.* In Part VII, the author relies on the opinions of many conductors and music educators concerning the rehearsal process.

Fuchs, Peter Paul, *The Psychology of Conducting.* Chapter 7: A View from the Pit—Opera and Related Arts; Chapter 8 is a brief discussion about soloists.

Garretson, Robert L., *Conducting Choral Music*, 8th ed. Chapter 6: Conducting Choral/Orchestral Works covers this area from the standpoint of the vocal director conducting choral/orchestral works.

Holmes, Malcolm H., *Conducting an Amateur Orchestra.* Chapter 4: Rehearsal Planning, Chapter 5: Detailed Rehearsals, Chapter 6: The Final Rehearsal.

Hunsberger, Donald and Roy E. Ernst, *The Art of Conducting*, 2nd ed. Chapter 13: Musical Theater deals with the conducting and rehearsing problems found in musical theater productions.

Labuta, Joseph A., *Basic Conducting Technique*, 5th ed. Chapter 13: The Instrumental Rehearsal provides ideas about how to rehearse the instrumental ensemble.

Leinsdorf, Erich, *The Composer's Advocate: A Radical Orthodoxy for Musicians.* On pp. 175–78, the author presents ten admonishments to the conductor about what should or should not happen in the rehearsal process.

Lisk, Edward S., *The Creative Director: Alternative Rehearsal Techniques.* The book is based
on the ideas of integrated and alternative rehearsing with emphasis on what happens in the
warm-up period.

Madsen, Clifford K., and Cornelia Yarbrough, *Competency-based Music Education.* On page
86 the authors provide a list of "Suggested Components for Ensemble Rehearsals" in developing a positive educational environment.

Moses, Don V., Robert W. Demaree, Jr., and Allen F. Ohmes, *Face to Face with an Orchestra.*
Part I: Working with an Orchestra assumes that you are a choral director.

Nowak, Jerry, and Henry Nowak, *Conducting the Music, Not the Musicians.* Chapters 27 and
28 address the problems of tuning, balance, sonority and ensemble seating arrangements, etc.

Prausnitz, Frederik, *Score and Podium (A Complete Guide to Conducting).* Chapter 14: Players
and Orchestra, Chapter 15: Orchestra and Conductor, Chapter 16: Orchestra Plus.

Rudolf, Max, *The Grammar of Conducting*, 3rd ed. Chapter 28: Rehearsal Techniques, Chapter
29: Conducting Opera and Chapter 30: Conducting Choral Works with Orchestra.

Wagar, Jeannine, *Conductors in Conversation.* Jeannine Wagar has interviewed 15 contemporary (professional) conductors about the various aspects of their lives and profession.

REPERTOIRE FOR PROJECTS AND ASSIGNMENTS

Full Orchestra, Chamber Orchestra or String Orchestra

Bach: Concerto for Two Violins in D minor (string orchestra)
Berlioz: Roman Carnival Overture
Bizet: L'Arlesienne Suite No. 2 (various movements)
Debussy: Danses sacrée et profane (harp soloist with strings)
Frescobaldi: Toccata in D minor for Orchestra (Kindler, arr.)

Concert Band or Wind Ensemble

Arnold: Prelude, Siciliano and Rondo (Paynter, arr.)
Barber: Commando March
Chance: Variations on a Korean Folk Song
Curnow: Where Never Lark or Eagle Flew
Erickson: Second Symphony for Band (various movements)

Miscellaneous or Small Ensembles

Gabrieli, G.: Symphoniae Sacrae (various selections in this series)
Mozart: Serenade No. 11 in E-flat (2 oboes, 2 clarinets, 2 bassoons, and 2 horns)

Part III

TECHNICAL PRIORITIES
AND TEACHING STRATEGIES

South Dakota State University Symphonic Band; James McKinney, Conductor

Chapter Eight

Intonation and Tuning

ESTABLISHING THE PITCH LEVEL

The problems of intonation never go away within any instrumental music ensemble.
The conductor deals with intonation problems in every rehearsal and should make
the players aware of these intonation problems during the rehearsal process. In score
study, the conductor should anticipate passages that may contain intonation problems
and need pitch adjustments. Sectional rehearsals (or with individual players) before
the full rehearsal can be helpful in improving intonation. Keeping the pitch level at
A=440 requires constant attention in the rehearsal process. This perpetuation of the
pitch level may require periodic tuning throughout the rehearsal process. The conductor may find it necessary to adjust the pitch level several times during every rehearsal
process. Likewise, the players should begin to take on the responsibility for good intonation within the ensemble. I list numerous books on intonation in the Recommended
Reading at the end of this chapter for investigation by the advanced conductor.

The mature ensemble should achieve fine intonation through careful listening, by
adjusting the pitch level, and with cooperation and awareness among the players.
With the younger ensemble, there must be a degree of tolerance by the conductor. As
the ensemble matures, the conductor should continually work for the improvement of
intonation. The players will respond and work to improve the intonation, but only if
the conductor shows some concern for this improvement. Below I offer many ideas
and suggestions for designing teaching strategies to improve this ensemble intonation
in the rehearsal process.

TEACHING STRATEGY NO. 1: PITCH LEVEL (MATURE ENSEMBLES)

It is important to establish a pitch level within the instrumental ensemble. The conductor can approach this pitch level tuning *in the traditional manner*. With the mature
orchestral ensemble, the procedure is for the oboist to sound a concert "A" (440) and
then the players tune their own instruments to this pitch. This is the common practice

161

for establishing a pitch level within the orchestral ensemble. In some cases, it may be broken down whereby the woodwinds tune first, followed by the brass, then the lower strings (violas, cellos, and basses) and finally the upper strings (violins). The same basic procedure works with the concert band ensemble. The clarinetist (or another instrumentalist) sounds a concert "B-flat" (456) or a concert "F" and the players then tune to this pitch. Some concert band conductors today prefer to use a concert F (and the concert A) for adjusting the pitch level within the ensemble.

An alternative to this procedure for establishing a pitch level within the mature ensemble is to use *an electronic tuning device* that can produce all the pitches of a chromatic scale in several octaves. Some suggest turning on this tuning device early (before the formal tuning) while the musicians assemble to make them aware of the importance of establishing this pitch level and playing with good intonation. Another use of the tuning device would be to position this device so that the players could individually check their own pitch level visually before the rehearsal process begins. Beyond this, during the rehearsal process the players will need to listen and adjust the pitch level as well as the other problematic pitches. I present other ideas concerning the use of a tuning device in the rehearsal process and individually tuning before or after the rehearsal process at the end of this chapter.

TEACHING STRATEGY NO. 2:
PITCH LEVEL (YOUNGER ENSEMBLES)

In the case of the less mature ensemble, it may be necessary for the conductor to establish the pitch level *by individually tuning each player* to the designated pitch. The conductor can do this with or without the aid of a tuning device. Usually the conductor will need a pitch comparison supplied by an instrumentalist, a pianist, an electronically produced pitch, or with the use of the tuning device in determining the deviation from the established pitch. This time-consuming procedure cannot take place in every rehearsal process. This situation would challenge the orchestra conductor to teach the young string player to tune the open strings (carefully) as soon as possible to alleviate this dilemma. Again, individual tuning by the orchestra conductor would consume a tremendous amount of rehearsal time with any large ensemble. Likewise, the concert band director should move toward the ideal situation of each player being able to tune accurately and adjust the instrument properly.

In some instances, *spot checks on intonation are allowable* throughout the rehearsal process, as long as they do not take away from the pace of the rehearsal process. If this procedure is used, the conductor should be teaching the players to (1) listen so that the players can eventually tune their own instruments accurately, (2) understand the procedure for adjusting the pitch on the instrument, that is, the moving of the tuning slide on the brass, adjusting on the woodwind instruments, or adjusting the tuning pegs on strings, and (3) produce the given pitch consistently with the proper breath support on wind instruments and with the string instruments comparing and adjusting the pitch with the other open strings. With this procedure, the conductor may want to check the entire ensemble over a period of several rehearsals.

TEACHING STRATEGY NO. 3:
COMPARISON/SECTION/CHOIR TUNING

Another procedure that conductors frequently employ for establishing the initial pitch level is *the careful tuning of the principal players or section leaders*; then time is allotted for the other players in the section to tune their instrument with a comparison of the pitch sounded by each principal player. The advantage here is that tone quality does not take away from or interfere in any way as it may when comparing the pitch with a different quality. This tuning procedure needs a more mature group because it assumes that the individual player can accurately tune the instrument. This particular approach may require more time during the rehearsal process, but should lead to better pitch level accuracy. This will place more responsibility on the section leaders or principals to establish the pitch level within their section. The idea of tuning within the various families (or choirs) can also be an effective procedure.

A similar procedure is *comparison tuning, done among the various players*. Examples of this might be the clarinet pitch compared to that of the French horn or the cello compared to the trumpet. This unique procedure creates sensitivity among the players to produce a blend of tone quality and reinforces the tuning experience in establishing the pitch level. This is a valid procedure because such tone quality and intonation adjustments are required during the actual ensemble performance. On frequent occasions, the players will be performing with these other instruments and must produce good intonation.

TEACHING STRATEGY NO. 4:
TUNING FROM THE BASS FOR THE PITCH LEVEL

Another frequent and recommended method of tuning is *tuning upward from the bass*. In other words, establish a solid pitch level with bass instruments in the ensemble. In the orchestra, accomplish this with the careful tuning of the basses, cellos, bass clarinet, bassoons/contrabassoon, trombones, and tuba. Likewise, in the concert band or wind ensemble, the bassoons/contrabassoon, bass clarinets, contrabass clarinets, baritone and bass saxophones, trombones, euphoniums, and tubas need to line up in terms of the pitch level. In this regard, the lower-pitched instrument players need to assume a certain responsibility for the intonation that will establish a good foundation for the entire ensemble.

From this established pitch level of the bass instruments, the middle-register instrument players (alto clarinet, English horn, alto and tenor saxophones, French horns, and violas) and then the soprano instrument players (piccolo, flutes, oboes, E-flat/B-flat clarinets, soprano saxophone, trumpets, cornet, and violins) can compare their pitch level on unison or octave tones. The theory behind this is that if the bass pitch is well established, then the other players can hear the pitch to adjust their pitch level as well as placing a particular pitch within the chord correctly. The bass voice of the ensemble can be a stabilizing factor (a pitch anchor, if you will) for the production of good intonation within the instrumental music ensemble.

TEACHING STRATEGY NO. 5: MISCELLANEOUS HINTS ON TUNING

Up to this point, the tuning strategies have been concerned with establishing a pitch level with the instrumental music ensemble. Moving forward, the maturing conductor must have the background information to solve intonation problems during the rehearsal process. Before proceeding with some specific intonation problems found in most ensembles, I offer some miscellaneous ideas and suggestions (hints) for the conductor to improve the tuning procedures for an instrumental music ensemble in the rehearsal process. Below are listed the elements that affect the quality of the intonation level established in the rehearsal process.

Tuning should take place in a quiet environment. If you hear a fine symphony orchestra tuning, you will note that there is not loud playing (or talking) occurring during this tuning procedure. If some members of an ensemble tune loudly, then the other members cannot hear themselves and therefore must play louder to check their tuning. The result is chaos that will not establish the pitch level. Likewise, tuning should take place without talking among the players; this detracts from the concentrated effort to listen and tune accurately. In tuning, play mezzo forte or less, but keep the sound well supported in the winds while tuning.

The tuning procedure should occur without vibrato. The use of vibrato only confuses the exact placement of the pitch level. Vibrato is generally produced as a fluctuation of pitch. Trying to tune when the pitch is wavering will only complicate the issue. Using vibrato in tuning simply makes the task more difficult to tune accurately. This suggestion is for the wind players only as the string players, of course, cannot apply vibrato in tuning the open strings.

String players need to be very meticulous in tuning the open strings on their instruments. This hardly seems necessary to mention, but in reality, there is much abuse here by string players. It does not make any sense to be careless with this tuning. The conductor should give the ensemble sufficient time to tune the open "A" as well as a comparison with the other open strings. If the open strings are not adjusted properly, then the placement of the finger on the string to produce a given pitch accurately cannot possibly be successful. With young ensembles, the conductor may find it worthwhile to check the various strings individually with the players (G, D, A, and E) for the violin section plus C with the violas and cellos and especially the 4th space open "E" with the violins.

The wind player has the unique problem *of producing the tuning pitch consistently.* This is particularly true with the brass instrument player because the pitch can vary considerably with the embouchure, the breath control, range, dynamics, and fatigue. It is an accepted practice for the brass player to produce the tuning pitch with scale notes leading up to the pitch (such as written notes G, A, B, and C for the B-flat trumpet and then sustain the tuning note C, which is concert B-flat, so that the embouchure will adjust into the tuning pitch). Especially with the brasses, "centering the tone" consistently is problematic in the tuning procedure. The player should produce the tuning pitch where it is on the instrument and then adjust with the tuning slide to the sounding pitch. Along with this consideration of centering the tone is the idea of what dynamic level should be employed for this tuning pitch. In general, it should be produced at a soft to medium dynamic level, but in all cases with proper breath support. The double horn poses further problems because of having to tune both sides of the French horn. I will further discuss the effects of dynamics on intonation.

Tuning to establish a pitch level *should eventually be the total responsibility of the individual player*. The player must learn to discriminate by listening for the "beats" when tuning and playing with the ensemble. The conductor must ensure that this happens by urging and encouraging the players to listen carefully; the player must understand the procedure for adjusting the pitch and be exacting in making these adjustments. The individual player's sense of pitch within the ensemble will vary, but with practice and maturity, most players are capable of making improvements with these adjustments. One of the most important tuning approaches is to make the individual player responsible for playing in tune.

A warm-up period before doing any serious or final tuning is necessary. (There might be justification for a preliminary tuning in some situations before the warm-up is completed.) This warm-up before tuning is imperative because it will give the players the opportunity to limber up and awaken those physical and mental powers required to produce the tone properly. The warm-up can take place on an individual basis or as a group. The conductor should not let the warm-up period become routine; this leads to boredom on the part of the players and takes away from the main purposes of doing the warm-up. Scales, intervals, chords, and chorales are useful as music material for intonation improvement, but they must be varied and played in a way that reaps maximum benefit from the time spent. Some tuning can take place during the warm-up period, particularly with unison scales, sustained notes, or chord playing. After the warm-up is completed, the players should be ready to produce a "true" tuning pitch. However, string players must tune the open strings before beginning the warm-up for obvious reasons.

Repeat the tuning during the rehearsal process. Under normal circumstances, the pitch will tend to go up and *periodic tuning will help the pitch level* from doing this. *If the rehearsal hall temperature changes* or is not at a comfortable level, the intonation may also become problematic. The conductor should keep watch over this matter and request tuning as needed in the rehearsal process. There should always be an available electronic sounding pitch for reference when tuning during the rehearsal process. Likewise, there should also be periodic tuning done during the concert performance. The conductor can plan this tuning before the concert performance to ensure that the pitch level stays in place. If he or she senses pitch problems during the performance, then more tuning may be necessary than originally planned. If the conductor tunes only at the beginning of the rehearsal process, the impression from the players is that they are now in tune; rather tuning should be a periodic procedure during both the rehearsal process and the concert performance.

When tuning individually, players should compare the pitch to an established pitch level. The tuning procedure here should be either (1) to have the player produce the note before the comparison note is sounded or (2) to play the note simultaneously with the established pitch level and listen for "beats." In this way, the player will not automatically adjust to the pitch level sounded. The player should then adjust the instrument, *rather than adjusting to the pitch level*. Likewise, today there is a popular trend among concert band conductors of having the ensemble sing or hum the tuning pitch and then tune to this pitch on the instrument. There are inherent dangers in this procedure in that the player will adjust the embouchure and air instead of adjusting the instrument itself to the proper pitch level.

The conductor should constantly remind the players (1) to listen to each other, (2) to listen for "beats" especially in unison and octave playing, and (3) to think of blending and matching of the pitches. This tends to put the listening and the instrument adjustment responsibility squarely on the players. It may be necessary to spend some time in the rehearsal process in making the players aware of this technique of "*listening for beats.*" As the "beats" become slower, the pitches begin to approach good intonation. Faster "beats" indicate that the pitches are farther apart.

In working for the improvement of intonation, the ensemble should *sometimes play without music* (scales, unison intervals, sustained notes, chords, etc.) during the warm-up period, which is an ideal time to use such a procedure. This procedure will allow the players to listen and adjust. Playing without music may require the use of hand signals or other gestures by the conductor. The advantage of this kind of playing is to take away the visual aspect (of the printed music) and emphasize to the players to concentrate on pitch placement through careful listening.

When tuning to a given pitch or playing in an ensemble, *blend is an important factor.* In making pitch comparisons, the player must attempt to blend the tone with the surrounding sounds. Poor blend can cause some deception with the player in making the correct pitch adjustment. This lack of blend may occur for several reasons, such as with the dynamic level, ensemble balance, or quality of the tone produced. Good tuning is unachievable in the rehearsal process unless there is this proper blend within the ensemble. This tuning and blend can best be achieved at a softer dynamic. Too often, players tend to tune at a louder dynamic. This causes the other players to have to play louder as well. Then the "domino effect" occurs. Listen to how a fine symphony orchestra or a fine concert band tunes at a rather quiet dynamic, and then emulate this approach with all instrumental music ensemble tuning in producing this intonation.

Tuning should not become so commonplace *that it becomes haphazard or careless.* Players should consider this to be of the greatest importance. For example, in an orchestral ensemble with young violinists, it is well to check the open E string separately and with young violists and cellists it is worthwhile to check the open C string separately. These tunings seem to be somewhat elusive for the string player, if not altogether treacherous. Likewise, the G, D, and A open strings can be checked individually or in unison before and after a comparison tuning of the open strings by the players. In the wind sections, the players must take care to produce the tone properly with good quality and blend in tuning. Again, do not condone careless tuning in the wind sections.

Tuning to several notes will establish where the pitch center really is. In some instances, the usual tuning pitch may not be the best note to establish this pitch level on a particular instrument. A compromise between various notes and registers may arrive at a more accurate placement of the pitch level for the particular instruments (a case in point would be the French horn). A common tuning pitch on the B-flat trumpet such as the concert F does not necessarily give the player the best note to adjust the pitch level since this note tends to be slightly sharp because of the 3rd partial of the harmonic series. The conductor and players must understand that tuning to one pitch in establishing the pitch level during the rehearsal process will not solve all of the intonation problems within the ensemble. Recently, the sounding of a concert "A" (for double-reeds and saxophones) followed by a concert "B-flat" has allowed the various players in an ensemble to select one or the other in discovering the best pitch level. Many concert bands use concert "F" as well for tuning.

By playing slowly and relatively soft, the players have an opportunity to hear the intonation better. When playing loud and fast, there is a tendency for the players to stop listening to themselves and ignore the resultant poor intonation. In the rehearsal process, a worthwhile procedure is to play some of the loud, climactic passages at a softer dynamic level to allow the players to listen and adjust the intonation. After that procedure, the conductor should then return the passages to the indicated dynamic level but also request the same good intonation. Likewise, at very soft dynamic levels, the intonation will tend to be unstable due to the lack of good breath support, embouchure control, or insufficient bow pressure and speed.

Transpositions Involved in Tuning

The conductor must be ready to indicate to the players the written note to play on the instrument in order to tune to the various concert pitches. With younger ensembles, the players may not totally understand the transpositions of going from the written notes to sounding pitches and will need this information to produce the proper tuning note. Eventually, the conductor should expect the players to have this background when he or she requests a concert pitch. In band or orchestra ensembles, only a few transpositions require different written notes from those of concert pitch. The conductor will need to know these various transpositions well to instruct the players of the adjustments necessary to produce the correct pitches. The player will need advice as to the interval of transposition and the change of key necessary to make these adjustments as the conductor requests concert pitches. Table 8.1 provides the transpositions that are necessary in order to be aware of with ensemble tuning.

For the orchestra and band ensemble, B-flat transpositions include soprano clarinet, bass clarinet (+ one octave), contrabass clarinet (+ two octaves), soprano saxophone, tenor saxophone (+ one octave), bass saxophone (+ two octaves), cornet or trumpet, and treble-clef baritone (+ one octave). The E-flat transpositions include sopranino clarinet (exception—minor 3rd up), alto clarinet, contra alto clarinet (+ one octave), alto saxophone, and baritone saxophone (+ one octave). The F transpositions include only English horn and French horn. All of the other instruments are concert pitch instruments.

Table 8.1.

Transpositions	Written	Sounding
B-flat transpositions (major 2nd down + 1 or 2 8va basso)	C	B-flat
E-flat transpositions (major 6th down + 1 8va basso or minor 3rd up)	C	E-flat
F transposition (perfect 5th interval down)	C	F

With which octave the player should produce the pitch may need reinforcement from the conductor. (When the conductor thinks the written note to be played, it will be the reverse interval process of the transposition from written to sounding; the conductor [and player] should then think from sounding to written.)

In orchestral music, trumpet parts are frequently played on instruments other than the B-flat instrument. Common instruments now used in orchestras are the C trumpet (sounding concert pitch), the D trumpet (sounding a major 2nd higher than the written pitch), the E-flat trumpet (sounding a minor 3rd higher than the written pitch), the piccolo trumpet in B-flat (sounding a minor 7th higher than the written pitch), and the piccolo trumpet in A (sounding a major 6th higher than the written pitch). However, the tuning notes on the French horn or English horn must be calculated based on a perfect fifth lower to discover the sounding pitch on these instruments. Clarinet parts, not unlike the trumpet, are played on the A clarinet (sounding a minor 3rd lower than the written pitch) and the C clarinet (sounding concert pitch). To find the written note in sounding the proper tuning pitch on these instruments, the rule is to compare the instrument key with concert pitch C to discover what the interval of transposition is and then reverse the process. Therefore, the tuning note will be the reverse process of the transposition from the written to sounding; the conductor must now be thinking the interval of transposition from sounding to written. (An example of these transpositions would be where the E-flat trumpet—sounding a minor 3rd higher—is tuning to a concert A in the orchestra, and therefore, needs to play a written F-sharp below this A to sound the proper concert pitch.) The key signature would need adjustment accordingly in the music.

TEACHING STRATEGY NO. 6: INTONATION AND TONE PRODUCTION

A well-produced tone has a much better chance of being played in tune than does a poorly produced tone. There is a recognized distinct connection between the tone quality and intonation. Both of these statements are true and influence producing good intonation. What can the conductor do about this relationship of tone production and intonation to improve these elements in the instrumental ensemble? In the rehearsal process, the conductor can continually remind the young wind player about those aspects that equate with good tone production, such as posture, embouchure, breath control, and articulation. The conductor can also encourage the players to study with a competent teacher (preferably a teacher who plays the instrument well). Finally, the conductor in the rehearsal process should always be urging the player to play with the best possible tone quality.

Below are several ideas the conductor can present to make the players aware of this existing relationship of tone and intonation:

1. Encourage the players to play with a beautiful, characteristic sound on the instrument.
2. Insist that the players produce the tone with the proper fundamentals. For example, in the case of woodwind and brass players, this would involve the embouchure,

breath control, and oral cavity. With the string players, it would mean bow control, bow speed and pressure, the relationship of the bow to the string, and vibrato.

3. Discourage the type of aggressive playing that leads to a lack of control and produces poor tone quality.

4. Caution the player against trying to play too softly or without intensity so that the tone quality deteriorates and poor intonation results.

5. Encourage the players to listen to the surrounding ensemble sounds to improve tone quality, and thereby produce better balance, consistent blend, and good intonation.

TEACHING STRATEGY NO. 7: INTONATION AND BALANCE

As with tone production and intonation, *there is a strong connection between balance and intonation.* The factor of proper balance within the instrumental music ensemble allows the player to hear and adjust the pitch. Poor balance in the ensemble will confuse the player in an effort to improve the intonation. Especially, good chordal balance is a crucial aspect in that the players will be able to place their particular pitch within the context of the chord. Use some rehearsal time, as needed, in tuning chords. Balance within the particular section is also critical for the improvement of intonation in the ensemble. In Chapter 10: Ensemble Sonority—Tone, Balance, Blend, Color, and Texture I provide additional information and ideas for improving and refining the balance priority with the instrumental music ensemble.

The conductor should realize that good intonation is difficult when the upper parts in a section are tripled or quadrupled. Place fewer players on the higher part because the projection is accomplished easily in this higher range, especially on the brass instruments. Such tripling or quadrupling of a single part makes it more difficult to play with good balance and intonation. However, because of the extreme ranges involved and the balance problems mentioned above, distributing the parts differently or eliminating players from these upper parts in a particular passage is a possible solution for improving some intonation problems.

TEACHING STRATEGY NO. 8: INTONATION AND AWARENESS

Awareness of the pitch through careful listening by the players will lead to improvement of intonation in the instrumental music ensemble rehearsal process and in the concert performance. During the rehearsal process, the conductor must find ways of making the players aware of these pitch problems. This strategy is an all-encompassing one. In the rehearsal process, the conductor needs to isolate passages for the players to be able to hear the intonation problems. This may involve slowing the passage down or sustaining chords for careful listening. The conductor should also point out passages where the players may need to adjust intonation. Some of the reasons for faulty intonation include not centering the tone properly, embouchure problems, poor breath support, forced tone quality, tight throat, poor equipment, not listening, and the unawareness of certain note tendencies, just to mention a few such items.

Intonation problems are both short-term and long-range issues. With short-term problems, the conductor must focus on specific passages that need attention in rehearsing the concert repertoire. The long-range aspect is that intonation problems will occur in all instrumental music ensembles and the conductor is responsible for finding solutions to these problems. Awareness is certainly the key to improving these problems. The conductor must be knowledgeable about these intonation problems and their solutions. However, the conductor must be careful not to place so much emphasis on intonation throughout the rehearsal process *that the players try too hard to adjust and become paranoid* about making these needed intonation adjustments. Such intonation adjustments may cause other performance aspects to deteriorate as well. (See Appendix D for intonation problems/solutions.)

What applications of this intonation teaching strategy can the conductor utilize to make the players more aware of pitch problems? Below are some suggestions:

1. Isolate out-of-tune chords and find which note(s) need adjustment. Do this by playing the chord and dropping out notes or by starting with a single note such as the root of the chord and adding the other tones.
2. Check unison and octave passages by isolating these lines and adjusting the pitch as needed. This occurs quite frequently in contemporary music.
3. Play short-note chords more sustained or (even) non-rhythmically to discover where the pitch problems are occurring.
4. Play loud chords softer to give the players a chance to adjust and then increase the dynamic level, working to maintain the intonation accuracy.
5. Stop and tune when the ensemble intonation seems unsettled. All of these procedures are geared toward making the player more aware of existing pitch problems and the importance of good intonation.

TEACHING STRATEGY NO. 9: INTONATION, TONE CONTROL, EXTREME REGISTERS, AND EXTREME DYNAMICS

The lack of tone control, extreme registers, and extreme dynamic levels are causes of poor intonation. Especially with the young player, the inability to control the instrument properly leads to many intonation problems. The best approach is for the conductor-teacher to prescribe to the players certain techniques or procedures to improve tone control on the instrument. These techniques will vary with the instrument involved. *Do some work in the warm-up period regarding tone control.* Place emphasis on producing and controlling the tone with ease and consistency. The extreme registers played on the instrument also cause considerable intonation problems. Most instruments will tend to play out of tune in these extreme registers. The conductor needs to know about these problems and be able to communicate their solutions to the players. Extreme dynamic levels also exaggerate intonation problems. Again, the control of the tone becomes a factor in handling these extreme dynamic levels.

Tone control involves many technical aspects of musical instrument performance. *Some of these technical aspects include* embouchure, breath, articulation, oral cavity, bow control, bow speed and pressure, bowing style, technical facility, and technical accuracy. As the student matures and progresses, all of these technical aspects should begin to improve so that there is better tone control on the instrument. Musical sensitivity in performance is also an important and crucial part of this tone control. Even if the player begins to develop better tone control on the instrument, musical sensitivity is necessary to guide in controlling the instrument music performance. Only when the player has gained the necessary tone control will the problems of intonation start to show signs of improvement. Once the player has good control of the tone production, then the adjustment of the intonation is much more feasible.

Extreme registers are causes of intonation problems on the various musical instruments. Part of this is due to effort necessary to produce these extreme registers. Correct tone production will help alleviate some of these problems. Woodwind players should be aware of the best fingerings to use in the extreme registers. String players must utilize higher positions and take care especially with the use of the fourth finger. Making the players aware of these problems is an initial step in the resolution of intonation problems. The total ensemble range from the lowest notes of the contrabass or tuba to the highest notes of the violin or piccolo can present difficult problems with playing in tune. The conductor must know intonation tendencies on the various instruments in a particular register as well as the "bad note" tendencies throughout their entire range.

Extreme dynamic levels affect intonation for various reasons. For example, adjustments must be made in the brass embouchure between the dynamic level of pianissimo and fortissimo, or the pitch of a given note will change. (The opening measure in the first trumpet part of the Wagner *Rienzi Overture* is a perfect example of a sustained concert "A" that must move gradually from an extremely soft to an extremely loud dynamic and back to an extremely soft dynamic without the pitch changing.) Likewise, over-blowing will result in poor intonation, causing a lack of tone control. With the younger ensemble trying to obtain a very soft dynamic, the tendency will be to produce the tone with insufficient air or bow pressure. This problem results in a poorly produced tone and will affect the intonation severely. Again, awareness of the problem on the part of the player is essential in making these adjustments. The conductor is responsible for making the players aware of these problems as well as offering solutions. The conductor in the rehearsal process should not demand more dynamically from the ensemble than what is realistic for the ensemble to play with good intonation.

TEACHING STRATEGY NO. 10:
INTONATION AND INSTRUMENT CONSTRUCTION

The conductor should encourage the players to obtain good quality instruments in fostering the best possible intonation within the ensemble. Due to the inherent problems of instrument construction and adjusting to the problems of equal temperament tuning, intonation discrepancies in the instrumental music ensemble are present. For example, the brass player is subject to the natural laws of the blown pipe (harmonic series) that does not necessarily line up with equal temperament tuning. The manufacturer can only hope to construct the instrument *so that the player can play it in tune with some adjustments.* Another problem for the brass player is that the larger valve combination can cause some pitch deficiencies. The construction of woodwind instruments is a problem of boring the holes on the instrument correctly, and the proper placement of these tone holes with the keys and pads on the instrument. The woodwind players must know the correct and alternate fingerings to bring the pitch in accordance with the tuning of the other musical instruments.

The trumpet should be equipped with movable first and third valve slides in order to adjust the intonation on tones that are sharp in pitch. French horn tuning is somewhat problematic because of the double-horn construction that requires both sides of the instrument to be tuned separately and matched with each other. The F-attachment on the trombone, likewise, requires adjusting the slide positions differently than on the B-flat instrument when playing with this F-attachment or the other various attachments. The employment of the 4th valve on the euphonium and tuba will help considerably to improve the intonation on these two instruments. It is also important for the brass players to be aware of the effect that mutes have on intonation. In some cases, the tuning slide will need adjustment when using the mute on the brass instruments. The woodwind players depend heavily on careful instrument construction and the use of alternate fingerings in terms of producing good intonation.

The teaching strategy involved here (as mentioned previously) is for the conductor to encourage players to obtain the best possible instruments. The conductor must deal with this on an individual basis and will not always be successful because of financial circumstances. Likewise, the physical condition of the instrument, mouthpiece, reed, strings, and bow can be the cause of considerable intonation problems. With the younger ensemble, the conductor must check these items periodically and provide a remedy if needed. Another strategy for intonation improvement is to pass out a sheet to the various players showing which notes tend to be out of tune on their instruments because of the instrument construction and how to adjust these pitches. The serious player would then go about systematically comparing each tone throughout the entire range of the instrument with a tuning device in order to discover which tones need adjustment as well as how much to adjust each tone on the instrument.

Starting with the basic philosophy of instrument construction, the manufacturer builds the wind instrument above the standard pitch. Therefore, the player tuning to concert "A," "B-flat," or "F" will have to pull the tuning slide, barrel joint, bocal, mouthpiece, or head joint out to achieve the proper tuning pitch. There must be some caution in the sense that pulling an extreme amount will cause the instrument to be out of tune with itself. If it is necessary to do this in arriving at the consensus pitch level, ask several questions:

- Is this a good note to use in tuning? Perhaps the solution is to tune to more than one pitch and find a compromise position for adjusting the tuning slide, barrel joint, bocal, mouthpiece, or head joint.
- Is the tone production causing a problem? Check embouchure, breath, oral cavity, throat, tongue placement, etc.

- Is the player using the equipment provided on the instrument properly to produce good intonation when making these adjustments? These are the tuning slides, mouthpiece, extra valves, barrel joint, bocal, etc.

TEACHING STRATEGY NO. 11:
INTONATION AND EQUAL TEMPERAMENT TUNING

The system of equal temperament, used presently in instrumental music ensembles for tuning and playing with other members of the ensemble, permits discrepancies in pitch to occur. The string players as well as the wind players must also be aware of the adjustments needed to be in agreement with the equal temperament tuning. After the pitch level in an ensemble is established, it is then necessary to pursue the ideas of tonality, note tendencies, and chord functions based on equal temperament tuning. That is, the ensemble must think and play in the key to improve intonation. Such items as raising the 3rd of the major chord or the 7th (as a leading tone) into the tonic note are problematic notes.

The melodic and harmonic relationships in equal temperament tuning require these adjustments. For example, certain notes in a chord need adjustment to make the chord harmonically pleasing and progressing to the next chord. The conductor must possess this knowledge in order to make the players aware of these adjustments. There are many book sources for acquiring this information. One idea that relates to this problem is that of resonance of a chord as discussed in the following paragraph. The conductor must always be alert to point out these problems and offer solutions to the players. Careful listening within the ensemble will make the players aware of these tendencies as well. I list some of these book sources at the end of this chapter.

TEACHING STRATEGY NO. 12: INTONATION AND RESONANCE

An ensemble that is badly out of tune *will definitely project no resonance* in the musical performance. Consequently, the ensemble tone will decrease in quality and projection. An in-tune chord will resonate much better and add a "live" quality to the sound of the ensemble. The conductor must constantly strive to encourage the players to achieve this kind of resonance in their performance. This pertains to the number and makeup of overtones produced, not the dynamic volume or decibels generated. The players need to listen to how they are placing their pitches within the chord. If all of the players try to listen and adjust the pitch precisely, the resonance will be astounding! In many instances, the "bad notes" in terms of intonation will cause poor intonation in a chord, and these need adjustment to improve the chord intonation (harmonically). A very fine barbershop quartet thrives on this resonance factor. Check out Meredith Willson's *The Music Man* School Board Barbershop Quartet for such resonance!

Playing in the center of resonance is the key to producing a beautiful tone on the instrument. If the player must adjust the embouchure to such an extent in trying to improve the intonation, playing out of the center of resonance will result in a poorly produced tone. In playing the instrument with good intonation, make the necessary adjustments in pitch within the "center of resonance." If the player cannot adjust the pitch properly with the embouchure to keep the tone within this center of resonance, then explore other methods of adjustment. For example, the trumpet player can make use of the first and third valve slides, the French horn player can adjust the right-hand position in the bell, the trombone player can adjust the slide position, and the euphonium and tuba can employ the fourth valve. Woodwind players have a number of methods for helping intonation other than the embouchure, including alternate fingerings, adding fingers on the right hand (clarinet) to regular fingerings, or adjusting the air stream.

The conductor in the rehearsal process should stress this idea of good tone quality, good balance, good blend, and "sounding like a single instrument" in striving to achieve this resonant, well-in-tune ensemble. Again, these qualities are possible only if the players are listening intensely to the surrounding sound and to what the conductor is emphasizing during the rehearsal process. The playing of chorales in the warm-up period can be a worthwhile procedure for making the ensemble players aware of the "center of resonance" factor involved.

TEACHING STRATEGY NO. 13:
INTONATION AND ROOM TEMPERATURE

The temperature in the rehearsal room or hall is a crucial aspect for producing good intonation. Brass and woodwind players will tend to play flat if the temperature is somewhat below 72°F. However, the string instruments will tend to go sharp in pitch in the same environment with these colder temperatures. For an orchestra, this will obviously generate poor intonation. Most professional orchestras will have placed in their performance contract a stipulation concerning the prevailing temperature and legally can refuse to play if the venue fails to meet this temperature requirement. Extreme room temperatures in the rehearsal environment will mean constant tuning checks in order to adjust the pitch level throughout the rehearsal process.

If the temperature is extreme in either direction, the player will experience some physical discomfort, resulting in the loss of concentration. This loss of focus will affect intonation and many of the other elements of performance. The general discomfort in either a too warm or too cold rehearsal environment will certainly discourage the players from producing fine music. Adequate temperature and humidity control in the rehearsal facility is essential.

If the temperature of the rehearsal room or concert hall deviates considerably below the standard 72°F, the brass player, during a long rest, may need to "warm up" the instrument by silently blowing air through it and keeping the mouthpiece in the hand before making the entrance. With long periods of rest (such as in orchestral playing) the brass player should try to keep the instrument and mouthpiece as close to normal room temperature as possible. In abnormal rehearsal room temperatures, it may also be necessary to tune often during the rehearsal process. (Of course, this procedure of periodic tuning should be a common one, even if the environment temperature is normal.)

TEACHING STRATEGY NO. 14: INTONATION AND ADJUSTING

Adjusting the intonation on the various instruments is a part of the background that the conductor must acquire from the serious study of these instruments. The course content of methods and pedagogy classes should include information on this topic. Numerous pedagogical books contain this information. Many of these intonation adjustments are due to "bad notes" on the instrument as discussed previously. The reference books at the end of this chapter concern adjusting the intonation in this way.

The conductor and players must be aware of *these so-called bad notes on the particular instruments.* This information is gathered together over time in working with these problems of intonation. The more painstakingly that this "bad note" information is acquired by the conductor, the more immediately will these adjustment be made during the ensemble rehearsal process. The players must be encouraged to make these "bad note" adjustments through mechanical means on the various wind instruments or with the player's embouchure and air stream. With string instruments, the proper placement of the left-hand fingers and careful tuning of the open strings will achieve this better intonation.

The conductor needs to know which *methods of adjustment* are available to the player in improving the intonation on the various instruments. The conductor should then make the players aware of these adjustment options. The following is a list of some common methods of adjusting intonation on the various instruments.

Flute: adjust cork, adjust head joint, roll instrument, move head, adjust embouchure, and adjust air stream.

Oboe: adjust reed, adjust air speed, alternate fingerings, and adjust embouchure.

Clarinet: adjust reed, adjust air stream, adjust mouthpiece, adjust the barrel or section, alternate fingerings, and adjust embouchure.

Bassoon: adjust reed, adjust air stream, adjust bocal length, alternate fingerings, and adjust embouchure (Andy Gump).

Saxophone: adjust reed, adjust mouthpiece on pipe, alternate fingerings, and adjust embouchure.

French horn: adjust embouchure, adjust air stream, adjust right-hand position in the bell, use double horn, and tune the double horn properly.

Trumpet: adjust embouchure, adjust air stream, alternate fingerings, adjust third-valve slide and first-valve slide.

Trombone: adjust embouchure, adjust air stream, adjust the slide position, and adjust the position with the F-attachment (or other attachments).

Euphonium/Baritone: adjust embouchure, adjust air stream, use compensating mechanism and fourth valve.

Tuba: adjust embouchure, adjust air stream, adjust movable slide, and use fourth valve.

Timpani: adjust pedal, adjust hand position, adjust tuning tension and tuning apparatus.

Strings: adjust left-hand position, adjust finger placement, and carefully tune the open strings.

The teaching strategy outlined in Table 8.2 (at the end of the chapter) reviews some ideas and provides suggestions in designing a teaching strategy for improvement of the instrumental music ensemble intonation.

TUNING DEVICES

There are two types of tuning devices available. One tuning device generates the various pitches of the chromatic scale electronically. The players then compare and match their tones with the sounding pitch level by listening for the "beats." This tuning device can be of great help in training the ear of the musician. The Peterson 570 tuner is an example of this tone-generated device. The conductor may wish to use a tone-generated tuner to sound a pitch rather than using a selected player to produce the pitch. Practicing with this tuning device will definitely aid the player in improving intonation. The second tuning device is the strobotuner or the more portable Korg AT-12 tuning device. With this tuning device, when producing the pitch the player is able to see whether the tone is being played flat or sharp in relationship to equal temperament tuning. The player then makes adjustments until the machine shows that the pitch is correct. With the Strobotuner, the student should first tune by listening and then check the accuracy by viewing the tuner windows.

The proper use of these tuning devices is the key to intonation improvement. Use the tuner to "show" players the tones that need to be adjusted and then the players should attempt to "hear" in making the adjustments during the rehearsal process and concert performance. In using the tuning device, the player should use the ears more and the eyes less. Presently, there are many small, portable tuners on the market that the student-player can purchase and use during individual practice to improve intonation. However, when practicing individually, players must depend mostly on the ear to produce good intonation. The availability of tuning devices has helped the serious musician to become aware of the "bad note" tendencies and the importance of careful tuning and adjusting. Finally, here are two thoughts in using this tuning device: (1) periodically the player should use the tuning device throughout the entire range of the instrument to check the pitch deviations, and (2) this procedure can be expedited by having another person note the discrepancies as these are played. (Then note these deviations on an intonation chart or graph as a reference for the intonation improvement of the individual player.)

PRACTICAL APPLICATION (DISCUSSION/DEMONSTRATION)

1. Discuss the tuning procedure with the mature ensemble in terms of establishing the pitch level. Demonstrate this procedure.
2. Discuss the tuning procedure with the younger ensemble in terms of establishing the pitch level. Demonstrate this procedure.
3. Discuss the ideas of spot checks, section tuning, and comparison tuning within the ensemble. Demonstrate these procedures.
4. Discuss the idea of tuning from the bass to establish the pitch level. Demonstrate this procedure.
5. Discuss the tuning problems concerning the dynamic level, vibrato, open strings, brass consistency, player responsibility, warming-up, and periodic tuning.

6. For the conductor, what items are involved with the transpositions of ensemble tuning notes? How do these transpositions vary between the concert band and the orchestral wind instruments? (Musical Example)
7. Discuss the intonation factors regarding tone production, balance, awareness, tone control, ranges, dynamics, instrument construction, equal temperament tuning, resonance, blend, and room temperature.
8. Discuss and demonstrate the physical adjustments that may be necessary with the various instruments for intonation improvement.
9. What would you (as a conductor) do to improve the intonation of an ensemble? (This is an all-encompassing question.)
10. List some rehearsal procedures and teaching strategies that might make the players more aware of intonation problems.
11. Continue to gain familiarity with the standard repertoire found in Appendix A through CD listening, score study, and guidance from the conducting teacher. (See Appendix G for assignment forms.)

IN THE REHEARSAL PROCESS (LAB) ENVIRONMENT

1. Demonstrate various tuning procedures to establish the pitch level of the ensemble.
2. Demonstrate procedures for tuning from the bass.
3. Demonstrate tuning procedures without the written music.
4. Demonstrate tuning procedures in listening for "beats."
5. Demonstrate tuning procedures by establishing better balance within the ensemble to improve intonation.
6. Demonstrate tuning procedures by establishing better blend within the ensemble to improve intonation.
7. Demonstrate ways of making players more aware of the intonation problems.
8. Demonstrate the effects of range and dynamics on intonation. Compare various instruments together and with a tuning device on the examples below. (Musical Example)
9. Demonstrate the resonance factor on intonation. Play a major chord and adjust the tuning until the proper resonance occurs.
10. Spend considerable time adjusting the physical aspects on the various instruments in tuning during the rehearsal process (lab) environment. (See Appendix D: Intonation solutions.)
11. Complete student conducting/rehearsing projects (in the rehearsal process lab environment).

RECOMMENDED READING

Benade, Arthur H., *Horns, Strings & Harmony.* This is an early, paperback book (1960) about the various acoustical properties of musical instruments.

Casey, Joseph L., *Teaching Techniques and Insights for Instrumental Music Educators.* Chapter 6: Teaching Musical Skills through Performance Experience.

Fabrizio, Al, *A Guide to the Understanding and Correction of Intonation Problems.* This book covers the following areas: tuning process, pitch tendencies, adjustments, and acoustical considerations for band instruments.

Garofalo, Robert J., *Improving Intonation in Band and Orchestra Performance.* Chapter 1: Understanding Intonation, Chapter 2: Tuning Guides and Intonation Charts for Each Instrument, Chapter 3: Acoustics of Musical Instruments, and Chapter 4: Strategies for Improving Intonation.

Holmes, Malcolm H., *Conducting an Amateur Orchestra.* This book is geared toward the problems encountered with amateur orchestras; one of the areas covered is that of intonation.

Janzen, Eldon A., *Band Director's Survival Guide.* Chapter 9: The Tuning Process devotes considerable space in terms of the procedures used in tuning the band ensemble.

Jurrens, James, *Tuning the Band and Raising Pitch Consciousness.* This book focuses on individual band instruments and their pitch discrepancies and tendencies.

Kohut, Daniel L., *Instrumental Music Pedagogy* (paperback version). Chapter 3: Tone Quality, Intonation and Blend. There is a Conclusion on page 119.

Lisk, Edward S., *The Creative Director: Alternative Rehearsal Techniques.* Chapter 4: Ensemble Tone Quality mostly covers intonation problems.

McBeth, W. Francis, *Effective Performance of Band Music: Solutions to Specific Problems in Performance of 20th-Century Band Music.* Solution I—Achieving Correct Ensemble Pitch and Balance. The author states, "Pitch is a direct result of balance."

Middleton, James, Harry Haines, and Gary Garner, *The Symphonic Band Winds (A Quest for Perfection).* Chapter 4: Intonation (by Gary Garner) for valuable information on intonation and tuning.

Pottle, Ralph R., *Tuning the School Band and Orchestra*, 8th printing. This is an early and basic book (1970) on the band and orchestra intonation.

Stauffer, Donald, *Intonation Deficiencies of Wind Instruments in Ensemble.* Chapter 8: Conclusions and Recommendations provides direction for the conductor of an instrumental music ensemble in the rehearsal process.

REPERTOIRE FOR PROJECTS AND ASSIGNMENTS

Full Orchestra, Chamber Orchestra, or String Orchestra

Barber: Adagio for Strings (difficult key)
Brahms—Variations on a Theme of Joseph Haydn (various movements)
Copland: The Quiet City (trumpet, English horn, and strings)
Dvořák: Czech Suite, Op. 39 (various movements)
Gershwin: Rhapsody in Blue (piano soloist and orchestra)

Concert Band or Wind Ensemble

Reed, A.: A Festival Prelude
Massenet: Phedre Overture
Benson: The Solitary Dancer
Bilik: American Civil War Fantasy
Chance: Incantation and Dance

Miscellaneous or Small Ensembles

Schuller: Symphony for Brass and Percussion (various movements)
Kurka—The Good Soldier Schweik Suite (various movements)

TEACHING STRATEGY TABLE

Table 8.2. Intonation

CONDUCTOR CONCERNS	PROBLEM AREAS	TEACHING STRATEGIES
Ensemble pitch level Tuning procedures	Tone production and control	Work for good tone production to help with the intonation improvement (embouchure, air, tonguing, bowing, etc.).
Various hints on tuning Transpositions for ensemble tuning		Center the tone, which is very important for intonation improvement with the ensemble.
	Listening	Use phrases such as "line up the pitch" and "match the pitch," which are important and effective ideas
Tone production Balance/Blend Awareness (listen)		Use the idea of "beat" elimination procedures to help improve both listening and intonation.
Tone control on the instrument		In tuning chords, sustain each chord for the players to listen in making the needed adjustments.
The extreme registers and extreme dynamic levels	Equipment	Use good instruments, mouthpieces, and reeds, which are important here.
Instrument construction		Use reeds (adjusted) for the double-reed instruments.
Equal temperament		Maintain moveable tuning slides on all the brass instruments.
Resonance Room temperature		Adjust the pedals accurately and balance the head tension on timpani to improve intonation.
Adjusting the instrument	Balance and blend	Get the balance right and then intonation will improve.
Tuning devices		Use blend, necessary in listening, to improve intonation. The comparison of pitches with other players makes this crucial.

(*continued*)

Table 8.2. (*continued*)

	PROBLEM AREAS	TEACHING STRATEGIES
	Tuning procedures	Use the electronic tuning device in many different ways to improve intonation.
		See spot check, comparison tuning, and tuning from the bass (in this chapter).
		See miscellaneous tuning hints (in this chapter).
		Check complete chromatic scale for "bad notes" on the various instruments.
		Pay constant attention to the ensemble intonation in the rehearsal process. Use careful initial tuning and periodic tuning in the rehearsal process.
		Avoid extreme registers and extreme dynamic levels, which may cause considerable intonation problems.
What other teaching strategies (suggested by the conducting teacher or students) could improve the ensemble intonation?		

Chapter Nine

Rhythms and Rhythm Patterns

I define rhythm as a general and all-encompassing term. Rhythm involves tempo, tempo changes, meter, pulse, accentuation, note/rest values, and various rhythms and rhythm patterns. With conducting patterns and gestures, the conductor has more physical control over these aspects of the performance than most of the other performance aspects. (In evaluating an audiotape recording of a rehearsal process or a concert performance, it becomes very evident whether the conductor is controlling these rhythmic aspects of the musical performance.) Poor ensemble precision will result in the performance if the pulse is unclear and/or the rhythms and rhythm patterns are incorrect.

The conductor shows the pulse with the conducting patterns, and the players must then play these rhythms and rhythm patterns clearly as well as physically feeling the pulse. Good conducting technique involves showing the pulse so that the ensemble can respond with the precise tempo (or tempo changes), correct meter subdivision, exact note and rest values, proper accentuation, and correctly played rhythms and rhythm patterns. A common characteristic of both good conducting technique and precise ensemble execution is flow in the conducting patterns. *The flow in the conducting patterns will encourage this precise rhythmic execution and emphasize the forward motion of the musical line by the ensemble.* Assuming that the players are watching the conductor, these conducting patterns and gestures should show and control the precision and tempo of the ensemble during both the rehearsal process and the concert performance. The flow in the conducting patterns should communicate to the ensemble precisely where to execute the anticipated pulse.

The precise performance of the basic rhythms and rhythm patterns helps to ensure a cohesive ensemble. The emphasis is on the adjective *precise.* In any ensemble, the careless playing of rhythm patterns will result in poor precision and a lack of clarity in the musical performance. It will also prevent success in other aspects of the musical performance. Indeed, the incorrect playing of a specific rhythm pattern by the ensemble may blur many other performance aspects. *Rhythm patterns must be understood as mathematical relationships* and evolved through the subdivision (meter beat) of the pulse. The conductor must find a way to eliminate the careless performance of rhythms and rhythm patterns.

IN THE REHEARSAL PROCESS

The secret to exact performance of these basic rhythm patterns is in feeling the pulse and understanding the subdivision of the beat. Great importance rests on the accurate performance of these basic rhythm patterns in auditioning players for major symphony orchestras as well as for many other first-rate instrumental music ensembles. This leads to the following conclusion: The training of young players in school ensembles must emphasize the correct performance of these basic rhythms and rhythm patterns. The conductor/teacher then must insist that the players are fundamentally sound about the production of these basic rhythms and rhythm patterns in the rehearsal process!

Training the ensemble to play these basic rhythms and rhythm patterns precisely should be one of the first and most important objectives in the rehearsal process. Considerable space in this chapter is devoted to the proper playing of these basic rhythms and rhythm patterns because of the importance of this rehearsal priority. It is also very important to realize as a conductor that rhythm errors can be "clouded" in the rehearsal process through poor balance, poor blend, and uncontrolled dynamic levels. Rhythms also involve the player's tone production and articulation control on the instrument. Much of the ensemble training to improve rhythms and rhythm patterns can take place during the warm-up segment of the rehearsal process. Beyond this approach, the conductor must insist when working on concert repertoire that these rhythms and rhythm patterns be played precisely and correctly. The ensemble training will then lead to the application of this learning transfer by the players to future rehearsals, performances, and ensembles.

The conductor might have the players play, tap, count, clap, model, or sing the rhythm patterns while the conductor conducts or have the players conduct, count, and sing the rhythm to make the connection between the pulse and the rhythm patterns. A chalkboard (or whiteboard) can be a very valuable aid in teaching these rhythms and rhythm patterns. The singing or counting of rhythm patterns by the conductor can be an expedient means of teaching these patterns, but this must not be to the detriment of the players' understanding of the rhythm patterns and the subdivision of the beat. Otherwise, this kind of teaching borders on rote presentation and will need frequent repetition in future rehearsals with very little learning transfer for the players. Some serious work then in the warm-up period may be necessary for the improvement of these rhythms and rhythm patterns.

ELEMENTS OF RHYTHM

Tempo and Tempo Changes

A clear preparatory beat to indicate the precise tempo at the beginning of a piece or section gives the ensemble a sense of security. The preparatory beat must show the initial pulse length or beat duration so that the ensemble can properly subdivide the first beat of music. The conductor often shows this preparatory beat poorly, and so it does not clearly define the duration of that first beat of music. With the flick of the right wrist, the conductor identifies when the preparatory beat begins. At this point, the conductor shows the length of the initial beat to the ensemble. I address the preparatory beat problem in Table 9.1, Teaching Strategy (The Precise Tempo), at the end of the chapter.

If the tempo changes either suddenly or gradually, the conductor must show the tempo change with very precise conducting patterns, perhaps aided by the use of the left hand. Many conductors are guilty of leisurely changing the tempo when the music calls for a sudden tempo change rather than showing this precise tempo change. See Table 9.2, Teaching Strategy (Sudden Tempo Changes). Likewise, the conductor must gauge gradual tempo changes to arrive at the new tempo indicated by the composer. In addition, these gradual tempo changes should be smooth in order to avoid an abruptness in the musical line. See Table 9.3, Teaching Strategy (Gradual Tempo Changes). Tables 9.2 and 9.3 also appear at the end of the chapter. Both the sudden and gradual tempo changes are concerned with these basic problems. I supply additional information on the subject of tempo and tempo changes in Chapter 12: Tempo and Ensemble Precision.

Meter, Pulse and Accentuation

Conducting patterns define bar lines for the players. The conductor must differentiate meter indications between simple meter and compound meter so that the players will mentally subdivide correctly. The initial preparatory beat becomes crucial in this designation. This will aid in the proper performance of various rhythm patterns within the designated meter. The players need to be thinking and feeling in the correct subdivision of the beat. Simple meter (dividing into twos) is more common than compound meter, where the feel is the subdivision of threes. The conductor should point out this special feeling of compound meter as opposed to the more common duple meter with the young players. Shifting from duple subdivision to triple subdivision requires the player to feel the difference and make this change to the triple subdivision.

With younger ensembles, the conductor may have to spend some rehearsal time on alla breve meter (cut-time), eighth-note pulse meters (such as 3/8 in 3, 4/8 in 4, or 6/8 in 6), and compound meters (3/8 in 1, 6/8 in 2, 9/8 in 3, and 12/8 in 4). Note and rest values in these meters will need reinforcement. Especially, the subdivision of 3s in compound meters will need repeated clarification for the young player who has generally not been exposed as intensely or frequently as with duple subdivision. Primarily, the young player needs to differentiate between the meter feeling of 2s and that of 3s. Table 9.4, Teaching Strategy (Designating Meters), and Table 9.9, Teaching Strategy (Compound Meters), at the end of the chapter suggest ways of accomplishing the teaching of these various rhythmic aspects.

The players must see as well as feel the pulse that the conductor indicates for the ensemble. The conductor must be sure that the beat is clear. What happens between the beats actually shows this clarity. The beat itself becomes secondary in importance to the preparation of the beat or pulse. If the conductor's patterns are hesitant or rushed, the pulse will be insecure for the ensemble. The players must understand the meter and have a feeling for the pulse within the designated meter so that they can play the subdivision of each pulse accurately. Table 9.5, Teaching Strategy (Pulse Beat and

Accentuation), at the end of the chapter offers some ideas and suggestions for indicating and showing pulse and accentuation.

Because the pulse is such a crucial aspect of the rhythmic feeling and the accurate performance of rhythms and rhythm patterns, during the rehearsal process the player may find it very helpful *to mark complicated measures or complex rhythmic passages with a vertical line (or slash)* to show where the precise point of the beat will fall. This vertical line or slash will indicate to the player where the pulse actually occurs in the printed music. The conductor should encourage this pulse marking procedure throughout the rehearsal process. By marking the music and then feeling the pulse, the players will no longer be guessing at the rhythms or rhythm patterns during the rehearsal process or in the concert performance.

In order to reinforce what the players see on the printed page, the conductor must also indicate accentuation or weight on a note. We have accents on the beat and on the fraction of the beat. These two possibilities need to be shown with entirely different types of gestures within the conducting patterns. The main consideration for the conductor is to realize that the gesture must occur before the moment of the accent. If this does not happen, the communication between the conductor and the players is ineffective. I discuss this idea in Table 9.5, Teaching Strategy (Pulse Beat and Accentuation), at the end of the chapter. There are numerous types of accents to consider: dynamic, agogic, metric, harmonic, pitch, pattern, and with embellishments. These shown accents may be notated in several different ways such as >, ^, –, *fp*, *sfz*, *rinf.*, *ten.*, and other such markings (Kohut 1996, 173–75). In much printed music, the composer may not have notated the accent, but rather it is assumed under the circumstance of the agogic, metric, harmonic, pitch, and pattern accents.

Note/Rest Values and Subdivision

Note and rest values in reality are mathematical problems. The player must perceive where the beats (pulses) fall in order to correctly execute the given rhythm or rhythm pattern. Again, the conductor becomes the important controlling factor through the conducting patterns in showing these pulses, and thereby obtaining the correct performance of these rhythms and rhythm patterns from the ensemble. Even though the players are observing the conducting patterns, they still must feel the pulse. Remember, the conductor is the guiding force in keeping all the players in the ensemble precisely together.

The correct subdivision of each beat is crucial in the understanding and playing of rhythm patterns. All musical beats divide into either 2s or 3s or the multiples of these subdivisions. The player must be able to "sense" the subdivisions within the context of the established pulse. The conductor should talk about ratios in explaining rhythm patterns. By anticipating where the next pulse will occur, the player is able to subdivide the beat correctly. In order for the players to execute the subdivision correctly, *the conductor must provide a clear pulse for the ensemble.* A part of this clear pulse in the conducting pattern is showing the difference between simple meter and compound meter. The conductor as well as the players must be aware of this subdivision in the rhythm patterns. If the conductor decides to verbally count before the beginning of a section, then in simple meter the counting should be "1 and 2 and" and in compound meter, the counting should be "**1**, 2, 3, **4**, 5, 6" and then continue to show the compound meter beat within the conducting pattern.

I should emphasize here that the concern is not just to play the rhythms or rhythm patterns, but also rather to play them very precisely. The goal is for the players to line up the rhythms and rhythm patterns so that the precision is perfect. With many rhythm patterns there are distortion tendencies, such as with the dotted-8th and 16th note pattern played like part of a triplet figure. The conductor needs to be aware of these error tendencies so that he or she can correct them quickly in the rehearsal process. I define these error tendencies in detail in this chapter. Table 9.6, Teaching Strategy (Note and Rest Values); Table 9.7, Teaching Strategy (Various Rhythm Patterns); and Table 9.8, Teaching Strategy (Various Rhythm Patterns) at the end of the chapter address the specific problems of note and rest values. It is important and necessary for the conductor and the players to be aware of the underlying rhythmic system involved with musical performance. The players must count rhythms and rhythm patterns and not depend on rote learning within their musical performance. The following section outlines this rhythmic system—that is, tempo beats, meter beats, and melodic rhythm patterns.

A RHYTHMIC SYSTEM

Tempo Beats, Meter Beats, and Melodic Rhythm Patterns

Having preliminarily covered tempo and tempo changes, meter, pulse, and accentuation, and now, note/rest values as a part of the whole area of rhythm, and before proceeding to the performance of these basic rhythm patterns, it is appropriate to bring all of this under one system. The concern here is for the conductor/teacher to have control of the ensemble in the rehearsal process regarding the above elements of tempo, tempo change, meter, pulse, accentuation, and note/rest values. Beyond this, an awareness of the rhythmic system that generates the production of precise rhythms and rhythm patterns is necessary. Dr. Edwin E. Gordon has defined this rhythmic system in his book *The Psychology of Music Teaching* as that of tempo beats, meter beats, and melodic rhythm patterns (1971, 66–69).

The tempo beats above everything else must be consistent and secure. The exception to this stability is when one pulse from the next pulse is condensed or stretched for expressive purposes. The conductor, in showing the conducting patterns, is actually distinguishing these tempo beats. The pulse is a point in time and has a specific tempo length until the next pulse occurs as determined by the conductor. The length of time between tempo beats allows for the subdivision of the beat as designated by the meter. This meter beat then overlays the tempo beat, resulting in a basic even subdivision of twos or threes. Once this meter beat is established, melodic rhythm patterns should then coincide with the tempo beats and the meter beats.

The meter beats are perhaps the least understood, especially by the young instrumentalist. In the early stages of instrumental study, much emphasis rests on the idea of how many pulses occur in a measure (tempo beats). Subsequently, the various basic melodic rhythm patterns are taught in simple meter as the student progresses. However, players seem to overlook that within the duration of a single pulse or beat there is a fundamental division of this beat depending on the meter designation. The young instrumentalist must acquire the feeling for threes as in compound meters of 3/8 in one, 6/8 in two, 9/8 in three, or 12/8 in four. The difficulty of this acquisition is that the student has been playing in duple subdivision up to this time. The young player needs to make a concerted effort to keep the triple subdivision going mentally in compound meters (or as waltz-time in one). This subdivision of the pulse, of course, can change from one beat to the next.

The melodic rhythm patterns likewise overlay the tempo beats and the meter beats. If the melodic rhythm patterns change from the expected meter beat designated, then the meter beat will change to accommodate the melodic rhythm pattern. Because of the consistency of the tempo beat, this element of the rhythmic system will not change to accommodate either the meter beat or the melodic rhythm pattern. The tempo beat will only change if there is an expressive reason for this change or the composer indicates in the music that the tempo should deviate from the consistency of this established tempo beat.

In the final analysis, the conductor must strive to control the tempo beat for the ensemble by showing a clear conducting pattern indication for the pulse. The conductor and players then must feel the meter beat together, that is, the subdivision of the single beat into twos or threes.

The players must perform the various melodic rhythm patterns precisely within the context of the tempo beats and the meter beats. In bringing this all together, the duration from one pulse to the next is involved. Within this one pulse length, the tempo beat is defined, the meter beat is imposed on the tempo beat, and then the melodic rhythm pattern is played within the framework of the tempo beat and meter beat. With these three ingredients in mind, this chapter continues with the various rhythmic teaching strategies. In the following sections I offer ideas and suggestions for designing these teaching strategies for the various basic rhythms and rhythm patterns.

DESIGNING RHYTHMIC TEACHING STRATEGIES

Designing Teaching Strategies for the Rehearsal Process

Note: All the tables referred to in this section appear at the end of the chapter. A preparatory beat must indicate the exact tempo conceived by the conductor as well as showing the attack, the meter designation, the dynamic level, and the basic style. See Table 9.1, Teaching Strategy (The Precise Tempo). The preceding preparatory beat must control a sudden tempo change. See Table 9.2, Teaching Strategy (Sudden Tempo Changes). A gradual tempo change requires the conductor to be sensitive and musical in gauging the speed of the tempo change. See Table 9.3, Teaching Strategy (Gradual Tempo Changes). With the preparatory beat, the conductor must show the difference between simple and compound meter for the ensemble. See Table 9.4, Teaching Strategy (Designating Meters). The clear indication of pulse and accentuation by the conductor is essential for the precision and musicality of the ensemble. See

Table 9.5, Teaching Strategy (Pulse Beat and Accentuation). The correct performance of note and rest values with an instrumental ensemble will help ensure good precision and allow the ensemble to be rhythmically cohesive. See Table 9.6, Teaching Strategy (Note and Rest Values). A number of basic rhythm patterns (in simple and compound meter) cause a lack of clarity or good precision in the ensemble. See Table 9.7, Teaching Strategy (Various Rhythm Patterns). A number of basic rhythm patterns (in simple and compound meter) cause a lack of clarity or good precision with the ensemble. See Table 9.8, Teaching Strategy (Various Rhythm Patterns).

Miscellaneous Rhythmic Reading Problems

I have not covered five other rhythmic problem areas under these basic rhythm patterns. These five rhythmic problems include (1) compound meters, (2) asymmetrical meters—see Table 9.9, Teaching Strategy (Compound and Asymmetrical Meters) below, (3) the anacrusis or "pick-up" notes, (4) tied notes, and (5) rests at the end of the chapter.

The anacrusis (or pick-up notes) usually occurs as an introduction to the first main note of the phrase. Consequently, *the anacrusis tends to be slighted* in terms of both the rhythmic accuracy and importance. The players must be alert to play the anacrusis with a rhythmically precise value and with a clear indication from the conductor. Although a single note or a group of notes (anacrusis) will generally not be on a strong beat or as important as the main note that follows, the "pick-up" notes should be played securely. This is a common error with many ensemble performances. Another common error happens to the anacrusis when the upbeat is in duple subdivision and the previously established triple subdivision or with the beat following the anacrusis. This distinction is vital to the musical performance.

Tied notes require the player to feel the pulse correctly in tempo. Rhythmic guessing on tied notes usually results in considerable inaccuracies. If the player feels the pulse continuously, then he or she will know when to release the tied note and proceed on to the next note or rhythm pattern. A rapid tempo can also be an inhibiting factor in the proper execution of tied notes. In this instance, the player should release the tied note just slightly before the actually value is complete so that the following note or notes are placed precisely in time. The same general problem may also occur with the sixteenth rest followed by three sixteenth notes.

Rests present rhythmic problems because of inaccurate counting, rushing the pulse and precision of entrance after the rest. As in playing notes, rest values also can be distorted. In ensemble playing, the conductor and players are more likely to rush the pulse with the silence of the rests. The precision of entrance after the rest involves the exact timing of the breath (winds), the bow (strings), or the stroke (percussion). In many classical and romantic works, at the end of the piece there are frequently isolated chords punctuated and separated by rests. These isolated chords must continue in a rhythmic manner, even when the conductor decides for dramatic effect to alter this tempo. The conductor must show strongly and distinctly with the preparatory beat for each of the isolated chords, and must execute these passive gestures between the isolated chords. This conducting technique will give the players more security and confidence in the performance of these isolated chords.

SUMMARY: RHYTHMIC READING PROBLEMS

The player in the ensemble must know exactly where the pulse (the tempo beat) will occur. Granted, while playing in an ensemble, the conductor is showing this pulse. However, for the player to subdivide there needs to be a physical feeling on the part of the player for the length of one beat. This feeling may be in the form of foot tapping or another system of counting. The important matter is that this should happen in the ensemble for the player to become an independent music reader. In many instances, the player depends completely on the visual aspect shown by the conductor, which leads to a somewhat nebulous pulse with the player (because the player, in music reading, may not see every pulse that the conductor provides).

The player needs to experience this feeling of the pulse when playing in an ensemble. Further, the player, when then confronted with a musical work beyond the conducted ensemble, will be confident about playing the selection correctly without depending on "outside" help. The player must be able to solve these rhythmic reading problems independently within the ensemble, in solo work, in chamber music, or in individual practice.

Subdividing the beat involves being aware of two main factors: (1) whether the beat divides into twos or threes as in either simple meter or compound meter (the meter beat), and (2) the recognition of specific rhythmic patterns (melodic rhythm pattern). The subdivision of the beat can be accurate only if the player precisely anticipates the next pulse. In order to subdivide the beat, the player must know the length of the beat (that is, pulse to pulse). It is important for the conductor and the player to realize that the subdivision of the beat is dependent on both the meter beat and the melodic rhythm pattern. Solving rhythmic reading problems in ensemble performance involves the tempo beat, the meter beat, and the melodic rhythm pattern.

PRACTICAL APPLICATION (DISCUSSION/DEMONSTRATION)

1. Demonstrate by singing or playing the examples below so that the notated rhythms and rhythm patterns are understood and performed precisely by the conducting students. What error tendencies are involved with each rhythm? (Musical Example)
2. Demonstrate the conducting of asymmetrical meter patterns so that the conducting students can understand and then practice them. Repeat each measure many times. Use various music materials for practice. (Musical Example)
3. Show accents on the beat and on the fraction of the beat. Repeat each measure many times. (Musical Example)
4. Conduct examples of sudden tempo change (slow to fast and fast to slow). (Musical Example)
5. Conduct examples of gradual tempo change (accelerando and ritardando). (Musical Example)
6. With the use of the VTR or mirror, practice conducting the preparatory beat in simple meter for clarity; consider the compound meter preparatory beat as well.
7. Discuss, demonstrate, and practice the idea of wrist "flick" as an essential part of defining the beginning of the preparatory beat.

8. Discuss, demonstrate, and practice starting the ensemble on a beat other than the first beat of the measure; also demonstrate starting on the fraction of the beat (three ways as designated in the book). (Musical Example)
9. Discuss the rhythmic system as outlined in this chapter (tempo beat, meter beat, and melodic rhythm pattern).
10. Discuss the miscellaneous rhythmic reading problems that I cite under that heading in this chapter.
11. Demonstrate the execution of passive and active gestures for the conductor. What would prompt the use of these passive and active gestures?
12. What are some of the basic rhythm patterns in simple or compound meter that are problems in performing precisely?
13. Continue to gain familiarity with the standard repertoire found in Appendix A through CD listening, score study, and guidance from the conducting teacher. (See Appendix G for assignment forms.)

IN THE REHEARSAL PROCESS (LAB) ENVIRONMENT

1. Demonstrate the important factors involved in showing a clear conducting pulse. Analyze the conducting technique and then practice.
2. Have the conducting student teach the following rhythm patterns in the rehearsal process lab. Discuss the error tendency problems with each pattern. (Musical Example)
3. Demonstrate showing accents on and off the beat with the ensemble. (Musical Example)
4. Demonstrate starting the ensemble on the fraction of the beat (three ways). (Musical Example)
5. Demonstrate procedures in making the players aware of the problems involved in compound meter or waltz time in one (subdivision of the beat into 3s).
6. Have the conducting student show the performance of the asymmetrical meter rhythms patterns in the rehearsal process lab. Where is the elongated beat? (Musical Example).
7. Demonstrate (during the warm-up period) with scales how to improve the performance of various rhythms and rhythm patterns, using the examples shown below (Musical Example).
8. Complete student conducting/rehearsing projects (in the rehearsal process lab environment).

RECOMMENDED READING

Casey, Joseph L., *Teaching Techniques and Insights for Instrumental Music Educators.* Chapter 10: Rhythm and Movement under Section VI gives an overview of the problems of rhythm in the rehearsal process.

Cowell, Richard, *The Teaching of Instrumental Music*, 3rd ed. The book covers many areas of instrumental music along with tempo, meter, and rhythm found under Chapter 6: Rehearsal Techniques.

Farkas, Philip, *The Art of Musicianship*. There are many perceptive ideas on the topic of rhythm in Chapter 5: Rhythm.

Gordon, Edwin, *The Psychology of Music Teaching*. Chapter 5: Rhythmic Teaching lays out the rhythmic system that I have advocated and adopted for this book.

Hunsberger, Donald, and Roy E. Ernst, *The Art of Conducting*, 2nd ed. Chapter 8: Asymmetrical Meters and Chapter 9: Conducting Supermetric Patterns.

Kohut, Daniel L., *Instrumental Music Pedagogy* (paperback version). Chapter Two: Teaching Musical Notation covers the rhythmic problems of reading and sight-reading music.

Lisk, Edward S., *The Creative Director: Alternative Rehearsal Techniques*. Chapter 5: Rhythmic Perception.

Long, R. Gerry, *The Conductor's Workshop: A Workbook on Instrumental Conducting*. Chapter 13: Unusual Rhythms and Meters covers the material concerning asymmetrical meters.

Schleuter, Stanley L., *A Sound Approach to Teaching Instrumentalists*. Chapter 4: Teaching Rhythmic Feelings (starting on page 52) adheres to the Edwin Gordon thesis of tempo beats, meter beats, and melodic rhythm patterns.

Starer, Robert, *Rhythmic Training*. The emphasis in this book is matching the various rhythms and rhythm patterns with the given pulse.

REPERTOIRE FOR PROJECTS AND ASSIGNMENTS

Full Orchestra, Chamber Orchestra, or String Orchestra

de Falla: The Three-Cornered Hat Suite, Part I (various movements)
Elgar: Enigma Variations (various movements)
Gershwin: Cuban Overture
Gould: An American Salute
Grieg: Piano Concerto in A minor (various movements)

Concert Band or Wind Ensemble

Ives: Variations on "America" (Rhoads, arr.)
McBeth: Masque
Milhaud: Suite française (various movements)
Nelhybel: Festivo
Nixon: Fiesta del Pacifico

Miscellaneous or Small Ensembles

Altenburg: Concerto for Seven Trumpets and Timpani
Martinů: La revue de cuisine (clarinet, bassoon, trumpet, violin, cello, and piano)

TEACHING STRATEGY TABLES

Table 9.1. The Precise Tempo

CONDUCTOR CONCERNS	PROBLEM AREAS	TEACHING STRATEGIES
The exact tempo secured by the preparatory beat	Conducting technique	Establish good eye contact with the ensemble at the beginning of the selection.
The wrist flick to start the preparatory beat		Do a wrist flick on the initial preparatory beat to show the length of the first beat.
The meter designation		Keep the flow in the preparatory beat; do not hesitate at the top of the preparatory beat; this will simply confuse the players.
The attack on the first note of the phrase, section, or piece	Training the ensemble	Train the ensemble to breathe with the preparatory beat in order to achieve a good attack.
The dynamic level		Train the ensemble to watch the conductor on all of the important preparatory beats.
The basic style		
The essence and spirit of the music	Tempo and attack	Conceive and think the tempo before beginning the preparatory beat.
The selected tempo (using the metronome)		Indicate the tempo and attack clearly and precisely for the ensemble.
		Show that the initial attack is always one of the most important aspects with any instrumental performance.
	Meter Designation	Show whether the first beat is divided into 2s or 3s (meter beat).
		In simple meter, show that the designation will be in 2s; in compound meter, it will be in 3s.
	Dynamic level	Demonstrate that the size and intensity of the preparatory beat will indicate the dynamic level to the ensemble.
		Use the left hand to indicate the dynamic level before executing the preparatory beat by turning the palm of the left hand up or down as a reminder to the players about this dynamic level.
		Demonstrate that this is not a part of the rhythmic aspect, but a part of the preparatory beat execution.

(*continued*)

Table 9.1.   (*continued*)

	PROBLEM AREAS	TEACHING STRATEGIES
	Basic Style	Show that the basic style does not interfere with the smoothness and clarity of the preparatory beat.
		After the initial attack, confirm the basic style with specific conducting patterns.
		Demonstrate that, in some cases, basic style may be part of the preparatory beat.
What other teaching strategies (suggested by the conducting teacher or students) could implement the preparatory beat?		

Table 9.2.   Sudden Tempo Changes

CONDUCTOR CONCERNS	PROBLEM AREAS	TEACHING STRATEGIES
The conducting technique involved	Conducting technique	Use good eye contact with the ensemble in reinforcing these sudden tempo changes.
The sudden tempo change with the preparatory beat into the new tempo		Use the left hand to clarify and reinforce these sudden tempo changes.
	Going from slow to fast	Show the preparatory beat for the new tempo on the last part of the last beat of the slow tempo going into the new faster tempo.
The execution of this preparatory beat into the new tempo		
Slow to fast tempo		Show the preparatory beat for the new tempo precisely and emphatically. The preparatory beat must not look hesitant or unsure.
Fast to slow tempo		
		Occasionally, there may be some pick-up notes into the new tempo; show these as part of the new tempo in most cases.
A precise tempo change executed into the new tempo	Going from fast to slow	The rebound of the first beat in the slow tempo will indicate this new tempo into the second beat of the slower tempo.
A metronomic indication change		In some instances, a fermata might delay or precede the downbeat of the new tempo, in which case, indicate the slow tempo with a specific and basic preparatory beat into the new tempo.
		In going from fast to slow, the conductor must be very clear in the conducting motion so that the precision of the ensemble remains intact.

Table 9.2. (*continued*)

	PROBLEM AREAS	TEACHING STRATEGIES
	The sudden tempo change	The sudden tempo change must be executed precisely, not gradually or hesitantly with either the conducting or playing.
		The conductor must reinforce the sudden tempo change during the rehearsal process so there is no confusion within the ensemble.
		Mirroring the right-hand conducting pattern with the left hand may reinforce these sudden tempo changes.
What other teaching strategies (suggested by the conducting teacher or students) could implement sudden tempo changes?		

Table 9.3. Gradual Tempo Changes

CONDUCTOR CONCERNS	PROBLEM AREAS	TEACHING STRATEGIES
The conducting technique involved	Conducting technique	The conductor must clearly indicate the beats during these gradual tempo changes.
		Gradual tempo changes require good eye contact between the conductor and the ensemble.
Speeding up	Speeding up	Make the patterns gradually smaller in order to cover the conducting space with the patterns when speeding up.
Slowing down		The energy level should increase and, perhaps, the merging of the beats might be necessary such as with 3 into 1.
Merging of the beats	Slowing down	Make the patterns gradually larger in order to cover the conducting space with the patterns when slowing down.
Subdividing of the beats		The energy level should decrease and, perhaps, the subdivision of beats might be necessary when slowing down.
Gradual tempo changes gauged	Merging of the beats	It may be necessary to merge the beats at some point, but do this smoothly and gradually. In some cases, the conductor may want to use a transition pattern.
Arriving at the new tempo on time		Before merging, gradually speed up the motion and then do a transition into the new pattern.
		Examples of merging are from 3 into 1 or 6 into 2 (use the Italian six-pattern here).

(*continued*)

Table 9.3.   (*continued*)

	PROBLEM AREAS	*TEACHING STRATEGIES*
	Subdividing of the beat	It may be necessary for the conductor to subdivide the beat at some point; do the transition smoothly and gradually.
		Before subdividing, slow down in the existing pattern and then begin to subdivide after that.
	Gradual tempo change gauged	What new tempo will then occur after the tempo change? The conductor must gauge the gradual tempo change to arrive at this new tempo on time.
		Experiment with when and where to make this gradual tempo change. Sometimes, a very slight difference as to where this gradual tempo change begins will be better musically and/or more comfortable for the ensemble.
What other teaching strategies (suggested by the conducting teacher or students) could implement gradual tempo changes?		

Table 9.4.   Designating Meters

CONDUCTOR CONCERNS	*PROBLEM AREAS*	*TEACHING STRATEGIES*
The conducting technique involved	Conducting technique	Mentally subdivide the preparatory beat into 2s or 3s depending on the meter or the initial rhythm pattern.
Simple meter designation with the preparatory beat		The conducting technique must continue to show the division of the beat into 2s or 3s so the players are comfortable with this subdivision of the beat.
Compound meter designation with the preparatory beat		The preparatory beat must indicate the tempo and the designated meter into 2s or 3s.
The division into 2s in simple meters		This meter problem frequently happens when beginning to conduct with the one-beat pattern in 2/4 or 3/4 meter.
The division into 3s in compound meters		After the preparatory beat is executed in designating the meter, the conductor must continue to show either the subdivision of 2s or 3s.
The proper preparatory beat to indicate this meter		
Continuing the subdivision of simple meter with the conducting pattern	Simple meter	In simple meter, the subdivision is mostly in 2s unless the composer indicates a change to triple subdivision.
Continuing the subdivision of compound meter with the conducting pattern		The players must keep the subdivision of 2s in mind when playing in simple meter.

Table 9.4. (*continued*)

	PROBLEM AREAS	TEACHING STRATEGIES
	Compound meter	In compound meter, the subdivision is mostly in 3s unless the composer indicates a change to duple subdivision.
		The players must keep the subdivision of 3s in mind when playing in compound meter.
	The preparatory beat	The preparatory beat is all-important in establishing the duration of the initial beat of the music.
		The preparatory beat should establish the subdivision of the beat into 2s or 3s. If this does not occur, the players will be confused as to the tempo or the subdivision of the first beat.
	In the rehearsal process	In the rehearsal process, it may be necessary to confirm the subdivision in compound meters with the young ensemble as the triple subdivision of the beat is not as familiar as that of duple subdivision.
		In the rehearsal process, when designating the triple subdivision, execute the pattern with uneven speed.
What other teaching strategies (suggested by the conducting teacher or students) could implement designating the meters?		

Table 9.5. Pulse Beat and Accentuation

CONDUCTOR CONCERNS	PROBLEM AREAS	TEACHING STRATEGIES
Conducting technique clarity in showing the ictus of the beat	Conducting technique	The preparatory beat at the beginning of a piece or section is a commitment to the selected tempo.
The rebound of the beat pattern		The player sees general motion; the conductor must indicate the pulse with this idea in mind.
The size of the beat pattern		Indicate a change in the pulse by a preparatory beat before this change occurs.
The conducting plane		
Conducting pattern flow		The beat must be "alive" and secure; it must not be hesitant, deceptive, or rushed.

(*continued*)

Table 9.5.   (*continued*)

CONDUCTOR CONCERNS	PROBLEM AREAS	TEACHING STRATEGIES
Conducting technique clarity in showing the ictus of the beat The rebound of the beat pattern The size of the beat pattern The conducting plane Conducting pattern flow	The pulse beat	Pulse is the "heartbeat" of music. With young ensembles, finger snaps with the left hand may aid at times during the rehearsal process.
		A clear tempo beat shown by the conductor allows the player to subdivide the meter beat properly.
		In slow tempos, the player tends to play after the pulse beat.
		In fast technical passages, the player tends to rush from one pulse beat to the next.
		There may be rhythmically complex passages where it would be advantageous for the players to mark the pulse beat with slashes or vertical lines to indicate exactly where the beat falls; they will then subdivide the beat properly.
	Accentuation	A proper preparatory beat must anticipate the accentuation.
		Show an accent on the beat with a stop on the rebound of the previous beat (that is, the gesture of syncopation).
		Show an accent on the fraction of the beat with a strong gesture on the beat preceding this accent.
		Conceive the degree of accentuation and show the proper emphasis with the conducting technique.
		Dictate strong and weak beats by meter and show them with the conducting patterns (by defining the bar-lines).
		Indicate accents on the printed music or imply them through the phrasing or nuances in terms of the various musical passages.
		It may be necessary on occasion to mark or highlight the accents in the music so the players do not miss these important aspects of the musical interpretation.
What other teaching strategies (suggested by the conducting teacher or students) could improve the pulse and accentuation?		

Table 9.6. Note and Rest Values

CONDUCTOR CONCERNS	PROBLEM AREAS	TEACHING STRATEGIES
The conducting technique clarity	Conducting technique	Good conducting technique is an essential element in the accurate performance of note and rest values.
Accurate performance of the note and rest values		The players must be alert and watching the conductor in order to perform these note and rest values properly with the conductor.
The tempo beat	Accurate performance	Recognition of the melodic rhythm patterns and the understanding of the mathematical relationships of note and rest values are important.
The meter beat		
The melodic rhythm patterns		
The subdivision of the beat into 2s or 3s		Slow and rhythmic practice in the rehearsal process will lead to a more secure rhythmic and accurate performance by the ensemble.
A note followed by a rest receiving full value unless otherwise indicated	Subdivision of the beat	The correct subdivision of the beat by the players will ensure the accurate performance of these melodic rhythm patterns.
Style modifications (legato, staccato, marcato, and tenuto) somewhat altering the actual written note values		Unless all the members of the ensemble feel the pulse and subdivide the beat together, precision problems will occur.
	Note values	An important rule: A note when followed by a rest receives full value unless there is a staccato dot or other indication to shorten that note.
Passive/active gestures		Style indications and/or the various articulation markings may modify note values.
Avoidance of playing in the rests		Do not shorten note values at the end of the phrase unless otherwise indicated. This is a very common error with the young instrumentalist.

(*continued*)

Table 9.6.   (*continued*)

	PROBLEM AREAS	TEACHING STRATEGIES
	Rest values	The conductor should show rest values for the whole ensemble with passive gestures.
		Show rest values for the whole ensemble with the correct amount of time and without rushing; otherwise, poor precision will result.
		Young players frequently pass over or ignore rests unless they are feeling the pulse beat rhythmically and properly.
		Playing during the rests mars many performances. During the rehearsal process, carefully consider and reinforce this aspect so that this does not occur in the concert performance.
	What other teaching strategies (suggested by the conducting teacher or students) could help achieve note and rest accuracy?	

Table 9.7.   Various Rhythm Patterns

CONDUCTOR CONCERNS	*PROBLEM AREAS*	TEACHING STRATEGIES
Error tendencies of the various rhythm patterns	Dotted quarter and eighth note (Notate and discuss this rhythm pattern.)	The error tendencies are shortening the length of the dotted quarter or playing the 8th note too late.
Various rhythms and rhythm patterns		Place the 8th note exactly on the "and" of the second pulse.
Subdivision of the beat		Think of a quarter note tied to an 8th note or four 8th notes with the first three 8th notes tied together (for the dotted quarter).
Specific rhythm patterns		To correct, sing, tap, count, clap, model, or play this pattern.
Dotted quarter and eighth note pattern	Dotted eighth and sixteenth note (Notate and discuss this rhythm pattern.)	The error tendency is to play this pattern with a ratio of 2:1 rather than 3:1. The 16th note tends to come too early in the pattern.
Dotted eighth and sixteenth note pattern		Think of four 16th notes with the first three notes tied together.
Eighth and two sixteenth note pattern		Realize that the 16th note is closer to the following note shown.
Two sixteenths and eighth note pattern		However, this rhythm pattern in jazz style is played with the ratio of 2:1. In this particular style, there is need for a smoother execution of this rhythm pattern.
Triplet pattern		
Feeling the pulse		To correct, sing, tap, count, clap, model, or play this pattern.
Watching the conductor		

Table 9.7. (*continued*)

	PROBLEM AREAS	TEACHING STRATEGIES
	Eighth and two sixteenths note (Notate and discuss this rhythm pattern.)	The error tendencies are to delay the first 16th note or play a weak second 16th note.
		Place the first 16th note exactly on the "and" of the beat.
		There must be firm articulation or bowing on both 16th notes.
		To correct, sing, tap, count, clap, model, or play this pattern.
	Two sixteenths and eighth note (Notate and discuss this rhythm pattern.)	The error tendencies are to anticipate the pulse or play the second 16th note weakly.
		Play the first 16th note exactly on the pulse beat.
		There must be firm articulation or bowing on both 16th notes.
		To correct, sing, tap, count, clap, model, or play this pattern.
	Triplet (Notate and discuss this rhythm pattern.)	The error tendency is to play the first two notes too fast as in duple subdivision instead of the correct triple subdivision.
		The feel for the triplet must be one of equal value on all three notes.
		There must be a shift to the feel of triple subdivision from that of duple subdivision.
		To correct, sing, tap, count, clap, model, or play this pattern.
What other teaching strategies (suggested by the conducting teacher or students) could assist in performing these patterns correctly?		

Table 9.8. **Various Rhythm Patterns**

CONDUCTOR CONCERNS	PROBLEM AREAS	TEACHING STRATEGIES
Error tendencies of the various rhythm patterns	Quarter tied to four 16ths or the 16th rest followed by three 16th notes (Notate and discuss these rhythm patterns.)	The error tendency is to be late with the first articulated 16th note after the tie or the rest.
Various rhythms and rhythm patterns		In fast tempo, place the first articulate 16th note almost on the beat.
Subdivision of the beat		In slow tempo, the mathematical ratio of the first 16th note must be precise.
Specific rhythm patterns		To correct, sing, tap, count, clap, model, or play this pattern.

(*continued*)

Table 9.8.   (*continued*)

CONDUCTOR CONCERNS	PROBLEM AREAS	TEACHING STRATEGIES
Quarter tied to four sixteenth notes Sixteenth rest followed by three sixteenth notes Dotted eighth, sixteenth and eighth Syncopated rhythm patterns The hemiola rhythm patterns Longer followed by shorter notes or rests Anacrusis, tied notes and rests Feeling the pulse Watching the conductor	Dotted 8th, 16th, and 8th (Notate and discuss this rhythm pattern in compound meter.)	The error tendency is to distort this rhythm pattern with the 16th note coming late.
		Place equal importance on all three notes to avoid slighting the 16th note in this rhythmic pattern.
		Think of playing this rhythm pattern like a triplet in all cases.
		Play the pattern, omitting the 16th note and then replace the 16th note with the same rhythmic feel.
		To correct, sing, tap, count, clap, model, or play this pattern.
	Syncopated and hemiola rhythms (Notate and discuss these rhythm patterns.)	The error tendency is disruption of the pulse when playing on the fraction of the beat.
		Feel the pulse in order to play the syncopated notes against the pulse.
		Think of the tied equivalents for the precise performance of these syncopated and hemiola rhythmic patterns.
		These two rhythm patterns are common in music and should be addressed during the rehearsal process.
		To correct, sing, tap, count, clap, model, or play these patterns.
	Longer/shorter notes and rests (Notate and discuss these rhythm patterns.)	The error tendency is the failure to sustain the longer note or to give proper value to the note or rest and anticipate where to place the next shorter note.
		Feel the pulse and wait for the time to occur before going on to the next shorter note after the longer note or rest.
		To correct, sing, tap, count, clap, model, or play these patterns.
What other teaching strategies (suggested by the conducting teacher or students) could implement performing these patterns correctly?		

Table 9.9. Compound and Asymmetrical Meters

CONDUCTOR CONCERNS	PROBLEM AREAS	TEACHING STRATEGIES
The error tendency in compound meter	Compound meters	The error tendency is the failure to keep the feeling of the 3s with the subdivision of the beat during the compound meter.
Dividing the beat into 3s in compound meter		Consider each beat as a measure in waltz time with the subdivision of 3s.
Conducting the eighth note in compound meter		Develop the "triple" feel on each pulse.
		The melodic rhythm patterns in compound meter mostly coincide with the feeling of the 3s.
Conducting the dotted quarter note in compound meter		If the tempo were quite slow then the conductor would conduct the 8th note pulse rather than combining three 8th notes into groups. In this situation of conducting 8th notes, the subdivision of these notes then becomes duple.
The error tendency in asymmetrical meter		
Keeping the eighth note pulse consistent in asymmetrical meter		To correct, sing, tap, count, clap, model, or play these various compound meter patterns.
Conducting the eighth note in asymmetrical meter	Asymmetrical meters	The error tendency is the failure to maintain the basic unit "feel" (8th notes mostly).
The regular beat vs. the elongated beat in asymmetrical meter		Keep the 8th notes consistent and regular in asymmetrical meter.
		Learn to feel the regular beat and the elongated beat.
		The conductor needs to show and differentiate clearly between the regular beat and the elongated beat for the benefit of the players and for the correct subdivision of this pulse.
		In slow tempo, conduct the 8th notes in asymmetrical meter either in duple or triple subdivision. Then the conducting pattern must be determined as to where the subdivision into 2s or 3s should occur.
		In fast tempo, find the elongated beats in the measure and then determine the conducting pattern from this subdivision.
		Mentally, the conductor and the players must keep the 8th notes consistent in performing these asymmetrical meters.
		To correct, sing, tap, count, clap, model, or play these various rhythms in asymmetrical meters.
What other teaching strategies (suggested by the conducting teacher or students) could improve the compound and asymmetrical meters?		

Chapter Ten

Ensemble Sonority: Tone, Balance, Blend, Color, and Texture

ENSEMBLE SONORITY

Correct and characteristic tone production by each ensemble member coupled with a good instrument reed, mouthpiece, or bow will establish a solid foundation for the development of good ensemble sonority. From this point, the players need the conductor's challenge and guidance in controlling tone, to meet the demands of the music and in realizing the conductor's ensemble sonority conception. The conductor must know what to ask for tonally from the various individual players, instrumental sections, and instrument families (or choirs). *This idea assumes that the conductor has conceived the kind of sonority he or she expects from the ensemble.* Then in the rehearsal process, the conductor and players should continue to work together to bring this sonority conception to fruition.

It is assumed that in most ensembles, good individual tone production has been achieved or is being developed by the players; much of this is done outside of the rehearsal process (perhaps with the exception of the very young ensemble). The conductor now faces the development of this ensemble sonority. Much will depend on the constitution of the ensemble in terms of instrumentation, player numbers, and ensemble strengths and weaknesses. This is where the elements of ensemble tone, balance, blend, color, and texture come together to create the ensemble sonority conceived by the conductor. The ensemble sonority develops during the rehearsal process through the proper warm-up procedures, careful tuning, the selection of the repertoire, and the rehearsing of this repertoire. To a certain extent, the composer (or arranger) is responsible for the sonority based on the orchestration of the parts. The conductor and players then must realize this orchestration in the rehearsal process.

The younger ensemble needs instruction and encouragement to work toward a well-blended and well-produced homogeneous sonority. That is, individualism needs to be subdued in favor of a more cooperative ensemble effort. Each player's goal must be to contribute to this ensemble sonority. Later, as the ensemble matures, one of its goals should be to develop a more distinctive sonority. The approach of the ensemble must be one of listening, concentration, and teamwork in which this sonority is developed during the rehearsal process. Without this cooperative attitude, it would be very difficult for the conductor to develop and produce the desired ensemble sonority.

For the more mature ensemble, the main task for the conductor is to explain clearly what is wanted in terms of the tone quality, balance, blend, color, and texture. Here we assume that the tone production and control by each player is acceptable. Then the conductor must work to achieve the tone quality (brilliant, dark, light, heavy, projected, etc.) among the individual players, sections, and families of instruments as dictated by the repertoire and in matching the ensemble sonority conceived by the conductor. The tone, balance, and blend of the ensemble sonority are somewhat dictated by the composer (or arranger), and in the rehearsal process the conductor then regulates these performance aspects. In addition, the conductor should always strive for transparency in the texture, for clarity of the musical line, and for varying tone color and texture in order to achieve the desired ensemble sonority.

The conductor needs to have a clear concept of the sonority for the particular ensemble. He or she should not leave this conception to "natural" development or "visionless" circumstance. *The ensemble sonority of the orchestra* is one of distinction between the prominence of the string family and that of the timbre in the winds and percussion. The core of the orchestra sonority is the string section. In the rehearsal process, the conductor dictates the balance and blend between the strings and the wind-percussion element after knowing and understanding the composer's orchestration from score study. Some experimentation may be necessary in the rehearsal process to discover the intentions of the composer.

In contrast, *the concert band ensemble sonority* does not have the same kind of core found in the string family of the orchestra. (Perhaps only in transcriptions of orchestral works is there a resemblance of this core found in the flutes, oboes, clarinets, trumpets, or alto saxophones due to assigning the various upper string parts to these instruments. Likewise, bassoon, bass clarinet, baritone saxophone, euphonium, and tuba take the cello and contrabass parts from the orchestra score.) This means that the concert band ensemble has a variety of tone colors all independent of each other. Early in the 20th century, the band was thought to be more of a blended ensemble, but through the untiring efforts of the more recent band composers and arrangers, works for this ensemble have become more colorful. Works for concert band such as Alfred Reed's *A Festival Prelude*, H. Owen Reed's *La Fiesta Mexicana*, and John Zdechlik's *Chorale and Shaker Dance* are examples of this turnabout in band composing and arranging.

To achieve this section sonority concept, it is a good strategy for the conductor to think in terms of the ensemble consisting of the various sections of the ensemble and focus on the development of each section as an independent cohesive unit during the rehearsal process. Certainly, sectional rehearsals are useful for the development of this section sonority concept as well as improving some immediate technical or musical problems in the selected repertoire. The conductor must view section sonority as an entity in itself, and yet balance and blend it properly with the rest of the ensemble. For example, the percussion section must work to form a unit that plays well together and balances with the total ensemble sonority. The balance and blend within and among the various sections of the ensemble should come about during the rehearsal process so that the desired ensemble sonority will result from this in the concert performance.

The conductor should then consider these various sections in the context of families or choirs of instruments involved. The violin sections, the viola section, the cello section, and the double bass section constitute the string family. The flute section, the oboe section, the clarinet section, the bassoon section, and the saxophone section are a part of the woodwind family. The horn section, the trumpet section, the trombone section, the euphonium section, and the tuba section are members of the brass family. The percussion section is an entity within itself including a variety of instruments. As within each instrumental section and between the various sections, the conductor should integrate these family (or choir) sonority concepts as a part of the total ensemble sonority.

The point here is that the conductor must consider the instruments producing the full ensemble sonority on several levels (i.e., families [or choirs], among the sections, within the sections, and with the individual players). The ensemble tone, balance, blend, color, and texture are all considerations that the conductor must influence on these various levels during the rehearsal process. Some sections play only a single line while others contain several parts. The conductor must decide exactly what the ensemble sonority should be at any given moment and work toward achieving this in the rehearsal process. In the final analysis, the conductor must strive to achieve in the ensemble sonority (1) well-produced individual tone qualities, (2) a proper balance and blend among the sections as well as within each section, (3) family (or choir) cohesiveness, and (4) the contrast in tone color and texture with the total ensemble during the rehearsal process.

The chart in figure 10.1 shows the elements and the general connection of ensemble sonority with ensemble tone, balance, blend, color, and texture. As the conductor rehearses to achieve the desired ensemble sonority, the various elements must be

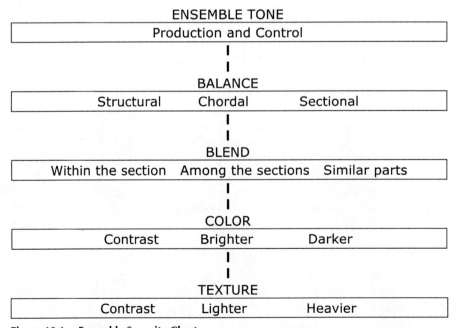

Figure 10.1.   Ensemble Sonority Chart

dissected and refined. Proper tone production and control, good balance, good blend, color contrast, and texture contrast must all be a part of the rehearsal objectives for the instrumental music ensemble. Without this proper tone, balance, and blend along with color and texture contrast, the ensemble sonority will lack variety and interest. The elements of ensemble sonority must keep their identity, and yet show this unity throughout the rehearsal process and into the concert performance.

The key to improving ensemble sonority is the awareness and sensitivity on the part of the conductor and the players to deal with these problems of ensemble tone, balance, blend, color, and texture. The conductor must detect and analyze what needs to happen to improve these elements and design teaching strategies for solving these ensemble sonority problems. The players, under the conductor's guidance and encouragement, can develop this needed tone control to adjust these elements of the ensemble sonority. The instructive adjustments of these elements for the ensemble sonority are the primary responsibility of the conductor. However, the players must also listen carefully and play sensitively in order to adjust these various ensemble sonority elements properly.

The conductor should encourage the players to become more sensitive to these ensemble sonority elements. Accomplish this by having the players listen and be involved in making these adjustments with the ensemble sonority elements. Young players in an ensemble tend to listen to themselves instead of to what is happening around them. These young musicians must learn to listen in order to improve precision, balance, blend, and intonation as well as the other performance sonority elements. The conductor is responsible for this ensemble sonority sensitivity during the rehearsal process. In some cases, the use of recordings for the players to hear fine performances can help to improve this sensitivity toward the various ensemble sonority elements.

ENSEMBLE TONE: PRODUCTION AND CONTROL

These ensemble sonority elements—ensemble tone, balance, blend, color, and texture—*are all closely connected to tone production and control* during the rehearsal process and in the concert performance. The conductor will need to devote considerable time during the rehearsal process to these elements, thus influencing the total performance of the ensemble. It is important for the conductor to address these performance elements and make the players aware of these elements while working on the concert repertoire in the rehearsal process. Give some attention to these five elements during the warm-up segment. The five elements involved in rehearsing the instrumental ensemble are inseparable; all five elements are involved with the tone production and control and the merging of these elements into the desired ensemble sonority.

Ensemble sonority is the collective result of individual tone quality and control. How the players produce the tone with their embouchure, breath, bow, stick, or mallet and so on will enhance or denigrate the outcome and the degree of refinement in the ensemble sonority. One important factor is the industry and application of the individual players to develop good tone quality and tone control on their instruments.

The concept of a characteristic tone on the instrument needs attention in the rehearsal process. Likewise, good instruction by a private teacher influences the development of this tone quality and control. Largely, tone production improvement must take place outside of the rehearsal process in private study, technique classes, and individual practice. The individual instrument itself (along with the mouthpiece, reed, bow, sticks, or mallets) is a determining factor in this tone production. A poor quality instrument will present limitations as to the degree of good individual tone production and control. The conductor can and should encourage the development and improvement of tone production and control during the rehearsal process. This procedure may mean that with the younger ensemble, the conductor will also need to emphasize how to achieve this improvement of tone production and control. With a more mature ensemble, the conductor must indicate to the players in the rehearsal process exactly what the desired sonority of a particular passage or section should be.

Generally, there is insufficient time in the rehearsal process to contend with all of the problems involved with tone production and control. It is not in the realm of this book to discuss the specific pedagogical approaches to improving tone production and control on the various instruments. However, the more individual players are producing an acceptable tone quality in the ensemble, the better the ensemble sonority will be. *Some work during the warm-up period can improve this ensemble tone and control.* It behooves the conductor to do what is necessary to see that the players in the ensemble are striving to produce an acceptable and characteristic tone quality. One way to improve individual tone production is to have the particular section listen and imitate the tone production of the section leader, assuming that this player's tone is a good model. Within the full ensemble, the conductor cannot work much with individuals during the rehearsal process; pacing and concentration with the whole ensemble would suffer. Throughout the rehearsal process, however, the conductor will need to work on tone production and control problems as the concert repertoire is rehearsed.

If the player is able to produce a beautiful sound on the instrument, it may lead to the desire to play more musically and enjoy practicing more. Modeling through recordings, teacher demonstrations, live performances, and peer imitation will accelerate the progress. This is why it is important for players to study with a teacher capable of producing a beautiful and characteristic sound. Through feedback from the teacher, the player can work to improve tone production measured against the correct concept. Common descriptions of poor tone production include airy, strident, bright, scratchy, gruff, and reedy sounds. Good tone production is beautiful, warm, projected, controlled, and centered.

Another aspect of good tone production *that needs fostering is tone projection.* Such concepts as airflow, spinning the tone, blowing through the horn (not just into the horn), and aiming the sound at distant targets are all ways of approaching tone projection development. Tone projection is especially crucial for the first chair player who is required to project the sound above the ensemble on frequent solo occasions. In some cases, however, the conductor will need to subdue the ensemble accompaniment to avoid covering up the solo line as opposed to asking the soloist to project more.

CONCEPTS OF TONE PRODUCTION

Qualities of good tone production include resonance, control, clarity, focus, consistency, and warmth. The tone quality must also have these characteristics: full sound, consistent among the registers, centered, unforced, free, and pure. It is important for the conductor and players to realize that register and volume affect tone quality. The player must learn the importance of striving to produce this "characteristic" tone on the instrument, even though there are many differences in concept involved here. By listening to numerous live performances and recordings, the player can gain a perspective and some insight into the quality of the sound produced on the particular instrument. In the rehearsal process, the conductor should take these individual tone production concepts and strive to produce this distinctive ensemble sonority. In some instances, a change of equipment (such as mouthpieces) might even be in order on specific instruments. With the young instrumentalist, producing an acceptable and characteristic sound may involve the actual tone production, and in this instance, there may need to be remedial work in order to rectify these tone production concepts.

With the young wind player, the conductor should promote the following tone production elements during the rehearsal process: posture, holding position, embouchure formation, breath use, throat relaxation, proper oral cavity, balance, blend, projection, and tone color variations. Some of these elements directly pertain to the younger ensemble. Other concerns for the wind players in the rehearsal process are reed quality (woodwinds), mouthpiece pressure (brass), condition of the mouthpiece and instrument, intonation, vibrato speed and depth, and other elements involved with the tone production and control. *For the more mature ensemble*, the wind tone production concepts might be of a more advanced level with concerns for musical interpretation.

For the string player, the following tone production elements are applicable during the rehearsal process: posture, holding position, finger placement, bow use, bow pressure, part of the bow used, amount of bow used, and bow placement on the string (near bridge or fingerboard). Other elements for the string players include the condition and adjustments of the instrument and bow, vibrato speed and depth, proper use of the bow, and other elements involved with improvement of the tone production. With the maturing ensemble, such items as bowing and bowing styles that I specify in the next chapter affect the tone production of the various string sections or the total string choir.

Because there are so many and varied instruments in the percussion family, the player needs to be schooled in a variety of playing techniques and as to how the sound is produced on the various percussion instruments. Some of these include stick size, mallet composition, adjustments needed for producing the desired tone on the various percussion instruments, striking position on the various instruments, and numerous other elements and techniques. In particular, the percussionist needs to develop tonal concepts that will match the artistry and musical sensitivity of the other instrumentalists in the ensemble. In the rehearsal process, the conductor will request from the percussion section the quality and volume of sound needed for good balance or blend with the rest of the ensemble. See Table 11.2, Teaching Strategy (Percussion Playing Techniques), in the next chapter for additional information on percussion instruments.

ENSEMBLE MATURITY DETERMINES TEACHING STRATEGIES

The conductor in the instrumental ensemble rehearsal process should have consider-able impact on the tone quality of individual players as well as control over the col-lective ensemble tone. With less mature ensembles, the conductor may need to devote some time to teaching in this area of tone production. Young players will need remind-ing of posture, instrument position, finger placement, embouchure formation, correct breathing procedure, and other basic tone production factors. With a more mature ensemble, the conductor would focus on musical aspects such as dynamics, phrasing, and other artistic demands of the music. This is the conductor's decision based on the performance and maturity level of the ensemble.

At a more advanced level, the conductor's duty to the players is to indicate spe-cifically the quality of the sonority desired, such as "darker," "brighter," "heavier," "lighter," "more vibrato," "more projected," etc. The extreme differences in teach-ing strategy application between the younger ensemble and the mature ensemble point out the wide background and versatility that the conductor should possess in working with these diverse ensembles. The more mature ensembles will want the conductor to be as specific as possible concerning the quality needed to bring the ensemble sonority in line with the conceived musical interpretation and the conduc-tor's conception of the ensemble sonority.

This may seem to be common sense, but it is crucial that the conductor be able to gear his or her approach and comments *to the appropriate ensemble level*. Fail-ure to do this properly will cause the young players to miss information about tone production necessary for their development. The more mature ensemble will become resentful if the conductor concentrates on basic tonal concepts rather than on the tone quality desired to enhance the musical interpretation of the work being rehearsed and performed. The mature player does not want to hear about how the conductor thinks the instrument should be played, but wants to know what the tone quality, style, bal-ance, blend, tone color, or the dynamics of given passage should be.

USE OF VIBRATO IN THE ENSEMBLE TONE

Vibrato enhances the beauty of the sound and adds warmth and intensity to well-pro-duced tones. Some instruments use vibrato most of the time. Others use it sparingly. The string player will use vibrato almost constantly. However, there are passages (sometimes indicated by the composer) where the string player will not use vibrato in order to create a "special" effect or mood. Likewise, the strings should avoid open strings in some circumstances, because vibrato cannot be applied on these open strings. In playing pizzicato, the string player must also be aware of the employment of vibrato. In numerous situations when the selection or phrase ends on a pizzicato, the string player should be encouraged to continue to use the vibrato in order for the tone to sustain the ring. The following wind players use vibrato most of the time to beautify the tone: flute, piccolo, oboe, English horn, bassoon, saxophone, trumpet, euphonium, and trombone, while the clarinet, horn, and tuba use vibrato much less frequently. The vibraphone has the option of using vibrato in the percussion section.

Most solo passages use vibrato to enhance and project the expressiveness of these solo instrument(s) as listed in the previous paragraph. Accompaniment chords and sustained notes requiring blend and stable intonation will not use vibrato. *The type of music will also dictate the use of vibrato.* A typical march or a fanfare on the brass instruments usually excludes vibrato. The clarinet might use vibrato in a stylistic way in realizing the jazz style and sonority. The player will make the initial determination about the use of vibrato; then if the conductor disagrees, the conductor has the final say on this ensemble sonority decision. It is important to realize that *a poor vibrato is unacceptable in any situation.* Vibrato must be taught carefully and produced well for its use either individually or within the ensemble in order for it to be effective.

The conductor will need to dictate (1) when the vibrato does not match his or her tonal concept, (2) whether to use vibrato at any given point, or (3) what degree of vibrato to employ. The degree of vibrato pertains to the *speed and the depth (or amplitude)* of the vibrato fluctuation. The speed of the vibrato may be increased to project intensity into the tone. Slowing the vibrato speed will result in a "calmness" of the sound. Of course, there are parameters here. A poorly produced vibrato will certainly not enhance the tone quality for these instrumentalists or for the ensemble sonority. In such instances, the conductor should rectify the situation by discouraging the use of such vibrato until its production is improved and controlled. Orchestra conductors are more conscious of the employment of vibrato than are concert band conductors. This is probably because of the predominance of the string family, which uses vibrato most of the time. However, the band conductor would enhance the ensemble sonority by giving attention to this matter during the rehearsal process and in preparation for the concert performance.

IMPROVING TONE CONTROL

Once the player produces the tone correctly, it is a matter of application (practice) by the player and maturation (in time) before the tone control is secure. The player must practice diligently and correctly to develop the needed tone control on the instrument. This serious application by the player over time will result in better tone control. In the rehearsal process, the conductor can accelerate this tone control process in several ways by (1) the selection of appropriate music for the ensemble, (2) challenging the potential expectations of the player's performance, (3) making the player aware of tone control problems on the specific instrument, (4) development of tone control during the warm-up period, and (5) designing teaching strategies for the improvement of tone control during the rehearsal process.

Much of what I have said concerning the ensemble tone, balance, blend, color, and texture *is dependent on this instrumental tone control.* The young player who has not gained this kind of tone control will have difficulties contributing to good ensemble tone, balance, blend, color, and texture within the ensemble. With the more mature player, the problem becomes one of awareness of and sensitivity to the other parts in the ensemble. The conductor must assess the maturity level for the potential tone control and design teaching strategies for this tone control improvement accordingly. Articulation can also be a factor in tone control; this is particularly true with brass instruments. If the tonguing on brass instruments is too strong, the tone control will be less than satisfactory. The use of "du" instead of "tu" will resolve this problem quickly. Likewise, the tongue placement for the attack can also cause some tone control problems with the articulation on all wind instruments.

Over-blowing on a brass instrument in loud passages may result in poor tone production and control. Much of the ensemble sonority is dependent on the balancing of the dynamic levels among the players, sections, and instrumental families. By the very nature of the specific instruments, the control factor is problematic. For example, the woodwind and string players can decrease the volume and control the security of the diminuendo to a greater degree than can most brass players, because of the way in which their tone is produced. This may be a consideration for the conductor in the musical interpretation.

Table 10.1, Teaching Strategy (Ensemble Tone Production and Tone Control), at the end of the chapter provides some ideas and suggestions for designing a teaching strategy to improve ensemble tone production and control.

ENSEMBLE BALANCE

The conductor does have considerable control over the balance aspect in the rehearsal process. By adjusting dynamic levels with the conducting patterns and gestures, verbal comments, and the written editing of the parts, the conductor can greatly influence the proper balance in the instrumental music ensemble. Tone quality, tone color, tonal intensity, balance, blend, intonation, instrument register, and instrument volume can all be factors in balancing the ensemble sonority. Some instruments simply can be played with more volume than other instruments. Sometimes certain sections are stronger than other sections in the ensemble because of numbers and/or prowess. In some cases, *the importance of these individual parts is not always recognized* (structural balance). To develop teaching strategies for improving ensemble balance, the conductor must realize the existence of five problematic areas of balance:

1. A balanced instrumentation
2. Potential dynamic ranges of the various instruments
3. Structural balance in the music (horizontal)
4. Chordal balance in the music (vertical)
5. Sectional balance in the music (within and among the various sections of the ensemble)

In order to have good and consistent balance in an instrumental music ensemble, the instrumentation must be sufficient to cover the parts uniformly in the performance of the selected repertoire. This assumes that the quality of performance by the players is such that they can adjust and play the individual parts in the proper context of the various works. *Striving for a balanced instrumentation with the instrumental music ensemble will solve many of the balance problems* encountered in the rehearsal process, and subsequently in the concert performance. In some instances, the conductor may be able to adjust certain dynamic levels or, during the rehearsal process, reduce the number of players on a given part. However, this is only a partial solution to the balanced instrumentation problem.

In addition to the above comments, *the conductor must distribute the parts among the players* in a manner that will allow for this better balance. Too often, the first parts are heard out of balance because of poor distribution of the various parts within the ensemble. In most instances, there needs to be fewer players on the first parts to achieve the proper balance in the ensemble, especially with the brass instruments. The conductor should insist on part distribution done so that proper balance will be possible. If the various parts in a section are doubled or tripled in the ensemble, then the quantity and quality of the distribution of the players must be considered in the light of how the general balance will be affected.

In the concert band today, the instrumentation is somewhat problematic in that there tends to be an over-supply of saxophones, trumpets, trombones, and percussion. Conversely, oboes, bassoons, and French horns are generally in short supply. This imbalance is due in part to the emphasis in school programs on jazz ensembles and marching bands. In the orchestral string family, there is a lack of violas and contrabasses, although this varies with the particular scenario. These deficiencies relate to the transfer of violin players to the viola, which sometimes does not happen, and the development of bass players is not always a priority. Careful planning and some foresight on the part of the conductor could remedy these instrumentation problems in today's ensembles.

POTENTIAL DYNAMIC RANGES OF THE INSTRUMENTS

In many instances the reason for poor balance in the instrumental music ensemble is *the players are unaware of or insensitive to this potential dynamic range* in relationship to the other instruments in the ensemble. The conductor must strive to develop this awareness and sensitivity in the players. For example, the dynamic potential of the trumpet is much greater than that of the flute. The trumpet player must be sensitive to this aspect of balance. The percussion section has the potential to overpower the entire ensemble. Part of the problem here is placing the percussion section at the back or to the left side of the ensemble, where hearing the other players in the ensemble is difficult. In some instances, the conductor simply accepts poor balance with the percussion section because this is so common in the ensemble sonority.

One way for the conductor to envision this balance problem is that if every part were marked at the same dynamic level, certain instruments would probably sound too prominent in the ensemble fabric, because of their potential dynamic range. For example, in the performance of a classical symphony, the trumpet, horn, and timpani dynamic level would overpower if played at the same conceived dynamic level marking as the rest of the ensemble. Therefore, the conductor must be aware of this and find ways of counteracting this inherent problem in the instrumental music ensemble. During the rehearsal process, the conductor should insist on the dynamic balance that will enhance the ensemble performance and coincide with the intent of the composer.

A fortissimo level in the brass family tends *to have different connotations* to the player than it does in the woodwind family, because of the potential dynamic range of the brass instruments. Therefore, the conductor must make the players aware of this problem and insist on making certain adjustments dynamically. Allowing a specific instrument, a whole section, or an entire family of instruments to play too strongly within the instrumental music ensemble will lead to considerable balance problems and certainly ruin the balance for the concert performance. This is not to say that in the orchestra, the string family is not the core of the ensemble or in the band, that the woodwind or brass family is not the core of this group at any given point. Rather, the music itself dictates the balance, based on the importance of the various assigned parts in the orchestration. The conductor should control and reinforce this structural, chordal, or sectional balance during the rehearsal process.

There appears to be more danger of poor balance *at the louder dynamic levels.* Some of this is due to the players not listening or adjusting at these louder dynamic levels. It is particularly noticeable on a crescendo as the dynamic potential of the various instruments "kick in," and such instruments as the trumpet, the trombone, and the percussion section begin to "win the battle." Loud, sustained horn passages can also cover important parts in the rest of the ensemble; likewise, the brass will tend to be harsh in loud passages in terms of the tone quality. Woodwinds and strings are hopelessly inferior in dynamic strength to the brass and percussion in loud passages. Louder string playing can be produced at the frog and/or with more frequent bow changes, but this may result in undesirable tone quality and with difficulty in the phrasing. The conductor should make the players aware of this problem concerning poor balance with loud dynamics during the rehearsal process in preparation for the concert performance.

The instrument registers, in conjunction with dynamic level potential, are also a factor as to whether a particular instrument can project the tone as needed. An example is the flute in the low register, in which it is difficult for the player to project a solo line even above a thinly scored accompaniment. The brass players have the inherent problem of overpowering the rest of the ensemble in their upper register due to the added effort of the applied air stream necessary to achieve these higher notes. Controlling the dynamic level in the upper register must be a priority for the brass player. The combination of dynamics and registers on the various instruments needs to be a concern for the conductor in producing a well-balanced ensemble.

STRUCTURAL BALANCE IN THE ENSEMBLE

In its simplest form, the structural balance involves the problem of *melody versus accompaniment.* As a performance rule, the melody must project above the accompaniment. The melody might exist in one or several instruments, one section, or within a family of instruments, such as in the string choir. Likewise, the accompaniment might reside in several different sections of the ensemble. A strategy to employ here is to mark the melody up one dynamic level or the accompaniment one dynamic level lower from the original marking. This could be marked in the parts before rehearsals begin or during the rehearsal process.

The conductor must constantly be aware of playing the melody prominently and not covering it up by the accompaniment. The negative circumstance of the accompaniment obliterating the melody occurs in performances more often than is realized. In a more complex musical form, several lines may need to project at various levels, or in some cases a poor decision may have been made as to which line is important. These balance problems are judgment calls on the part of the conductor, made after serious and careful study of the musical score and astute listening during the rehearsal process. Sometimes, however, the conductor neglects the inner voices in an effort to project the melody. Sustained chords may cover the melodic line also.

The main consideration in terms of structural balance is those instrumental parts in the ensemble *that either need to be projected or subordinated.* The conductor must take great care that structural balance in a musical selection is accomplished. Structural balance must be geared toward bringing out what should be heard. In score study, the conductor will make some decisions about which part(s) should be the most prominent. The conductor asking the ensemble during the rehearsal process to bring out the moving parts can be an initial step to setting up the proper structural balance. Structural balance is both a conductor and a player responsibility and problem. The conductor must strive to emphasize the important parts in the rehearsal process in preparation for a successful concert performance. Subsequently, the player must make musical decisions about the importance of the assigned part and learn to adjust the dynamic level for the proper balance with the rest of the ensemble. This musical sensitivity by the player can save considerable rehearsal time as well. The conductor can save rehearsal time at the beginning by asking the ensemble this question, "How important is your part at any given moment in the music?" This will help make the player aware of the structural balance and of his or her responsibility to make these decisions. The conductor and players might think in terms of layers of sound to envision the proper structural balance. However, the inner parts (or lines) that move might need to be played more prominently as well.

CHORDAL BALANCE IN THE ENSEMBLE

The chordal balance, whether the chord is long or short, must be a consideration for the conductor. This kind of balance will affect greatly the ensemble sonority. In most cases, the notes of a chord should sound equal in volume. An example of this is playing a chord on the organ. The players achieve much of this good balance through careful listening and adjusting for the proper balance. There might be other situations when a certain note in the chord needs more prominence for phrasing or melodic reasons, but in general, all the notes in a chord need to blend homogeneously. A popular theory today advocates that a chord should *be produced tonally as in a pyramid (or trapezoidal) fashion* with the bass note being the most prominent and the other notes above then played proportionately softer as the parts get higher. Final chords of a piece often do not balance well, especially in the case of loud chords or at loud dynamic levels.

One of the most abused balance problems occurs within a section *when the strong players are all on the first part.* Here the note is usually higher (tessitura) and will project with the result that the other parts are barely heard, if at all. The conductor must design teaching strategies to make the players aware of these problems, and thereby become more sensitive in their playing. Again, by stressing the idea of careful listening and adjusting dynamically to the other parts in the ensemble, the conductor can achieve better chordal balance. Isolating chords and adjusting the balance are activities that need to take place in the instrumental music ensemble rehearsal process. The conductor can foster some awareness regarding ensemble balance during the warm-up period through playing chords, lyric pieces, and chorales. Blend is a strong consideration in solving these problems.

Solving the problems of exposed or transparent passages in music is one of the situations that demands careful attention by the conductor. In many cases, the problem is not only one of balance, but also of clarity, precision, and intonation. We find that many of these transparency problems exist in contemporary music. The conductor should solve these problems in the rehearsal process because these transparencies are so "touchy" for the players and so noticeable to the listening audience. Unless the conductor rehearses such passages meticulously, the ensemble will present the concert performance negatively to the audience. The conductor should check the doubling of solo lines by several instruments for pitch, rhythm, phrasing, and so forth. Specific examples of this are unison and octave passages in the woodwinds and strings, or perhaps with the correct partials production on the brass instruments.

SECTIONAL BALANCE IN THE ENSEMBLE

Good balance (and blend) starts within each section of the ensemble and then combines with the other sections. This suggests a rehearsal strategy to improve the balance aspect beginning by getting each section balanced (and blended) and then balancing the various sections. Therefore, sectional balance has two aspects to consider: (1) balance within each section, and (2) balance among the various sections of the ensemble. With this approach, the concern is that each section must be balanced (and blended) whether there are a single part or several parts within the section. After employing this procedure, then apply the second procedure of balance and blend among the various sections in terms of the selected repertoire.

The control of the balance within a section assumes playing more than one part at a time. However, if the section is a single part, the conductor must also consider the blend among the players. Therefore, a single player predominating would also require some remedial attention from the conductor. This sectional balance could also be the same as chordal balance. Especially in the brass family sections, the danger of poor balance exists because of the high tones (which require more physical effort to produce) being projected too strongly. The conductor frequently assigns the first part in a section to the more competent players; they tend to play the part more aggressively. I advocated previously for having more players on the lower parts to balance the projection of the first part. Ultimately, the balance within the section depends on the skill of the players to control the dynamic levels (as well as the musical sensitivity) with the other players in the section. *Each section needs to strive for "section pride."*

The conductor can and should control the balance among the various sections of the ensemble by gestures and/or specific instructions in the rehearsal process. The left-hand palm held upward to a section indicates increasing the volume. The left-hand palm turned downward indicates that a particular section should decrease the volume. This, of course, assumes that the players are watching the conductor for guidance. If the players do not respond to these gestures, then the conductor must stop and verbally explain his or her intentions to the players, followed by repetition of the passages until achieving the proper balance. Again, if the ensemble is listening and sensitive to the surrounding sonority, rehearsal time can be saved in adjusting the balance among the various sections. *The conductor must take this responsibility for the balance among the sections* because of the conceived musical interpretation through score study and from the position on the podium that allows the conductor a better aural perspective of the total ensemble balance than it does for the individual player within the ensemble.

ENSEMBLE BALANCE IN THE REHEARSAL PROCESS

In the rehearsal process, the conductor has three basic options in controlling the balance of the ensemble: (1) through the conducting patterns of the right hand, (2) through the gestures of the left hand, and (3) by verbal comments directed to the appropriate section or individuals of the ensemble. The sectional rehearsal can be of value in adjusting the balance within the individual section, but the full ensemble rehearsal process will give the conductor the opportunity to adjust the balance among the various sections and families. The conductor must act as a catalyst in controlling the dynamic levels of the various sections during the rehearsal process in preparation for the concert performance. Finally, after achieving good balance within each section of the ensemble, *place the focus on the balance among the various sections of the ensemble.* In a sense, what must eventually happen in the rehearsal process is a progression of improved balance and sensitivity from the individual players, to within the section, to among the various sections, to the family (or choir), and finally to the whole ensemble. The conductor should evaluate the balance of the ensemble in the rehearsal process in terms of this progression.

Throughout much of music history, *the composer has left the problems of balance to the conductor and players.* It is necessary in many cases to edit the dynamic levels to achieve the proper balance. This editing, for the most part, should take place before the rehearsals begin in order to save time during the rehearsal process. However, the conductor cannot anticipate everything. In the rehearsal process, the player should be prepared to change these dynamic levels in the music in order to achieve the proper balance. At least through the classical period in music, composers marked all the instrumental parts at the same dynamic level in a given passage. It was then the total responsibility of the conductor and players to adjust the balance in order to achieve the proper musical interpretation of the given work.

Table 10.2, Teaching Strategy (Ensemble Balance), shown at the end of the chapter, gives some ideas and suggestions for designing a teaching strategy to improve the ensemble balance.

ENSEMBLE BLEND, TONE COLOR, AND TEXTURE

Ensemble Blend

I define blend as the relationship between two or more instrumental voices. When good blend occurs, the sound between the two or more players has a likeness in quality, volume, and pitch. It is certainly necessary to have this blend when two or more players are playing on the same part. Likewise, if there were two or more players on different parts, the music would dictate the nature of this blend. As a part of a sustained chord, there should be a blend and balance of the instrumental parts. In terms of sectional balance and ensemble sonority, the problems of blend should be foremost in the minds of the conductor and players. In many instances, striving for good blend is a secondary goal in instrumental music ensembles. This should not be the case; blend is an important and significant factor in the ensemble sonority. With this idea in mind, there are circumstances throughout almost any musical selection where blend is a very important factor for the instrumental music ensemble as well as for the musical interpretation.

Sensitivity to blend is an important consideration. If the player is duplicating a part with one or several other players on the same instrument, then there is no doubt that blend is crucial. We want the part to sound as if it were one player. If the player has a part to project as a melodic line, then blend is not necessarily appropriate. The exception to this is when the players are performing a solo line with several different instruments; then the matching of pitch, tone quality, and dynamic level is necessary among these soloists. The player needs to be sensitive to the other instruments playing the same solo line to adjust the tone quality, intonation, and dynamic level. *Sensitivity to blend is mainly a problem of the conductor listening and then adjusting the sound within the ensemble sonority.*

For many years, it was felt that blend was what the concert band should strive for, while the orchestral ensemble diversified in tone color. This concept has changed considerably due to band composers and arrangers striving to discover more color possibilities within the concert band sonority. The point is that there are places in the music where blend is important and other places to project the tone for structural balance and coloristic purposes. *Projection on an instrument comes through the vibrato, dynamics, and tonal intensity.*

Blend is a very important part of ensemble playing. The conductor must be vigilant to influence players from disrupting the ensemble blend. This usually occurs when the particular instrumentalist is playing too aggressively. With the encouragement of the conductor, players should develop the skill, control, and musical sensitivity to adjust between a passage that calls for a nice blend and one that needs to project to enhance the compositional structure and/or a special tone color within the ensemble.

Balance and blend are frequently connected components of the musical performance. However, with the instrumental ensemble, the final decision about the correct blend and balance must be with the conductor.

Tone projection is somewhat the opposite of blend in the ensemble. This part of ensemble performance would require the player(s) to rise above the ensemble sonority in order to be heard. *Too frequently, the rest of the ensemble covers the melodic line in the ensemble sonority.* The conductor must be aware of this and discourage it in the rehearsal process. The individual player or section of the ensemble can project the tone in many ways. Tone projection occurs through the employment of vibrato, tonal intensity, and stronger dynamics. Tone projection is an important part of ensemble performance and in achieving the proper ensemble sonority.

Table 10.3, Teaching Strategy (Ensemble Blend, Tone Projection and Color, and Texture Contrast), at the end of the chapter, furnishes ideas and suggestions for designing a teaching strategy to improve ensemble blend and tone projection.

Tone Color and Texture Contrast

Although I have devoted much of this chapter to ensemble tone, balance, and blend in the instrumental music ensemble, the conductor must not ignore the ideas of tone color and texture contrast. A performance without this color and texture contrast can be a rather bland and uninspiring one. There are numerous ways to achieve this tone color and texture contrast: by dynamics, style, orchestration, instrumentation, and changing the tone color or texture, and throughout by emphasizing the various lines. Balance and blend in the instrumental ensemble sound are very necessary, but these must not be the only ingredients. *Contrasts in tone color and texture should also be a necessary priority for the conductor in the rehearsal process.* Through the selected repertoire, the conductor can realize this tone color and texture contrast in the rehearsal process and in the concert performance as well.

At first, the younger ensemble needs to learn blending the tones to make a homogenized sound. However, at some point the conductor must present and foster the idea of tone color contrast in performance. The composer or arranger dictates the tone color for a given work; it is then the conductor's duty to realize this orchestration during the rehearsal process. In the rehearsal process, the conductor must strive to bring out as much tone color contrast as possible for the interest and excitement of the player and for the listener in realizing the musical interpretation. Mutes are one way to achieve tone color contrast in the brass. In the strings, the use of mutes, bow placement on the string (sul tasto or sul ponticello), and passages played on one string such as G or D can contrast the tone color. The use of vibrato (or no vibrato) creatively can enhance the tone color contrast along with that of tonal intensity. Directional instruments (trumpets, cornets, and trombones) can produce tone color contrast by positioning their bells into the stand or above the stand. The conductor must strive to achieve as much tone color contrast as possible in the rehearsal process and then subsequently in the concert performance.

Texture contrast may involve the heaviness, lightness, thickness, or transparency of the orchestration. The complexity of the various lines as well as the performance quality in terms of the style, articulation, tone color, and the dynamic levels conceived may affect the texture contrast. In the rehearsal process, the conductor can explain texture contrast verbally or relate it through visual imagery to the players. The selection of concert repertoire also has a strong bearing on the texture contrast in the concert programming. The complexity of the texture in a work will have a direct effect on the tempo and clarity of the musical line in the performance. In dealing with both tone color and texture contrast, the conductor can be a creative force in the rehearsal process. For example, by raising the bells of directional brass (trumpets, cornets, and trombones), the conductor can achieve this projection of the sound with energy and vitality; conversely, lowering the bells into the stand will allow for quiet playing without resorting to poor breath support and the subsequent intonation problems. This is just one example of what players can do to affect the texture of the ensemble sonority. *The use of soloists and the programming of smaller ensembles* inserted in the concert performance can give the impression of this texture contrast as well.

PRACTICAL APPLICATION (DISCUSSION/DEMONSTRATION)

1. Discuss some ideas about formulating ensemble sonority conceptions in terms of ensemble tone, balance, blend, color, and texture in the rehearsal process.
2. Describe the general ensemble sonority concepts for the orchestra, the chamber orchestra, the string orchestra, the concert band, the wind ensemble, the brass ensemble, the woodwind ensemble, and the percussion ensemble. What should dominate? How will you go about achieving these desired sonorities?
3. Consider the various aspects of individual, section, and choir sonority.
4. Discuss the elements involved with ensemble sonority. (See figure 10.1.)
5. List some of the tone control problems that you (as a conductor) might expect to encounter during the rehearsal process. (See Appendix C.)
6. Discuss the three types of ensemble balance (structural, chordal, and sectional).
7. Why is it so important for the conductor to "solve these transparencies" in the rehearsal process? (Musical Example)
8. What teaching strategies would you use in order to achieve better ensemble tone and control?
9. What teaching strategies would you use to achieve better ensemble balance and blend?
10. What teaching strategies would you use to achieve better tone color and texture contrast?
11. Continue to gain familiarity with the standard repertoire found in Appendix A through CD listening, score study, and guidance from the conducting teacher. (See Appendix G for assignment forms.)

IN THE REHEARSAL PROCESS (LAB) ENVIRONMENT

1. Demonstrate ways to brighten and darken the ensemble tone. (Musical Example)
2. Demonstrate procedures for achieving proper balance with the ensemble (structural, chordal, and sectional).

3. Demonstrate the use of vibrato for enhancing ensemble tone.
4. What ways or procedures would you use in balancing the instrumentation of the ensemble? Demonstrate these procedures.
5. What ways or procedures would you use for developing blend within the ensemble? Demonstrate these procedures.
6. What should the conductor do or say to make the players more aware of what to listen for in terms of the general ensemble sonority?
7. What should the conductor do or say to make the players more aware of ensemble tone color and texture contrast?
8. Complete student conducting/rehearsing projects (in the rehearsal process lab environment).

RECOMMENDING READING

Green, Elizabeth A. H. *The Dynamic Orchestra.* Chapter 1: Sound (The Ear) and with an important summary on pp. 57, 58, and 59.
Janzen, Eldon A., *The Band Director's Survival Guide.* Chapter 7: Analyzing the Sound of Wind Groups and Chapter 8: Teaching the Concert Band Sound.
Kahn, Emil, *Conducting.* Chapters 11 through 16 address various aspects of the tone produced in the orchestra or band ensemble.
Kennan, Kent, *Orchestration.* This is one of the standard books used in college orchestration courses. The book represents an overview.
Kohut, Daniel L., *Instrumental Music Pedagogy* (paperback version). Chapter 8: Ensemble Rehearsal Procedure under D. Wind-Percussion Tone Color.
Kohut, Daniel L., *Musical Performance: Learning Theory and Pedagogy.* Part III (chapters 9–12) focuses on tone production.
Long, R. Gerry, *The Conductor's Workshop: A Workbook on Instrumental Conducting.* Chapter 4: Orchestral Balance is a rather short chapter but makes some significant points about the problems of ensemble balance.
Prausnitz, Frederik, *Score and Podium (A Complete Guide to Conducting).* Chapter 14: Players and Orchestra investigates the role of the player in the orchestra, and emphasizes ensemble sonority.
Rimsky-Korsakov, Nicolas, *Principles of Orchestration.* Part I, chapters 1–4, address the problems of sonority in the orchestra. Part II provides full scores from some of Rimsky-Korsakov's compositions.

REPERTOIRE FOR PROJECTS AND ASSIGNMENTS

Full Orchestra, Chamber Orchestra, or String Orchestra

Bach: Suite No. 3 in D Major (2 oboes, 3 trumpets, timpani, continuo, and strings)
Beethoven: Egmont Overture
Brahms: Academic Festival Overture
Dukas: The Sorcerer's Apprentice
Glinka: Russlan and Ludmilla Overture

Concert Band or Wind Ensemble

Bennett: Suite of Old American Dances (various movements)
Dello Joio: Variants on a Medieval Tune (various movements)
Giovannini: Overture in B-flat
Hanson: Chorale and Alleluia
Jenkins: American Overture for Band

Miscellaneous or Small Ensembles

Ellis, Merrill: Mutations (for brass quintet, film, tape, and slides)
Milhaud: La création du monde (chamber orchestra: no viola)

TEACHING STRATEGY TABLES

Table 10.1.   Ensemble Tone Production and Tone Control

CONDUCTOR CONCERNS	PROBLEM AREAS	TEACHING STRATEGIES
Producing the characteristic tone on the instrument	Ensemble tone production	Strive for good individual tone quality; achieve correct tone production from the ensemble.
Ensemble sonority development		Encourage beautiful, controlled ensemble tone production.
Good balance and blend		Work on ensemble tone in the warm-up period with chorales and lyric pieces.
Good intonation Tone control		Encourage the securing of good equipment (and maintaining it in satisfactory condition).
Structural, sectional, and chordal balance		Strive for good balance and blend in the rehearsal process to improve ensemble tone and the ensemble sonority.
Tone projection The ensemble tone not forced or strident		Strive to achieve good intonation; the relationship between the ensemble tone and intonation is crucial.
	Ensemble tone control	Encourage the ensemble to play with an aggressive sound but always with good tone control.
Ensemble sonority concepts A clear conception by the conductor of the ensemble sonority		Do not sanction forced, strident, and uncontrolled playing.
		Always strive for warmth in the various sounds produced and good ensemble tone production and control.
Vibrato application (tone projection)		With good tone control, the players can then produce many of the performance aspects properly.
Tone color and texture contrast		With good tone control, the player is able to conform to the rest of the ensemble in producing the desired sonority.

Table 10.1. (*continued*)

	PROBLEM AREAS	TEACHING STRATEGIES
	Ensemble sonority	Use modeling and imitation with live performances and recordings to develop the concept of good ensemble sonority.
		The conductor should have a clear concept of what the overall ensemble sonority should be.
		The proper use of vibrato can enliven the ensemble sonority. However, this vibrato use must always be tasteful. Make the vibrato a part of the tone.
		Sonority balance is an important part of ensemble tone production and control. Stress tone production and control in the rehearsal process.
		Stress the idea of blend in order to achieve tone color contrast as well as texture.
What other teaching strategies (suggested by the conducting teacher or students) could improve ensemble sonority?		

Table 10.2.   Ensemble Balance

CONDUCTOR CONCERNS	PROBLEM AREAS	TEACHING STRATEGIES
Ensemble balance (playing sensitively and listening to the other parts)	Instrumentation	Strive for an ideal standard instrumentation sufficient to cover all of the parts adequately.
Parts distribution		Place more players within a section on the lower parts for better ensemble balance.
Structural balance (melody vs. accompaniment)	Playing ability	When possible, player personnel should be of similar playing ability and performance level.
Sectional balance (within and among the sections)		Place strong players on each of the parts within the section.
Chordal balance	Ensemble balance	Make the players aware of the various problems and solutions that are involved in good ensemble balance.
What is the importance of each individual part in the music?		Compare the ensemble balance in "tutti" passages to that of an organist sustaining chords. (The idea of chordal balance with more players on the lower parts such as 2 on first, 4 on second, and 6 on third is a worthwhile concept.)
Dynamic levels (dynamic contrast and relativity)		

(*continued*)

Table 10.2. (*continued*)

CONDUCTOR CONCERNS	PROBLEM AREAS	TEACHING STRATEGIES
Transparent passages (rehearsed carefully) Always listen for the melody Sustained or accompanying parts covering the melody Consider how to bring out the moving parts	Ensemble balance (*continued*)	The conductor must encourage careful listening and sensitive playing to improve the ensemble balance.
		Listen down to the bottom of the ensemble for better balance, but rehearse from the bottom upward for better balance.
		Divide the players with good leadership ability among the various parts in a section.
		Make players aware of the structural balance by playing the melody, countermelody, and accompaniment separately in order to make the players aware of the importance of their parts.
		Request that players consider how important their part is at any given moment as to whether they must back off or project the part.
	Dynamic level	Sustained notes may cover up a moving part; have the sustained notes back off and/or project the melody or moving parts.
		The idea of "if you cannot hear the melodic line, you are playing too strongly" is a worthwhile concept for helping with the balance among the parts and with the players.
		Judge balance from a distance by getting away from the ensemble—as within the audience area to listen and judge the balance.
What other teaching strategies (suggested by the conducting teacher or students) could improve ensemble balance?		

Table 10.3. Ensemble Blend, Tone Projection and Color, and Texture Contrast

CONDUCTOR CONCERNS	PROBLEM AREAS	TEACHING STRATEGIES
Working on blend in the warm-up period Playing chorales and lyric pieces to improve blend Calling attention to passages that need blend during the rehearsal process	Ensemble blend	Work on ensemble blend during the warm-up period with chorales and sustained chords.
		Play chorales and other lyric pieces to improve the blend.
		Strive to develop good ensemble blend within each section and within each choir (strings, woodwinds, and brass, as well as the percussion section).

Table 10.3. (*continued*)

CONDUCTOR CONCERNS	PROBLEM AREAS	TEACHING STRATEGIES
Tone projection sonority Vibrato, dynamics, and intensity for tone projection Tone color with the directional instruments Thinking of the color spectrum in varying this tone color Darkening and brightening of a chord Considering the thickness of the orchestration Using soloists and small ensembles to achieve this texture contrast	Tone projection	In contrast to the blend, the tone projection is involved with solo playing within the ensemble.
		There may be other situations where an entire section or choir will need to be projected.
		Tone projection is produced with the air on wind instruments, the bow stroke, bow speed, and bow pressure with strings, and the stroke intensity on the percussion instruments.
		Enhance tone projection with vibrato and tonal intensity, and through the various selected dynamic levels.
	Ensemble tone color contrast	Create contrast in the ensemble tone color by raising the bell above the stand or by lowering the bell into the stand with the directional instruments (trumpets and trombones).
		In terms of tone color, the conductor should think about the color spectrum and such qualities as light, dark, vibrant, brilliant, sonorous, mysterious, etc.
		The percussion section, when played sensitively, can enhance the tone color of the ensemble.
		Having the lower-pitched instruments project stronger will darken a chord.
		Players should learn to darken or brighten the sound by various physical techniques on their individual instruments.
	Ensemble texture contrast	Realize the texture contrast by following the composer's indications closely.
		Texture contrast involves the thickness of the orchestration as well as the dynamic level.
		In thinly scored passages, clarity, technical accuracy, and intonation of the individual lines become very important rehearsal aspects.
What other teaching strategies (suggested by the conducting teacher or students) are there for blend, tone projection and color/texture contrast?		

Chapter Eleven

Articulation and Bowing

WIND AND PERCUSSION ARTICULATION

Articulation pertains to *how we enunciate* in musical performance. The beginning of a note may be forcefully played or barely perceptible. There are many degrees between these two extremes. Articulation on the wind instruments includes the options of tonguing and slurring notes. Articulation on the string instruments relates to the use of the bow and bowing styles. Articulation on the percussion instruments involves the selection of sticks and mallets as well as the strength of the stroke and where to place the stroke on the instrument. The conductor must be aware of all of these possibilities, and communicate to the players in the rehearsal process the articulation according to the musical indications and emotional content of the music.

When terms such as leggiero, scherzo, or delicately appear at the beginning of a passage, the conductor must insist on light articulation. The conductor should show this lightness of articulation with a small pattern (using the wrist and without much forearm tension or movement in the patterns). Likewise, if terms such as marcato, pesante, or forceful appear in the music, the conductor must show a larger, stronger beat pattern to indicate heavier articulation. The conductor can show the ensemble other aspects of articulation, such as tenuto, in which the beat pattern must have an extremely lucid motion with strong definition of the ictus. In general, the conductor should indicate the weight and style of the articulation with right-hand patterns in the same way in which conductors usually communicate dynamic levels to the players. The left-hand gestures can also reinforce the articulations shown by the conducting patterns in the right hand.

As with all conducting patterns and gestures, the conductor must communicate clearly before the articulations occur. The conductor should be able to show with patterns and gestures the strength differences between this regular accent > and the "caret" (^) accent. The conductor must show stronger accents such as the *sforzando* with even more exaggerated gestures before they occur. The stylistic conducting patterns of staccato, legato, marcato, and tenuto can influence the ensemble performance dramatically if the players are watching and responding to these conducting patterns and gestures. If the conductor indicates these articulations clearly and the players do not respond adequately to these patterns and gestures, then additional verbal comments and detailed work in the rehearsal process may be necessary.

An important vocal technique for the conductor to develop is the *articulation of very fast, rhythmic passages in modeling or demonstrating* these passages for the ensemble during the rehearsal process. This is workable with the use of double- or triple-tonguing vocal articulations. The double-tonguing vocal articulation uses the syllables of "ta-ka," while the triple tonguing uses "ta-ta-ka." Many occasions will arise when this type of vocal presentation is effective in the rehearsal process. Likewise, employ the use of various vocal syllables for emphasis or accents in modeling to demonstrate the variety of articulation possible with the instrumental ensemble. Such vocal syllables as "tee," "tah," "du," or variations of these syllables can be used for reinforcing these articulations. This kind of modeling and demonstration will require the conductor to be innovative and creative.

SLURRING IN WIND ARTICULATION

The other problematic consideration in wind articulation involves slurring notes. Here the options are less problematic, once the player starts the initial note of the slur. However, one glaring problem occurs frequently in slurring, pertaining to the final note of a slur. *There seems to be a natural tendency to shorten the value of this last note of the slur.* The result is an abrupt, unmusical effect. Players must make an effort to play this final note of the slur with sufficient duration. In fast passages, this problem can lead to an uneven sound and may even distort the rhythmic aspect of the passage. This problem might seem to be a minor consideration, but many technical passages are played poorly due to this distortion involving the very last note of the slurred articulation.

Slurring marks and phrase marks can be easily confused. In some instances, the conductor will need to make these decisions for the ensemble. If there are double markings in the music, then the longer marks will indicate a phrase, while the shorter marks will show the articulations in the phrase. Romantic period composers tended to use the phrase mark, especially in the string parts. (Here it is necessary for the concertmaster or conductor to place the bowings in the parts indicating these bowing changes during the phrase.) The conductor must oversee that the wind players are executing the articulation as indicated by the composer in the music. In very early music (Renaissance and Baroque), few articulations were ever shown. The players were expected to supply these articulations. In some instances, this has allowed modern editors of these works to overstep their boundaries. In general, players should perform the articulation uniformly within the ensemble and consistently from passage to passage. (One exception occurs when the composer has intentionally articulated the strings and the winds differently on the same passage.)

AFFECTED PRIORITIES IN ARTICULATION

Poor articulation can be a reason for precision problems, especially within the performance of rapid tempos. The conductor needs to know the limitations that the players have on a particular instrument in terms of articulation speed. This may necessitate a change of articulation in order to negotiate the passage properly and precisely. With the brass instruments, flute, and piccolo, the conductor might request the use of double or triple tonguing or possibly slurring two notes and tonguing two notes in a series of four fast-articulated notes. With woodwind instruments, the conductor might suggest slurring in groups of four or even slurring the whole series of notes together. However, these articulation changes must be done carefully so as not to negate the composer's intentions or render the passage unmusical.

The tone production can deteriorate with the articulation of fast, short notes. The action of the tongue in wind playing coupled with the air stream *will affect the quality of the tone production.* In general, the player must be aware of this danger with fast articulation and compensate for this problem with a more legato approach so that the tone remains firm and secure. As fast articulation requirements occur, the player must adjust the process of "tonguing" on the wind instruments to one of lightness and smoothness. The tongue must stay relaxed so that fast or light articulation will be possible. When playing loud on fast, articulated passages it may be necessary to decrease the volume slightly in order to play musically. In fast-tongued passages, there is a tendency to try to shorten the note length, but the player should instead play the notes smoothly to avoid a rather brittle and unmusical articulation.

There is a rather close relationship between articulation, style, and general musical expression. In confronting articulation problems in the rehearsal process, the conductor needs to consider this relationship. In executing the articulation, there are two main concerns: the beginning of the note (attack) or its continuation to the next note (as in slurring). The four basic styles in musical performance are staccato, legato, tenuto, and marcato. In executing these styles, there are three major considerations: (1) the beginning (articulation), (2) the end (duration), and (3) the needed emphasis (weight). The musical expression relationship relates to this emphasis and the emotional aspects of performing music. In this context, it is apparent that articulation, style, and musical expression *are a complete and total package.* The players should make constant adjustments of the articulation so that it is compatible with the demands of the music. Part of what the conductor must show in the conducting patterns and gestures or address verbally in the rehearsal process concerning articulation, by its very nature, will involve stylistic and musical expression considerations. I address these matters in detail in Chapter 14: Style and Musical Interpretation.

It is literally impossible to separate articulation from phrasing because both affect dramatically the interpretation of the music. When the conductor verbalizes to the ensemble about the articulation, it is difficult to avoid referring to the length of the notes and the shape or decay of these notes. Certainly, these phrasing considerations largely determine the shape and decay of notes. In particular, the degree of accent or emphasis presents problems for the conductor and players in musical performance. The conductor must show these accents (on and off the beat) before they occur, and the players will need to execute these accents within the context of the music. In confronting the problems of phrasing, the conductor must consider the beginning of the note, the decay (or lack of decay) of the note, and the end of the note to produce the proper style. An example of this is the baroque string style, in which there is little or no decay but some spacing between notes of longer duration because of the type of bow used in that particular musical period.

INACCURACIES IN ARTICULATION

One of the many problems that occur frequently in the rehearsal process is the inaccurate performance of articulations. Philip Farkas, in his *Art of Musicianship*, states that you can only do two things to notes in wind performance, that is, either tongue them or slur them (1976, 29.). This seems simple enough. However, this particular inaccuracy problem exists within many ensembles. For example, if there are only four notes slurred in a passage, then the player must slur only four notes. This problem usually occurs because the player, distracted by other music reading items, does not observe the articulation written in the music or else is simply careless in performing the correct articulation. The teaching strategy here must be *to make the player aware of these articulation inaccuracies.* By pointing out these errors when they occur, the conductor should encourage the player to be more concerned and meticulous about this performance aspect.

Causes of poor articulation on initial attacks can be technical problems, such as tongue position, tight throat, restriction of the air stream, and the lack of reed response (woodwinds) or lip response (embouchure) on the brass instruments. Excessive or hard tonguing results in an explosive or unmusical attack accompanied by the possibility of "splitting" the tone and losing the tone control as found with the brass instruments. With younger ensembles, there is a tendency to tongue too strongly, resulting in poor tone production. Along with this comes tone distortion and poor intonation. The tongue position must be checked and perhaps an adjustment should be made to a "la" or "da" rather than a "ta." Such strong articulation occurs frequently at loud dynamic levels. With percussionists, the initial attack problem may be a visibility problem, and they may need to position the instruments for better sight lines. The cause of poor ensemble articulation and precision on the initial attack may also be an unclear preparatory beat execution by the conductor, or the ensemble members are not watching the conductor carefully enough. The players need to breathe with this initial preparatory beat.

TWO ARTICULATION CONSIDERATIONS

No matter how many notes may be slurred together, the last note of the slur will tend to be shortened excessively. The player must take care that this last note of the slur does not lose its tone quality or pitch. This final note of the slur may affect the tempo and rhythm of the passage. In very fast rhythmic or technical passages, abruptness at the end of the slur may lead to a distortion of the rhythm pattern. The solution is to be aware of this problem and give enough duration to this final note of the slur so that it does not distort the rhythmic aspect, the tone quality, or pitch of this last note and/or the articulation of the following note.

The question arises as to how short a note can be played without the distortion of pitch and quality. Many conductors keep asking the ensemble for shorter and/or crisper articulations. The conductor must not carry this to ridiculous lengths. It is important for the players to be aware of these limits in terms of musicality. Wind instrumentalists must temper fast-tongued passages with good breath support and a relaxed, legato tonguing process. Otherwise, the pitch and tone quality of the passage will be unacceptable musically. The tongue release is effective on the woodwind instruments, but the brass player should use the tongue release only in extreme cases to shorten the note length. If the composer intended mostly a percussive effect without much regard for pitch and tone quality, then the players might be justified in using a tongue release, producing an articulation that is somewhat void of good pitch and tone quality. This occurs very infrequently, however.

ARTICULATION TERMS AND MARKINGS

Many musical terms influence the degree of articulation. The conductor should develop a working vocabulary of these terms and be able to relay their meaning to the players in terms of the proper articulation. Of course, many of these terms are also style and musical expression indications. The conductor should not assume that the players know these terms. The following are common terms that affect the articulation and should be discussed and demonstrated:

Legato—Smooth and sustained
Staccato—Detached and light
Marcato—Detached and heavy
Tenuto—Held, sustained for full value
Alla marcia—In the style of a march
Cantabile—In a singing style
Decisivo—Decisively
Delicatamente—Dainty; light articulation
Dolce—Sweet, smooth, gentle
Drammatico—Dramatic, somewhat exaggerated
Elegante—Graceful, polished
Grandioso—Grand, noble
Maestoso—Majestic, stately
Pesante—Heavy, ponderous
Leggiero—Light, delicate
Rinforzando (*Rinf.*)—Reinforced, accented
Scherzando—Jesting, playful

This list could be much longer and include equivalent terms in other languages as well as Italian. Consult a music dictionary when a term is unknown. Remember that the composer has placed a term in the music to guide and influence the articulation and style as well as the musical interpretation of the work. I supply this brief listing simply to point out the importance of knowing and being aware of these terms in how they affect the interpretation of a musical work.

Besides musical terms to indicate the articulation, expression markings in the music guide the conductor and players. The following are some of the markings that influence the articulation and should be discussed and demonstrated:

Staccato dot
Staccatissimo mark
Legato mark
Sostenuto (*sost.*)
Tenuto (*ten.*)
Accent (normal)
Strong accent (caret)
Sforzando (*sfz*)
Rinforzando (*rinf.*)
Forte-piano (*fp*)
Sforzato(*sf*)
Slur mark with staccato dots (slurred staccato)
Slur mark with legato marks (slurred tenuto)
Slur mark with accents (slurred accents)
Tenuto/staccato marks (tenuto staccato)

ARTICULATION ELEMENTS

Just as in the consideration of style, the start of the note, the length of note, and the end of the note must be considerations in proper articulation. The start of the note may begin very gently, very forcefully, or with various degrees between these two extremes. *The length of a note will depend on the rhythmic value of the note, the general style of the passage, and/or the articulation marking shown in the music.* The weight of the note depends upon the dynamic level, the music expression marking, or where it might occur within the phrase. The basic style and the dynamic level may influence the end of the note also. The conductor must consider the various aspects of articulation in score study and reinforce them with the players during the rehearsal process.

PRODUCTION OF ARTICULATION

Some notes should decay quickly, while others will have little decay. Decisions about the decay of notes must be based on the style, articulation markings, the musical period, and the conductor's judgment. The conductor and players should work together to develop as much variety in articulation and style as possible to meet the musical demands of the composer. This decay of notes is a factor to consider with the elements of both articulation and style. For example, in the baroque string style there is very little decay of the notes because the bow remains on the string. The wind instruments must then imitate this style.

The staccato dot or staccatissimo mark relates to the tempo and the style of the piece. This marking is not an absolute. The staccato dot did not become prevalent in music until the Classical period. This is not to say that music before this period was performed only in a semi-legato or legato style. However, composers began to use the dot and other such markings during the time of Haydn and Mozart. If such markings appear in editions of earlier music, it is the work of an editor. The performance of a staccato indication should be with thoughtful consideration and *not simply thinking that the note should be short.* Rather, the staccato dot is an indication of separation from the note that follows, and in most instances also denotes a light attack of the note. In numerous instances, ensembles (and conductors) tend to ignore the staccato dot, and therefore, an incorrect or uneven staccato style occurs within the instrumental music ensemble. Staccatissimo is a sharp and dry staccato.

The legato dash on a note can be interpreted in several ways: (1) sustained full value, (2) increased duration, (3) slight emphasis, (4) a soft, smooth beginning to the note, (5) a sustained sound to the end of the note, or (6) as an indication that the note should be articulated. The decision in articulating a legato dash would depend greatly on the context of the note within the phrase. The conductor should dictate this decision through patterns and gestures or verbally in the rehearsal process. Leaving this decision to the players will invite articulation differences. One of the most difficult styles to achieve within the instrumental music ensemble is *a "true" sustained legato style; players frequently tend to space fast notes.*

The various accent markings are somewhat confusing, and in some cases used inconsistently. The regular or common accent indicates a dynamic change. The notes surrounding the accented note should be softer in volume than the accented note(s). Especially with younger ensembles, there is a tendency to start the note with an explosive attack (by using more tongue force, extreme bow pressure, or an inordinate amount of percussion stroke) instead of the next dynamic louder to realize the marked accent. The "caret" accent (^) when compared to the regular accent, generally means that it should be played more strongly than the regular accent. All of this is relative to the context of the note in the music. In some instances, there might be a space before the accent. The caret accent is sometimes interpreted to be a shorter duration (such as in jazz interpretation), but there is inconsistency in the use and meaning of this accent. Consider this accent to be an indication of highlighting the note. The other accents, such as *sfz* (sforzando), *rfz* (rinforzando), *fp* (forte-piano), and *sf* (sforzato) should be played in good musical taste and are dependent on the musical period and the musical effect desired. In rehearsing the instrumental music ensemble, *the conductor must insist that all the players observe the accents uniformly*; otherwise, the effect is one of unevenness.

The combination of the slur and staccato dot, the slur and legato dash, and the slur and accent are likewise confusing. These articulations do not appear to have universal agreement. Musicians usually interpret the combination of the slur and the staccato dot to be played with a soft attack of somewhat sustained value. The combination of the slur and the legato mark is, perhaps, the most controversial of these combined articulations. The question is whether the notes should be articulated or slurred. The answer probably lies in the context of the music and which way sounds best. There is general agreement that the notes should be sustained full value. However, in string playing, this articulation indicates that the bow should move in one direction only and with the louré style of bowing. The combined articulation of the slur and the accent mark should be slurred with a "pushy" feeling with the breath on each note. The combination of the legato dash and staccato dot are interpreted with a slight space and "lift" to the note on which it appears.

TECHNICAL PERFORMANCE OF ARTICULATION

How these articulations are performed technically on the various instruments must be a concern for the conductor. With young players, the conductor must understand the pedagogical implications of the articulation on various instruments. With a more mature ensemble, the conductor's concern should be with the degree of the articulation as well as the quality of the musical articulation. The young wind player tends to equate the forcefulness of the articulation with the tonguing (or articulation) process. In most instances, the weight of the articulation should be accomplished by using breath on wind instruments. With the percussionist, the motion and the speed of the selected stick or mallet are factors in articulating properly.

It is important for the conductor to make the players aware of the variety of articulations that are possible on the wind, string, and percussion instruments. In the early stages of training an ensemble, the focus is on getting everyone to articulate together (precision). However, as the ensemble matures, the conductor should begin to refine the articulations as they correlate with the demands of the music. These articulations may include everything from a sharp, percussive attack to a very soft "du" beginning of the note. The wind player must learn to adjust this articulation on the particular instrument and still maintain the security and response. The percussionists will need to gain knowledge about the stick and mallet selection, the "hot-stove stroke," the stroke placement on the instrument, and the musical sensitivity to balance and blend with the rest of the ensemble.

It is important for the players to realize that everyone in the ensemble needs to articulate with a similar quality or the results will be erratic and uneven. Uniformity, consistency, and evenness are the keys here. With younger groups, there is a tendency to articulate too forcefully in loud passages. The results are a general loss of tone control, poor ensemble sound, and questionable rhythmic precision. The conductor must indicate to mature players the quality of the sound and/or the evenness of articulation needed on a particular passage. In describing the kinds of articulations needed, the conductor might use such words as lighter, heavier, pointed, softer, forceful, clear, and clean.

SPEED, CLARITY AND PRECISION IN ARTICULATION

Extreme articulation speed becomes a problem of precision. Some players are unable to maintain the required articulation and stay in tempo. The conductor may decide to slow the tempo in order to be playable for the ensemble or suffer the consequences in terms of ensemble precision. Another solution is changing the articulation to alleviate the problem, but apply such procedures with good musical taste. These are difficult choices. However, maintain the tempo selected in the rehearsal into the performance. Tempo changes during the performance could spell disaster. In some cases, it may be necessary to abandon such concert repertoire. An example of this fast articulation problem appears in the final movement of the Rimsky-Korsakov *Scheherazade* where double tonguing and triple tonguing in the brass are frequently required. With this example, it would be impossible to make articulation changes because of the effects and tempos demanded in the movement. Clarity is involved with speed and precision in the musical performance.

As in pronouncing or enunciating words, articulation in musical performance becomes more difficult as the speed increases. The conductor must address clarity and precision of articulation in the rehearsal process. Fast articulation on the various instruments will present problems for the conductor to resolve. In most ensembles, the brass players are expected to have developed the technique of double and triple tonguing in order to perform fast, articulated passages. Woodwind players (except for piccolo and flute, who can use multiple tonguing) generally are not expected to develop multiple-tonguing techniques. If the tempo of the passage is too severe for single tonguing, it may be necessary to change the articulation so that there are fewer continuously articulated notes in order to maintain the selected tempo.

DESIGNING TEACHING STRATEGIES
FOR THE REHEARSAL PROCESS

Table 11.1, Teaching Strategy (Wind Articulation), offers ideas and suggestions for designing a teaching strategy in solving wind articulation problems. Table 11.2, Teaching Strategy (Percussion Playing Techniques), presents ideas and suggestions for designing a teaching strategy in identifying and solving percussion technique problems. Both tables are located at the end of the chapter

BOWINGS AND BOWING STYLES

Bowings and bowing styles are the manner in which string players articulate in music. The conductor of an orchestral ensemble needs to have considerable background in this area. I strongly recommend that the orchestra conductor should have this experience and background on the string instruments. Beyond this, the conductor should acquire pedagogical knowledge on the proper use of the bow and the bowing styles in relationship to the musical periods. With study and consultation, conductors who do not play a string instrument can develop expertise in selecting and dictating bowings and bowing styles. In general, the conductor should make decisions about bowings and bowing styles based on the musical period, on-the-string or off-the-string bowings, part of the bow to use, bow placement on the string, and in consideration of the technical level of the players involved. Tempo, dynamics, note emphasis, and the desired effects influence the bowing and the bowing style choices.

With the orchestral ensemble, the young player needs to be encouraged to use as much bow as possible. The tendency is to be tentative in moving the bow on the string. The result is a less satisfactory tone. The request for a "full bow" is a reminder to the players in producing a good sound. At some point in the rehearsal process, the player may need more information as to the part of the bow to use on a particular passage. The young player should be expected to mark these with a pencil in the music—frog (F), lower half (LH), middle (M), upper half (UH), and tip (T). There are also many other fundamental performance aspects, such as posture, holding the instrument, holding the bow, bow placement on the string, bow pressure and speed, wrist movement, and flexibility of the bow arm along with the related elbow position and motion in bowing that may need attention in the rehearsal process. *These bowings need to be marked in the music by the conductor (or concertmaster) before the rehearsals begin.*

The conductor must know *how using the various bowings and the bowing styles will sound.* The conductor must also be aware of what part of the bow to use to produce the desired sound or to articulate a given passage successfully. Bow pressure and bow speed are also factors that influence the sound produced. The use of the bow near the bridge (sul ponticello) or toward the fingerboard (sul tasto) will moderate the tone quality in contrast to the usual placement of the bow on the string. In asking for certain bowings in the rehearsal process, the conductor must know the technical level of the ensemble to avoid going beyond their present training. On string instruments, the beginning of the tone is often insecure because the bow is not placed on the string delicately to start the note, resulting in a bouncing of the bow off the string on the initial attack. The quality of the attack on string instruments is also dependent on what part of the bow is used. Stronger attacks will demand placing the bow closer to the frog with a down-bow. When a lighter attack is required, the player should place the bow on the string near the tip with an up-bow. Bowing styles should receive some attention in both the warm-up period and when the various bowing styles are required in the music.

BOWINGS ON THE STRING INSTRUMENTS

The down-bow begins the tone closer to the frog of the bow and consequently tends to produce a stronger sound initially. The result of an up-bow is that the tone begins closer to the tip of the bow and the beginning of the tone is softer and less articulate. *The string player should be prepared to use down-bow (⊓) and up-bow (v) in various notational and rhythmic situations.* The conductor, in consultation with the concertmaster and the principal players in the string sections of the orchestra, should determine the bowings before rehearsals begin. During the rehearsals, these bowings may change to accommodate tempo, articulation, phrasing, and dynamics. There are numerous options in bowing a specific passage; the conductor should make a determination based on his or her conception from the musical score. Take care with the cello and bass (at the frog) in that the sound at the beginning of a down-bow is not rough and unmusical, especially in loud passages. There are specific bowing principles to employ in determining up-bow and down-bow. I list these principles below.

Uniformity of bowing within each string part solidifies and organizes the sound produced. In most instances, there should be uniformity of bowing among the various string parts, depending on the rhythmic similarity. However, the cellos and basses may not coincide with the violins and violas, because of the technical characteristics of these instruments or as the various parts demand. There are a few, rare circumstances where "free bowing" may be employed to achieve a more continuous sound, which has been associated with the "Philadelphia" sound defined by that orchestra's former conductor, Leopold Stokowski. Uniformity of bowing ranks as *the single most important aspect of orchestral string performance* and must be specified and reinforced during the rehearsal process. The player should adhere to the printed bowing indications (by the composer or arranger) unless other factors make these bowings less effective. In this case, the conductor or the concertmaster should make a determination to change the bowings to improve the musical effect.

There are specific established bowing principles in orchestral performance. The conductor should be knowledgeable concerning these bowing principles. In order to place bowings in the orchestra music, the conductor should be completely aware of these bowing principles. In chapter 6 of *The Dynamic Orchestra*, Elizabeth A. H. Green (1987, 111–27) provides a comprehensive explanation of bowing uniformity, as follows:

1. The note on the first beat of the measure is down-bow.
2. If there is an odd number of bows before the bar line, start with an up-bow; if there is an even number of bows before the bar line, start with a down-bow.
3. A slur over the bar line is taken down-bow.
4. In repeated rhythmic motifs interspersed with rests, the note present with the greatest stress takes the down-bow.
5. In passage-work of even, unslurred notes, starting on a beat, the first of the four is taken down-bow.
6. When the bowing does not arrive properly on the down-bow, accommodation is usually made by playing the last note of the measure on an extra up-bow.
7. The dotted-eighth-with-sixteenth is generally played on one bow, or "linked," regardless of how it is printed.
8. In 4/4, forte, the isolated syncopated half note, unslurred, is taken on a new down-bow, especially if accented and preceded by an unslurred quarter note.
9. The last note of a crescendo passage (or group of notes, if slurred) is taken up-bow with the climax note on the down-bow.
10. Forte whole-note trills are often played down-up (two bows), in order to sustain the forte throughout.
11. Three- and four-note chords are usually played with a succession of down-bows.
12. The up-bow is used for the beginning of a piece that needs an immediate crescendo on a long note, or for the note(s) before a climax note, on the following bow. The climax note comes down-bow.

There are some exceptions to these bowing principles. Likewise, there are bowings employed by the mature ensemble that a young, inexperienced string player cannot execute. In the case of the fine professional player through the development of good bow control, more options and "artistic" bowings are available. The conductor should acquire many more details in determining these bowings. The concertmaster can be of help to the conductor as to whether the players are capable of executing these "artistic" bowings.

BOWING STYLES ON THE STRING INSTRUMENTS

Types of bowing styles include on-the-string bowings (legato, détaché, martelé, slurred staccato, staccato and louré) and off-the-string bowings (staccato, spiccato, sautillé, staccato volanté, and ricochet). Following are some of the bowing styles to be discussed, demonstrated, and/or shown with a musical example by a proficient string player for the benefit of the conducting student in class:

1. Détaché (on-the string)—to be demonstrated with a musical example
2. Louré or portato (on-the-string)—to be demonstrated with a musical example
3. Tremolo: (bowed and fingered) (on-the-string)—to be demonstrated both ways
4. Martelé (on-the-string)—to be demonstrated with a musical example
5. Slurred staccato (on-the-string)—to be demonstrated with a musical example
6. Staccato (as a generic term: either on-the-string or off-the-string)—to be demonstrated both ways
7. Spiccato or "brush stroke" (off-the-string) to be demonstrated both ways
8. Sautillé (off-the string)—to be demonstrated with a musical example
9. Staccato volanté (off-the-string)—to be demonstrated with a musical example
10. Ricochet (off-the-string)—to be demonstrated with a musical example

The development of bowing styles is crucial in order to convey and execute the musical interpretation and the intentions of the composer. An ensemble that is incapable of producing off-the-string bowing styles may be unable to play works from the classical period through the contemporary period properly. This span of music demands the use of the "brush stroke" or spiccato bowing style on many occasions. Likewise, knowledge concerning the Baroque string style, in which the bow remains on the string but is stopped to produce space between the longer notes, will need to be stressed by the conductor in order to produce this correct musical period style. In both the romantic and contemporary period music, the player must be ready to mix the various bowings and bowing styles as dictated by the composer in order to produce the usual sounds as well as the many unusual special effects modern music demands.

STRING TERMS, TECHNIQUES, AND SPECIAL EFFECTS

All of the following string terms should be part of the vocabulary of the orchestral conductor in order to communicate these to the players in the rehearsal process: divisi, double stops, frog, tip, full bows, shifting positions, hooked or linked bowings, staggered bowings, vibrato, non-vibrato, as it comes, law of compensation, arco, and various types of pizzicato. Likewise, the following terms pertaining to bowing styles and special effects are also part of the orchestral vocabulary for the string student: legato, détaché, martelé, staccato, portato or louré, spiccato, sautillé or saltando, flautando, a punta d'arco, col legno, sul ponticello, sul tasto, repeated notes, successive down-bows or up-bows, starting with the bow on the string, linked or hooked bowing, recovering the bow, chords, modo ordinario, bowed or fingered tremolo, portamento, glissandi, and harmonics (natural and artificial). A string specialist should discuss and demonstrate these and other terms for the benefit of the conducting students.

The conductor needs to be aware of certain other aspects of string playing beyond the bowings and the bowing styles. These include such items as play with firm, left-hand fingers on a soft, rapid passage for clarity, and the use of the brush stroke with off-the-string bowings. In soft passages, other instructions by the conductor may be needed (use upper part of the bow, play near the fingerboard, turn stick of bow toward fingerboard, use less bow hair, use less bow pressure, use slow bow speed and small amount of bow in reducing the speed). In loud passages, contrary instructions may be in order (use lower part of bow, play nearer the bridge, play with flat bow, use more bow pressure, and use faster bow speed). In producing the crescendo on a note, use up-bow on the attack; with the diminuendo, use down-bow to start the attack. Change the bow direction on sustained notes without undue accenting. For speed, use the lower-middle part of the bow (or the balance point). Use the tip or near the tip with rapid speed for the tremolo. Discuss such techniques for the benefit of the conducting students in class.

Special effects on string instruments should receive the attention of the conductor in the rehearsal process as well as those dealing with these special effects on wind and percussion instruments. A few of these special effects on string instruments that need to be considered in the rehearsal process are ponticello or sul ponticello, tasto or sul tasto, bowed tremolo, fingered tremolo, artificial harmonics, natural harmonics, glissandi, portamento, pizzicato, left-hand pizzicato, legno or col legno, and many more special effects. It is very important that the conductor knows how to produce these special effects and what the resulting sound will be. (I provide sources for these special effects in Appendix D.)

SUMMARY: BOWINGS AND BOWING STYLES

I offer these bowings and bowing styles as some of the possibilities used by string players in achieving the proper articulation for a particular passage. In general, the conductor needs to encourage the string player to play more aggressively, especially in louder passages. The conductor should have a working knowledge of these bowings and bowing styles in order to develop strategies for use in the instrumental music ensemble rehearsal process. Reinforce these bowing strategies during the rehearsal process. It is important that the conductor knows what sound will be produced by these various bowings and bowing styles. Without this background, the conductor will be unable to conceive and communicate the desired sound or know how to achieve these techniques or special effects with the string players.

Even though most of the time, the bowing on the strings instruments and the articulation of the winds coincide, there are exceptions in the repertoire. For example, the strings may be playing legato while the winds are playing staccato. In the majority of these situations, the composer has indicated this for the purpose of effect. The conductor must realize the composer's intentions and reinforce this relationship between the strings and the winds. On some occasions, it might be necessary to adjust the articulation of the winds from the standpoint of sheer execution or with the strings to adjust the bowing because the player is unable to control the bow as demanded in the music. However, before making these changes, the conductor should give strong consideration regarding the integrity of such adjustments.

Table 11.3, Teaching Strategy (Bowings and Bowing Styles), at the end of the chapter provides ideas and suggestions for designing teaching strategies to improve bowings and bowing styles on string instruments.

PRACTICAL APPLICATION (DISCUSSION/DEMONSTRATION)

1. Discuss and demonstrate the various kinds of articulation on the wind instruments, the playing techniques on the various percussion instruments, and the bowings and bowing styles on the string instruments.
2. Demonstrate and practice conducting these four musical styles (staccato, legato, tenuto, and marcato). Also, modify these four styles as in the rehearsal process through the conducting technique or with conductor demonstrations (verbalizing or singing).
3. Discuss and demonstrate the problems involved with partial accuracy, large interval skips, lip slurring, and legato tonguing (trombone) on the brass instruments.
4. Have a string player demonstrate the following bowing styles, so that the student conductor will be able to ask for these specific techniques in the rehearsal process: détaché, martelé, spiccato, louré, ricochet, sautillé, and staccato.
5. Take the Violin I part from a classical symphony (Haydn or Mozart), and based on the bowing principles of Elizabeth Green, apply these in marking down-bow and up-bow (Mozart: Symphony No. 40 in G minor).
6. Discuss and demonstrate how the following wind articulation symbols are played: (a) staccato dot, (b) staccatissimo mark, (c) legato or tenuto mark, (d) regular accent, (e) caret accent, (f) legato mark with staccato dots, (g) the slur mark with staccato dots, (h) the slur mark with tenuto mark, and (i) the slur mark with accents. (Musical Example)
7. Continue to gain familiarity with the standard repertoire found in Appendix A through CD listening, score study and guidance from the conducting teacher. (See Appendix G for assignment forms.)

IN THE REHEARSAL PROCESS (LAB) ENVIRONMENT

1. Demonstrate conducting the ensemble with various styles in the rehearsal (lab) environment. Practice these!
2. Demonstrate how to show on-the-beat accents, using the "gesture of syncopation" and the contrasted style changes (Menotti: *Amahl and the Night Visitors*).

3. Discuss the teaching strategies that might achieve better wind articulation clarity on fast passages.

4. Demonstrate the following bowing styles during the rehearsal process lab: détaché, martelé, louré, spiccato, sautillé, and staccato. (Musical Example)

5. Demonstrate the following string special effects during the rehearsal process lab: tremolo, sul ponticello, sul tasto, and col legno. (Musical Example)

6. Discuss and demonstrate how to achieve uniformity of bowing (the down-bow, the up-bow, the part of bow used, and the pressure and speed of the bow).

7. Complete student conducting/rehearsing projects (in the rehearsal process lab environment).

RECOMMENDED READING

Farkas, Philip, *The Art of Musicianship*. In Chapter 6: Articulation, the author addresses certain articulation markings for wind instruments.

Green, Elizabeth A. H., *Orchestral Bowing and Routines*. This book contains the various basic bowings as well as the more advanced (artistic) bowings.

Green, Elizabeth A. H., *Teaching Stringed Instruments in Classes*. This book is based on the idea of teaching stringed instruments from the very beginning level.

Kjelland, James. *Orchestral Bowings: Style and Function*. The author justifies the orchestral bowings in terms of style and function. Chapter 2 covers bow strokes and classification and Chapter 3 covers bow direction.

Kohut, Daniel L., *Instrumental Music Pedagogy* (paperback version). Chapter 4: Bowing and Articulation. Starting on page 133 the book deals with wind instrument articulation.

Long, R. Gerry, *The Conductor's Workshop: A Workbook on Instrumental Conducting*. Chapter 5: Articulation.

McBeth, W. Francis, *Effective Performance of Band Music: Solutions to Specific Problems in the Performance of 20th Century Band Music*. Solution II: Achieving Correct Performance of Dynamic and Articulation Markings.

Rabin, Marvin, and Priscilla Smith, *Guide to Orchestral Bowings through Musical Styles*. A practical book (1984 and revised in 1990) on the subject of orchestral bowings and bowing styles with an accompanying video.

Weisberg, Arthur, *The Art of Wind Playing*. Chapters 1–7 cover Dynamics and Intonation, Tonguing (Single and Double), Vibrato, Technique, Breathing, Style (Renaissance through Contemporary), and Interpretation.

REPERTOIRE FOR PROJECTS AND ASSIGNMENTS

Full Orchestra, Chamber Orchestra, or String Orchestra

Beethoven: Symphony No. 5 (First movement)
Britten: Young Person's Guide to the Orchestra (with narrator)

Ives: The Unanswered Question (four flutes, trumpet, and strings)
Gershwin: Porgy and Bess: A Symphonic Picture for Orchestra
Haydn: Symphony No. 104 "London" (various movements)

Concert Band or Wind Ensemble

Grainger: Lincolnshire Posy (various movements)
Holst: Suite No. 1 in E-flat Major (various movements)
Mailman: Liturgical Music (various movements)
McBeth: Chant and Jubilo
Persichetti: Divertimento for Band (various movements)

Miscellaneous or Small Ensembles

Ives: Calcium Light Night (flute, clarinet, bassoon, two trumpets, trombone, timpani, two percussion, piano, and strings)
Persichetti: Serenade No. 1, Op. 1 (flute, oboe, clarinet, bassoon, 2 horns, 2 trumpets, trombone, and tuba)

TEACHING STRATEGY TABLES

Table 11.1.   Wind Articulation

CONDUCTOR CONCERNS	PROBLEM AREAS	TEACHING STRATEGIES
Tongue position with wind players	Tonguing	Keep the back of the tongue relaxed and articulate lightly (even in loud, fast passages).
Use of multiple tonguing on fast passages for the brass and flute/piccolo		Use multiple tonguing (double tonguing and triple tonguing) for the brass when this is applicable.
The various kinds of wind articulations		If necessary, change the articulation (to alleviate severe articulation problems). Be sure to do this in good taste.
Vocal articulation modeling for the conductor		Keep the fast articulation in time by slightly accenting the first note of each pulse.
Last note of the slur tending to be shortened		Correct the tongue placement or position for the wind player if this is the problem.

(continued)

Table 11.1. (*continued*)

CONDUCTOR CONCERNS	PROBLEM AREAS	TEACHING STRATEGIES
Lip slurring on brass instruments The legato-tongue technique on trombone for slurring Articulation production Thinking of tonguing smoothly on fast, staccato passages Using the breath, not the tongue to produce loud, articulated passages	Slurring	To avoid a loss of quality or pitch, do not shorten the last note of the slur. This may cause rhythmic problems as well.
		Lip slurring on brass instruments is especially problematic in producing a smooth connection between slurred notes. I strongly recommend using the tongue arch with the "tah-oo-ee" syllables—but do not allow the choking off of high notes.
		In some cases, slurring may provide an alternate solution to fast, articulated notes; this eliminates the finger-tongue coordination on some passages.
		Although there is no universal agreement, when shown with the staccato dot, tenuto mark, or accent the player must perform the slur in a certain manner.
	Special articulation problems	The wind player must depend on the breath to sustain fast, articulated passages.
		The trombonist has a special problem in slurring; the player must develop the legato tongue technique to solve such slurring problems.
		On wind instruments, when playing fast, articulated passages, think smoothly rather than staccato; this articulation problem can then lead to a rather "brittle" articulation and style.
		Decrease the louder dynamic levels, if necessary; these passages are more difficult to maintain when involving this very fast articulation.
What other teaching strategies (suggested by the conducting teacher or students) could improve wind articulations?		

Table 11.2. Percussion Playing Techniques

CONDUCTOR CONCERNS	PROBLEM AREAS	TEACHING STRATEGIES
The various percussion playing techniques The choice of sticks, mallets, or hammers The part of the instrument that is struck Balance and precision between the percussion section and the rest of the ensemble Basic percussion instruments World music percussion instruments Special effect percussion instruments Unusual percussion instruments	Conductor concerns	Conductor concerns with the percussion include timpani tuning, buzz roll on snare drum, muffling or muting, drum head tension, sticks, mallets, hammers, and playing techniques on the various percussion instruments.
		There is a particular concern for the conductor as to what part of the instrument to strike with regard to dynamics and tone color or for crash cymbals in producing the proper sound.
		The balance or the delayed sound between the percussion section and the rest of the ensemble is a constant concern for the conductor because of tendencies by the percussionist to overpower or drag tempo.
	Basic percussion instrument playing techniques (to be demonstrated)	The basic percussion instruments include timpani or kettledrums, snare drum, bass drum, crash cymbals, suspended cymbal, triangle, woodblock, xylophone, marimba, vibraphone, glockenspiel or orchestra bells, chimes or tubular bells, and gong or tam-tam.
	World music percussion instrument playing techniques (to be demonstrated)	World music percussion instruments (including Latin-American rhythm instruments) include tambourine, castanets, claves, cowbell, conga drums, bongo drums, temple blocks, timbales, guiro, maracas, and various other kinds of drums.
	Special effect percussion instrument playing techniques (to be demonstrated)	Percussion instruments for special effects include sleigh bells, whip, sandpaper blocks, log drum, bird whistle, rattle, ratchet, celesta, auto horns, and other instruments designated by the composer.
	Unusual percussion instrument playing techniques (to be demonstrated)	Unusual percussion instruments might include anvil, brake drums, recorder, thunder sheet, wind machine, crotales, marching machine, various whistles, sirens, cello or bass bow on vibraphone, and other instruments designated by the composer.
	Percussion articulation	The reason for this discussion about the various percussion instruments is that the tone on most percussion instruments is produced through articulation.
What other teaching strategies (suggested by the conducting teacher or students) could pertain to the percussion instruments?		

Table 11.3.   Bowings and Bowing Styles

CONDUCTOR CONCERNS	PROBLEM AREAS	TEACHING STRATEGIES
Down-bow and up-bow for uniformity Baroque style bowing Spiccato or "brush stroke" bowing in the classical period Other bowing styles needed	Bowings	Execute Baroque style bowing with on-the-string bowings.
		Use linked or hooked bowings on dotted 8th and 16th note rhythm patterns and with other related meters and rhythms.
		Staggered bowing is done on both the outside and the inside.
		The bow, elbow, and wrist must have some flexibility so that the bow remains perpendicular to the neck and the strings.
The part of the bow to be used The speed and pressure of the bow Sul ponticello bowing Sul tasto bowing Tremoli bowing Pizzicato playing	Bowing styles	Spiccato bowing (or the brush stroke) begins in the Classical period of music.
		The conductor should specify the type of bowing according to the sound desired, perhaps then moderated by the technical level of the ensemble.
		Select the part of the bow that will allow effective execution of the bowing style. Designate this in the music for young players.
		Indicate the bowing style for the players in order to be consistent.
		The speed and pressure of the bow on the string may need to be determined for certain passages.
Fingerings and positions Special effects in string playing	Fingerings and positions	Fingerings may be necessary to avoid open strings for vibrato use and for appropriate position use.
		The lower positions are used in orchestral playing more often than in solo playing.
	Special effects	Sul ponticello is usually played at the tip of the bow and very close to the bridge. Sul tasto is played at the middle of the bow and closer to the fingerboard.
		Pizzicato can be performed in a number of different ways. The danger with pizzicato is in the rushing of the pulse, and thereby, poor precision results.
		When performing tremoli, the bow speed should be executed very rapidly in order provide the excitement of this special effect.
		Some other special effects include harmonics, glissandi, col legno, portamento, and non-vibrato.
What other teaching strategies (suggested by the conducting teacher or students) could improve bowings and bowing styles?		

Part IV

MUSICAL PRIORITIES
AND TEACHING STRATEGIES

South Dakota State University Civic Symphony; Dr. John Brawand, Music Director and Conductor

Chapter Twelve

Tempo and Ensemble Precision

TEMPO AND ENSEMBLE PRECISION RELATIONSHIP

Tempo and ensemble precision in musical performance are closely related areas. This is the main reason for grouping these two performance elements together. Many of the performance problems that occur in the area of ensemble precision are due to the selected tempo or the change of tempo by the conductor. Precision sometimes is referred to as "ensemble" in describing the desired cohesiveness of the group rhythmically. This performance aspect should rank very high in the priorities because the quality of ensemble precision will seriously affect many of the other performance elements as well. If the ensemble precision is inadequate, it will affect such elements as intonation, rhythm, balance, blend, articulation, and bowing. Ensemble precision is a very important element in musical performance in conjunction with the tempo and tempo changes!

The right tempo is a crucial part of the musical interpretation for a given work. Much has been written *about selecting this "right" tempo.* A review of some of these ideas might be helpful for the advanced conductor. Tempos are determined in many different ways. Selecting the tempo that will communicate the composer's intentions must be the main goal for the conductor. Tempo selection factors include the composer's written indications or metronome markings, the performance level of the ensemble, the musical period, the specific style of the composer, the complexity of the harmony and counterpoint, the rhythmic demands, and many other factors that I delineate later in this chapter.

The main connection between the tempo and precision problems is speed. If the tempo is too fast or too slow for a particular piece, the performance will not be satisfying for the players or the audience. If the tempo is too extreme, poor precision will result because of inadequate technical facility or lack of tone control within the ensemble. Having adequate conducting technique, insistence by the conductor that the players watch, the exact performance of rhythm and rhythm patterns, and the development of adequate technical facility and accuracy from the ensemble should result in superior precision with the ensemble. However, the conductor must constantly be aware of poor precision or "pull," which may occur between the conductor and the ensemble so that he or she can resolve these situations in the rehearsal process. If there is good visual communication between the conductor and the ensemble, the problems of ensemble precision should be minimal. Likewise, the problems involved with the changes of tempo and performance flexibility should not be major concerns if the conductor is communicating well visually with the ensemble.

It is vital to establish this communication between the conductor and the ensemble from the beginning. This involves the placement of the conductor and ensemble so there is this direct communication. The conductor must be so well prepared through score study that this communication is inevitable and the ensemble will watch the conductor and be guided in terms of tempo, tempo changes, flexibility, rubato, dynamics, nuances, accents, phrasing, style, and musical interpretation. These aspects assume that the conductor is prepared and ready for the rehearsal process.

TEMPO SELECTION FACTORS

The following are considerations in selecting the "right" tempo (to be discussed in the following paragraphs of this chapter):

• Metronome markings
• Recordings
• Music periods and composers
• The critical bar theory
• Ensemble performance level
• Acoustical characteristics of the performance facility
• The music itself (Richard Wagner called this the "Melos")

In considering these various tempo selection factors, several of these factors may influence the conductor at one time. *One factor may modify another factor* or several of the factors might be a strong consideration on the final decision as to the "right" tempo. For example, the metronome marking is certainly a strong and significant factor because of its specific designation, but the ensemble performance level may curtail achieving this marking. Another example is that in listening to several recordings of the piece, there may be considerable differences in tempo selection, and therefore another factor might influence the final decision by the conductor in terms of the tempo. The conductor needs to integrate all of these factors into making the final decision.

TEMPO TERMS

The tempo terms used by a composer give a general indication of the tempo of the composition. The conductor should be familiar with most of these frequently used tempo terms and have a music dictionary at hand to look up the unfamiliar ones. Never leave the meaning of these terms to chance or an "educated" guess. Most of these terms are in a foreign language. The most familiar tempo terms are in Italian. French and German terms are generally less familiar and may require the use of a music dictionary. A common list of tempo terms from slow to fast include grave, larghissimo, largo, larghetto, lento, adagio, adagietto, andante, andantino, moderato, allegretto, allegro, vivace, presto and prestissimo. Some moderating terms that change the above-mentioned tempo terms include ben, ma non troppo, piu, meno, rubato, molto, guisto, alla, un poco, assai, sempre, animato, quasi, sehr, subito, and many more terms in various languages. In addition to these moderating terms, there are also terms that indicate a change of tempo, such as accelerando, stringendo, ritardando, rallentando, ritenuto, allargando, Tempo I, a tempo, calando, morendo, perdendosi, ad libitum, a piacere, poco a poco, largemente, con anima, and many others.

The tempo modifiers of the various tempo terms are also crucial in the selection of the tempo, as is the case with defining and knowing the various tempo terms. Always consider these modifiers in the tempo selection. Because most of the modifying terms are in a foreign language, as are the tempo terms, the use of a music dictionary is imperative. These modifiers are crucial in arriving at the "right" tempo; otherwise, there is no purpose in having such terms in the score. Examples of these modifiers connected with a tempo term include allegro moderato, allegro molto, allegro assai, and allegro con moto. The worst scenario is for the conductor to guess at the meaning of tempo terms or modifiers, and thereby mar the performance through this lack of important knowledge.

METRONOME MARKINGS

The metronome marking is a more exacting presentation of the composer's intentions than that of a tempo term. However, metronome markings, on occasion, have proven to be incorrect or sometimes miscalculated by the composer. Unfortunately, in many instances, the designated metronome markings are published and such markings are then difficult to change. The conductor should consider the metronome marking as an exact indicator of the tempo, but be prepared to adjust the tempo selection if other factors dictate that a change would be more effective. Often, the composer or arranger provides a range in the metronome marking to follow, such as 72–80.

The maturing conductor (as well as the experienced conductor) should spend time developing the ability to produce these various metronomic markings with the conducting patterns. This is all very important *when going from the rehearsal process to the concert performance.* Even after considerable conducting experience, the conductor needs to check constantly that these markings are being followed. Recording the rehearsal process can be an aid in checking these metronome markings. Table 12.1 below provides a procedure for developing this ability to "hit the mark." When working with metronome markings, be careful that the note values indicated for the specific tempo are correct. Compound meter metronome markings can also be somewhat deceiving because of the triple subdivision feel.

RECORDINGS

For the conductor, listening to recordings could be a worthwhile guide in selecting the "right" tempo. The more recordings heard of a single work, the better perspective the conductor will have in determining the tempo. Selecting recordings by reputable conductors and ensembles is certainly an important consideration here. However, there is some danger in the use of recordings to determine tempo. The professional ensemble will generally be able to play the work at whatever tempo the conductor chooses. To adhere exactly to some of these professional ensemble tempos with a younger ensemble could be disastrous for the performance and discouraging to the ensemble. Common sense is necessary in such circumstances. If the ensemble is incapable of playing the selection at a tempo reasonably close to what is indicated by the composer, then the conductor might want to consider whether or not the selection should be programmed or whether its technical/musical demands are of value for the younger ensemble at the present time.

By listening to recordings, the conductor will be able to identify the "traditional tempo." With works that have "stood the test of time," the conductor should be knowledgeable about these traditional tempos and changes of tempo. In listening to several recordings of the same work, the conductor can gain a perspective on these tempos or changes of tempo. It is unwise for a conductor to program and perform in concert *such works that are tradition-bound without knowing the performance history.* An example of this would be a Johann Strauss Waltz in which certain tempo rubatos are traditional. Contemporary works are less treacherous as long as one follows the notation and instructions of the composer.

MUSICAL PERIODS AND COMPOSERS

The various musical periods (baroque, classical, romantic, and contemporary) are a determining factor in tempo selection as is the individual composer. (Because the metronome was invented during the time of Beethoven, metronome markings that appear before this time are those of an arranger or editor and not those of the composer.) As an example of the musical period influence, the Mozart (classical) allegro indications are generally performed faster than are those of the Handel (baroque) allegro indications. Likewise, certain composers seem to demand slower or faster tempos in many of their works. It is valuable for the conductor to not only listen to the specific recording of a selected work but to also be familiar with other works by that particular composer. This will provide a certain perspective for the conductor in selecting the "right" tempo.

The whole area of performance practice is one that the maturing conductor needs to pursue for authenticity. Performance practices should not only include the tempo but also style, dynamics, articulation and bowing, and certainly the correct performance of trills, mordents, appoggiaturas, turns, grace notes, and other ornamentation. Another factor in performance practice is the number of players used in the performance of a specific work. There are differences of opinion as to the number of players to use in modern-day performances of baroque and classical period music. I will consider all of these performance aspects in more detail in Chapter 14: Style and Musical Interpretation. It is crucial that the conductor be knowledgeable in the area of performance practice of the various musical periods to produce these authentic performances. Then in the rehearsal process, the conductor needs to communicate these performance practices to the ensemble. There are several fine sources on performance practice listed at the end of this chapter (under the Recommended Reading).

THE CRITICAL BAR THEORY AND TEMPO MODIFICATION

In almost any musical composition, there is a passage or several measures of music that will largely determine the appropriate tempo for the ensemble. In his book *The Art of Musicianship*, the late Philip Farkas elaborated on the idea of the critical bar theory (1976, 19). This tempo selection factor may be in terms of the flow of the piece or because of certain technical or rhythmic demands required. At any rate, the critical bar theory will help the conductor determine what the "right" tempo should be and then begin the specific section or composition at that tempo or else modify the tempo slightly for this critical bar passage.

It is important for the conductor to evaluate constantly *whether the initial tempo will need to be modified at certain points* even though the composer has not indicated this in the music with a tempo term change. However, this is not to say that the conductor has license to change tempo randomly or without justifiable reasons. An example of this idea is in the finale of Dvořák's Symphony No. 9, *From the New World*, in which the tempo indication is allegro con fuoco (lively with fire). This tempo term generally prevails throughout the movement. However, playing some of the sections at the opening tempo of this movement would make the music feel rushed and uncomfortable. Such a situation taken at face value would bring doubt to the listener that the conductor has captured the essence and spirit of the music in certain sections of this particular work.

ENSEMBLE PERFORMANCE LEVEL

Consider the capability of the instrumental music ensemble in determining a reasonable yet functional tempo. Virtuoso recorded performances are abundantly available, but the tempos, especially fast ones, may not be realistic for some groups. There are, of course, tempo parameters in terms of programming works that cannot be played close to an acceptable tempo. If the tempo must be slowed for technical reasons to a point where the essence and spirit of the work is lost, consideration should be given to changing the concert repertoire. Likewise, playing a work or movement at such a slow tempo that breathing, bowing, and the sustained quality of the work breaks down, then consider moving the work forward at a slightly faster tempo.

It is not an easy decision to delete a selection from the program, especially if the ensemble has been rehearsing it for some time. However, failure by the conductor to make this decision could result in a disaster for the ensemble in the concert performance. This particular situation should dictate to the conductor as early as possible that he or she must make a decision about this problem to avoid wasting valuable rehearsal time on the particular selection. If the conductor decides to go ahead with the work, two problems might result: (1) an attempt to play at the indicated tempo with the consequence of great technical inaccuracy in the performance, or (2) playing at a slower tempo with the danger of losing the essence and spirit of the work and leaving the conductor and ensemble open for criticism about the tempo selection in the concert performance.

PERFORMANCE FACILITY

The physical performance facility is a factor in determining the correct tempo. A very "live" room may require the tempos to be slightly slower, while a hall with a "dry" resonance will demand a brisker tempo. Temper this acoustical factor with the other tempo factors listed above. It is also important for the conductor *to understand the difference in the response* when going from the orchestra to the concert band. The string response is generally a bit delayed in relationship to the pulse. The concert band response is slightly quicker. This string response will seem strange at first in comparison to that of an ensemble primarily of wind and percussion instruments. However, these response differences can and will be quickly resolved with some conductor time in front of either of these ensembles.

There are times when the music must be allowed to "breathe" and "sound," which might dictate a slower tempo, a change of tempo, or tempo rubato. There are other specific places in the music where, because of the dynamics, loud dynamic resonance must have time to subside before continuing at a softer dynamic level. These decisions are based on the acoustics of the performance facility as well. The conductor must consider especially the clarity of the concert performance in terms of the performance facility, and to some extent, this determines tempos and tempo fluctuations. For these reasons, it becomes critical that the conductor has scheduled a rehearsal or two in the performance facility (if the rehearsals are in a different location from the concert) to solve these problems before the concert performance. The acoustics of the performance hall do and should influence these tempo determinations by the conductor.

THE MUSIC ITSELF

Richard Wagner, the famous German composer and conductor, contended that if the conductor understood the music (or Melos), the "right" tempo would be selected. Wagner concluded that singing was the best way to find this true tempo. This is certainly valid and authoritative advice. Nonetheless, the conductor should consider other factors in tempo selection along with this to modulate what conclusions were determined through inner singing. By inner singing while studying the score, the conductor should be able to find a tempo that would work in bringing the music to proper fruition.

The music itself as a factor in determining the "right" tempo might be called "musical intuition or instinct" on the part of the conductor. The mistake would be to believe that musical intuition or instinct is the only way to determine the correct tempo.

Temper musical intuition with knowledge and the traditional tempo of a given work. It would be wrong for the conductor to assume that his or her instinct is more reliable than the composer's metronome marking or other tempo indications. The conductor should attempt to grasp the essence and spirit of the work in the quest for selecting the "right" tempo. *In many and most cases, the selection of tempo depends upon the actual "flow" of the music.*

Richard Wagner's other statement about tempo selection—that it is the only duty of the conductor—might appear to be somewhat oversimplified. However, there is considerable validity as to the importance of tempo selection in the success of the concert performance. Because of the importance of this duty, the conductor should carefully consider the tempo throughout the rehearsal process, so that the ensemble is prepared to play at this tempo during the concert performance. (I do not suggest always playing the selections up to the perceived or designated tempo in rehearsals.) Slow rehearsing is sometimes necessary to achieve many of the performance aspects in the rehearsal process before returning to the "right" tempo. In preparation for the concert performance, the conductor must reinforce this in the rehearsal process with whatever tempo he or she has selected for the concert performance.

CONDUCTING SPECIFIED TEMPOS

Achieving this "right" tempo is a difficult task for the conductor. Experience is certainly a good teacher in this area, but concerted and intelligent effort on the part of the conductor is also necessary. In order to be able to produce these given metronome indications, intense practice with a metronome by the conductor will be required. It is extremely important for the conductor to match up these numerical indications with the essence and spirit of the music. Consequently, there are both technical and musical aspects involved in arriving at the "right" tempo. The conductor may find that the tempos are too fast, causing considerable technical errors. Likewise, a very slow tempo may cause musical problems due to a lack of the sustaining prowess of the instrumental music ensemble. In both cases, this could be a challenge for the conductor and the ensemble to develop more technical accuracy or work to improve the sustained sound of the ensemble in the rehearsal process. The conductor must be able to achieve the metronome marking as indicated by the composer or adjust this tempo to adhere to the other factors involved in selecting this "right" tempo. Table 12.1 will help in developing this specific skill in finding and conducting the various tempos indicated in the music with the use of the metronome markings.

Using a stopwatch (or iPod) or a regular watch, practice conducting and counting the metronome markings shown in table 12.1. When you have mastered these markings consistently, begin to check the common tempo indications with a metronome. Some frequently used metronome markings in music for the pulse are 52, 60, 72, 80, 88, 92, 96, 100, 108, 112, 120, 126, 132, 138, 144, 152, and 160. As you begin to conduct music and indicate tempos, frequently check the various tempos with a metronome. With sufficient practice, the conductor will be able to develop quite precise accuracy.

Table 12.1. Timing Chart of Metronome Markings

Duration in seconds of 10 beats (11 pulses)	Duration in seconds of one beat marking	Metronome
15	1.5	40
12	1.2	50
10	1.0	60
7.5	.75	80
6	.6	100
5	.5	120
3.75	.375	160
3	.3	200

It is important to point out that the skill of indicating the metronome marking precisely is one that the conductor must reinforce throughout his or her career, leaving nothing to chance. Checking with the metronome must be a continuous activity for the working conductor. Recording rehearsals and comparing the metronome markings with the replay of the recording can be an effective method for the conductor to gain this confidence. However, the music must always make sense at the selected tempo.

REHEARSING AT SLOW TEMPOS

A common strategy used by conductors in the rehearsal process is to slow down a passage or section to solve either technical or musical problems. The technical difficulty may be fingering facility, articulation speed, intonation accuracy, or rhythmic precision. The musical problems may be ensemble precision, style, musical expression, and so on. Three cautionary suggestions in using this strategy are (1) when the technical or musical problem is solved, then return the passage or section to the proper tempo within the context of the selection, (2) watch that in slowing a passage down in tempo, other problems do not occur because of this strategy (for example, with the slower tempo, problems of breathing with the wind players and bowing with the string players may surface), and (3) rehearsing too long at a slow tempo will make it more difficult to finally establish the required faster tempo.

By slowing down the tempo from the prescribed indication of the composer, the conductor can achieve better precision and clarity with the ensemble. When such passages or sections are then secure in terms of precision and clarity, reinstate the designated tempo. Rehearsing at a slower tempo can also improve technical facility and accuracy along with intonation accuracy. In many cases, by slowing down the tempo, the ensemble will be able to assimilate what the problem is and will correct the problem without the conductor having to stop the ensemble for comments or demonstrations. This will also indicate to the players where they may need to spend their individual practice time, ultimately saving rehearsal time.

FINAL THOUGHTS ON TEMPO SELECTION

The conductor must be vigilant in attempting to discover the "right" tempo(s) for a work. *Realistically speaking, the tempo selection in musical performance is crucial.* A top priority for the conductor must be the selection, maintenance, and variance of this tempo. The developing conductor may not see this importance at first. When the conducting student begins the conducting study in the college curriculum or even earlier, there is little attention devoted to conducting at the "right" tempo. However, after gaining some conducting experience in front of an ensemble, the tempo selection should begin to gain importance and soon, much time and effort should be devoted to the problem of the "right" tempo. In the final analysis, the tempo at any given juncture depends on the idea of the concert performance being an artistic and authentic presentation.

In the selection of tempo, the number of beats conducted in a measure is a critical consideration also. The fact that the meter shows 4/4 or common time meter is no assurance that it is best conducted in four beats to the measure. If the tempo is very fast, then the four-pattern may be too "fussy" and frantic. Conducting the 4/4 meter in two beats per measure will result in more flow and clarity. The same would be the case in 3/4 meter as to whether to conduct in three or one. It would depend on the tempo and the emphasis needed on each beat. Likewise, choices will need to be made with compound meters (3/8, 6/8, 9/8, and 12/8). More beats per measure will give a certain sense of control, but may give the players a feeling of "nervousness" in the conducting patterns. Fewer beats may cause a lack of precision, especially if the pulse beat is quite slow or the ensemble is insecure rhythmically. An example of this is to be found in the "Storm" section of the Rossini *William Tell Overture* that is designated alla breve (or cut-time). If conducted in two beats per measure, the rhythmic and precision aspects can become very unstable. Conducting this section in four beats per measure solidifies this particular section (especially the "raindrops" in this part of the overture!).

The character of the music is a strong determining factor in tempo selection. The conductor must strive to capture the essence and spirit of the music. Thereby, the music will take on the proper character and the players will communicate the emotional content to the audience. *Certain types of music demand a characteristic tempo, such as that of a particular dance.* Examples of such dances are the sarabande, mazurka, waltz, or tango. In another example, rags are often played too fast when musically they should have a bit of "stickiness" to them. It behooves the conductor to find the appropriate tempo for these pieces.

It is important to realize that in slower tempos, one can employ rubato more reasonably, while in faster tempos, maintain a strict pace. *This idea of tempo rubato versus strict tempo will certainly influence the choice of tempos.* Likewise, playing at a strict tempo with slow passages can cause the listener to miss the expressiveness of the work. For example, a tempo rubato could give the slow passage some impetus and the correct feeling of intensity and drive. Fast tempos will automatically have a sense of drive, but a tempo rubato in this situation might also be a disruptive element in such a musical interpretation. The conductor will need to conceive the selection of tempo carefully based on the use of tempo rubato or strict tempo. You will find examples of both strict tempo and tempo rubato in a selection such as Gershwin's *Rhapsody in Blue*.

ENSEMBLE PRECISION

Ensemble precision problems exist for many reasons. Poor precision in an ensemble usually results for some of the following reasons:

1. Inadequate communication between the conductor and the ensemble on the preparatory beat/downbeat at the beginning of a work, section, or phrase
2. Poor conducting technique in indicating these attacks, showing releases, and in the handling of fermatas
3. Failure to maintain the tempo set by the conductor
4. Lack of attention (in watching the conductor) and/or rhythmic instability on the part of the players
5. Inaccurate playing of rhythms and rhythm patterns
6. Problems of tempos and tempo changes (sudden or gradual)
7. Inadequate technical facility and accuracy by the players in performing the selected repertoire
8. Early or late entrance after rests (cueing may help considerably here)

The conductor is largely responsible for achieving good precision with the ensemble. Some instrumental music ensembles, especially in Europe, have rehearsed so diligently that a conductor is not necessary. However, during the rehearsals and the performance someone is in charge. These groups need an occasional "nod" or other indication from the appointed leader to achieve a precise attack or release. A string quartet, woodwind quintet, or brass quintet does not use a conductor. There is no doubt that a specific member of these ensembles is responsible for indicating the pulse (at various points) just as the conductor does with the larger instrumental ensemble.

Beyond setting the tempo for the ensemble, the conductor is responsible for the rhythmic aspects of indicating attacks, releases, and changes of tempo. As I mentioned earlier, the conductor does have more conducting control over this part of the performance than many of the other technical or musical aspects. To some extent, the conductor has conducting control over dynamic levels, balance, phrasing, style, and musical interpretation. Of course, all of this is assuming that the players are watching and are playing sensitively to the conductor's patterns and gestures. In the rehearsal process, these rhythmic performance aspects involving ensemble precision should receive serious attention. Consequently, the rehearsal process must be a time *for solidifying this rhythmic control over the ensemble.*

Even if the conducting technique is superb, the conductor will be ineffective in front of the ensemble unless the players are watching and responding sensitively to the conducting patterns and gestures. Ensemble precision problems would be extremely difficult to solve in an uncontrolled or undisciplined scenario. This lack of control by the conductor will be frustrating to the players as well. *The ensemble wants this guidance*; the players do not want to be guessing as to where the pulse is. Therefore, the conductor must impose the conducting patterns and gestures on the ensemble by being very clear and expressive, and by insisting that the players watch the conductor. Only in this way can precision problems be resolved in the ensemble rehearsal process and then transferred successfully to the concert performance. In many instances, the conductor takes for granted that the ensemble is watching. This certainly may not be the case. Be sure the sight lines to the podium are good for every ensemble member.

INADEQUATE COMMUNICATION AT THE BEGINNING

Poor ensemble precision will result when there is inadequate communication between the conductor and players. What is involved here is the clarity of the conductor's preparatory beat and the response from the players on the downbeat. Precision problems may occur at the beginning of a piece, section, or phrase that starts on a fraction of the beat. *This is always a treacherous situation.* I discussed this in more detail in Chapter 4: Conducting Technique. In most cases, the conductor should avoid using the phrase, "One, two, ready, play" during the rehearsal process except to simply establish the tempo of a passage that needs detailed work; thereafter return to the silent preparatory beat and downbeat when you play this passage. The problem with the preparatory beat and downbeat is that the ensemble must start together and gain the momentum instantly from silence.

Several factors are involved in this initial communication with the ensemble. Eye contact between the conductor and the players is essential. It is a good idea for the conductor *to memorize the first few measures* of any selection conducted, to establish eye contact with the ensemble. In this regard, the conductor should realize that he or she does not have to produce any specific sounds, as the players are required to do. Therefore, the memorization involves the tempo, meter, starting count, style, and dynamic level in those first few measures of music. This would not seem to be an extremely difficult task for the conductor, but would involve careful score study and practice. This would also apply at the beginning of a new section or phrase. *The technique of audiation is crucial for the conductor in hearing the whole phrase.*

The conductor should wait until the ensemble is attentive with instruments in playing position. This waiting period should be neither too short nor too long. If there is insufficient time to get the instruments in playing position, the lack of readiness to play and frustration on the part of the players will result. If beginning takes too much time, then the players who already have their instruments in playing position become impatient. The conductor will visually scan the ensemble to see that the players are ready to begin; then the preparatory beat and the downbeat should follow.

The preparatory beat is one of the most important gestures the conductor must execute in leading an instrumental music ensemble. The clarity of the preparatory beat should be unmistakable. The flick of the wrist for the preparatory beat should be executed with subtlety, precision, and clarity to define the beginning of the preparatory beat. (There is some danger especially when starting a slow, quiet piece because the motion is generally smaller and less emphatic.) The conductor must insist that with this flick of the wrist, the ensemble will take a synchronized breath with the preparatory beat motion. In this way, the communication between conductor and ensemble is assured and effective. The preparatory beat is subtle in the sense that it is a passive, not active, gesture.

The downbeat is an active gesture that indicates to the player that the sound should begin. However, the preparatory beat and the downbeat gesture is a collective feeling between conductor and players in achieving this initial attack. The conductor must be in touch with the ensemble visually and psychologically, and not just routinely go through pedantic motions of the preparatory beat and the downbeat. Through the conductor's facial expression, slight movements of the head, and inhaling, the conductor can greatly enhance this communication. In some cases, the conductor may choose to use the "delayed beat" technique wherein the beat is shown and then the ensemble will respond after this pulse. This needs rehearsal by the ensemble and the conductor. Particularly in slow tempos, this technique is quite effective.

The next beat after the downbeat is very important as this truly establishes the pulse and tempo of the piece. The problem here is that the preparatory beat and downbeat show the distance between one pulse and the next in establishing the tempo. However, the following beat after the downbeat will then confirm this choice of tempo. This is not to imply that the preparatory beat and downbeat should be tentative and then establish the tempo after that. The preparatory beat and downbeat gestures should be decisive; however, the ensemble will appreciate this exact pulse indication on the beat following the downbeat.

In summary, the preparatory beat and downbeat gestures are crucial in establishing the initial attack and tempo. After considerable experience, both the conductor and the players tend to take this all for granted. *The result is a poor attack.* The conductor needs to check periodically that the preparatory beat is clear. The use of the VTR or a mirror can be an important visual aid in determining this clarity. Likewise, the players must be alert in watching the conductor. It is important for the conductor to remind the ensemble about taking a breath with the preparatory beat (even the string, keyboard, and percussion players should do this!). This initial attack problem is always difficult because, in a sense, the ensemble is starting at zero in terms of momentum. It is essential for the conductor to be communicating well with the ensemble through eye contact and with this conducting clarity.

POOR CONDUCTING TECHNIQUE

I have alluded to this whole area of conducting technique under the heading of Inadequate Communication. However, I need to stress that a clear conducting technique is necessary to obtain an accurate and positive response from the ensemble. Having good conducting technique is just as important as the player having good technical facility and accuracy on the instrument. For precision of attacks and releases and in handling fermatas, the conductor must be the guide for the ensemble. If the conductor is unclear with these conducting patterns and gestures, this will become quite apparent to the players quickly. This inadequate conducting will lead to a loss of credibility for the conductor and a lack of confidence on the part of the ensemble.

The conductor who attempts to lead an ensemble without adequate conducting technique will not find success even if he or she is an outstanding musician and instrumentalist. *Controlling the ensemble well and obtaining the desired response from the ensemble are two very important goals for every conductor.* These goals are unachievable without a clear conducting technique. The ensemble will not respond properly to careless or poorly developed conducting technique. If the advanced conductor has not yet developed a sound conducting technique, then more remedial work in this area is crucial. (See Appendix F.)

The ensemble execution on attacks, releases, and in handling fermatas will expose poor conducting technique quickly. I have covered initial attacks, releases, and fermatas in previous chapters. There are many factors involved concerning this poor conducting technique. Some of these factors go back to the initial conducting training or the lack of such training. However, many of these poor conducting techniques develop over time *due to the acquisition of bad conducting habits* or through the lack of effort on the part of the conductor to maintain a clear conducting technique. It is very important for the conductor to evaluate the conducting technique periodically to keep this conducting technique sharp and clear in order to communicate precisely with the ensemble. Many conductors have had no success or very limited success because of these various conducting technique problems.

The release does not seem to be as high on the priority list with instrumental conductors as it is with vocal conductors. This is probably because the vocalist must deal with text and the enunciation of consonants at the end of the phrase. However, the instrumental conductor should take just as much care with the releases as does the vocal director. The key to a proper release is in the preparation. The preparation of the release telegraphs the intentions of the conductor about when the release will occur and the character of the release. The speed of the release must not be a "surprise" for the players or a ragged release will result. The character of the release will vary tremendously from a very soft, subtle release to a loud, sharp cut-off, depending on the musical requirements. In any case, the release must be prepared and shown clearly. If the conductor releases the final note of the composition or phrase with one single "beat" gesture, it may be necessary in the rehearsal process to *come to a consensus with the ensemble in terms of this final note length.* Likewise, some conductors tend to release in a "circular" fashion and this may cause some confusion with the players. Instead, he or she should execute the release in a clockwise or counterclockwise downward motion. The release may also stay within the pattern by the pulse showing below the conducting plane. The left-hand release can be a very effective gesture; this leaves the right hand ready for the continuation of the music. Releases (or breaks) must come on the beat even if the music actually ends on a fraction of the beat. Examples are Holst's *The Planets* and Gershwin's *Rhapsody in Blue* and *An American in Paris.*

Fermatas in reality are a cessation of the rhythmic pulse and may follow a tempo change. (In many cases, a tempo change occurs as the fermata is approached.) Consequently, the precision of the ensemble during the appearance of a fermata can be problematic. Often a *poco ritardando* (written or unwritten) precedes this fermata along with the spacing of the notes. Take care to ensure that the ensemble follows the patterns of the conductor into the fermata. Then the release of the fermata is another crucial aspect as is the continuation of the music after the fermata. The handling of fermatas requires careful consideration of both attacks and releases. The continuation of the music after a fermata usually involves the resumption of a specified tempo.

The conductor must carefully conceive and then precisely execute all of this in order for the ensemble to be able to follow these patterns and gestures. This is a situation wherein conducting practice is very important for the conductor.

MAINTAINING THE TEMPO

Once the tempo is established, it becomes imperative to maintain the tempo unless the composer's indications (accelerando, ritardando, fermatas, etc.) or musical considerations (phrasing and musical interpretation) dictate a change in the tempo. On the surface, this may all seem apparent. However, in actual practice a failure to maintain the tempo can lead to poor precision with the ensemble. Even though there may be subtle tempo changes, there should be a feeling of maintaining the established tempo. *If there is a rhythmical "pull" within the ensemble*, it may very well be due to the lack of maintaining the tempo. The correction of this lack of tempo maintenance falls directly on the shoulders of the conductor. In the rehearsal process, this problem of maintaining the tempo must be addressed and procedures taken to achieve this tempo maintenance. An example is the fast section (with after-beats) of the Shostakovich *Festive Overture*.

The conductor is responsible for maintaining the tempo. Good communication, with eye contact and clear conducting patterns and gestures can keep this problem minimal. Certain players in the ensemble can be of help or a hindrance in maintaining the tempo. The contrabass (or tuba) section and the percussion section are examples of such sections. *The conductor should use larger patterns to counteract rushing and conduct with smaller patterns to counteract dragging the tempo.* In the rehearsal process, the conductor should continue to conduct at a conceived tempo even if the players rush or drag the established tempo. This will indicate to the players the "error of their ways" and they will need to catch up or slow down accordingly. The conductor should not adjust the patterns or gestures to this rushing or dragging of the tempo in the rehearsal process. In the concert performance, the conductor must strive to maintain the tempo in such circumstances but should not carry this to the point of causing chaos with the ensemble precision. Rather, the conductor should firm the beat pattern (with more vertical motions) to help the players rhythmically and to realize exactly where the pulse is occurring.

If the ensemble begins to speed up or slow down, the conductor must simply keep the tempo steady to maintain the flow. In the rehearsal process, this is the way to counteract precision problems, and in such circumstances, the players rushing or slowing down will have to adjust or suffer the consequences of not being with the rest of the ensemble. In the concert performance, the conductor must carefully attempt to guide the ensemble back to the established tempo with good conducting flow and without causing precision problems.

Rushing the pulse is a common problem, especially with younger ensembles. With very young ensembles, it might be due to sheer excitement during the rehearsal process or concert performance. This rushing occurs for a number of reasons. One reason is the poor performance of rhythmic note values. Often, rushing the pulse results from "grabbing" at a group of notes instead of keeping the group of notes rhythmic and precise. Another rushing problem involves the lack of technical facility or reading prowess of the players. Loud and fast-articulated notes sometimes tend to encourage rushing. Likewise, there is a tendency to increase speed on the crescendo and to decrease speed on the diminuendo. With the string player, *there is a tendency to rush on pizzicato passages.*

Technical difficulties in the music, rhythmic problems on the wind instruments, or bowing and fingering problems with the string sections may cause *unwanted slowing of the pulse.* There is a natural tendency to slow down in difficult passages because of the lack of technical prowess. In the case of a rhythmic problem that slows down the tempo, the conductor will need to insist on precise, rhythmic execution. Likewise, bowing indications may need revision. Dragging the pulse may also occur because the players cannot keep up with the indicated tempo of the conductor. In such circumstances, the conductor will need to decide on a particular course of action. Either the whole tempo will need to be slower or detail work on the passage will be necessary to improve the technical facility and accuracy. Soft, slow, and sustained notes tend to encourage slowing down or dragging the pulse. Fast tempo after-beats may cause the tempo to slow down as well.

This information about maintaining the tempo is not to imply that the ensemble must sustain a selected tempo rigidly (like a metronome). However, where the music indicates strict tempo (guisto), as in a march, the conductor must impose this on the ensemble. In other circumstances, the conductor may only need to give the impression of strict tempo. The decisions by the conductor concerning rigidity of tempo are made after careful score study and thoughtful consideration of the essence and spirit of the work. The music itself should dictate this tempo rigidity to the conductor. What is at stake here is the musicality of the performance.

Actually, tempo flexibility ranks very high in terms of achieving musicality and musical expression in the performance of music as far as the conductor is concerned. In this regard, the conductor should have strong control over the ensemble in producing this musicality and the musical expression. The conductor must conceive tempo flexibility and reinforce it during the rehearsal process. It should not keep changing throughout the rehearsal process. Otherwise, the players will tend to become confused as to what may happen next and how the conductor wants the music to sound. A very strong influence concerning tempo flexibility is the musical period. Certainly, the conductor has more license in tempo flexibility in the romantic period than the baroque or classical periods of music.

PLAYER ALERTNESS AND RHYTHMIC STABILITY

Not only does poor precision result *from the lack of attention on the part of the players*, but also many other performance problems tend to surface. In general, the ensemble will be unable to project finesse or musicality in the rehearsal process or in the concert performance when good precision is lacking. For example, precision has a direct relationship with style and balance. In cases where the feeling of pulse or correct rhythms may become erratic within the ensemble, there is usually a rehearsal procedure or teaching strategy that will be helpful in maintaining this rhythmic stability. In the rehearsal process, the conductor should point out these stabilizing factors to the players. The key to good precision for the player is watching the conductor and listening to the rest of the ensemble simultaneously.

What can the conductor do to gain the alertness needed in both the rehearsal process and the concert performance? In the short term, the conductor must make every effort to keep the players interested and excited about what they are doing. Long-range solutions include the conductor having the respect of the ensemble through careful planning and preparations, demanding good technical execution, displaying superb musicianship, and establishing his or her leadership with the ensemble. Once the respect from the ensemble is established, then the conductor can expect and will get the cooperation and effort needed from the ensemble to produce this superior precision. The ensemble should be motivated internally to achieve this kind of ensemble precision.

The causes of rhythmic instability within the ensemble are quite varied. *The conductor, in order to arrive at a proper solution, should analyze this rhythmic instability.* The cause of the instability might be a particular section or several sections of the ensemble. It might be failure to watch the conductor or careless playing of rhythms and rhythm patterns. Whatever the reason for the problem might be, the conductor will need to institute the solution. If the conductor finds that the players are untrained in watching the conductor or in responding properly to the patterns and gestures, then remedial work may be necessary in these performance areas. Perhaps the conductor will need to prioritize and rehearse some basic rhythms and rhythm patterns during the warm-up period. The percussion section may require some sectional rehearsals in order to establish a solid foundation of rhythmic stability for the ensemble. There could be many other reasons for this rhythmic instability, but the conductor will need to solve these problems for the ensemble to achieve good precision. These specific rehearsal objectives should be reflected in the teaching strategies that the conductor might employ during the rehearsal process.

Table 12.2, Teaching Strategy (Player Alertness and Rhythmic Stability), at the end of the chapter offers ideas and suggestions for designing such a teaching strategy to improve player alertness and rhythmic stability.

PRECISION PROBLEMS CAUSED BY
INACCURATE RHYTHMS AND RHYTHM PATTERNS

I covered the problems of inaccurate rhythms and rhythm patterns detail in chapter 9. The cohesiveness of the ensemble is dependent on all of the members playing rhythms and rhythm patterns accurately. Poor execution of these rhythms and rhythm patterns causes ensemble precision problems. Therefore, *a rhythmic system must be in place* in the rehearsal process so that poor rhythmic execution can be resolved effectively and efficiently. In training an ensemble to be a cohesive unit, one of the main duties of the conductor is to instill the importance of the absolute correct performance and interpretation of these rhythms and rhythm patterns. Once the rhythm problems are resolved, there will be a good foundation established to proceed to other performance problem areas such as intonation, balance, blend, articulation, style, and phrasing.

Rhythmic precision is a crucial factor in any ensemble performance. The rehearsal process solidifies rhythmic ensemble precision. The conductor must constantly reinforce and confirm the importance of ensemble precision. Watching the conductor to know exactly where the pulse occurs and then playing the rhythms and rhythm patterns precisely must be a continuous priority for the conductor and the ensemble. Spending rehearsal time counting, playing, or singing these rhythmic passages while the conductor shows the pulse is one way of improving this rhythmic precision with the ensemble.

PRECISION PROBLEMS WITH TEMPOS AND TEMPO CHANGES

The selected tempos can cause precision problems. I covered the whole area of tempo selection in detail earlier in this chapter. These ensemble precision problems are connected to the tempo selection process strongly. A selected tempo that is too fast or too slow can be very disconcerting for the ensemble and negatively affect the concert performance. In some cases, the problem is that the ensemble simply does not have the technical prowess to play the selected repertoire at the proper tempo. The problem might be that the ensemble has not developed the musicianship to perform a slow, lyric piece adequately. In these situations, the ensemble has not developed the sustained musical line to bring such a work to fruition. Whatever the reason for these problems of precision with the ensemble, the tempo may be a factor in this ensemble precision.

Whether the tempo change is sudden or gradual, a change of tempo may result in poor precision within the ensemble. If the conductor realizes this danger, then he or she will take greater care to show these changes precisely. For example, approaching the fermata in many cases requires a change of tempo before arriving at the point of the fermata. A further example of this problem might be that on a sudden tempo change, the preparatory beat into the new tempo is not clear and precise. The conductor should conceive and solidify these changes of tempo in the rehearsal process with the ensemble. The conductor must always remember to prepare for these changes in tempo by this preparatory conducting gesture.

A precise preparatory beat should indicate a sudden tempo change before the change occurs. The conductor should not wait until the new tempo arrives to show what the change of tempo will be. In changing suddenly from slow to fast tempo, the preparatory beat must show the new tempo on the last half of the pulse value of the slow tempo. This is necessary in order to give proper value to the final beat of this slow tempo. In changing suddenly from fast to slow tempo, the preparatory beat is the rebound of the first beat of the new tempo. After arriving on this first beat of the new tempo, the gesture must now reflect a change of pulse length into the second beat. A *ritenuto* marking (suddenly slower) is an example of this application.

The conductor must indicate *gradual tempo changes such as accelerando and ritar-dando* so that speeding up or slowing down of the pulse is secure. In the *accelerando*, the conductor must make the change smoothly, especially if showing fewer beats per measure at some point is necessary. Likewise, in the *ritardando*, the conductor must gradually slow down before starting a subdivided beat pattern. He or she must establish these gradual tempo changes during the rehearsal process. Certainly, solidifying these tempo changes becomes one of the main priorities of a final dress rehearsal. In making gradual tempo changes, the conductor should determine when it is most comfortable to go with more or fewer beats in the conducting pattern, and then modulate them to avoid any abruptness in the musical line.

Tempo rubato is defined as "a style of playing in which one note may be extended at the expense of another, for purposes of expression" (Lee, *Music Theory Dictionary*, 1966). The term rubato literally means "robbed." The precision of the ensemble can be damaged if not all of the players are alert and ready for these changes of tempo. *Rubato may occur in the melodic line only or with the whole ensemble.* Often in accompanying a soloist, the ensemble will maintain a steady tempo while the soloist uses rubato to enhance the musical interpretation. The musical period and style impose parameters on how much rubato to use with a specific musical interpretation. If rubato is used often and inappropriately, the ensemble will gradually become insecure with the precision. The ensemble should not employ rubato in the concert performance unless the conductor has carefully configured and reinforced it during the rehearsal process. Always use tempo rubato tastefully.

If a tempo is changed from the way the ensemble is used to playing, it may also be necessary to revise such elements as the general style, phrasing, amount of emphasis, or note length. Slower tempos may require the style to be more sustained and emphatic and the phrasing to be more deliberate; faster tempos may need more spacing of the notes and a lighter style with the phrasing more straightforward. If the style and phrasing changes are not made with the tempo changes, the result may be a loss of vitality or an incorrect stylistic interpretation of the music. *For example, equal-valued notes in a ritardando must become more sustained as the tempo slackens.*

When a precision problem occurs due to a tempo change, have the players count out loud while the conductor conducts the passage ("conduct and count" procedure). This will encourage the players to watch the conductor and understand the problem in the context of the tempo change. With this procedure, the players will feel and understand where the musical pulse occurs and how they will need to adjust and subdivide the rhythm patterns within the tempo change. Tempo changes (either gradual or sudden) can be a disruptive element in ensemble precision. The conductor should show these changes clearly and securely, and the players must be attentive in watching the conductor's patterns and gestures in order to respond properly to these tempo changes. In some cases, it may even be necessary in the rehearsal process to slow down the tempo in order to improve these musical aspects in preparation for the concert performance. After this improvement, return the passage to the prescribed tempo.

Table 12.3, Teaching Strategy (Tempos, Tempo Changes, Rubato, and Nuances), at the end of the chapter provides ideas and suggestions for designing a teaching strategy to improve tempos, tempo changes, tempo rubato, and nuances.

INADEQUATE TECHNICAL FACILITY AND ACCURACY

Inadequate technical facility and accuracy within the ensemble will lead to poor precision. The conductor must consider the collective technical prowess of the ensemble along with the demands of the music. If the selection being rehearsed or performed is too demanding for the ensemble's present technical facility and accuracy, then precision problems will undoubtedly result. Selections that make fewer technical demands on the ensemble will ensure fewer precision problems. With very difficult music, the players are diverted from such performance elements as precision, intonation, articulation, bowing, and so on. The technical elements may also overwhelm the attention of the players regarding all of the details of the various musical elements. Consequently, the players cannot focus on listening across the ensemble for such problems as tone, balance, blend, style, and musical expression.

How much control or responsibility the conductor can have in improving the technical skills of the ensemble members in the rehearsal process is somewhat limited. Perhaps the conductor can influence this area during the warm-up period. Similarly, the repertoire selection may challenge the players to increase their technical prowess. The conductor-teacher can make specific suggestions during the rehearsal process and encourage the players to develop more technical facility and accuracy. In many cases, the lack of good technical facility and accuracy may be due to the absence of good study materials, poor practice habits, and incorrect practice procedures. The conductor should emphasize these problems during the rehearsal process for the benefit of the members of the ensemble. The players should accomplish much of this development through private teachers and serious application in their individual practice. However, the conductor can act as a catalyst by encouraging the players to study privately and practice correctly and diligently.

The lack of good precision in the ensemble may be an indication to the conductor that the selection of music may be making technical and musical demands beyond the performance level of the ensemble or even that of the ensemble's potential. In many instances, the conductor misjudges the performance level and the potential of the ensemble and selects music that the ensemble is incapable of performing well. *The conductor must realize that a musical challenge is just as important as a technical challenge.* This philosophy will then lead to more emphasis on fine, fundamental playing rather than just "chasing the notes and rhythms" in the rehearsal process or even in the concert performance! The conductor should give careful consideration to this kind of program building.

EARLY OR LATE ENTRANCES AFTER RESTS

Early or late entrances after rests become a disruptive factor in ensemble precision. In some cases, the counting of rests before the entrance or a lack of rhythmic understanding causes the problem. Generally, however, it is due to a lack of careful listening and not feeling the pulse with the rest of the ensemble during the rests. When the players enter early or late, the precision results are not unlike a locomotive lurching forward, causing a chain reaction with the rest of the cars on the track. Until the ensemble *stabilizes and synchronizes* this pulse movement, precision on entrances will remain erratic.

Some of the precision problems with early and late entrances after rests are due to the lack of good preparation by the players before the entrance. The wind player must "time" the inhalation of the breath. It is important to realize that there needs to be sufficient time to take the breath, set the embouchure, and exhale into the instrument. In many cases, the string player should have the bow on the string (especially if it is a rather quick entrance) instead of trying to control the placement of the bow on the string from above the string. The percussionist will need to feel the pulse and be ready to enter at the exact moment of execution. In general, the player making the entrance must be mentally and physically coordinated with the rest of the ensemble. The conductor preparing the cue in these instances can help the precision and character of the entrance. *However, the player must not become too dependent on the conductor for the cueing.*

In all cases, the conductor should execute the cueing by a preparatory gesture before the point of entrance; in addition, he or she should make eye contact with the individual player or section before presenting this preparatory gesture. This preparatory gesture must always be rhythmic and precise. The preparatory gesture should reflect the character (dynamic level, articulation, and general style) of the entrance. By showing the cue in this manner, the conductor can avoid early or late entrances after rests. The left hand, right hand, head, and eyes can all contribute to the proper cueing of the entrance. *In contrast, a pointing gesture by the conductor is a rather poorly conceived motion for indicating a cue.*

PRACTICAL APPLICATION (DISCUSSION/DEMONSTRATION)

1. Practice indicating specified metronome markings (such as 60, 72, 88, 96, 104, 112, 120, 132, 144, and 160).
2. Gauge with the metronome and consider musically the various tempo terms: grave, lento, largo, larghetto, adagio, andante, andantino, moderato, allegretto, allegro, vivace, presto, and prestissimo.
3. Practice changes of tempo—merging from three into one (accelerando) and subdividing from four into eight (rallentando). (Musical Example)
4. Design a four-measure rhythmic phrase (see below) containing different rhythm patterns. Conduct the class as they sing (use "tah") or play the rhythm patterns. Make corrections with the ensemble. (Musical Example)
5. Continue to gain familiarity with the standard repertoire found in Appendix A through CD listening, score study, and guidance from the conducting teacher. (See Appendix G for assignment forms.)

IN THE REHEARSAL PROCESS (LAB) ENVIRONMENT

1. Have the students conduct the ensemble to establish these metronome markings: 60, 72, 88, 96, 104, 112, 120, 132, 144, and 160.

2. Show rehearsal procedures used in isolating a technical passage (play slowly, play rhythmically, and return to the specified tempo). (Musical Example)
3. Conduct the ensemble without music. Indicate the meter and have the ensemble count or play (on a single pitch). Change the tempo, style, and dynamics.
4. Conduct the ensemble, demonstrating the proper technique in executing the preparatory beat, downbeat, and after the downbeat in establishing the tempo and precision.
5. Conduct the ensemble, demonstrating sudden tempo changes—slow to fast and fast to slow. (Musical Example)
6. Conduct the ensemble, demonstrating the release (which beat, precision, and character?). Do not rush the release. (Musical Example)
7. Conduct the ensemble, demonstrating handling fermatas in three ways: (a) one beat break, (b) more than one beat break, and (c) "sliding" fermata. (Musical Example: count 4 before releases)
8. Conduct the ensemble, demonstrating the proper way to show cues with conductor preparation (to prevent early or late entrances). (Musical Example)
9. Complete student conducting/rehearsing projects (in the rehearsal process lab environment)

RECOMMENDED READING

Dorian, Frederick, *The History of Music in Performance.* Chapter 5: Tempo and Metronome contains information about the "right" tempos and the use of the metronome in this regard.

Farkas, Philip, *The Art of Musicianship.* Chapter 4: Tempo offers ideas and concepts about selecting the "right" tempo. The author feels that this right tempo is one of the most important duties of the conductor.

Green, Barry, and W. Timothy Gallwey, *The Inner Game of Music.* Chapter 14: Ensemble Playing connects with the awareness strategy that is explained in Chapter 4: The Power of Awareness.

Kahn, Emil, *Conducting.* Part 4, Chapter 18: Tempo refers to the following aspects of tempo: markings, tempo and temperament, rubato, endings, and the metronome.

Leinsdorf, Erich, *The Composer's Advocate: A Radical Orthodoxy for Musicians.* Chapters 5 and 6 in this book pertain to the choice of the right tempo and chapter 7 delineates the conductor's role in the rehearsal process.

Marsh, Robert Charles, *Toscanini and the Art of Conducting.* In this paperback book about Toscanini, there are frequent references in Chapter 3: Toscanini's Musicianship concerning the subject of tempos.

Rudolf, Max, *The Grammar of Conducting*, 3rd ed. In Part 4, Chapter 32: Choice of Tempo, there is a detailed discussion about selecting tempos, tempo modification, tempo relations, and metronome indications.

Schuller, Gunther, *The Compleat Conductor.* A Philosophy of Conducting (starting on page 3) covers many salient points about tempo and tempo modification.

Wagner, Richard, *On Conducting*, 2nd ed. On page 20, Wagner states, "The whole duty of a conductor is comprised in his ability always to indicate the right tempo." The rest of the book attempts to confirm this statement.

REPERTOIRE FOR PROJECTS AND ASSIGNMENTS

Full Orchestra, Chamber Orchestra, or String Orchestra

Barber: Overture to the "School of Scandal"
Beethoven: Symphony No. 5 (4th movement)
Chausson: Poem for Violin and Orchestra
Copland: Rodeo: Four Dance Episodes (various movements)
Harris: Symphony No. 6 (various movements)

Concert Band or Wind Ensemble

Reed, A.: Armenian Dances, Part I or Part II (various movements)
Rimsky-Korsakov: Procession of the Nobles (Leidzen, arr.)
Sheldon, R.: Visions of Flight
Smith, C.: Symphony No. 1 for Band (various movements)
Stravinsky: Symphonies of Wind Instruments (various movements)

Miscellaneous or Small Ensembles

Schoenberg: Pierrot lunaire, Op. 21 (Sprechstimme; 1 flute-piccolo, 1 clarinet (bass
   clarinet.), piano, violin, viola, and cello)
Varése: Ionisation (12 percussion and piano

TEACHING STRATEGY TABLES

Table 12.2.   Player Alertness and Rhythmic Stability

CONDUCTOR CONCERNS	PROBLEM AREAS	TEACHING STRATEGIES
Clear and musical conducting technique for the players to watch	Conducting technique	The conductor must acquire a very clear conducting technique. Otherwise, the players will stop watching the conductor.
		Playing with good ensemble precision comes from the leadership of the conductor.
Tempo selection factors		
Watching the conductor		Conducting initial attacks of the phrase must always be a major concern for the conductor.
Ensemble precision		
Emphasizing the musicality	Watching the conductor	Occasionally, the conductor should make some changes in tempo, style, or dynamics to see if players are watching. (Do not do this frequently; the players will begin to feel deceived.)
Good eye contact with the ensemble		
Good player sight lines to the conductor		Emphasizing musicality in the rehearsal process should be a way of getting the players to watch the conductor.

Table 12.2. (**continued**)

CONDUCTOR CONCERNS	PROBLEM AREAS	TEACHING STRATEGIES
The conducting plane always visible to the players	Watching the conductor (*continued*)	Monotonous-looking conducting will not cause players to watch.
		Simply exclaiming, "watch" will not necessarily be an effective means for player alertness.
Keeping patterns and gestures centered	Conductor communication	If the conductor expects the players to watch, then he or she must make good eye contact with the ensemble to establish this communication.
Encouraging players to listen to each other		The conductor must think of guiding the sound of the ensemble and not just conducting and reading the score.
Players becoming accurate and independent music readers	Sight lines to the conductor	The conductor must insist that the players have good sight lines to the podium. This may mean some adjustments in the seating arrangement of the ensemble.
		The conductor must see to it that the conducting plane is always visible for the players. This may mean lowering the conductor's stand or adjusting the plane.
		The conductor must keep the patterns and gestures centered so that all of the players can see them clearly.
		Encourage the players to watch the conductor and listen. In this way, the ensemble will come together as a cohesive unit.
What other teaching strategies (suggested by the conducting teacher or students) could improve player alertness and rhythmic stability?		

Table 12.3.   Tempos, Tempo Changes, Rubato, and Nuances

CONDUCTOR CONCERNS	PROBLEM AREAS	TEACHING STRATEGIES
Conceiving the tempo	Tempos	The preparatory beat sets the tempo. The conductor must conceive this tempo before making the preparatory gesture.
Practicing the conceived tempos with metronome markings		In score study, the conductor should conceive and practice the tempos in preparation for the rehearsal process.
Reinforcing tempo changes with the ensemble in the rehearsal process		The conductor should check these tempos with a metronome throughout the rehearsal process and be consistent with the selected tempo into the concert performance.

(*continued*)

Table 12.3. (*continued*)

CONDUCTOR CONCERNS	PROBLEM AREAS	TEACHING STRATEGIES
Keeping tempos and tempo changes consistent between the rehearsal process and the concert performance Thinking musically when using the tempo rubato Reinforcing the tempo rubato during the rehearsal process Conceiving the nuances in score study and reinforcing them with the ensemble in the rehearsal process	Tempo changes	Conduct tempo changes so there is no doubt with the players as to these tempo changes and their extent.
		Work on tempo changes (sudden or gradual) in the rehearsal process so that the players will know what to expect in the concert performance.
		These tempo changes may need some experimenting as to when to change in the music and what will work best for the ensemble.
	Tempo rubato	Reinforce tempo rubato in the rehearsal process so the players are not deceived during the concert performance.
		The conductor must always be thinking musically when using tempo rubato in the musical interpretation. Tempo rubato should be tasteful.
	Nuances	Without these nuances music can begin to sound very mechanical and void of any real emotions in the rehearsal process and in the concert performance.
		The conductor should conceive nuances during score study and reinforce them with the ensemble in the rehearsal process.
		These nuances can best be described when listening to the great jazz trumpeter Louis Armstrong play or sing. His performances have "soul."
What other teaching strategies (suggested by the conducting teacher or students) could improve tempos, tempo changes, rubato, and nuances?		

Chapter Thirteen

Phrasing and the Musical Line

PHRASING

Phrasing is one of the elements in ensemble performance that the conductor must conceive, initiate, and dictate. He or she cannot leave it to the members of the ensemble to decide. The conductor should show by patterns and gestures and/or indicate verbally in the rehearsal process where the phrase begins, where the phrase ends, the contour of the phrase, the climax of the phrase, and the other dynamic and stylistic considerations in the phrasing. The conductor must shape and define phrases with the conducting technique. This assumes and implies that the players are watching the conductor. *Phrasing involves a musical idea.* Phrases in music must make sense just as sentences do in writing or speaking. Uniformity in phrasing among the players is essential for a fine ensemble performance. In the concert performance, the conductor must define the phrasing for the players and the listeners. However, this will only happen if the conductor has communicated this to the players during the rehearsal process.

The composer indicates this molding and punctuation of the phrase; this requires the conductor to study the score and bring this information to the attention of the players in the rehearsal process. If the composer's phrasing indications are unclear, then the conductor should decide on this molding and punctuation. The conductor must discover the length of the phrase and then indicate this to the players in the rehearsal process. There may be times in the rehearsal process when the conductor will want to experiment with the phrasing to decide what is best. By considering where the wind player must take the breath, the conductor makes the phrasing decision in the ensemble rehearsal process. Likewise, the players may experiment with the phrasing and be able to give the conductor some feedback and insight about the possibilities of the phrase. If the phrasing makes sense for the listener, then the conductor and players have succeeded in phrasing properly. The string player, pianist, and percussionist should also think about phrasing even though the breath is not a defining factor in the phrasing as with wind instruments. The string player, in many cases, will define the phrase with the bowing or the bowing style employed and the percussionist should then copy the phrasing of the wind and string player. The percussionist must listen carefully during the rehearsal process and be sensitive to the phrasing of the wind and string players.

The selection of music material for concert programming by the conductor can strongly affect the awareness and development of good ensemble phrasing. Likewise, when the conductor emphasizes phrasing in the rehearsal process, the players will begin to be aware of the importance of proper phrasing. The conductor, when conducting expressively and showing phrase beginnings, contours, climaxes, musical expression, and endings, will reinforce these items for the player in the rehearsal process. The conductor will be effective in teaching the ideas of phrasing by using analogy, metaphor, or imagery. In addition, the use of visual strategy, such as a chalkboard to diagram phrase contour (that is, the profile of the musical line) can be helpful to reinforce the idea of this phrasing in musical performance.

Developing the musical line so there is continuity and forward motion within the phrase must be an important facet of the conductor's strategy. The shaping of the phrase pertains to making the musical line cohesive and yet variable to reflect the intentions of the composer. Two main areas in phrasing to foster are *the sustained musical line and the spacing of notes*, with the concept that the phrase must seem to be "glued together." The sustained musical line, while not easily achieved, does lead to the cohesiveness and forward flow of the phrase. Likewise, the spacing of notes is critical in certain musical styles; however, the phrase must still have a sense of the musical line. Silence can be a very important part of making music; it differentiates the phrases and enhances the dramatic aspect. If the conductor has proficiency on the piano, showing the phrasing and musical line on this instrument can be effective in the rehearsal process. Likewise, the idea of audiation by the conductor can greatly influence the phrasing and musical line wherein the phrase is heard an instant before the conducting or playing of the phrase begins.

Phrasing and articulation are related in that the phrase involves the grouping of notes and also in terms of the length and weight of these notes. Whether they are sustained or spaced notes, the conductor must strive to make the phrase cohesive and to define the phrasing for the players and the audience. The weight of the various notes can aid in defining the phrase. The emphasis on notes is comparable to the way we speak in that we stress certain words to clarify the meaning. An effective orator uses the same kind of emphasis (and subtleties), as does the expressive conductor or musician. This phrasing and articulation of notes will give meaning and dramatic effects to both the phrase and the musical line.

It is easy for the instrumental conductor to ignore or overlook the phrase continuity and division of the music into phrases for several reasons:

1. The instrumental music conductor tends to think in terms of bar lines and conducting patterns, especially in contemporary music where the meters change quite frequently.
2. In instrumental music, there is no text to indicate phrases and phrase endings as in vocal music.
3. The instrumental conductor, unlike the player or vocalist, does not have to produce the phrase with the actual pitches. Consequently, the focus tends to become a rhythmic one rather than one of phrasing and emphasis.

4. The string (and percussion) players in the orchestral ensemble will be able to continue the music indefinitely without the division into phrases; the wind player, however, must breathe to produce the tone and in this way is able to define the end of the phrase. Therefore, the conductor needs to insist on good phrasing from all the members of the ensemble.
5. The complexities of the band or orchestra score can be overwhelming for the evolving conductor; this causes the phrasing to become a secondary issue in score study as well as during the rehearsal process or concert performance.
6. In instrumental music, the expressive qualities of the phrase are not always as obvious; they are with the provided text and the phrasing in vocal works.

The point is that the instrumental conductor, with all of the other elements of musical performance to consider in the rehearsal process, often does forget about the phrasing and the musical line. However, it is extremely important to understand how phrases make up the composition, how the phrases fit together, and *how it all unfolds to convey various musical ideas.*

ELEMENTS OF PHRASING

The phrase is comparable to the sentence in writing or speaking. If a phrase is to make sense to the players and audience, the conductor must indicate the phrases with the conducting patterns and gestures or verbally in the rehearsal process to make certain that the players understand these phrasing elements. What parts or elements of the phrase should the conductor convey with the conducting patterns and gestures or delineate for the players verbally during the rehearsal process?

1. The beginning of the phrase (with the preparatory beat showing the precise attack, tempo, meter, dynamic level, and style)
2. The end of the phrase (to indicate the release, a breathing place, release of tension, or an appropriate musical pause)
3. The contour of the phrase (as indicated or implied by the composer)
4. The climax (or important "peak" notes) of the phrase
5. The dynamic level and nuances of the phrase (as these change)
6. The pulse fluctuation (tempo and nuances) of the phrase (as these change)
7. The style, weight (or strength) of the notes, and the musical expression indications within the single phrase

THE BEGINNING OF THE PHRASE

With the preparatory beat, the conductor should not only indicate the attack, tempo, meter, style, and dynamic level, but also the character of the articulation. The character of the articulation involves the dynamic level, style, and precision with this initial beginning of the phrase. However, there is more to it than just the three elements of tempo, style, and the dynamic level. The beginning of the phrase needs to be shown with a clear preparatory beat and downbeat in which the conductor and players breathe together to ensure a good attack. *This certainly requires a psychological as well as a visual communication between the conductor and players.* Only if the players are watching and alert to the conductor's preparatory gesture and the conductor is "in sync" psychologically with the ensemble (at the beginning of the phrase) will this attack be secure.

There must be a psychological communication between the conductor and the players that somewhat defies explanation. The conductor must have eye contact with the ensemble and the ensemble must respond to the conductor's patterns and gestures appropriately. This involvement means that the player should be seeing these patterns and gestures and preparing in some way to play the first note of the phrase as indicated by this gesture. *The player preparation for the beginning of the phrase depends on the particular instrument.* For the wind player, the preparatory beat means taking the breath with this gesture. With the string player, the preparatory beat means putting the bow in position above or on the appropriate string. The percussionist should be in position to activate the stick (or mallet) on the specific percussion instrument and make contact at the exact moment of the downbeat. In the rehearsal process, the conductor has the options and the opportunity to communicate verbally with the players in addition to expressing his or her intentions through the conducting technique. Table 13.1, Teaching Strategy (The Beginning of the Phrase), at the end of the chapter presents ideas and suggestions for designing a teaching strategy on showing the beginning of the phrase for the ensemble.

THE END OF THE PHRASE

The end of the phrase must be prepared just as carefully as the beginning of the phrase. There must be a preparation for the release of the final note of the phrase just as there is at the beginning of the phrase. The final note must be released with a sensitivity dictated by the music. Many conductors do not understand this. Such conductors are only concerned about showing a precise release. This leads to an abrupt release (then poorly executed by the ensemble). The conductor must indicate the release "in tempo" unless the pulse has ceased as in the case of a fermata. If the release is on a fermata, then the conductor must define the preparatory beat for the release well so the players are not confused about exactly where the release should occur.

The end of the phrase must have the feeling of rest, that is, a relief from the intensity of the phrase. This will help the listener to make more sense of the phrase. The pause at the end of the phrase is brief in most cases, but must give the definite impression of ending the phrase. Tapering the end of the phrase involves inflection, dynamics, tone control, and perhaps the vibrato. The conducting gestures must reflect these subtleties, and in most instances, reinforce them in the rehearsal process. Frequently, the string player will be encouraged to continue the vibrato motion after the release of the tone with the bow or on a pizzicato.

The conductor may alter the conducting pattern of the phrase ending depending on whether the music continues or stops. In most cases, if the music continues, the conductor should stay in the pattern and show the release on the indicated pulse. However, if the music does stop, the conductor will adjust the conducting pattern to produce the release on this final pulse. The conductor may taper the phrase ending or end it rather abruptly, depending on the composer's indications and intentions. Here the conducting gestures should reflect a musical decision by the conductor. The ensemble, through the conductor's clear patterns or gestures, should achieve the character and uniformity of the release at the end of a phrase. Therefore, this places the responsibility on the conductor to show the release of the phrase clearly and sensitively.

The impact of *the final phrase of a piece* is vital in terms of leaving the proper emotional impression with the audience. In many cases, the composer has indicated dynamically exactly what is wanted. However, the tempo, tempo change, articulation, note emphasis, and lengths may not be as clearly indicated as is the general dynamic level. For example, the final cadence chords of a symphony or concerto may traditionally involve a ritardando or delay of the last chord even though there is no ritardando or ritenuto indicated by the composer. The conductor will need to consider the kind of impact that this last phrase and ending note should communicate to the listener. The last phrase may end with great bravura, with a quiet fading, or with some degree between these two extremes. If the conductor has adequate conducting technique and thinks musically, the visual indication to the ensemble for communicating the impact of this final phrase should be correct as well as dramatic. Only if the players are watching and playing with musical sensitivity will the ensemble nuance reflect this proper phrase ending. The rehearsal process will give the conductor an opportunity to confirm or change this musical interpretation of the final phrase. Table 13.2, Teaching Strategy (The End of the Phrase), at the end of the chapter contains ideas and suggestions for designing a teaching strategy concerning the end of the phrase.

THE CONTOUR AND CLIMAX OF THE PHRASE

The composer has initially conceived the phrase. Through score study, the conductor must determine the rise and fall of the phrase, the tension and relaxation of the phrase, and where the important point(s) are in the phrase. The conductor has control over certain aspects of the phrase while conducting. The conductor can show the tempo, dynamics, and style that the composer has indicated and/or the changes that the conductor might make in shaping the phrase. In the rehearsal process, the conductor solidifies these phrasing determinations with the players. The conductor must make these decisions and then see that there is a total consensus among the players about the contour of the phrase. Accelerando, ritardando, rubato, crescendo, diminuendo, accent, vibrato, and tonal intensity can communicate *the motion and direction of the phrase*.

There might be instances where the soloist would interpret the contour of the solo line without the conductor's guidance, in which case the conductor would be concerned about the ensemble's precision and balance. However, in a phrase where the whole ensemble is directly involved, the players need this guidance to achieve uniformity in the phrase contour. *The conducting patterns and gestures should reflect how the conductor wants the phrase contour to be performed.* Here, the left hand technique may figure strongly in showing the contour of the phrase dynamically while the right hand continues to show pulse. This is an example where the two hands need to be ambidextrous in showing separate gestures. The conductor's right hand might also affect the phrase by showing the pulse, in which hurrying or stretching the pulse beat in interpreting the phrase defines the phrase contour.

The contour within each phrase should be considered, because this dictates flow and tension-relaxation, and helps define the climax (or pivot-point) of the phrase. This flow gives forward motion and direction to the phrase contour. Within a composition, there is also a definite relationship between and among the phrases. This relationship will establish a pattern, help communicate the essence and spirit of the music, and provide emotional impact for the listener. In the final analysis, the conductor must consider the contour of an entire piece in order *to give this direction and emotional impact to the musical performance.* Table 13.3, Teaching Strategy (The Phrase Contour), at the end of the chapter offers ideas and suggestions for designing a teaching strategy concerning the phrase contour for the ensemble.

The climax of the phrase tends to give shape and definition to the phrase. The conductor determines where this climax will occur in the phrase and then reinforces this in the rehearsal process. Once this is determined from score study, there are numerous ways to highlight the climax: (1) crescendo-diminuendo, (2) accelerando-ritardando, (3) ritardando into the climax, (4) tension-relaxation, (5) forward flow toward the climax, (6) tone quality intensity, (7) use of vibrato, (8) tenuto and rubato, (9) emphasis on the climax (peak note or notes), and (10) space before the climactic note. The phrase climax and/or the important peak notes shown by the conductor are somewhat problematic. It is not always the highest note of the phrase. It could be the lowest note. It might be a note that is foreign to the key. An anticipatory note of the same pitch might precede the climax. Perhaps the best way to decide on the climax is to sing the phrases during score study (and use inner singing).

Comparing the phrase climaxes for how strongly to perform a particular climax and to ascertain the relationship of the phrases to each other is the conductor's task. The dynamic range of the piece may modify this phrasing as well. The composer will indicate with the various dynamic levels where the strongest climax will be in a particular piece. Look for these indications and then work to discover how much emphasis to place on the various climaxes. With this approach, there will be less danger of playing all the climaxes too strongly, and thereby failing to reveal the inner phrase structure. Table 13.4, Teaching Strategy (The Phrase Climax), at the end of the chapter provides ideas and suggestions for designing a teaching strategy to achieve the proper phrase climaxes for the ensemble.

TEMPO, DYNAMICS, STYLE AND
MUSICAL EXPRESSION WITHIN THE PHRASE

Within the phrase, the composer may indicate tempo fluctuations (accelerando-ritardando), dynamic changes (sudden or gradual), style changes, and other indications of musical expression, such as accents, fermatas, pauses, and so on. The conductor should show this musicality within the phrase with proper gestures. However, when the players do not respond to these gestures in the rehearsal process, then the conductor must persist and demonstrate verbally or by singing how the ensemble should execute this musicality. The conductor's patterns and gestures should indicate the phrasing and the energy level throughout the phrase. In addition to all of these details, the conductor must see that the phrasing is apparent to the players, and subsequently will be to the audience in the concert performance. It is worthwhile for the conductor to spend considerable time rehearsing each phrase to make the players aware of thinking about the phrase in musical performance. Table 13.5, Teaching Strategy (Musical Expression in the Phrase), at the end of the chapter presents ideas and suggestions for designing a teaching strategy for the careful observation of musical expression markings in the phrase.

OTHER ASPECTS OF PHRASING

There are other aspects of phrasing that the conductor should keep in mind during the rehearsal process:

1. When the phrase is too long to complete in one breath or when sustained bowing is required, "staggered" breathing or bowing in the ensemble may be necessary. The conductor should arrange this carefully.
2. Sustained tones need to have direction. This is accomplished by tonal intensity, vibrato, or dynamic changes.
3. Follow the rule of reiteration (as proposed by Philip Farkas) wherein a repeated passage, phrase, or figure is never played the same way (1976, 10).
4. Carefully taper phrase; give full value to the final note of the phrase (unless otherwise indicated by a staccato dot or other style marking).
5. Rehearse in phrases. (As an outcome, correct a wrong-note or rhythm error within the context of the phrase.)
6. A series of repeated tones will usually indicate a dynamic increase toward or a dynamic decrease away from a theoretical point.
7. The conductor need not sing well, but should be able to deliver to the ensemble the conception of how the phrase should sound.
8. Let the melody "sing" and "soar" to enhance the phrasing and the musical line.

THE MUSICAL LINE

Developing the musical line is a part of the musical interpretation. This pertains to the physical and psychological connection of notes that make up the phrases. There must be a feeling of continuity as a phrase is rehearsed and performed. Much of this continuity comes from understanding the phrase and the reality of the musical performance. The phrase must have direction and flow by which these notes are moving within the phrase. The direction builds tension toward the climax and then relaxation away from the climax. How this tension and relaxation are generated in the phrase is dependent on the conductor's conception of the phrase and the effectiveness in the rehearsal process to communicate this to the players. The flow pertains to the continuity and direction of the notes within the phrase. The ensemble must nurture the musical line during the rehearsal process.

If the player slurs the entire phrase, the problem is less severe; the performer has no choice but to connect notes. However, this is an exception from the general rule in a musical composition. The musical line needs a sense of unity and connection (even when the style is staccato or marcato). The musical line must have forward motion and this sense of connection. The conductor needs to be concerned about this connection of the notes within the phrase. One subtle aspect is that the conducting patterns and gestures have a "flow," so that the players will sense this connection in the phrase. At times in the rehearsal process, it may be necessary to remind the players about the flow and connection of notes within the phrase. The conductor can do this by singing or modeling the phrase and/or through conductor demonstrations.

There is frequently confusion when the composer indicates a slur marking over the whole phrase in an effort to connect the series of notes as a phrase. The dilemma here *is in the articulation of the notes.* If there are two sets of slur indications, then it is safe to assume that the composer intended the longer slur to be a phrase marking. However, if there is only the one extended phrase marking, the conductor must decide how the players will articulate or bow it. This problem frequently appears in the romantic-period music of such composers as Brahms and Wagner, where the slur marking is used to indicate the phrase. Especially for the string player, the decisions concerning the bow changes become critical. If necessary, the conductor must consider these details of bowing and articulation and mark them in the music before the rehearsal process begins.

To give the musical line impetus, it may need variation in tempo in order to achieve the desired musical expression. The forward motion of the line is achieved through tempo, flow, intensity, emphasis, and dynamic change. In most cases, the composer has conceived and indicated in the musical score what the "look" of the musical line should be. In studying the score, the conductor should assimilate what the composer has shown and then relay this to the players in the rehearsal process. In addition, the bar line is an important factor in emphasizing strong and weak beats to give the musical line emphasis and direction.

The ensemble can greatly enhance *the flow of the musical line* with fewer conducted beats per measure. Very rapid conducting patterns tend to obstruct this flow. An example of this is conducting a Strauss waltz in three beats as opposed to one beat to a measure. Of course, there are other factors involved here as well. If the tempo is quite slow, then fewer beats may mean that the conductor will have considerable more difficulty controlling the tempo, showing accents, and being precise with various indications of pulse. Supermetrics and melded gestures are a prototype of this in that the conductor omits pulses to allow for this flow. A further example of this would be, when in a faster tempo, the isolated 3/8 bar is elongated into one pulse rather than in three very rapid pulses in order to keep the eighth notes in time (as often in contemporary music).

The conductor must not allow the musical line to become distorted *because of technical difficulties in tone production or flexibility.* The line should be constituted on musicality and not based on or influenced by technical problems. With the brass instruments, these problems may pertain to large skips in that extreme physical change of the embouchure and air are necessary in executing these skips. This can lead to a sudden change of the dynamic level, and thereby cause the note to project or "jump" out of the phrase. Likewise, unless there is a dramatic indication by the composer, the musical line should generally have an evenness of intensity in terms of the tone production. It is a common error by many players to increase the dynamic level on long, sustained tones in the upper register or even to do a rather quick "swell" because of the technical demands, or erroneously for the purpose of musical expression.

CONCEIVING THE PHRASE AND THE MUSICAL LINE

In executing a phrase, the conductor should have a conception of how the phrase is going to sound before playing it (through audiation in score study). Then the conductor and players must find a way to connect notes so that the phrase is a cohesive unit. Even if the phrase requires staccato or marcato style, the player must "bring the notes together" to give the impression of a connected musical line. The contour or profile of the musical line should create interest, direction, and musical expression in the phrase. The conductor should also consider the creative dynamic levels between the phrases, and point this out to the players during the rehearsal process, such as in terraced dynamics in baroque music.

The music must give the sense of moving forward. There may be some exceptions to this, when the music is intentionally static or hesitant in nature, but generally, the phrase should have this forward motion. The conductor and players generate this forward motion in many ways during the rehearsal process. The conductor must keep the feeling of a "live" beat so that the players respond accordingly. A beat that shows little or no impulse or energy will certainly not "electrify" or "inspire" the ensemble to keep the musical line moving forward. The variance in the speed of the conducting patterns and gestures can invigorate the players to produce this forward motion in the musical line.

One of the great conductors of the 20th century, Arturo Toscanini, indicated on many occasions that one of the most difficult aspects for the instrumental music ensemble to perform well was a sustained musical line. "Sostenuto, sostenuto" was his plea in many rehearsals. *The musical interpretation involves the idea of a sustained musical line as well as the forward flow and the direction of the phrase.* The conductor must strive to produce this sustained musical line in the rehearsal process to transmit this quality to the players and subsequently to the audience in the concert performance. The conductor is responsible for showing this sustained musical line with the conducting patterns and gestures. One of the main reasons for including the idea of the musical line in this chapter is to reinforce the importance of this sustained musical line and its impact on the concert performance. Table 13.6, Teaching Strategy (Developing the Musical Line), at the end of the chapter lists ideas and suggestions in designing a teaching strategy for developing the musical line for the ensemble.

PRACTICAL APPLICATION (DISCUSSION/DEMONSTRATION)

1. Discuss and then demonstrate by conducting the beginning, the contour, the climax, the musical expression, and the ending of this phrase. (Von Suppé: Light Cavalry Overture)
2. Are there other phrasing possibilities for the above phrase? Consider other phrases as well.
3. Discuss the "rule of reiteration." See "Other Aspects of Phrasing" above.
4. Discuss and demonstrate conducting phrase endings. (Musical Example)
5. Discuss this rule: Sustain the note full value before a rest (unless otherwise indicated by a staccato or accent mark). (Musical Example)
6. What are the advantages and disadvantages of conducting more and fewer beats in a measure for the musical line development? (Musical Example: Beethoven Egmont Overture)
7. Why is rehearsing in phrases a good strategy? When is rehearsing in phrases not necessarily a good strategy?
8. Continue to gain familiarity with the standard repertoire found in Appendix A through CD listening, score study, and guidance from the conducting teacher. (See Appendix G for assignment forms.)

IN THE REHEARSAL PROCESS (LAB) ENVIRONMENT

1. Demonstrate conducting the beginning of the phrase in the rehearsal process environment. (Consider tempo, dynamics, and style). (Musical Example)
2. Demonstrate conducting the end of the phrase in the rehearsal process environment. (Consider tempo, dynamics and style) (Musical Example)
3. Demonstrate conducting and achieving the phrase contour in the rehearsal process environment. (Musical Example)
4. Demonstrate conducting and achieving the phrase climax in the rehearsal process environment. (Musical Example)
5. Demonstrate in various ways how to achieve the musical line and the flow of the phrase with the ensemble in the rehearsal process environment. (Select the musical example.)
6. Demonstrate the conducting patterns and gestures to enhance the "sweep" of the musical line in the rehearsal process environment. (Musical Example)
7. Complete student conducting/rehearsing projects (in the rehearsal process lab environment)

RECOMMENDED READING

Casey, Joseph L., *Teaching Techniques and Insights for Instrumental Music Educators*. Chapter 5, Part 1 under Audiation presents ideas for the conductor or player in terms of hearing the phrase before conducting or playing the phrase.

Dorian, Frederick, *History of Music in Performance*. Chapter 4: Phrasing and Dynamics elaborates on the historical as well as the execution of the phrasing and articulations in this particular chapter.

Farkas, Philip, *The Art of Musicianship*. Chapter 2: Phrasing covers the areas of defining the phrase, the climax or pivot-point of the phrase, and the methods used in achieving the tension and relaxation in the phrase.

Harris, Frederick, Jr., *Conducting with Feeling*. There are several sections in this book that allude to the areas of phrasing and the musical line.

Kohut, Daniel L., *Instrumental Music Pedagogy* (paperback version). In Chapter 5: Phasing and Interpretation, the author deals with melodic grouping, musical line, large intervals, accents and rhythmic interpretation, and jazz style and interpretation.

Nowak, Jerry, and Henry Nowak, *Conducting the Music, Not the Musicians*. This textbook is based on the idea of conducting phrases in music. There are many exercises offered for the conducting student to experience this approach.

Thurmond, James Morgan, *Note Grouping: A Method for Achieving Expression and Style in Musical Performance*. Chapter 13: Phrasing and the Musical Line is where the emphasis is in terms of note grouping.

REPERTOIRE FOR PROJECTS AND ASSIGNMENTS

Full Orchestra, Chamber Orchestra, or String Orchestra

Holst: St. Paul Suite (strings) (various movements)
Hovhaness: Mysterious Mountain Symphony (various movements)
Janáček: Sinfonietta (large brass instrumentation in first movement)
Mendelssohn: Symphony No. 4 "Italian" (various movements)
Kabalevsky: Overture to "Colas Breugnon," Op. 24

Concert Band or Wind Ensemble

Schuman, W.: Chester Overture (from New England Triptych)
Shostakovich: Festive Overture (Hunsberger, arr.)
Ticheli: Vesuvius
Wagner: Elsa's Procession to the Cathedral (Caillet, arr.)
Williams, C.: Symphonic Suite (various movements)

Miscellaneous or Small Ensembles

Stravinsky: Ebony Concerto (clarinet and jazz orchestra)
Reynolds: Theme and Variations for Brass Choir and Percussion

TEACHING STRATEGY TABLES

Table 13.1.   The Beginning of the Phrase

CONDUCTOR CONCERNS	PROBLEM AREAS	TEACHING STRATEGIES
Good communication with the ensemble at the beginning of the phrase Clarity with the preparatory beat Breathing with the preparatory beat Modeling the beginning of the phrase for the ensemble Conceiving the articulation and bowing at the beginning of the phrase Indicating dynamic levels with the size of the preparatory beat and the use of the left hand Reinforcing the style with the use of the left hand	Conducting technique	Discover ways of getting the players to watch the conductor at the beginning of the phrase.
		The conductor should have good eye contact with the ensemble at the beginning of the phrase in order to obtain a precise attack from the whole ensemble.
	Preparatory beats	Emphasize to all the players the importance of taking the breath with the preparatory beat (even though string and percussion players do not need to breathe!).
		Insist that the players observe the dynamics and basic style with the preparatory beat.
		The preparatory beat clarity is crucial; do not be tentative with this gesture especially on the beginning of soft, slow phrases.
	Phrasing	Teach phrasing effectively through modeling and imitation in the rehearsal process. The conductor can model this by singing, playing on piano, or playing on another instrument.
		The conductor should also breathe with the players at the beginning of the phrase.
	Articulation and bowing	Consider the articulation and/or bowing at the beginning of the phrase during score study and reinforce this with the ensemble in the rehearsal process.
		The conductor must decide the emphasis or weight of the first note of the phrase, and then demonstrate with the proper emphasis in the rehearsal process.

Table 13.1.   (*continued*)

	PROBLEM AREAS	TEACHING STRATEGIES
	Dynamic level and/or style	The conductor should indicate the dynamic level with the size of the preparatory beat. The left hand can also help indicate the style and dynamic level by turning the palm of the hand up or down.
		What dynamic level and/or other dynamic markings are indicated at the beginning of the phrase? There could be both a dynamic level indicated and a marking on the first note of the phrase such as an accent.
What other teaching strategies (suggested by the conducting teacher or students) could help secure the beginning of the phrase?		

Table 13.2.   The End of the Phrase

CONDUCTOR CONCERNS	PROBLEM AREAS	TEACHING STRATEGIES
Good communication with the ensemble on the release of the phrase A clear preparation for the release of the phrase The character of the release along with good precision Vocalize the phrase releases for awareness with the ensemble Phrase endings tending to go flat in pitch Avoiding "chopping off" the end of the phrase Reinforcing these phrase endings with the ensemble during the rehearsal process String players continuing the vibrato after the release	Conducting technique	Discover various ways to get the players to watch the conductor.
		The conductor should have good eye contact with the ensemble.
		Taper phrase endings with a specific conducting gesture with either the right or left hand.
	Phrasing	Emphasize to all the wind players to take a breath at the end of the phrase to define the phrase.
		Indicate to the ensemble the end of the phrase with the clear and proper release motion.
		Look for cadences that will define phrases endings in score study.
		Mark in the score and the wind parts phrase endings.
		Phrase endings can be effectively taught through modeling and imitation or demonstrations during the rehearsal process.

(*continued*)

Table 13.2. (***continued***)

	PROBLEM AREAS	TEACHING STRATEGIES
	Releases	Be insistent that the players are sensitive to the phrase release by watching the conductor.
		The conductor can vocalize these phrase releases in the rehearsal process to make the players aware of these phrase releases.
		Give careful attention to the release to accomplish it with the proper character, dynamics, and uniformity.
	Intonation	The phrase ending tends to go flat in pitch because of the lack of breath support and control on the release.
		Carefully tune final chords and maintain pitch on the release with the ensemble.
	Note and rest values	Avoid "chopping off" the ends of phrases. This is where the conductor must show the precise release motion.
		Notes followed by a rest receive full value unless otherwise indicated by a staccato mark or another indication.
		The conductor must indicate precisely and musically when and how the phrase should end.
		These phrase endings may need to be reinforced frequently during the rehearsal process.
	Vibrato	String players need to keep vibrating at the end of certain phrases and let the sound die.
What other teaching strategies (suggested by the conducting teacher or students) could assist in executing the phrase ending?		

Table 13.3.   The Phrase Contour

CONDUCTOR CONCERNS	PROBLEM AREAS	TEACHING STRATEGIES
The conducting technique involved in shaping the phrase contour Showing phrase contour with tempo, dynamics, intensity, and relaxation Inner singing to discover the phrase contour Analyze pitch movement to discover phrase contour Shaping the phrase with both energy and relaxation Reinforcing the right-hand patterns with left-hand gestures to indicate the phrase contours Observing the markings of the composer in shaping the phrase contour Considering the profile of the musical line	Conducting technique	Show with patterns and gestures the tempo, dynamics, and style changes in achieving the phrase contour.
		Increase or decrease the size of the conducting pattern to indicate the intensity or relaxation of phrase contour.
	Phrase contour	Through modeling and imitation, show the ensemble how the phrase contour should sound. If this is ineffective, then the conductor should demonstrate the phrase contour.
		Sing or indicate verbally what note or notes to emphasize in producing these various phrase contours.
		By inner singing during score study, the conductor can discover these phrase contours.
		Analyze pitch movement in score study to discover how the phrase contour should sound.
	Shaping the phrase	Think about the intensity and relaxation of the phrase in shaping the phrase contour.
		The conductor should indicate with the conducting patterns or the left-hand gestures how he or she will shape the phrase contour in the rehearsal process as well as in the concert performance.
		Shape the phrase with dynamics, tempo changes, tonal intensity, articulation, tone color changes, and vibrato.
		By carefully observing the markings of the composer in score study, the conductor should be able to conceive this shaping and contour of the phrase.
	Visual and verbal aids	There can be many shapes and contours to the phrase; show these on a chalkboard or with other visual aids. With a single line drawn on the chalkboard, the conductor can show the profile of the line and emphasize with thicker lines the various intensities during the phrase.
		Employ descriptive words and verbal "pictures" to enhance the "look" of the phrase contour.
What other teaching strategies (suggested by the conducting teacher or students) could aid in achieving the proper phrase contour?		

Table 13.4.   The Phrase Climax

CONDUCTOR CONCERNS	PROBLEM AREAS	TEACHING STRATEGIES
Considering how the climax of the phrase will be approached and then left	Conducting technique	Indicate by conducting patterns and left-hand gestures how to achieve the climax of the phrase (approaching and leaving the climax of the phrase).
Deciding in score study where the climax of the phrase actually occurs		Conduct the climax with a clear preparatory beat before the climactic note.
Deciding how strongly to conduct and play the climax of the phrase	Highlighting the climax	In many instances, the conductor should show with the conducting technique a dramatic preparatory gesture or a hesitation before the climatic note with the use of a slight ritardando and/or spacing before the climatic note.
Deciding which of the phrase climaxes should be the most dramatic	Score study	Decide in score study where the climax of the phrase will occur and how strongly to conduct and play this climax.
Vocalizing both the phrase contour and climax for the players		Through score study, determine which of the phrase climaxes need to be the most dramatic and how to execute these various climaxes.
Playing the climatic note down-bow for emphasis, weight, and impact	Modeling and vocalizing	With a model (conductor or player) demonstrate where and how to produce the climax of the phrase.
With young ensembles, reinforcing these climaxes during the rehearsal process		Vocalize in the rehearsal process where the climax of the phrase will occur.
		By vocalizing, the conductor can simultaneously show both the contour of the phrase and the climax of the phrase.
	Strings	In most instances, the climactic note should be played down-bow for emphasis, weight, and impact; therefore, bowings need to be conceived so that this does happen in the progression of up-bows and down-bows.
	Marking the climax	With younger ensembles, it is important to mark the music as a reminder to the players that this climax is an important note in the phrase. There may be a need to show how to achieve the climax with the phrase contour.
		The climactic note may be marked in the instrumental parts with an X above this note to reinforce this for the younger ensemble.
What other teaching strategies (suggested by the conducting teacher or students) could help in achieving the phrase climax?		

Table 13.5. Musical Expression in the Phrase

CONDUCTOR CONCERNS	PROBLEM AREAS	TEACHING STRATEGIES
Considering the musical expression indications shown within the phrase by the composer Observing and performing these musical expression indications by the composer Modeling and demonstrating the musical expression for the ensemble Using the "conduct and count" procedure to show the musical line Feeling the tension and relaxation in the phrase Observing that dynamics and nuances are part of the musical expression Tempo fluctuations, stretching beats and rubato as part of the musical expression Reinforcing the musical expression during the rehearsal process	Conducting technique	Show with conducting patterns and left-hand gestures the composer's specified indications for the musical expression.
		There are many things that the conductor must consider and produce with the conducting technique concerning the musical expression shown in the phrase.
	Modeling and imitation	Through the model and imitation procedure, the conductor can perform or sing how the musical expression should sound.
	Musical expression produced	In many instances with young ensembles, the conductor will need to show how to produce the musical expression on the various instruments.
		The conductor will need to explain and/or demonstrate various elements of musical expression to the players.
	Conducting and counting	Have the ensemble count verbally, emphasizing musical expression, while the conductor shows these changes in the conducting technique.
		Counting passages can also help the precision as well as the musical expression of the ensemble because the players are now watching the conductor.
	Tension and relaxation	The conductor can sing, verbalize, or otherwise demonstrate the feeling of tension and relaxation in the phrase.
		Realize nuances in the phrase through the tension and relaxation in the phrase.
	Dynamic changes	Through sensitive playing, the percussion section can be very effective in producing musical expression with the crescendo, diminuendo, and various accents.
		Long notes and repetitive figures should have some directions dynamically.
	Tempo changes and rubato	Tempo fluctuations, stretching beats, and rubato are important aspects of musical expression.
		These changes in tempo must be reinforced in the rehearsal process so that they do not surprise the players during the concert performance.
What other teaching techniques (suggested by the conducting teacher or students) could be useful in achieving musical expression in the phrase?		

Table 13.6. Developing the Musical Line

CONDUCTOR CONCERNS	PERFORMANCE AREAS	TEACHING STATEGIES
Molding the musical line in the rehearsal process Modeling and demonstrating the musical line Singing and verbalizing to help realize the musical line Feeling the "sweep" of the musical line Moving the musical line forward Thinking musically to help sustain the phrasing and the musical line Rehearsing in phrases to sustain the musical line Showing the phrasing and the musical line in both the rehearsal process and the concert performance	Conducting technique	Conduct with "flow" in the conducting patterns to produce the precision and musicality with the ensemble.
		The conducting patterns and gestures by the conductor should reflect the change of energy as dictated in the music.
		The conductor should focus the conducting technique on molding the musical line in the rehearsal process and in preparation for the concert performance.
	Modeling and imitation	Use a model for the ensemble to imitate, showing the musical line as the conductor has conceived it.
		In terms of the musical line, listen to some fine musicians in how they phrase music.
		The conductor should give the ensemble specific feedback in developing the musical line.
	Singing and verbalizing	Sing or verbalize how the musical line should sound in terms of style and the musical conception.
		A sustained musical line is a singing line not unlike what the conductor does with inner singing in score study.
	Forward motion of the musical line	Feel the "sweep" of the musical line. This may involve fewer or more beats per measure. Both the right hand and the left hand can contribute to this forward motion of the musical line.
		Show the forward motion of the musical line in the "flow" of the conducting technique.
	Tone control	Stress the idea of tone control with the use of breath control and bow control in sustaining and moving the musical line forward.
		The conductor thinking musically will help sustain the breathing, bowing, and phrasing of the musical line.

Table 13.6.   (*continued*)

	PERFORMANCE AREAS	TEACHING STATEGIES
	Rehearse in phrases	Rehearsing in phrases makes for a better understanding of the musical structure for the players.
		The correction of errors can be isolated and improved on through the rehearsing in phrases.
		The conductor and players should still think about phrases, and not just about meter changes or bar-lines in contemporary music.
What other teaching strategies (suggested by the conducting teacher or students) could help in developing the musical line?		

Chapter Fourteen

Style and Musical Interpretation

How should this sound? This is the all-encompassing question, but it primarily refers to the areas of style and musical interpretation. After the conductor gets beyond the more mundane aspects of musical performance, *the question arises as to the proper style (note length and note emphasis) and the musical interpretation.* Here the conductor must make critical decisions for the ensemble. If the conductor left these aspects to the individual players in the ensemble to decide, the results would be chaotic. The conductor must communicate style and musical interpretation through conducting patterns and gestures or with verbal comments and demonstrations in the rehearsal process and subsequently be reinforced in all of the following rehearsals as necessary.

This is where music imagery becomes so critical for the conductor as to how to rehearse the music. This imagery comes from meticulous score study and in conceiving the style and musical interpretation. Then the conductor must communicate to the ensemble exactly the music imagery that he or she conceived in score study. There may be occasions when the conductor will find that the conception is incorrect, or at the very least surprising. In this case, the conductor should do more score study and research to clarify this conception. During the rehearsal process, the conductor needs to bring this clear conception along with adequate conducting technique to reflect how the music should sound. There must be a physical and psychological connection from the musical conception in the mind of the conductor *to the conducting hands, arms, and baton to communicate the proper style and musical interpretation for the instrumental music ensemble.*

DEFINING STYLE

Style in musical performance has several connotations. In a specific sense, style relates to note length and emphasis (i.e., staccato, marcato, legato, and tenuto). Style also refers to the musical period historically and strongly connects to what is known as the performance practice of the period. Style also involves tempo, articulation, phrasing, and dynamics. Maintaining the correct style throughout a work is a difficult task for the conductor especially with a younger ensemble. Finally, the term, "style" could reflect and define the essence and spirit of the music. The conductor should strive to grasp this essence and spirit in bringing forth the proper performance contrast and authenticity.

Style and tempo are closely related. Tempo is an important part of any musical interpretation. The style may need to be adjusted if the tempo is adjusted. For example, if the selected tempo is very rapid, it may be necessary to produce a staccato style that is lighter and crisper than if the tempo selected were more moderate. Certainly there are numerous other factors in the musical interpretation, but if the correct tempo and style are achieved, the musical results will tend to be very positive. Many conductors place great emphasis (and rightly so) in the rehearsal process on achieving the proper style, and this certainly has a strong connection with the selected tempo.

Style can also be used in a very general sense of being distinctive. The virtuoso soloist in musical performance is striving for this uniqueness of style. It is important to realize that the style in solo playing as opposed to ensemble performance is somewhat different. However, the stylistic concerns in the ensemble are not ones of virtuosity as in solo playing. Ensemble playing has more to do with the uniformity of ensemble performance than with the virtuosity of solo playing. Therefore, in the rehearsal process, the focus is on the priorities of intonation, precision, balance, blend, articulation, phrasing, and a uniform style along with the musical interpretation.

DEFINING MUSICAL INTERPRETATION

I define musical interpretation as the realization of a musical work in performance. It is a term used to represent almost everything that can be done in a musical performance, such as nuances, flexibility, precision, and so on. Musical interpretation involves the performance of a work so that the players and the audience understand what the composer was trying to communicate musically. The parameters of this book will not allow a detailed discussion of specific works. The conductor should seek this out through the many available resources on musical interpretation. However, musical interpretation should be distinctive and authentic.

The study of musical interpretation is a lifelong process. One acquires it by (1) serious music study and research, (2) listening to quality performances, (3) careful personal score study, and (4) actual performance experience. Musical interpretation involves the elements of performance, authenticity, imagination, and musical sensitivity. Conductors and players are obligated in practicing the art of music to attend concerts and hear all kinds of musical performances. In many cases, musicians limit their horizons by listening only to music in their specific area. Brass players listen to brass performances or string players attend only orchestra or string quartet concerts. The instrumental conductor has much to gain in listening to vocal performances, chamber music performances, and so on. Live performances are especially encouraged as well as the acquisition of an extensive record library. Likewise, the study of various musical scores by the conductor is essential in gaining a perspective on the repertoire.

Musical interpretation should be based on the music itself (as notated by the composer), the traditions of the musical period, and the imagination, creativity, and musical sensitivity of the conductor. There is considerable latitude in musical interpretation, but it must be done in such a way as to reflect intelligence, research, understanding, and musical taste. The extremes in musical interpretation are, perhaps, always of a precarious rationale. The conductor should strive to interpret and realize the music with the composer's intentions as the most important goal. If the composition were a relatively recent work, the most authentic interpretation might be one conducted by the composer. (This is assuming that the composer is an adequate conductor and the ensemble is competent and well rehearsed.) This is not to say that other conductors and ensembles would be incapable of producing an authentic interpretation of the work. The important point here is that the conductor understands the composer's intentions for writing the work and then strives to interpret the composition as the composer intended it to be performed musically.

MUSICAL INTERPRETATION IN THE REHEARSAL PROCESS

The factors involved in musical interpretation are numerous, but the conductor must seriously pursue these during the rehearsal process in preparation for the concert performance. *The right tempo is the primary consideration in all situations.* After the tempo selection, phrasing needs careful consideration; this determines the structure and the sense of the musical interpretation. Beyond this, the style, the dynamics, the nuances, and other musical expressions are important considerations in dealing with the musical interpretation during the rehearsal process. These items of musical interpretation must be reinforced in the rehearsal process after the conductor has conceived the musical interpretation through meticulous score study, extensive research, and then coming before the ensemble ready to communicate this conception to the ensemble.

The conductor's conception should be somewhat personal, but based on solid musicianship. This musicianship involves research concerning the composer, the selection, and the musical period involved. Then the conductor should study and incorporate the details of the musical score into this conception. As the rehearsals continue, there may be some changes in the conception especially after hearing the ensemble in the rehearsal process. However, the conductor should make these changes in the early stages of these rehearsals. Dress rehearsals are not the appropriate time to make these changes for the obvious reason that the concert performance may suffer from player insecurity.

THE FOUR BASIC STYLES

The four basic styles in musical performance are staccato, marcato, legato, and tenuto. Staccato style is light and detached. Marcato style is heavy and detached (most of the time, depending on the tempo). Legato style indicates a smooth, sustained execution of the music. Tenuto style translates to ultra legato. A further step in realizing these four basic styles is to develop some flexibility in these style changes with varying degrees of these styles. Common errors in stylistic performance include "clipping" note values (especially at the end of phrases), always playing faster notes separated, and poor uniformity of note length among the players. It is important for the conductor to realize *that tempo (or speed) of the piece does affect the selected style.*

If the conductor is able to show these four basic styles in the conducting patterns with the reinforcement in the left-hand gestures, and attain from the players the proper response to these patterns and gestures, he or she has taken a significant step in terms of producing the appropriate style. It is not enough just to conduct these styles in the rehearsal process, however. There will be times when these styles must be rehearsed meticulously to obtain the desired articulation and note length. In many of these situations, the imitation of the conductor's vocalization of these styles is, perhaps, the most efficient procedure for obtaining the correct style. Once this is done, the conductor's patterns and gestures then act as a reminder to the ensemble of the particular style desired.

Many conductors approach the rehearsal process *with the idea of solidifying the style* of the work before other priorities are considered. The philosophy here is that if the style is played correctly and uniformly, many of the other performance aspects, such as balance, blend, and intonation, will fall into place. This is also a large part of capturing the essence and spirit of the music. It is important for the maturing conductor to keep this in mind throughout the rehearsal process and into the concert performance. It is very easy for the ensemble to slip into a general "semi-legato" style and never recover from it. Staccato style is frequently ignored or gradually becomes longer as the performance continues. The conductor must keep reminding the players of the numerous possibilities in terms of this variation in style.

REHEARSING THE FOUR BASIC STYLES

Finally, the conductor must teach and rehearse these basic styles with the younger ensemble. Failure to do this leads to uninspired, dull performances. The easy thing to do with an ensemble is to allow the players to play everything "semi-legato" and "mezzo-forte." The warm-up period is a perfect opportunity to begin teaching these four basic styles. The lack of style and changes in musical style usually occur with a less motivated group (which reflects on the conductor and what is happening in the rehearsal process). Style can be diagrammed on the chalkboard and vocalized by the conductor. With younger ensembles, in teaching these four basic styles, it may be necessary to provide some technical information about the articulation, note length, and other performance aspects during the rehearsal process. It is helpful for the conductor to speak in musical terms in teaching these four basic styles.

One of the main concerns in achieving the correct style *is note length.* This involves the amount of space (or silence) between notes. Staccato and sometimes, marcato dictate the detaching of notes. Often accents, after-beats, syncopated notes, and isolated notes are played too long. In rehearsing the instrumental ensemble, the conductor must make these decisions with the thought of achieving a uniformity of style. Some of the players cannot be playing semi-legato while others are playing staccato with the expectation of achieving a uniformity of execution by the ensemble. The tempo is also a factor in the decision about note length. There is a tendency for extremely short notes to lose tone quality and pitch. Both the conductor and the players must realize this problem in order to counteract this rather unmusical effect.

There are many factors involved with the proper weight (or stress) on the note. Written accents, unwritten accents, dynamic level, general style (such as marcato style) and the phrase climax are some of the considerations in how much weight a note should receive. The conductor will have the final say in these matters. The musicianship of the conductor will certainly affect these decisions. *Good conducting technique is vital in showing the weight of the notes through the gesture of syncopation.* This gesture of syncopation is also very useful in that it can dictate many of the different performance aspects to the instrumental music ensemble. Conductors whose technique is too heavy and exaggerated will find it difficult to vary the weight of these notes. If the players are watching and sensitive to the proper weight of the patterns and gestures of the conductor, the ensemble performance will then turn into an exciting, musical experience.

It is important for both the conductor and players to realize that at any given moment in the music *two contrasting styles may be present.* For example, the melody may be in a legato style while the accompaniment might be rhythmic and staccato in style. Each part may need separate rehearsing. The question arises as to which style to conduct. The answer depends on the group and what the conductor decides will be the most effective way of achieving this style contrast. The style indication should then be conducted consistently from the rehearsal process through the concert performance so there is no confusion on the part of the players.

MODIFYING THE FOUR BASIC STYLES

It is also important for both the conductor and players to understand that these four basic styles are just that—basic. There are many degrees between these four basic styles, determined by the context of the music. How long or short, how much emphasis there should be, and the articulations of a note are all questions that the conductor must wrestle with in the rehearsal process. Staccatissimo, secco staccato, and ben marcato are some of the terms that denote these degrees between the basic styles. Max Rudolf, in his *The Grammar of Conducting*, cites six conducting styles: "non-expressivo, light-staccato, full-staccato, espressivo-legato, marcato and tenuto" (1995). With a musically sensitive ensemble, the conductor should be able to obtain these stylistic differences. Even more degrees of the basic styles may be refined during the rehearsal process.

To a point, the conductor should be able to show these various styles with the conducting patterns and gestures. However, if the player response to the patterns and gestures is not an appropriate one, then the conductor must resolve the problem verbally in the rehearsal process. *Vocalization by the conductor to show the style is one of the most effective and efficient means used in the rehearsal process.* If the players learn to listen carefully to the conductor and then imitate the conductor's vocalizing, much time will be saved in the rehearsal process. A less efficient or effective method is simply having the players execute the style and then make the correction if it needs to be longer or shorter, lighter or heavier, and so on. This tends to waste time in the rehearsal process. The players may need to mark their parts if the conductor indicates such style changes. Having a pencil ready to mark the music so that the player remembers the requested changes is very important in terms of the learning transfer. In some situations, it may be necessary to indicate to the players how to mark such changes in the music.

STYLISTIC TERMS, MARKINGS, AND TEACHING STRATEGIES

It is important to know the definitions of the various stylistic terms and markings. During score study, the maturing conductor (as a musician) should undertake considerable research to understand the meaning of these stylistic terms and markings. Only in this way will the conductor be able to lead the ensemble properly. Then, within the context of the music, the conductor should determine and realize these terms and markings in the rehearsal process. If the developing conductor is unaware of the definition of the stylistic term or is unsure of the execution of the particular style marking, he or she should consult a musical dictionary in order to apply the correct definition or execution during the rehearsal process.

As with tempo terms, the composer usually supplies *stylistic terms* that dramatically affect the musical interpretation. These terms are placed in the music to give the conductor a general idea of the style and mood of the composition. The following are just a few examples of these stylistic terms: agitato, alla marcia, allegretto, animato, appassionato, bravura, brilliante, cantabile, deciso, deliberato, dolce, espressivo, funèbre, con fuoco, giocoso, guisto, grandioso, grazioso, lugubre, leggiero, maestoso, pesante, religioso, risoluto, scherzando, sonore, sostenuto, spiritoso, tranquillo, and vigoroso. With many of these stylistic terms, the meaning can be gleaned from the foreign word. However, the conductor should consult a music dictionary for the definitions if in doubt. The conductor should not take a chance on being wrong!

In the rehearsal process and concert performance, *the conductor and the players often simply ignore* the stylistic markings. Unless the conductor insists on playing these markings correctly and uniformly, the players may not observe these style indications. There are not many stylistic markings to be aware of, but these few markings are used frequently in music performance. The staccato dot, the legato (or tenuto) dash, the marcato accents (> and ^) and sometimes a combination of these markings are shown in the music. In addition, the slur may be added to these markings, causing the type of articulation to change. Again, these markings will need to be reinforced in the rehearsal process as to the exact note length and weight (stress) desired by the conductor. Table 14.1, Teaching Strategy (The Music Period Style and Interpretation), at the end of the chapter presents ideas and suggestions for designing a teaching strategy to achieve the proper style and execution.

MUSICAL PERIOD STYLES AND PERFORMANCE PRACTICES

With the instrumental music ensemble, the main stylistic considerations are those of four distinct periods in instrumental music. These four periods are the baroque (1600–1750), the classical (1750–1825), the romantic (1825–1900) and the contemporary (1900–present). As with all historic periods, there are some crossover times from one period to another. This certainly affects the style that the conductor and players must project in their performance. Not all composers who have written in a specific period reflect that musical period. For example, Jean Sibelius composed in the style of the romantic period, although he wrote many of his works in the contemporary period. Therefore, consider the individual composer when interpreting music stylistically. Performance practice includes the areas of articulation, dynamics, tone, rhythm, tempo, melody, and ornamentation (such as the mordant, trill, turn or gruppetto, and grace notes).

Listed below are some of the main characteristics of these various musical periods. The conductor should *strive for authenticity* in the musical interpretation. Only through acquired musicianship and detailed research will the conductor be able to justify the choices in tempo, style, and musical interpretation of a particular work in a specific musical period. By knowing the characteristics and general style of these musical periods, the conductor can begin to lead the ensemble in scholarly interpretations and present authentic performances. Performance practice in these various periods is an important part of this musical interpretation.

THE BAROQUE PERIOD

The following are some of the main characteristics of the baroque period in music that would influence the instrumental music ensemble rehearsal process and the concert performance:

1. With the baroque string style (because of the type of bow used at that time), there were no off-the-string bowings; spacing of the notes was executed by stopping the bow on the string.
2. Terraced dynamics (mainly piano [*p*] and forte [*f*] dynamics) prevailed, the repetition of phrases done with the opposite dynamic level.
3. Stately tempos were the fashion (polyphonic music demanded these tempos to ensure clarity of the various musical lines); extremes in tempos were to be avoided.
4. The characteristic or traditional performance in terms of tempo, style, dynamics, and ornaments (starting trills on the top notes, turns, mordents, appoggiaturas, ornaments on the beat, etc.), established performance practice.
5. The basso continuo was the foundation of the orchestral composition, harpsichord or organ reinforced with cello, bassoon, or string bass.
6. Concerto grosso, fugue, chorale prelude, operatic overtures, instrumental parts (from oratorios), solo concertos, miscellaneous instrumental pieces, and dance suites represented the type of compositions for the instrumental music ensemble.

7. Tone color was not a strong consideration for the baroque composer, except in selecting solo parts; instruments were used as voice lines, not as sources of instrumental color particularly.
8. Polyphony, structural balance, and a steady line was the rule.
9. Tone quality and texture is somewhat thick and heavy.
10. General style is that of breadth and continuity (broad détaché bowing in the strings).
11. Orchestra instrumentation did not include clarinet, trombone (except with sacred music), percussion (except timpani), and the number of wind parts was minimal.
12. Cadence awareness in the performance of baroque music dictates the phrasing and the tempo change on the final phrase (a slight ritardando and a pause before the final note was required). Overlapping of phrases was a common characteristic of this period.

In conducting and rehearsing music in the baroque period, the conductor needs to keep in mind the main characteristics of this period. These characteristics include the baroque string style, the balance of the various multiple lines (polyphony), the phrasing, the traditional idea of the ritardando and pause just before the final note of a movement or piece, the terraced dynamics of forte and piano, and the idea of stately tempos and broad execution of the style and notes (détaché). Along with these performance characteristics is the conductor's knowledge of the numerous ornamentations that were prevalent in the baroque period. These ornaments include the correct execution of trills, mordents, turns (gruppettos), appoggiaturas, and other such ornamentation.

THE CLASSICAL PERIOD

The following are some of the main characteristics of the classical period in music that would influence the instrumental music ensemble rehearsal process and the concert performance:

1. String bowing style of staccato and spiccato (because of the type of bow used, the music of the period was performed often with off-the-string bowings when required). Bowing styles included spiccato and "brush" stroke bowing.
2. Crescendo, diminuendo, and sudden dynamic changes occurred (but using the same dynamic indications for all of the parts was still common).
3. Tempos at fast speeds (allegro) were played brightly. Homophonic music was the rule; slow tempos were legato and lucid.
4. The correct performance of ornaments was an important consideration (as it was in the baroque period).
5. Orchestral writing and instrumentation expanded and solidified. (The flute and clarinet appeared, as did some horn, trumpet, trombone, and percussion parts—although limited mostly to timpani until Mozart and Haydn.)
6. Musical form was very important; music was highly structured (architecture).

7. Articulation was light (staccato dot or *sforzato*) and the texture was transparent (sustained notes must not cover up moving parts); sharp, clean and precise attacks prevailed.
8. The composer became more specific in the score as to intent.
9. The basso continuo disappeared and the five-part string writing began.
10. Types of instrumental compositions included rondo, minuet, divertimento, serenade, scherzo, operatic overture, theme and variations, sonata (sonata-allegro), solo concerto, symphony, and suite.
11. The key words in musical interpretation were restraint, transparency, and beauty of tone.
12. Projection of the melody was important (for the structural balance).

Although a number of elements carried over from the baroque period, the classical period of Haydn and Mozart has some very distinct and characteristic changes. These main changes *included the tourte bow*, which allowed the player to execute off-the-string bowings and more bowing styles, the indications by the composer of dynamic variances, a more transparent style due to the homophonic nature of the classical period, additional instruments in the orchestra, musical form became more important, and the basso continuo of the baroque period dissolved. The conductor must still be aware of the correct performance of ornaments and the performance practice of the classical period.

THE ROMANTIC PERIOD

The following are some of the main characteristics of the romantic period in music that would affect the instrumental music ensemble rehearsal process and the concert performance:

1. Tone color and texture became important considerations in this period (This change occurred in part through new and additional instruments in the ensemble, extreme dynamics, sudden dynamics, extreme ranges, and some harmonic innovations.)
2. Expanded dynamic levels, special effects, and more musical expression developed. (Long crescendos and diminuendos needed to be gauged and controlled; special effects are produced with various bowing styles and techniques such as sul ponticello, sul tasto, pizzicato, col legno, and harmonics, as well as stopped horn, mutes, special percussion effects, more varied percussion instruments, and striking dynamic contrasts with big climaxes.)
3. More rubato and sudden tempo changes led to more "dramatic" music.
4. More rhythmic complexity, some changes in meter, and sudden and unexpected pauses evolved.
5. Programmatic or descriptive music (such as the tone poem) appeared.
6. Expanded forms (the symphonic poem as well as other expanded multi-movement compositions) developed.

7. Expanded phrase length and melodies, lyricism, and asymmetrical phrase structure began.
8. Large, sonorous ensemble tone (grand and powerful) prevailed.
9. Emphasis on tone color of the individual solo instruments developed.
10. Composers used more vibrato to expand the emotional quality of the music.
11. Ensemble instrumentation was larger and more varied (partly because of the improvement and invention of instruments, including piccolo, English horn, bass clarinet, contrabassoon, valved brass, trombone, tuba [serpent or orpheclide], varied percussion instruments, harp, and piano).
12. Types of compositions included opera, symphonic tone poem, symphonic variations, virtuoso (solo) concerto, symphony, waltz, nocturne, the romantic overture, and large choral-orchestra works.

Because of the expanded instrumentation and the desire of the composers of this period to achieve more color and freedom in musical composition and performance, the conductor should exaggerate the elements of tempo, dynamics, style, and special effects. In general, the orchestration of romantic period compositions greatly increased in terms of instrument numbers and individual parts. All of this complicated the rehearsal process environment because the conductor now had to deal with more parts in the score and then bring all of these elements to fruition in preparation for the concert performance. The conductor now needed to be ready to conduct and rehearse larger forces, although these expanded forces provided for more variety and some very exciting musical performances.

THE CONTEMPORARY PERIOD

The following are some of the main characteristics of the contemporary period in music that influence the instrumental music ensemble rehearsal process and the concert performance:

1. Rhythmic, asymmetrical, and shifting meter complexity evolved, as well as cross-rhythms.
2. Harmonic dissonance (often unresolved) appeared.
3. Variable and new instrumentation developed.
4. Fragmentation of the melodic line; lines are angular and disjunctive.
5. Atonality, polytonality, polymeter, and polydynamics prevailed.
6. Style diversity in composition evolved, including Neo-baroque, Neo-classical, Neo-romanticism, Impressionism, Nationalism, aleatory, jazz (improvisation), electronic, serial (or twelve-tone), and minimalism.
7. Experimental music or new music (often difficult technically and demanding special instruments, techniques, and equipment) arose.
8. The composer became very specific with the score indications, requiring adherence to the composer's instructions.
9. Emphasis on the use of percussion instruments with the ensemble prevailed.

10. Types of compositions included programmatic music, symphony, suite, solo concerto, concert overture, variations, contemporary opera, contemporary ballet, chamber music of unusual combinations, and various dances.

The conductor should *adhere to the indications of the composer.* The composer is quite specific as to what is intended in the contemporary composition. Likewise, the conductor must become knowledgeable about the many new instruments and techniques involved in contemporary music. The conductor needs to become very skilled in terms of meter changes and asymmetrical meter conducting. Additionally, the conductor should be aware of the percussion section as many of the "new" sounds come from this section with various instruments. Much of the contemporary music needs "settling" time because of the technical and rhythmic demands made upon the players.

TRANSITIONAL PERIODS OF MUSIC AND THE INDIVIDUAL COMPOSERS

All of the items listed above pertain to the interpretation of music in these specific musical periods. These characteristic lists and summaries represent a small portion of the knowledge the conductor must possess in order to interpret the music from these four periods properly. There are, in addition to these four periods of instrumental music, some transitional periods such as the Rococo and Impressionistic periods that need consideration along with these transitional periods and the specific composers in interpreting the music properly within the context of the musical period and in the life and works of the specific composer. Likewise, there are other transitional periods and compositional styles to consider, such as nationalism, expressionism, neo-classical, serial, and minimalism.

The individual composer is certainly a consideration in terms of the style and musical interpretation of his or her works. A comparison of J. S. Bach and Hector Berlioz would not only cross the musical periods, but each individual composer was trying for entirely different ways of composing within the context of these musical periods. There could be many other comparisons made about the individual composers. The developing conductor must be aware of these individual differences through score study and research on the composer and familiarity with their musical output. Whatever piece might be at hand, the maturing conductor should also listen (live performances or CDs) to other works by the same composer in order to capture the style and intended musical interpretation for that individual composer. Brahms should sound like Brahms! Bernstein should sound like Bernstein!

THE ESSENCE AND SPIRIT OF THE MUSIC

"How should this sound?" This question confronts the advanced conductor again when trying to grasp the essence and spirit of the music. Essence is defined as "a basic trait or set of traits that define and establish the character of something; the most central and material part" (Roget's *Thesaurus*, 1988). The essence of a serenade would be that of a calm, quiet, and peaceful mood. The spirit of the music relates to the vitality or driving force of the music in performance. Is the spirit of the work slow, fast, humorous, happy, sad, dramatic, and so on? A common tactic used by many conductors is to exclaim, "The music must dance!" as an attempt to capture this distinct spirit in the music. Lack of success in capturing this essence and spirit of the music with the ensemble will result in ordinary, unexciting performances. The essence and spirit involves the overall mood of the selection. There are many adjectives such as arrogant, violent, brassy, tender, etc. that could describe the mood. Some composers have employed vamps in their music in order to set the mood of the piece, such as in Bernstein's "Symphonic Dances from *West Side Story*."

In some cases, it is very clear what the essence and spirit of the music should be. For example, a John Philip Sousa march immediately dictates to the conductor a marcato style with certain strategically placed accents and/or implied dynamics. The form is very standardized: introduction, first strain, second strain, and trio. (After the conductor has rehearsed and performed several of these marches, there is no excuse for keeping the head and eyes in the score, and yet this is a common occurrence with even experienced conductors.) In contrast and as a further example, the first movement of a classical symphony has a fairly standard form, but is perhaps more complex in capturing the essence and spirit of the work because within this movement the essence and spirit may change several times as themes are introduced. The essence and spirit of the work will tend to dictate to the conductor the various dynamic levels, dynamic ranges, musical expression, tempo, tempo changes, style, and articulation. When the conductor has a clear concept of the essence and spirit of the music and is able to communicate this in the rehearsal process, the ensemble should then play with the correct "feeling for the music" in the concert performance.

It is important for the conductor to determine exactly the essence and spirit of the music before rehearsals begin. In score study, the conductor must ask many questions. In some cases, the type of music may immediately indicate this essence and spirit. For example, is it a tango, a nocturne, a march, a waltz, a scherzo, or a minuet? Then the conductor should interpret the work in the characteristic manner. Making such determinations allows the conductor to better perceive the compositional style and the composer's intentions. Sometimes it is not easy to make this determination. In programmatic music, the conductor must think "about the story." Adjectives supplied by the composer, such as majestic, somber, playful, and so on might indicate clues to the essence and spirit. *Discovering this essence and spirit of the work should be one of the conductor's first preparations for the rehearsal process.*

IN THE REHEARSAL PROCESS

The conductor must see "the big picture" and not get caught up in the details of the notes, rhythms, or even the phrases. This is not to say that in the rehearsal process there is no need for careful, detailed rehearsing. Rather, the conductor must be aware of what he or she is trying to project to the players and later on to the audience. This

involves the essence and spirit of the music and the conductor's re-creation of it. Much
of the conductor's success depends upon how well the essence and spirit of the work
is projected to the players in the rehearsal process.

First, the basic style needs to be shown with patterns and gestures, and in some
instances, the ensemble may need further verbal instruction as to how to accomplish
this either technically or musically. Then address the details such as tempo changes,
accents, dynamic contrast, phrasing, and articulation. The conductor needs to convey
the emotional intensity of the music. For example, the final notes (or measures) of
various works are important in terms of closure and impact for the listening audience.
The conductor must carefully conceive these final endings. An example of this closure would be at the end of the Beethoven *Symphony No. 5* wherein the punctuated
C major chords must have direction and emotional impact. Finally, the conductor,
through patterns and gestures or conductor demonstrations in the rehearsal process,
will communicate the emotions of the music to the ensemble. The music itself will
determine in what sequence the conductor should accomplish all of this. For example,
in programmatic music, the conductor should be thinking about what the composer is
conveying. The conductor must always remain in physical control; it is easy to let the
emotions of the music distort the conducting patterns and gestures. If this happens,
*then both the conducting technique and the emotional gestures involved begin to lose
the necessary clarity.* In summary, the four steps in capturing and communicating the
essence and spirit of the music to the instrumental music ensemble are:

1. The establishment and/or modification of the basic styles (staccato, legato, marcato, or tenuto) at any given point in the music
2. Rehearsing the details of the work (tempo, tempo changes, articulation, accents,
   dynamics, phrasing, etc.)
3. Bringing out the essence and spirit of the passage, phrase, or section in the rehearsal process and in the concert performance with the proper conducting patterns
   and gestures
4. Then projecting the big picture that the conductor communicated to the ensemble
   in the rehearsal process and to the listener during the concert performance

VERBOSITY IN THE REHEARSAL PROCESS

The use of description and imagery in the rehearsal process can be very effective, but
the conductor must be careful *that these approaches do not lead to verbosity.* There is
a dangerous tendency for many conductors to "paint pictures" verbally in the rehearsal
process while attempting to capture the essence and spirit of the music. Some of this is
certainly valid, especially in specific instances such as programmatic music or where
the composer is actually trying to relate or describe an image. However, this verbalization may be carried much too far by the conductor and this leads to boredom for the
ensemble as well as time wasted in the rehearsal process. As a rule, in the rehearsal
process the conductor should deliver only specific information about the technical
and musical aspects of the work verbally. There is a danger of wasting time in the

rehearsal process simply by talking too much. Effective conductors show this with conducting patterns, gestures, and by singing to make their points or in correcting the various problems through other means than talking.

Along the same line, however, the conductor would do well to let the players know exactly what the composer's intentions were in writing the piece. There may be historical, musical, or programmatic significance of the piece that will lead to a better performance. As conductors, we supply detailed program notes to the audience but sometimes neglect explaining the essence and spirit of the music to the ensemble. The conductor should give the needed information to the players for a better musical interpretation during the rehearsal process. The conductor should suggest, "Here are a couple of ideas on interpreting this piece," rather than telling or demanding these details from the ensemble. In some cases, the composer may supply information about the piece at the front of the score as to its significance and interpretation.

INTERPRETATION STUDY

The Conductor and Interpretation Study

Musical interpretation involves score study, research, and listening to the music (live and/or recorded). *The conductor's goal must be to interpret the music as closely as possible to the composer intention.* This involves research into the composer and the work at hand as well as being a competent conductor to bring the composition to fruition. The fine conductor will strive to make the musical interpretation as creative and interesting as possible. Proper tempo and tempo changes, creative phrasing, and dynamic contrast are some elements that will begin to shape the interpretation into a musical and exciting performance. Musical interpretation is a monumental area of consideration. The study of musical interpretation should be a lifelong endeavor for all conductors and musicians. The various periods of music and individual composers need in-depth research. In the various graduate-level conducting courses or seminars, musical interpretation of specific works should be one of the main topics of discussion.

Even after the conductor has studied the musical score and conceived the musical interpretation, there is no real promise that this musicality will pervade the concert performance. However, the competency and credibility of the conductor hinges on the musical interpretation and on the musicality that he or she has acquired and brings before the ensemble in the rehearsal process. *Only if the conductor has developed a high level of competency in the conducting technique and in the rehearsing of the ensemble* will this musical interpretation succeed in the concert performance.

The conductor must take responsibility (or blame) for the musical interpretation. Likewise, the conductor's teaching and control of the ensemble in the rehearsal process is reflected in the concert performance. The skills and knowledge of the conductor to impose the conceived musical interpretation on the ensemble is paramount to the success of the concert performance. The conductor must always be comparing the actual playing by the ensemble to his or her conceived musical interpretation. Only then, through careful rehearsing, will the conductor achieve the desired musical interpretation from the ensemble in the concert performance.

A final point about conducting technique and musical interpretation: If the conducting technique has been developed to the point of being clear and automatic, then the conductor is able to focus on the musical interpretation. *In such a situation, the conducting technique is no longer a studied, physical process, but becomes subservient to the musical considerations of the conductor.* The conductor must practice technique until it is clear and automatic. However, even after this practice, it might be of value for the conductor to check periodically, through videotaping, for clarity in the conducting technique. The constant changing of meters and the existence of asymmetrical meters in a work (mostly found in contemporary music) are two areas that the conductor needs to practice so that he or she masters the mechanical aspects and can concentrate on the musical interpretation.

The Conductor's Education in Musical Interpretation

Most any serious music study relates to the musical interpretation. Music theory, music history and literature, conducting technique, the serious study and performance on a particular instrument, and ensemble experience should be incorporated into the educational background of a conductor. The conductor then brings to the rehearsal process all of his or her educational background, performance skills, and conducting ability to enhance the musical interpretation in the rehearsal process and the concert performance.

Music theory instruction gives the conducting student information about melody, harmony, rhythm, and musical form and structure along with training the ear to detect and correct errors in the rehearsal process. *Great emphasis should rest on aural training* for any music career preparation. The training of conductors should also include keyboard skills. In auditioning to be accepted into most graduate conducting programs the requirements usually involve both aural skills and keyboard competency.

The study of music history and literature supplies the musician with information about the composers, the literature, and the musical periods. This knowledge is essential for the conductor. In all cases, it is the responsibility of the conductor to select music for programs. Having good background in music literature and ensemble repertoire is necessary to provide a perspective for the conductor in selecting music for performances. The conductor must also know the styles and performance practice of the various periods of music to interpret the selected repertoire properly.

Private study on a chosen instrument provides invaluable information concerning musical interpretation. It is unimaginable that an instrumental music conductor could be very successful if he or she never experienced playing a musical instrument in a quality ensemble. The conductor would have little musical sensitivity toward such an instrumental music ensemble performance. Even after a player has become a full-time conductor, there are many reasons for continuing to perform on his or her major instrument. Among these reasons is the appreciation for what is involved with the actual performance in an instrumental music ensemble.

Authenticity involves performing the music as the composer intended. In this sense, there are many factors to consider. Score study, knowledge about the composer and the musical period, performance practice of the period, and other interpretative details are some of these factors. To be certain of an authentic interpretation of the work being prepared, the conductor should obtain two or more reputable recordings to gain a perspective on the musical interpretation of the work at hand. If no recordings are available, then listening to other works by the same composer and gleaning the general style and possible musical interpretation might be in order.

All four of these areas are necessary to enhance the level of musical interpretation by the conductor. As mentioned previously, the conductor should develop a high level of competency in both the conducting technique and rehearsing skills. It is the main purpose of this book to help the developing conductor achieve these goals. However, the conductor is only ready to pursue his or her conducting career in instrumental music if he or she has devoted considerable time and effort to musical interpretation through serious study of music theory, music history and literature, conducting/ rehearsing, and considerable instrumental performance in a quality ensemble.

PRACTICAL APPLICATION (DISCUSSION/DEMONSTRATION)

1. Discuss and demonstrate the four basic musical styles and the modification of these basic styles. What might influence these styles? Listen and adjust.
2. Discuss the meaning of the various style terms listed under the heading "Stylistic Terms, Markings, and Teaching Strategies" in this chapter.
3. Discuss style, performance practice, and general interpretation characteristics of the baroque period.
4. Discuss style, performance practice, and general interpretation characteristics of the classical period.
5. Discuss style, performance practice, and general interpretation characteristics of the romantic period.
6. Discuss style, performance practice, and general interpretation characteristics of the contemporary period.
7. What is the essence and spirit of the music?
8. How will the techniques of music imagery and inner singing (or inner hearing) for the conductor affect the score study, the rehearsal process, and the concert performance?
9. Continue to gain familiarity with the standard repertoire found in Appendix A through CD listening, score study, and guidance from the conducting teacher. (See Appendix G for assignment forms.)

IN THE REHEARSAL PROCESS (LAB) ENVIRONMENT

1. Demonstrate the procedures for communicating the conductor's interpretation of the music at hand during the rehearsal process environment. (Musical Example)
2. Demonstrate the rehearsal procedures for reinforcing the four basic musical styles with the ensemble during the rehearsal process.

3. Demonstrate vocalizing the style and/or note lengths with the ensemble during the rehearsal process.
4. Demonstrate the ideas for bringing forth the characteristics of a particular period of music (baroque, classical, romantic, and contemporary) with the ensemble during the rehearsal process.
5. Demonstrate the rehearsal procedures for communicating the essence and spirit of the music in the rehearsal process. (Select the Musical Example.)
6. Demonstrate communicating the emotions of the music in the rehearsal process environment. (Select the Musical Example from the Repertoire.)
7. Complete student conducting/rehearsing projects (in the rehearsal process lab environment).

RECOMMENDED READING

Dart, Thurston, *The Interpretation of Music.* This early book (1954) discusses musical interpretation and especially style in the 18th century that is applicable for the string and wind music of this time.

Dorian, Frederick, *History of Music in Performance.* Chapter 2: The Baroque, Chapter 3: Rococo and Enlightenment, chapters 4 and 5 on the Classical period, Chapter 7: Classical Romanticism and Chapter 8: Power and Virtuosity.

Green, Elizabeth A. H., *The Dynamic Orchestra.* Chapter 3: Interpretation (The Mind) is very brief, but there are numerous points made about interpretation.

Kahn, Emil, *Conducting.* Pages 155–59 of this book discuss ornamentation, which is frequently not addressed properly for advanced conductors.

Leinsdorf, Erich, *The Composer's Advocate: A Radical Orthodoxy for Musicians.* The author has many important ideas on musical interpretation that should be considered by the maturing conductor.

McBeth, W. Francis. *Effective Performance of Band Music: Solutions to Specific Problems in the Performance of 20th Century Band Music.* Solutions VII: Interpretation of Twentieth-Century Band Music is quite brief, but makes some substantial points about the interpretation of contemporary band music.

McElheran, Brock, *Conducting Technique for Beginners and Professionals.* Chapter 20: Thoughts on Interpretation; on page 102 there is a Performance Chart that suggests choices of interpretation.

Rudolf, Max, *The Grammar of Conducting*, 3rd ed. See Part 4 on Interpretation and Style, which is rather extensive.

Scherchen, Hermann, *Handbook of Conducting.* Scherchen's main premise is "to interpret all music . . . exactly as its composer intended it to be played."

Schuller, Gunther, *The Compleat Conductor.* In Part 2, Gunther Schuller goes into great detail about many of the masterworks. He believes that works should be "realized" rather than "interpreted."

Voxman, Himie, *Baroque and Classical Music.* This pamphlet was published by the G. Leblanc Corporation. The main consideration here is the performance of trills, mordents, appoggiaturas, rhythmic practices, and tempo in these musical periods.

REPERTOIRE FOR PROJECTS AND ASSIGNMENTS

Full Orchestra, Chamber Orchestra, or String Orchestra

Humperdinck: Prelude to Hansel and Gretel
Beethoven: Piano Concerto No. 5 (Emperor) (various movements)
Dvorak: Symphony No. 8 in G Major (various movements)
Gershwin: An American in Paris
Respighi: Ancient Airs and Dances, Suite III (string orchestra)

Concert Band or Wind Ensemble

Camphouse: A Movement for Rosa
Breydert: Suite in F for Band
Reed, A.: The Hounds of Spring
Yontz: Scherzo for a Bitter Moon
Zdechlik: Chorale and Shaker Dance

Miscellaneous or Small Ensembles

Gounod: Petite symphonie (1 flute, 2 oboes, 2 clarinets, 2 bassoons, and 2 horns) (various movements)
Piston: Divertimento for Nine Instruments (flute, oboe, clarinet, bassoon, and string quintet)

TEACHING STRATEGY TABLE

Table 14.1. The Music Period Style and Interpretation

CONDUCTOR CONCERNS	PROBLEM AREAS	TEACHING STRATEGIES
Considering and showing the four basic styles with the conducting technique	Conducting technique	Show with conducting patterns and gestures the various musical styles; indicate the weight of notes on accents, *sfz, fp, sf*, etc.
Vocalizing the note lengths and weight for efficiency in the rehearsal process		Work on the four basic styles and their modification in the warm-up period of the rehearsal process.
Emphasizing the importance of the correct articulations		Without music (on scales or a single pitch), show the four basic styles and have the ensemble respond to these stylistically in the warm-up period.

Table 14.1.   The Music Period Style and Interpretation

CONDUCTOR CONCERNS	PROBLEM AREAS	TEACHING STRATEGIES
Marking bowings and breathing in the instrumental parts Communicating with the players concerning the period style and performance practice Interpreting the music distinctively and authentically Keeping the composer's intentions the most important part of the musical interpretation	Note length and emphasis	Stress the importance of note length and emphasis to achieve a "uniform" style.
		The idea of verbalizing or vocalizing note lengths will save considerable rehearsal time versus having the players experiment with how long or short a note should be played.
	Articulation	Emphasize to the players the proper articulation and musical sensitivity involving the beginning of the note.
	Bowing and bowing styles	Mark the bowings, part of the bow to use, and bowing style in the parts before the rehearsal process begins. On occasion, you may need to make changes during the rehearsal process.
	Period style considerations	Communicate to the players the necessary information concerning the style of the particular musical period in order to obtain an authentic performance.
		Communicate the baroque period style of on-the-string bowing to the string section as well as to the winds in terms of note length with little or no decay of the notes.
		In the classical period, off-the-string bowing such as the brush stroke or spiccato are employed for fast, rhythmic passages.
		In both the romantic and contemporary periods, there are many bowing styles needed and determined by the expressive qualities within these two specific musical periods.
What other teaching strategies (suggested by the conducting teacher or students) could communicate music period style and interpretation?		

Chapter Fifteen

Dynamics, Nuances, and Musical Expression

DYNAMICS AND NUANCES

Dynamics and nuances in music are a part of the total musical expression package. *Many performances lack dynamic contrast or specific musical expression.* For the conductor, the main consideration is to make the players aware of and sensitive to the dynamics and nuances through conducting patterns and gestures or with verbal comments during the rehearsal process. The conductor also has some visual control over the dynamics and nuances through the conducting patterns and gestures in the actual concert performance, but must refine and solidify these with the ensemble previously in the rehearsal process. In music, there are written and implied dynamics. The conductor must deliver implied dynamics during the rehearsal process, and perhaps add them as written dynamics for the ensemble in some cases.

Nuances have a different connotation than just dynamics or dynamic levels. There is more subtlety with nuances. These nuances, sometimes described as "shadings," can also involve tempo, intensity, and phrasing. In a sense, nuances are a part of dynamics, but occur within the dynamic level of a given passage. Nuances convey emotions in the music, and significantly affect the audience. A tapering of the final note of a piece is an obvious example of the use of nuance in music. *Nuances are an important part of any musical performance.* The conductor must discover these nuances through score study and inner singing and then rehearse these various nuances to succeed in the concert performance.

In his book *The Art of Musicianship*, Philip Farkas lists six situations involving the adjustment of dynamic levels with the ensemble: (1) the importance of the passage, (2) association with other performers, (3) tone color desired, (4) size of the ensemble, (5) size of the auditorium, and (6) placement in the group (1976, 14–15). All of these situations relate to balance and blend, which I discussed in chapter 10: Ensemble Sonority. The point is that dynamic adjustment is always crucial in developing a well-balanced ensemble in conjunction with the desired nuances of the particular composition and within the ensemble itself.

Dynamics play a strategic part in the musical phrasing as well. Once the emotional peak of the phrase has been determined, the gradual or sudden dynamics can set the

307

phrase in relief. A sudden forceful dynamic level at the beginning of the phrase will cause a dramatic effect to occur. Likewise, the end of the phrase may taper off for a gradual and subtle ending. The conductor must guide the ensemble dynamically toward and away from these peaks to ensure meaningful phrasing. All of this dynamic phrasing should be rehearsed carefully during the rehearsal process in preparation for the concert performance. Importantly, the phrase is defined and executed *through both tempo fluctuations and dynamic variations.*

The proper performance of dynamics, therefore, influences more than just the dynamic level itself. The dynamics are involved with balance, blend, and phrasing—elements very important in a musically expressive performance. The players must listen carefully and adjust the dynamic level to produce this expressive performance. In the rehearsal process, the conductor should insist on these dynamic levels in preparation for the concert performance. It is much safer technically to play a medium dynamic level throughout, but if this is allowed the musically expressive performance will not be achieved. Such dynamics as *fp* are treacherous elements to perform consistently, especially on brass instruments because of the nature of the harmonic series and the wind-blown pipe. *Tone control becomes a very important factor in such performances.* However, a musically expressive performance requires that the players, shown by the conductor, control these dynamics and nuances.

DYNAMIC CONTRAST

Few instrumental ensembles explore or utilize the entire dynamic range from pianissimo to fortissimo. The main consideration here is the contrast. There are a number of reasons for the lack of dynamic contrast in ensemble performance:

1. Problems arise when playing extremely loudly or softly. When the conductor demands the extreme dynamic ranges, the other performance elements such as intonation, tone quality, tone control, balance, blend, and articulation can become problematic.
2. Loud dynamics are frequently attained (even if out of control), but very soft dynamics seldom are achieved.
3. Some instruments have limitations in terms of the dynamic range.
4. The performance and maturity levels of the ensemble are factors in producing and controlling these extreme dynamics.
5. In order to produce extremely loud or extremely soft dynamics, more effort and control are required from the players.

In the rehearsal process, the conductor must reinforce the various dynamic levels desired from the ensemble. As mentioned above, this can lead to other problems in tone production and control. The conductor must be cautious not to demand dynamic contrast that is beyond the present performance level of the ensemble. He or she cannot expect younger groups to produce the same amount of contrast as a more mature ensemble. However, in the rehearsal process the conductor should strive to develop the various dynamic levels from *pp* (pianissimo) to *ff* (fortissimo), but always with the awareness that there are limitations depending on the maturity and performance level of the ensemble.

Problems of intonation, tone control, tone color, balance, blend, and articulation appear when the conductor demands extreme dynamic levels. It is easier and safer to play at a medium dynamic level. In Chapter 8: Intonation and Tuning, I discussed the effect of extreme dynamics on intonation. Likewise, tone control is affected by extremely loud or soft playing. It is more difficult to control the tone because greater effort is used in achieving these extreme dynamic levels. The other problem in this situation is that the characteristic sound of the instrument tends to change with the performance of extreme dynamics. Balance and blend sometimes become distorted at these extreme dynamics because of the capabilities of the player and capacities of the particular instruments to be played at these extreme loud or soft dynamics. *Articulation at the extreme dynamic levels can also be problematic.* In soft passages, the security of attack and response becomes more treacherous. At loud dynamic levels, the force of the articulation becomes a problem and causes loss of tone control (especially with the various wind instruments). In 1962, Paul R. Lehman did a study concerning dynamic contrast. The study concluded that

> in a musical context a variation in intensity of five decibels or even more can go unnoticed by the human ear. If differences in loudness must exceed a minimum of five decibels to be perceptible, a question follows: What range of intensity variation across the spectrum of all six dynamics would allow recognition of each individual step from pianissimo to fortissimo? The first is to propose that a six-decibel change in intensity is perceptible; on this assumption the total dynamic range from pianissimo to fortissimo must be at least 30 decibels, or a thousand fold increase in acoustical power. In practice a good musician should be able to vary his or her intensity even more than that. (Patterson 1974)

This study was conducted with individual instruments; therefore, the conclusion about listener perception of distinct dynamic levels is not completely valid for the entire instrumental music ensemble. However, this study does point out the importance of encouraging the players to develop and control these six dynamic levels (*pp, p, mp, mf, f, ff*). *Certain players will have more difficulty than others in producing and controlling this dynamic range.*

Some instruments simply can be played stronger than others can. For example, the flute has a relatively small dynamic range in comparison to that of the trumpet. Therefore, the trumpet player should realize this and be made aware of this problem in the ensemble balance. The percussion section of an instrumental ensemble is capable of obliterating the rest of the ensemble because of the capacity of the percussion instruments to generate many decibels of sound. Leadership from the conductor and musically sensitive playing on the part of the ensemble must counteract these differences. This is certainly an important reason for fostering the idea of listening and musical sensitivity in the rehearsal process.

Playing softly, especially with the younger ensemble, tends to become problematic unless the tone is produced correctly at this dynamic level. *However, consistent pianissimo is difficult to achieve with most ensembles, except for the professional en-*

semble. The tone control involved in playing softly becomes somewhat "risky," especially with wind and string players. The natural tendency is to decrease the air stream in volume and speed with the wind player, or lighten the bow pressure or decrease the bow speed with the string player. The results are a loss of good tone quality and insecurity of intonation. Because of these problems, the conductor should never demand a softer dynamic than the group is capable of controlling. The wind player needs good breath control, light tonguing, and effective vibrato maintenance. String players need to know about taking more notes under one bow, playing near the fingerboard, playing at the tip of the bow, and changing bow pressure and speed. Likewise, the percussionist needs a controlled wrist action, proper stroke placement on the instruments, and sensitivity toward the total ensemble balance.

Loud playing in many cases will result in a loss of tone control, balance problems, and intonation problems. *There is a natural tendency for the players to stop listening when playing at loud dynamic levels.* The ensemble tone can also become very strident in quality with loud passages. This will result in many tone and balance problems. In terms of balance, the players who possess the largest dynamic potential will be able to overpower the rest of the ensemble. The conductor should see to it in the rehearsal process that this kind of playing is controlled and that good balance and intonation prevail. Frequently at the end of a piece, the loud dynamic level becomes a problem in terms of the tone control, balance, blend, and intonation.

Soft playing has a tendency to cause the ensemble to slow the tempo down; loud playing may cause the ensemble to rush the pulse as well as the various rhythmic patterns. The conductor must guard against these tendencies and maintain a steady tempo in the rehearsal process in preparation for the concert performance. This is not to say that in specific passages where the dynamic level increases or decreases, the tempo must remain exactly metronomic. If the music dictates a forward flow or a relaxation of tempo in terms of the phrasing and/or dramatic impact, such tempo fluctuations may then be justified.

Likewise, the conductor and players must realize that *each instrument has its own peculiarities in the various registers.* Brass players will tend to play louder in the upper register because of the effort required to produce these notes, especially when large intervallic skips are involved. The fine brass player should spend considerable time in individual practice and in the rehearsal process listening and controlling in order to balance the upper register with the other registers. The low register of the flute, for example, is very difficult to project. The euphonium, tuba, and bass trombone have tone and control problems in the low register, although they can play with considerable force in this register. These register peculiarities do require adjustment in dynamic levels. The conductor must study the idiosyncrasies of the instruments in designing teaching strategies to control these various dynamic levels.

A performance by a fine professional ensemble is an example of how the maturity factor comes into play. The mature ensemble is capable of producing all of the dynamic levels and controlling them. The conductor in the rehearsal process must encourage as much contrast in the dynamic level as the ensemble is able to produce and at the same time realize the limitations and problems associated with these extreme dynamic levels. *In most cases, achieving dynamic contrast relates to technically controlling the sound.* To go suddenly from a soft dynamic to a loud dynamic or vice versa also involves tone control, proper articulation, and musical sensitivity.

DYNAMIC RELATIVITY

A commonly heard statement is, "Dynamics are relative." This is certainly a true statement and good advice for both the conductor and the players. There are two important areas of dynamic relativity involved here: (1) contrast in the dynamics, and (2) balance and blend in the ensemble. Even if the conductor had a machine that could show a specific dynamic level of a measurable quantity in decibels, dynamics are still considered relative. In the instrumental ensemble, there are no absolutes in dynamic levels. *The conductor must measure and control these levels.* In the rehearsal process, the conductor evaluates and establishes these levels with the ensemble. If the performance then moves to a different place, the conductor may need to reevaluate the concert hall regarding dynamic levels in order to accommodate the difference in acoustics between the rehearsal room and the concert hall. One of the main problems confronting the players is that they see only one dynamic marking on the music. The conductor must make the players aware that they may need to temper this one dynamic marking by the collective dynamic level of the ensemble; in some cases, this would depend on the importance of the individual part.

The conductor must show these differences of dynamic levels in the rehearsal process in preparation for the concert performance. The ensemble should learn to respond to the conducting patterns and gestures the same way in the rehearsal process as in the concert performance. *In the rehearsal process, many conductors exaggerate these conducting patterns and gestures in order to achieve the dynamic contrast.* This leads to over-conducting and if continued into the concert performance is certainly a distraction for the audience. The conductor needs to be more economical and consistent in the conducting motions so that the ensemble will respond consistently and appropriately to the patterns and gestures in both the rehearsal process and in the concert performance. Therefore, the conductor must not confuse the players with conducting patterns and gestures indicated in the rehearsal process and then altered during the concert performance.

The balance and blend in the instrumental music ensemble involve the careful adjustment of these dynamic levels. Through listening, the players must be sensitive to making these needed adjustments. Other performance aspects involved are tonal intensity, tone color, and intonation. Again, in the rehearsal process the conductor must establish these various performance aspects if there is any hope for a successful concert performance. The conductor must balance the various parts with musical sensitivity and dynamic relativity in mind. Achieving a blended ensemble tone will necessitate sensitivity on the part of the players by adjusting the indicated dynamic level to accommodate the sound of the total ensemble. The conductor is responsible for developing this musical sensitivity and dynamic relativity with the players during the rehearsal process.

A final point about dynamic contrast and relativity pertains to the idea that a dynamic marking such as an indicated accent should be played according to the prevailing dynamic level. If the accent appeared in a soft passage, then the volume of the accented note would (generally) be less than if it occurred in a louder passage. Likewise, an accent in the classical period would indicate more restraint than if it appeared in a romantic period composition. In other words, the degree of dynamic change must be musically tasteful and understood in the context of the music. The control of the tone is obviously the key to musical sensitivity in playing dynamics properly. *Contrast and relativity* are the two elements that pose problems in the performance of dynamics. The conductor and the players alike must strive to produce this dynamic contrast through clear conducting technique and controlled playing, along with the realization that the dynamics are always relative within the instrumental music ensemble.

GRADUAL DYNAMICS

The problem in the playing of gradual dynamics is gauging the length of the crescendo or diminuendo. With the crescendo, the tendency is to increase the volume too soon, causing the eventual dynamic level marking to be attained too early. With the diminuendo, the tendency is also to decrease the volume too soon, arriving early at the softer dynamic indication. Likewise, the diminuendo is often simply ignored. In both situations, there is a tendency to execute these gradual dynamic changes unevenly. Balance throughout the crescendo or diminuendo is a critical aspect of the musical performance. Examples of this occur in such works as Rossini overtures and Wagner operatic excerpts. The percussion section can greatly enhance the effectiveness of these gradual dynamics by increasing or decreasing the dynamic level at the proper time during the crescendo or the diminuendo.

These gradual dynamics may occur over a very short time or continue for a relatively long period. It is important for the conductor and the players to discern the length of the gradual dynamics, and increase or decrease the volume steadily. The instrumental players who have great potential for dynamic range, such as the brass and percussion, must be careful not to get to a loud dynamic level too soon on a crescendo or to soften too quickly on a diminuendo. If the length of the gradual dynamic is such that the conductor will run out of space for showing this dynamic change with the left hand, then he or she can repeat the gesture to achieve this gradual dynamic effect. This conducting procedure is executed by bringing the left hand up on the crescendo and then repeating the crescendo motion if needed, or bringing the left hand down on the diminuendo and repeating the diminuendo motion if needed. *This recovery of the left hand must be rather inconspicuous or these gradual dynamic indications may be uneven.*

Especially in romantic and contemporary period music, composers sometimes use polydynamics, wherein the opposite gradual dynamics occur simultaneously (e.g., where one section has a crescendo and another section has a diminuendo). *The rehearsal process will be a time in which to work out these problems of polydynamics.*

The conductor must decide which dynamic indication to show in the rehearsal process and in the concert performance by the conductor's patterns and gestures and then adhere to this consistently during the rehearsal process, with no attempt to show both of these dynamic changes. By isolating the two parts or the various sections and rehearsing for the proper dynamic change with each part or section, the conductor will decide which part to show with the left-hand gestures in the concert performance.

Another related problem with gradual dynamics is when a crescendo/diminuendo is shown as a swell < >; the level of the loudest point must be determined and rehearsed by the conductor. This level will vary depending on the appropriate dynamic for the particular work. For example, there would not be as much of a crescendo in a serenade as there would be in a march. The original dynamic level indicated by the composer influences the extent of such a crescendo. Likewise, returning to the original dynamic level is problematic. On many occasions, particularly with younger ensembles, after they have achieved a loud dynamic, they ignore the softer dynamic level. The conductor must not allow this. In general, the younger ensemble will tend to stay louder rather than return to the softer indicated level. *The "swell" can be a very expressive dynamic* if observed consistently by the whole ensemble. The proper use of the percussion instruments involved (especially timpani, snare drum, or suspended cymbal) can produce this crescendo/diminuendo to enhance the beautiful effect of the swell.

SUDDEN DYNAMICS AND ACCENTS

Players have a tendency to anticipate sudden dynamics. Subito (or sudden) dynamics should have an element of "surprise." Perhaps the most famous example is the Haydn *Symphony No. 94 in G Major*, appropriately subtitled the "Surprise" Symphony. The listener anxiously awaits the sudden loud chord, but the player must not anticipate it; otherwise, the sudden dynamic change will be ineffective. Whether the sudden dynamic goes from soft to loud or loud to soft, the player must not anticipate it with a gradual dynamic toward the new level before the "surprise" occurs. *However, the conductor should show with the patterns and gestures an instant before the sudden dynamic* that there is this change in dynamics. In addition, there is the problem in ensemble performance whereby not all of the players will observe these sudden dynamics equally. The conductor must reinforce this uniformity with the players in the rehearsal process. Sudden loud dynamics must be controlled so that the sound is not harsh or unmusical. Young instrumentalists will find some problems with these musical demands. In all cases, the sudden dynamic must be played with sensitivity and within the context of the existing dynamic level. A further refinement with sudden dynamics is to balance and blend this dynamic effect so that there is an evenness of sound within the ensemble.

In many cases, accents represent a sudden dynamic change. There are many kinds of accents involved in the musical expression. Daniel Kohut lists seven types of accents in his book, *Instrumental Music Pedagogy*: dynamic accent, agogic accent (duration), metric accent (primary and secondary), harmonic accent (dissonance), pattern accent, syncopation accent, and embellishments (1996, 173). Some of these accents are subtle and less conscious accents than are the dynamic accent or a *sforzando*. The conductor must consider all of these accents, however, and when called for, indicate them with the proper patterns or gestures to the ensemble. Accents will vary in weight depending on the dynamic level, where they might occur in the phrase, or through the various indications of the composer. Accents on notes with the idea of being "bell tones" can be played with weight and strong attacks on the notes and then immediately sustained more softly.

Especially with sudden loud dynamics, there is a tendency to articulate the attack of the initial loud dynamic too forcefully. The player's articulation should generally not become harsh in quality in such a situation, but rather should achieve the loud dynamic with controlled tone production. With the wind player, the air stream should increase in volume, but not necessarily the tongue force. The string player should increase the bow speed and pressure. The percussionist will use a more forceful stroke with the stick (or mallet) but with a "hot stove" effect to avoid the initial harsh attack on the change of dynamics. Sometimes, the conductor tends to perpetuate this unwanted accent in an effort to make the change to the sudden dynamic level. The conductor must take care not to over-conduct such passages whereby the ensemble distorts the sound in trying to match the visual pattern or gesture.

The execution of sudden soft dynamics also involves the idea of tone production and control on the instrument. The young player will have some problems with this sudden dynamic change. The sudden soft dynamic will tend to either be ignored or due to the lack of tone control will result in poor tone production. On wind instruments, this tone control may affect the tone quality and intonation. The bow control with string players will lack the finesse to produce a suddenly soft sound well. When the percussionists observe the sudden dynamic, they should be able to execute this without too much difficulty. The conductor must show this sudden soft dynamic before it is time to execute this dynamic change; otherwise, there is a danger that the player will only give token notice to this dynamic change. The conductor has three options here: (1) change the size of the beat just before the dynamic change, (2) use the left hand with the palm turned down just the instant before the dynamic change, or (3) move the conducting plane higher an instant before the dynamic change to confirm the soft dynamic level for the players. All three of these options can be employed at the same time if the conductor feels the need to reinforce this dynamic change with the ensemble.

MAINTAINING THE DYNAMIC LEVEL

Maintaining the dynamic level would seem to be an easy thing to do. Unfortunately, it is not. *Soft dynamics tend to get louder.* The reverse, however, is not always true with loud dynamics. Very loud dynamics seem to maintain themselves, unless physical endurance (breath, embouchure, and energy) wanes. Along the same line, though, a sustained loud note at the end of a section or piece will tend to deteriorate for these stated reasons. In all of this, it behooves the conductor to be vigilant in maintaining the indicated dynamic level. An example of maintaining a *pp* (pianissimo) dynamic level is found in the transition from the third to the fourth movement of the Beethoven

Symphony No. 5, in which the tendency is to allow the pianissimo dynamic level to move toward a louder dynamic level and thus destroy the sudden majesty of the crescendo just before the beginning of the final movement. Maintaining this soft dynamic level will necessitate careful rehearsing by the conductor. It will not just happen on its own accord, especially with a less mature group.

In summary, the ability of an ensemble to play with a consistent, sustained sound of equal volume represents an important performance aspect. Variations involved with musical expression can succeed only if this consistent, sustained sound is present in the instrumental music ensemble performance. Until this sound and control is well established with the ensemble in the rehearsal process, musical expression (that is, playing loud or soft or with various shadings) will lack the tone production necessary to make these changes for effective musical expression. One of the difficult things for the conductor to get an ensemble to produce is a sustained musical line. However, it must be a major goal for any ensemble to achieve. Only then will the tone production remain solid throughout. This sustained quality is noticeable in the top professional orchestras and concert bands.

The maturing conductor will need to develop two basic styles of conducting *to produce this consistent, sustained sound with the ensemble*—that is, the legato pattern and the tenuto pattern. The legato pattern should have a decided smoothness to the motion; the conducting motions are curved as opposed to straight. The legato pattern will not be as telling in terms of the exact ictus, and therefore should not be employed for long periods. The look of the pattern will be horizontal rather than vertical, and in this sense the motion toward the ictus will not have as much clarity as in a regular non-espressivo pattern. Likewise, the tenuto pattern will have some of the same characteristics of the legato pattern, but should show the ictus clearly, in that there is a "click" executed on each beat (or pulse). Also, the left hand can be used for the sustaining quality by simply turning the palm upward as in a crescendo gesture, but without any further movement of the left hand.

CONCEIVING THE DYNAMIC RANGE

Not every selection played will have the same dynamic range. The conductor may need to curtail a serenade in its dynamic range. This is not to say that there should be little or no dynamic contrast, but the calm and quiet of a serenade should not be interrupted by an exaggerated fortissimo. In contrast, a dramatic work of great emotional content will demand a larger dynamic range from *pp* to *ff*. If the work were from the classical period in music, then restraint dynamically would be the rule. Much depends on the nature of the work and the composer's intent. The texture of the work might also give the conductor a clue as to the dynamic range. Works of great delicacy and finesse would indicate a smaller, softer dynamic range, while heavy, more ponderous pieces would generally indicate to the conductor a larger dynamic range. The composer will give some help in this decision by the dynamic levels indicated in the music, but in the final analysis, the conductor should decide on the extent of this dynamic range.

Through score study, the conductor must discover and conceive the softest and loudest dynamic levels in a piece. Then, in the rehearsal process, the conductor will *make the players aware of the dynamic boundaries of the work.* They will accomplish this by watching the conductor and listening carefully to the surrounding ensemble sound. If these procedures do not effectively achieve the desired results, then the conductor must verbally adjust the dynamic range during the rehearsal process. Failure by the conductor to establish this dynamic range will distort the musical interpretation of the work. If the conductor has trained the group to watch and respond to the size of the conducting patterns and gestures, then the conductor should be able to control these dynamic levels with the conducting technique.

The conductor should indicate in the rehearsal process by left-hand gestures if the dynamic range needs adjusting. The left-hand gesture with the palm turned down should show the player, section, or entire ensemble that the sound may need to be decreased in volume. Likewise, the left-hand gesture with the palm turned upward should show the player, section, or entire ensemble that the sound must increase in volume. If this left-hand gesture does not bring a definite response from the players involved, the conductor may need to stop the ensemble and verbally indicate the intentions of such a gesture. *The ensemble might easily ignore this left-hand gesture,* especially if the ensemble has not learned to watch the conductor and play sensitively. Unfortunately, the players may not see this left-hand gesture as being very specific, and therefore may ignore it. In many instances, if the conductor uses the left hand constantly to mirror the right hand, then this gesture will be less effective in showing this dynamic range.

AWARENESS AND SENSITIVITY TO DYNAMICS, NUANCES, AND MUSICAL EXPRESSION

Because dynamics are relative and yet need to be contrasted, the players must be aware of the dynamic balance and be sensitive to the problems of adjusting the numerous and frequently changing dynamic levels in the rehearsal process and the concert performance. The tone control of the instrument at the various dynamic levels requires skill development. The wind player controls dynamics with the air column and embouchure. The string player uses bow speed, bow length, and bow pressure. The percussionist uses stroke placement and force on the particular instrument to produce the required dynamic levels.

There are many problems to consider in a full ensemble performance with balancing and contrasting the dynamic levels. In the instrumental ensemble performance, many aspects involve great sensitivity on the part of both the conductor and the players. Some of the problems involved in these dynamic levels may pertain to eliminating players on a part. At times it may be necessary to reduce the number of players on a single part by eliminating the doubling or tripling on that part. There may be instances when the conductor, for the sake of the dynamic levels, intonation, or clarity, will find that fewer players on a part will solve some of these problems.

If the conductor approaches the ensemble rehearsal with a sense of musicality and shows this musical sensitivity with the proper patterns and gestures, the ensemble will respond musically to the various dynamic levels. This is assuming that the ensemble response is the result of watching the conductor's patterns and gestures. On the other hand, if the conducting technique is not well developed, the response by the group, even though they may be watching the conductor, will be erratic and somewhat bland. In combination with the conducting technique, the conductor may find it necessary to verbally instruct the ensemble as to what is wanted in terms of dynamic contrast and at the same time make the players aware of these problems concerning the balance and blend during the rehearsal process.

In many cases, especially with younger ensembles, players ignore dynamic and musical expression markings because of the technical problems encountered. If this is the prevailing situation, then the conductor should consider the possibility that the selection being rehearsed is too difficult for the ensemble at present. An easier, less technically demanding selection, played with a sensitivity toward the dynamics and musical expression, is of much greater value for the ensemble as well as for the ears of the audience. The challenge for the instrumental music ensemble should not always be just a technical challenge, but should also be a musical one. Table 15.1, Teaching Strategy (Dynamics and Nuances), at the end of the chapter offers ideas and suggestions for designing a teaching strategy for dynamic contrast, dynamic relativity, awareness, and musical sensitivity.

MUSICAL EXPRESSION AND MUSICIANSHIP

As mentioned at the beginning of this chapter, dynamics and nuances are two aspects of the ensemble musical expression. The conductor and players must have acquired a musical expression vocabulary and know how to perform the various terms and markings of musical expression. I covered some of this material in previous chapters under articulation and bowing, tempo and ensemble precision, style and musical interpretation, and phrasing and the musical line. All of these elements are part of what is termed *musicianship*. The maturing conductor must continue to improve on the musicianship throughout his or her entire career. In so doing, the conductor hopes to pass this on to the players through the conducting patterns and gestures and through verbal instruction in the ensemble rehearsal process.

The conductor must show a commitment to the music through emotional involvement in the rehearsal process. Through expressive conducting technique and good score preparation, the conductor should be able to convince the players to play in this musical manner. How expressively players interpret the music is influenced by how they feel about the music. If the conductor shows this emotional intensity in the rehearsal process, it will be contagious among the players, just as is the idea of conductor enthusiasm for the music. *One criterion for selecting pieces is that the conductor is committed to the music.* It is difficult to show or express emotional intensity with a work to which the conductor is somewhat indifferent. The conductor should show the emotion of the music, such as happy, sad, excited, and so on in such a conducting and rehearsing scenario.

The idea of tempo modifications should be a large part of the whole picture of musical expression for the conductor. I dealt with these areas of musical expression in Chapter 12: Tempo and Ensemble Precision and in Chapter 13: Phrasing and the Musical Line. However, these tempo modification issues are extremely important in terms of the emotional variations and musical expression in both the rehearsal process and the concert performance. The composer usually indicates tempo fluctuations in the music. There are, of course, exceptions to this, but in general, the conductor should adhere to the printed score in this regard. Stretching of beats would be more the conductor's prerogative in that the composer would not necessarily indicate them in the musical score. The composer may or may not indicate Tempo rubato (discussed in the above-mentioned chapters). In general, slow tempo selections will lend themselves better to the application of this tempo modification. Fast tempo selections would by necessity be less likely to use these tempo modifications in the musical interpretation.

Although I included vibrato in Chapter 10: Ensemble Sonority—Tone, Balance, Blend, Color, and Texture, I need to mention it here, especially in terms of what the vibrato can do emotionally in the ensemble performance. *Intensification of the vibrato or relaxation of the vibrato can enhance the emotional quality of the passage.* In a few situations, when the composer or conductor requests no vibrato, the music can take on a bleak or sinister quality. Finally, the vibrato is used to increase the beauty of the sound and in this sense, enhance the musical expression. Especially in melodic and solo passages, the conductor should encourage or insist upon the use of vibrato (with the proper depth and speed).

In some cases, musical expression terms appear at the beginning of a piece or section. For example, terms such as cantabile, scherzando, and giocoso would indicate musical expression at the start of the section or piece, while other terms are placed at specific points in the music to designate a change from what has been happening previously. Examples of this include calando, crescendo, diminuendo, sul ponticello, and sul tasto. *These musical terms and markings* are crucial for the conductor and players in capturing the essence and spirit of the music. The musical period, the existing dynamic levels, the type of composition, and many other factors will influence the performance of these expression markings. The musical expression markings generally are shown over a note or over a group of notes such as with a crescendo marking or a style indication.

The musical expression terms noted in this chapter should be part of the musician's vocabulary. The conductor must not overlook these terms or assume that the players know their meaning. I present a very brief listing of musical expression terms with the definitions as given here:

Affettuoso: with emotion
Alla marcia: in the style of a march
Amore: with tenderness
Calore: with warmth
Agitato: agitated
Con brio: with spirit, brilliantly
Cantabile: in a singing style

Dolce: Sweetly
Con fuoco: with fire
Giocoso: Joyfully
Grazioso: Gracefully
Leggiero: Lightly
Morendo: Dying away
Perdendosi: Dying away
Pesante: Heavy
Sostenuto: Sustained

This is a short list of musical expression terms that the conductor and players need to be aware of during the rehearsal process. There are many more terms in various languages that must be considered in the performance of the music as well. The conducting teacher may want to expand on this list for general student information.

Many of the musical expression markings relate to dynamics and articulation. The following examples of familiar markings may need to be discussed:

Crescendo: becoming gradually louder
Diminuendo: becoming gradually softer
Regular accent >: with stress
"Caret" accent ^: stronger than the regular accent
sfz: short for sforzando (with a strong accent)
rinf.: abbreviation for rinforzando (with a sudden loud accent)
fp: loud, then immediately soft
Staccato dot: detached and light
Secco staccato: dry staccato
Tenuto or sostenuto mark: sustained
Fermata (or hold): approach, length, and release need to be considered

Articulations often involve the slur: in combination with staccato dot, for example lightly tongued; in combination with sostenuto mark, for example either tongued or slurred; or in combination with the accent mark, for example slurred with breath push.

Again, this is a very short list of musical expression markings to observe in the performance of music. The conducting teacher may wish to expand on this list during the class meetings for general student information.

The wind player produces and controls dynamics, nuances, and musical expression by the variance of the air column and the embouchure. The articulation (tongue) may also be a factor in the production of dynamics, nuances, and musical expression. The string player uses the bow on the string to produce variations in dynamics, nuances, and musical expression. The bow stroke on the string will vary in length, the part of the bow used, the bow speed and pressure, the bow near the bridge (sul ponticello), or the bow toward the fingerboard (sul tasto) to produce variations in dynamics, nuances, and musical expression. Additionally, the number of notes produced under one bow is a factor dynamically. If a louder dynamic level is required, then a change of bow resulting in fewer notes under one bow may be necessary. Many notes played under a single bow result in a softer execution of the musical passage. The percussionist is able to produce and control the dynamics, nuances, and musical expression with various sticks and mallets, by the point of contact between the stick (or mallet) and the instrument, and also with the force of the stroke. Because the percussionist must become competent on a variety of instruments, the techniques of tone production and tone control on the various percussion instruments need serious practice and study. Only in this way will the player be able to attain the needed tone production and control. With younger ensembles, it may be necessary for the conductor to instruct the players technically in producing this musical expression.

Why should these three elements be combined in the conducting and rehearsing of the instrumental music ensemble? *Dynamics, nuances, and musical expression should be produced and controlled by the conductor for the ensemble in the rehearsal process.* The conductor must consider the idea of dynamics and nuances (or shadings) as a part of the entire musical expression picture. These dynamics and nuances should be produced with the variance of intensity and energy. In extremely loud passages, the ensemble tone must not be allowed to become strident and poorly balanced with the rest of the ensemble; in soft passages, the tone must not become "anemic" and out of tune. Dynamics, nuances, phrasing and musical expression should not come only after the notes and rhythms are learned, but should be realized throughout the rehearsal process. The performance of musical expression should begin right away on a new work. How much the conductor immediately demands will depend on the performance and/or maturity level of the ensemble. If in the rehearsal process, musical expression is delayed until the notes and rhythms are in place, adjustments to the dynamics, nuances, musical expression and in the musical interpretation of the work will need to be made later. Philip Farkas carefully defines and discusses all of these areas of musical expression in his book, *The Art of Musicianship* (1976).

The conductor and players must carefully observe musical expression indications. The difference between an average performance and a truly outstanding one may very well be in the details of the musical expression that the conductor and the ensemble realize in the rehearsal process and subsequently in the concert performance. A performance void of musical expression would certainly leave the listener disappointed. The observation of musical expression terms and markings found in the printed music are extremely important for the performance success of the ensemble and must certainly be reinforced with the ensemble during the rehearsal process. Table 15.2, Teaching Strategy (Musical Expression), at the end of the chapter presents ideas and suggestions for designing a teaching strategy for the observance and improvement of musical expression.

PRACTICAL APPLICATION (DISCUSSION/DEMONSTRATION)

1. Discuss the conducting and playing problems involved in achieving good dynamic contrast.
2. Dynamics are relative. What does this involve for the conductor and players?

3. Describe the problems in conducting and playing gradual dynamics and then demonstrate. (Select the Musical Example from the Repertoire.)
4. Describe the problems in conducting and playing sudden dynamics and then demonstrate. (Select the Musical Example from the Repertoire.)
5. Discuss the various kinds of accents. (See "Dynamic Relativity" above.)
6. How are accents shown on the beat? Demonstrate. (Select the Musical Example from the Repertoire.)
7. How are accents shown off the beat? Demonstrate. (Select the Musical Example from the Repertoire.)
8. Select a musical phrase. Discuss the musical expression involved. Demonstrate the dynamics, nuances, and musical expression by conducting this phrase. (Select the Musical Example from the Repertoire.)
9. Continue to gain familiarity with the standard repertoire found in Appendix A of this book through CD listening, score study, and guidance from the conducting teacher. (See Appendix G for assignment forms.)

IN THE REHEARSAL PROCESS (LAB) ENVIRONMENT

1. Demonstrate by conducting the various dynamic levels with the use of pattern size, left hand use, or the emotional intensity with the conducting patterns in the rehearsal process. (Select the Musical Example from the Repertoire.)
2. Demonstrate by conducting how to achieve the proper balance with left-hand use or verbally with the ensemble during the rehearsal process. (Select the Musical Example from the Repertoire.)
3. Demonstrate by conducting how to achieve sudden or gradual dynamics with the left hand in the rehearsal process environment. (Select the Musical Example from the Repertoire.)
4. Demonstrate by conducting how to enhance the musical expression and nuances with the left hand in the rehearsal process environment. (Select the Musical Example from the Repertoire.)
5. Complete student conducting/rehearsing projects (in the rehearsal process lab environment).

RECOMMENDED READING

Farkas, Philip, *The Art of Musicianship*. Chapter 3: Dynamics deals with the various aspects of ensemble dynamics. Chapter 9: Ensemble Playing (in the next to last paragraph) alludes to the idea of dynamics being relative.

Green, Barry, and W. Timothy Gallwey, *The Inner Game of Music*. Chapter 14: Ensemble Playing has much to do with the feelings and expression in the music.

Green, Elizabeth A. H., *The Dynamic Orchestra*. In Chapter 1: Sound (The Ear), there are references to dynamic adjustment, solo passages, and dynamic projection. There is an overview of this chapter on pp. 57–59.

Harris, Frederick, Jr., ed., *Conducting with Feeling.* Chapter 5: Communicating Musical Feeling does not necessary speak directly to dynamics, nuances, or musical expression, although these areas of musical expression must be considered a part of the whole idea of communicating the musical feeling.

Lisk, Edward S., *The Creative Director: Alternative Rehearsal Techniques.* Chapter 6: Dynamics deals with various dynamic indications as well as various color shifts. There are charts to show these dynamic indications and color shifts.

Maiello, Anthony, *Conducting Nuances.* The author uses the term "Nuances" to include all the various physical and subtle aspects of the conducting technique.

McBeth, W. Francis, *Effective Performance of Band Music: Solutions to Specific Problems in the Performance of 20th Century Band Music.* Solution II: Achieving Correct Performance of Dynamic and Articulation Markings summarizes the various ideas on dynamic and articulation markings.

Scherchen, Hermann, *Handbook of Conducting.* Chapter 3: Orchestral Playing and Conducting deals with intensification, dynamics, style, and the importance of singing in orchestral conducting.

Wagar, Jeannine, *Conductors in Conversation.* The organization of this book is based on interviews with specific orchestra conductors who answer the questions posed in the section about balancing orchestral sound in unfamiliar halls.

REPERTOIRE FOR PROJECTS AND ASSIGNMENTS

Full Orchestra, Chamber Orchestra, or String Orchestra

Beethoven: Symphony No. 8 (various movements)
Bernstein: Overture to "Candide"
Bizet: Carmen Suite No. 1 (various movements)
Britten: Matinee Musicales, Op. 24 (after Rossini) (various movements)
Dvořák: Cello Concerto in B minor (various movements)

Concert Band or Wind Ensemble

Chance: Incantation and Dance
Del Borgo: Do Not Go Gentle into that Good Night
Giannini: Symphony No. 3 (various movements)
Herman: North Sea Overture
Holsinger: To Tame the Perilous Skies

Miscellaneous or Small Ensembles

Copland: Appalachian Spring Ballet Suite (original instrumentation for 13 instruments)
Stravinsky: Octet for Wind Instruments (flute, clarinet, 2 bassoons, 2 trumpets, and 2 trombones)

TEACHING STRATEGY TABLES

Table 15.1. Dynamics and Nuances

CONDUCTOR CONCERNS	PROBLEM AREAS	TEACHING STRATEGIES
Developing and using the six pattern sizes to indicate the dynamic levels Reinforcing the dynamic levels by marking the instrumental parts Establishing both dynamic contrast and dynamic relativity within the ensemble during the rehearsal process	Conducting technique	Work to develop six pattern sizes to coincide with the six dynamic levels of the ensemble.
		Insist that the players watch the size of the beat pattern and also the left-hand dynamic gestures.
		Do not place the conducting patterns and gestures outside of the visual range (conducting box) for the players.
		Conduct with as much musicality as possible to make the players aware of dynamics and nuances.
Producing gradual dynamics with smoothness in the volume change Sudden dynamics immediate and precise	Dynamic contrast	Establish dynamic levels with the ensemble from (*pp*) pianissimo to (*ff*) fortissimo for this dynamic contrast and conduct this way.
		Highlight dynamic markings in the parts in order to bring out this dynamic contrast.
Soft dynamics played securely Loud dynamics controlled	Dynamic relativity	Key words for playing dynamics are contrast and relativity.
		Dynamic relativity involves playing with sensitivity in conjunction with all of the other instrumental parts.
Nuances involving the phrasing, tempo, intensity, and relaxation Discovering nuances through score study, music imagery, and inner singing	Dynamic awareness	Have the players in the rehearsal process reinforce or change these dynamic marks if needed.
		The conductor should be able to change the dynamics with the pattern size or left-hand use.
		The rehearsal process is the time to establish this awareness with the players in terms of both the dynamic contrast and relativity.

Table 15.1. (*continued*)

	PROBLEM AREAS	TEACHING STRATEGIES
	Dynamic sensitivity	Gauge and produce gradual dynamics without sudden changes in volume.
		Sudden dynamics should be a "surprise" to the listener.
		Maintain good balance in the ensemble as the dynamic level changes.
		With soft dynamics, the tone must remain secure.
		With loud dynamics, maintain the tone control.
	Nuances	Nuances in terms of these dynamics are somewhat subtle but important for expression.
		Nuances can be discovered through score study, music imagery, and inner singing.
What other teaching strategies (suggested by the conducting teacher or students) could improve the dynamics and nuances?		

Table 15.2. Musical Expression

CONDUCTOR CONCERNS	PROBLEM AREAS	TEACHING STRATEGIES
Thinking and conducting expressively during the rehearsal process and concert performance Making the conducting motion before the musical expression will occur	Conducting technique	Think and conduct musically always in the rehearsal process and in the concert performance.
		The arms, hands, and baton should create this musical expression to guide the players.
		What happens between the beats is the key to musical expressive conducting.
Using proper articulation to promote the desired musical expression Using accents as an important part of the musical expression	Play a recording	After working on a piece in the rehearsal process, play a professional recording of the work for the young ensemble to give them this musical expression concept of the work.
	Articulation	Stress the importance of various types of articulations in the ensemble rehearsal process.
Changing tone color to enhance the musical expression		Work on articulation in the warm-up period of the rehearsal process to improve this part of the musical expression package.

(*continued*)

Table 15.2. (*continued*)

CONDUCTOR CONCERNS	PROBLEM AREAS	TEACHING STRATEGIES
Considering texture contrast as important for the audience (in terms of programming) Using the variance of the tempo to give meaning to the musical expression	Dynamics and accents	Stress the importance of the dynamics and accents as a part of the musical expression during the rehearsal process.
		With the younger ensemble, it may be necessary to instruct as to how to execute and play the various accents.
	Balance and blend	Stress the importance of listening to improve balance and blend in the rehearsal process.
		All the players must respond to the various aspects of balance and blend or the results will be uneven musical expression.
	Tone color and texture contrast	Tone color contrast will enhance the excitement and musical expression of the ensemble performance. The more tone color contrast the conductor can bring out with the ensemble, the more expressive and exciting the concert performance will be.
		The variance of the texture during the rehearsal process will certainly enhance the concert performance. This can be accomplished in a number of ways: the selection of repertoire, programming of soloists and smaller ensembles, and careful rehearsing of the composer's orchestration intentions.
	Tempo and tempo changes	Vary the tempo as indicated in the musical score or as the music demands such tempo changes.
What other teaching strategies (suggested by the conducting teacher or students) could improve the musical expression?		

Part V

THE CONDUCTOR
IN THE 21ST CENTURY

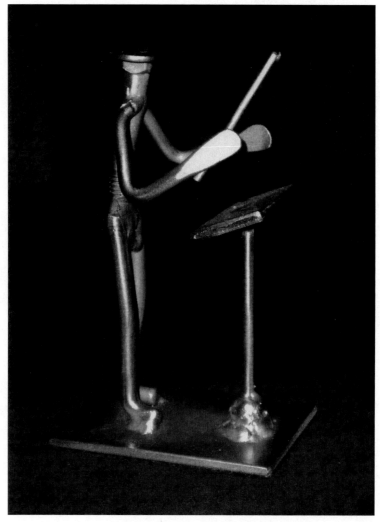

21st-Century Conductor Statuette

Chapter Sixteen

Conducting and Rehearsing Contemporary Music

CONTEMPORARY MUSIC AND ITS COMPLEXITIES

Contemporary music performances demand special approaches, adapted conducting technique, and appropriate teaching strategies. Some traditional conducting techniques can be employed, but others may need to be created to accommodate the technical and musical complexities of contemporary music. The conductor should be aware of these complexities and realize that contemporary music generally requires more "settling time" than does the music of earlier periods. Rehearsal continuity is an important factor because of the irregular nature of this music and the complexities presented to the conductor and players. This is the reason for including a separate chapter on this subject.

Contemporary music involves non-traditional notation, parts in score form, explanatory legends, new performance techniques (somewhat foreign to the training and experience of the players), new instruments, new techniques on the standard instruments, new conducting techniques, prerecorded sounds with the ensemble, stage movement, dancers incorporated with the ensemble, player movement within the ensemble, narrator, actors, special stage lighting, slide and film projection, MIDI synthesizer and sequencer, to name just a few of these innovations. The conductor, as the leader of the ensemble, must understand these new ideas to the extent that he or she is able to explain and nurture the proper execution of these innovations in the rehearsal process. *In score study, the conductor should analyze the unique problems involved with the particular contemporary work.*

In many contemporary works, the conductor becomes somewhat of a "supervisor" or "manager" in overseeing that the piece is properly performed. The conductor must come to the rehearsal prepared to show and explain to the players the performance aspects that they need to address. In some cases, the conductor will need to adapt the conducting technique from the standard technique. The main duties of the conductor may be to show beginnings and endings of sections with some cueing and dynamic indications for balance; especially in aleatoric music or improvisatory musical styles provide a certain freedom for the players. There may be instances when the main conducting gestures will be to show the passage of time in seconds by mouthing numbers or with the use of hand signals.

With all of the obstacles found in contemporary music, the inevitable question might be asked, "Why should this music be performed?" The answer to this question is that there are many fine contemporary composers writing challenging and accessible music for instrumental music ensembles. Only if this music is performed for audiences will the music of today be recognized as a significant contribution and legacy for future generations. The conductor should play contemporary music in conjunction with earlier music *so that the audience will be more responsive and open-minded to the contemporary music.* Sometimes, verbal comments by the conductor during the concert performance about a contemporary work can promote interest for the audience as to what to listen for in the music. The conductor should not depend on the entire audience reading the printed program notes. Some brief comments by the conductor may help the audience to be more receptive to this music. In some cases, if the composer is available to conduct his own composition, this can be an exciting event for the players.

THE COMPLEXITIES OF CONTEMPORARY MUSIC

In score study, the conductor should first discover these complexities in the music so that there can be a thorough understanding of these complexities. These complexities translate into technical and musical problems that need to be resolved in the rehearsal process. The conductor should design teaching strategies to communicate and implement solutions for these problems with the ensemble. These technical and musical problems appear frequently in contemporary music, and the conductor and players must contend with the following complexities:

1. Complex rhythmic organization
2. Melodic and harmonic complexities
3. Extreme technical demands on the players
4. Performance techniques and special effects
5. New notation and composer instructions
6. Changing and asymmetrical meters
7. New instruments and unusual instrumental techniques
8. Music theater presentations (multimedia and staging)

In dealing with contemporary music, there is no substitute for exploring this complex music as a player in an instrumental music ensemble. Much of this music requires a strong technical background in performance. Only with this background can the conductor appreciate or know about the technical demands that are made upon the player. If this background is lacking, the conductor will not understand these complexities and what the ensemble needs to accomplish during the rehearsal process. A secure rhythmic background is also required because of the rhythmic complexity of contemporary music. This rhythmic complexity also involves changing and asymmetrical meters that will challenge the conductor constantly in contemporary music. There has also developed a new system of notation (nontraditional) that the conductor should be knowledgeable about and be able to explain to the players in the rehearsal process. This notation represents a broad spectrum of notational innovations by the composer. (See Appendix D: Instrumental Techniques, Intonation, and Special Effects.) Finally, in many contemporary compositions, the composer requests the playing of standard instruments with unusual techniques and some special effects. Again, the conductor must study the score in great detail in order to be prepared to help the players to properly perform these required techniques and the special effects in contemporary music.

CONTEMPORARY MUSIC PERFORMANCE PROBLEMS

Complex Rhythmic Organization

The conductor and players of contemporary music will face complicated rhythmic patterns, polyrhythms, and new rhythmic organization. This will require the conductor to study the score with the greatest scrutiny in preparation for the rehearsal process. The conductor must be ready to articulate this complex rhythmic organization to the players. The players must be aware of the rhythmic problems, and be prepared to study and practice their parts diligently. Many contemporary composers, in their efforts to notate what they want rhythmically, strive to show note and rest durations with precise values. This translates into further rhythmic complexity in music reading. Additionally, aleatoric and improvised passages occurring in contemporary music will need attention in the rehearsal process. Syncopation abounds in contemporary music in which pulse, meter, and rhythms are rearranged. Therefore, the conductor should be ready to confront these many meters, rhythms, and rhythm patterns in the rehearsal process.

So much of contemporary music requires the conductor to have a strong background rhythmically, it would seem impossible for the conductor to cope with the rhythmic complexities of contemporary music without this kind of rhythmic background. Changing and asymmetrical meter in contemporary music is an example in which the conductor must possess this solid rhythmic foundation. Unless the conductor understands and feels the consistency of the common subdivision (such as eighth- or sixteenth-note values) in asymmetrical meter, the chances of showing a secure pulse are remote. Tempo changes and tempo relationships often pose rhythmic problems in contemporary music. Finally, there is great complexity alone in the rhythms and rhythm patterns found in contemporary music. The conductor must be ready through serious score study *to detect and correct these rhythmic problems during the rehearsal process.*

Melodic and Harmonic Complexities

Melodic and harmonic trends such as disjunctive and angular melodic lines (Klangfarbenmelodie), unusual melodic doublings, atonal harmonic techniques, microtones, thin and exposed scoring, octave and fifth tunings, and fragmentation of the melodic line are some of the complexities in contemporary music. For the conductor and players, these complexities present problems to be solved beyond those found in music of the previous musical periods. Composers such as Webern and Berg saw fit to fragment the melodic line frequently. Schoenberg and his followers in initiating serial music began a new era harmonically. Debussy explored various harmonic systems such as the use of the pentatonic scale in his imaginative compositions. The conductor and players must confront polychords, non-triadic sonorities such as quartal harmony, secundal harmony, polytonality, atonality, and extreme dissonances in the rehearsal process and in the concert performance. The tuning of frequent dissonance is a major concern for the conductor and players in contemporary music. Large interval skips are especially demanding with brass players because of the partial accuracy problem. Along with this is the lack of a tonal center and the performance in the extreme registers of the various instruments. All of these melodic and harmonic changes with contemporary music present unique rehearsal and performance problems.

The conductor must detect and correct tonal problems in the rehearsal process by studying the score carefully and applying that study to the ensemble's performance in the rehearsal process. During this score study, the conductor may find it necessary to play tonally or harmonically difficult passages on the piano to reinforce the music imagery. A passage may be entangled to so many dissonances and complex harmonic issues that the conductor will be unable to hear this clearly in the mind. The problem may be a large interval skip or the density of a chord. The important point here is for the conductor to detect and correct these tonal and harmonic problems in the rehearsal process. Because of the melodic and harmonic complexities of many contemporary works, the conductor will probably need to spend considerable time in score study in preparation for the rehearsal process.

Extreme Technical Demands on the Players

Contemporary music perhaps reflects life in the 20th century. The complexities and demands of this music are extreme. With the advent of a work such as Stravinsky's *Rite of Spring* in the early part of this past century, the demands made upon the players of contemporary music are here to stay. Besides having to possess great technical facility, players must be willing to devote long hours of practice time to achieve the technical accuracy that is required of live performances, recordings, radio, and television. Audiences have come to expect this perfection. For this reason and several others that will be evident by the end of this chapter, many players are hesitant to put themselves in this precarious position. *Here the conductor must show some patience and perseverance with the players to give them a sense of confidence.* Because of the complexity and freedom of contemporary music, the cooperation of the players is crucial in the rehearsal process. Such elements as those found in aleatory and improvisational passages require the players to take more chances, with the outcome being less certain. When the technical demands are extreme, the conductor should allow more rehearsal time to attain a good performance. In some instances, the conductor may find it necessary to precede regular rehearsals with individual attention or some sectional rehearsals to resolve these special problems before the full rehearsal.

A further problem in contemporary music is that at least some composers are less concerned about writing in a way that will enhance the sound and the execution on a particular instrument; they are satisfied to leave this to the technical and musical skills of the player. However, there is a fallacy here in that the players may not perform the music the way the composer intended. Many of these composers are more concerned about the musical line and effects desired rhythmically and tonally *than whether or not the passage is actually idiomatic and comfortable on the various instruments.* These complexities may become even more acute for the players as contemporary composers write and realize their works on the computer. The computer will accept whatever the composer specifies and is able to duplicate this in sound through such software as Finale and Sibelius.

With the advent of writing music with the computer (which can now be played back out of the computer), a further danger is in the composing of contemporary music that becomes so technically, rhythmically, or tonally difficult that the performance demands are almost humanly impossible. If these new works move in this extreme direction, few if any conductors or players will embrace these works because of the amount of rehearsal time involved in preparing such works for a performance. *A positive aspect of this technology, however, is that the score and parts can be reproduced quickly and cleanly with tremendous efficiency on the computer.* Editing of the score and parts may require some time and patience by the composer. This does mean, however, that composers will not have to spend half of their "artistic lifetime" copying scores and parts. The transposition of the parts is easy once the score is in the computer.

Performance Techniques and Special Effects

The conductor and players of contemporary music are required to learn new performance techniques and special effects as notated by the composer. *The conductor must be the catalyst in cultivating these new techniques and special effects in the rehearsal process* and in developing teaching strategies to achieve proper execution of these techniques and special effects. In many instances in the performance of contemporary music, more score study and more rehearsal time is demanded than for the standard repertoire because of the appearance of these new performance techniques and special effects. In some instances, the composer explains how to perform these special techniques in preliminary instructions at the beginning of the score or at the point in the music where these unusual technical problems and special effects occur. The conductor must come to the rehearsal prepared to illuminate for the players how to perform these techniques and special effects. For example, Bartók indicates five different ways to play the cymbals in his *Concerto for Two Pianos, Percussion and Orchestra.* I have addressed these performance techniques and special effects in contemporary music in the listing of the Recommended Reading at the end of this chapter.

Special effects, created on either standard instruments or new instruments, are a part of the contemporary music scene. It would be ludicrous to attempt to list all of the special effects that contemporary composers might devise in communicating the music to their audiences. The possibilities are unlimited and mostly dependent on the creativity of the composer. The conductor will need to explain (or demonstrate) in the rehearsal process the special effects desired with the standard instruments. Special effects produced on new musical instruments will require *the availability of these instruments and the development of new playing techniques.* First, the conductor and eventually the players in the rehearsal process must deal with the composer's wishes in terms of these special effect requirements in contemporary music.

New Notation and Instructions

The contemporary composer has found that traditional notation breaks down in attempting to notate sounds and special effects in contemporary musical expression. *In some cases, the composer provides instructions.* This may be in the form of a "legend," a table of definitions, or an explanation in the music of this nontraditional notation. The conductor and players should adhere to these instructions in the performance of the work. If the composer gives no instructions in the music, then the conductor must research this new notation and be prepared to explain to the players what the composer intended. Occasionally, the conductor and players find it necessary to invent or "interpret" the new notation that lacks instructions by the composer. Additional score study time may be required because of this new notation or the lack of instructions about the notation. (See Appendix D: Instrumental Techniques, Intonation, and Special Effects.)

The instructions provided by the composer will give the conductor insight as to how to interpret the music. The authenticity of the work is dependent on the adherence to these instructions. These instructions may supply answers to such areas of performance as tempo, rhythm, balance, articulation, dynamics, phrasing, improvisation, and many other performance aspects. The performance of the nontraditional notation shown in the score and parts at the beginning or in the various places when this notation appears is also a crucial part of the instructions and must be seriously studied by the conductor in preparation for the rehearsal process. These instructions are critical to the musical interpretation. Some of these notation problems may include microtones, glissandi, indeterminate pitch, highest and lowest, rhythmic durations, proportionate durations, unordered elements, tremoli, half-valve sounds, muting, flutter-tongue, pointillistic music, and spatial notation.

Changing and Asymmetrical Meters

The compositional devices of changing and asymmetrical meters began to appear mostly at the beginning of the contemporary period. However, these devices have now become commonplace in contemporary music. When the meter changes, there are two possibilities for the conductor to consider: (1) the pulse (tempo beat) may stay the same, or (2) the pulse (tempo beat) changes to accommodate the new meter. In the early 20th century, it was not unusual for the meter to change but the pulse (tempo beat) to stay the same. However, as time went on, the second possibility became more prevalent, where the pulse changes to accommodate the new meter. Usually the composer will indicate by note value equations whether the tempo beat is to remain constant or should change.

In many instances, the composer will indicate above the bar line which note value equals which note value at the point where the meter changes. If there is no indication from the composer, the conductor must apply logic and rationality or follow a model (reliable recording or live performance) as to which possibility to apply. In recent times, the general rule for meter changes is to keep the "common note value" going, that is to say, that eighth note equals eighth note or other designated note values. The composer uses the meter change to shift the regular accents at bar lines. With this second option, the conductor and players should think of this common note value when the meter changes and keep the eighth note (or other note value) constant.

Conducting 5/8 or 7/8 meters in fast tempo is the basis of understanding the problems of executing asymmetrical meters. *In general, the conductor must divide the measure into regular beats and elongated beats.* Regular beats refer to those applied in simple meter. Elongated beats would be extended to half again the value of the regular beat in most instances. The options for conducting 5/8 meter are two (2+3 and 3+2); the options for 7/8 are three (2+2+3, 2+3+2, and 3+2+2). If the principle of regular and elongated beats is understood, then any asymmetrical meter pattern can be devised. For example, 11/8 might be conducted in a five-pattern (or frame) as four regular beats and one elongated beat. Where this elongated beat would appear in the pattern depends on the composer's notation in the music. Determine the conducting pattern by the number of rhythmic groupings in the measure combining regular beats and elongated beats as notated.

The conductor, when confronted with asymmetrical meter, will need to decide the pulse length and note value (tempo beat). For example, in 5/8 meter the choices are five pulses (8th notes) or two pulses (2+3 or 3+2). In 7/8 meter, the choices are seven pulses (8th notes) or three pulses (2+2+3, 2+3+2 or 3+2+2). It will depend largely on the tempo of the piece. However, this is not the only factor involved. Fewer tempo beats would help the phrasing and the musical line, while more tempo beats would provide better clarity and rhythmic security. If the tempo were such that showing more tempo beats would cause the pattern to become flustered in appearance or to slow the tempo, then the decision should be made for fewer tempo beats or a very modified five-pattern or seven-pattern.

Conducting changing and asymmetrical meters is one of the most important conducting techniques for the advanced conductor to develop because so much of contemporary music contains this meter fluctuation. In order for the conductor to help the players, the patterns for the regular beats and elongated beats must be executed clearly *with a distinguishable difference between these unequal beats.* The key to conducting or playing these meters or rhythmic patterns precisely is to keep the basic unit (eighth note, etc.) pulsating in the mind. Another technique for the conductor to keep the basic unit precise is "tonguing" the basic unit (eighth notes, etc.) as if playing a wind instrument. Thinking the subdivision of the meter beat in contemporary music is also very essential. Another aspect of this is found in metric modulation or tempo modulation in works of contemporary composers such as Elliot Carter. Examples of polytempo are found in Charles Ives's *The Unanswered Question*, in which the string orchestra is conducted without regard for the soloists and in Einojuhani Rautavaara's *Concerto for Birds and Orchestra*, in which the last movement of the work requires two conductors to keep specific choirs of instruments proceeding at different tempos and yet coordinated with the prerecorded tape or disk.

New Instruments and Unusual Instrumental Techniques

Modern technology is beginning to bring forth new instruments. Composers are experimenting with these to find different sounds. Primarily among these is the electronic synthesizer, which can duplicate various wind, string, and percussion tone qualities on the keyboard through the employment of MIDI (Musical Instrument Digital Interface). These electronic string, wind, and percussion instrument sonorities are being perfected and used to produce extraordinary sounds within the instrumental music ensemble. For some time, the percussion section of the instrumental music ensemble has been an environment where new and unusual instruments have been employed. This continues to be the case. Many of the special effects created by the composer tend to be orchestrated within the percussion section of the ensemble. The conductor must become knowledgeable about these new instruments and the techniques involved in playing them properly in the context of the instrumental music ensemble.

The conductor will need to have a grasp of these instrumental techniques used in contemporary music. Examples of such techniques would include multiphonics, the altissimo register, special string effects, and other such unusual instrumental techniques. In certain cases, these rather unusual techniques are simply a different way of producing tones on the common instruments of the band or orchestra. In other cases, the new instrumental techniques connect to electronically generated instruments or new instruments that are the product of modern technology and would require unusual instrumental techniques, with tone production called for in the contemporary music scores. In the score, the contemporary composer should indicate to the conductor and players how to execute these new techniques requested in the music.

Music Theater (Multimedia and Staging)

The term *music theater* has now evolved to identify those works that encompass more than a conductor and ensemble in performance. These presentations may involve other artistic media. Although multimedia presentations seem to come and go with the times, some significant contemporary works classify as multimedia. The use of film or video projection, prerecorded tapes (or CDs), dance, lighting, and other artistic media combine with music to create these attractive and unusual presentations. The contemporary opera and American musical theater verge on being multimedia presentations at times. *The conductor must learn to be flexible and inventive in this rehearsal and performance environment.*

At least partially in an effort to create a more attractive presentation, contemporary composers have written works that involve movement or staging of musicians during the performance. This may include the conductor as well as the players. It may also involve lighting, scenery, and costumes. Modern technology such as television cameras and monitors often enhance and solve problems of sight and sound with these presentations. Examples of such works are George Crumb's *The Time and the River* and his *Ancient Voices of Children.*

Avant-garde music can encompass multimedia, staging, electronic tape, aleatoric music, serial, minimalism, and other compositional styles. Some examples of this type of modern music are Raautavara's *Concerto for Birds*, Hovhaness's *And God Created Great Whales*, Ives's *Unanswered Question*, Merrill Ellis's *Mutations for Brass Quintet and Conductor*, Elliott Carter's *Concerto for Orchestra*, and György Ligeti's *Atmosphères*. This whole area of avant-garde music (or new music) must be considered from the standpoint that each work presents new and innovative approaches in music composition and performance.

Table 16.1, Teaching Strategy (Conducting Contemporary Music), provides ideas and suggestions for designing a teaching strategy in the conducting of contemporary music. Table 16.2, Teaching Strategy (Rehearsing Contemporary Music), offers ideas and suggestions for designing a teaching strategy in the rehearsing of contemporary music. These are both located at the end of the chapter.

PRACTICAL APPLICATION (DISCUSSION/DEMONSTRATION)

1. Select a contemporary instrumental ensemble score that contains numerous meter changes. Practice conducting these meters. (Select the Musical Example from the Repertoire.)
2. Select a contemporary instrumental ensemble score that contains asymmetrical meters. Practice conducting these meters. (Select the Musical Example from the Repertoire.)
3. Discuss some of the new notational signs found in contemporary music scores: microtones, glissandi, indeterminate pitch, rhythmic duration, unordered elements, tremoli, pointillistic, and spatial notation. (Appendix D)
4. Discuss the problems encountered in the performance of contemporary music theater and avant-garde works.
5. Discuss philosophically why contemporary music should be performed. (What are the objections to performing this music?)
6. What is the role of the conductor in fostering performances of "new music"? Would this help encourage commissioning and premiere performances?
7. Continue to gain familiarity with the standard repertoire found in Appendix A through CD listening, score study, and guidance from the conducting teacher. (See Appendix G for assignment forms.)

IN THE REHEARSAL PROCESS (LAB) ENVIRONMENT

1. Conduct changing meter passages with the ensemble. (Be sure to keep thinking of the phrase; select the Musical Example from the Repertoire.)
2. Conduct asymmetrical meter passages with the ensemble. (Be sure to keep thinking of the phrase; select the Musical Example from the Repertoire.)
3. Conduct and rehearse some rhythmically difficult passages of contemporary music with the ensemble. (Select the Musical Example from the Repertoire.)
4. Conduct and rehearse some technically difficult passages of contemporary music with the ensemble. (Select the Musical Example from the Repertoire.)

5. Conduct and rehearse passages of contemporary music involving some new performance techniques or special effects with the ensemble. (Select the Musical Example from the Repertoire.)
6. Complete student conducting/rehearsing projects (in the rehearsal process lab environment).

RECOMMENDED READING

Blade, James, *Orchestral Percussion Techniques*, 2nd ed. This is an important resource for contemporary percussion techniques.

Camphouse, Mark, *Composers on Composing for Band*. This book brings the composer and conductor of contemporary band music to the same page.

Cope, David, *New Directions in Music*. This book gives an overview of contemporary music and was originally and specifically written for the composer.

Dallin, Leon, *Techniques of Twentieth Century Composition*. This book categorizes the various special effects (such as microtones, Sprechstimme, fragmentation, and electronic tapes) in contemporary music.

Fink, Robert, and Robert Ricci, *The Language of Twentieth Century Music*. This book is set up in a dictionary form and defines various terms associated with the music of the 20th century.

Green, Elizabeth A. H., and Nicolai Malko, *The Conductor and his Score*. Chapter 8: The Contemporary Score contains some of the common music notation found in contemporary music on pp. 116–18.

Hunsberger, Donald, and Roy E. Ernst, *The Art of Conducting*. Chapter 12: Contemporary Music shows on pp. 135 and 136 some of the notation used by contemporary composers.

Labuta, Joseph A., *Basic Conducting Techniques*, 5th ed. A number of musical examples by contemporary composers could be used from this book. Transposed parts are also provided in the 5th edition of this book. In the 6th edition, these parts are online.

McBeth, W. Francis, *Effective Performance of Band Music: Solutions to Specific Problems in the Performance of 20th Century Band Music*. Solution VII—Interpretation of Twentieth-Century Band Music briefly covers this area.

Prausnitz, Frederik, *Score and Podium (A Complete Guide to Conducting)*. Chapter 13: Perspectives: The View from Our Century provides considerable information about 20th-century conducting and performance problems.

Read, Gardner, *Contemporary Instrumental Techniques*. This book covers many of the problems in the conducting and rehearsing of contemporary music.

Schuller, Gunther, *The Compleat Conductor*. There is no better source for the conducting of contemporary music than this book written by an author who has been a professional hornist, conductor, composer, educator, and writer.

Vermeil, Jean, *Conversations with Boulez (Thoughts on Conducting)*. This book delves into the areas of contemporary avant-garde music or New Music.

Weisberg, Arthur, *Performing Twentieth-Century Music: A Handbook for Conductors and Instrumentalists*. Areas covered include: (1) Elements of 20th-Century Rhythm, (2) Rewriting/Composite Rhythms, (3) Metronome/Metric Modulation, and (4) The Basics of Conducting/Preparing the Score.

REPERTOIRE FOR PROJECTS AND ASSIGNMENTS

Full Orchestra, Chamber Orchestra, or String Orchestra

Holst: The Planets (seven movements)
Debussy: Prelude to the Afternoon of a Faun
Ginastera: Estancia: Four Dances, Op. 8a
Stravinsky: Firebird Suite (various movements)
Bernstein: Symphonic Dances from "West Side Story"

Concert Band or Wind Ensemble

Reed, H. Owen: La Fiesta Mexicana (three movements)
Bielawa: Spectrum (tape and new notation)
Husa: Music for Prague 1968 (special effects and fragmentation)
Markis: Aegean Festival Overture (asymmetrical meters)
Schuller: Meditations for Band (fragmentation)

Miscellaneous or Small Ensembles

Stravinsky: L'histoire du soldat (asymmetrical meters) (clarinet, bassoon, cornet, trombone, percussion, violin, and double bass)
Barber: Capricorn Concerto for Flute, Oboe, Trumpet and Strings: 2/2/1/1/1

TEACHING STRATEGY TABLES

Table 16.1. Conducting Contemporary Music

CONDUCTOR CONCERNS	PROBLEM AREAS	TEACHING STRATEGIES
Changing meters or asymmetrical meters presenting conducting technique problems in contemporary music Differentiating the regular beat from the elongated beat Keeping the eighth note "feel" going in the asymmetrical meters	Changing meters	With changing meters, players appreciate good conducting technique and a clear pulse, resulting in a rhythmically precise performance.
		Practice these meter changes (daily) for the works to be conducted in the rehearsal process and in the concert performance.
	Asymmetrical meters	With asymmetrical meters, define the pulse precisely.
		Show the specific difference between the regular beat and the elongated beat.

(continued)

Table 16.1.   (***continued***)

CONDUCTOR CONCERNS	PROBLEM AREAS	TEACHING STRATEGIES
If needed, verbally explaining or demonstrating the conducting of asymmetrical meter Cueing if necessary with fragmentation of the musical line Adjusting the conducting technique somewhat for contemporary music More score study in contemporary music because of the complexities involved	Asymmetrical meters (*continued*)	Think the basic unit; think about the subdivision of each beat. "Tongue" the basic unit to maintain rhythmic evenness.
		Practice the asymmetrical meters until you can do them smoothly, precisely, and accurately.
		When the tempo is slow or moderate, show the elongated beat in an abbreviated 3-pattern to help players to subdivide.
		It is the responsibility of both the conductor and players to keep the basic unit precise and even.
	Verbal explanations	Verbally explain and demonstrate conducting patterns that may be causing confusion for players.
		With younger ensembles, there may be a need to introduce these changing and asymmetrical meters for the first time.
	Cueing	Cueing may become quite crucial because of the fragmentation of the musical line in contemporary instrumental music.
	Phrasing	Even though meters are changing or asymmetrical, phrasing should still be a major concern.
		Marking the score, bar grouping, and phrase indications can help with contemporary music also.
	Sudden tempo changes and the ensemble precision	Careful preparation of the sudden tempo changes to preserve the ensemble precision is important.
	Unique aspects of contemporary music	These unique aspects may require the conductor to adapt and adjust the conducting technique to meet the various demands of contemporary music.
What other teaching strategies (suggested by the conducting teacher or students) could implement conducting of contemporary music?		

Table 16.2.   Rehearsing Contemporary Music

CONDUCTOR CONCERNS	PROBLEM AREAS	TEACHING STRATEGIES
Following the composer's instruction carefully	Score Study	There should be meticulous study of contemporary musical scores because of the complexity.
Separating out the various unique rehearsal elements		The composer's instructions to the conductor should be observed and assimilated.
Very active percussion parts in contemporary music		Separate the various unique rehearsal elements that need detailed rehearsing in the contemporary musical score.
Working on the rhythms, technical passages, and special effects		Marking the score and parts can be of tremendous help in the rehearsing of contemporary instrumental music.
More rehearsal "settling time" for contemporary music		Pay special attention to percussion parts; they usually play prominent roles in much of contemporary music.
Aleatoric passages demanding more freedom from the conductor	In the rehearsal process	Rehearse specific areas discussed as problematic in chapter 16.
Exposed lines and passages requiring very careful rehearsing		Anticipate the passages that need attention before the rehearsal process begins.
Large interval skips posing difficulty for the brass players		Specific work on complex rhythms, special effects, and other technical passages may be necessary in the rehearsal process.
Introducing to the ensemble the most attainable passages first in the contemporary music selections		More rehearsal "settling time" may be necessary with much of the contemporary music.
		Players may need detailed explanations by the conductor concerning various performance aspects of contemporary music.
		Use the "count and conduct" procedure with complex rhythmic passages in contemporary music.

(*continued*)

Table 16.2. (*continued*)

	PROBLEM AREAS	*TEACHING STRATEGIES*
	Aleatory music	In aleatory music, the conductor must give more control and freedom to the players.
		Have the ensemble play without a conductor at times to test the security of the performance.
	Special problems in contemporary music	Exposed lines and passages require careful rehearsing in contemporary music because of the thin texture of the ensemble.
		Large and difficult interval skips cause problems for brass players in contemporary music.
		Instead of working through the entire piece, introduce to the ensemble the more attractive passages and sections at first.
What other teaching strategies (suggested by the conducting teacher or students) could assist in rehearsing contemporary music?		

Chapter Seventeen

Conductor Profile and Self-Evaluation

CONDUCTOR PROFILE

This chapter pertains to what a conductor should try to accomplish in the rehearsal process and during his or her conducting career. *There needs to be a growth pattern as a conductor*, with little or no stagnation throughout the conducting career. The growth pattern entails many aspects that I have previously discussed in this book. The maturing conductor can return to this chapter on various occasions to evaluate his or her progress. The conductor profile can act as a check on both the positive aspects and the negative ones. Other guidelines could be advanced in this conductor profile section. The impact with the conductor profile should be in terms of the quality of the self-evaluation.

This book has attempted to present information of lasting value for the advanced conductor in determining the top priorities, using effective rehearsal procedures, and designing teaching strategies for rehearsing the instrumental music ensemble. It is difficult to separate the actual conducting from rehearsing *because good conducting technique can eliminate much of the verbal explanations* and strongly influence the procedures used during the rehearsal process. The ensemble must learn to respond to the conducting technique. If the maturing conductor has acquired good conducting technique, then the rehearsing of the instrumental music ensemble is on a firm foundation. The conductor can spend the rehearsal process time performing music rather than constantly stopping the ensemble for corrections, verbal comments, or conductor demonstrations.

I have not attempted in this book simply to clone the evolving conductor into an experienced, successful conductor. Designing rehearsal procedures and teaching strategies is a very personal issue. Much depends on the personality, creativity, and musical background of the conductor. However, it is hoped that some of the ideas and suggestions presented in this book will help the maturing conductor begin to develop effective rehearsal procedures and design creative teaching strategies. *In too many instances, the rehearsal process has been left to chance in the advanced collegiate conducting courses.* This book is an attempt to better prepare the developing conductor to conduct and rehearse through a more systematic conducting curriculum following the initial conducting course.

BE ORGANIZED AND PREPARED

The organizational aspect for the conductor is paramount. The ensemble will not respond positively in the rehearsal process if the conductor appears to be disorganized. In most cases, the players will notice immediately and disparage the disorganized conductor. The organization of the conductor *involves many preparations before rehearsals begin.* Certainly, the conductor must establish the general order of importance in this regard. These preparations will go far in gaining the respect (and yes, the admiration) of the ensemble. The conductor must take care of these organizational details, perhaps using a checklist to guarantee addressing all of these items. In the next few paragraphs, I list some of these important items as a guide for the conductor.

The most important preparation is score study. Conscientious score study involves many hours of work and isolation. Do not come to the rehearsal process unprepared! Even an experienced conductor who has already conducted a particular piece many times in performance should study the score. The ensemble can accomplish much more in the rehearsal process when the conductor has the details of the score fresh in mind and can offer to the ensemble insights about the performance of the music. Score preparation by the conductor means that the conductor will know what to accomplish in the rehearsal process and in future rehearsals. As conductors, we expect the players to prepare their parts before the rehearsal process begins. How can the conductor demand this of the players without having given many hours to the serious study of the scores?

Next in importance is the preparation of the music for the players before the rehearsal process begins. Bowings and/or fingerings must be marked in the string parts. Breathing (phrasing) and style (articulation) markings may be necessary in the wind parts. If the key changes frequently, for example as in George Gershwin's *An American in Paris*, it may be necessary to mark these changes in some way. It is also helpful to provide sufficient rehearsal numbers or letters in the music. Having a starting point from which to count measures so that all of the players can find their place does save valuable rehearsal time. In some cases, each measure could be numbered. Rehearsal time can and should be saved by examining the parts for printed errors as well. Although this music preparation is time-consuming for the conductor, such preparation avoids much wasted rehearsal time. Each player needs to have a pencil to mark additional requests, corrections, or changes during the rehearsal process.

The next preparations are the conductor's rehearsal plan and schedule and the teaching strategies for the rehearsal process. What is the game plan? Designate the amount of time to be devoted to each specific selection and the segments in the rehearsal process. This will not always work out exactly because of unexpected circumstances in the rehearsal process. Adjustments will be necessary for future rehearsals. *Then the rehearsal objectives must be in place to guide the conductor.* This detailed plan would include passages that need attention, areas of performance (priorities) that should be improved and refined, and the most efficient procedures and teaching strategies for the conductor to employ. There should also be a comprehensive (overall) plan based on the number of rehearsals before the concert performance.

If it is the first rehearsal in preparation for a concert performance, the conductor might assume that most of the rehearsal process will be devoted to familiarizing the players with the selected repertoire as an ensemble. (If the situation is such that the players will have the music in advance and are expected to prepare the music before coming to this first rehearsal, then the procedures can go beyond acquainting the players with the music.) In subsequent rehearsals the conductor should have the advantage of knowing exactly what needs to be rehearsed. *Overlook no details.* I recommend recording the rehearsal process when possible. If this is not feasible, then the conductor should plan for the following rehearsal immediately after the rehearsal process so that he or she remembers the details for the next rehearsal. If the time between rehearsals is considerable, this lack of rehearsal continuity will affect the rehearsal planning and preparation. There are many other preparations to be accomplished either by the conductor or delegated to other staff members or student personnel, including

1. Obtaining the music (purchase or rental)
2. Cataloging purchased music or checking in rental music
3. Placing music in folders (with a pencil for marking)
4. The general preparation of the rehearsal facility (see chapter 2)
5. Availability of needed special instruments (piano, harp, percussion, etc.)
6. Availability of tuning devices, recording equipment, chalkboard, mutes, cello stops, etc.

This rehearsal organization and these preparations are necessary for the success of the rehearsal process and for the improved performance level of the ensemble. The point is that completing these preparations saves a tremendous amount of time during the rehearsal process. These preparations also include the rehearsal plan and schedule (strategy) and the teaching strategies that the conductor must conceive, execute, and reinforce with the ensemble. Even though the conductor may find some of these preparations to be rather routine and mundane, they are a necessary part of being organized, being prepared, and showing strong leadership with the ensemble. The ensemble conductor must have definite ideas about what should happen in the rehearsal process and then proceed to accomplish these items.

PERSONAL PREPARATION

I have stressed personal and long-range preparation for the conductor throughout this book. However, the personal preparation is probably the least considered after conductors find gainful employment and are out there "practicing the art and craft." The conductor needs to develop a "five-year plan" (or whatever period chosen) with specific goals in his or her development as a conductor and leader of an instrumental music ensemble. The growth must be as a person, a teacher, a musician, and a conductor. Leadership of the ensemble involves personality, sensitivity toward the players, and most certainly musicianship. Conductors must be willing to "pay their dues" in this personal preparation.

These conductor goals should be realistic. It would be quite unrealistic to aspire to a specific conducting position in a certain length of time. Rather, these goals should be attainable with sustained effort and determination on the part of the conductor. The goals may be quite varied. *These goals must be formulated based on where the conductor is presently and what needs to be achieved in order to be a more competent and successful conductor.* The conductor should always aspire to the artistic details; it is not enough just being organized and efficient in the rehearsal process. It often happens that the conductor relegates score study and musical details to a later time and then never completes them. As examples of these goals, the conductor must strive to improve any weaknesses (such as in the conducting technique), acquire more music knowledge, develop rehearsal skills, learn the standard repertoire, investigate new works, and be ready to grasp various conducting opportunities as they become available. With the advanced conductors, there should certainly be some consideration for the ideas of networking and entrepreneurship in order to promote the conducting career. Develop career path details such as biographies, interview skills, marketing strategies, resumes, promo kits, grant proposals, and contact lists.

Depending on the goals defined for improvement, the conductor must now determine how to achieve these goals within the timetable of the plan. Following are a few suggestions: (1) continually listening to all kinds of music (acquiring and augmenting a diverse CD library), (2) attendance at rehearsals, performances, workshops, instrumental clinics, instrumental master classes, music conventions, and conducting symposiums, (3) advanced study at collegiate institutions or with a master conductor, (4) personal study and research, (5) performing on an instrument in a quality ensemble, and (6) musical growth as a conductor through intensive score study and practice. The focus should constantly be on musical interpretation. An agenda for accomplishing the goals in this plan needs to be spelled out and then executed as conceived.

BE A TEACHER (MAKE PLAYERS AWARE)

As I mentioned in the preface, the leader of an ensemble is an organizer, teacher, and conductor. Teaching is defined as the act, process, or art of imparting knowledge and developing skills. In the instrumental rehearsal process, this act, process, and art has to exist based *on what is actually heard in the rehearsal process*; otherwise, there will be little or no improvement in the performance level of the ensemble. Rehearsing an instrumental music ensemble involves being both a conductor and a teacher. Most of the teaching will be involved with showing (by conducting patterns and gestures) or communicating with the players (verbally, playing, or singing) what should be transpiring in the rehearsal process. Teaching ability in the classroom is somewhat different from what goes on in the rehearsal hall. In the classroom, the content would include much more cognitive learning; this is not to say that this kind of learning does not happen in the rehearsal process. However, in the rehearsal process much depends on the sounds produced as music covers time and space. Consequently, there is more aesthetic education in the rehearsal process than in the academic classroom. Above all else, the conductor should be a teacher and not a drillmaster. *Do not teach by rote.* The primary responsibilities of the conductor are fostering playing skills, disseminating needed information, developing musicianship, and promoting artistic performance.

Player awareness is the key to effective rehearsal progress. The conductor should insist on certain behavior from the ensemble and make this clear to the players from the very start. Likewise, the conductor must make the players aware of both technical and musical problems (and the solutions) throughout the rehearsal process. Verbal explanations or comments by the conductor in the rehearsal process should center on this awareness aspect. The main objectives of the rehearsal process, beyond rehearsing the selected repertoire, are to improve various performance aspects of the ensemble (such as intonation, precision, balance, phrasing, etc.). This can take place only if the players are made aware of the problems to be solved. Teaching in the rehearsal process is a combination of the conducting technique and the rehearsal comments. The teaching by the conductor in the rehearsal process should always be linked to musicianship and musical sensitivity.

If the players learn what is expected of them in the rehearsal process, in most cases, they will be able to adjust their parts in relationship to the rest of the ensemble. This awareness strategy also involves listening and musical sensitivity on the part of the players. This strategy can be useful in improving many performance aspects. Intonation, balance, dynamics, and style are four priorities that could be improved with this awareness strategy. There are numerous ways throughout the rehearsal process to promote this awareness strategy, including conducting, singing, modeling and imitation, verbal comments, isolating places for the players to hear, and through specific feedback from the conductor as well as many other such awareness strategies.

When the conductor stops the ensemble to make a correction or improve the performance in some way, the awareness of the problem must be the primary consideration. *However, too much verbal analysis by the conductor will lead to wasted time in the rehearsal process.* In order to make these corrections, the teaching strategy employed is important. In any case, the conductor should try to make the players aware of the problem and then provide a reasonable solution. (For example, the conductor has stopped the group because the phrasing is not uniform and is therefore unacceptable. Now the conductor has a number of options available for solving the problem, depending on the reason for the problem. Perhaps the conductor might verbally explain where the wind players should take the breath, sing or play the phrase for the players to imitate what is wanted in the phrasing, have the phrase played by an ensemble member, correct a technical error in the phrase, or consider the various musical expressions or nuances within the phrase.) Realistically, the conductor cannot possibly anticipate every problem that might come up in the rehearsal process. In some instances, the conductor would find it beneficial to delay the solution until the next rehearsal process and in the intervening time find an effective solution to the problem.

When the Conductor Stops the Ensemble

For most players, one of the most frustrating occurrences in the rehearsal process is for the conductor to stop the ensemble and say, "Let's do that again." The perplexity with this statement is that the conductor has not made the players aware of the reason for asking for the repetition. If it is for reasons of familiarity or to solidify the passage or section, then the conductor should indicate this specifically to the ensemble. *In general, the conductor needs to make the ensemble aware of the reason for stopping.* By stopping at the appropriate places, the conductor will send the right message to the players, enhancing the conductor's credibility. When the conductor does not stop for what should be obvious problems, the players may assume that the conductor's standards are questionable or that the conductor is unaware of the problem. Some of the specific circumstances in which the conductor might want to stop and make the players aware of the particular problem, as well as to offer a solution to the problem follow.

1. Note and rhythmic errors
2. Balance and blend among the parts (or the various sections or choirs)
3. Intonation discrepancies
4. Poor ensemble tone quality
5. Dynamic level desired
6. To adjust the articulation or bowing
7. To suggest the proper and consistent style among the players
8. Phrasing and other such musical problems
9. Poor precision within the ensemble
10. Musical expressions and nuances needed

Many of these stopping points during the rehearsal process involve the rehearsal priorities that I have discussed in this book. Making the players aware of these problems and their solutions will lead to the improvement of the ensemble performance. In some instances, if the players are aware of the problems, they can and will make the needed adjustment themselves. Depending on the maturity and performance level of the ensemble, the conductor as a teacher has the responsibility to see that in the rehearsal process he or she gives the players solutions to the problems as they present themselves. The next few sections deal with the conductor being credible, specific, insistent, and consistent in the rehearsal process through the proper use of the conducting technique and rehearsing skills; this relates directly to making the players aware of these performance problems.

BE CREDIBLE

The conductor cannot necessarily depend on the ensemble responding immediately to the conductor, even when the conductor is reputable and a proven success in the field. The conductor must appear credible in the minds of the ensemble; he or she must seem "worthy of being believed." Trust and sincerity are two key facets in that credibility. Gaining credibility comes through knowledge and preparation. No matter what the decorum of the rehearsal process is or the makeup of the ensemble is like, *the conductor must come before the group thoroughly prepared.* As the rehearsals progress, it will become apparent to the ensemble that the conductor knows what he or she is doing technically and musically. This involves detecting errors, making corrections efficiently and effectively, making musical judgments decisively, and in general, controlling the rehearsal process for the best use of the allotted time. Always display clear conducting technique. The conducting patterns and gestures should communicate to the players and later to the audience (in the performance) that the conductor is credible. The conductor should always try to use effective procedures in the rehearsal process for the purpose of ensemble progress. Knowledge of instrumental techniques and performance concepts must be a concern for the conductor in the rehearsal process; knowledge about instrumental pedagogy is especially important with younger ensembles. These procedures will involve hard and serious work, being energetic and enthusiastic, and being committed to the rehearsal process objectives as well as to the ensemble performance goals. Above everything else, the conductor needs to show that he or she is committed to the music being rehearsed.

Credibility must be earned. The conductor will not necessarily gain respect just by being a "nice person." The ensemble will judge the conductor's effectiveness rather quickly, although this may or may not be a fair evaluation. Over a longer period of rehearsal time, this negative evaluation may prove to be absolutely incorrect. However, the conductor must be ready from the beginning to present to the ensemble his or her competency as a conductor. *Be yourself as a conductor.* Do not put on "airs." The conductor's image should be one of honesty and integrity. The players must trust what the conductor is doing. As a conductor, do not be afraid to laugh at yourself; this will help your credibility. Be "up front" with the players. The conductor needs to show strong leadership, sincerity, sympathy, integrity, patience, trust, respect, and confidence with the ensemble. A simple example such as knowing the score well so that the conductor can have good eye contact with the ensemble will lead to this credibility and respect from the group. It is extremely important that the conductor share the performance credit with the ensemble as well as expressing this to the general public following the concert performance.

Qualities of a Credible Conductor

How the conductor shows these various qualities will depend strongly on the individual personality, background, and musicianship of the conductor. *General behavior by the conductor is also an important factor in being credible.* For the evolving conductor, it is important to develop the skills necessary to be a good conductor. Hoping that the ensemble will respond in a positive manner is not enough, however. The conductor must act and speak in a sincere way that will cause the ensemble to believe that what is happening in the rehearsal process is worthwhile. Admit your mistakes as a conductor in the rehearsal process. Do not place the blame somewhere else in order to cover up your own mistakes. The conductor should prepare carefully so that mistakes are minimal in the rehearsal process. The conductor needs to make thoughtful decisions based on a quality background of musical experience. Also, the conductor needs to be assertive because problems need to be resolved directly in the rehearsal process.

The conductor will gain credibility because of his or her preparation for the rehearsal process. Being credible means that the preparation has been thorough and meticulous. This involves detailed score study, research into the composers and the music periods of the selections, designing teaching strategies for solving problems, and thereby, in achieving a musical interpretation of the work that is considered to be authentic. *Authenticity is a part of being credible* and will do much toward gaining the respect of the ensemble (and the audience). Authenticity involves the performance practices (such as tempo, style, dynamics, and embellishments) employed during the particular musical period. Preparation and authenticity represent steady steps toward conductor credibility. In terms of authenticity, the developing conductor should refer to the material presented in Chapter 14: Style and Musical Interpretation.

In order for the conductor to gain this credibility, he or she must have developed organizational skills. As the leader of an ensemble, the conductor will need to be organized in many aspects: the personal time, the rehearsal preparations, the music, the personnel, the performances, and the rehearsal process to mention just a few. The organization of time is crucial for conductors because they must be prepared in spite of a busy schedule. Organize all of the music in several ways (the obtaining of the music, score study, marking the music, the distribution of the parts to the players, etc.) in preparation for the rehearsal process. Personnel organization with most ensembles involves much time and effort on the part of the conductor. The organization of the concert schedule and performances by the conductor as well as many other details are necessary for the realization of these events. The rehearsal process must be organized to maximize the benefits from the rehearsal time. If these aspects are not well organized, the conductor will certainly lose credibility with the ensemble in the rehearsal process and with the audience in the concert performance.

Professionalism as a conductor (and teacher) relates to being competent. The players expect the conductor, as a leader of an ensemble, to be professional in the rehearsal process and in the concert performance. The idea of professionalism involves many things. Professionalism pertains to how the conductor relates to and treats people— players, colleagues, and the public. Professionalism pertains to how well the conductor can conduct, rehearse, and perform music properly with the ensemble. Professionalism pertains to the extent of this preparedness and the quality of the conductor's work. In this regard, conductors simply must know what they are trying to accomplish in the rehearsal process! This credibility is involved in what you say and do in most all venues as a conductor. *Finally, constructive criticism by the conductor is the only way to proceed within the rehearsal process in order to be professional regarding the instrumental music ensemble.*

BE SPECIFIC

General comments in the instrumental music rehearsal process are of little value in achieving the rehearsal objectives. The more specific and exacting the conductor can be in articulating problems and solutions, the less wasted time in the rehearsal process. General comments lead to confusion and frustration on the part of the players. In most cases, the players want to know exactly what the problems are as well as the proposed solutions. *The conductor should be as clear and "to the point" as possible.* The conductor should isolate problems and offer specific solutions for these performance problems. The conductor should avoid being *condescending or philosophical* in the rehearsal process; this wastes time.

A comment by the conductor such as "I do not like the tone quality of the clarinet section" does very little if anything to improve the sound of the clarinet section, especially with a younger ensemble. Specific instructions are necessary concerning the problem and the solution. If it is a technical problem in the ensemble, the conductor must stress those fundamental aspects that will lead to tone improvement, such as the use of the air, the embouchure formation, reed quality, etc. If it is a musical problem, then the conductor needs to specify the tone quality desired with such words as darker, brighter, louder, softer, less strident, etc. With the younger ensemble, the solution may need to be accompanied with pedagogical information in order to achieve the desired results. The conductor should not point out problems without offering a specific solution during the rehearsal process. Through demonstrations, modeling (and imitation), or verbal comments, the conductor should identify the problems and propose the specific solutions.

Teaching Strategies are Necessary

Problems in the rehearsal process may be solved through demonstrations, modeling (and imitation), or verbal comments. Imitation in the rehearsal process can be an efficient and effective teaching tool. Many times, verbal comments will be inadequate and result in generalities that lead to little progress during the ensemble rehearsal process. Modeling by the conductor or members of the ensemble can prove to be an efficient procedure for improving certain performance aspects. For example, if the conductor wishes to improve the quality of tone produced in the cello section, he or she might ask the principal player to model this quality of tone for the rest of the section. The cello section, following the modeling by the principal cellist during the rehearsal process, should then strive to imitate this model in every way possible.

The conducting patterns and gestures can represent another idea for being specific in the rehearsal process. Clear, precise conducting patterns and gestures with an alert (watching) ensemble will send a specific indication to the players. This will partially eliminate the need to stop the ensemble for comments, modeling, or demonstrations. If comments are necessary to clarify or solve a problem in the rehearsal process, the conductor should make every effort to be as succinct with these comments as possible. *Long, drawn-out explanations waste much time in the rehearsal process.* The conductor should try to find a few words with a specific message in solving these problems during the rehearsal process. All of the teaching strategies need to be specific so that they are effective and efficient during the rehearsal process. This can happen through score study, planning, and the various preparations for the rehearsal process. These preparations include the order and timing of the selections to be rehearsed, identifying passages that need to be improved, and all of the other rehearsal objectives to be achieved during the rehearsal process.

BE INSISTENT

The messages that the conductor sends to the players are critical in the long-range plan of developing a cohesive, musical ensemble and in the effective rehearsing of the concert repertoire. If the message is that the conductor is willing to accept mediocrity, the ensemble will respond accordingly. Conversely, if the conductor sends the message that he or she will only accept the highest standards of performance, then the ensemble will strive to reach those standards. The words to describe being insistent as a conductor in the rehearsal process include correctness, musicality, drive, determination, unyielding, uncompromising, tenacity, persistence, confrontational, committed, patience, impatience, perseverance, and being genuine.

How are these messages sent? The conductor does it in many ways. In general, these messages are sent through a projection of an attitude and are psychologically transmitted. It is a message from one rehearsal to another. In many different ways, the conductor is saying to the players, "I want this ensemble to be the very best group possible." *The conductor must show a strong commitment in taking care of problems in the rehearsal process.* The conductor should not ignore problems like an ostrich sticking its head in the sand. If the conductor does not have a solution to the problem, it may be necessary to delay the solution until the next rehearsal process. However, the conductor should not just hope that the problems will go away or that the players will solve them. These problems do not solve themselves, and therefore, may persist even through the concert performance! As mentioned, persistence in getting things done is a quality the conductor must show during the rehearsal process. If this means that the pace of the rehearsal process slows down, then it still must happen until the problem is solved.

All ensemble musicians have experienced the situation wherein the conductor spends 15 minutes of rehearsal time on four measures of music or works with a specific section for a similar length of time. In both procedures, the players not involved in the rehearsal process may become inattentive and even bored. Do not use these rehearsal procedures too frequently. However, these procedures are delivering the right message in that the conductor wants this passage played correctly and musically. By sending this message, the attitude of the conductor should be reflected in the work ethic and positive attitude of the players. Likewise, the conductor who spends half of the rehearsal process working on intonation is risking some criticism from the players. However, such a procedure does send a strong message that the conductor wants the ensemble to be able to play in tune.

In the Rehearsal Process

There is little question what message is the correct one for the conductor to send the players in the rehearsal process. It is a question of the activity, the procedure (strategy), and its frequency. *Common sense plays an important part here.* The conductor must sense when "enough is enough." Based on the amount of rehearsal time available before the concert performance, the conductor must be sensitive at any given point in the rehearsal process as to when to change the activity or procedure. There must always be a certain balance between patience and impatience in rehearsing the ensemble during the rehearsal process.

The conductor should always be insistent about the details of the musical performance and take care of them in the rehearsal process. There should be no compromise in getting these details correct. It is easier to follow the path of least resistance and gloss over some of the details that will require time and effort to set them right. Likewise, other details in terms of preparation, score study, and rehearsal planning must receive attention before the rehearsal process begins. The players will understand the conductor's insistence concerning the details; this will strengthen the conductor's credibility. *The concert performance will meet expectations if the conductor is insistent on accurate and musical playing in the rehearsal process.*

BE CONSISTENT

There are three main areas where consistency is important for the conductor in the rehearsal process:

1. Attitude of the conductor in the rehearsal process
2. Relationship between the conductor and the players
3. Consistency in the conducting technique during the rehearsal process and into the concert performance

The conductor needs to appear consistent in attitude from day to day and from one rehearsal process to another. If the conductor is inconsistent, the players will not know exactly what is to be expected. Wrong messages will be sent to the players by this inconsistent attitude. The conductor must be reliable in the rehearsal process. From one rehearsal process to the next, the conductor must remain steadfast and not vary emotionally to the point that this consistency wavers much. This is not to say that the conductor should be suave or serene no matter what transpires in the rehearsal process, but the rehearsal process should not seem as if the conductor is on an emotional roller coaster either.

In the Rehearsal Process

The conductor must reflect a consistency in attitude and mood in the rehearsal process. In this regard, the players want to know what to expect from moment to moment and from rehearsal process to rehearsal process. If the conductor displays erratic behavior in the rehearsal process, the players will become confused as to how to respond. This is not to say that no matter what happens, the conductor should show no negative emotion or positive enthusiasm. *The rehearsal process will have its peaks and valleys.* What it does mean is that the conductor must make great effort to respond to what occurs in the rehearsal process with consistency. As much as possible, minimize outside influences concerning the conductor during the rehearsal process. In terms of behavioral demeanor, emotional character, and steadfast purpose, the conductor must strive for consistency. The rehearsal process needs to have intensity with full concentration from both the conductor and the players.

The second important aspect of consistency is in the relationship between the conductor and the players. *In the rehearsal process, the conductor needs to be in control.* This does not mean being a dictator in style. Especially with a younger ensemble, the players must learn to accept the discipline necessary to carry on an effective rehearsal process. As the ensemble matures, a certain amount of "give and take" is allowable if it equates with an environment that is conducive to effective learning and making good music. At the semi-professional and professional levels, it becomes more of a businesslike relationship with both conductor and players assuming the responsibility for fine ensemble performance. In general, the relationship moves from one of imposed discipline in the rehearsal process to one of self-discipline and self-motivation. At whatever the performance level, the relationship between the conductor and the players should be one of cooperation and mutual respect. The conductor should not allow ego to get in the way or to hold a grudge in terms of the relationship with the players. The conductor should treat all of the players as fairly as possible. Some ideas, words, and phrases to describe being consistent might include optimistic, positive, patient, caring, responding well under stress, the same standards for all players, and in general, a consistent approach by the conductor toward the players.

Third, the conductor must *make every effort to conduct consistently* during the rehearsal process and into the concert performance. If the conductor is inconsistent in this regard, the players become very insecure as to what will happen in the concert performance. The players have enough to be concerned about without having the added problem of not knowing what the conductor is going to do. For example, if the conductor varies the handling of a fermata from one rehearsal process to the next, when the performance comes around the ensemble will only be able to guess what may happen. In such an instance, disaster could strike and the ensemble would lack good precision if not "crash and burn!" The conductor will certainly lose credibility with the ensemble if the conducting technique is erratic during the rehearsal process and this continues into the concert performance.

BE FLEXIBLE AND SPONTANEOUS

Flexibility is a quality that the conductor needs to possess or develop in supervising and managing the rehearsal process. Occasionally, the conductor will find the situation of the rehearsal process somewhat stressful. The conductor who rigidly adheres to a rehearsal plan may find the results to be unsuccessful. Even though the conductor has planned carefully, it is important to have some flexibility as the rehearsal continues. If it does not exactly follow the preconceived plan throughout, it may be possible after a slight deviation to return to the original rehearsal plan. The conductor should "go with the flow," if the direction is constructive. The conductor should respond with some flexibility to what is happening in the rehearsal process. *This flexibility should lead to spontaneity on the part of the conductor.* This spontaneity should begin to appear in the form of enthusiasm for what is transpiring in the rehearsal process and for the improved performance level of the ensemble. Following are four examples of conductor flexibility in the rehearsal process:

1. The conductor should react in a manner that is comparable to the material Teflon, that is, nothing "sticks" to him or her. If the activities or pace of the rehearsal process are not going according to the rehearsal plan, the conductor must "shift gears" without appearing dismayed or flustered.
2. When the rehearsal process begins to show signs of stress because of any number of problems, the use of humor, a change of pace, or a different rehearsal direction can often turn the rehearsal process into a very productive session.
3. The player has just missed an important passage and the conductor is about to react negatively to the player. Instead, the conductor diverts his or her attention to another problem with the ensemble to give the player in question an opportunity to regain composure.
4. The conductor should be prepared to settle for what happens in the rehearsal process, after giving it his or her "best shot." This does not imply giving up. It may mean that this problem will need confronting in the next rehearsal process.

In the Rehearsal Process

The very nature of the rehearsal process in itself demands flexibility on the part of the conductor. *Things do not always go as planned.* The experienced conductor, who studies the score well and then reacts to what occurs in the rehearsal process, but has no rehearsal plan, is showing what might be considered the ultimate in flexibility. This can work if the conductor's background, experience, and musicianship are superior. Sometimes in the rehearsal process it is necessary to change planned procedures to keep the rehearsal interesting and the ensemble progressing. Likewise, the conductor should make the rehearsal somewhat unpredictable so that it does not become routine for the players. The conductor should be flexible in dealing with the players. The conductor should be receptive to new ideas that will demand this flexibility. The conductor must listen to what is actually happening in the rehearsal process in order to adjust the segments, priorities, procedures, and teaching strategies as needed.

The purpose of this book has been to guide the developing conductor in designing teaching strategies. The above paragraph may seem contrary to this purpose. However, the rehearsal plan and schedule will ensure an organized and productive rehearsal process, rather than a groping and reacting approach to the rehearsal process. The conductor needs to have this rehearsal plan and schedule, but keep the options open and be flexible as the rehearsal process unfolds. Adaptability is a key word in rehearsing the instrumental music ensemble. The conductor must conceive and design teaching strategies to ensure the success of these rehearsal objectives. The conductor must deal with many things in the rehearsal process including issues such as ego, attitude, compromise, and confrontation.

Part of being spontaneous is "letting yourself go" somewhat; be as creative and imaginative as possible. If this means straying from the rehearsal plan or the anticipated teaching strategies that you conceived before the rehearsal process began, so be it. The conductor should avoid teaching everything the same way, because students learn in many different ways. The conductor must remain in the "experimental" mode; try different things in the rehearsal process. Humor in the rehearsal process may spark this spontaneity. This procedure can also relax a tense atmosphere and allow for energized progress from the ensemble. Of course, this humorous approach must not be too long or too frequent with the results being a loss of concentration within the ensemble. Subsequently, the discipline of the ensemble should not be lost through this spontaneity.

BE CONFIDENT AND ENTHUSIASTIC

These two qualities—confidence and enthusiasm—are necessary for good leadership. I have said little in this book about leadership even though the book is directed toward being the leader of an ensemble. If this were a psychological treatise, rather than a practical study guide, then the book would need a chapter or more on this topic. *However, these two qualities are important in gaining the respect of the ensemble.* The conductor needs to "look and act the part." Do so through communicating this confidence with the ensemble. Eye contact is important in the rehearsal process so that the players feel this connection. The conductor's confidence should be reflected in the conducting patterns and gestures. Likewise, the enthusiasm shown by the conductor in rehearsing the ensemble is an important aspect of this physical and psychological leadership.

If the conductor's background, score study, and preparations have been thorough, then the confidence necessary to project such an atmosphere should be there. For the maturing conductor there will certainly be some trepidation at the beginning of the career. However, this lack of confidence should dissipate after a few rehearsals and the confidence in one's ability will eventually surface, if the preparation has been adequate. Even if the ensemble does not respond 100 percent to what the conductor does, the conductor will still achieve some of the rehearsal objectives because of this pre-rehearsal planning and preparation. With this preparation before the rehearsal process, *the players should respond positively just from the conductor's efforts in this regard.*

This confidence and enthusiasm from the conductor allow the taking of risks in the rehearsal process and even in the concert performance. Playing a little too fast, playing a little too slow, playing a little too loud, and playing a little too soft will project the conductor and the ensemble into a more creative world of performance. This must always happen with the best musicianship in mind, that is, in good taste. This risk-taking should make for much more exciting and inspired performances. Likewise, when the conductor shows the enthusiasm for the music performed, the ensemble will tend to "catch" this enthusiasm for the performance of the music and be ready to follow the conductor in taking these risks during the rehearsal process and the concert performance.

Confidence

The conductor must project this confidence based on his or her background and preparation for the rehearsal process. *Usually an arrogant attitude is a sign* that the conductor is trying to hide a lack of preparation or to prove something to the ensemble. The ensemble will discover this attitude very quickly—even with very young players! An attitude of disdain or arrogance probably relates to the conductor's own self-esteem, but is certainly not an attitude that will motivate the players or produce great musical performances. It is always a worthwhile goal to strive for a perfect technical performance, but what is more important is to have the music be exciting and inspirational to the players and the audience. This involves being as musical as one can possibly be.

The background of the conductor is crucial in terms of confidence. This involves the quality of preparation throughout the conductor's academic training as well as during the musical training of the conductor. I focused this book on these two areas of training for the maturing conductor. If the advanced conductor has placed serious emphasis on both the academic training and the musical training during the formal education, then confidence during the rehearsal process will be apparent. The advanced conductor should have developed skills to a high proficiency level on a musical instrument as well as being immersed in all of the study necessary for being a successful person, teacher, musician, and conductor.

The conductor must find sufficient time for planning and preparation of the rehearsal process. Not everything will necessarily go just as planned. However, if most of the plans are realized, the rehearsal process will be considered a success and beneficial for the technical and musical progress of the ensemble. This successful rehearsal process will give the conductor additional confidence. When the conductor and players are involved in this type of rehearsal process and are aware of the progress made in the rehearsal process, the confidence level of the conductor should continue to soar.

Enthusiasm

This book has focused attention on the idea of designing teaching strategies for rehearsing the instrumental music ensemble. In so doing, the conductor must not forget about projecting enthusiasm and spontaneity in the rehearsal process. The amount of enthusiasm and spontaneity shown in the rehearsal process has a direct relationship to the conductor's energy level. In this regard, it behooves the conductor to keep the personal energy level as high as possible. (Avoiding extreme physical fatigue is important to keep the conductor's positive outlook.) This would involve maintaining this positive attitude, keeping in shape physically and mentally, and avoiding "burn-out." The problem of so-called burn-out occurs when the expected results of work done does not seem to be rewarding or satisfying to the conductor in comparison to the amount of time, work, and energy consumed. *The conductor needs to be passionate about his or her work.* By being committed to and excited about the music, the conductor cannot help but project this enthusiasm to the players. Conductor enthusiasm stimulates the players. This is one reason that the selection of good music by the conductor is so important. The conductor must realize that his or her show of enthusiasm is rather contagious with the players and does result in player enthusiasm!

The planning of teaching strategies should not cause the conductor to eliminate one of the most important elements that will influence the ensemble, which is his own enthusiasm for the music and the accomplishments of the group. *Enthusiasm and vitality are important ingredients in the rehearsal process.* This comes from being optimistic. The conductor should keep the players invigorated and responsive. This does not imply that the conductor should always project to the players that "life is wonderful" every moment of the rehearsal process. In reality, the rehearsal process is a time of confrontation and the working out of problems. There is inherent adversity in the rehearsal environment. Things do not always go smoothly or as anticipated. However, if the conductor realizes this and can still maintain the ambiance of enthusiasm in the rehearsal process, the ensemble should respond positively. From time to time, the conductor should notice and contemplate the kind of "feedback" received from the players on this matter. Is there visible enthusiasm from the players during the rehearsal process?

The conductor should guard against the rehearsal process becoming methodical and dull. There would seem to be a disparity between strategy planning and spontaneity that must be bridged. In designing teaching strategies, the conductor is attempting to anticipate problems and rehearsal situations. This would not necessarily foster spontaneity. Again, the conductor will need to show some flexibility in the employment of the various teaching strategies to create an aura of unpremeditated actions and verbalization in the rehearsal environment. The conductor can even create enthusiasm in the rehearsal process by the conducting patterns and gestures. If the patterns and gestures seem to be showing a lack of enthusiasm for the music or what is happening in the rehearsal process, players will notice this rather quickly. However, if the patterns and gestures appear to be "alive" and promoted by the conductor's enthusiasm for the music at hand, the players will respond accordingly.

In summary, these two qualities—confidence and enthusiasm—relate to motivation. *The conductor needs to be a motivator.* I made some points in chapter 3 about motivation, and if this book mainly focused on leadership, psychology, discipline, and motivation, then considerable space would need to be devoted to these areas of concern. However, as stated in the preface, the parameters of this book do not necessarily emphasize these specific areas. Books listed at the end of this chapter are excellent sources for further study. Because these are broad areas, the given scenario would determine and modify specific motivational devices. However, the conductor sharing the credits and rewards with the members of the ensemble is an example of this confidence and enthusiasm for the rehearsal process and the concert performance. Preparing the ensemble well in the rehearsal process will show this confidence and enthusiasm from both the conductor and the ensemble. Words describing this confidence and enthusiasm of the conductor include dynamic, charismatic, great vitality, positive attitude, intense passion, and unrelenting energy.

BE CREATIVE

Being creative involves looking at things in different ways. Because we are dealing with an art form, there is not just one way of approaching the rehearsal process or the musical performance. In writing about rehearsal procedures, it would be of little value simply to list the various approaches used in the past. These approaches could certainly be a guide, but each conductor needs to develop his or her own rehearsal procedures.

The conductor needs to "personalize" the approach to rehearsing the instrumental music ensemble. By looking at things in a different light, so to speak, the conductor will approach the rehearsal process in a more creative manner. As a single example, the use of original music material during the warm-up period could be a creative part of the rehearsal process. By personalizing the rehearsal process, the conductor will find this to be a challenge in coming up with new ways to guide the ensemble and in being creative.

Throughout the rehearsal process, the conductor must strive to change the routine. There are certainly aspects of the rehearsal process that need to be consistent for the players, such as the warm-up period and the tuning procedures. However, even these segments need to be changed somewhat and kept as interesting as possible for the players. If the rehearsal process becomes uninteresting for the players, then all of these activities begin to lose their purpose and focus. There are many different ways to rehearse these technical and musical passages and get good results. *The conductor must continually look for these alternative ways.* The priorities discussed throughout this book suggest many teaching strategies. There are times when the conductor actually needs to experiment in the rehearsal process to discover some of these creative rehearsal procedures and teaching strategies.

Creativity in the Rehearsal Process

Following is a list of some ideas for creative activities that the conductor might investigate for use before and during the rehearsal process:

- Creating a unique rehearsal environment and aura
- The warm-up period (original material)
- Tuning procedures (vary these procedures)
- Conceiving the rehearsal plan and schedule
- Use of effective teaching strategies
- Establishing the rehearsal priorities for the ensemble
- Different seating arrangements for the ensemble
- Designing creative rehearsal segments and procedures
- Pacing the rehearsal process for better player interest and concentration
- The use of audiovisual aids (recordings, posters, pictures, PowerPoint, etc.)
- The use of creative verbal descriptions and comments in the rehearsal process
- Varying and controlling the stylistic considerations for the ensemble
- Defining the phrase for the players in the rehearsal process
- Conceiving exciting musical interpretations
- Always promoting musicianship within the ensemble
- Creative and artistic conducting for a better musical interpretation
- Playing with more dynamic contrast, nuances, and musical expression

The conductor can also be creative in many other ways with the following items:

- The selecting of rehearsal and concert repertoire
- Program building with the various types of programs

- Selecting unique repertoire
- Printed concert programs (attractive!)
- Concert publicity
- Selection of guest, faculty, or student soloists
- Varying the medium in concert programming (soloists and smaller ensembles)
- Premiere performances
- Commissioning of new works
- Bringing in guest composers, conductors, and soloists
- Performing music with soloists and/or chorus
- Performing music with dancers
- Use of special lighting effects in the concert performance

As a leader of an instrumental music ensemble, the conductor should be creative. This will result in inspired music making. The music itself can dictate and guide creativity in the rehearsal process. The conductor should allow for freedom in the rehearsal process among the players with this creativity. By engaging players in making musical decisions, the conductor can promote this experimentation and freedom. In a sense, I directed this whole book toward being creative in the designing of teaching strategies. I have not attempted to say, "do this," but rather to present ideas and suggestions for designing these teaching strategies to be used in the instrumental music rehearsal process. *Part of the idea of the conductor being creative is through brainstorming, networking, being flexible, and elaborating on various musical ideas.* The conductor should be imaginative and open to taking risks. The conductor who is creative and musical is certainly striving to reach a higher artistic level of ensemble performance.

BE MUSICAL

I purposefully left this section toward the end of the book. The idea of being musical is to leave this as the "parting shot" for the advanced conductor. With all of the distractions and elements in conducting and rehearsing the instrumental music ensemble that the conductor faces, it is easy to put the musical aspect aside. In some cases, musicality is simply never addressed before the concert performance. (Rather, I would suggest overlooking other aspects if necessary to keep the musicality in the ensemble rehearsal process.) It is rare to hear school ensembles project this musicality. *The musicality should be a part of every rehearsal process* and not an added ingredient in the last rehearsal or two. It is too late then. Making such drastic changes at the end only leads to confusion in the players.

When this musicality is present in a performance, the conductor is the guiding force and the main reason for its existence. The conductor must show dynamics, nuances, phrasing, musical expression and style, and capture the essence and spirit of the music. In the final analysis, the conductor is the artistic force of the ensemble—creative, refined, skillful, and above all else, musical. *Only if the conductor is musical and artistic will the ensemble reflect these qualities.* Therefore, it behooves the maturing conductor, through serious study on an instrument, to take the necessary opportunities to be exposed to this musicality and then come before the ensemble with an attitude of promoting and guiding this artistic performance.

Musicianship in the Rehearsal Process

The conductor must be a sound and sensitive musician, developed through previous study and musical performance. The conductor who stops playing a musical instrument when becoming a conductor is in danger of losing this musical sensitivity. *The conductor should show this inspirational leadership.* In this way, his or her work will take on a special dimension that is rare among conductors. There are just too many untrained and unmusical conductors out there. There are also conductors with developed skills going through the motions of being a conductor who for various reasons are putting forth little effort to communicate this musicality to the ensemble. Occasionally, a conductor conducts musically! This musicianship comes from within oneself and the results are that the patterns and gestures (and rehearsing skills) reflect this special quality of musicianship. This musicality sets the conductor apart from the majority of conductors. This is why I have written this book!

There is something about having to actually produce music physically that will keep the conductor appreciative and aware of what the player is going through to perform music expressively in an instrumental music ensemble. This will give the conductor a measurement for what to expect in the rehearsal process. The conductor should become involved in the music, and yet keep the reality of the rehearsal process in order to detect and solve technical and musical problems. *Even though technical detailed work is repetitious, the result should be musical.* Avoid tapping the music stand with the baton to either keep the pulse or solicit the attention of the ensemble in the rehearsal process because it is unmusical. The conductor should strive to be musical with everything he or she does in the rehearsal process. Conductors should draw upon all of their background and musical training in the conducting and rehearsing of the instrumental music ensemble. By observing conductors who are musical in the rehearsal process and concert performance, the maturing conductor can become much more effective in terms of these rehearsal procedures. The conductor should use as much musical vocabulary as possible in the rehearsal process. *The conductor should always be striving for this "musical" performance, and not just a technically perfect one.* In producing music, there is no substitute for a conductor who is an expressive musician and is able to conduct and verbalize this expressiveness to the ensemble in the rehearsal process.

The imagination of the conductor is the basis for staying musical with the ensemble in the rehearsal process. To capture the essence and spirit of the music, the conductor must be free of encumbering aspects in the rehearsal process. He or she can accomplish this by preparing these aspects so that they do not interfere with the musical imagination. Through meticulous score study and conducting practice, these diverting aspects become less troublesome and allow the conductor to concentrate on the musicality aspect during the rehearsal process. Creative phrasing is an example of such mental-physical activity. The focus in the rehearsal process and the concert performance should be on what you are producing musically.

This attitude of musicality should permeate the conductor's thinking while preparing the score for the rehearsal process (and, of course, in the concert performance). This kind of thinking and attitude should be reflected in all of the actions taken in the rehearsal process, because the final product must be musical. The conductor must solve technical problems early enough in the rehearsal progression so that there is sufficient rehearsal time for fostering this musicality and solving these musical problems.

I have frequently implied in this book that imitation is a great teaching strategy in rehearsing the instrumental music ensemble. *The players tend to imitate and reflect the musicianship of the conductor.* It is difficult for the conductor to be musical unless he or she has developed that musicianship through the reality of quality instrumental music performance. This makes a strong case for serious study on a musical instrument in the early training of the developing conductor. Also listening to great music (live or recorded) sensitively played will certainly enhance the conductor's musicianship. While the conductor is practicing conducting the various selections, the concentration should be on the conducting technique, but in the rehearsal process and concert performance the focus should be on the musicianship.

GUIDELINES AND SELF-EVALUATION

I present these conductor guidelines as general principles for the rehearsing of the instrumental music ensemble. When in doubt, the developing conductor should revert to these ideas as a way of evaluating the effectiveness of his or her conducting and rehearsing skills. These guidelines can serve as a checklist of items and motivational devices in striving for excellence as a conductor.

The following guidelines for self-evaluation are necessary so the maturing conductor has a basis for progressing in his or her career as a conductor:

1. Be organized and prepared
2. Be a teacher
3. Be credible
4. Be specific
5. Be insistent
6. Be consistent
7. Be flexible and spontaneous
8. Be confident and enthusiastic
9. Be creative
10. Be musical!

Using these Guidelines in the Rehearsal Process

The conductor must consider all of these guidelines in light of the particular situation. The conductor's self-evaluation in using these guidelines should allow for such items as the ensemble performance level, the ensemble potential, and the conductor's growth. For the evaluation to be valid, the conductor must be as realistic and honest as possible about the progress of the ensemble, the realization of the rehearsal objectives, and the achievement of the formulated performance goals. If these guidelines are employed in this specific way, they should point the conductor in the proper direction. These guidelines all relate to the development and improvement of the conductor in the rehearsal process. The conductor must continually evaluate and question what is happening in the rehearsal process.

Self-evaluation is a difficult and soul-searching process. The use of an audio or video recording employed during the rehearsal process or in the concert performance can be an aid in this evaluation. The recording of the rehearsal process gives the conductor the opportunity to hear and/or view the rehearsal process without the many distractions that might occur during the actual rehearsal time. A recording made of the concert performance will also serve as an indicator of how successful the results of the rehearsal process were. Taping the rehearsal process answers at least some of the following questions: (1) what and where are the problems with this ensemble, (2) what teaching strategies might the conductor employ, and (3) is the rehearsal time being spent effectively and efficiently? Other information that can be garnered from taping the rehearsal process include the avoidance of skipping necessary teaching points, the effect of modeling, the general ensemble attitude, the errors missed in the rehearsal process, the effectiveness of the corrections made, and (especially with videotaping) the conducting technique. In general, the rehearsal process taping will tend to answer the question about the rehearsal process objectives achieved. Likewise, some sort of evaluation by the conductor should occur after every rehearsal process to affirm what has taken place. The employment of this taping can help to evaluate the whole rehearsal process, the concert performance, and (most especially) the conductor!

Before, During and After the Rehearsal Process

Beyond this concrete evidence of the recording, the conductor must depend upon his or her own judgment to evaluate the degree of achievement. Ultimately, the success of the conductor is reflected in the concert performance of the ensemble. Following is a list of items, activities, and procedures to use for qualitative self-evaluation before, during, and after the rehearsal process:

1. Score study and preparation (pre-rehearsal)
2. The warm-up procedure (and materials)
3. The tuning procedure (and periodic tuning)
4. Playing time versus talking time in the rehearsal process
5. The number of times stopped in the rehearsal process
6. The frequency of attention to musicality
7. Player attitude in the rehearsal process
8. Conductor attitude in the rehearsal process
9. The playing of new works to improve the reading aspect
10. Detailed work on specific passages in the rehearsal process
11. Effectiveness of the rehearsal segments and procedures
12. Effectiveness of the verbal comments (solutions to problems)

13. Pacing of the rehearsal process by the conductor
14. The overall performance of the ensemble in the rehearsal process
15. The specific response of the ensemble to the conducting technique
16. The conducting technique clarity (and conductor's eye contact)

Finally, the conductor-teacher should first look inward as a possible reason for poor ensemble results. From this personal feedback (self-evaluation), the conductor should then strive to improve the conducting technique, the rehearsal procedures, and the teaching strategies, which should result in the raising of the ensemble performance level. As the conductor gains valuable experience in front of the ensemble, he or she should conceive and develop a stockpile of teaching strategies. In this way, the conductor will be ready to solve these technical and musical problems in the rehearsal process. The conductor should always be thinking about the quality of the musical experience fostered within the ensemble during the rehearsal process.

PRACTICAL APPLICATION (DISCUSSION/DEMONSTRATION)

1. Develop your own additional qualitative items for the conductor profile and self-evaluation to apply before, during, and after the rehearsal process. These qualitative items may differ somewhat from those proposed in the book.
2. What kind of activities or procedures in the rehearsal process would lead to better player understanding and awareness? (This is an all-encompassing question!)
3. Show and/or discuss by some role playing (as a conductor during the rehearsal process) to reinforce the various guidelines below:
    a. Be credible
    b. Be specific
    c. Be insistent
    d. Be consistent
    e. Be flexible and spontaneous
    f. Be confident and enthusiastic
    g. Be creative
    h. Be musical
4. Continue to gain familiarity with the standard repertoire found in Appendix A through CD listening, score study, and guidance from the conducting teacher. (See Appendix G for assignment forms.)

IN THE REHEARSAL PROCESS (LAB) ENVIRONMENT

1. Assign student conducting/rehearsing projects throughout the semester (or year) to give the students opportunities to stand in front of an ensemble and make it all happen in the rehearsal process (lab) environment.
2. Using a VTR to show and to critique each student conductor will be an invaluable experience for the conducting student. These student conducting/rehearsing projects should be a regular part of the rehearsal process (lab) environment if possible.

3. Complete student conducting/rehearsing projects (in the rehearsal process lab environment).

RECOMMENDED READING

Battisti, Frank L., *The Winds of Change: The Evolution of the Contemporary American Wind Band/Ensemble and its Conductor.* Chapter 16: Beyond Music Teaching and Conducting: Leadership is a brief chapter that presents some important ideas to supplement the conductor profile.

Battisti, Frank L., *On Becoming a Conductor.* This recent book (2007) covers many important areas about becoming a conductor.

Dalby, Max F., *Band Rehearsal Techniques.* Chapter 6: Evaluation addresses the evaluation of the band director and the instrumental music program in the public schools.

Fuchs, Peter Paul, *Psychology of Conducting.* Chapter 12: The Ten Questions that are posed with a number of successful professional conductors concerning various topics on conducting and rehearsing.

Goldman, Richard Franko, *The Wind Band.* Chapter 10: The Conductor and Teacher has some great thoughts about the conductor as a teacher in front of the wind band in the rehearsal process.

Green, Barry, and W. Timothy Gallwey, *The Inner Game of Music.* Chapter 4: The Power of Awareness is an important chapter for the musician and the conductor-teacher.

Harris, Frederick Jr., ed., *Conducting with Feeling.* The Coda of this book (starting with page 84) summarizes the ideas and thoughts that relate to the personal and professional growth of conductors.

Lisk, Edward S., *The Creative Director: Alternative Rehearsal Techniques.* Chapter 8: Success Techniques pertain to Guideline No. 2 of this chapter, "Be a Teacher (Make Players Aware)."

Middleton, James A., Harry Haines, and Gary Garner, *The Symphonic Band Winds (A Quest for Perfection).* See chapter 8 on Continuing Personal Growth as a Teacher and Musician, written by James A. Middleton.

Peters, G. David, and Robert F. Miller, *Music Teaching and Learning.* Chapter 10: Assessment provides personal and professional assessment of the music conductor and is aimed at the public school music conductor.

Prausnitz, Frederik, *Score and Podium (A Complete Guide to Conducting).* Chapter 15: Orchestra and Conductor illuminates the relationship between the orchestral players and the conductor.

Rudolf, Max, *The Grammar of Conducting*, 3rd ed. This is one of the most comprehensive books on conducting and rehearsing available and should be in the library of every practicing conductor.

Wagar, Jeannine, *Conductors in Conversation.* The organization of this book is based on interviews with 15 contemporary professional conductors.

Wittry, Diane, *Beyond the Baton.* The section on Character Development (for the conductor) suggests the following: a positive outlook, integrity, humility, discipline, persistence, and a passion for the art form.

Zander, Rosamund Stone, and Benjamin Zander, *The Art of Possibility.* Benjamin Zander, a well-known conductor along with his wife, who is an executive coach and family systems therapist, have combined their backgrounds to write this book on dealing with people in various musical performance scenarios.

Chapter Eighteen

Coda

From Rehearsal Process to Concert Performance

Following are some ideas to consider in preparation for the transition from the rehearsal process to the concert performance. The conducting teacher may want to add items to this list from his or her own conducting background and experience, and discuss these various items below with the students at some point during the conducting class:

PERFORMANCE CONSISTENCY

Conducting Technique Consistency

Keep the conducting technique consistent from the rehearsal process through the concert performance. Do not change the conducting technique in the concert performance from that used during the rehearsal process.

Consistency between the Rehearsal Process and the Concert Performance

The conductor should reinforce the technical and musical aspects of the performance during the rehearsal process. Then in the concert performance, the players will feel confident about their performance. Again, the conductor must be consistent in every way possible when going from the rehearsal process to the concert performance.

Tempo Consistency

The conductor should reinforce tempos from the later rehearsals and then replicate them during the concert performance. A different tempo on the concert performance from what was rehearsed can certainly generate errors and cause many problems for the ensemble.

Conductor Changes Lead to Player Confusion

Keep in mind that conductor changes during the concert performance from what the ensemble had come to expect from the rehearsal process will confuse the players rather than help the ensemble to play better in the concert performance. There are opportunities in the rehearsal process to change various performance aspects as the rehearsals progress, but do not initiate these changes during the final dress rehearsal or just before the concert performance in most cases.

THE PERFORMANCE VENUE

Performance Hall

If the performance hall is different from the rehearsal hall, then there may be changes that should be made during the rehearsals at the new location especially in terms of tempos, styles, dynamics, balance, or other such performance aspects. Tempos may need adjustment because of the acoustics in the performance hall.

Seating Arrangement

Ideally, the rehearsal environment can be duplicated in the performance hall. There may need to be certain adjustments if the seating arrangement is different when moving from the rehearsal environment to the performance hall in order to accommodate the space provided. If the ensemble has been rehearsing on risers or platforms, then this should certainly continue in the performance hall.

Acoustics

In many cases, the players will need time to become acclimated to variations in acoustics moving from the rehearsal environment to the performance hall. This is why it is important to have one or more rehearsals in the performance hall before the concert performance presentation.

Players Hearing and Seeing the Conductor

Because so much depends on the players being able to hear each other, the ensemble needs to have sufficient time in the performance hall to adjust for any differences between the rehearsal environment and the concert venue. There may be a need to adjust the seating in order for all the ensemble members to see (sight lines) the conductor clearly.

Performance Aspects Affected

Until the players have adjusted to the new sounds in the performance hall, such performance aspects as precision, balance, blend, dynamics, and intonation may be somewhat insecure (if not completely suspect) in the concert hall environment. Sound checks in the performance hall are a necessary part of this preparation.

Attractive Performance Venue

The performance venue should be as clean and attractive as possible. Both the players and the audience will appreciate this aspect of the concert environment. In some cases, flowers, plants, banners, or holiday decorations can give the performance venue uniqueness during the concert performance.

THE REHEARSAL PROCESS

The Importance of the Rehearsal Process

The concert performance should and will reflect what the rehearsal process accomplished. Never assume that certain technical or musical passages will take care of themselves through repetition. (In the early rehearsals, the conductor may allow time for the players to make corrections on their own during these times of repetition.) Eventually however, the conductor may find it necessary to step in and make these changes at some point if they continue to be incorrect or unmusical before the concert performance.

The Musical Interpretation Reinforced during the Rehearsal Process

The conductor must come to the rehearsal process with a clear image of how the music should sound. On occasion, the conductor will alter this conception after hearing the reality of an earlier rehearsal process. However, when the conceived musical interpretation is then resolved, this must be strongly reinforced with the ensemble during the rehearsal process in preparation for the concert performance.

ENTRANCES, APPLAUSE, BOWS, AND EXITS

Entrances Planned

Preliminary planning before the dress rehearsal process is necessary in terms of entrances on and exits off the stage for the ensemble, concertmaster, and soloist(s). In most cases, this review would take place during the final dress rehearsal.

Conductor Entrance

The conductor should not enter casually. When the conductor comes onto the concert stage initially, many of the ensembles traditionally stand to acknowledge his or her entrance. At this point, the conductor's score for the first selection will already be on the music stand and opened to the appropriate page. The conductor will indicate to the ensemble to be seated and then give the ensemble sufficient time to prepare for the downbeat. At this point, the conductor may want to give the ensemble some time to focus before the first selection of the concert performance.

Bows Planned

The conductor needs to anticipate and plan bows for the ensemble, for the soloist(s), and for the conductor. Some of this might change during the concert performance, but at least conceive a plan.

Players Face the Audience on Bows

It is effective to have the ensemble members face directly out to the audience when the conductor asks the players to stand in acknowledging the applause. This seems to be more prevalent in the concert band ensemble than in the symphony orchestra presently. There might be occasions to have the entire ensemble bow.

Encores and Applause

Encores must also be anticipated and planned for during the rehearsal process with the whole ensemble as well as when a guest soloist is involved. (In certain situations, the soloist may indicate to the conductor to have the ensemble stand and acknowledge the applause as well.)

Concertmaster and Ensemble Recognition

The handshake with the concertmaster (or with the principal clarinetist in the concert band) by the conductor is the recognition of appreciation for the performance by the ensemble. The conductor should not over-use this gesture, but relegate it to after the final selection in most instances. In some situations, the conductor may also extend the hand to the principal second violinist, the principal violist, and the principal cellist as well. A similar gesture is also appropriate with the concert band's front row.

Conductor and Soloist Recognition by the Ensemble

On rare occasions, the conductor or soloist receives a "shuffling" of the feet by the instrumental music ensemble to express and acknowledge their appreciation for the outstanding work done on a particular piece or concert. The soloist may also receive applause from the ensemble, and in the case of the orchestra, by a visual sign from the string section with the tapping of the bow on the sheet music, by tapping right hand on the leg or by hand clapping with the rest of the ensemble. The concert band members would show this appreciation with hand clapping.

Exits Planned

Exits may need planning as well, especially if the next selection requires fewer or more playing personnel or other groups such as chorus, soloist(s), dancer(s), or the conductor exit. This should all be done efficiently so that the "plot" does not "drag."

SOLOISTS, ENSEMBLES, CHORUS AND DANCERS

Accompanying the Soloist (or Small Ensemble)

There may be some music stands, chairs, instruments, and equipment that need to be moved before the soloist or small ensemble can enter and begin. These logistics need to be resolved as efficiently and expertly as possible. Then, give the soloist or small ensemble time to tune carefully if needed. The conductor should be positioned so that there can be visual contact between the conductor and soloist(s) or small ensemble. The conductor must make sure that the soloist (or small ensemble) is ready to begin the selection. Bows at the end may need prior discussion to avoid any awkwardness in the whole presentation. The conductor should follow behind the soloist (or small ensemble) on the entrance and exit.

Soloists within the Ensemble Acknowledged

The conductor should acknowledge the prominent soloist(s) within the ensemble following a specific selection in the program. These names may need to be written on the last page of the score (or on a separate sheet) so there are no omissions. This procedure could also take place in score order. In certain compositions, it may be necessary to acknowledge entire sections. Some conductors find it convenient to start on one side of the ensemble and designate the soloists with a sweep to the other side of the ensemble. In any case, the soloists should know in advance of these procedures.

Soloists, Small Ensembles, Chorus, or Dancers

If a soloist, small ensemble, chorus, or dancers are part of the program, then consider space and logistics in relationship to the performance stage. Larger soloist instruments such as a piano, two pianos, or a small ensemble setting will need considerable space. In addition, entrances, exits, or positioning of chorus members or dance personnel must receive careful planning. Such matters as risers and chairs for the chorus are important considerations when performing extended choral and orchestra works such as an oratorio.

TUNING THE ENSEMBLE

General Tuning Procedure

The tuning procedure must be the same from the rehearsal process to the concert performance. Periodic tuning during the concert may be necessary also. In most cases, the concertmaster and principal oboist (or principal clarinetist in the concert band) would be responsible for this procedure during the concert performance. The person sounding the tuning pitch should have an electronic tuner to ensure accuracy.

Orchestra Tuning Specifics

The audience applauds the entrance of the concertmaster at symphony concerts. The concertmaster would then indicate to the principal oboist to sound a concert A (440).

Various sections of the orchestra proceeds to tune to this pitch. The common order of tuning is the woodwinds, followed by the brass, then the lower strings, and completed with the upper strings. The concertmaster or the conductor controls the periodic tuning during the concert performance.

Concert Band Tuning Specifics

In the concert band performance, the principal clarinetist would enter to the audience applause and control the tuning procedure. The usual tuning is to a concert B-flat (456) although many ensembles are now using both concert B-flat and concert A (440) as well as a concert F for tuning. The principal clarinetist or the conductor controls the periodic tuning during the concert performance.

THE AUDIENCE

Late Audience Entering

If the first selection is relatively short, then late audience may enter after this first selection. If the first work on the program has several movements, then the late audience may come in at the end of the first movement.

Controlling the Audience Applause between Movements

The conductor has a certain amount of control over the applause between movements of a selection. By not allowing the hands to come down immediately at the end of a movement, the conductor can keep the audience from applauding between these movements of the selection.

Controlling the Audience Applause at the End of a Selection

There are also various ways of controlling the applause at the end of a selection with the conductor returning to the podium promptly or by acknowledging soloists within the ensemble while the audience is still applauding.

Audience Distractions

Concertgoers should turn off cell phones, pagers, and other electronic devices when entering the concert hall. An announcement in the printed program should help this situation, or else have this announced before the concert begins or have signs placed at the doors. Likewise, flash photography and video cameras can be distractions.

THE CONCERT AURA

Concert Lighting

The use of concert lighting in the performance can be very effective in special programs (such as holiday concerts, young people's concerts, and pops concerts). This should be planned and executed during the dress rehearsal in order to acclimate the performers to these light changes (which might include the need for stand lights). Audience lighting will also need to be controlled throughout the concert performance.

Speaker, Narrator, or Conductor

A speaker can introduce the musical selections or may be a part of the actual performance in certain works. If the narrator is designated in a specific selection, then sufficient time must be allowed during the rehearsal process to coordinate the narration with the music. If the conductor chooses to speak to the audience, then the conductor must be well prepared to articulate the information about the music, the ensemble, or other such matters.

Sound System

If there is speaking to be done from the stage during the performance, the sound system must be integrated during the dress rehearsal so that there are no surprises for the performers or conductor. Those speaking to the audience must be well prepared in their presentations.

Recording

Recording of performances must be as unobtrusive as possible. Recording personnel movement and microphone placement in the performance hall should not be a distraction to the ensemble or to the audience. This is also true with the videotaping of the concert performance.

Stage Manager

A stage manager (with additional personnel) may be necessary for moving equipment at the dress rehearsal and during the concert performance. This may involve moving chairs, music stands, and instruments as well as other needed equipment. (The piano lid should be up for the soloist.) Otherwise, these logistic problems are left for the conductor or players to handle. At any rate, these logistic changes need to be planned and executed efficiently in the concert performance. Equipment personnel must be appropriately dressed.

Lighting and Sound Technicians

Lighting and sound technicians need to be at the final dress rehearsal and the concert performance. These technicians should be familiar with the facility in order to make the lighting and sound adjustments as needed.

CONCERT PROMOTION

Concert Publicity and Promotion

The conductor or assigned personnel need to initiate and control publicity and promotion of the concert performance through various channels (newspaper advertisements, news articles and pictures, television, radio, direct mail, web sites, e-mail, Facebook, ads, fliers, posters, and other sources of advertising).

Concert Tickets

The sale and purchase of concert tickets must be addressed in terms of general admission or reserved seating as well as the printing of the tickets. General admission would involve ticket sellers, ticket takers, and program distribution. Reserved seating would involve ticket sellers, ticket takers, and program distribution, plus ushers to assist with seating in the performance facility.

Box Office

The conductor must establish early on locations where concert tickets will be obtainable for purchase and advertise as to price and availability. Convenience for the audience is the most important consideration. Having tickets available at several locations may benefit this procedure.

Concert Program

The concert program should be initiated by the conductor and include the ensemble personnel involved with special designation as needed, conductor photo/biography, biographies/photos of soloists, program selections and movements, composer's full names (also arrangers) and dates, program notes, and announcements of upcoming concerts and events, as well as the advertising of sponsorship and the listing of patrons. The printed program should be as attractive as possible with the application of some artistic design or artwork in color and/or computer-generated materials.

MISCELLANEOUS ITEMS

Handling the Music

There should be a system set up to handle the music. If the music is purchased, then it needs to be checked in, indexed, and placed in the music library for future use. Forms should be available (either written or entered into the computer) for quick access when needed. If the music is rented, then it must be returned promptly with all parts accounted for, marks erased, and sent back to the rental library. Rental libraries usually provide forms to check in this material when sending the music back.

Concert Touring

Concert touring with the ensemble involves additional organization. This activity includes tour scheduling, transportation of personnel, movement of the necessary instruments and equipment, plus lodging and food arrangements for ensemble personnel throughout the tour. The conductor may need to designate or hire a tour manager in this situation.

Assistant Conductor or Auditors

In certain scenarios, an assistant conductor or auditors (with scores) can be a tremendous help to the conductor during the rehearsal process and before the concert performance. The assistant conductor or auditor(s) can listen during the rehearsal process to detect errors or problems that need to be resolved before the concert performance. The conductor may also hear these problems, but such reinforcement can be a confirming element. Before the performance, an assistant conductor could take care of numerous duties so the conductor can focus on the musical aspects.

Conductor Podium/Stand

The height and placement of the conductor podium/stand must be a consideration when moving from the rehearsal space to the performance hall. In all cases, the clarity of sight lines from the players to the conductor is the crucial aspect and may very well involve the height and placement of the conductor podium and stand. In some cases, the podium and stand will need to be moved slightly away from the ensemble in order to achieve better sight lines.

Extra Stand for the Conductor Scores

The first selection of the concert should be on the conductor's stand, open to the appropriate page of the score. The remainder of the scores could be on an extra stand behind the conductor's stand (or some conductor stands have a lower shelf), readily available for the conductor to access the next selection. If the conductor leaves the stage after a selection, then a member of the ensemble could easily place the next selection on the conductor's stand. This will prevent the conductor from having to shuffle through scores when he or she returns to the stage in preparation for the next selection.

Multiple Performances of a Concert

The advantages of multiple performances of a concert are that the players become more confident about their individual performance and each performance will be a challenge in playing with more musicality. In some situations, additional performances will mean that more people will be able to attend the performance. Certain performances (such as operas, ballets, and musical theater productions) are often presented several times.

Providing Program Notes Verbally

It is important to consider the possibility that the conductor might say a few well-chosen words about the selection to be played in the concert performance. The conductor, however, must be well prepared so the presentation is concise and accurate. Perhaps not every selection will need introduction by the conductor. Another approach is to have a speaker talk about the selections. In both instances, whether it is the conductor or a speaker, there should be amplification so the entire audience can hear well. Particularly, unfamiliar or new works might need some explanation or even some musical demonstration.

Ensemble Concert Etiquette

There may be a need with some ensembles to remind them of the expected proper concert etiquette. This pertains to respect for their fellow musicians, the conductor, and the audience. This etiquette might involve proper playing posture and position, appropriate dress or uniforms, professional attitude, and cooperation, and thereby being a helpful person in the concert environment.

* * *

The conducting teacher may need to discuss some other items for the benefit of the conducting student in terms of going from the rehearsal process to the concert performance. (Most of this information is seldom seen in print or discussed in other music courses.)

Appendix A

Score Study and Program Building with Standard Repertoire

The rationale behind these listings of instrumental ensemble music material is to present some of the frequently performed and representative works of the various instrumental media. I do not intend these lists to be comprehensive in nature; rather, they are selected lists for the purposes of score study and program building. Omissions are unintentional. The conducting teacher may want to expand and tailor these listings to fit the needs of the advanced conductor.

These listings can also serve as a guide for students in acquiring repertoire. Large scores and miniature scores (as well as CD recordings) of these works are available. I have considered the periods of music, significant composers, and various compositional styles. I have also included some works that I indicated as easy and medium in difficulty. Finally, these listings can aid in a general discussion of instrumental music ensemble literature, and establish for the maturing conductor a familiarity with much of the standard repertoire. (Many students enter college with very little or no background in instrumental music ensemble repertoire.)

SCORE STUDY AND PROGRAM BUILDING REPERTOIRE FOR ORCHESTRA, CHAMBER ORCHESTRA, AND STRING ORCHESTRA

Adams, John (b. 1947)

Tromba lotana
Short Ride in a Fast Machine
The Chairman Dances (Foxtrot for orchestra)

Adler, Samuel (b. 1928)

Elegy for String Orchestra

Albéniz, Isaac (1860–1909)

Iberia (Arbós, arr.)

Albinoni, Tomaso Giovanni (1671–1750)

Adagio in G minor, Op. 5, No. 4 (Strings and continuo)

Anderson, Leroy (1908–1975)

Trumpeter's Lullaby (Solo trumpet or trumpet trio) (Pops Concert)
Bugler's Holiday (Trumpet trio) (Pops Concert)
Sandpaper Ballet (Pops Concert)

Irish Suite (Pops Concert)
Sleigh Ride (Holiday Concert)
(Many other light classical selections)
  (Holiday and Pops Concerts)

Arnold, Malcolm (1921–2006)

Four Cornish Dances, Op. 91
Four Scottish Dances, Op. 59
Tam O'Shanter Overture, Op. 51

Arutunian, Alexander (b. 1920)

Concerto for Trumpet and Orchestra in
  A-flat Major

Bach, Johann Christian (1735–1782)

Concerto in C minor for Viola, Clarinet, and
  Orchestra

Bach, Johann Sebastian (1685–1750)

Brandenburg Concerto No. 2 in F Major,
  BWV 1047 Brandenburg Concerto No. 3
  in G Major, BWV 1048
Brandenburg Concerto No. 4 in G Major,
  BWV 1049
Brandenburg Concerto No. 5 in D Major,
  BWV 1050
Concerto for Two Violins in D Minor, BWV
  1043
Christmas Oratorio for Chorus and Soloists
  SATB, BWV 248
Cantata No. 51, for Soprano, Trumpet,
  Strings, and Continuo
Concerto in C minor for Violin and Oboe,
  BWV 1060
Orchestral Suite No. 3 in D Major, BWV 1068

Barber, Samuel (1910–1981)

Adagio for Strings, Op. 11
Overture to the "School for Scandal," Op. 5
Intermezzo from "Vanessa"
Concerto for Violin and Orchestra, Op. 14
Essay No. 1, Op. 12
Essay No. 2, Op. 17

Medea's Meditation and Dance of
  Vengeance, Op. 23a

Barlow, Wayne (1912–1996)

The Winter's Passed (Oboe and Strings)

Bartók, Béla (1881–1945)

Concerto for Orchestra, Sz.116
Music for Strings, Percussion and Celesta,
  Sz.106
Divertimento for Strings (1939), Sz.113
The Miraculous Mandarin Suite, Op. 19
Romanian Folk Dances for String Orchestra,
  Sz.56 (Easy)
Five Pieces for Younger Orchestra (Easy)

Beethoven, Ludwig Van (1770–1827)

Coriolanus Overture, Op. 62
Egmont Overture, Op. 84
Leonore Overture No. 2, Op. 72a
Leonore Overture No. 3, Op. 72b
Overture to Fidelio, Op. 72c
King Stephen Overture, Op. 117
Symphony No. 1 in C minor, Op. 21
Symphony No. 2 in D major, Op. 36
Symphony No. 3 in E-flat major, Op. 55
Symphony No. 4 in B-flat major, Op. 60
Symphony No. 5 in C minor, Op. 67
Symphony No. 6 in F major "Pastorale,"
  Op. 68
Symphony No. 7 in A major, Op. 92
Symphony No. 8 in F major, Op. 93
Symphony No. 9 in D minor, Op. 125
Piano Concerto No. 3 in C minor, Op. 37
Piano Concerto No. 4 in G major, Op. 58
Piano Concerto No. 5 in E-flat major, Op. 73
Violin Concerto in D major, Op. 61
Triple Concerto in C Major for Violin, Cello,
  Piano, and Orchestra, Op. 56

Bellini, Vincenzo (1801–1835)

Overture from "Norma"
Concerto in E-flat Major for Oboe and
  Orchestra (Also for trumpet and orchestra)

Berg, Alban (1885–1935)

Three Pieces for Orchestra, Op. 6
Concerto for Violin

Berlioz, Hector (1803–1869)

Symphonie fantastique, Op. 14
Roman Carnival Overture, Op. 9
Benvenuto Cellini Overture
Romeo and Juliet, Dramatic Symphony,
   Op. 17 (Various movements)
Requiem, Op. 5 (Tenor soloist, chorus,
   brass choirs, and large orchestra)
Harold in Italy, Op. 16 (Viola solo and
   orchestra)
Hungarian (Rakoczy) March
Les nuits d'été, Op. 7 (Mezzo-soprano and
   orchestra)

Bernstein, Leonard (1918–1990)

Overture to "Candide"
Chichester Psalms for Soloists, Chorus, and
   Orchestra
Symphonic Dances from "West Side Story"
Selections from "West Side Story" (Various
   arrangements)
Fancy Free Suite (Galop, Waltz, and Danzon)
Slava! (Orchestra with pre-recorded tape)
Divertimento for Orchestra (Various
   movements)

Bizet, George (1838–1875)

Carmen Suite No. 1 (Various movements)
Carmen Suite No. 2 (Various movements)
L'Arlesienne Suite No. 1 (Various
   movements)
L'Arlesienne Suite No. 2 (Various
   movements)
Symphony No. 1 in C Major
Children's Games Suite (Young People's
   Concert)

Bloch, Ernest (1880–1959)

Concerto Grosso No. 1 (Solo piano and
   strings)

Proclamation for Trumpet and Orchestra
Schelomo: Hebraic Rhapsody (Solo cello
   and orchestra)

Bock, Jerry (1928–2010)

Fiddler on the Roof Selections (Pops
   Concert)

Böhme, Oskar (1870–1938)

Trumpet Concerto in F Minor, Op. 18 (rev.
   and ed. by Foss)

Bolcom, William (B. 1938)

Commedia for (Almost) 18th-Century
   Orchestra
Songs of Innocence and of Experience
   (Large forces involved here)

Borodin, Alexander (1833–1887)

Polovetsian Dances from "Prince Igor"
Symphony No. 2 in B minor
In the Steppes of Central Asia

Brahms, Johannes (1833–1897)

Academic Festival Overture, Op. 80
Tragic Overture, Op. 81
Variations on a Theme by Joseph Haydn,
   Op. 56a
Alto Rhapsody, Op. 53 (Alto soloist, men's
   chorus, and orchestra)
Symphony No. 1 in C minor, Op. 68
Symphony No. 2 in D Major, Op. 73
Symphony No. 3 in F Major, Op. 90
Symphony No. 4 in E minor, Op. 98
Piano Concerto No. 2 in B-flat Major, Op. 83
A German Requiem, Op. 45 (Soprano and
   baritone soloists, chorus, and orchestra)

Britten, Benjamin (1913–1976)

Young Person's Guide to the Orchestra (with
   narrator), Op. 34 (Young People's Concert
   or without the narrator)

A Simple Symphony, Op. 4 (String
  orchestra)
Matinées Musicales (After Rossini), Op. 24
Soirées Musicales (After Rossini), Op. 9
Serenade for Tenor, Horn and Strings, Op. 31
Four Sea Interludes from Peter Grimes,
  Op. 33A
War Requiem, Op. 66 (Chorus, boys' choir,
  and two orchestras)

Bruch, Max (1838–1920)

Violin Concerto No. 1 in G minor, Op. 26
Kol Nidrei for Cello and Orchestra, Op. 47

Bruckner, Anton (1824–1896)

Symphony No. 4 in E-flat major "Romantic"
Symphony No. 7 in E major
Symphony No. 9 in D minor
Te Deum (SATB soloists and orchestra)

Canteloube, Joseph (1879–1957)

Chants d'Auvergne (Voice and orchestra in
  four volumes)

Chabrier, Emmanuel (1841–1894)

España Rhapsody
Joyeuse marche

Chadwick, George (1854–1931)

Symphonic Sketches (Various movements)

Chaminade, Cécile (1857–1944)

Concertino for Flute and Orchestra in D
  Major, Op. 107

Chausson, Ernest (1855–1899)

Poème, Op. 25 (Violin and orchestra)
Symphony in B-flat Major, Op. 20

Chávez, Carlos (1899–1978)

Symphony No. 2 (Sinfonia india)

Chopin, Frédéric (1810–1849)

Andante Spianato and Grande Polonaise
  Brillante, Op. 22
Piano Concerto No. 1 in E minor, Op. 11
Piano Concerto No. 2 in F minor, Op. 21

Cimarosa, Domenico (1749–1801)

The Secret Marriage Overture
Oboe Concerto in C minor (with string
  orchestra)

Copland, Aaron (1900–1990)

The Quiet City (Trumpet, English horn, and
  strings)
"Billy the Kid" Ballet Suite
Rodeo: Four Dance Episodes
Appalachian Spring Ballet Suite (Full
  orchestra)
Lincoln Portrait for Speaker and Orchestra
Old American Songs, Set I (Medium Voice
  and orchestra)
The Red Pony (Film Suite for orchestra)
El Salón México (Ballet Suite)
Clarinet Concerto
Symphony No. 3
Variations on a Shaker Melody (Medium)
An Outdoor Overture

Corelli, Arcangelo (1653–1713)

Concerto Grosso in G minor, Op. 6, No. 8
  (Christmas Concerto)
Suite for String Orchestra (Medium)

Corigliano, John (B. 1938)

Gazebo Dances
The Red Violin: Chaconne for Violin and
  Orchestra (Film music)

Couperin, François (1668–1733)

Overture and Allegro from "La Sultana" Suite (Milhaud, orch.)

Cowell, Henry (1897–1965)

Ballad for String Orchestra (Medium)
Hymn and Fuguing Tune No. 2 for Strings (Medium)

Creston, Paul (1906–1985)

Concertino for Marimba and Orchestra
Dance Overture, Op. 62

Crumb, George (B. 1929)

Echoes of Time and the River: Four Processionals for Orchestra
A Haunted Landscape (Avant-garde)

Debussy, Claude (1862–1918)

Danses sacrée et profane (Harp and Strings)
La mer
Prelude to the Afternoon of a Faun
Printemps, Symphonic Suite
Three Nocturnes
Première Rhapsody for Clarinet and Orchestra
Ibéria

Delibes, Léo (1836–1891)

Coppelia: Suite No. 1
Sylvia: Ballet Suite

Delius, Frederick (1862–1934)

The Walk to the Paradise Garden
On Hearing the First Cuckoo in Spring
Summer Night on the River

Dello Joio, Norman (1913–2008)

Concertino for Clarinet and Orchestra
Five Images for Orchestra (Medium) (Young People's Concert)
Air for Strings (Easy)

New York Profiles
Night Flight to Madrid (Medium)

Diemer, Emma Lou (B. 1927)

Festival Overture (Medium)

Dittersdorf, Karl Ditters Von (1739–1799)

Tournament of Temperments (Medium)
Sinfonia Concertante for String Bass, Viola, and Orchestra (Medium)

Dohnányi, Ernö (1877–1960)

Variations on a Nursery Song for Piano and Orchestra, Op. 25
Concert Piece for Cello and Orchestra

Dukas, Paul (1865–1935)

The Sorcerer's Apprentice (Pops Concert)
Symphony in C Major
Villanelle (Solo horn and orchestra)

Dvořák, Antonín (1841–1904)

Czech Suite in D Major, Op. 39
Concerto in B minor for Cello and Orchestra, Op. 104
Symphony No. 8 in G Major, Op. 88
Symphony No. 9 in E minor (From the New World), Op. 95
Serenade in E, Op. 22 (Strings)
Romance in F minor, Op. 11 (Violin and orchestra)
Carnival Overture, Op. 92
Nocturno for String Orchestra, Op. 40 (Medium)
In Nature's Realm, Op. 91
Slavonic Dances, Op. 46, No. 8 (Medium)

Elgar, Edward (1857–1934)

Serenade in E minor for String Orchestra, Op. 20
Enigma Variations, Op. 36

Cello Concerto in E minor, Op. 85
Pomp and Circumstance March No. 1, Op. 39
Sea Pictures, Op. 37 (Contralto solo and
orchestra)
Cockaigne, Concert Overture
In the South, Concert Overture
Introduction and Allegro, Op. 47 (Solo string
quartet and strings)

Enesco, Georges (1881–1955)

Rumanian Rhapsody No. 1 in A Major,
Op. 11

Falla, Manuel De (1876–1946)

Spanish Dance No. 1 from "La Vida Breve"
Ballet Suite from "El Amor Brujo"
Nights in the Gardens of Spain (Solo piano
and orchestra)
Three Dances from "The Three-Cornered
Hat," Suite No. 2

Fauré, Gabriel (1845–1924)

Pavane for Orchestra and (optional) Chorus,
Op. 50
Elegie for Cello (or viola) and Orchestra,
Op. 24
Suite from Pelléas et Mélisande, Op. 80

Franck, César (1822–1890)

Symphony in D minor
Symphonic Variations for Piano and
Orchestra
Psyché et Eros

Frescobaldi, Girolamo (1583–1643)

Toccata in D minor for Orchestra
(Kindler, arr.)

Gershwin, George (1898–1937)

An American in Paris
Rhapsody in Blue (Solo piano and orchestra)

Concerto in F for Piano and Orchestra
Porgy and Bess: Symphonic Picture for
Orchestra (Bennett, arr.)
Cuban Overture
Variations on "I Got Rhythm" (Solo piano
and orchestra)
Lullaby (String orchestra)

Giannini, Vittorio (1903–1966)

Symphony No. 2
Concerto for Trumpet and Orchestra

Gillis, Donald (1912–1978)

Short Overture to an Unwritten Opera
(Medium)
The Man Who Invented Music for Narrator
and Orchestra (Medium) (Young People's
Concert)
January, February, March! (Medium)
(Young People's Concert)

Ginastera, Alberto (1916–1983)

Estancia: Four Dances, Op. 8a
Variaciones Concertantes, Op. 23

Glazunov, Alexander (1865–1936)

Saxophone Concerto in E-Flat Major,
Op. 109

Glière, Reinhold (1875–1956)

Russian Sailors' Dance from "The Red
Poppy" ballet (Medium)

Glinka, Mikhail (1804–1857)

Russlan and Ludmilla Overture

Gould, Morton (1913–1996)

American Salute
The Cowboy Rhapsody (Young People's
Concert or Pops Concert)

Spirituals in Five Movements for Orchestra
Fall River Legend: Ballet Suite (1961 version)
Latin-American Symphonette
Pavane (Medium)

Gounod, Charles (1818–1893)

Faust Ballet Suite

Grainger, Percy (1882–1961)

Irish Tune from County Derry (2 horns and
   strings)

Granados, Enrique (1867–1916)

Intermezzo from "Goyescas"

Granjany, Marcel (1891–1975)

Aria in Classic Style (Solo harp and strings)

Grieg, Edvard (1843–1907)

Piano Concerto in A minor, Op. 16
Peer Gynt Suite No. 1, Op. 46
Peer Gynt Suite No. 2, Op. 55
Holberg Suite, Op. 40 (Strings)
Two Elegiac Melodies, Op. 34
Norwegian Dances, Op. 35
Symphonic Dances, Op. 64
Symphony in C minor

Griffes, Charles Tomlinson (1884–1920)

The White Peacock

Grofé, Ferde (1892–1972)

Grand Canyon Suite (Pops Concert)
Mississippi Suite (Pops Concert)

Grundman, Clare (1913–1996)

Two Sketches for Orchestra (Medium)
Three Carols for Christmas (Medium)

Guilmant, Alexandre (1837–1911)

Morceau Symphonique for Trombone and
   Orchestra

Handel, George Frederic (1685–1759)

The Messiah, HWV 56 (SATB soloists,
   chorus, and orchestra)
Water Music Suite (Hardy, arr.)
Royal Fireworks Music Suite, HWV 351
   (Hardy, arr.)
The Faithful Shepherd Suite (Beecham, arr.)

Hanson, Howard (1896–1981)

Symphony No. 1, Op. 21 "Nordic"
Symphony No. 2, Op. 30 "Romantic"
Song of Democracy for Chorus and
   Orchestra

Harris, Roy (1898–1979)

Symphony No. 3 in One Movement
Symphony No. 6 "Gettysburg"

Haydn, Franz Joseph (1732–1809)

Trumpet Concerto in E-Flat Major
Cello Concerto in C Major
Cello Concerto in D Major
Symphony No. 45 in F-sharp minor
   (Farewell)
Symphony No. 88 in G Major
Symphony No. 94 in G Major (Surprise)
Symphony No. 100 in G Major (Military)
Symphony No. 104 in D Major (London)
(Many more symphonies and concertos)

Herbert, Victor (1859–1924)

March of the Toys (Holiday concert)
Concerto for Cello and Orchestra, Op. 30,
   No. 2
Victor Herbert's Favorites (Sanford, arr.)
   (Pops Concert)

Hindemith, Paul (1895–1963)

Mathis der Maler Symphony
Symphonic Metamorphoses of Themes by
　Carl Maria von Weber
Concert Music for Strings and Brass, Op. 50
　Five Pieces for String Orchestra, Op. 44,
　No. 4 (Easy)
Trauermusik for Solo Viola and String
　Orchestra

Holst, Gustav (1874–1934)

The Planets, Op. 32 (with women's choir on
　last movement)
St. Paul's Suite, Op. 29, No. 2 (String
　orchestra) (Medium)
Brook Green Suite (String orchestra)
　(Medium)
The Perfect Fool: Ballet Music

Honegger, Arthur (1892–1955)

King David (Soloists SAT, chorus,
　and speaker)
Pacific 231

Hovhaness, Alan (1911–2000)

Fantasy on Japanese Wood Prints, Op. 211
　(Xylophone and orchestra)
Mysterious Mountain Symphony, Op. 132
And God Created Great Whales, Op. 229,
　No. 1 (pre-recorded tape)
Prayer to St. Gregory, Op. 62b (Trumpet and
　strings) (Medium)
Psalm and Fugue Op. 42a (Medium)
Armenian Rhapsody No. 2, Op. 51 (Medium)
(Many more symphonies)

Hummel, Johann Nepomuk (1778–1837)

Concerto for Trumpet and Orchestra in
　E-Flat Major (or E Major)

Humperdinck, Engelbert (1854–1921)

Prelude to Hansel and Gretel

Husa, Karel (b. 1921)

Apotheosis of This Earth (with chorus)
　(Originally for concert band)
Concerto for Brass Quintet and String
　Orchestra

Ibert, Jacques (1890–1962)

Concertino da Camera (Alto saxophone
　and orchestra)
Divertissement
Escales (Ports of Call)

Indy, Vincent d' (1851–1931)

Symphony on a French Mountain Air
　(Solo piano and orchestra)

Ippolitov, Ivanov (1859–1935)

Caucasian Sketches, Op. 10

Ives, Charles (1874–1954)

The Unanswered Question, S.50 (4 flutes,
　trumpet, and strings)
Variations on "America" (Orch. William
　Schuman)
Symphony No. 4, S.4 (with chorus and
　orchestra)
The Circus Band (Unusual instrumentation)

Janáček, Leoš (1854–1928)

Sinfonietta (Extensive brass in the first
　movement)

Kabalevsky, Dmitri (1904–1987)

Overture to "Colas Breugnon," Op. 24
The Comedians Suite, Op. 26 (Medium)
　(Young People's Concert)

Kalinnikov, Basil S. (1866–1901)

Symphony No. 1 in G minor

Kern, Jerome (1885–1945)

Symphonic Selections from "Showboat"
  (Bennett, arr.) (Pops Concert)
Symphonic Selections from "Roberta"
  (Bennett, arr.) (Pops Concert)

Khatchaturian, Aram (1903–1978)

Concerto for Violin and Orchestra
Three Dances from the "Gayaneh" Ballet
  (includes Sabre Dance)
Masquerade Suite for Orchestra

Kleinsinger, George (1914–1982)

Tubby, the Tuba with narrator (Young
  People's Concert)
Symphony of Winds with narrator
  (Young People's Concert)

Kodály, Zoltán (1882–1967)

Háry János Suite

Kurka, Robert (1921–1957)

Concerto for Marimba and Orchestra

Lalo, Edouard (1823–1892)

Symphonie Espagnole, Op. 21 (Violin and
  orchestra)
Cello Concerto in D minor

Larson, Libby (b. 1950)

Overture for the End of a Century

Ligeti, György (1923–2006)

Atmosphères (Avant-garde)

Liszt, Franz (1811–1886)

Les Preludés, S.97
Piano Concerto No. 1 in E-flat Major, S.124

Loewe, Frederick (1901–1988)

My Fair Lady Selections (Bennett, arr.)
  (Pops Concert)
Camelot Selections (Bennett, arr.) (Pops
  Concert)
Brigadoon Selections (Bennett, arr.) (Pops
  Concert)

Macdowell, Edward (1861–1908)

Piano Concerto No. 2 in D minor, Op. 23

Mahler, Gustav (1860–1911)

Symphony No. 1 in D Major "Titan"
Symphony No. 2 in C minor "Resurrection"
Symphony No. 5 in C-sharp minor (contains
  Adagietto for Strings and Harp)
Das Lied von der Erde (alto or baritone and
  tenor soloists)
Songs of a Wayfarer (solo voice, medium
  and orchestra)

Marcello, Benedetto (1686–1739)

Concerto in D minor for Oboe and Strings

Mascagni, Pietro (1863–1945)

Intermezzo from "Cavalleria Rusticana"
  (Medium)

Massenet, Jules (1842–1912)

Phèdre Overture (Medium)
Thaïs: Méditation for Violin (or Flute) and
  Orchestra (Medium)

Mayuzumi, Toshirō (1929–1997)

Concertino for Xylophone and Orchestra

Mcphee, Colin (1900–1964)

Tabuh-Tabuhan (Orchestra with two solo
  pianos)
Nocturne

Mendelssohn, Felix (1809–1847)

Hebrides Overture (Fingal's Cave), Op. 26
A Midsummer Night's Dream Overture,
  Op. 21
Symphony No. 3 in A minor (Scottish),
  Op. 56
Symphony No. 4 in A Major (Italian), Op. 90
Symphony No. 5 in D Major (Reformation),
  Op. 107
Concerto in E minor for Violin and
  Orchestra, Op. 64
Ruy Blas Overture, Op. 95

Menotti, Gian Carlo (1911–2007)

The Sebastian Ballet Suite
Excerpts from "Amahl and the Night
  Visitors" (Holiday Concert)

Milhaud, Darius (1892–1974)

Concerto for Percussion and Small
  Orchestra, Op. 109
Suite provençale, Op. 152b
Suite française, Op. 248 (originally for band)

Mozart, Wolfgang Amadeus (1756–1791)

Impresario Overture, K.486
Marriage of Figaro Overture, K.492
Magic Flute Overture, K.620
The Abduction from the Seraglio Overture,
  K.384
Don Giovanni Overture, K.527
Concerto for Clarinet in A major, K.622
Concerto No. 1 in G Major for Flute, K.313
Violin Concerto No. 5 in A Major, K.219
Concerto No. 21 for Piano in C Major,
  K.467
Concerto for Two Pianos in E-flat Major,
  K.365
Concerto for Bassoon in B-flat Major, K.191
Concerto for Flute and Harp in C Major,
  K.299
Concerto for Horn No. 3 in E-flat Major,
  K.447
Symphony No. 40 in G minor, K.550
Symphony No. 41 in C Major, K.551
Eine Kleine Nachtmusik, K.525
Exaltate Jubilate for Soprano Solo and
  Orchestra, K.165
Requiem (SATB soloists, chorus and
  orchestra), K.626
(Many more symphonies and concertos)

Mussorgsky, Modest (1839–1881)

Pictures at an Exhibition (Ravel, orch.)
Night on Bald Mountain (Rimsky-Korsakov,
  orch.)
Prelude to "Khovantchina" (Rimsky-
  Korsakov, orch.)
Hopak from "Fair at Sorochinsk" (Easy)

Nelhybel, Vaclav (1919–1996)

Movement for Orchestra (Medium)
Music for Orchestra (Medium)
Passacaglia for Strings (Medium)

Nicolai, Otto (1810–1849)

Merry Wives of Windsor Overture

Nielsen, Carl (1865–1931)

Little Suite for Strings, Op. 1
Symphony No. 5, Op. 50

Offenbach, Jacques (1819–1880)

Overture to "Orpheus in the Underworld"
La Belle Helena Overture
La vie Parisienne Overture (Dorati, arr.)
  (Pops Concert)

Orff, Carl (1895–1982)

Carmina Burana (Soloists, chorus and
  orchestra)

Pachelbel, Johann (1653–1706)

Canon for Strings and Continuo (Medium)

Penderecki, Krzysztof (B. 1933)

To the Victims of Hiroshima (Threnody)
(String orchestra)

Persichetti, Vincent (1915–1987)

The Hollow Men (Trumpet solo and string
orchestra)

Piazzolla, Astor (1921–1992)

Four, For Tango (String orchestra)
Two Tangos (with accordian)
(Many more tangos)

Piston, Walter (1894–1976)

The Incredible Flutist Suite
Three New England Sketches
Sinfonietta (chamber orchestra)

Ponchielli, Amilcare (1834–1886)

La Gioconda: Dance of the Hours

Poulenc, Francis (1899–1963)

The Story of Babar, the Little Elephant (with
narrator) (Young People's Concert)
Concerto for Two Pianos and Orchestra in
D minor
Gloria in G (Solo soprano, chorus, and
orchestra)

Previn, Andre (B. 1929)

Overture to a Comedy

Prokofiev, Sergei (1891–1953)

Peter and the Wolf, Op. 67 (with narrator)
(Young People's Concert)
Symphony No. 1, Op. 25 (Classical)
Lieutenant Kiji Suite, Op. 60 (opt. baritone
voice)
Piano Concerto No. 3 in C Major, Op. 26

Romeo and Juliet Suite No. 1, Op. 64bis
March and Scherzo from "The Love for
Three Oranges"

Puccini, Giacomo (1858–1924)

I crisantemi (The Chrysanthemums) for
String Orchestra

Rachmaninoff, Sergei (1873–1943)

Rhapsody on a Theme of Paganini, Op. 43
(Piano and orchestra)
Symphony No. 2 in E minor, Op. 27
Piano Concerto No. 1 in F-sharp minor, Op. 1
Piano Concerto No. 2 in C minor, Op. 18
Piano Concerto No. 3 in D minor, Op. 30

Rautavaara, Einojuhani (B. 1928)

Concerto for Birds and Orchestra (with pre-
recorded tape)

Ravel, Maurice (1875–1937)

Pavane pour une infante défunte
Daphnis and Chloé Suite No. 2
La Valse
Bolero
Piano Concerto in G Major
Le Tombeau de Couperin
Mother Goose Suite (Young People's
Concert)

Reed, H. Owen (B. 1910)

La Fiesta Mexicana (originally for concert
band)

Respighi, Ottorino (1879–1936)

Pines of Rome
Fountains of Rome
La boutique fantasque Suite (After Rossini)
The Birds (Gil uccelli)
Ancient Airs and Dances, Suite III (String
orchestra)

Revueltas, Silvestre (1899–1940)

Sensemayá

Rimsky-Korsakov, Nikolai (1844–1908)

Capriccio Espagnol, Op. 34
Le Coq d'or Suite: Introduction and
    Wedding March
Scheherazade, Symphonic Suite, Op. 35
Russian Easter Overture, Op. 36

Rodgers, Richard (1902–1979)

Oklahoma Selections (Bennett, arr.) (Pops
    Concert)
The Sound of Music: A Symphonic Picture
    (Bennett, arr.) (Pops Concert)
Victory at Sea, Symphonic Scenario
    (Bennett, arr.) (Pops Concert)
South Pacific Selections (Bennett, arr.)
    (Pops Concert)
Carousel Selections (Bennett, arr.) (Pops
    Concert)
The King and I Selections (Bennett, arr.)
    (Pops Concert)

Rodrigo, Joaquín (1901–1999)

Concierto de Aranjuez (Solo guitar and
    orchestra)

Rossini, Gioacchino (1792–1868)

Largo al Factotum (Baritone soloist with
    orchestra)
La Scala di Seta (The Silken Ladder)
    Overture
William Tell Overture
L'italiana in Algeri Overture
Barber of Seville Overture
La Cenerentola (Cinderella) Overture
La Gazza Ladra (The Thieving Magpie)
    Overture
Semiramide Overture

Roussel, Albert (1869–1937)

Symphony No. 3 in G minor, Op. 42
Sinfonietta for Strings, Op. 52

Saint-Saëns, Camille (1835–1921)

Carnival of the Animals (Two solo pianos,
    cello, and orchestra) (Young People's
    Concert)
Introduction and Rondo Capriccioso, Op. 28
    (Violin and orchestra)
Havanaise, Op. 83 (Violin and orchestra)
Danse macabre, Op. 40
Symphony No. 3 in C minor, Op. 78 (Organ
    Symphony)
Piano Concerto No. 2 in G minor, Op. 22
Morceau de Concert (French horn and
    orchestra)

Sarasate, Pablo de (1844–1908)

Zigeunerweisen (Gypsy Airs), Op. 20
    (Violin and orchestra)

Satie, Erik (1866–1925)

Gymnopédies No. 1 and 3 (Debussy, orch.)

Schoenberg, Arnold (1874–1951)

Verklärte Nacht, Op. 4 for Strings (1943)
Chamber Symphony No. 1, Op. 9b
Chamber Symphony No. 2, Op. 38

Schreiner, Adolph (1847–1921)

The Worried Drummer (Young People's
    Concert or Pops Concert)

Schubert, Franz (1797–1828)

Symphony No. 5 in B-flat Major, D. 485
Symphony No. 8 in B minor (Unfinished),
    D. 759
Symphony No. 9 in C Major "The Great,"
    D. 944

Rosamunde Overture, D.644
Mass No. 2 in G Major, D.167 (Chorus and
STB soloists)

Schuller, Gunther (B. 1925)

Journey into Jazz for Narrator, Jazz
Ensemble, and Orchestra
Seven Studies on Themes after Paul Klee

Schuman, William (1910–1992)

American Festival Overture
New England Triptych
Newsreel in Five Shots (Medium)

Schumann, Robert (1810–1856)

Piano Concerto in A minor, Op. 54
Symphony No. 1 in B-flat Major (Spring),
Op. 38
Symphony No. 4 in D minor, Op. 120 (1851
revision)
Violin Concerto in D minor, WoO 23
Cello Concerto in A minor, Op. 129
Concert Piece for Four Horns and Orchestra,
Op. 86

Scriabin, Alexander (1872–1915)

The Poem of Ecstasy, Op. 54 (Large
instrumentation)

Sessions, Roger (1896–1985)

The Black Maskers Ballet Suite

Shostakovich, Dmitri (1906–1975)

Age of Gold Ballet Suite, Op. 22a
Festive Overture, Op. 96
Symphony No. 1 in F minor, Op. 10
Symphony No. 5 in D minor, Op. 47
Symphony No. 10 in E minor, Op. 93
Concerto No. 1 for Piano, Trumpet and
Strings, Op. 35
Cello Concerto No. 1 in E-flat Major, Op. 107

Sibelius, Jean (1865–1957)

Symphony No. 1 in E minor, Op. 39
Symphony No. 2 in D Major, Op. 43
Symphony No. 5 in E-flat Major, Op. 82
Finlandia, Op. 26
Swan of Tuonela, Op. 22 (English horn and
orchestra)
Concerto in D minor for Violin and
Orchestra, Op. 47
Romance in C for Strings
Pohjola's Daughter (Tone poem), Op. 49

Smetana, Bedřich (1824–1884)

Overture to "The Bartered Bride"
The Moldau (Symphonic poem)
From Bohemia's Forests and Meadows

Spohr, Ludwig (1784–1859)

Concerto No. 1 in C minor for Clarinet,
Op. 26

Starer, Robert (1924–2001)

Dalton Set for Young People (Easy) (Young
People's Concert)
Six Variations on 12 Notes (Easy) (Young
People's Concert)

Still, William Grant (1895–1978)

Symphony No. 1 (Afro-American
Symphony)
Festive Overture (Large instrumentation)

Strauss, Franz (1822–1905)

Concerto for Horn and Orchestra in C minor,
Op. 8

Strauss, Johann, Jr. (1825–1899)

Tales from the Vienna Woods, Op. 325
Emperor Waltzes, Op. 437
Overture to Die Fledermaus

Thunder and Lightning Polka, Op. 324
Beautiful Blue Danube Waltz

Strauss, Richard (1864–1949)

Till Eulenspiegel's Merry Pranks, Op. 28
Death and Transfiguration, Op. 24
Don Juan, Op. 20
Thus Spake Zarathustra, Op. 30
Le Bourgeois Gentilhomme Suite, Op. 60
Alpine Symphony, Op. 64 (Large
    instrumentation including Wagner tubas)
Eine Heldenleben, Op. 40
Horn Concerto No. 1 in E-flat, Op. 11
Der Rosenkavalier Waltzes, Op. 59

Stravinsky, Igor (1882–1971)

Suite No. 1 for Small Orchestra
Suite No. 2 for Small Orchestra
Firebird Ballet Suite (1919 version)
Petrouchka Ballet Suite (1947 revision)
Rite of Spring Ballet Suite
Circus Polka (Composed for a Young
    Elephant) (Young People's Concert)
Concerto for Piano and Wind Instruments
Symphony in Three Movements
Symphony in C

Tartini, Giuseppi (1692–1770)

Trumpet Concerto in D Major

Tchaikovsky, Peter Ilyich (1840–1893)

Romeo and Juliet Overture-Fantasy (1880)
1812 Overture, Op. 49
Francesca di Rimini Overture, Op. 32
Capriccio Italien, Op 45
Nutcracker Ballet Suite, Op. 71a (Holiday
    Concert)
Swan Lake Ballet Suite, Op. 20
Sleeping Beauty Ballet Suite, Op. 66a
Rococo Variations for Cello and Orchestra,
    Op. 33

Piano Concerto No. 1 in B-flat minor, Op. 23
Violin Concerto in D Major, Op. 35
Serenade for Strings, Op. 48
Symphony No. 2 in C minor (Little Russian),
    Op. 17
Symphony No. 4 in F minor, Op. 36
Symphony No. 5 in E minor, Op. 64
Symphony No. 6 in B minor (Pathetique),
    Op. 74
Orchestra Suite no. 1, Op. 43
Eugene Onegin Waltz
Russian Chorale and Overture (Isaac, arr.)
    (Easy)
Marche Slave, Op. 31

Telemann, Georg Philipp (1681–1767)

Concerto for Trumpet in D Major (two
    oboes, strings and continuo)
Concerto for Viola in G Major (strings and
    continuo)
Don Quixote Suite (strings and continuo)
Suite in A Minor (flute, strings and continuo)

Thompson, Randall (1899–1984)

Symphony No. 2 in E minor

Toch, Ernest (1887–1964)

Pinocchio: A Merry Overture (Young
    People's Concert)
Circus Overture (Young People's Concert)

Towers, Joan (B. 1938)

Fanfare for the Uncommon Woman for
    Orchestra
Tambor

Turina, Joaquín (1882–1949)

La procession del Rocio, Op. 9
Danzas Fantásticas

Vaughan Williams, Ralph (1872–1958)

Fantasia on Greensleeves (Two flutes, harp, and strings) (Holiday Concert)
Serenade to Music (Solo voices, chorus, and orchestra)
The Wasps Overture
Symphony No. 2 in G Major (London)
Fantasia on a Theme of Thomas Tallis (Double string orchestra)
Concerto in F minor for Tuba and Orchestra
The Lark Ascending (Solo violin and chamber orchestra)

Verdi, Giuseppe (1813–1901)

La Forza del Destino Overture
Prelude to Act I "La Traviata"
Overture to "Nabucco"
The Sicilian Vespers Overture
Requiem (SATB soloists, chorus, and orchestra)

Vivaldi, Antonio (1678–1741)

The Four Seasons, No. 1-4, Op. 8
Gloria in D Major (Soloists SSA, chorus, and orchestra)
Concerto in C for Two Trumpets, Strings, and Continuo
(Many more concertos for various soloists and combinations)

Wagner, Richard (1813–1883)

Prelude to Die Meistersingers
Ride of the Walkyrie from "Tannhauser"
Siegfried Idyll
Prelude to Act III "Lohengrin"
Rienzi Overture
Prelude and Liebestod from "Tristan und Isolde"
Wesendonck Songs (Soprano and orchestra)

Walton, William (1902–1983)

Façade Suite No. 1
Façade Suite No. 2
Crown Imperial, Coronation March

Ward, Robert (B. 1917)

Jubilation: An Overture

Warlock, Peter (1894–1930)

Capriol Suite (String orchestra or full orchestra)

Weber, Carl Maria Von (1786–1826)

Der Freischütz Overture
Oberon Overture
Concertino for Clarinet and Orchestra, Op. 26
Concerto No. 1 in F minor for Clarinet and Orchestra, Op. 73
Concerto No. 2 in E-flat Major for Clarinet and Orchestra, Op. 74
Concerto for Bassoon and Orchestra in F Major, Op. 75
Invitation to the Dance (Berlioz, orch.)

Webern, Anton (1883–1945)

Passacaglia, Op. 1
Six Pieces for Orchestra, Op. 6 Five Pieces for Orchestra, Op. 10

Weinberger, Jaromir (1896–1967)

Polka and Fugue from "Schwanda"

Whear, Paul (B. 1925)

Catskill Legend (Medium)

Williams, John (B. 1932)

Olympic Fanfare (Pops concert)
Star Wars: Symphonic Suite (Pops Concert)

Willson, Meredith (1902–1984)

Symphonic Impressions from "The Music Man" (Hayman, arr.) (Pops Concert)

Wolf-Ferrari, Ermanno (1876–1948)

Overture to "The Secret of Suzanne"

Yardumian, Richard (1917–1985)

Armenian Suite (Full or chamber orchestra)
Cantus animae et cordis (Strings)

Zwilich, Ellen Taaffe (B. 1939)

Celebration for Orchestra (Large orchestra)

For Additional Orchestra Repertoire Sources

See David Daniels: *Orchestral Music: A Handbook*, 4th ed.
See *Orchestra Music Guide* (The Instrumentalist Company).
See Richard Eldon Yaklich: *An Orchestra Guide to Repertoire and Programming.*

SCORE STUDY AND PROGRAM BUILDING REPERTOIRE FOR CONCERT BAND AND WIND ENSEMBLE

In this category, the conductor must make the decision as to which selections are suitable for performance by the wind ensemble as opposed to the full symphonic band. Base this decision on ensemble texture desired, instrumentation required (and available), and your experienced judgment in terms of presentation. It is important to realize that with the contemporary composers, there may be works that I have not listed because of their recent publication. The young conductor must continue to investigate the various new works by contemporary composers for all of these ensembles.

Adams, John (B. 1947)

Short Ride in a Fast Machine (Odom, arr.)
Grand Pianola Music (wind ensemble, 2
     pianos and 3 female voices)

Alford, Kenneth (1881–1945)

Colonel Bogey March (Fennell, ed.)
The Vanished Army March
The Purple Carnival March
Army of the Nile March
(Many more marches)

Amram, David (B. 1930)

King Lear Variations

Anderson, Leroy (1908–1975)

A Trumpeter's Lullaby (Trumpet solo or
     trio) (Pops Concert)
Bugler's Holiday (Trumpet trio) (Pops
     Concert)
Sandpaper Ballet (Pops Concert) (Medium)
(Many other light selections)

Arnold, Malcolm (1921–2006)

English Dances, Op. 71 (Johnston or
     Paynter, arr.)
Four Scottish Dances, Op. 59 (Paynter, arr.)
Four Cornish Dances, Op. 91 (Marciniak, arr.)
Prelude, Siciliano, and Rondo, Op. 80
     (Paynter, arr.)
Tam O'Shanter Overture, Op. 51
     (Paynter, arr.)

Bach, Johann Sebastian (1685–1750)

Fantasia in G Major (Goldman-Leist, arr.)
Prelude & Fugue in G minor
     (Moehlmann, arr.)
If Thou Be Near (Moehlmann, arr.)
Jesu, Joy of Man's Desiring (Leidzèn or
     Reed, arr.) (Medium)
Come, Sweet Death (Leidzèn or Reed, arr.)
Toccata and Fugue in D minor (Leidzèn, arr.)
Little Gigue in G minor (Cailliet, arr.)
     (Medium)
Sheep May Safely Graze (Reed, arr.)
(Many more transcriptions)

Badings, Henk (1907–1987)

Concerto for Flute and Wind Orchestra
Symphony in C

Bagley, Edwin Eugene (1857–1922)

National Emblem March (Fennell, ed.)

Balay, Guillaume (1871–1942)

Au Pays Lorrain Overture (Chidester, arr.)

Barber, Samuel (1910–1981)

Commando March

Barnes, James (B. 1949)

Trail of Tears
Yorkshire Ballad (Medium)
Symphony No. 2, Op. 44
Symphony No. 3, Op. 89
Invocation and Toccata
(Many more contemporary works for band)

Bartók, Béla (1881–1945)

For Children (Finlayson, arr.) (Medium)
Four Pieces for Band (Suchoff, arr.)
    (Medium)

Bassett, Leslie (B. 1923)

Designs, Images and Textures
Sounds, Shapes and Symbols

Beecham, Sir Thomas (1879–1961)

March for Band

Beethoven, Ludwig Van (1770–1827)

King Stephen Overture, Op. 117
    (Cailliet, arr.)
Egmont Overture, Op. 84 (Tobani, arr.)
(Many more transcriptions)

Bennett, Richard Rodney (B. 1936)

Morning Music
The Four Seasons
Concerto for Trumpet and Wind Orchestra

Bennett, Robert Russell (1894–1981)

Suite of Old American Dances
Down to the Sea in Ships
Symphonic Songs for Band

Benson, Warren (1924–2005)

The Leaves are Falling
The Solitary Dancer
Symphony for Drums and Wind Orchestra
Rememberances
Meditation on "I am for Peace"
Helix for Tuba and Band
Symphony No. 2
(Many more contemporary works for band)

Bergsma, William (1921–1994)

March with Trumpets

Berlioz, Hector (1803–1869)

Grand Symphonie Funèbre et Triomphale,
    Op. 15 (Goldman, arr.)
Beatrice and Benedict Overture, H. 138
    (Henning, arr.)
Roman Carnival Overture, Op. 9
    (Godfrey, arr.)
Rakoczy March from "The Damnation of
    Faust" (Smith, arr.)

Bernstein, Leonard (1918–1990)

Danzon from "Fancy Free" (Krance, arr.)
Overture to "Candide" (Beeler or
    Grundman, arr.)
West Side Story Selections (Duthoit, arr.)
Slava! (Grundman, arr.)
Profanation (Scherzo) from Jeremiah
    (Bencriscutto, arr.)
Divertimento (Grundman, arr.)

Symphonic Suite from "On the Waterfront"
(Duker, arr.)

Bielawa, Herbert (B. 1930)

Spectrum (Band and pre-recorded tape)
Prisms

Bilik, Jerry (B. 1933)

American Civil War Fantasy
Symphony for Band

Binge, Ronald (1910–1878)

Cornet Carillion for Three or Four Cornets
and Band (Werle, arr.)

Bock, Jerry (1928–2010)

Selections from "Fiddler on the Roof"
(Various arrangements)

Borodin, Alexander (1833–1887)

Polovetsian Dances from "Prince Igor"
(trans. Hindsley)

Brahms, Johannes (1833–1897)

Academic Festival Overture, Op. 80
(Hindsley, arr.)
Blessed Are They, from A German Requiem,
Op. 45 (Buehlman, arr.)

Breydert, Frederick M. (B. 1909)

Suite in F for Band

Bright, Houston (1916–1968)

Prelude and Fugue in F minor
Concerto Grosso (Soloists—flute, clarinet
and oboe)

Broege, Timothy (B. 1947)

The Headless Horseman
Sinfonia III "Hymns and Dances"
Sinfonia VI
(Many more contemporary works for band)

Bukvich, Daniel (B. 1954)

Symphony No, 1 "In Memoriam Dresden"
(Avant-garde)

Cacavas, John (B. 1930)

Days of Glory (Easy)
Gallant Men March (Medium)
Star Spangled Spectacular (The Music of
George M. Cohan) (Pops Concert)
American Sea Rhapsody (Medium)
(Many more light contemporary works for
band)

Camphouse, Mark (B. 1954)

The Shining City (Narrator and band)
Three London Miniatures (Medium)
A Movement for Rosa
In Memoriam
Whatsoever Things for Symphonic Band
(Many more contemporary works for band)

Carter, Charles (B. 1926)

Overture for Winds (Medium)
Symphonic Overture (Medium)
Overture in a Classical Style (Medium)

Catel, Charles-Simon (1773–1830)

Overture in C (R. F. Goldman, arr.)

Chance, John Barnes (1932–1972)

Incantation and Dance
Variations on a Korean Folk Song

Elegy
Blue Lake Overture
Introduction and Capriccio for Piano and 24
  Winds
Symphony No. 2
(Many more contemporary works for band)

Coates, Eric (1886–1957)

Knightsbridge March
London Suite

Colgrass, Michael (B. 1932)

Urban Requiem
Old Churches (Medium)
Winds of Nagual

Copland, Aaron (1900–1990)

An Outdoor Overture
Lincoln Portrait for Narrator and Band
  (Beeler, arr.)
Emblems
Variations on a Shaker Melody
The Red Pony (Film Suite)
El Salón México (Hindsley, arr.)

Corelli, Arcangelo (1653–1713)

Sarabanda and Gavotte from "Christmas
  Concerto" (Gordon, arr.) (Medium)

Corigliano, John (B. 1938)

Gazebo Dances (Corigliano, arr.)

Cowell, Henry (1897–1965)

Shoonthree
Hymn and Fuguing Tune No. 1
Celtic Set

Creston, Paul (1906–1985)

Celebration Overture, Op. 61
Prelude and Dance, Op. 69

Zanoni, Op. 40
Concertino for Marimba and Band, Op. 21b

Curnow, James (B. 1943)

Legend and Sundance
Rejouissance
Where Never Lark or Eagle Flew
Fiddle Tunes from the American Revolution
Fantasia on "Ein Feste Burg"
(Many more contemporary works and
  arrangements for band)

Daehn, Larry (B. 1939)

With Quiet Courage (Medium)
As Summer was Coming In (Easy)

Dahl, Ingolf (1912–1970)

Sinfonietta for Concert Band
Concerto for Alto Saxophone and Wind
  Orchestra

Daugherty, Michael (B. 1954)

Niagara Falls

Deak, Csaba (B. 1932)

Five Short Pieces for Symphonic Band

Del Borgo, Elliot (B. 1938)

Do Not Go Gentle into That Good Night
Symphonic Essay
Rituale
(Many more contemporary works for band)

Della Cese, David (1856–1938)

L'Inglesina (The Little English Girl) March

Dello Joio, Norman (1913–2008)

Fantasies on a Theme of Haydn
Scenes from "The Louvre"

Variants on a Medieval Tune
Satiric Dances for a Comedy by
   Aristophanes

De Nardis, Camille (1857–1951)

Universal Judgment (Cafarello, arr.)

Dvořák, Antonín (1841–1904)

Serenade in D minor, Op. 44
Finale from the "New World" Symphony,
   Op. 95 (Leidzén, arr.)

Elgar, Edward (1857–1934)

Nimrod from "Enigma Variations," Op. 96
   (Wright, arr.)

Erb, Donald (1927–2008)

Space Music
Stargazing

Erickson, Frank (1923–1996)

Air for Band (Easy)
Second Symphony for Band
Toccata for Band (Medium)
Concertino for Trumpet and Band
(Many more contemporary works and
   arrangements for band)

Ewazen, Eric (B. 1954)

Celtic Hymns and Dances
Legacy for Symphonic Band

Fauchet, Paul (1881–1937)

Symphony in B-flat (Gillette/Watson, arr.)

Fillmore, Henry (1881–1956)

The Klaxon March
Americans We March (Fennell, ed.)
His Honor March (Fennell, ed.)

Rolling Thunder March
The Footlifter March
(Many more marches)

Frescobaldi, Girolamo (1583–1643)

Toccata (Slocum, arr.)

Fucik, Julius (1872–1916)

Entry of the Gladiators March (Circus march)

Ganne, Louis (1862–1923)

The Father of Victory March

Gershwin, George (1898–1937)

An American in Paris (Krance, arr.)
Selections from "Porgy and Bess" (Robert
   Russell Bennett, arr.)
Rhapsody in Blue (Grofé, orch.)
Strike Up the Band (Lowden or Barker, arr.)
Catfish Row (Hunsberger, arr.)

Giannini, Vittorio (1903–1966)

Fantasia for Band (Medium)
Symphony No. 3
Preludium and Allegro
Variations and Fugue

Gigout, Eugène (1844–1926)

Marche des Rogations (Rhodes, arr.)
   (Medium)

Gillingham, David (B. 1947)

With Heart and Voice
Heroes, Lost and Fallen
Waking Angels
(Many more contemporary works for band)

Gillis, Don (1912–1978)

Symphony No. 5 1/2 (Bainum, arr.)
Tulsa (Portrait in Oil) (Ford, arr.)

Giovannini, Cesar (B. 1925)

Sonatina for Band (Easy)
Overture in B-flat for Band

Glière, Reinhold (1875–1956)

Russian Sailor's Dance from the "Red
  Poppy" (Vinson, arr.) (Medium)

Goldman, Edwin Franko (1878–1956)

On the Mall March
On Parade March
(Many more marches)

Gossec, François Joseph (1734–1829)

Military Symphony in F (R.F. Goldman—
  Leist, arr.)
Classic Overture in C (R.F. Goldman, arr.)

Gould, Morton (1913–1996)

American Salute (Lang, arr.)
Symphony No.4 "West Point" for Band
Symphony for Band
St. Lawrence Suite (2 solo antiphonal
  trumpets needed)
Prisms
Ballad for Band

Gounod, Charles (1818–1893)

Faust Ballet Music (Winterbottom, arr.)

Grainger, Percy (1882–1961)

Handel in the Strand (R. F. Goldman, arr.)
Irish Tune from County Derry (Kent, arr.)
Lincolnshire Posy (Fennell, arr.)
Children's March, Over the Hills and Far
  Away (Erickson, arr.)
Hill Song No. 2
Australian Up-Country Dance (Bainum, arr.)
Molly on the Shore
Colonial Song
Shepherd's Hey (Clark and Schmidt, ed.)

The Power of Rome and the Christian Heart
Ye Banks and Braes O'Bonnie Doon
Sussex Mummers' Christmas Carol
Country Gardens (Clark, arr.)

Grantham, Donald (B. 1947)

Southern Harmony
Kentucky Harmony

Gregson, Edward (B. 1945)

Festivo
Metamorphoses

Grieg, Edvard (1843–1907)

The Last Spring, Op. 34 (Wilson, arr.)
  (Medium)

Grundman, Clare (1913–1996)

American Folk Rhapsody No. 1 (Medium)
American Folk Rhapsody No. 2 (Medium)
American Folk Rhapsody No. 3 (Medium)
American Folk Rhapsody No. 4 (Medium)
Fantasy on American Sailing Songs
  (Medium)
An Irish Rhapsody (Medium)
Hebrides Suite (Medium)
(Many more contemporary works for band)

Guilmant, Alexandre (1837–1811)

Morceau Symphonique (Solo for trombone
  and band) (Shepard, arr.)
Choral March and Fugue (Righter, arr.)

Hall, R. B (1858–1907)

Officer of the Day March (Gore, ed.)

Handel, George Frederick (1685–1759)

Music for the Royal Fireworks
  (Mackerras, arr.)
Water Music (Kay, arr.)

Aria and Fugue (Osterling, arr.) (Medium)
An Occasional Suite (Osterling, arr.) (Easy)
Song of Jupiter (Anderson, arr.) (Easy)
(Many more transcriptions)

Hanson, Howard (1896–1981)

Chorale and Alleluia, Op. 42
Laude
Symphony No. 2 "Romantic" (Second
    Movement) (Goldberg, arr.)
Dies Natalis
(Many more works for band)

Hanssen, Johannes (1874–1967)

Valdres—Norwegian March (Bainum, arr.)
    (Trumpet soloist needed)

Harbison, John (B. 1938)

Olympic Dance
Three City Blocks

Hartley, Walter (B. 1927)

Sinfonia No. 4 (Medium)
Concerto for Saxophone
Concerto for 23 Winds
Capriccio for Trombone and Band

Haydn, Franz Joseph (1732–1809)

St. Anthony Divertimento (Wilcox, arr.)
Concerto in E-flat Major for Trumpet and
    Band (Duthoit, arr.)
(Many more transcriptions for band)

Hazo, Samuel (B. 1966)

Perthshire Majesty (Medium)
Home are the Sailors
(Many more contemporary works for band)

Herbert, Victor (1859–1924)

Victor Herbert Favorites (Lake, arr.) (Pops
    Concert)

Hermann, Ralph (1914–1994)

Belmont Overture (Medium)
North Sea Overture
Concerto for Trumpet and Band

Hindemith, Paul (1895–1963)

Symphony in B-flat
Symphonic Metamorphosis on Themes by
    von Weber (Wilson, arr.)
Konzertmusik, Opus 49 (Piano, harp, and
    winds)
Concert Music for Wind Orchestra, Op. 41

Holsinger, David (B. 1945)

Liturgical Dances
To Tame the Perilous Skies
Havendance
In the Spring at the Time When Kings Go
    Off to War
On a Hymnsong of Lowell Mason (Easy)
On a Hymnsong of Philip Bliss (Medium)
(Many more contemporary works for band)

Holst, Gustav (1874–1934)

Suite No. 1 in E-flat Major
Suite No. 2 in F Major
Hammersmith, Prelude and Scherzo, Op. 52
Mars from "The Planets" (Holst, arr.)
Jupiter from "The Planets" (Holst, arr.)
A Moorside Suite in E-flat (Jacob, arr.)
Dance of the Spirits of Fire (from The
    Perfect Fool), Op. 39 (Harpham, arr.)

Hovhaness, Alan (1911–2000)

Suite for Band
Symphony No. 4 for Wind Orchestra, Op. 165
Symphony No. 14 for Winds "Ararat" Op. 94

Husa, Karel (B. 1921)

Music for Prague 1968
Apotheosis of This Earth
Concertino for Percussion and Wind
    Ensemble

Al Fresco
Smetana Fanfare
(Many more contemporary works for band)

Iannaccone, Anthony (B. 1943)

After a Gentle Rain
Sea Drift
Images of Song and Dance No. 1
(Many more contemporary works for band)

Ippolitov, Ivanov (1859–1935)

Procession of the Sardar (Engman, arr.)
  (Medium)

Ives, Charles (1874–1954)

The Circus Band (Elkus, arr.)
Variations on "America" (Rhoades, arr.)
Decoration Day (Elkus, arr.)
Country Band March (Sinclair, arr.)
(Many more works transcribed for band)

Jacob, Gordon (1895–1984)

William Byrd Suite
Music for a Festival (Combined with brass
  choir)
An Original Suite for Band
Old Wine in New Bottles
(Many more works for band)

Jager, Robert (B. 1939)

Second Suite for Band
Third Suite for Band
Celebration!
Sinfonia Noblissima
Symphony No. 2
Shivaree
(Many more contemporary works for band)

Jenkins, Joseph (B. 1928)

American Overture for Band
Symphonic Jubilee

Jewell, Fred (1875–1936)

E Pluribus Unum March
Supreme Triumph March
The Screamer March
(Many more marches)

Kabalevsky, Dimitri (1904–1987)

Overture to Colas Breugnon (Hunsberger, arr.)

Kalinnikov, Basil S. (1866–1901)

Symphony No. 1: Finale (Bainum, arr.)

Kelterborn, Rudolph (B. 1931)

Miroirs

Kennen, Kent (1913–2003)

Night Soliloquy (Flute and band)

Khachaturian, Aram (1903–1978)

Armenian Dances (Satz, arr.)

King, Karl (1891–1971)

Hosts of Freedom March
Barnum and Bailey's Favorite March
Purple Pageant March (Paynter, ed.)
(Many more marches)

Krenek, Ernst (1900–1991)

Dream Sequence, Op. 224
Symphony No. 4, Op. 34

Lagassey, Homer (1902–1990)

Sequoia (Tone Painting)

Laplante, Pierre (B. 1943)

In the Forest of the King (Medium)
Overture on a Minstrel Tune (Easy)

American Riversongs
(Many more contemporary works for band)

Larsen, Libby (B. 1950)

Concert Dances
Sun Song

Latham, William (1917–2004)

Three Chorale Preludes (Medium)
Brighton Beach March (Medium)
Serenade for Band (Medium)
Court Festival (Medium)
Proud Heritage March (Medium)
(Many more contemporary works for band)

Leemans, Pierre (1897–1980)

Belgian Paratroopers March (Wiley, arr.)

Lopatnikoff, Nicolai (1903–1976)

Concerto for Wind Orchestra, Op. 41

Lo Presti, Ronald (1933–1985)

Elegy for a Young American
Pageant Overture
(Many more contemporary works for band)

Luigini, Alexandre (1850–1906)

Ballet Egyptien, Op. 12 (Holmes, arr.)

Mahr, Timothy (B. 1956)

Endurance
The Soaring Hawk
Daydream
(Many more contemporary works for band)

Mailman, Martin (1932–2000)

Liturgical Music for Band, Op. 12
Exaltations, Op. 67

Geometrics No. 2 for Band, Op. 29
(Many more contemporary works for band)

Makris, Andreas (1930–2005)

Aegean Festival Overture
Mediterranean Holiday

Marcello, Benedetto (1686–1739)

Psalm 18 (Whitney, arr.) (Easy)
Psalm 19 (Whitney, arr.) (Easy)

Margolis, Bob (B. 1921)

Terpsichore
Color
(Many more contemporary works for band)

Maslanka, David (B. 1943)

A Child's Garden of Dreams
Symphony No. 2
Symphony No. 3
Symphony No. 4 (In One Movement)
(Many more contemporary works for band)

Massenet, Jules (1842–1912)

Meditation from "Thaïs" (Harding, arr.)
Phédre Overture (Cailliet, arr.)
Le Cid (Ballet Music) (Reynolds, arr.)

Mayuzumi, Toshirō (1929–1997)

Music with Sculpture
Concerto for Percussion and Band

McBeth, W. Francis (B. 1933)

The Seventh Seal, opus 50
Chant and Jubilo, opus 25
Kaddish, opus 57
Masque, opus 44
Beowulf: An Heroic Trilogy, opus 71

Of Sailors and Whales: Five Scenes from
   Melville, opus 78
Caccia, opus 62
Canto (Easy)
(Many more contemporary works for band)

Mcphee, Colin (1900–1964)

Concerto for Wind Orchestra (Unusual band
   instrumentation)

Mctee, Cindy (B. 1953)

Circuits
Soundings

Méhul, Étienne (1763–1817)

Overture in F Major (Smith, arr.)

Meij, Johan De (B. 1953)

Symphony No. 1 "The Lord of the Rings,"
   V. Hobbits

Mendelssohn, Felix (1809–1847)

Overture for Band, Op. 24 (Greissle, arr.)

Mennin, Peter (1923–1983)

Canzona for Band

Messiaen, Olivier (1908–1992)

Et Expecto Resurrectionem Mortuorum

Miaskovsky, Nicolai (1881–1950)

Symphony No. 19, Op. 46

Milhaud, Darius (1892–1974)

Suite française, Op. 248b
West Point Suite for Band, Op. 313

Morrissey, John J (1906–1990)

Four Episodes for Band (Easy)
Music for a Ceremony (Medium)
(Many more works for band)

Mozart, Wolfgang Amadeus (1756–1791)

Cosi Fan Tutti Overture, K.588 (Moehlmann,
   arr.) (Medium)
Marriage of Figaro Overture, K.492
   (Slocum, arr.)
The Impresario Overture, K.486 (Barnes,
   arr.) (Medium)
Ave Verum Corpus, K.618 (Buehlman, arr.)
   (Easy)
Air and Alleluia (Kinyon, arr.) (Easy)
(Many more works transcribed for band)

Musgrave, Thea (B. 1928)

Journey Through a Japanese Landscape
   (Marimba soloist)

Mussorgsky, Modest (1839–1881)

Night on Bald Mountain (Paynter, arr.)
Hopak from "Fair at Sorochinsk" (Isaac, arr.)
   (Easy)
(Many more works transcribed for band)

Nelhybel, Vaclav (1919–1996)

Sine Nomine
Festivo (Medium)
Chorale for Symphonic Band (Medium)
Symphonic Movement
Trittico
Estampie (with antiphonal brass)
(Many more contemporary works for band)

Nelson, Ron (B. 1929)

Rocky Point Holiday
Te Deum Laudamus

Passacaglia (Homage to B-A-C-H)
Morning Alleluias for the Winter Solstice
(Many more contemporary works for band)

Nixon, Roger (1921–2009)

Fiesta del Pacifico
Reflections
Elegy, Fanfare and March
(Many more contemporary works for band)

Offenbach, Jacques (1819–1880)

Ballet Parisien (Isaac, arr.) (Medium)

Orff, Carl (1895–1982)

Carmina Burana: Suite (Krance, arr.)

Osterling, Eric (1926–2005)

Bandology March (Medium)
Totem Pole March (Medium)
(Many more marches)

Penderecki, Krzysztof (B. 1933)

Pittsburgh Overture

Persichetti, Vincent (1915–1987)

Pageant for Band, Op. 59
Psalm for Band, Op. 53
Divertimento for Band, Op. 42
Masquerade for Band, Op. 102
Symphony No. 6 for Band, Op. 69
Serenade for Band (Medium)
Chorale Prelude: So Pure the Star, Op. 91
Parable IX for Band, Op. 121
(Many more contemporary works for band)

Piston, Walter (1894–1976)

Tunbridge Fair: Intermezzo for Symphonic
  Band

Ployhar, James (1926–2007)

Devonshire Overture (Easy)
Korean Folk Song Medley (Medium)
May Day Carol (Easy)
Impressions of a Scottish Air (Easy)
(Many more easy works for band)

Poulenc, Francis (1899–1963)

Suite française (d'après Claude Gervaise)

Press, Jacques (B. 1930)

Wedding Dance ("Hasseneh") (Johnston, arr.)

Prokofiev, Sergei (1891–1953)

March, Op. 99 (Yoder, arr.) (Trumpet soloist
  needed)
Athletic Festival March, Op. 69 (R.F.
  Goldman, arr.)

Reed, Alfred (1921–2004)

Armenian Dances, Parts I and II
A Festival Prelude
Russian Christmas Music
Alleluia! Laudamus Te
First Suite for Band
Second Suite for Band
Third Suite for Band
Fourth Suite for Band
The Hounds of Spring, A Concert Overture
  for Winds
Rushmore, A Symphonic Prologue for
  Winds
Symphonic Prelude (Black is the Color of
  My True Love's Hair)
(Many more contemporary works for band)

Reed, H. Owen (B. 1910)

La Fiesta Mexicana
For the Unfortunate
Heart of the Morn (Medium)

Respighi, Ottorino (1879–1936)

Pines of the Appian Way (Leidzèn, arr.)
La Boutique Fantasque after Rossini
   (Godfrey, arr.)
Huntingtontower Ballad

Reynolds, Verne (B. 1926)

Scenes
Concerto for Band

Riegger, Wallingford (1885–1961)

Dance Rhythms for Band

Rimsky-Korsakov, Nicolas (1844–1908)

Procession of the Nobles from Mlada
   (Leidzèn, arr.)

Rodgers, Richard (1902–1979)

The Sound of Music (R. R. Bennett, arr.)
Victory At Sea (R. R. Bennett, arr.)
Gaudalcanal March (Leidzèn, arr.)
Selections, Carousel (Leidzèn, arr.)
Selections from "The King and I" (R. R.
   Bennett, arr.)
(Many more musical selections transcribed
   for band)

Rodrigo, Joaquín (1901–1999)

Adagio for Wind Orchestra

Rogers, Bernard (1893–1968)

Three Japanese Dances

Rossini, Gioacchino (1792–1868)

Barber of Seville Overture (Duthoit, arr.)
L'italiana in Algeri Overture (Kent, arr.)

La Gazza Ladra Overture (Cailliet, arr.)
(Other opera overtures transcribed for band)

Russell, Armand (B. 1932)

Theme and Fantasia
(Many other contemporary works for band)

Saint-Saëns, Camille (1835–1921)

Pas Redouble, Op. 86 (trans. Arthur
   Frackenpohl)
Marche Militaire Française, Op. 60
   (Hindsley, arr.)

Sallinen, Aulis (B. 1935)

Chorale

Schmitt, Florent (1870–1958)

Dionysiaques, Op. 62 (Difficult and large
   instrumentation)

Schoenberg, Arnold (1874–1951)

Theme and Variations, Op. 43a

Schuller, Gunther (B. 1925)

Meditation for Concert Band
Study in Textures
Diptych for Brass Quintet and Concert Band
Song and Dance (Violin and wind ensemble)
On Winged Flight: A Divertimento for Band
Symphony No. 3, "In Praise of Winds"
(Many other contemporary works for band)

Schuman, William (1910–1992)

New England Triptych
George Washington Bridge: An Impression
   for Band
Newsreel Suite
Chester Overture

When Jesus Wept
Be Glad Then America
American Festival Overture

Schwantner, Joseph (B. 1943)

. . . And the Mountains Rising Nowhere for
  Band (Avant-garde)
From a Dark Millennium for Wind Ensemble
  (Avant-garde)
(Other contemporary works for band)

Seitz, Roland (1867–1946)

March Grandioso
Salutation March
The World is Waiting for the Sunrise
  (Alford, arr.)
(Many other marches for band)

Sheldon, Robert (B. 1954)

Beyond the Higher Skies, op. 62
Fall River Overture, op. 18
Visions of Flight, op. 30
Fanfare and Intermezzo, op. 24
(Many other contemporary works for band)

Shostakovich, Dmitri (1906–1975)

Festive Overture, Op. 96 (Hunsberger, arr.)
Finale from "Symphony No. 5 in D minor,"
  Op. 47 (Righter, arr.)
Folk Dances (Reynolds, arr.)
Prelude, Op. 34 (Reynolds, arr.)

Smith, Claude T. (1932–1987)

Joyance
Symphony No. 1 for Band
Emperata Overture
Incidental Suite
Anthem for Winds and Percussion
God of Our Fathers
(Many other contemporary works for band)

Smith, Robert W. (B. 1958)

Credo
Incantations
On Eagle's Wings
Inchon
(Many other contemporary works for band)

Sousa, John Philip (1854–1932)

Stars and Stripes Forever March
Washington Post March
El Capitan March
Semper Fidelis March
Hands Across the Sea March
Black Horse Troop March
King Cotton March
The Thunderer March
Fairest of the Fair March
(Many more marches for band)

Sparke, Philip (B. 1951)

Celebration
Dance Movements
Music for a Festival
(Many more contemporary works for band)

Stamp, Jack (B. 1954)

Fanfare for a New Era
Cloudsplitter
Prayer & Jubilation
(Many more contemporary works for band)

Strauss, Richard (1864–1949)

Serenade, Opus 7
Suite in B-flat, Opus 4
Sinfonia in F
Sonatina in E-flat
Allerseelen (Davis/Fennell arr.) (Medium)

Stravinsky, Igor (1882–1971)

Symphonies of Wind Instruments (1947
  version)

Circus Polka (Raksin, arr.) (Young People's Concert)
Concerto for Piano and Wind Instruments (rev. 1950)

Strouse, Charles (B. 1928)

Selections from "Annie" (Higgins, arr.) (Pops Concert)

Sullivan, Arthur (1842–1900)

Pineapple Poll—Ballet Suite (Duthoit, arr.)

Suppé, Franz Von (1819–1895)

Light Cavalry Overture (Fillmore, arr.)
Poet and Peasant Overture (Kent, arr.)
Morning, Noon and Night in Vienna Overture (Fillmore arr.)

Swearingen, James (B. 1947)

Novena, Rhapsody for Band (Easy)
Covington Square for Band (Easy)
Invicta for Band (Easy)
Exaltation for Band (Easy)
Flight of Valor (Easy)
(Many more easy contemporary works for band)

Tchaikovsky, Peter Ilyich (1840–1893)

Dance of the Jesters (trans. Ray Kramer)
Finale from Symphony No. 4 in F minor, Op. 36 (Safranek, arr.)
1812 Overture, Op. 49 (Williams, arr.)
(Many more works transcribed for band)

Texidor, Jaime (1884–1957)

Amparito Roca (Winter, arr.)

Thomson, Virgil (1896–1989)

A Solemn Music

Ticheli, Frank (B. 1958)

Amazing Grace
Cajun Folksongs II
Shenandoah (Medium)
Vesuvius
Postcards
Sun Dance
Loch Lomond (Medium)
An American Elegy
Cajun Folksongs (Medium)
Blue Shades
(Many more contemporary works for band)

Tschesnokov, Pavel (1887–1944)

Salvation is Created (Houseknecht, arr.)
Two Chorales

Tull, Fisher (1934–1994)

Toccata
Sketches on a Tudor Psalm
The Final Covenant
(Many more contemporary works for band)

Turina, Joaquín (1882–1949)

La Procession du Rocio, Op. 9 (A. Reed, arr.)
Five Miniatures (Krance, arr.)

Van Der Roost, Jan (B. 1956)

Suite Provençale
Canterbury Chorale
(Many more contemporary works for band)

Varèse, Edgard (1883–1965)

Octandre (Wen-chung, rev.) (Small instrumentation)

Vaughn Williams, Ralph (1872–1958)

English Folk Song Suite
Toccata Marziale

Rhosymedre, Prelude on a Welsh Hymn Tune
Flourish for Wind Band (Medium)
Sea Songs

Verdi, Giuseppe (1813–1901)

Prelude to Act I of "La Traviata"
  (Falcone, arr.)
La Forza del Destino (Lake, arr.)
Nabucco Overture (Caillet, arr.)

Vivaldi, Antonio (1678–1741)

Concerto in B-flat for Two Trumpets and
  Band (Originally in C)
Concerto for Piccolo and Band in C
(Many more concertos transcribed for band)

Wagner, Richard (1813–1883)

Elsa's Procession to the Cathedral
  (Caillet, arr.)
Invocation of Alberich (Cailliet, arr.)
Trauersinfonie (Leidzèn, arr.)
Awake (Houseknecht, arr.) (Medium)
Introduction to the Third Act of "Lohengrin"
  (Hindsley, arr.)
Entry of the Gods into Valhalla
  (Godfrey, arr.)
(Many more works transcribed for band)

Walton, William (1902–1983)

Crown Imperial, Coronation March
  (Duthoit, arr.)
Orb and Septre (Richardson, arr.)

Ward, Robert (B. 1917)

Jubilation Overture
Prairie Overture

Ward, Samuel A. (1847–1903)

America, The Beautiful (Dragon, arr.)
  (with optional chorus)

Washburn, Robert (B. 1928)

Symphony for Band

Weill, Kurt (1900–1950)

Three Penny Opera Suite (Various
  arrangements)

Weinberger, Joseph (1896–1967)

Polka and Fugue from Schwanda
  (Bainum, arr.)

Whear, Paul (B. 1925)

Stonehenge Symphony

Whitacre, Eric (b. 1970)

October
Ghost Train Triptych
Sleep
Cloudburst
(Many more contemporary works for band)

White, Donald (B. 1921)

Miniature Set for Band

Williams, Clifton (1923–1976)

Symphonic Suite
Symphonic Dance No. 3, "Fiesta"
Dramatic Essay for Trumpet and Band
Fanfare and Allegro
Festivals
The Sinfonians March
Caccia and Chorale
Variation Overture (Medium)
(Many more contemporary works for band)

Williams, John (B. 1932)

The Cowboys (Curnow, arr.)
Star Wars Trilogy (Hunsberger, arr.)
  (Pops Concert)
Olympic Fanfare (Curnow, arr.)

Willson, Meredith (1902–1984)

Selections from "The Music Man" (Lang, arr.)
The Music Man Selections (A. Reed, arr.)
  (Medium)
Seventy-six Trombones March (Lang, arr.)
(Many more musical selections transcribed
  for band)

Wood, Haydn (1882–1959)

Mannin Veen

Work, Julian (B. 1910)

Portraits from the Bible

Youtz, Gregory (B. 1956)

Scherzo for a Bitter Moon
Fireworks

Zdechlik, John (B. 1937)

Chorale and Shaker Dance
Celebrations
Psalm 46
Grand Rapids Suite
(Many more contemporary works for band)

Zwilich, Ellen Taaffe (B. 1939)

Ceremonies

For Additional Band Repertoire Sources

See Frank L. Battisti's *The Winds of Change: The Evolution of the Contemporary American Wind Band/Ensemble and its Conductor.* See *Band Music Guide* (The Instrumentalist) for additional band music. Much repertoire for the band can be discovered on the Internet if the specific composer or title is known or identified.

SCORE STUDY AND PROGRAM BUILDING REPERTOIRE FOR MISCELLANEOUS OR SMALL INSTRUMENTAL ENSEMBLES

I have not categorized this material under orchestra, chamber orchestra, string orchestra, concert band, or wind ensemble, but it can be conducted. This music material below could be used in the rehearsal process (lab) environment for conducting/rehearsing projects because of the smaller instrumentation involved. Most of this material would need individual practice before class begins because of the difficulty involved. Many of these works could be programmed in conjunction with band and orchestra concert performances. These works could act as a change of texture rehearsed outside of the full ensemble rehearsal process. Some of the smaller ensembles could also be used as recital repertoire.

Adler, Samuel (B. 1928)

Music for Eleven (2 flutes, oboe, clarinet,
  bass clarinet, bassoon, 4 percussion and
  timpani)
Preludium for Brass and Percussion
  (3 trumpets, 3 horns, 3 trombones,
  euphonium, tuba, and percussion)
Divertimento for Brass and Timpani
  (3 trumpets, 3 horns, 3 trombones,
  euphonium, tuba, and timpani)

Altenburg, Johann Ernst (1734–1801)

Concerto for Seven Trumpets and Timpani
  (King, arr.)

Anderson, Leroy (1908–1975)

Suite of Carols for Brass Choir (4 horns,
  4 trumpets, 4 trombones, euphonium,
  and tuba)

Suite of Carols for Woodwind Choir (piccolo, 2 flutes, 2 oboes, English horn, 3 clarinets, alto clarinet, bass clarinet, 2 bassoons, contrabassoon, and contrabass)

Arnell, Richard (1917–2009)

Ceremonial and Flourish for Brass
 (3 trumpets, 4 horns, and 3 trombones)

Baldwin, David (B. 1948)

Concerto for Seven Trumpets and Timpani

Barber, Samuel (1910–1981)

Capricorn Concerto, Op. 21 for Flute, Oboe, Trumpet, and Strings (2/2/1/1/1)
Mutations from Bach (4 horns, 3 trumpet, 3 trombones, tuba, and timpani)

Bassett, Leslie (B. 1923)

Nonet for Winds, Brass and Piano (flute, oboe, clarinet, bassoon, horn, trumpet, trombone, tuba, and piano)

Beethoven, Ludwig Van (1770–1827)

Octet for Winds, Op. 103 (2 oboes, 2 clarinets, 2 horns, and 2 bassoons)
Rondino in E-flat Major for Winds, (2 oboes, 2 clarinets, 2 horns, and 2 bassoons)

Berg, Alban (1885–1935)

Kammerkonzert for Piano, Violin and 13 Winds (piano solo, violin solo, piccolo, flute, oboe, English horn, E-flat clarinet, A clarinet, bass clarinet, bassoon, contrabassoon, trumpet, 2 horns, and trombone)

Berlioz, Hector (1803–1869)

Recitative and Prayer from "Symphonie Funèbre et Triomphal," Op. 15

(Woods, arr.) (4 horns, 4 trumpets, 3 trombones, baritone, and tuba)

Bernard, Emile (1845–1902)

Divertissement for Winds, Op. 36 (Double woodwind quintet)

Bernstein, Leonard (1918–1990)

Mass: Three Meditations (Solo cello plus unusual instrumentation)
Prelude, Fugue and Riffs (Solo clarinet, 5 trumpets, 4 trombones, 2 alto saxes, 2 tenor saxes, baritone sax, 2 percussion, piano, and solo double bass)

Bird, Arthur (1856–1923)

Serenade for 10 Winds, Op. 40 (Double woodwind quintet)

Boulez, Pierre (B. 1925)

Le marteau sans maître (The Hammer without a Master) (alto voice, alto flute, xylorimba, vibraphone, guitar, viola, and percussionist)

Britten, Benjamin (1913–1976)

The Sword in the Stone (flute, clarinet, bassoon, trumpet, trombone, percussion, and harp)

Casella, Alfredo (1883–1947)

Serenata (trumpet, clarinet, bassoon, violin, and cello)

Chávez, Carlos (1899–1978)

Toccata (6 percussion)

Chou Wen-Chung (B. 1923)

Soliloquy of a Bhiksuni (Solo trumpet, 4 horns, 3 trombones, tuba, timpani, and 2 percussion)

Clarke, Jeremiah (1674–1707)

The Prince of Denmark's March (Trumpet
  Voluntary) for Seven Trumpets and
  Timpani (Marlatt, arr.)

Colgrass, Michael (B. 1932)

Concerto for Timpani (3 trumpets,
  3 trombones, tuba, and timpani)

Copland, Aaron (1900–1990)

Fanfare for the Common Man (4 horns,
  3 trumpets, 3 trombones, tuba, timpani,
  and 2 percussion)
Appalachian Spring Ballet Suite (Original
  instrumentation for 13 instruments—flute,
  clarinet, bassoon, piano, and minimum
  strings: 2/2/2/2/1)
Ceremonial Fanfare (4 horns, 3 trumpet,
  3 trombones, and tuba)

Cowell, Henry (1897–1965)

Sinfonietta (Flute, oboe, clarinet, bassoon,
  horn, trumpet, trombone, 4 violins, viola,
  cello, and double bass)
Rondo (3 trumpets, 2 horns, and 3 trombones)

Crumb, George (B. 1929)

Ancient Voices of Children (Soprano, boy
  soprano, oboe, mandolin, harp, amplified
  piano, toy piano, and 3 percussion)
  (Avant-garde)
Unto the Hills (Song Cycle for voice,
  percussion quartet, and amplified piano)

Debussy, Claude (1862–1918)

Le martyre de Saint Sébastien: Two Fanfares
  (6 horns, 4 trumpets, 3 trombones, tuba,
  and timpani)

Donato, Anthony (1909–1990)

Nonet (3 trumpets, 3 trombones, and
  3 percussion)

Donizetti, Gaetano (1797–1848)

Sinfonia for Winds in G minor (Flute,
  2 oboes, 2 clarinets, 2 bassoons, and
  2 horns)

Druckman, Jacob (1928–1996)

Dark Upon the Harp (Mezzo-soprano soloist,
  horn, 2 trumpets, trombone, tuba, and
  2 percussion)

Dukas, Paul (1865–1935)

Fanfare from "La Peri" (3 C trumpets,
  4 horns, 3 trombones and tuba or the
  Delon Lyren arrangement for 4 B-flat
  trumpets, and 2 B-flat fluegelhorns)

Dvořák, Antonín (1841–1904)

Serenade, Op. 44 (2 oboes, 2 clarinets,
  2 bassoons, optional contrabassoon,
  3 horns, cello, and string bass)

Ellis, Merrill (1916–1981)

Mutations for Brass Quintet, Conductor,
  Film, Tape, and Slides (Multimedia and
  avant-garde)

Enesco, Georges (1881–1955)

Symphonic/Dixtour (2 flutes, oboe, English
  horn, 2 clarinets, 2 bassoons, and 2 horns)

Ewazen, Eric (b. 1954)

Fantasia (7 trumpets)
Sonoran Desert Harmonies (8 trumpets)
Symphony in Brass (4 trumpets, 4 horns,
  3 trombones, bass trombone, tuba, and
  2 percussion)
Grand Canyon Octet (8 horns or 8
  trombones)
Legend of the Sleeping Bear (8 horns)
A Western Fanfare for Brass Orchestra
  (4 trumpets, 6 horns, 3 trombones, bass
  trombone, tuba, and 2 percussion)

Fauré, Gabriel (1845–1924)

Nocturne, Op. 33 (Groview, trans.) (Flute,
  2 oboes, 2 clarinets, 2 bassoons, and
  2 horns)

Françaix, Jean (1912–1997)

Seven Dances from the Ballet "Sophie"
  (Double woodwind quintet)

Gabrieli, Giovanni (1554/7–1612)

Sacrae Symphoniae (Various selections for
  brass choirs)
Sonata Piano e Forte (Horn, 2 trumpets,
  4 trombones, baritone horn, and tuba)

Gillingham, David (B. 1947)

Serenade for 10 Winds and Percussion
  (Songs of the Night) (Flute-piccolo, oboe,
  clarinet, bassoon, 2 trumpets, 2 horns,
  trombone, tuba, and 3 percussion)

Goessens, Eugene (1893–1962)

Fantasy, Op. 40 (Flute, oboe, 2 clarinets,
  2 bassoons, 2 horns, and trumpet)

Gounod, Charles (1818–1893)

Petite symphonie, Op. 90 (Flute, 2 oboes,
  2 clarinets, 2 bassoons, and 2 horns)

Grainger, Percy (1882–1961)

Australian Up-Country Tune (Bainum,
  arr.) (2 trumpets, 2 horns, 2 trombones,
  euphonium, and tuba)

Handel, George Frederick (1685–1759)

Three Pieces (4 trumpets, horn, 4 trombones,
  tuba, and timpani)

Harbison, John (B. 1938)

Music for 18 Winds (2 flutes-piccolo,
  2 oboes, 2 clarinet, alto sax, 2 bassoons,
  4 horns, 2 trumpets, 2 trombones, and tuba)

Harris, Roy (1898–1979)

Concerto for Amplified Piano, String Bass,
  Brass and Percussion (Solo piano, string
  bass, 4 horns, 3 trumpets, 3 trombones,
  baritone, tuba, and percussion)

Hartley, Walter (B. 1927)

Sinfonia No. 3 for Brass (5 trumpets, 4 horns,
  3 trombones, euphonium, and tuba)
Canzona (8 trombones)

Haydn, Franz Joseph (1732–1809)

Octet in F (2 oboes, 2 clarinets, 2 horns, and
  2 bassoons)

Hindemith, Paul (1895–1963)

Wind Septet (Flute, oboe, clarinet, bass
  clarinet, bassoon, horn, and trumpet)
Octet (Clarinet, bassoon, horn, violin,
  2 violas, cello, and double bass)

Horvit, Michael (B. 1932)

Antique Suite (2 trumpets, 2 horns,
  2 trombones, euphonium, and tuba)

Hovhaness, Alan (1911–2000)

Khaldis: Concerto for Piano, Trumpets, and
  Percussion, Op. 91 (Piano, 4 trumpets, and
  percussion)
Tower Music, Op. 159 (Flute, oboe, clarinet,
  bassoon, 2 horns, 2 trumpets, trombone,
  and tuba)
Mountains and Rivers without End, Op. 225
  (Flute, oboe, clarinet, trumpet, trombone,
  harp, and 3 percussion)

Husa, Karel (B. 1921)

Divertimento for Brass Ensemble and
   Percussion (2 or 4 horns, 3 trumpets,
   3 trombones, tuba and 2 percussion)
Intradas and Interludes for Seven Trumpets
   and Percussion

Indy, Vincent D' (1851–1931)

Suite in the Olden Style, Op. 24 (Trumpet,
   2 flutes, 2 violins, viola, and cello)
Chanson et danses, Op. 50 (Flute, oboe,
   2 clarinets, 2 bassoons, and horn)

Ives, Charles (1874–1954)

Calcium Light Night for piccolo, clarinet,
   cornet, trombone, bass drum, and 2 pianos
   (4 players)
Tone Roads No. 1 (Flute, clarinet, bassoon,
   and strings: 2/2/2/1/1)
Tone Roads No. 3 (Flute, clarinet, trumpet,
   trombone, percussion, piano, and strings:
   2/2/2/1/1)
Over the Pavements, S.82 (Flute-piccolo,
   clarinet, bassoon, trumpet, 3 trombones,
   bass drum, cymbals, and piano)

Jacob, Gordon (1895–1984)

Interludes from "Music for a Festival"
   (4 trumpets, 3 trombones, and timpani)
Trombone Octet (8 trombones)
Canterbury Flourish for Eight Trumpets
Divertimento in E-flat Major (2 oboes,
   2 clarinets, 2 horns, and 2 bassoons)
Old Wine in New Bottles (Double woodwind
   quintet and 2 trumpets)

Janáček, Leoš (1854–1928)

Sokol Fanfare (9 trumpets, 2 bass trumpets
   or 2 trombones, 2 tenor tubas or 2
   baritones, horn or trombone, and timpani)
   (first movement of the *Sinfonietta*)

Jones, Samuel (B. 1935)

Festival Fanfare (5 horns, 3 trumpets,
   3 trombones, and tuba)

Krommer, Franz (1759–1831)

Octet-Partita, Op. 57 (2 oboes, 2 clarinets,
   2 bassoons, and 2 horns)

Kurka, Robert (1921–1957)

The Good Soldier Schweik Suite (2 flute-pic,
   2 oboes-E.H., 2 clarinet-bass clarinet, 2
   bassoons, double bass, 3 horn, 2 trumpets,
   trombone, timpani, and percussion)

Larsen, Libby (B. 1950)

North Star Fanfare (4 horns, 3 trumpets,
   3 trombones, and tuba)

Lo Presti, Ronald (1933–1985)

An Overture and a Finale (8 trumpets)

Martinů, Bohuslav (1890–1959)

La revue de cuisine (Clarinet, bassoon,
   trumpet, violin, cello, and piano)
Rondi (Trumpet, oboe, clarinet, bassoon,
   piano, and 2 violins)

Mcphee, Colin (1900–1964)

Concerto for Piano and Wind Octet (Piano
   solo, 2 flutes, oboe, clarinet. bassoon,
   horn, trumpet, and trombone)

Mendelssohn, Felix (1809–1847)

Octet in E-flat Major for Strings, Op. 20
   (4 violins, 2 violas, and 2 cellos)
Nocturne, Op. 61 (Hogwood, arr.) (Flute,
   2 oboes, English horn, 2 clarinets,
   2 bassoons, 2 horns, and trumpet)

Messiaen, Olivier (1908–1992)

Oiseaux exotiques (Exotic Birds) for solo
piano, winds, and percussion (Solo piano,
2 flutes-piccolo, oboe, 4 clarinets, bassoon,
2 horns, trumpet, and 7 percussion)

Milhaud, Darius (1892–1974)

La création du monde (2 flutes, oboe,
2 clarinets, bassoon, horn, 2 trumpets,
trombone, alto sax, timpani, percussion,
piano, 2 violins, cello, and double bass)
Concertino d'été (Viola solo, flute, oboe,
clarinet, bassoon, horn, trumpet, 2 cello,
and double bass)
Dixtour d'instruments à vent, Op. 75 (Little
Symphony No. 5) (2 flute-piccolo,
2 oboes-English horn, 2 clarinets-bass
clarinet, 2 bassoons, and 2 horns)

Mouret, Jean-Joseph (1682–1738)

Rondo from "Suites de symphonies"
(4 trumpets, 4 horns, 4 trombones, tuba,
and timpani)

Mozart, Wolfgang Amadeus (1756–1791)

Serenade No. 10 in B-flat Major, K.370a
(2 oboes, 2 clarinets, 3 bassoons +
contrabassoon [or double bass], 4 horns,
and 2 basset horns)
Serenade No. 11 in E-flat Major, K.375
(2 oboes, 2 clarinets, 2 bassoons, and
2 horns)
Serenade No. 12 in C minor, K.388 (2 oboes,
2 clarinets, 2 bassoons, and 2 horns)
Divertimento in E-flat Major, K.166
(4 oboes + 2 English horns, 2 clarinets,
2 bassoons, and 2 horns)
Divertimento in B-flat, K.186 (4 oboes +
2 English horns, 2 clarinets, 2 bassoons,
and 2 horns)
Divertimento in C Major, K.188 (2 flutes,
5 trumpets, and timpani)

Nelhybel, Vaclav (1919–1996)

Three Intradas (3 trumpets, 2 horns,
3 trombones, and tuba)
Chorale for Brass and Percussion
(3 trumpets, 2 horns, 3 trombones,
baritone, tuba, and 3 percussion)

Perle, George (1915–2009)

New Fanfares (4 horns, 3 trumpets, and
3 trombones)
Serenade No. 2 for Eleven Players (Flute,
oboe, clarinet, bassoon, trumpet, tenor sax,
percussion, piano, violin, viola, and cello)

Persichetti, Vincent (1915–1987)

Serenade No. 1, Op. 1 (Flute, oboe, clarinet,
bassoon, 2 horns, 2 trumpets, trombone,
and tuba)

Pierné, Gabriel (1863–1937)

Pastorale variée dans le style ancien, Op. 30
(Flute, oboe, clarinet, 2 bassoons, horn,
and trumpet)

Piston, Walter (1894–1976)

Divertimento for Nine Instruments (Flute,
oboe, clarinet, bassoon, and string quintet)

Poulenc, Francis (1899–1963)

Suite française (2 oboes, 2 bassoons,
2 trumpets, 3 trombones, percussion,
and harpsichord)

Purcell, Henry (1659–1695)

Funeral Music for Queen Mary, after
Purcell (Stucky, arr.) (2 flutes, 2 oboes,
2 clarinets, 2 bassoons, 4 horns,
3 trumpets, 3 trombones, tuba,
3 percussion, harp, piano, and celesta)

Symphony from Act IV from "The Fairy
Queen" (Olcott, arr.) (8 trumpets)
(2 Movements)

Raff, Joachim (1822–1882)

String Octet in C Major, Op. 176 (4 violins,
2 violas, and 2 cellos)
Sinfonietta for 10 Winds, Op. 188 (Double
woodwind quintet)

Rautavaara, Einojuhani (B. 1928)

Requiem in Our Time (4 trumpets, 4 horns,
3 trombones, baritone, tuba, timpani, and
percussion)
Octet for Winds (Flute, oboe, clarinet,
bassoon, English horn, 2 trumpets, and
trombone)

Ravel, Maurice (1875–1937)

Introduction and Allegro (Solo harp, flute,
clarinet, 2 violins, viola, and cello)

Read, Gardner (1913–2005)

Sound Piece, Op. 82 (4 trumpets, 4 horns,
3 trombones, baritone, 2 tubas, timpani,
and percussion)

Reger, Max (1873–1916)

Serenade in B-flat Major (2 flutes, 2 oboes,
2 clarinets, 2 bassoons, and 4 horns)

Reinecke, Carl (1824–1910)

Octet in E-flat Major, Op. 216 (Flute, oboe,
2 clarinets, 2 horns, and 2 bassoons)

Reynolds, Verne (B. 1926)

Theme and Variations for Brass Choir
and Timpani (3 trumpets, 3 horns,
3 trombones, baritone, tuba, and timpani)

Riegger, Wallingford (1885–1961)

Nonet for Brass (3 trumpets, 2 horns,
3 trombones, and tuba)

Rorem, Ned (B. 1923)

Sinfonia for 15 Wind Instruments and
Percussion (Piccolo, 2 flutes, 2 oboes,
English horn, 4 clarinets, 2 horns,
3 bassoons, and percussion)

Ruggles, Carl (1876–1968)

Angels (Muted 4 trumpets and 3 trombones)

Saint-Saëns, Camille (1835–1921)

Septet, Op. 6 (E-flat trumpet, piano,
2 violins, viola, cello, and double-bass)

Sallinen, Aulis (B. 1935)

Serenade (Woodwind quartet and brass
quartet)

Schmitt, Florent (1870–1958)

Lied and Scherzo, Op. 54 (Solo horn, piccolo,
flute, oboe, English horn, 2 clarinets,
2 bassoons, and horn)

Schoenberg, Arnold (1874–1951)

Pierrot lunaire, Op. 21 (Sprechstimme;
flute-piccolo, clarinet-bass clarinet, piano,
violin, viola, and cello)

Schubert, Franz (1797–1828)

Octet in F Major, D. 308 (2 oboes,
2 clarinets, 2 horns, and 2 bassoons)

Schuller, Gunther (B, 1925)

Symphony for Brass and Percussion, Op.
  16 (6 trumpets, 4 horns, 3 trombones,
  baritone, 2 tubas, timpani, and percussion)
Fanfare (12 trumpets)

Seeboth, Max (1904–1967)

Suite for Seven Brass Instruments
  (4 trumpets and 3 trombones)

Shulman, Alan (1915–2002)

Top Brass, Six Minutes for Twelve (4 horns,
  4 trumpets, 3 trombones, and tuba)

Sibelius, Jean (1865–1957)

Canzonetta, Op. 62a (Stravinsky, arr.)
  (2 clarinets and bass clarinet, 4 horns,
  harp, and double bass)

Spohr, Ludwig (1784–1859)

Septet in A minor, Op. 147 (Horn, flute,
  clarinet, bassoon, piano, violin, and cello)
Octet in E Major, Op. 32 (Clarinet, 2 horns,
  violin, 2 viola, cello, and double bass)
Nonet in F Major, Op. 31 (Flute, oboe,
  clarinet, bassoon, horn, violin, viola, cello,
  and double bass)

Strauss, Richard (1864–1949)

Serenade in E-flat for 13 Winds, Op. 7
  (2 flutes, 2 oboes, 2 clarinets, 2 bassoons,
  tuba, double bass, and 4 horns)
Suite in B-flat Major, Op. 4 (2 flutes,
  2 oboes, 2 clarinets, 2 bassoons,
  contrabassoon, and 4 horns)

Stravinsky, Igor (1882–1971)

Octet for Wind Instruments (Flute, clarinet,
  2 bassoons, 2 trumpets, and 2 trombones)

L'histoire du soldat (Clarinet, bassoon,
  cornet, trombone, percussion, violin, and
  double bass)
Ebony Concerto (Solo clarinet, 5 saxes,
  4 clarinets, bass clarinet, horn, 5 trumpets,
  3 trombones, guitar, bass, piano, drum set,
  and harp)
Eight Instrumental Miniatures for Fifteen
  Players (2 flutes, 2 oboes, 2 clarinets,
  2 bassoons, horn, 2 violins, 2 violas and
  2 cellos)
Ragtime for 11 Instruments (flute, clarinet,
  horn, cornet, trombone, cimbalom,
  percussion, 2 violins, viola, and double
  bass)

Tomasi, Henri Frédien (1901–1971)

Fanfares liturgiques (4 horns, 3 trumpets,
  3 trombones, tuba, timpani, and
  2 percussion)

Tower, Joan (B. 1938)

Second Fanfare for the Uncommon Woman
  (4 horns, 3 trumpets, 3 trombones, tuba,
  timpani, and 3 percussion)
Third Fanfare for the Uncommon Woman
  (2 brass quintets)
Black Topaz (flute, clarinet, trumpet,
  trombone, 2 percussion, and piano)

Tull, Fisher (1934–1994)

Segments (8 trumpets)
Variations on an Advent Theme (6 trumpets,
  4 horns, 4 trombones, 2 baritones, 2 tubas,
  percussion, and timpani)

Uber, David (1921–2007)

Nocturne for Trumpet Choir (9 trumpets)
Liturgy for Brass Choir and Timpani, Op.
  50 (4 trumpets, 2 horns, 3 trombones,
  baritone, tuba, and timpani)

Varèse, Edgard (1883–1965)

Ionisation (12 percussion and piano)
Intégrales (2 flutes-piccolos, oboe, 2 clarinet,
  E-flat clarinet, horn, 2 trumpets,
  3 trombones, and 4 percussion)
Octandre (Flute-piccolo, oboe, clarinet,
  E-flat clarinet, bassoon, horn, trumpet,
  trombone, and double bass)

Villa-Lobos, Heitor (1887–1959)

Bachianas Brasileiras No. 1 (8 cellos)
Bachianas Brasileiras No. 5 (Soprano and
  8 cellos)

Vinter, Gilbert (1909–1969)

Blazon (8 trumpets)

Walton, William (1902–1983)

Façade (with reciter, flute-piccolo, clarinet/
  bass clarinet, trumpet, alto saxophone,
  percussion, and 1 or 2 cellos) (39 minutes)

Façade 2 (with reciter, flute-piccolo, clarinet,
  trumpet, alto saxophone, percussion, and
  cello) (12 minutes)

Weill, Kurt (1900–1950)

Suite from "Threepenny Opera" (Keyboards,
  2 clarinets, 2 trumpets, trombone,
  percussion, banjo, and guitar)
Concerto for Violin and Wind Instruments
  (Violin, 2 flutes/piccolo, oboe, 2 clarinets,
  2 bassoons, 2 horns, trumpet, timpani,
  percussion, and double basses)

Weinberger, Jaromir (1896–1967)

Concerto for Timpani with Four Trumpets
  and Four Trombones (4th part on tuba
  also)

Zwilich, Ellen Taafee (b. 1939)

Concerto (Solo trumpet, flute, 8 clarinets,
  percussion, double bass, and piano)

For Additional Smaller Ensemble Repertoire Sources

See Paul G. Anderson, "Brass Ensemble Music Guide" (*The Instrumentalist*)
See Lyle Merriman and Himie Voxman, "Woodwind Ensemble Music Guide" (*The
  Instrumentalist*)
See George N. Heller, *Ensemble Music for Winds and Percussion Instruments: A Catalog*
See David Daniels, *Orchestral Music: A Handbook* (Fourth Edition)
See William Scott, *A Conductor's Repertoire of Chamber Music Compositions for Nine to
  Fifteen Solo Instruments*

SCORE STUDY AND PROGRAM BUILDING REPERTOIRE
FOR MUSICAL THEATER PRODUCTIONS (PIT ORCHESTRA)

Although the young conductor may begin his or her conducting career in front of a band, orchestra, or other instrumental ensemble, at some point it may be desirable or necessary to conduct a pit orchestra (or a smaller ensemble) accompanying a musical production, opera (operetta), or ballet (or modern dance group).

Adler, Richard, and Jerry Ross

Damn Yankees (1955)
Pajama Game (1954)

Andersson, Benny, and Bjorn Ulvaeus

Mamma Mia! (1999)

Bacharach, Burt

Promises, Promises (1968)

Bart, Lionel

Oliver! (1963)

Berlin, Irving

Annie Get Your Gun (1946)

Bernstein, Leonard

West Side Story (1957)
Candide (1956)
Wonderful Town (1953)
On the Town (1944)

Bock, Jerry

Fiddler on the Roof (1964)

Brooks, Mel

The Producers (2001)

Cohan, George M.

George M! (1968)

Colman, Cy

Sweet Charity (1965)

Flaherty, Stephen

Seussical, the Musical (2000)
Ragtime (1998)

Gershwin, George

Porgy and Bess (1935)
Crazy for You (1991) [Originally "Girl
   Crazy" (1930)]

Gesner, Clark

You're a Good Man, Charlie Brown (1967)

Goggin, Dan

Nunsense (1985)

Grieg, Edvard

Song of Norway (1944)

Hamlisch, Marvin

A Chorus Line (1975)

Hart, Larry

Pal Joey (1940)
Boys from Syracuse (1938)

Herman, Jerry

Mame (1966)
Hello, Dolly! (1964)

Holmes, Rupert

The Mystery of Edwin Drood (1987)

Jacobs, Jim, and Warren Casey

Grease (1972)

John, Elton

The Lion King (1997)

Kander, John

Cabaret (1966)
Chicago (1975)

Kern, Jerome

Show Boat (1927)
Roberta (1933)

Lane, Burton

Finian's Rainbow (1947)

Larson, Jonathan

Rent (1996)

Leigh, Mitch

Man of La Mancha (1965)

Leosser, Frank

Guys and Dolls (1950)
How to Succeed in Business without Really
 Trying (1961)
The Most Happy Fella (1956)

Loewe, Frederick

Brigadoon (1947)
Camelot (1960)
My Fair Lady (1956)
Paint Your Wagon (1951)
Gigi (1973)

MacDermot, Galt

Hair (1968)
Two Gentlemen of Verona (1971)

Menken, Alan

Beauty and the Beast (1994)

Merrill, Bob

Carnival (1961)

Miller, Roger

Big River (1985)

Porter, Cole

Anything Goes (1934)
Can-Can (1953)
Kiss Me, Kate (1948)

Rodgers, Richard

Carousel (1945)
Cinderella (1957)
Oklahoma! (1943)
South Pacific (1949)
The King and I (1951)
The Sound of Music (1959)

Rodgers, Mary

Once Upon a Mattress (1959)

Romberg, Sigmund

The Desert Song (1926)
The Student Prince in Heidelberg (1924)

Schmidt, Harvey

110 in the Shade (1963)
I Do! I Do! (1966)
The Fantasticks (1960)

Schonberg, Claude-Michel

Les Misérables (1986)
Miss Saigon (1989)

Schwartz, Stephen

Godspell (1971)
Pippin (1972)
Working (1978)
Wicked (2003)

Shaiman, Marc

Hairspray (2002)

Sondheim, Stephen

A Funny Thing Happened on the Way to the
 Forum (1962)
A Little Night Music (1973)
Company (1970)
Into the Woods (1987)
Sweeney Todd, The Demon Barber of Fleet
 Street (1979)

Strouse, Charles

Bye Bye Birdie (1960)
Applause (1970)
Annie (1977)

Styne, Jule

Funny Girl (1964)
Gypsy (1959)
Sugar (1972)
Bells are Ringing (1956)

Tesori, Jeanine

Thoroughly Modern Millie (2002)

Warren, Harry

Forty-Second Street (1980)

Webber, Andrew Lloyd

Jesus Christ Superstar (1971)
Cats (1982)
Phantom of the Opera (1988)
Evita (1979)
Joseph and the Amazing Technicolor
    Dreamcoat (1969)
Sunset Boulevard (1993)

Weill, Kurt

The Three-penny Opera (1959)
Berlin to Broadway (1972)

Wildhorn, Frank

Jekyll and Hyde (1990)

Willson, Meredith

The Music Man (1950)
The Unsinkable Molly Brown (1960)

Wright, Robert, and George Forrest

Kismet (1953)

Yeston, Maury

Phantom (1991)

Youmans, Vincent

No, No, Nanette (1925)

SCORE STUDY AND PROGRAM BUILDING REPERTOIRE FOR OPERA AND OPERETTA PRODUCTIONS (OPERA ORCHESTRA)

Again, this is not a comprehensive listing, but rather a representative one. This listing can be used to search for possible opera or operetta programming and for possible ideas for concert opera productions with orchestra or for opera workshop presentations.

Argento, Dominick

Postcard from Morocco (1971)

Barber, Samuel

Vanessa (1957)

Beethoven, Ludwig Van

Fidelio, Op. 72 (1805)
Bellini, Vincenzo
Norma (1813)

Bizet, Georges

Carmen (1875)

Britten, Benjamin

Albert Herring (1947)
The Turn of the Screw (1954)
Peter Grimes (1945)

Copland, Aaron

The Second Hurricane (1937)
The Tender Land (1954)

Donizetti, Gaetano

The Daughter of the Regiment (1840)
Lucia di Lammermoor (1835)
The Elixir of Love (1832)
Don Pasquale (1810)

Gershwin, George

Porgy and Bess (1935)

Glass, Philip

Einstein on the Beach (1976)
The Juniper Tree (1986)

Gounod, Charles

Faust (1869)

Herbert, Victor

Babes in Toyland (1903)
Naughty Marietta (1910)
The Fortune Teller (1898)

Humperdinck, Engelbert

Hansel and Gretel (1893)

Lehar, Franz

The Merry Widow (1907)

Leoncavallo, Ruggero

I Pagliacci (1892)

Mascagni, Pietro

Cavalleria Rusticana (1890)

Massenet, Jules

Manon (1884)
Thaïs (1894)

Menotti, Gian Carlo

Amahl and the Night Visitors (1951)
The Consul (1950)
Help, Help, The Globolinks! (1968)
The Medium (1946)

Mozart, Wolfgang Amadeus

Don Giovanni (1787)
The Magic Flute (1791)
The Marriage of Figaro (1786)
Cosi Fan Tutte (1790)

Offenbach, Jacques

La Perichole (1868)
Orpheus in the Underworld (1858)
The Tales of Hoffman (1881)

Prokofiev, Sergei

The Love for Three Oranges (1921)

Puccini, Giacomo

Turandot (1926)
La Bohème (1896)
Madame Butterfly (1904)
Tosca (1900)
Gianni Schicchi (1918)

Purcell, Henry

Dido and Aeneas (1689)
The Fairy Queen (1692)

Rossini, Gioacchino

Cinderella (1817)
The Barber of Seville (1816)
The Italian Girl in Algiers (1813)

Smetana, Bedřich

The Bartered Bride (1866, rev. 1870)

Strauss, Johann

Die Fledermaus (1874)

Strauss, Richard

Elektra (1909)
Der Rosenkavalier (1911)
Salome (1905)

Sullivan, Arthur

H.M.S. Pinafore (1878)
The Mikado (1885)
The Pirates of Penzance (1879, revised 1981)
Trial by Jury (1875)

Vaughan Williams, Ralph

Riders to the Sea (1932)

Verdi, Giuseppe

La Traviata (1853)
Rigoletto (1851)
Aida (1871)
La Forza del Destino (1862)
Il Trovatore (1853)

Wagner, Richard

Lohengrin (1850)
Die Meistersinger von Nurnberg (1868)
Parsifal (1882)
Tannhäuser (1845)
Tristan und Isolde (1865)

Weill, Kurt

Down in the Valley (1948)

Weinberger, Jaromir

Schwanda, the Bagpiper (1927)

SCORE STUDY REPERTOIRE AND PROGRAM BUILDING FOR BALLET AND MODERN DANCE MUSIC (PIT ORCHESTRA)

The conductor may find it desirable (or necessary) to conduct a ballet orchestra or an instrumental ensemble for a ballet or modern dance group. The ballet repertoire is quite standard. However, the repertoire for modern dance groups is particularly varied and open, as many concert selections (or movements from concert selections) and dance selections can and are used for this repertoire. Therefore, the listing under this category would be unlimited for the repertoire in modern dance presentations.

Adams, John

The Chairman Dances (1985)
Grand Pianola Music (1982)

Antheil, George

Ballet Mecanique (1925)

Barber, Samuel

Medea, Op. 23 (1946)
Souvenirs, Op. 28 (1952)

Berlioz, Hector

The Troyens Ballet (1863)

Bernstein, Leonard

Fancy Free Ballet (1944)
The Age of Anxiety (1949)

Copland, Aaron

Appalachian Spring Ballet (1944)
Rodeo Ballet (1942)

Billy the Kid Ballet (1938)
El Salón México Ballet (1943)

Debussy, Claude

The Afternoon of a Faun (1894)

Delibes, Leo

Sylvia Ballet (1876)
Coppelia Ballet (1870)

Falla, Manuel De

El Amor Brujo Ballet (1915)
The Three-Cornered Hat Ballet (1916)

Glazunov, Alexander

Raymonda Ballet (1898)

Glière, Reinhold

The Red Poppy Ballet (1927)

Gould, Morton

Fall River Legend Ballet (1947)
Tap Dance Concerto (1952)

Gounod, Charles

Faust Ballet (1859)

Holst, Gustav

The Perfect Fool Ballet (1920–22)

Khachaturian, Aram

Gayneh Ballet (1942)
Spartacus Ballet (1956)

Lully, Jean Baptiste

Le Triomphe de L'amour (1681)

Massenet, Jules

Le Cid Ballet (1885)
Manon Ballet ((1884)

Menotti, Gian Carlo

Sebastian Ballet (1944)

Piston, Walter

The Incredible Flutist Ballet (1938)

Prokofiev, Sergei

Cinderella Ballet (1945)
Romeo and Juliet Ballet (1938)

Rimsky-Korsakov, Nicolai

The Snow Maiden Ballet (1882)

Rossini, Gioacchino—Respighi

La Boutique Fantasque (1919)

Schubert, Franz

Incidental Music to Rosamunde (1823)

Schuman, William

Judith (1949)
Undertow (1945)

Sessions, Roger

The Black Maskers Ballet (1923)

Shostakovich, Dmitri

The Age of Gold Ballet (1930)
The Bolt Ballet (1931)

Stravinsky, Igor

Firebird Ballet (1910)
Petroushka Ballet (1911)
Rite of Spring Ballet (1913)
The Fairy's Kiss (1928)
Pulcinella Ballet (1920)
Agon (1957)

Tchaikovsky, Peter Ilyich

Swan Lake Ballet (1877)
Sleeping Beauty Ballet (1890)
Nutcracker Ballet (1892)

Walton, William

The Quest Ballet (1943)

MODERN DANCE REPERTOIRE

As mentioned above, this repertoire could encompass almost any piece that an artistic director, choreographer, or dance teacher might choose to use for modern dance music. A representative listing of this material would be of little value for the advanced conductor because of this diversity in the present-day modern dance music repertoire.

Appendix B

An Outline of Conducting and Rehearsing Problems

This checklist and review of the conducting and rehearsing problems found within the rehearsal process are a summary of chapters 4, 8, 9, 10, 11, 12, 13, 14, 15, and 16 in this book. The idea behind this summary is to present the information in a condensed form so that the maturing conductor can periodically review this material as he or she continues to gain competency as a conductor. With all of the information and the conducting/rehearsing skills involved, it becomes quite easy to forget about or overlook some of these important elements. The conducting teacher should take the conducting students through these conducting and rehearsing problems (below) in class before beginning these student conducting/rehearsing projects.

I. Conducting Problems (refer to chapter 4)
    A. Conducting stance and position
    B. Conducting clarity (with the patterns and expressive gestures)
    C. Conducting flow and communication with the ensemble
    D. Basic conducting elements (and the subsequent problems)
        1. Conducting the various patterns and the subdivisions of these patterns
        2. Conducting meters (simple, compound, changing, and asymmetrical)
        3. Executing preparatory beats properly
        4. Indicating releases clearly
        5. Handling fermatas
        6. Cueing as needed
        7. Indicating dynamic levels, nuances, and ensemble balance
        8. Showing styles, accents, phrasing, and musical expression
        9. Using the left hand effectively
       10. The score study necessary in order to implement this conducting technique
    E. Recurring conducting problems
        1. Tempo selection
        2. Differentiating the counts in the conducting patterns
        3. Unclear and/or "fussy" conducting patterns and gestures
        4. Precision problems on the initial attacks

5. Precision problems on tempo changes
6. Proper conducting of the phrase and the musical line
7. Poor musical interpretation (score study is needed here)
8. Lack of style indications (and contrast) in the conducting technique
9. Lack of dynamic contrast in the conducting technique
10. Ignoring musical expression (such as accents and other stylistic markings) in the conducting technique
11. Not showing musicality with the conducting technique
12. Lack of aggressive and authoritative conducting technique
13. Not keeping the right hand turned over to maintain the plane
14. Over-conducting
15. Using small gestures too much, causing a lack of clarity
16. Not keeping patterns or gestures centered or focused
17. Keeping the head and eyes in the score too much
18. Unclear preparatory beats and releases
19. Not showing the compound meter beat subdivision clearly
20. Not communicating either good precision or musicality
21. Not handling fermatas properly and musically
22. Poor execution in subdividing, merging, and melding the patterns
23. Too little or too much cueing
24. Ineffective use of the left hand (and meaningless gestures)
25. Not being creative with the conducting patterns and gestures (such as the dynamics indications, gestures of syncopation, and the passive/active gestures)

II. Rehearsing Problems
   A. Intonation and Tuning (refer to chapter 8)
     1. Tuning (to establish the pitch level)
     2. Periodic tuning (throughout the rehearsal process)
     3. Tuning from the bass
     4. Listening carefully in order to adjust the pitch
     5. Knowing transpositions involved in ensemble tuning
     6. Encouraging good tone production to help the intonation accuracy
     7. Physically adjusting the pitch on the various instruments
     8. Balance and blend factors in tuning
     9. Tone control, extreme registers, and extreme dynamic levels affecting the intonation
    10. "Bad notes" on the various instruments
    11. Solving the transparencies in terms of pitch
    12. Resonance and centering pitches factors in securing good intonation
   B. Rhythm and Rhythm patterns (refer to chapter 9)
     1. Simple and compound meter rhythmic problems
     2. Exact and precise rhythms and rhythm patterns
     3. The subdivisions and ratios in rhythms and rhythm patterns
     4. Tempo beats, meter beats, and melodic rhythm patterns
     5. Watching the conductor for the pulse and flow
     6. Ignoring the accents as indicated in the music (or as implied)
     7. Changing and asymmetrical meters
     8. Anacrusis, tied notes, and rests can be rhythmic problems

C. Ensemble Sonority (refer to chapter 10)
   1. Poor ensemble tone production
   2. Tone control problems
   3. Tone production concepts
   4. Balance problems
   5. Blend problems
   6. Tone projection for the structural balance and the proper sonority
   7. Tone color contrast
   8. Texture contrast
   9. Use of vibrato to enhance ensemble sonority
   10. Individual, section, and family (or choir) sonority concerns
D. Articulation and Bowing (refer to chapter 11)
   1. Articulation and style are closely connected
   2. Poor observation of articulation terms and markings
   3. Poor performance of percussion playing techniques
   4. Slurring and tonguing as indicated in the music (winds)
   5. Poor performance of the various indicated articulations
   6. Negotiating fast articulated passages
   7. Bow use (placement, pressure and speed)
   8. Lack of unison bowing in the string sections
   9. Incorrect and/or inconsistent bowing styles
   10. Poor production of string techniques and special effects
E. Tempo and Ensemble Precision (refer to chapter 12)
   1. Tempo and ensemble precision are closely related
   2. Lack of the precise tempo indicated by the conductor
   3. Tempo that is too fast or too slow for the ensemble prowess
   4. Tempo rigidity, flexibility, or instability problems
   5. Rhythm patterns played inaccurately, causing precision problems
   6. Rhythmic instability within the ensemble (watch the conductor)
   7. Improper selection of the number of beats in a measure
   8. Poor ensemble precision (especially on initial attacks)
   9. Lack of clarity due to poor ensemble precision
   10. Poor communication between the conductor and ensemble
   11. Late or early entrances are disruptive in the musical line
   12. Lack of cueing the entrances to improve ensemble precision
F. Phrasing and the Musical Line (refer to chapter 13)
   1. General lack of attention to the phrasing
   2. Not taking the breath at end of the phrase (winds)
   3. Phrase endings not given proper rhythmic value
   4. Staggered breathing or bowing when needed
   5. Planned bowing in the string sections for better phrasing
   6. Rehearse in phrases to achieve accuracy and continuity
   7. Lack of attention to the dynamics and the climax of the phrase
   8. The arch or phrase contour is ignored
   9. Lack of forward motion in the musical line
   10. The development of the sustained musical line in the ensemble not pursued diligently enough

G. Style and Musical Interpretation (refer to chapter 14)
1. Lack of attention to the correct style
2. Musical period characteristics are ignored
3. The performance practices of the various musical periods are ignored
4. Poor realization and/or modification of the four basic styles
5. Stylistic terms and markings are not given much attention
6. Not capturing the essence and spirit of the music
7. Little attention given to the details of the musical interpretation
8. Conductor's musical conception not well communicated to the ensemble in the rehearsal process
9. The composer's intentions not well communicated to the ensemble in the rehearsal process
10. Lack of emotions (or feelings) in the music
H. Dynamics, Nuances, and Musical Expression (refer to chapter 15)
1. Lack of dynamic contrast in the ensemble performance
2. Subtle nuances ignored or nonexistent
3. Musical expression not a top priority for the ensemble
4. Rubato and nuances not necessarily a part of the ensemble musical expression
5. Dynamics are uncontrolled, causing poor balance and blend
6. The employment of vibrato not well conceived by the conductor or produced within the ensemble
7. General lack of emotional involvement with the music
8. Ignoring dynamic terms and markings
9. Not watching or responding to the conductor with the dynamics, nuances, or musical expression
10. Crescendo and diminuendo not executed gradually and gauged carefully by the conductor
11. Sudden dynamics not done with an element of "surprise"—not anticipated, but carefully prepared by the conductor
12. Musical sensitivity and dynamic relativity not hand in hand with achieving an "artistic" performance
I. Conducting and Rehearsing Contemporary Music (refer to chapter 16)
1. Conducting changing and asymmetrical meter
2. Sufficient score study (for contemporary music)
3. Knowledge of contemporary music special effects notation
4. Complex rhythms and rhythm patterns
5. Needed special instruments and equipment availability
6. Extreme technical demands made upon the players
7. Fragmentation, minimalism, and other compositional styles
8. Performance techniques and special effects not properly produced
9. Use of new and unusual instrumental techniques
10. Multimedia presentations (coordination of the elements)
11. Composer instructions followed
12. Explaining conducting patterns and gestures when needed
13. Special attention to exposed passages in many cases

14. Percussion parts scrutinized by the conductor (contemporary composers utilize these instruments frequently)
15. Contemporary music requiring more "settling time" as opposed to the more traditional music rehearsing
16. Giving players more freedom in aleatory music, because of the improvisatory nature of this compositional style
17. Attention to the musical phrasing and playing with good intonation important factors in the conducting and rehearsing of contemporary music

Appendix C

An Outline of Technical Problems Encountered in the Ensemble Rehearsal Process

This outline is not all-inclusive, but does provide a checklist and review for the conductor of the many technical problems encountered in the instrumental music ensemble rehearsal process. This outline is expected to help the maturing conductor to realize the numerous problems that confront the conductor in the rehearsal process. With serious study and extensive experience, the conductor should add to this list of technical problems and be able to offer solutions to problems encountered in the rehearsal process. The conducting teacher should take the conducting students through these technical problems and discuss or demonstrate them during the class period.

I. Technical problems encountered in the rehearsal process
    A. Reading prowess (refer to chapter 3: Essential No. 8)
        1. Keys and key signatures
        2. Rhythm and meter problems
        3. Feeling the pulse and subdividing the beat properly
        4. Too-fast tempo for the present technique or reading prowess of the ensemble
        5. Articulation and bowing problems
        6. Accidentals, clefs, and transpositions (for orchestra)
        7. Reading in note groups and musical patterns for better accuracy and fluency
        8. Range problems (especially on the brass instruments)
        9. Miscalculation of partials with the brass instruments
      10. Large interval flexibility needed (especially with brass instruments)
    B. Technical facility and accuracy on the various instruments
        1. Correct practice habits (how to practice)
        2. Practicing slowly and rhythmically at first
        3. Developing reading accuracy, facility, and fluency (gradually)
        4. Developing a precise and steady beat (metronome/tapping foot)
        5. Practicing scales, arpeggios, and technical etudes
        6. Correcting technical errors within the context of the phrase
        7. Fingers/tongue coordination (for winds) or bow/left-hand fingers coordination (for strings) by practicing slowly and rhythmically

    8. Deciding if it is a rhythmic problem or a technical problem

    9. Reading the next note group while playing the previous note group to avoid "surprises"

C. Note (and rest) accuracy

    1. Key signatures and accidentals

    2. Correct partials and large intervals on the brass instruments

    3. Rhythmic accuracy with all instruments

    4. Centering pitches for better note accuracy and intonation

    5. Fingers and tongue coordination with wind instruments

    6. Bow and left-hand fingers coordination with string instruments

    7. Developing the correct playing techniques on the various percussion instruments

    8. Rests counted accurately (watch the conductor)

    9. Accuracy in the musical performance

    10. Good tone control on the instruments essential

D. Intonation accuracy (refer to chapter 8)

    1. Establishing the pitch level carefully

    2. Periodic tuning during the rehearsal process

    3. Isolating passages for intonation improvement

    4. Careful listening and listening for "beats"

    5. Tuning from the bass

    6. Vibrato use, dynamics, etc.

    7. Awareness of the "bad notes" on the particular instrument

    8. Emphasizing good tone production to improve intonation

    9. Muting with brass, causing some intonation problems

    10. Proper positioning of valve slides on the brass instruments

E. Rhythmic accuracy (refer to chapter 9)

    1. Feeling the pulse (the heartbeat of music)

    2. Tapping the foot in individual practice

    3. Metronome use in individual practice

    4. Subdividing the beat correctly and accurately

    5. Practicing slowly for rhythmic accuracy

    6. Watching the conductor (for the pulse)

    7. Tempo beats, meter beats, and melodic rhythm patterns important components of this rhythmic accuracy

F. Ensemble sonority (refer to chapter 10)

    1. General ensemble sonority (conductor's conception)

    2. Tone quality production

    3. Tone control problems

    4. Balance and blend problems

    5. Tone color and texture contrast

    6. Dynamics, nuances, and musical expression

G. Articulation and bowing (refer to chapter 11)

    1. Playing correct articulation as shown in the music

    2. Observing and performing a variety of articulations

    3. Uniformity of articulation among the wind players

    4. Correct tongue placement for the proper articulation

5. Encouraging the development of double and triple tonguing for the brass instruments and flute/piccolo
6. Selection of sticks and mallets on the various percussion instruments
7. Proper techniques on the various percussion instruments
8. Bowing uniformity in the string sections
9. Bowing styles not properly executed in the string sections

H. Teaching strategies (for solutions to the above problems)
1. Teaching strategies planned before the rehearsal process
2. Responding properly to technical problems that may occur during the rehearsal process
3. With younger ensembles, employing pedagogical solutions
4. Varying the teaching strategies depending on the reason for the problem
5. Teaching strategies to refine the various priorities with the ensemble

II. Specific technical problems within the various sections and choirs of the instrumental music ensemble (an overview of these problems)

A. Woodwinds
1. Correct embouchure for the various woodwind instruments
2. Correct, alternate, and trill fingerings
3. Correct tongue placement
4. Multiple tonguing on flute and piccolo
5. Reed quality and adjustments (except flute and piccolo)
6. Air speed and volume control
7. Vibrato (with the exception of the clarinet family)

B. Brasses
1. Correct embouchure for the various brass instruments
2. Accuracy in partials (overtones) production
3. Proper tongue placement and oral cavity
4. Air speed and volume control
5. Adequate range and endurance
6. Flexibility (intervals, lip slurs, and excessive mouthpiece pressure)
7. Vibrato (except on French horn and tuba)
8. Lip slurring with tongue position change (tah-oo-ee)
9. Large dynamic range (must be controlled and balanced)

C. Percussion
1. Choice of sticks, mallets, hammers, etc.
2. Organization and placement of instruments and equipment
3. Striking position on the instrument
4. Various rudiments and playing techniques involved
5. Dampening of the sound
6. Use of multiple mallets and the playing grip on mallet instruments
7. Maintenance of instruments and equipment
8. Large dynamic range (must be controlled and balanced)

D. Strings
1. Correct holding of the instrument and playing position
2. Uniformity of the bowing stroke
3. Correct bow use (pressure, speed, and placement)

    4. Careful tuning of the A string (and comparison with the other open strings)

    5. Fingerings, string crossings, position shifts, and harmonics

    6. Correct and consistent bowings and bowing styles

III. Technical problems relating to each individual instrument

  A. Flute (and piccolo)

    1. Thin tone quality (embouchure formation and air)

    2. Intonation (especially in the upper and lower registers)

    3. Finger-tongue coordination (slow practice needed here)

    4. Correct, alternate, and trill fingerings

    5. Vibrato and tone projection

    6. Instrument adjustment for intonation improvement

    7. Multiple tonguing

  B. Oboe (and English horn)

    1. Reed quality and response (adjustments)

    2. Centering the tone and breath pressure control

    3. Tongue placement for proper articulation

    4. Embouchure formation and control

    5. Vibrato and tone projection

    6. Intonation improvement by centering the tone

    7. Correct, alternate, and trill fingerings

    8. Instrument and reed adjustments for intonation improvement

    9. Harmonics useful on the oboe

    10. English horn parts usually very soloistic in nature

  C. Clarinets (sopranino, soprano, alto, bass, contralto, and contrabass)

    1. Reed quality and response (adjustments)

    2. Mouthpiece and reed selection

    3. Tongue placement for the proper articulation

    4. Throat-register intonation and tone quality

    5. Embouchure formation and control

    6. Barrel length or rings for intonation improvement

    7. Correct, alternate, and trill fingerings

    8. Tongue release (when needed)

    9. Transpositions (for A and C clarinet parts in orchestra)

    10. Reading in treble and bass clef on bass clarinet

    11. Bass clarinet, contralto clarinet, and contrabass clarinet crucial in establishing a good pitch level for the ensemble

  D. Bassoon (and contrabassoon)

    1. Reed quality and response (scrape and wire adjustment)

    2. Tongue placement for the proper articulation

    3. Embouchure formation and control

    4. Reading in bass and tenor clef

    5. Vibrato and tone projection

    6. Correct, alternate, and trill fingerings

    7. Three bocal lengths

    8. Instrument and reed adjustments for intonation improvement

    9. Bassoon and contrabassoon crucial in establishing a good pitch level for the ensemble

E. Saxophones (soprano, alto, tenor, baritone, and bass)
    1. Reed quality and response
    2. Mouthpiece and reed selection
    3. Embouchure formation and control
    4. Tongue placement for the proper articulation (low register)
    5. Vibrato and tone projection
    6. Correct, alternate, or trill fingerings
    7. Intonation adjustments
    8. Large dynamic range (must be controlled and balanced)
    9. Poor intonation (due to incorrect lip tension)
    10. Tenor, baritone, and bass saxophones crucial in establishing a good pitch level for the band ensemble
F. French horn (single, double, and descant)
    1. Correct playing/holding position and mouthpiece placement (2/3 upper lip)
    2. Correct right hand position in the bell
    3. Tongue placement for the proper articulation
    4. Proper use of the double horn and the tuning of both sides
    5. Pitch placement (workable) slides and partial accuracy
    6. Stopped horn: distant/brassy (on the F side; read half-step down)
    7. Bass clef reading (octave) and many transpositions (for orchestra)
    8. Large dynamic range (must be controlled and balanced)
    9. Multiple tonguing
    10. Lip slurring with tongue position change (tah-oo-ee)
    11. Left-hand fingers on the flat tip of the valves
    12. Replacing valve strings periodically and other such maintenance
    13. Straight and transposing mutes
G. Trumpet (cornet and flugelhorn)
    1. Correct partials and technical accuracy
    2. Embouchure formation and control (1/2 upper lip)
    3. Tongue placement for the proper articulation
    4. High register and endurance (even mouthpiece pressure)
    5. Many transpositions (for orchestra)
    6. Playing the various trumpets (B-flat trumpet, C trumpet, B-flat or A piccolo trumpets, E-flat/D trumpets, cornet, and flugelhorn)
    7. Vibrato (hand or lip)
    8. Intonation adjustment with (workable) slides, embouchure, and air
    9. Large dynamic range (must be controlled and balanced)
    10. Multiple tonguing
    11. Lip-slurring with tongue position change (tah-oo-ee)
    12. Mutes (straight, cup, Harmon and many others)
H. Trombone (alto, tenor, and bass)
    1. Slide position accuracy and alternate positions
    2. Legato tonguing technique (for slurring)
    3. Mouthpiece placement on embouchure (2/3 upper lip)
    4. F-attachment (or with other attachments) slide adjustments
    5. Vibrato (jaw or slide)

6. Tenor and alto clef reading (for orchestra and solo performance)
7. Large dynamic range (must be controlled and balanced)
8. Glissandi (or smear) proper execution
9. Multiple tonguing
10. Lip-slurring with tongue position change (tah-oo-ee)
11. Bass trombone performance (extreme low register fostered)
12. Pedal tones
13. Mutes (straight, cup, Harmon, and many others)
14. Tenor trombone and bass trombone crucial in establishing a good pitch level for the ensemble

I. Euphonium/baritone
1. Intonation accuracy (compensating mechanism)
2. Use of fourth valve for intonation improvement
3. Both bass and treble clef reading
4. Tone control in the low register
5. Mouthpiece placement on embouchure (2/3 upper lip)
6. Vibrato (jaw)
7. Tone production (requires a larger amount of air)
8. Large dynamic range (must be controlled and balanced)
9. Multiple tonguing
10. Lip-slurring with tongue position change (tah-oo-ee)
11. Euphonium/baritone crucial in establishing a good pitch level for the band ensemble

J. Tuba (Sousaphone)
1. Centering the tone
2. Tone control in the low register
3. Clean articulation
4. Flexibility and technical facility development
5. Use of the fourth valve or a tuning slide for better intonation
6. Tone production (requires a larger amount of air)
7. Large dynamic range (must be controlled and balanced)
8. Multiple tonguing (mostly on solo performance)
9. Lip-slurring with tongue position change (tah-oo-ee)
10. Various pitched tubas (BB-flat, E-flat, CC, and F) all concert-pitched instruments (the fingering changes)
11. Tuba/Sousaphone crucial in establishing a good pitch level for the ensemble

K. Timpani
1. Smooth single-stroke roll (faster speed on higher drums)
2. Careful tuning of pitches on the various drums
3. Choice of mallet
4. Drum size and range on timpani
5. Striking position on the tympani head
6. Muffling or dampening the sound
7. Instrument and equipment maintenance
8. Large dynamic range (must be controlled and balanced)

L. Percussion (concerned with many instruments)
    1. Execution of the rudiments (rudimental and buzz rolls)
    2. Desired sounds and effects on the various instruments
    3. Playing techniques and muting on the various instruments
    4. Dynamic level compared with the rest of the ensemble
    5. Tension of drum heads (and snares) for proper sound
    6. Size and depth of snare drum, bass drum, and other membrane instruments
    7. Choice of sticks, mallets, and other striking equipment
    8. Bass drum (mallet, stroke placement, rolls, and muffling)
    9. Cymbal size (weight, thickness, tone color, striking, and roll)
    10. Bells (mallets), chimes (hammers), and tam-tam (mallet)
    11. Large dynamic range (controlled and balanced)
    12. Large skips and reading prowess on keyboard instruments
    13. Development of multiple-mallet keyboard performance
    14. Use of pedal and the mallet dampening technique on vibraphone
    15. Instrument and striking equipment maintenance
M. Keyboard instruments (piano, harpsichord, organ, and celesta)
    1. Instrument placement within the ensemble
    2. Player positioned to watch the conductor
    3. Balance problems with the ensemble
    4. Properly tuned instruments
    5. The orchestra or band should tune to the piano with the soloist
    6. Registration on harpsichord and organ
N. Harp
    1. Tuning
    2. Use of the pedals (and the inherent sight-reading problems)
    3. Glissandi (one or both hands)
    4. Arpeggiated chords (one or both hands)
    5. Harmonics
    6. Dampening
O. Violin (and Viola)
    1. Playing position and left hand position
    2. Accurate tuning and finger placement on the fingerboard
    3. Proper bow use (pressure, speed, placement, and direction)
    4. Finger and bow coordination
    5. Correct and consistent bowing style
    6. Vibrato
    7. Special string techniques
    8. Fingerings, position shifts, string crossings, and harmonics
    9. Reading in alto and treble clef on viola
P. Cello (and Contrabass)
    1. Playing position and left-hand position
    2. Accurate tuning and finger placement on the fingerboard
    3. Proper bow use (pressure, speed, placement, and direction)
    4. Finger and bow coordination
    5. Correct and consistent bowing style

 6. Vibrato
 7. Special string techniques
 8. Fingerings, position shifts, string crossings, and harmonics
 9. Reading in bass, tenor, and treble clef on cello
10. Reading in bass and tenor clef on contrabass
11. Cello and contrabass crucial in establishing a good pitch level for the orchestral ensemble

Appendix D

Instrumental Techniques, Intonation Problems/Solutions, and Special Effects for the Individual Instruments

For each individual instrument, there are instrumental techniques, intonation problems/solutions, and special effects that need proper execution. Unless the conductor understands how these various instrumental techniques, intonation problems/solutions, and special effects are actually produced and sound, this all becomes useless information. In preparation for the rehearsal process, the conductor during score study must devise teaching strategies for these various instruments. Only by having an extensive pedagogical background will the conductor come to understand the production of these performance aspects in order to design the appropriate teaching strategies for the rehearsal process. Live demonstrations of these performance aspects are the best way to acquire this information. The conducting teacher, with the help of other instrumental teaching specialists or proficient players on the various instruments, should discuss and demonstrate these topics for the benefit of the conducting students in class.

FLUTE (PICCOLO)

Instrumental Techniques

Vibrato, double-tonguing, triple-tonguing, trills, and tremoli (seldom)

Intonation Solutions

Adjust tuning plug, adjust head joint, breath support, adjust embouchure, roll instrument, head or jaw movement, add fingers, and "bad notes" adjusted

Special Effects

Glissandi, flutter-tongue, portamenti (seldom), and harmonics (seldom)

OBOE (ENGLISH HORN)

Instrumental Techniques

Vibrato, trills, tremoli (seldom), and harmonics

Intonation Solutions

Vary lip tension, adjust reed, amount of reed in the mouth, playing position, alternate fingerings, fork fingering, finger shading, harmonics, bocal (English horn), and "bad notes" adjusted

Special Effects

Glissandi, flutter-tongue and portamenti (seldom)

CLARINET (BASS CLARINET)

Instrumental Techniques

Trills, transpositions (in the orchestra or the purchase of A clarinet or C clarinet), and tremoli (seldom)

Intonation Solutions

Amount of mouthpiece in the mouth, adjust reed, adjust barrel, adjust middle joint, adjust bell, alternate fingerings, throat register, finger shading, embouchure-lipping, added fingers, half hole, rings, and "bad notes" adjusted

Special Effects

Glissandi, flutter-tongue, multiphonics, multiple tonguing (seldom), portamenti (seldom), harmonics (seldom), and vibrato (jazz)

BASSOON (CONTRABASSOON)

Instrumental Techniques

Vibrato, trills, and tremoli (seldom)

Intonation Solutions

Amount of reed in mouth, adjust reed or wire, bocal length, added fingers, embouchure-lipping, "Andy Gump" embouchure setting, drop jaw on low notes, and "bad notes" adjusted

Special Effects

Glissandi, flutter-tongue, and portamenti (seldom)

SAXOPHONE

Instrumental Techniques

Vibrato, trills, and tremoli (seldom)

Intonation Solutions

Amount of mouthpiece in the mouth, adjust reed, varying lip tension, adjust mouthpiece on cork, alternate fingerings, added fingers, and "bad notes" adjusted

Special Effects

Glissandi, flutter-tongue, and portamenti (seldom)

TRUMPET (CORNET OR FLUGELHORN)

Instrumental Techniques

Vibrato, double-tonguing, triple-tonguing, lip slurs, lip trills, transpositions (orchestra), trills, lip trills, shakes, and fall-offs

Intonation Solutions

Adjust tuning slide, adjust air stream, adjust embouchure, third-valve slide, first-valve trigger, larger valve combinations, third partial notes, fifth partial notes, sixth partial notes, "bad notes" adjusted, extreme registers and extreme dynamics, alternate fingerings, and playing with mutes

Special Effects

Muted (straight mute, cup mute, Harmon mute, and many others), glissandi (half-valved or fingered), flutter-tongue, off-stage performance (seldom), plunger mute, hand in the bell (seldom), and bells up (seldom)

FRENCH HORN

Instrumental Techniques

Double-tonguing, triple-tonguing, lip slurs, right hand position in the bell, trills, lip trills, transpositions (orchestra), stopped horn, and bass clef reading (and the octave difference)

Intonation Solutions

Adjust embouchure, adjust air stream, tuning both sides of the horn and the valve slides, right hand in the bell adjustment, larger valve combinations, fifth partial notes, sixth partial notes, "bad notes" adjusted, extreme registers, extreme dynamics, alternate fingerings, double horn tuning, and playing with mute (straight, transposing, and hand-stopped)

Special Effects

Muted (Straight mute and transposing mute or stopped horn), bells up, flutter-tongue, off-stage performance (seldom), glissandi (half-valved or fingered) and vibrato (for mostly solo purposes)

TROMBONE

Instrumental Techniques

Vibrato, double-tonguing, triple-tonguing, F-attachment (or other attachments) use, legato tonguing technique (for slurring), lip slurs, and both tenor clef and alto clef reading (with orchestra)

Intonation Solutions

Adjust tuning slides (B-flat and attachments), adjust embouchure, adjust air stream, (mostly) adjust slide positions, alternate positions and the slide adjustments for the various attachments, extreme registers, and extreme dynamics

Special Effects

Flutter-tongue, glissandi or smears, muted (straight mute, cup mute, Harmon mute, and many others), plunger mute (seldom), and hand in the bell (seldom)

EUPHONIUM/BARITONE

Instrumental Techniques

Vibrato, double-tonguing, triple-tonguing, lip slurs, and both bass clef and treble clef reading

Intonation Solutions

Adjust tuning slide, adjust embouchure, adjust air stream, use of compensating mechanism, alternate fingerings and the fourth valve use, extreme registers, and extreme dynamics

Special Effects

Flutter-tongue, muted (straight mute), glissandi (seldom), trills (mostly solo performance), and tremoli (seldom)

TUBA/SOUSAPHONE

Instrumental Techniques

Double tonguing, triple tonguing, lip slurs, and vibrato

Intonation Solutions

Adjust tuning slide, adjust embouchure, adjust air stream, drop jaw, alternate fingerings, and fourth valve or tuning slide use while playing

Special Effects

Flutter-tongue, glissandi (seldom), muted (straight mute), and trills (mostly solo performance)

TIMPANI

Instrumental Techniques

Interval recognition, dampening, stick types (soft to hard), methods of striking, single-stroke rolls, roll speed, and "hot stove" stroke

Intonation Solutions

Careful tuning with pedal, lug tuning, learn and sing intervals, tuning fork use, adjust for even tension of drum head, and use of the tuning device on the instrument

Special Effects

Pedal glissandi (seldom)

PERCUSSION (NO INTONATION PROBLEM/SOLUTIONS)

Mallet Instruments

Instrumental Techniques

Stick types, rolls, trills, tremoli, vibrato (vibraphone), and pedal (vibraphone), multiple-mallet grip, and various other special techniques on the keyboard instruments

Special Effects

Glissandi

Cymbals

Instrumental Techniques

Dampening or choking, method of striking, and cymbal size (diameter, thickness, and tone color)

Special Effects

Scraping on suspended cymbal or the use of unusual beaters

Snare Drum

Instrumental Techniques

Stick types, method of striking, snares or no snares, wire-brush, and trap set technique

Special Effects

Rim-shot and muffled

Bass Drum

Instrumental Techniques

Stick type, method of striking, and dampening

Special Effects

Rolls (with mallets)

Gong, Tambourine, and Triangle

Instrumental Techniques

Method of striking, beater types, and playing techniques

Special Effects

Roll on tambourine and roll on triangle

OTHER PERCUSSION INSTRUMENTS

Instrumental Techniques

There are an unlimited numbers of percussion instruments that need to be considered here in terms of the playing techniques.

Special Effects

Through the imagination of the composer and the availability of the instruments (see the Contemporary Music Special Effects and Notation Bibliography below in this chapter)

HARP

Instrumental Techniques

Glissandi (one hand or two hands), chords and arpeggios (one hand or two hands), harmonics, enharmonics, dampening, trills, tremoli, and the seven pedal combinations

Intonation Solutions

Careful initial tuning and re-tuning when needed

Special Effects

Non-arpeggiated and like a guitar

KEYBOARD (CELESTE, HARPSICHORD, ORGAN AND PIANO)

Instrumental Techniques

Scales, arpeggios, chords, tremoli, trills, and registration change (for harpsichord and organ)

Intonation Solutions

Careful initial tuning and re-tuning when needed

Special Effects

Glissandi, embellishments, tone clusters, plucking strings in piano, prepared piano, and amplified piano

STRINGS

Instrumental Techniques

Strike with bow, au talon, punta d'arco, full bow, middle of the bow, balance point, successive down-bows, successive up-bows, pizzicato (arpeggiated, chords, glissando, and left-hand technique with slap, snap, and thumb), harmonics, tremoli (bowed and fingered), col legno, sul ponticello, sul tasto, and trills

Intonation Solutions

Careful tuning, string comparisons (perfect fifths or perfect fourths on double bass), left hand and arm positions, finger placement on fingerboard, position shifts, finger sliding, and harmonics use for tuning on cello and double bass

Special Effects

Muted, natural harmonics, artificial harmonics, divisi, glissandi, staggered bowing, chords, double stops, and non-vibrato

Please note: In addition to these intonation problems/solutions, there will also be "thin" and "stuffy" notes found on the various woodwind instruments including that of the throat register of the clarinet and with the large valve combinations and upper register on brass instruments. These notes need to be addressed and discussed by the conducting teacher or instrumental specialist for the benefit of the conducting students in class.

CONTEMPORARY MUSIC SPECIAL EFFECTS AND NOTATION BIBLIOGRAPHY

In contemporary music, these special effects and the notation are almost unlimited (especially in the percussion section of the ensemble). In most instances, the composer will supply some information in the score as to how to execute these special effects. Listed below are references to consult for these special effects and the notation that are commonly used by the contemporary composer:

Fink, Robert, and Robert Ricci, *The Language of Twentieth Century Music* (1975). This book is set up in dictionary form and deals with the various compositional aspects of 20th-century music.

Green, Elizabeth A. H., and Nicolai Malko, *The Conductor and his Score* (1969). See chapter 8: The Contemporary Score. The authors show many examples of musical notation and list what is called "Somewhat standardized symbols."

Hunsberger, Donald, and Roy E. Ernst, *The Art of Conducting* (1992). See chapter 12: Contemporary Music. The authors list contemporary notational symbols on pp. 135 and 136.

Lawson, Colin (ed.), *The Cambridge Companion to the Orchestra* (2003). See chapter 4: From Notation to Sound. The example used here is that of the Lutoslawski's *Cello Concerto* with the explanation by the composer.

Read, Gardner, *Contemporary Instrumental Techniques* (1976). Part I illustrates generalized techniques of extended ranges, muting, glissandi, harmonics, percussive devices, microtones, amplification, and extra musical devices.

Read, Gardner, *Thesaurus of Orchestral Devices* (1953). Parts II through VII cover orchestral devices for woodwind instruments, brass instruments, percussion instruments, keyboard instruments, harp, and string instruments.

Risatti, Howard, *New Music Vocabulary (A Guide to Notational Signs for Contemporary Music)* (1975). The entire book covers general notational material and specifically for strings, percussion and harp, woodwinds, brass, and voice.

Stone, Kurt, *Music Notation in the Twentieth Century: A Practical Guidebook* (1980). This book covers music notation of the 20th century thoroughly and has many musical examples and excerpts to confirm this notation.

Appendix E

Recommended Conducting and Rehearsing Videos

Numerous videos are available for the advanced conductor to gain valuable insights in terms of the conducting technique and rehearsing skills. The insights presented in these videos have both positive and negative features. Take care to sort out what is effective and what is ineffective for use by the maturing conductor. The following is a representative listing with general descriptions of these available videos.

VHS

The Art of Conducting: Techniques of Conducting (various conductors)

Films for the Humanities & Sciences, FFH 4602. Conductors in this video are Fritz Reiner conducting the New York Philharmonic and the Chicago Symphony, George Szell conducting the Cleveland Orchestra, Herbert von Karajan, and Leonard Bernstein. Selections include excerpts from the Tchaikovsky *Violin Concerto*, Beethoven's *Seventh Symphony*, the Brahms *Academic Festival Overture*, Debussy's *La Mer*, Shostakovich's *Fifth Symphony*, and Mahler's *Fourth Symphony*. This video shows the distinct contrast in conducting style between the Fritz Reiner/George Szell approach and the animated, virtuosic conducting of Herbert von Karajan and Leonard Bernstein. Duration: 36 minutes.

The Development of a Conductor: Simon Rattle on the Record

Films for the Humanities & Sciences, FFH 3868. Simon Rattle began his conducting career at a very early age and won an international conducting competition at the age of 19. He began conducting the Birmingham Symphony Orchestra shortly after this success and has remained with this ensemble throughout his career. Having started learning contemporary repertoire first as a percussionist, Rattle tends toward this type of repertoire but, of course, programs the standard orchestral repertoire as well. His conducting is very creative and he fosters the idea that "the concern must be for the sound produced." Duration: 58 minutes.

Leonard Bernstein: In Rehearsal (Stravinsky, *The Rite of Spring*)

Kultur 1446. Hi-fi Dolby System. This video shows Leonard Bernstein conducting the Schleswig-Holstein Music Festival Orchestra in rehearsals for Stravinsky's *Rite of Spring*. The Orchestra consists of young professionals and so it is a matter of Bernstein molding the ensemble into his conception of this very difficult work. At the beginning, Bernstein asks for a G Major scale to which he changes tempo, dynamics, and style in order to get the ensemble to watch the conductor. He then explains to the ensemble the "essence and spirit" of the piece to be rehearsed. The important aspect during the rehearsal is "to get the sound right." He shows with the conducting technique how he wants this to sound. At one point, Bernstein suggests using all downbows to make the sound more agitated and at another time he says, "I don't feel the jazz." He uses humor at several points to break the tension of the rehearsal process. He also uses analogy with the music and cartoon figures from the Walt Disney film *Fantasia*. Leonard Bernstein always shows great emotion, energy, and musicality in his conducting and rehearsing. Duration: 60 minutes.

Bruno Walter: The Maestro, The Man

Video Artist International 69407. This video shows Bruno Walter rehearsing the Brahms *Symphony No. 2 in D* (first and fourth movements) with the Vancouver International Festival Orchestra. This video was produced in 1958, so the visual aspect is not particularly attractive. However, Walter's conducting and rehearsing techniques are very apparent—expressive conducting, showing the bowings for the string section, insisting on the correct style in the woodwinds, rehearsing without a score, always having concern for the accompanying parts, and knowing the score quite meticulously. On the other side of the coin, he does not always keep the beat pattern centered or focused and there is too much cueing done by pointing, which causes "fussiness" in the conducting style. In the interview between the two movements of the symphony, Bruno Walter bemoans the fact that it is not easy to learn to be a conductor because your instrument is the orchestra (or band) and those ensembles are in short supply for the conducting student. He also stresses the idea that the musician must have sincerity and "spirit" in order to be a conductor. Duration: 58 minutes.

Hermann Scherchen: In Rehearsal (J. S. Bach: *Art of the Fugue*)

Video Artist International 69408. This video shows Hermann Scherchen rehearsing the J. S. Bach *Art of the Fugue* (orchestrated by Hermann Scherchen) with the CBC Toronto Chamber Orchestra in 1966. Initially he explains the structure of the work to the orchestra. Hermann Scherchen's conducting style can be described as very clear and precise. He tends to use a lot of wrist motion and controls the various lines with the use of the left hand and arm. He also tends to be very careful about initiating the tempo. He sometimes lacks visible motion with the small patterns. He also tends to turn the right hand over, and therefore loses the conducting plane. He is very insistent about ensemble precision and the correct subdivision of the beat. Scherchen continues to conduct while verbally rehearsing the ensemble to achieve the continuity of the music. He seems to be slightly too severe at times in relationship with this fine professional chamber orchestra. His book, *Handbook of Conducting*, is one of the best conducting books ever written! Duration: 58 minutes.

Leonard Bernstein Conducts *West Side Story*: The Making of the Recording

Deutsche Grammaphon Video, 072 206-3. NTSC Dolby System. This video shows Leonard Bernstein both in rehearsal with the singers and with the full orchestra and cast. He does not record in sequence, but has a well-planned strategy for getting this recording made. There is considerable "back and forth" throughout the video between the Maestro and the people recording. Bernstein seldom looks at the score and knows exactly what he wants from the singers and the orchestra. Between rehearsals and recording sessions, he spends a tremendous amount of time listening to "play-backs" and this prompts him to exclaim, "you see before you a tired, aging Maestro." However, when he rehearses and conducts he expends unbelievable energy. He spends much time in the video taking care of details, such as more guitar in listening to the playback and getting the balance right with the tambourine and maracas in the "Cha-Cha." Bernstein is shown rehearsing "Maria" with the piano accompaniment and the soloist (José Carreras) and then with the orchestra with careful attention to the interpretative details. He also shows great dynamic contrast with the orchestra in accompanying "Officer Krupke." Note the very moving rendition of "Tonight" between Anita (soloist Tatiana Troyanos) and Maria (soloist Kiri Te Kanawa). Duration: 1 hour, 29 minutes.

Maestros in Moscow, Moscow Philharmonic (Conducted by Lawrence Leighton Smith and Dmitri Kitayenko)

Kodak Video Programs, CAT 833 1399. The interesting aspect of this video is in the American conductor Lawrence Leighton Smith conducting Russian music and Russian conductor Dmitri Kitayenko conducting American music in a concert with the Moscow Philharmonic and hosted by actor Gregory Peck. This video also shows many scenes from Russian culture, interspersed with a jazz jam session! The video opens with music from Copland's *Appalachian Spring Ballet Suite*. Maestro Smith conducts the Glazunov *Concert Waltz in E-flat*; Griffes's *The White Peacock*, conducted by Maestro Kitayenko, follows. Following this is Piston's *The Incredible Flutist Suite* and the Mussorgsky *Prelude to "Khovanshchina."* Maestro Kitayenko then conducts the string orchestra version of Gershwin's *Lullaby for Strings*, and the final work on the program is Glinka's *Russlan and Ludmilla Overture*. There are some interesting conducting aspects in this video: Maestro Smith conducts mostly with a very high conducting plane while Maestro Kitayenko conducts with a low conducting plane; both conductors have clean conducting technique. Maestro Smith mirrors the right hand with the left even during the crescendo gesture. Maestro Kitayenko lets the solo players have a good deal of freedom with musical interpretation. Maestros Smith and Kitayenko both find it necessary to fluctuate between three and one (*Concert Waltz*) and two and one (*Russlan and Ludmilla Overture*) in order to improve the flow. Duration: 72 minutes.

The Art of Conducting: Great Conductors of the Past

Teldec Video. VHS Hi-fi 4509-95038-3. NTSC Dolby System. At the beginning of this video are some quick segments by Toscanini, Szell, Bernstein, Barbirolli, and Beecham. Then Richard Strauss is shown conducting his own *Till Eulenspiegel*. Felix Weingartner then conducts the von Weber *Der Freischutz Overture* completely through. Bruno Walter conducts a brief section of Mozart's *Symphony No. 40 in G minor* and rehearses a bit of the Brahms *Second Symphony in D Major.* With this unfamiliar orchestra, he confirms where the various instrumental parts are located in the orchestra setup. Maestro Otto Klemperer was quite severe and authoritative with the orchestra. In conducting the Beethoven *Symphony No. 9*, his beat pattern and conducting plane are very low, making it almost impossible for the ensemble to see the pulse. Maestro Furtwangler seemed unconcerned about tempo or precision in conducting the Wagner *Die Meistersinger Overture*. Toscanini then conducts Verdi's *La Forza del Destino* and shows wonderfully clear conducting technique while the NBC Symphony Orchestra plays with great virtuosity! Stokowski talks about achieving the intentions of the composer. He uses no baton, but makes both hands very expressive. The Stokowski sound is very luscious and has freedom to breathe. Isaac Stern reiterates in an interview that Koussevitzky "yelled and cajoled until he got what he wanted" and Reiner conducted "mostly with the eyes." George Szell talked about how he was able to build the Cleveland Orchestra. Maestro von Karajan seldom looks at the orchestra when he is conducting. The conducting is very powerful. Isaac Stern described Bernstein's conducting as "an eruption of creativity and sheer emotion." Duration: 1 hour, 57 minutes.

The Art of Conducting: Legendary Conductors of a Golden Age

Teldec Video, 95710-3, Unitel. NTSC Dolby System, c. 1997. This video shows many conductors from Europe and Russia. Some are better known than others. There are two different performances of Richard Strauss's *Till Eulenspiegel's Merry Pranks* on this video by Wilhelm Furtwangler and later by Sergiu Celibidache. Compare these performances with those of Zubin Mehta and Richard Strauss on other available videos. Erich Kleiber has an elegant interpretation of the Johann Strauss Jr. *Blue Danube Waltz* on this video. Charles Munch with the Boston Symphony performs parts of Debussy's *La Mer*, the Ravel *Daphnis et Chloe Suite No. 2*, and the Berlioz *Symphonie fantastique*. His interpretation shows a real passion for French music. Sergiu Celibidache conducts the Beethoven *Egmont Overture* with great energy followed by excerpts from the Richard Strauss *Till Eulenspiegel's Merry Pranks* and the Dvorak *Symphony No. 9 (New World)*. The video concludes with the Russian conductor Evgeny Mravinsky rehearsing and conducting the first and last movements of Tchaikovsky's *Symphony No. 5*. (This recording is also available on DVD.) Duration: 1 hour, 55 minutes.

Leonard Bernstein: *Beethoven Symphony No. 5 & 6* and the *Leonore Overture No. 3*

Wiener Philharmonik, Deutsche Grammmophon Video, 072 201-3. NTSC. This video begins with a performance of the *Leonore Overture No. 3*. Maestro Bernstein brings the work to a triumphant ending! This is followed by a performance of Beethoven's *Symphony No. 6 (Pastoral)*. Bernstein has little concern for the patterns and more concern about the musical phrasing, style, and accents. This is a good introduction to the Bernstein conducting, more geared to the musical interpretation than in showing the proper conducting technique. Using no scores on any of these three performances, he obviously "sees" the scores through music imagery (or a photographic memory)! In the second movement "By a Brook," it is interesting to watch and hear the rubato and nuance indications used by Bernstein. Bernstein dramatically indicates sudden dynamics in describing thunder and lightning in the Storm scene. The sustained musical line is evident from the orchestra at the end of the Symphony. Maestro Bernstein dramatically and forcefully conducts the opening passage of Beethoven's *Symphony No. 5*. It is obvious from the beginning of the first movement that Bernstein knows exactly what he wants from the orchestra. In the second movement, he gets the "noble" quality from the brass and timpani. He then slows the tempo for even more impact at the end of this movement. Bernstein sustains the pianissimo at the end of the third movement with the quick crescendo into the Finale. In the fourth movement, he adds two trumpets to the ensemble for more intensity. Duration: 1 hour, 42 minutes.

Leonard Bernstein: Young People's Concerts with the New York Philharmonic (*The Sound of an Orchestra*)

Sony Classical, SHV 57440. This video, produced in December 1965, is in black and white. It is a part of a series of Young People's Concerts by Leonard Bernstein and the New York Philharmonic from Lincoln Center in New York City. Because these concerts are geared toward children, this video does show a format for Young People's Concerts and emphasizes certain points concerning the importance of performing music according to the intention of the composer and musical period. The concert begins with a rather poor interpretation (on purpose) of the Haydn *Symphony No. 88 (Largo)* and then continues with the correction of this performance. Bernstein stresses the importance of dynamics, phrasing, vibrato, and rubato. The corrected performance can be compared with the performance of this movement in the video done by Christoph von Dohnanyi and The Philharmonia Orchestra just below. Maestro Bernstein emphasizes that "the composer always comes first" with the interpretation of a work. This means that the conductor must research and perform this music as the composer intended it to sound. Characteristics of the musical period and the individual composer must always have primary considerations. Bernstein makes a comparison between German and French composers and their styles using the Brahms *Symphony No. 1* followed by Debussy's *Ibéria*. He then turns to the contemporary period with the performance of Stravinsky's *L'histoire du soldat* for seven diverse instruments and emphasizes the style as being clear and dry. He concludes the concert with a demonstration of American Music using the Gershwin *An American in Paris* jazzy trumpet solo and Copland's *Hoe-down from the Rodeo Suite*. Duration: 54 minutes.

CONDUCTING/REHEARSING VIDEOS (DVD)

Christoph von Dohnanyi: In Rehearsal with The Philharmonia Orchestra (Haydn, *Symphony No. 88 in G*)

Spektrum TV/RM ARTS, c. 1998; www.image-entertainment.com. The Maestro has many interesting approaches during the rehearsal process. For example, here are some quotes: "Can you listen for it?" "That was beautiful," "Everyone listen to the cellos," and "you have to deal with it" if it does not match the interpretation. The Maestro is a congenial conductor and deals with the problems in a calm, intellectual way. He uses inner singing, even audibly, throughout the rehearsal process. In fast passages, he tends to slow the tempo in order to improve the precision and intonation. He gives players feedback while continuing to conduct. Throughout the video, various player opinions are interspersed between the rehearsing. At one point, the Maestro discusses the idea of the conductor also being a composer as was the case with Franz Joseph Haydn, and indicates that this is a real advantage in terms of the performance. He ends with a statement about how important it is for the composer to have a sense of humor in his music, as does Haydn in the fourth movement of this symphony. This is a beautifully produced video in color with numerous camera angles to view the conductor and players. Duration: 58 minutes.

Georg Solti: The Making of a Maestro

Image Entertainment. ID9288RADVD. NTSC Dolby System, c. 1997. There are numerous excerpts conducted by Sir Georg Solti in this video. These excerpts show the tremendous energy and passion possessed for the music by the Maestro. He had worked with Arturo Toscanini, Bruno Walter, Richard Strauss, Igor Stravinsky, Benjamin Britten, and Béla Bartók. He was, at first, mostly an opera conductor in Budapest, Bavaria, Munich, London, and many other venues. Then Solti came to Chicago and built the Chicago Symphony Orchestra into one of the top ensembles in the world. This video has some real clues as to how he was able to do all of this! Duration: 92 minutes.

Zubin Mehta: In Rehearsal (R. Strauss, *Till Eulenspiegel's Merry Pranks*), Israel Philharmonic

Image Entertainment. RAssociates. ID9254RADVD. NTSC Dolby System. This video shows Zubin Mehta rehearsing the Richard Strauss *Till Eulenspiegel* tone poem with the Israeli Philharmonic Orchestra in 1996. He points out that the two main themes are in the famous horn solo followed by E-flat sopranino clarinet solo (very mischievous) in denoting Till. He constantly reminds the orchestra about what is going on in the "story." He also reminds them about playing the accents and the awareness of "color."

At one point, he says "have fun with it." The video is an interesting study as to how the orchestra members and conductor interact. Zubin Mehta has wonderful conducting technique and it is especially noticeable that the conducting flow is an important part of his conducting technique. This DVD is somewhat difficult to obtain because of the limited copies produced. Duration: 55 minutes.

Vaclav Neumann: In Rehearsal (Beethoven, *Leonore Overture No. 3* and Smetana, *Overture to the Bartered Bride*) Sudfunk-Sinfonieorchester

Arthaus Musik 101 059. Even though this video is in black and white, it is a strong presentation because after rehearsing the ensemble, Maestro Neumann is shown conducting the concert performance. It also has English, French, and German subtitles. Vaclav Neumann is a very encouraging, sincere, and yet demanding conductor. The Sudfunk Symphony Orchestra is a very fine ensemble of professional players. Throughout the rehearsal process, the conductor explains the meaning and story involved with the opera. He is very careful not to let the orchestra build the crescendo too soon by saying "save." He also talks a lot about "energy, sensitivity, and pianissimo." In fortissimo passages, the right hand technique is somewhat stiff with the elbow retreating behind his body and no wrist action. He shows very clear accents throughout. He uses descriptive words such as "blissful" and "love" to set the mood. At one point, he describes the flute and oboe duet as "an intimate conversation." Neumann feels that Beethoven writes the crescendo in the Coda of the *Lenore Overture No. 3* like no other composer has ever written. In the performance, he does not use a score. Maestro Neumann takes the tempo in *The Bartered Bride Overture* at a tremendous speed, really causing the bass players to scramble. He mentions that the overture was written before the opera. He states that "you have to be a sprinter" in this overture. At one point the conductor suggests that "you need to be more diabolical" and in another place "like a cat, treading softly." Maestro Neumann sums up this overture by calling it "whirling music." Duration: 1 hour, 39 minutes.

Carlos Kleiber: Beethoven *Symphonies 4 & 7*, Concertgebouw Orchestra of Amsterdam

Phillips Video Classics, B0003880-09. (UNITEL, 1983). This video is a unique presentation by Carlos Kleiber in that it is obvious from watching him that he is using inner singing through the facial expression and his mouth movement throughout both of these symphony performances. He is less concerned about conducting patterns and gestures and more concerned about the musicality and the emotions to be conveyed in the music of the performances. He achieves great dynamic contrast from the orchestra. At times, he shows very sharp attacks in these symphonies. He indicates to the orchestra at the beginning of the third movement what the tempo will be before the downbeat—it is more like a scherzo than a minuetto. He gives two beats before the finale begins because of the rapidity of the tempo and this then erupts into a virtuoso finale! The Beethoven *Seventh Symphony* with the dotted 8th/16th/8th note patterns are played cleanly throughout. Kleiber makes a precise transition from the poco sostenuto to the vivace in the first movement. He communicates well with the orchestra even though his conducting technique is somewhat unorthodox. There is great energy displayed in the last movement from both the conductor and orchestra. All of this amounts to some very exciting performances! Duration: 72 minutes.

Frederick Fennell Remembered: The Tokyo Kosei Wind Orchestra with Frederick Fennell Conducting

Winds BOD—7002. Frederick Fennell was one of America's finest conductors and conducting teachers of the 20th century. This video is a single concert with the Tokyo Kosei Wind Orchestra and the repertoire includes the Howard Hanson *Chorale and Alleluia*, the Clifton Williams *Symphonic Suite*, Igor Stravinsky's *Suite from the Ballet "The Firebird,"* and the William Walton *Crown Imperial, Coronation March* among others. Such conducting elements as subdivision, eye contact, phrasing, nuances, facial expression, releases, accents, conducting flow, left hand uses, unity of precision, and musicianship from Dr. Fennell at the age of 90 are remarkable in this video! Duration: 94 minutes.

Allen McMurray: Conducting from the Inside Out, Disk Three (Kindred Spirits Featuring Allen McMurray, H. Robert Reynolds, Craig Kirchoff, and Richard Floyd)

GIA DVD-665. H. Robert Reynolds is shown rehearsing a collegiate ensemble from the University of Colorado–Boulder on the Percy Grainger *Colonial Song* and the first movement of Gustav Holst's *First Suite in E-flat*. Richard Floyd rehearses this ensemble on the Jan Van de Roost *Suite Provençale*. Craig Kirchoff also rehearses the same ensemble on Dimitri Shostakovich's *Prelude* and finally, Allan McMurray is shown rehearsing the second movement (Intermezzo) of the Gustav Holst *First Suite in E-flat*. At the beginning of each section, the conductor presents his philosophy on rehearsing and performing music. The video is an interesting contrast of conducting and rehearsing styles by four very reputable collegiate band conductors. Duration: 2 hours.

Master Conductors: "A Legacy of Wisdom" (featuring Fennell, Hindsley, and Revelli)

GIA DVD-708. This video was filmed in 1986 at the University of North Texas at a music conference. Mark Hindsley (former conductor at the University of Illinois), William Revelli (former conductor at the University of Michigan), and Frederick Fennell (founder and former conductor of the Eastman Wind Ensemble) are three highly regarded wind conductors of the 20th century. At the beginning, the three are conducting briefly with these personal observations: Hindsley shows accents very well and has very clear patterns, Revelli uses inner singing while conducting, and Fennell uses wonderful facial expressions and his eyes to communicate to the ensemble.

Mark Hindsley makes a good point that the literature is limited for the band and for this reason he has done a tremendous amount of transcribing of orchestral literature for the band. He feels that there is a real need for variety in the literature. William Revelli makes points about the interpretation of the score, competent conducting, personal musicianship, having talent as a conductor, instrumental study, singing, a confident attitude, study, sacrifice, and knowing the instrument transpositions. Frederick Fennell suggests that when conducting you are really playing your instrument and the conductor should have a strong personality and emotional involvement with the music. Revelli stresses the importance of the rehearsal process, score study, and hard work. Hindsley emphasizes that in the rehearsal, "You need to know what you want." Fennell states emphatically that the score is the great teacher! Revelli feels that the key to being a good conductor is in singing (solfège). As these sessions continue, Fennell makes a wonderful point about what will correct itself and what will not correct itself in the rehearsal process. It is a question of listening to what is happening. He also suggests that the conductor needs a time frame for the rehearsal, even though this may not always work out as planned. Revelli brings up the importance of selecting the right tempo. He suggests going to every concert (or rehearsal) you can to watch the conductor. He also mentions that the sound is important (and compares it to the human voice). He stresses the idea that the conductor is the intermediary between the composer and the audience along with the fact that as a conductor, we always need to be a student! Revelli also brings up the idea of conducting with nuances and inflections. The conductor must demand perfection! This video represents the first of a series of DVDs dedicated to history's greatest conductors of the Wind Band. Duration: 1 hour 16 minutes.

Pierre Boulez: In Rehearsal (Berg, *Three Pieces, Op. 6* and Boulez, *Notations I–IV*), Vienna Philharmonic Orchestra

Image Entertainment, IDO848RADVD. Pierre Boulez rehearses Alban Berg's *Three Pieces for Orchestra, Op. 6* and his own composition *Notations I–IV* with the Vienna Philharmonic Orchestra. Boulez uses no baton, but shows clear beats in the rhythmic complexities of these pieces. He has many players and groups individually play their parts to confirm the precision, check for wrong notes, or adjust the balance. It is obvious that both the score and parts have each measure numbered to make for efficiency in rehearsing. Boulez also is shown in conversation about the various aspects of orchestral performance. At one point, he has the trumpets play to confirm the intonation without the flutter-tongue. At times, he will go through a whole movement and then "take it apart" for the details. While rehearsing his *Notations* he states, "this is how I subdivide this passage" and then shows this subdivision. He does not take the movements in order of the performance (on the video), but after playing the first movement he then skips to the second movement because it is the most difficult and will be performed as the final movement. He conducts with a lot of subdivision to solidify the rhythmic aspects. Duration: 57 minutes.

* * *

Many of these videos are available from Shattinger Music Company in St. Louis, Missouri. Numerous videos are also available that I do not list here, as well as other videos that will certainly be produced in the future. The conducting teacher should have some of these videos available for student viewing. After showing a video in class, there could be a discussion by the conducting teacher and the conducting students or given as a written assignment for the conducting students as to what has transpired in the video.

In addition to these videos, there are also YouTube presentations on the various web sites with bands, orchestras, and smaller ensembles. These YouTube presentations could be useful for the analysis of the compositions, for the quality of the performances, or for the competency of the conductors. Care should be taken in using these YouTube presentations in the sense that these presentations will vary considerably in terms of the performance quality, the recorded sound, and the picture clarity. These YouTube presentations may be enlarged on the computer or projected on to a larger screen for classroom use.

The conducting teacher, with these videos and YouTube presentations, should discuss these various conducting/rehearsing aspects for the benefit of the conducting students. This will require considerable research on the part of the conducting teacher in preparation for the class presentation of these videos and for the various YouTube sites.

Appendix F

Student Project Evaluations (Conducting and Rehearsing)

The purpose behind this listing is to provide comments for use by the conducting teacher in evaluating, maintaining, or improving conducting technique and rehearsing skills. With developing conductors, this listing will remind them of those performance areas that they need to evaluate periodically. It is necessary for all conductors to keep the conducting technique as clear and sharp as possible throughout their conducting careers. The conducting teacher should discuss or demonstrate the instructions below in detail for the benefit of the conducting student (before these student conducting/rehearsing projects begin).

MECHANICS

1. Stance and posture
   a. The feet should be approximately 12 inches apart with one foot slightly forward.
   b. The conductor must not tap the foot, bend the knees, or display poor posture.
   c. There should be equal weight on both feet for body balance.
   d. The conductor should be standing tall.
2. Attention position
   a. The "ready" or attention position must look like the conductor is ready to execute the preparatory beat.
   b. The hands should be about 18 inches apart in readiness to execute this preparatory beat (with or without the use of the left hand).
3. Arms position
   a. There is a tendency for the arms to be too close to the body, causing a poor conducting position.
   b. The arms need to be "up and out" at the 4:00 and 8:00 positions.
   c. The basic forearm position needs to be nearly parallel to the floor.
   d. If the player can see most of the inside forearm of the conductor from the front, then the angle of the forearm and upper arm is incorrect.

    e. The angle of the forearm and upper arm of the conductor should be an obtuse angle, not an acute angle from the side view.

    f. The arms' position must never extend straight out as this causes the patterns and gestures to look contrived, stiff, and awkward.

4. Elbows

    a. Holding both elbows too close to the body distorts the entire conducting position.

    b. In general, the elbows need to be "forward and away" from the body.

    c. In many cases, if there is too much elbow movement in the patterns, then this movement should be transfer to the wrist.

5. Wrists

    a. There must be flexibility in the wrist, but not "floppiness."

    b. The wrists must not twist in the pattern motion, but keep the palm of the right hand parallel to the floor; this twisting of the right hand will cause the baton to point upward with a loss of a clear ictus.

    c. The wrist must not allow the right hand to droop downward or point upward as this distorts the flow of the conducting patterns.

    d. If the right wrist is stiff, the whole arm and elbow will move more, resulting in a lack of clarity and flow in the conducting patterns.

6. Baton grip

    a. Hold the baton with the thumb and forefinger beyond the baton handle with the forefinger curled around the baton; the other fingers should be curled as well, but not gripping the baton handle.

    b. By having the last three fingers of the right hand extended downward, there is a tendency to bend the hand and wrist downward as well.

    c. Point the baton at approximately 45 degrees to the left; if the baton is pointed straight with the arm, the wrist will be stiff and curtail the flow in the conducting motion.

    d. Do not place the forefinger on top of the stick as this gives the impression of stiffness in the conducting motion and tends to point the baton downward.

7. Baton or no baton

    a. Most instrumental conductors use a baton.

    b. Choose a baton that has the balance point just beyond the baton handle.

    c. On rare occasions, the instrumental conductor might choose to use no baton on a very lyric movement where the style is legato or tenuto.

    d. The conductor who decides to use no baton should have the fingers slightly apart, but certainly not use the forefinger as an extension of the right hand.

8. Conductor's stand/podium

    a. The conductor's stand must not block the players' vision in seeing the ictus of the beat pattern.

    b. The conductor's stand/music may be slightly slanted, yet nearly parallel to the floor.

    c. Do not place the stand so the conductor can view the music more easily; there is a good chance that the stand will cover up much of the beat pattern for the players.

    d. The podium height and placement must be a consideration in order for the players to see the conducting patterns and gestures clearly and easily.

CONDUCTING PATTERNS

1. Conducting Patterns
   a. Show conducting patterns firmly, aggressively, and with clarity.
   b. Center conducting patterns for the players to respond to the leadership of the conductor; do not turn your back on the players.
   c. The two-pattern and three-pattern will tend to slide to the right because neither pattern moves toward the ictus on the left.
   d. The conducting patterns should not have extra bounces, circles, curls, etc. that will distort the clarity of the patterns; these motions are often referred to as being "fancy" or "fussy."
   e. If the conducting motion becomes too vertical, it is difficult to distinguish which beat of the conducting pattern is being shown.
   f. If the conducting motion becomes too horizontal, it is difficult to distinguish where the ictus is being placed.
   g. The "non-espressivo" or neutral pattern can be effective at certain times just in order to show the clarity of the pattern.
2. Pattern size and plane
   a. The conductor must show aggressive patterns, but not so large that the patterns become distorted.
   b. If the patterns become too small, the ensemble will not respond positively to these small patterns when used over a long period.
   c. The size of the conducting patterns should change according to the dynamic level and for achieving this dynamic contrast.
   d. If the conducting plane is too high (around the face of the conductor), the motion of the beats will be toward the players and difficult to interpret.
   e. If the conducting plane is too low, the danger is that the players will be unable to see the bottom of the beat (ictus).
   f. If the conducting plane keeps changing constantly, the players will be confused as to where the ictus in the conducting pattern will be placed.
3. One-beat pattern
   a. The clockwise motion (for the conductor) is preferable because this shows the motion of the beat as a preparatory beat for the downbeat (outside to inside).
   b. The one-beat pattern must show the subdivision of the beat into 2s or 3s.
4. Two-beat pattern
   a. It is too easy to let the two-beat pattern look like a "half-moon" or a "U-shape" (rather than the correct "backward J" or "fish hook"); such wrong pattern motion will not define well which is the first beat or the second beat.
   b. The two-beat pattern will tend to move too far to the right and out of the conducting box.
5. Three-beat pattern
   a. On the rebound of the second count, the motion should be "up and over" rather than retracing the second beat so that the pattern is symmetrical.
   b. The three-beat pattern will tend to move too far to the right and out of the conducting box.

6. Four-beat pattern
   a. On the rebound of the third count, the motion should be "up and over" rather than retracing the third beat so that the pattern is symmetrical.
   b. The four-beat pattern does move to the left on the second count, but be sure not to then place first count and the third count at the same point.
7. Six-beat pattern or other beat patterns
   a. The German six-beat pattern defines each ictus well; this pattern must be practiced to remain consistent. The sixth count should be "up and over."
   b. The Italian six-beat pattern should be used when merging from six beats into two beats (as this pattern outlines the two-beat pattern).
   c. Other beat patterns may also prove to be problematic in terms of clarity.

STYLES

1. Staccato Style
   a. Straight lines show the staccato style with a "flick" on each ictus.
   b. The staccato style pattern is generally small to indicate lightness.
   c. The staccato style might be described as "flicking water off of the baton."
   d. The staccato style pattern is executed mostly with the wrist and some slight movement of the forearm.
2. Legato Style
   a. The legato style needs flow and more horizontal movement.
   b. However, if the movement becomes too horizontal in this style, there will be less clarity with the pulse.
   c. In legato style, the movement in the patterns must be curved, not straight.
   d. The legato style pattern will probably be slightly larger because more distance between beats is required.
3. Marcato Style
   a. The marcato style is similar to the staccato style except that there needs to be more weight and emphasis on the beats.
   b. In the marcato style, there will be less wrist "flick" and slightly more forearm intensity and movement than with the staccato style.
4. Tenuto Style
   a. The tenuto style might best be described as ultra legato.
   b. The tenuto style motion is very fluid with a wrist "flick" on the ictus.
   c. The tenuto style is quite uneven and "sticky" in movement speed.
   d. The tenuto style might be comparable to practicing underwater in a swimming pool where there is "resistance" between beats—like pulling taffy.

CONDUCTING TECHNIQUE

1. Preparatory beats
   a. The conductor should be looking at the ensemble when executing the preparatory beat and downbeat at the beginning.

    b. There should be a full preparatory beat before the music begins. The preparatory beat should be executed from the outside to the inside.

    c. The execution of the preparatory beat begins with a "wrist flick" to designate the beginning of the preparatory beat.

    d. The preparatory beat should show meter designation, tempo, attack, dynamic level, and the basic style.

2. Releases

    a. Releases must always be shown with a preparatory beat.

    b. Releases must be shown on a beat, not on a fraction of the beat and in tempo (except for certain circumstances such as with fermatas).

    c. The conductor must not ignore releases or the results will be poor releases by the whole ensemble.

    d. Releases should show the precision, the dynamic level, and the "character" of the release.

3. Fermatas

    a. In holding the fermata, the right hand should continue to move in order to sustain the sound; the left hand may also be used here as well.

    b. There are three basic ways of handling fermatas: (1) no break between the fermata and the following note, (2) one-beat break between the fermata and the following note, or (3) more than one-beat break between the fermata and the following note.

    c. The conducting pattern direction after the fermata poses some problems and must be planned and practiced by the conductor in order to arrive on the correct beat that follows.

4. Cueing

    a. The cues must be prepared in order to be effective—no sudden cues.

    b. Most cues are done with the eyes of the conductor accompanied by the appropriate gesture.

    c. Showing a clear pattern and then letting the players enter on their own and at the proper time is better than doing a fast series of cues.

    d. Pointing as a cue is not a proper gesture; rather the eyes, right hand, left hand, or head nod should be an "invitation" to the players.

    e. It is helpful to go through a rehearsal without cueing occasionally, so that the players will not become dependent on the conductor for these cues.

    f. The idea of cueing is not to show where the player or section should enter, but rather to show precision, dynamic level, and the character of the entrance.

5. Showing accents

    a. To be effective, accents must always be shown with a preparation by the conductor before the accent occurs.

    b. Accents on the beat should be shown by the gesture of syncopation. This gesture of syncopation is executed with a stop on the rebound of the previous beat before the accent occurs.

    c. Accents off the beat should be shown by a strong gesture on the beat before the accent occurs.

    d. The conductor must show the weight of the accent by the strength of the pattern or gesture.

LEFT-HAND USE

1. Left-hand position (at rest)
   a. The left hand should be in "ready" position in front of (but not touching) the body.
   b. The left hand must not hang down at the side as this gives the conductor a look of indifference for both the players and the audience.
   c. Keep the left hand motionless until it is ready for a specific duty.
   d. The left hand should not move as a "pulse" motion with the right hand.
2. Left-hand movement
   a. The left hand should be independent of the right hand as much as possible—as in ambidextrous conducting. The conductor should practice this independence of the two hands.
   b. Keep the left hand from showing the pulse except when mirroring the right hand.
   c. Do not move the right hand and left hand in parallel motion; the motion should always be in contrary motion.
   d. Do not cross the left-hand over right-hand patterns under any circumstance.
3. Left-hand duties
   a. Use the left hand for independent duties such as the crescendo, diminuendo, cueing, balancing, accents, releases, phrasing, etc. with the exception of when it is mirroring the right hand.
   b. The left hand should be turning pages of the score, but then returned to the "ready" position.
   c. The left hand should also be used for dynamics, nuances, and musical expression.
   d. Many conductors wrongly use the left hand hardly at all except for turning the pages of the score or the mirroring of the right hand.

DYNAMICS

1. Showing dynamics
   a. When showing dynamics or adjusting the balance, bring the left hand forward to establish the attention of the ensemble.
   b. Do not pull the left hand back toward the body for the diminuendo; this movement feels good to the conductor, but is ineffective for the players.
   c. In showing soft dynamics or on a diminuendo, there is a danger that the left hand will move too low, causing the gesture to be obscured from the ensemble. Keep the left hand visible and "out in front."
2. Sudden dynamics
   a. Sudden dynamics must be shown with the left hand before they happen.
   b. Sudden soft dynamics can be shown with a higher conducting plane, the size of the conducting pattern, the use of the left hand, or a combination of all three.
   c. The conductor should show the sudden loud dynamics an instant before with the use of the left hand and/or by the size of the beat pattern.
3. Gradual dynamics
   a. The conductor must gauge the length of the crescendo or diminuendo to judge how rapidly or slowly it should be executed.

b. If the gradual dynamic is very long, then the conductor may need to repeat the left hand conducting gesture for the gradual dynamic change several times.

c. The conductor must show with the left hand the gradual dynamic moving up or down smoothly; this must be practiced in conjunction with the right-hand beat patterns.

4. Crescendo and Diminuendo
   a. The left hand and arm must move smoothly in making these gestures.
   b. The left hand and arm should be away from the body for these gestures to be effective for the ensemble.
   c. The left hand and arm must be in a comfortable-looking position, not a "poised" position.
   d. With the crescendo, the left hand should be turned somewhat upward; with the diminuendo, the left hand should be turned somewhat downward.
   e. Practice the conducting patterns with the right hand and arm and at the same time executing the crescendo and diminuendo with the left hand and arm.
   f. If the left hand and arm are too close to the body on the crescendo or diminuendo movement, the motion of these gestures looks very ineffective and awkward.

METERS AND TEMPOS

1. Changing and Asymmetrical Meters
   a. These meters must be executed precisely to show the pulse and the conducting pattern.
   b. There is a tendency to be looking at the score more with the changing and asymmetrical meters, resulting in poor communication with the ensemble and a lack of attention to the phrasing by the conductor.
   c. In developing the asymmetrical meter conducting technique, there must be a clear distinction between the regular beat and the elongated beat.
   d. If the tempo is somewhat slow, the elongated beat may be subdivided to help the clarity of the asymmetrical meter for the ensemble.

2. Fast tempos
   a. The conductor must reduce the pattern size to cover less distance quickly in order to keep the clarity in the patterns—or else show fewer beats in a bar.
   b. Avoid a frantic look with fast tempo conducting.

3. Slow tempos
   a. The conductor must increase the pattern size to cover more distance slowly in order to keep the clarity in the patterns—or else subdivide the beat pattern.
   b. Avoid a nebulous look with slow tempo conducting by clicking on the ictus.

4. Changes of tempo
   a. When going suddenly from slow to fast, the last half of the last beat of the slow tempo must show the preparation for the new, faster tempo.
   b. When going suddenly from fast to slow, the rebound into the second beat of the new, slower tempo shows the speed of the slower tempo.
   c. When slowing down gradually, slow down in the regular pattern first and then begin to subdivide the beat after that in executing the slower tempo.

SUBDIVISION AND MERGING PATTERNS

1. Subdivision into 2s and 3s
    a. Keep the basic conducting pattern clear by placing the subdivision close to the main beat and in the opposite direction of the following main beat.
    b. The subdivision beat should be smaller than the main beats to keep the basic conducting pattern clear. On the final beat of the subdivision in compound meter, use the "Christmas tree" pattern with the triple subdivision.
    c. The subdivision may also be executed by stopping on the ictus and waiting; the music (and tempo) will dictate this type of subdivision.
    d. The subdivision may also be divided into 3s as dictated with the compound meter or the notation of the composer.
2. Merging patterns
    a. Examples of merging patterns are going from 3 into 1 or 6 into 2; these patterns need to be practiced so that a smooth transition can be made.
    b. Sometimes it is necessary to decrease or increase the number of pulses in a bar to achieve more flow or to help in executing the change of tempo.

MELDING GESTURES AND SUPERMETRICS

1. Melding gestures
    a. Melding gestures are basically not showing the ictus of all the beats in the conducting pattern and melding through the beat on to the following beat.
    b. The melding gesture can also be used in handling fermata situations; the ensemble must be aware of these gestures.
2. Supermetrics
    a. Supermetrics are used for the same general purposes as those of melding gestures where no attempt is made to show the basic beat pattern.
    b. Supermetrics are used to improve the conducting flow and to sustain the quality of the phrase. These changes may need to be marked in the score for consistent use during the rehearsal process and the concert performance.

SCORE SHEET FOR EVALUATING CONDUCTING TECHNIQUE

Name _____ Repertoire _____ Date _____

Performance Areas	Good	Fair	Poor	*Comments
Mechanics				
Stance and posture				
Attention position				
Arms position				
Elbows				
Wrists				

Baton grip				
Baton or no baton				
Conductor's stand/podium				
Conducting patterns				
Conducting patterns				
Pattern size & plane				
One-beat pattern				
Two-beat pattern				
Three-beat pattern				
Four-beat pattern				
Six-beat pattern (others)				
Styles				
Staccato style				
Legato style				
Marcato style				
Tenuto style				
Conducting technique				
Preparatory beats				
Releases				
Fermatas				
Cueing				
Showing accents				
Left hand				
Left hand position (at rest)				
Left hand movement				
Left hand duties				
Dynamics				
Showing dynamics				
Sudden dynamics				
Gradual dynamics				
Crescendo & Diminuendo				
Meters and tempos				
Changing & Asymmetrical				
Fast tempos				
Slow tempos				
Changes of tempo				

Subdivision and merging gestures				
Subdivision into 2s & 3s				
Merging gestures				
Melding gestures & supermetrics				
Melding gestures				
Supermetrics				

PERFORMANCE AREAS FOR REHEARSING SKILLS TO BE EVALUATED, MAINTAINED, OR IMPROVED

Some of the student evaluation projects should include the rehearsing skills as well as the conducting technique. Therefore, the following section emphasizes those items involved in rehearsing the instrumental music ensemble. However, not all of these various items would necessarily be a part of a single student evaluation project. Videotaping is the best way to evaluate these projects. In some cases, these evaluations might be useful as both conducting technique projects and rehearsing skills projects. The conducting teacher should discuss or demonstrate the instructions below in detail for the benefit of the conducting students (before these student conducting/rehearsing projects begin).

Rehearsing the Ensemble

1. Communicating
   a. By having the "head and eyes in the score" most of the time, there is little or no chance of communicating with the ensemble; instead, the conductor should be relating to the ensemble.
   b. There are many circumstances where the conductor needs to be communicating physically, psychologically, visually, and verbally with the ensemble in the rehearsal process.
   c. Meticulous score study must precede the rehearsal process for the conductor to be ready to communicate well with the ensemble.
2. Score reading/conducting
   a. The conductor should memorize at least the first few bars of each section in order to communicate well with the ensemble.
   b. The full score at first may present some problems for the maturing conductor in terms of communicating with the ensemble. Meticulous score study must be done to compensate for this problem.
   c. Conducting and reading the score at the same time is somewhat problematic in that the arms and hands will tend to get in the way of seeing the score.
   d. The conductor must not distort (or change) the conducting position and motions by pulling the arms and hands back toward the body or by raising the conductor's stand to compensate for not seeing the score clearly.
3. Phrasing
   a. Show the phrase endings and be careful of the initial attack on the next phrase.

   b. The conductor must indicate the phrase contour and the phrase climax.

   c. The conductor must be aware of showing the proper style and musical expression within each phrase.

4. Conducting flow

   a. The conductor must show this conducting flow in the conducting patterns and gestures through the musical expression movement and indications.

   b. Choppy and distorted conducting patterns will not show this flow.

   c. The opposite of flow is hesitancy; the player needs to know exactly where the next pulse will be placed.

   d. The wrist movement, stick flexibility, and motion speed show and determine this conducting "flow" physically.

5. Interpreting the music

   a. Make your musical interpretations distinctive and authentic.

   b. There may be a lack of musical expression and emotion in the conducting.

   c. There may be a lack of intensity and relaxation in the conducting.

   d. Refer to chapter 14: Style and Musical Interpretation for more details.

6. Score study and preparation

   a. The conductor must devote much of the preparation time for the rehearsal process in the reading, study, and preparation of the musical score.

   b. There is little hope for a successful rehearsal process unless the conductor is well prepared. The conductor must know the score very well and what to rehearse during the rehearsal process.

   c. If the conductor has not studied the musical score thoroughly or prepared for the rehearsal process, it becomes obvious to the players that the conductor is not ready to rehearse the ensemble. This decreases conductor credibility.

In the Rehearsal

1. Use of the rehearsal time

   a. By preparing well before the rehearsal process, the conductor can save considerable time; as a result, the ensemble will be much more cooperative and responsive.

   b. Refer to the two sections on "Saving Time" and "Wasting Time" in the rehearsal process found in chapter 3: The Ten Essentials of the Rehearsal Process Scenario—Essential No. 3. What needs to be done in the rehearsal process?

2. Rehearsal pacing

   a. Rehearsal pacing may take some time to figure out depending on the maturity and performance level of the ensemble.

   b. Rehearsal pacing does not always mean that you are going at an extremely fast rate; there are times when the ensemble must have time to digest the information or begin to achieve the proposed skills involved.

   c. Frequent stopping will tend to slow the pace of the rehearsal process.

3. Listening and sensitivity

   a. The conductor must be a good listener in the rehearsal process in order to hear what is happening; in this way, the conductor can correct errors, adjust the balance or blend, and produce the conceived musical interpretation.

b. The ensemble members must listen to fit their parts into the ensemble fabric properly. The conductor must promote this listening and sensitivity.

c. Listening is critical in terms of intonation, precision, balance, blend, phrasing, and musical interpretation. The conductor must make the players aware of these performance areas.

d. Led by the conductor, the players must perform with sensitivity; if the conductor does not conduct musically and sensitively, the players will not play with any musical sensitivity.

4. Watching the conductor

a. The conductor must train the ensemble and insist that the ensemble watch the conductor. Some of this can happen during the warm-up period.

b. If the conductor has his "head and eyes" in the score, the players will likewise only look at their music. The conductor must give players a reason to watch.

c. It is crucial to watch the conductor in order to establish good precision and musicality in the rehearsal process and certainly during the concert performance.

5. Detect/correct errors

a. This is an important duty for the conductor. In some cases, the players will detect and correct errors, but in the final analysis, the conductor must be responsible for seeing that this occurs in the rehearsal process.

b. Standing in front of the ensemble, the successful conductor hears what is happening and detects and corrects these errors in the rehearsal process.

6. Continuity and details

a. Continuity and details must be resolved in the rehearsal process. The conductor must see that each selection is prepared both in terms of continuity and in the details of the performance.

b. The conductor must seam one section to the following section and prepare the ensemble to know what is coming next in the music.

c. The details of the musical performance are crucial, starting with good score study and preparation by the conductor.

7. Teaching strategies

a. If the conductor knows the score and the ensemble performance level, he or she can anticipate the teaching strategies before the rehearsal process begins.

b. If the conductor is unprepared to cope with a particular problem, then the solution can wait until the next rehearsal to allow the conductor time to design a new teaching strategy to solve the problem or for the players to practice their parts.

c. Refer to chapters 8–16 on designing teaching strategies.

Rehearsal Segments

1. Warm-up period

a. The warm-up period is very important for educational or amateur ensembles in that it sets the environment and climate for the entire rehearsal process.

b. The warm-up should be interesting and varied for the players.

c. During the warm-up period, many performance aspects can be worked on for the improvement of the ensemble.

2. Tuning and periodic tuning

a. Serious tuning by the ensemble should take place after the warm-up period because players should have made certain adjustments during the warm-up.

    b. Throughout the rehearsal process, the pitch level should be checked periodically.

    c. There are many different ways of checking the tuning; this changes somewhat with the ensemble's progress and needs. See chapter 8: Intonation and Tuning.

3. Rehearsing repertoire

    a. Rehearse each selection meticulously in preparation for the concert performance. Some works will need more rehearsal time than others.

    b. The recording of the rehearsal process can be a great help in deciding which selections need more rehearsal time and what to rehearse.

    c. There are numerous approaches to rehearsing the concert repertoire. The conductor should decide this in the pre-rehearsal planning, during score study, and in configuring the rehearsal plan and schedule.

4. Detailed work on passages

    a. Especially with younger educational ensembles, detailed work on passages in the rehearsal process will be a necessity.

    b. However, as a conductor, do not become a drillmaster where repetition is the sole means of solving performance problems.

    c. Detailed work on passages can lead to rote learning rather than understanding the performance aspects of the passage.

5. Problem solving

    a. There are all kinds of problems to be solved in the rehearsal process—some are technical problems and some are musical problems; some of these rehearsal problems have little to do with the music being performed, but must be solved for the progress of the ensemble.

    b. Some of these problems may need to be solved outside of the full rehearsal process in sectional rehearsals or through individual attention.

    c. However, the conductor is responsible for solving these problems within the rehearsal process for the most part.

Developmental Areas

1. Music reading (sight-read)

    a. This is a very important part of the rehearsal process and the conductor must be diligent about pursuing this performance area.

    b. If the ensemble can read fluently and accurately, then the conductor can begin the rehearsal at a much higher level of performance.

    c. Much of the responsibility for good reading lies with the individual player, but in the rehearsal process, the conductor should promote this music reading aspect in every way possible.

2. Promoting musicianship

    a. Musicianship involves numerous performance areas; work on some of these areas during the warm-up period.

    b. The conductor must think musically throughout the rehearsal process as well as in the concert performance.

    c. Musicianship and musical sensitivity go hand in hand. With both of these ingredients promoted, the rehearsal should result in an artistic performance.

3. Improving the priorities

    a. Such priorities as precision, ensemble tone, balance, blend, intonation, articulations, rhythms, and style can be refined in the warm-up period.

b. In some cases, the refining of certain priorities will take a longer time than with other priorities. The conductor must be insistent but patient.
c. Many of the priorities will become apparent while rehearsing the concert repertoire; these refinements will need to be pursued in order for the ensemble to reach a higher performance level.

Rehearsal Procedures

1. Verbalizing by the conductor
    a. Keep verbalizing during the rehearsal process to a minimum. The two qualities to keep in mind in verbalizing are accuracy and conciseness.
    b. Some verbalizing must take place in the rehearsal process, but the ensemble is there to play and rehearse efficiently and effectively.
    c. Verbalizing tends to slow the pace of the rehearsal process. Long explanations by the conductor can lead to a loss of concentration and focus by the ensemble.
2. Modeling and imitation
    a. The modeling and imitation procedure is a very effective teaching tool.
    b. The modeling and imitation procedure may be done by the conductor or by a selected member (or section) of the ensemble.
3. Conductor demonstrations
    a. Demonstrations by the conductor usually involve verbalizing, explaining, and/ or the vocal performance of a particular passage.
    b. In some instances, the conductor might sing and conduct the passage simultaneously to supply both the audio and visual.
    c. The modeling and imitation procedure can be combined with demonstrations by the conductor.
4. Feedback by the conductor
    a. Feedback by the conductor is a very important part of the rehearsal process.
    b. The player needs the conductor to say whether the passage is acceptable or unacceptable as played.
    c. If the passage is unacceptable, the conductor must decide whether to pursue the solution immediately or delay it for the following rehearsal (to give the players time to practice).
5. Performance concepts
    a. During the rehearsal process, the conductor must be aware and alert to teaching performance concepts (especially with the younger ensemble).
    b. The conductor should teach these performance concepts through conducting, verbalizing, modeling, feedback, and demonstrations.
    c. These performance concepts are too numerous to delineate here, but it will become apparent what needs to be done during the rehearsal process if the conductor's background, preparation, and listening skills are adequate.
    d. By teaching these performance concepts in the rehearsal process, the conductor is reinforcing these ideas for effective learning transfer with the players.

SCORE SHEET FOR EVALUATING REHEARSING SKILLS

Name _____ Repertoire _____ Date _____

Performance Areas	Good	Fair	Poor	*Comments
Rehearsing the ensemble				
Communicating				
Score reading/conducting				
Phrasing				
Conducting flow				
Interpreting the music				
Score study & preparation				
In the rehearsal				
Use of the rehearsal time				
Rehearsal pacing				
Listening & sensitivity				
Watching the conductor				
Detect/correct errors				
Continuity & details				
Teaching strategies				
Rehearsal segments				
Warm-up period				
Tuning & periodic tuning				
Rehearsing repertoire				
Detailed work on passages				
Problem solving				
Developmental areas				
Music reading (sight-read)				
Promoting musicianship				
Improving priorities				
Rehearsal procedures				
Verbalizing by conductor				
Modeling & imitation				
Conductor demonstrations				
Feedback by conductor				
Performance concepts				

Note: The conducting teacher should refer to the Performance Areas and Score Sheets above; first, check the good, fair, or poor columns on the score sheets and then add a letter identification for the comments (a, b, c, d, e, f, or g in the various performance areas) or else provide written comments on these score sheets. All of these ideas must be practiced, corrected (if needed), or improved on by the advanced conductor in order to establish these performance areas for the conducting technique and the rehearsing skills. *The two Score Sheets may be duplicated for individual student evaluations.*

A NOTE TO THE CONDUCTING TEACHER

One of the things that makes conducting evaluations difficult is that not every item will be evaluated with each student conducting/rehearsing project, because the various conducting patterns and gestures or the rehearsing situations will happen only periodically. Therefore, the "good, fair, or poor" scale for evaluation is somewhat subjective, and should be used more for the benefit of the conducting student's improvement than to giving a specific grade for each of these performance areas. This is the reality of the conducting evaluation. The final grading will need to be based on a general grade or numerical weight for these various conducting/rehearsing projects along with other items such as knowledge of the repertoire (see Appendix A for the repertoire and Appendix G for the repertoire assignments), midterm and final examination grades, quality contributions in the classroom, and the conducting and rehearsing improvements made by each student during the semester.

Videotape both the conducting and rehearsing projects so that the conducting teacher can carefully review these projects and objectively evaluate them. This will be of great benefit for the conducting student's improvement during the semester (or year). This will mean that the conducting teacher must devote time to the review of these projects with individual critiques for the students to improve both the conducting and rehearsing. For example, the conducting teacher might wish to view each taping twice (using a remote). The first time through, the conducting teacher might check the rating of "good, fair, or poor" for each category involved with the critique, and then with the second viewing, add comments (identify these comments by the letters provided or else with written comments) that apply from the performance areas listed in this appendix.

The idea behind this book has been to continue the education of the conducting student beyond the basic conducting course. The focus has been on what happens in the rehearsal process scenario. Certainly, both the conducting and rehearsing are a large part of this whole scenario. The conducting technique, in combination with the rehearsing aspects in the rehearsal process, will strongly determine the success or failure of the conductor's career.

It is my contention that the various areas of rehearsing have not been handled very well in the past, but rather left to the practical experience of the developing conductor in front of the ensemble. I hope this book as a part of the conducting curriculum will prepare the maturing conductor to better understand and handle situations in the given instrumental music rehearsal process scenario.

I have tried to provide as much flexibility as possible in sequencing the various aspects of the conducting and rehearsing study. The conducting teacher can sequence these activities, discussions, demonstrations, projects, and assignments in many different ways (see Appendix I). Many conducting books supply the necessary information but fail to provide these activities, projects, assignments, and opportunities to develop the conducting technique and rehearsing skills in producing competent conductors. I hope that this book will change the way conducting teachers and conducting students approach the study of conducting and rehearsing with the instrumental music ensemble.

Appendix G

Listening and Score Study Analysis Assignment Forms

LISTENING ASSIGNMENT FORM

(Select from the end of the various chapters or Appendix A.)

Suggested: Five standard works for band and five standard works for orchestra or a combination of both—to be turned in to the conducting teacher for grading purposes. (Recordings needed)

COMPOSER, COMPOSITION, MOVEMENT (and composer dates and/or composition date):

MUSICAL PERIOD AND CHARACTERISTICS OF THE PERIOD INVOLVED (refer to chapter 14):

ESSENCE AND SPIRIT OF THIS WORK (refer to chapter 14):

COMPOSITIONAL CHARACTERISTICS OF THIS COMPOSER (research):

WHAT OTHER WORKS DID HE OR SHE COMPOSE? (research):

SPECIAL OR INTERESTING ASPECTS OF THIS COMPOSITION (research or listen):

OTHER COMMENTS ABOUT THIS WORK (listen):

This page may be duplicated for the 10 assignments.

SCORE STUDY ANALYSIS ASSIGNMENT FORM

(Select from the end of the chapters or Appendix A.)

Suggested: Five standard works for band and five standard works for orchestra or a combination of both—to be turned in to the conducting teacher for grading purposes. (Musical scores needed)

COMPOSER, COMPOSITION, MOVEMENT
(and composer dates and/or composition date):

_____

INSTRUMENTATION AND ORCHESTRATION PARTS:

_____

CLEFS AND TRANSPOSITIONS INVOLVED:

_____

FORM, THEMES, AND FLOW CHARTS INVOLVED:

_____

COMPLEX METERS AND/OR RHYTHMS IDENTIFIED:

_____

PERIOD CHARACTERISTICS, PHRASING ASPECTS, OR BAR GROUPING:

_____

DYNAMICS, NUANCES, ACCENTS, AND MUSICAL EXPRESSION:

_____

STYLE, MUSICAL INTERPRETATION ASPECTS, OR SOLOISTS WITHIN THE ENSEMBLE NEEDED:

_____

CONDUCTING PROBLEMS AND SOLUTIONS:

_____

_____

PLAYING PROBLEMS AND POSSIBLE TEACHING STRATEGIES:

_____

_____

This page may be duplicated for the 10 assignments. (See Chapter Five.)

Appendix H

Creating the Rehearsal Process (Lab) Environment in the Conducting Curriculum

One of the most difficult, but very important aspects of teaching conducting and rehearsing is in creating a rehearsal process (lab) environment in which the students can actually apply the information and skills in a practical way. The conducting teacher must make every effort to create this rehearsal process (lab) environment for the conducting students. (See the bibliographical list in Music Material Found in Other Conducting Books, at the end of this appendix.) Below are some possible situations to implement in order to create this environment within the conducting curriculum:

1. *Use a regularly scheduled full band and/or orchestral ensemble.* This particular situation would be the most beneficial for both the student conductors (practical conducting and rehearsing experience) and for the players (to gain ensemble repertoire and to develop their music reading prowess).
2. *Use a slightly smaller ensemble than the band or orchestra ensemble* (which might present problems because of the band and orchestra required instrumentation). However, even if the instrumentation were somewhat lacking, this could still be a worthwhile conducting/rehearsing experience.
3. *Within the conducting class, form as large an ensemble as possible* (this might also present problems of instrumentation for the band and orchestra repertoire). Music materials are available for C, B-flat, E-flat, and F instruments, plus alto clef (viola) and percussion parts. (See the Rehearsal Problem Charts below.)
4. *Within the conducting class, use a chamber music ensemble.* A woodwind quintet, brass quintet, string quartet, or larger ensemble could be used for the students to conduct and solve problems that might occur in this rehearsal process (lab) environment. There are also music materials available that are scored in three or four parts (C score), but may need to be transposed. (See the Rehearsal Problem Charts below.)
5. *Within the conducting class, form various instrumental ensembles* as listed in Appendix A under Score Study and Program Building Repertoire for Miscellaneous or Small Instrumental Ensembles for the students to solve conducting and rehearsing problems within this rehearsal process (lab) environment. (See the Rehearsal Problem Charts below.)

6. *Use recordings, a piano reduction, or a two-piano reduction* (however, these rehearsal process [lab] environments have conducting limitations and no real rehearsing possibilities).

REHEARSAL PROBLEM CHARTS

Below are charts indicating rehearsal problems, reasons for the problems, and possible solutions to the problems as a starting point for class discussion and for practical application in the rehearsal process (lab) environment as referred to above in the rehearsal environments 3, 4, and 5.

Table H.1.

REHEARSAL PROBLEM	REASON FOR THE PROBLEM	SOLUTION TO THE PROBLEM
Wrong Notes and Inaccuracies	Keys and key signatures	Work on various keys in the warm-up period (scales, broken 3rds, and arpeggios). Refer to Lisk 1987, 18–25.
	Accidentals	Work on carrying the accidentals through the measure in many different situations.
	Partials (brass)	Stress partial accuracy in the warm-up period (brass only in this part of the warm-up period).
	Fingerings	Make the strings and the various woodwind instruments aware of the fingering problems involved.
	Uneven runs	In many cases, these uneven runs are rhythmic problems rather than just technical problems.
	Large interval skips	This is a particular problem with the brass instruments (practicing intervals and octave skips will help this problem). Feel these pitches at the embouchure.
Poor Intonation	Ensemble pitch level	Careful tuning in the warm-up period and periodic tuning will help the ensemble intonation.
	In specific passages	Isolate these passages and then adjust the pitches.
	Ensemble tone production problems	Embouchure, air, tongue, bow use, instrument, etc.

Table H.1. (*continued*)

REHEARSAL PROBLEM	REASON FOR THE PROBLEM	SOLUTION TO THE PROBLEM
	"Bad notes" on the instrument	Make players aware of these "bad notes" and how to adjust them.
	Players not listening	Stress listening in many different ways throughout the rehearsal process.
	Extreme registers causing some intonation problems	Make players aware of extreme register intonation problems.
	Extreme dynamic levels causing some intonation problems	Make players aware of extreme dynamic level intonation problems and the solutions.
Rhythmic Instability	Lack of correct rhythm and rhythmic subdivision	Work on rhythms and rhythm patterns subdivision in the warm-up period frequently.
	Not seeing and feeling the pulse together	Watch the conductor and feel the pulse as a group.
	With specific instrumental sections or choirs	Work with these sections or choirs to produce the rhythms and rhythm patterns correctly.
	On specific passages	Isolate the passages and correct the rhythmic problems.
	Changing and asymmetrical meters	Work on the understanding and execution of the various meters.
	Compound meters	Feel the subdividing into 3s in compound meter.
	Accentuation	The conductor must show these accents and the players must read and play them.

Table H.2.

REHEARSAL PROBLEM	REASON FOR THE PROBLEM	SOLUTION TO THE PROBLEM
Poor Ensemble Tone Production	Uneven ensemble tone	Stress balance and blend throughout the rehearsal process.
	Poor structural balance	Explain the structure of the melody, countermelody, and accompaniment.
	Brass over-blowing	Make brass players aware of these tone and balance problems.

(*continued*)

Table H.2.   (*continued***)**

REHEARSAL PROBLEM	REASON FOR THE PROBLEM	SOLUTION TO THE PROBLEM
	Lacks tone color change	Explain the sonority needed in a particular passage (a descriptive explanation may be necessary).
	Lacks texture clarity	Rehearse each line carefully and then put the lines back together.
	Percussion too strong for the rest of the ensemble	The conductor must stress to the percussion section to be more dynamically sensitive.
	Vibrato application	Explain when to use vibrato and also request the speed and depth of the vibrato needed.
	Chord balance and blend	Make players aware of these problems, and then adjust these chords.
Poor Articulation or Bowing	Incorrect articulation (winds and percussion)	Make players aware of these articulation errors and problems.
	Ignoring articulation markings	Point out to the players these articulation markings.
	Inconsistent articulations among the players	Rehearse these passages for better articulation consistency.
	Poor production of these articulations	Explain and/or demonstrate these articulations. (Discuss.)
	Poor bow use	The conductor should suggest certain bowing adjustments.
	Poor production of the string techniques	Explain and/or demonstrate how to improve these various string techniques. (Discuss.)
	Incorrect bowing style	Détaché, martelé, spiccato, louré, etc. must be executed properly. (Have these demonstrated.)

Table H.2. **(*continued*)**

REHEARSAL PROBLEM	REASON FOR THE PROBLEM	SOLUTION TO THE PROBLEM
Poor Ensemble Precision	Poor initial attack	The conductor should execute a clear preparatory beat and the players should watch to improve precision of these initial attacks.
	Poor tempo change	Use the "conduct and count" procedure to improve this.
	Not watching the conductor	Stress watching the conductor throughout the rehearsal process.
	Poor rhythms and rhythm patterns	Work on the rhythms and rhythm patterns in the warm-up period.
	Unclear pulse by the conductor	Show conducting patterns more clearly (rebound is important).
	Tempo rushes or drags	Isolate the problem and work for a steady tempo.
	Entrances are early or late	Conductor should prepare cues better and the players should watch the conductor more.

Table H.3.

REHEARSAL PROBLEM	REASON FOR THE PROBLEM	SOLUTION TO THE PROBLEM
Poor Phrasing and Style	Not breathing at phrase endings or watching out for the phrase endings	Mark phrase endings in the music and watch the conductor for the release indications.
	Not releasing the phrase together	Watch for the conductor's phrase release preparatory motion.
	Unaware of the phrase contour	Explain or show by conducting how to do the phrase contour.
	Ignoring the phrase climax	Show where the phrase climax is with the conducting gestures or mark the climax in the music.
	Inconsistent style among the players	Show or explain the style needed here; rehearse this aspect, and perhaps mark the music.
	Inconsistently keeping to the style	The conductor must remind the players about this problem.
	Failure to observe correct music period style	Consider the style of the baroque, classical, romantic, and contemporary periods.

(*continued*)

Table H.3.   (*continued*)

REHEARSAL PROBLEM	REASON FOR THE PROBLEM	SOLUTION TO THE PROBLEM
Poor Dynamics, Nuances, and Musical Expression	Poor balance at the loud dynamic levels	Players need to listen more at the loud dynamic levels and adjust.
	Players are unaware of nuances as indicated by the conductor	Watch the conductor and play these nuances with much more sensitivity in the rehearsal.
	Ignoring the musical expression indications in the phrase	Make players more aware of these musical expression indications in the music.
	More dynamic contrast needed in the performance	Show this with the conducting patterns and gestures.
	Gradual dynamics are played unevenly	Rehearse these gradual dynamics (such as with that of the crescendos and diminuendos).
	Poor balance and blend confusing ensemble dynamic levels	Strive to make the players more aware of these balance and blend problems within the ensemble dynamic levels.
	Poor production of the musical expression (such as the forzando or accent)	Explain, model, or demonstrate these musical expression markings for the ensemble.

Note: Many other conducting and rehearsing problems (see Appendixes B and C for more specific problems) should be resolved during these rehearsal process labs. The above charts are simply a way of getting these activities started and open for discussion and demonstration.

The below list is an attempt to identify various music materials that are useful in the conducting classroom or in the rehearsal process (lab) environment. The main logistic problems here are that from one conducting class to the next, there will be an unpredictable number of students available in the conducting class and the instrumentation will probably change each semester. There may be a need to bring in additional players as well. This will require considerable planning by the conducting teacher in order to have the ensemble in place for the conducting students to conduct and rehearse.

MUSIC MATERIAL FOUND IN OTHER CONDUCTING BOOKS FOR SMALLER CLASSROOM ENSEMBLES

Bailey, Wayne, *Aural Skills for Conductors.* The author detects and corrects note errors, rhythmic errors, intonation errors, balance/dynamic errors, and articulation errors in this book. The exercises are excerpts of works from vocal, choral, wind, and string repertoires. The exercises will need to be transposed from the score. There is a 30-minute cassette tape available for conducting teachers with both correct and incorrect versions of the selected exercises.

Bailey, Wayne, *Conducting: The Art of Communication.* This book has numerous exercises in three- and four-part writing for conducting practice. The transposed parts are available with a CD-ROM of the finale files; these are free of charge to adopting instructors. From these files, the instructor can create MP3 files for individual student practice.

Butts, Carrol M., *Troubleshooting the High School Band: How to Detect and Correct Common and Uncommon Performance Problems.* This book contains a number of sections with transposed parts to be played in unison/octaves for solving sight-reading rhythmic problems, volume control, lip slur control, ties, rests, pick-up notes, balance (chords) problems, precision on attacks, precision on releases, and style. These examples could also be useful in the warm-up period with younger bands.

Curtis, Larry G., and David L. Kuehn, *A Guide to Successful Instrumental Conducting.* This textbook covers the basic conducting technique and then supplies basic and intermediate etudes for practicing these techniques, scored for single-line instruments (which may be found in the conducting class) for flute, clarinet, horn, trumpet, trombone, percussion, violin, viola, cello, and bass.

Hunsberger, Donald, and Roy E. Ernst, *The Art of Conducting*, 2nd ed. Starting in the Overview with Excerpts for chapter 4 on page 190 there is a wealth of music material available. Most of the instrumental examples have the parts transposed for B-flat voices, E-flat voices, and (sometimes) F voices and piano. These examples could be useful in an advanced conducting course, especially those examples involved with changing and asymmetrical meters.

Kohut, Daniel L., and Joe W. Grant, *Learning to Conduct and Rehearse.* There are 17 instrumental music examples starting on page 145, scored in four parts and occasionally with added percussion parts. The parts would need to be transposed for the B-flat, E-flat, and F instruments.

Labuta, Joseph A., *Basic Conducting Techniques*, 5th ed. Starting with Part III on page 107, these excerpts are scored in four parts and occasionally with some added percussion parts. In this 5th edition, the parts have been transposed for the B-flat, E-flat, and F instruments. In the 6th edition, these transposed parts are online.

Long, R. Gerry, *The Conductor's Workshop: A Workbook on Instrumental Conducting.* This book contains many very short music examples specifically geared to solving some conducting technique problems. The examples are scored in three (C) parts and would need to be transposed for the B-flat, E-flat, and F instruments.

Maiello, Anthony, *Conducting: A Hands-On Approach (Music Examples by Jack Bullock).* Music examples are found throughout this book and the parts are supplied in score form for C treble-clef instruments, B-flat instruments, E-flat instruments, and F instruments plus alto clef (viola), C bass-clef instruments, and piano. The examples would be playable from the score within the conducting class.

Nowak, Jerry, and Henry Nowak, *Conducting the Music, Not the Musicians.* Most of the music examples are scored for full orchestra or band, but if the lab ensemble has fair instrumentation, many examples could be used by the student conductor in gaining some practical conducting and rehearsing experience. There are no separate transposed parts here; however, these could be read from the score in the lab environment. There is a keyboard part provided with these examples as well.

Phillips, Kenneth H., *Basic Techniques of Conducting.* Some of the music examples are scored for C treble-clef part, B-flat part, alto clef (viola) part, F part, E-flat part, and C bass-clef part. Even though the examples are geared toward the basic technique of conducting, this book does supply a few examples for conducting instrumental groups combined with choral ensembles.

Ross, Allan A., *Techniques for the Beginning Conductors*. These music examples are scored for many and varied ensembles including one- or two-piano reductions. There are transposed parts provided for some of the examples. Most of the book is concerned with conducting technique, score reading, and terminology.

Rudolf, Max, *The Grammar of Conducting*, 3rd ed. These music examples are mostly in condensed score form or reduced for the piano. The examples would need to be rescored into multiple parts and then transposed for the transposing instruments. The music examples are very brief in most cases.

Shepherd, William, *A Conducting Workbook*. Most of the music examples in this workbook are a single (or double) line; however, a C treble-clef part, B-flat part, E-flat part, F part, and C bass-clef part are provided in most cases. These music examples could be of great value, particularly in working on changing and asymmetrical meters.

Spradling, Robert, *Error Detection: Exercises for the Instrumental Conductor*. This text includes 43 instrumental scores with exercises that include note, rhythm, expression, and random errors within the instrumental parts. Students will conduct from accurate scores while class members perform from parts that have these errors embedded in them. Conductors learn to identify and effectively solve the errors as a part of developing efficient rehearsal techniques.

See Appendix A in this book under the section Score Study and Program Building Repertoire for Miscellaneous or Small Instrumental Ensembles for additional music material for the conducting/rehearsing projects with the smaller ensembles. This music material would need to be purchased over a period of time (or borrowed from other music libraries) to accommodate the instrumentation available in the present conducting class.

Appendix I

Class Activities, Discussions, Demonstrations, Projects, and Assignments for Advanced Conductors

Within most conducting courses, the conducting teacher has excellent information to relate to the conducting student, but does not necessarily proceed with these various activities, discussions, demonstrations, projects, or assignments in order to deliver this information and develop these skills with the advanced conductor. The following list suggests ways of delivering this information and developing skills for the advanced conductor. There are numerous ways to sequence these items.

1. Complete conducting/rehearsing projects with the full ensemble (orchestra or band).
2. Complete conducting/rehearsing projects with the smaller ensembles (see Appendix H and/or Appendix A under Miscellaneous or Small Instrumental Ensembles).
3. Conduct with recordings (but realize that this has limited value in that there is no control of the music by the conductor and no real rehearsing possibilities).
4. Discuss and/or demonstrate the statements and questions posed in the Practical Application sections at the end of the chapters—after assigning these chapters to be read.
5. Conduct and/or demonstrate the musical examples from the In the Rehearsal Process (Lab) Environment sections starting with chapter 8—after assigning these chapters to be read.
6. Chapter 4: Conducting Technique provides various conducting demonstrations at the end of most sections for use by the conducting teacher and students.
7. Review chapter 5: Score Study, Music Imagery, and Inner Singing and discuss in detail various facets of score reading, study, and preparation including music imagery, bar grouping, inner singing, and making flow charts.
8. Review chapters 1 and 6 and discuss and/or demonstrate how to employ the listed segments and procedures in the rehearsal process.
9. In chapters 8–16, review the various Teaching Strategy Tables and add other possible teaching strategies to these tables. (See the Teaching Strategy Tables at the end of these various chapters.)
10. Review the items proposed in chapter 17: Conductor Profile and Self-Evaluation and add other important self-evaluation items to those listed.

11. Complete the forms for Listening Assignments and Score Study Analysis Assignments found in Appendix G. Start an annotated computer file of these works for your own personal use.
12. During the class period, listen to recordings, observe scores, and discuss the details in some of the Standard Repertoire found in Appendix A. Start an annotated computer file of these works for your own personal use.
13. Discuss the Conducting and Rehearsing Problems found in Appendix B.
14. Discuss and have demonstrated the Technical Problems Encountered in the Rehearsal Process for each instrument found in Appendix C.
15. Discuss and have demonstrated the Instrumental Techniques, Intonation Problems/Solutions, and Special Effects for each instrument found in Appendix D.
16. View some of the videos found in Appendix E and discuss with the conducting students what particularly important items have transpired during these various conducting/rehearsing videos. Observe YouTube performances as well.
17. Review with the conducting students the items found in the Student Project Conducting/Rehearsing Evaluations: Performance Areas for both the conducting technique and rehearsing skills in Appendix F (before beginning the student conducting/rehearsing projects).
18. Discuss the items found in chapter 18: Coda—From Rehearsal Process to Concert Performance with the conducting students. (There may be other issues that the conducting teacher and the students need to bring up as well.)
19. Discuss and/or demonstrate problem solving in the rehearsal process found in the Appendix H under the Performance Problem Charts (before beginning the student conducting/rehearsing projects).
20. Administer a midterm exam and final exam—written, practical, or both.

A NOTE TO THE CONDUCTING TEACHER

By the very nature of the conducting course, there are many subjective aspects. Therefore, it behooves the conducting teacher to have as many objective ways in which to evaluate the conducting students throughout the semester (or year) during the conducting course.

Certainly, the conducting teacher can use these various activities and assignments in any number of ways to enhance the education of the student conductor. It is important for the students to know how they are doing in the class periodically. In this way, the student can learn what needs improvement in their approach to conducting and rehearsing the instrumental music ensemble.

As much as possible, explain the grading system at the beginning of the course so that the students will know exactly what they need to accomplish. There should be considerable weight placed on the practical student conducting/rehearsing projects with the ensembles simply because this is the main point of the conducting course.

Bibliography

ORCHESTRA

Adey, Christopher. *Orchestral Performance: A Guide for Conductors and Players*. London: Faber and Faber Limited, 1998.

Green, Elizabeth A. H. *The Dynamic Orchestra*. Englewood Cliffs, NJ: Prentice-Hall, 1987.

Holmes, Malcolm H. *Conducting an Amateur Orchestra*. Cambridge, MA: Harvard University Press, 1951.

Kjelland, James. *Orchestral Bowing: Style and Function*. Van Nuys, CA: Alfred Publishing Co., 2003.

Lawson, Colin, ed. *The Cambridge Companion to the Orchestra*. New York: Cambridge University Press, 2003.

Moses, Don V., Robert W. Demaree Jr., and Allen F. Ohmes. *Face to Face with an Orchestra*. Princeton, NJ: Prestige Publications, 1987.

Rabin, Marvin, and Priscilla Smith. *Guide to Orchestral Bowings through Musical Styles*. Madison, WI: University of Wisconsin, 1984 (rev. 1990).

CONCERT BAND

Battisti, Frank L. *The Winds of Change: The Evolution of the Contemporary American Wind Band/Ensemble and its Conductor*. Galesville, MD: Meredith Music Publications, 2002.

Butts, Carrol M. *Troubleshooting the High School Band: How to Detect and Correct Common and Uncommon Performance Problems*. West Nyack, NY: Parker Publishing Company, 1981.

Dalby, Max F. *Band Rehearsal Techniques: A Handbook for New Directors*. Northfield, IL: The Instrumentalist Publishing Company, 1993.

Janzen, Eldon A. *Band Director's Survival Guide*. West Nyack, NY: Parker Publishing Company, 1985.

McBeth, W. Francis. *Effective Performance of Band Music: Solutions to Specific Problems in the Performance of 20th Century Band Music*. San Antonio, TX: Southern Music Company, 1972.

Middleton, James, Harry Haines, and Gary Garner. *The Symphonic Band Winds: A Quest for Perfection*. San Antonio, TX: Southern Music Company, 1986.

Whitwell, David. *A New History of Wind Music*. Evanston, IL: Instrumentalist Company, 1972.

CONDUCTING TECHNIQUE

Atherton, Leonard. *Vertical Plane Focal Point Conducting*. Muncie, IN: Ball State University, 1989.

Bailey, Wayne. *Conducting: The Art of Communication*. New York: Oxford University Press, 2009.

Battisti, Frank L. *On Becoming a Conductor*. Galesville, MD: Meredith Music Publications, 2007.

Boult, Adrian C. *A Handbook on the Technique of Conducting*. Oxford, UK: Hall the Publisher Limited, 1949.

Curtis, Larry G., and David L. Kuehn. *A Guide to Successful Instrumental Conducting*. Dubuque, IA: William C. Brown Publishing Company, 1992.

Demaree, Robert W. Jr., and Don V. Moses. *The Complete Conductor*. Englewood Cliffs, NJ: Prentice-Hall, 1995.

Fuchs, Peter Paul. *The Psychology of Conducting*. New York: MCA Music, 1969.

Garretson, Robert L. *Conducting Choral Music*. 8th ed. Upper Saddle River, NJ: Prentice-Hall, 1998.

Green, Elizabeth A. H. *The Modern Conductor*. 6th ed. Englewood Cliffs, NJ: Prentice-Hall, 1997.

Green, Elizabeth A. H. *The Modern Conductor Workbook*. Englewood Cliffs, NJ: Prentice-Hall, 1964.

Hunsberger, Donald, and Roy E. Ernst. *The Art of Conducting*. 2nd ed. New York: Alfred A. Knopf, 1992.

Instrumentalist Magazine, *Conductor Anthology Vol. I and II*. Northfield, IL: The Instrumentalist Publishing Company, 1989.

Kahn, Emil. *Conducting*. New York: Free Press, 1965.

Labuta, Joseph A. *Basic Conducting Technique*. 5th ed. Upper Saddle River, NJ: Prentice-Hall, 2004.

Leinsdorf, Erich. *The Composer's Advocate: A Radical Orthodoxy for Musicians*. New Haven, CT: Yale University Press, 1981.

Long, R. Jerry. *The Conductor's Workshop: A Workbook on Instrumental Conducting*. Dubuque, IA: William C. Brown Company Publishers, 1971.

Maiello, Anthony. *Conducting: A Hands-On Approach*. Miami, FL: Warner Bros. Publications, 1996.

Maiello, Anthony. *Conducting Nuances*. Chicago: GIA Publications, 2008.

Malko, Nicolai. *The Conductor and His Baton: Fundamentals of the Technique of Conducting*. Copenhagen: Hansen, 1950.

Marsh, Robert Charles. *Toscanini and the Art of Conducting*. New York: Collier Books, 1954.

McElheran, Brock. *Conducting Technique for Beginners and Professionals*. New York: Oxford University Press, 1966.

Nowak, Jerry, and Henry Nowak. *Conducting the Music, Not the Musician*. New York: Carl Fischer, LLC, 2002.

Noyes, Frank. *Anthology of Musical Examples for Instrumental Conducting*. Dubuque, IA: Wm. C. Brown Company Publishers, 1961.

Phillips, Kenneth H. *Basic Techniques of Conducting*. New York: Oxford University Press, 1997.

Prausnitz, Frederik. *Score and Podium: A Complete Guide to Conducting*. New York: Norton, 1983.

Ross, Allan A. *Techniques for Beginning Conductors*. Belmont, CA: Wadsworth, 1976.

Rudolf, Max. *The Grammar of Conducting: A Comprehensive Guide to Baton Technique and Interpretation.* 3rd ed. New York: Schirmer Books, 1995.

Scherchen, Hermann. *Handbook of Conducting.* New York: Oxford University Press, 1989.

Schuller, Gunther. *The Compleat Conductor.* New York: Oxford University Press, 1997.

Shepherd, William. *A Conducting Workbook with CD-Rom Video.* Belmont, CA: Wadsworth, 2002.

Wagner, Richard. *On Conducting.* London: The New Temple Press, 1869.

Wood, Sir Henry J. *About Conducting.* London: Sylvan Press, 1945.

REHEARSING

Kohut, Daniel L., and Joe W. Grant. *Learning to Conduct and Rehearse.* Englewood Cliffs, NJ: Prentice-Hall, 1990.

Lisk, Edward S. *The Creative Director: Alternative Rehearsal Techniques.* Ft. Lauderdale, FL: Meredith Music Publications, 1987.

Read, Gardner. *Thesaurus of Orchestral Devices.* London: Sir Isaac Pitman & Sons, LTD, 1953.

Spradling, Robert. *Error Detection: Exercises for the Instrumental Conductor.* New York: Carl Fischer, 2010.

Weerts, Richard. *Handbook of Rehearsal Techniques for the High School Band.* West Nyack, NY: Parker Publishing Company, 1976.

PEDAGOGY

Blade, James. *Orchestral Percussion Techniques.* 2nd ed. London: Oxford University Press, 1961.

Casey, Joseph L. *Teaching Techniques and Insights for Instrumental Music Educators.* Chicago: GIA Publications, 1991.

Colwell, Richard J., and Thomas Goolsby. *The Teaching of Instrumental Music.* 3rd ed. Englewood Cliffs, NJ: Prentice-Hall, 1992.

Farkas, Philip. *The Art of Musicianship.* Bloomington, IN: Musical Publications, 1976.

Green, Elizabeth A. H. *Teaching String Instruments in Class.* Englewood Cliffs, NJ: Prentice-Hall, 1966.

Kohut, Daniel L. *Instrumental Music Pedagogy.* Champaign, IL: Stipes Publishing, 1996.

Moore, E. C. *Playing at Sight* (Pamphlet). Kenosha, WI: LeBlanc.

Starer, Robert. *Rhythmic Training.* New York: MCA Music, 1969.

Voxman, Himie. *Baroque and Classical Music* (Pamphlet). Kenosha, WI: LeBlanc.

Weisberg, Arthur. *The Art of Wind Playing.* New York: Schirmer Books, 1975.

SCORE STUDY

Battisti, Frank L., and Robert Garofalo. *Guide to Score Study for the Wind Band Conductor.* Galesville, MD: Meredith Music Publications, 1990.

Forseth, James O., and Richard F. Grunow. *MLR Instrumental Score Reading Program.* Chicago: GIA Publications, 1997.

Green, Elizabeth A. H., and Nicolai Malko. *The Conductor and His Score*. Englewood Cliffs, NJ: Prentice-Hall, 1975.

Jacob, Gordon. *How to Read a Score*. London: Boosey & Hawkes, 1944.

REPERTOIRE

Anderson, Paul G. *Brass Ensemble Music Guide*. Evanston, IL: The Instrumentalist Company, 1978.

Bernstein, Leonard. *Young People's Concerts*. New York: Anchor Press/Doubleday, 1970.

Camphouse, Mark, ed. *Composers on Composing for Band*. Chicago: GIA Publications, 2002.

Daniels, David. *Orchestral Music: A Handbook*. 4th ed. Lanham, MD: Scarecrow Press, 2005.

Fennell, Frederick. *Time and the Winds*. Kenosha, WI: LeBlanc, 1954.

Goldman, Richard Franko. *The Wind Band*. Boston: Allyn and Bacon, 1961.

Goodman, A. Harold. *Instrumental Music Guide*. Provo, UT: Brigham Young University Press, 1977.

Heller, George N. *Ensemble Music for Wind and Percussion Instruments: A Catalog*. Washington, DC: Music Educators National Conference, 1970.

Instrumentalist Magazine. *Band Music Guide*. Northfield, IL: The Instrumentalist Company, 1996.

Instrumentalist Magazine. *Orchestra Music Guide*. Evanston, IL: The Instrumentalist Company, 1966.

Merriman, Lyle, and Himie Voxman. *Woodwind Ensemble Music Guide*. Evanston, IL: The Instrumentalist Company, 1973.

Scott, William. *A Conductor's Repertoire of Chamber Music Compositions for Nine to Fifteen Solo Instruments*. Westport, CT: Greenwood Press, 1993.

Wittry, Diane. *Beyond the Baton*. New York: Oxford University Press, 2007.

Yaklich, Richard Eldon. *An Orchestra Guide to Repertoire and Programming*. Lewiston, NY: E. Mellen Press, 2003.

TEACHING

Bailey, Wayne. *Aural Skills for Conductors*. Mountain View, CA: Mayfair, 1992.

Gordon, Edwin E. *The Psychology of Music Teaching*. Englewood Cliffs, NJ: Prentice-Hall, 1971.

Labuta, Joseph A. *Teaching Musicianship in the High School Band*. West Nyack, NY: Parker, 1972.

Madsen, Clifford K., and Cornelia Yarbrough. *Competency-Based Music Education*. Englewood Cliffs, NJ: Prentice-Hall, 1980.

Peters, G. David, and Robert F. Miller. *Music Teaching and Learning*. New York: Longman, 1982.

Schleuter, Stanley L. *A Sound Approach to Teaching Instrumentalists*. Kent, OH: Kent State University Press, 1984.

Walker, Darwin E. *Teaching Music: Managing the Successful Music Program*. 2nd ed. New York: Schirmer Books, 1998.

20TH-CENTURY MUSIC

Dallin, Leon. *Techniques of Twentieth Century Composition.* Dubuque, IA: William C. Brown Company, 1957.

Fink, Robert, and Robert Ricci. *The Language of Twentieth Century Music.* New York: Schirmer Books, 1975.

Hart, Philip. *Conductors: A New Generation.* New York: Charles Scribner's Sons, 1979.

Read, Gardner. *Contemporary Instrumental Techniques.* New York: Schirmer Books, 1976.

Risatti, Howard. *New Music Vocabulary (A Guide to Notational Signs for Contemporary Music).* Urbana: University of Illinois Press, 1975.

Stone, Kurt. *Music Notation in the Twentieth Century: A Practical Guidebook.* New York: Norton, 1980.

Vermeil, Jean. *Conversations with Boulez (Thoughts on Conducting).* Portland, OR: Amadeus Press, 1989.

Weisberg, Arthur. *Performing Twentieth-Century Music: A Handbook for Conductors and Instrumentalists.* New Haven, CT: Yale University Press, 1993.

INTONATION

Benade, Arthur H. *Horns, Strings & Harmony.* Garden City, NY: Anchor Books/Doubleday, 1960.

Fabrizio, Al. *A Guide to the Understanding and Correction of Intonation Problems.* Galesville, FL: Meredith Music Publications, 1994.

Garofalo, Robert J. *Improving Intonation in Band and Orchestra Performance.* Galesville, MD: Meredith Music Publications, 1996.

Jurrens, James. *Tuning the Band and Raising Pitch Consciousness.* San Antonio, TX: RBC Publications, 1991.

Pottle, Ralph. *Tuning the School Band and Orchestra.* 8th printing. Hammond, LA, 1970.

Stauffer, Donald, *Intonation Deficiencies of Wind Instruments in Ensemble.* Washington, DC: Catholic University of America Press, 1954.

MUSICAL PERFORMANCE

Copland, Aaron. *Music and Imagination.* Cambridge, MA: Harvard University Press, 1980.

Dart, Thurston. *The Interpretation of Music.* London: Hutchinson, 1954.

Dorian, Frederick. *The History of Music in Performance.* New York: Norton, 1942.

Harris, Frederick Jr. *Conducting with Feeling.* Galesville, MD: Meredith Music Publications, 2001.

Kohut, Daniel L. *Musical Performance: Learning Theory and Pedagogy.* Englewood Cliffs, NJ: Prentice-Hall, 1985.

Thurmond, James Morgan. *Note Grouping: A Method for Achieving Expression and Style in Musical Performance.* Galesville, MD: Meredith Music Publications, 1982.

GENERAL

Green, Barry, and W. Timothy Gallwey. *The Inner Game of Music*. New York: Anchor Press/ Doubleday, 1986.

Kennan, Kent. *The Technique of Orchestration*. Englewood Cliffs, NJ: Prentice-Hall, 2002.

Patterson, Blake, "Musical Dynamics." *Scientific American* 231, no. 5 (November 1974): 78–95.

Rimsky-Korsakov, Nicolas. *Principles of Orchestration*. New York: Edwin F. Kalmus, 1912.

Taubman, Howard. *The Maestro: The Life of Arturo Toscanini*. New York: Simon & Schuster, 1951.

Wagar, Jeannine. *Conductors in Conversation: Fifteen Contemporary Conductors Discuss Their Lives and Profession*. Boston: G.K. Hall, 1991.

Walter, Bruno. *Of Music and Music-Making*. New York: Norton, 1961.

Zander, Rosamund Stone, and Benjamin Zander. *The Art of Possibility*. New York: Penguin Group, 2000.

Index